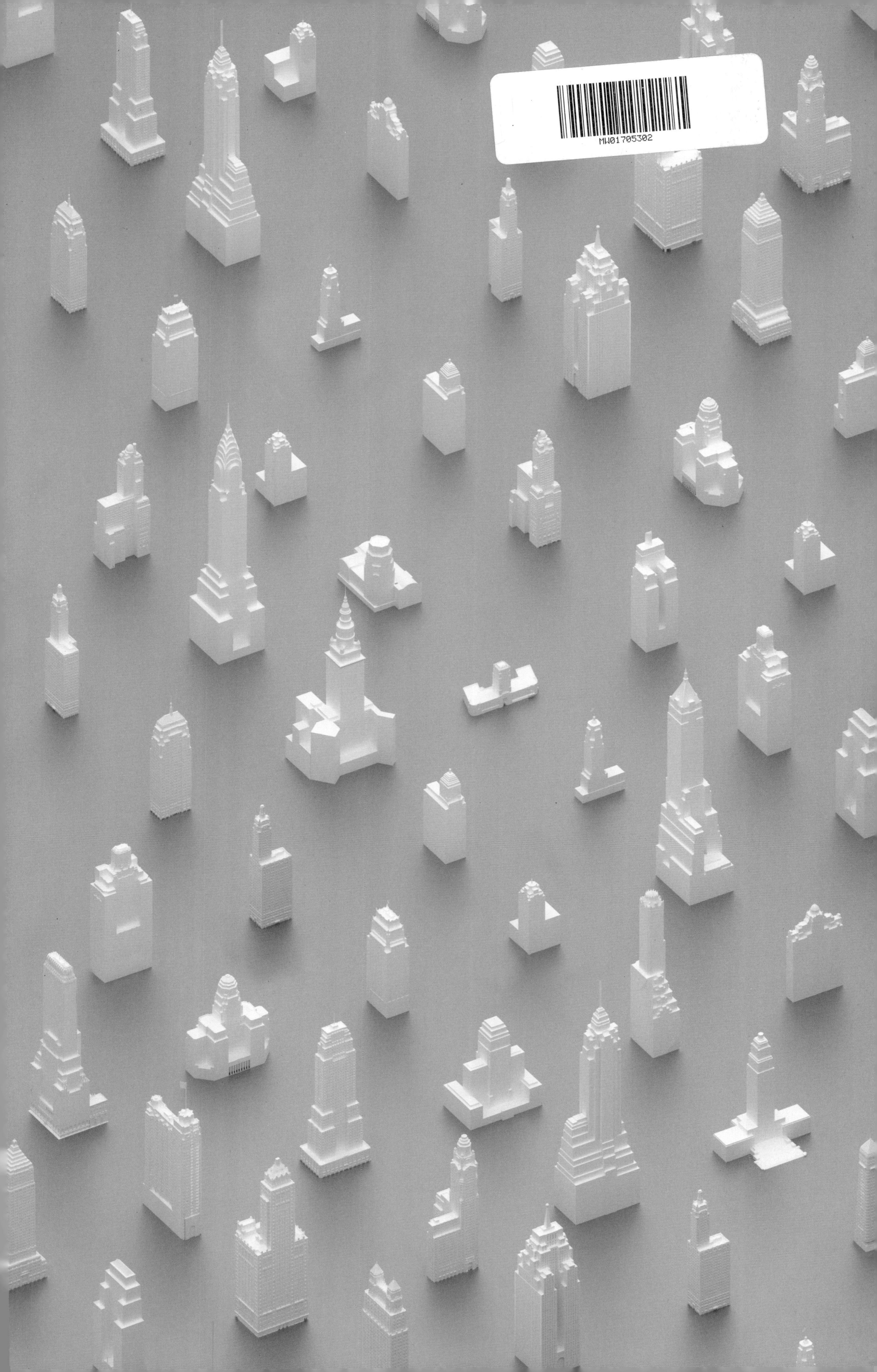

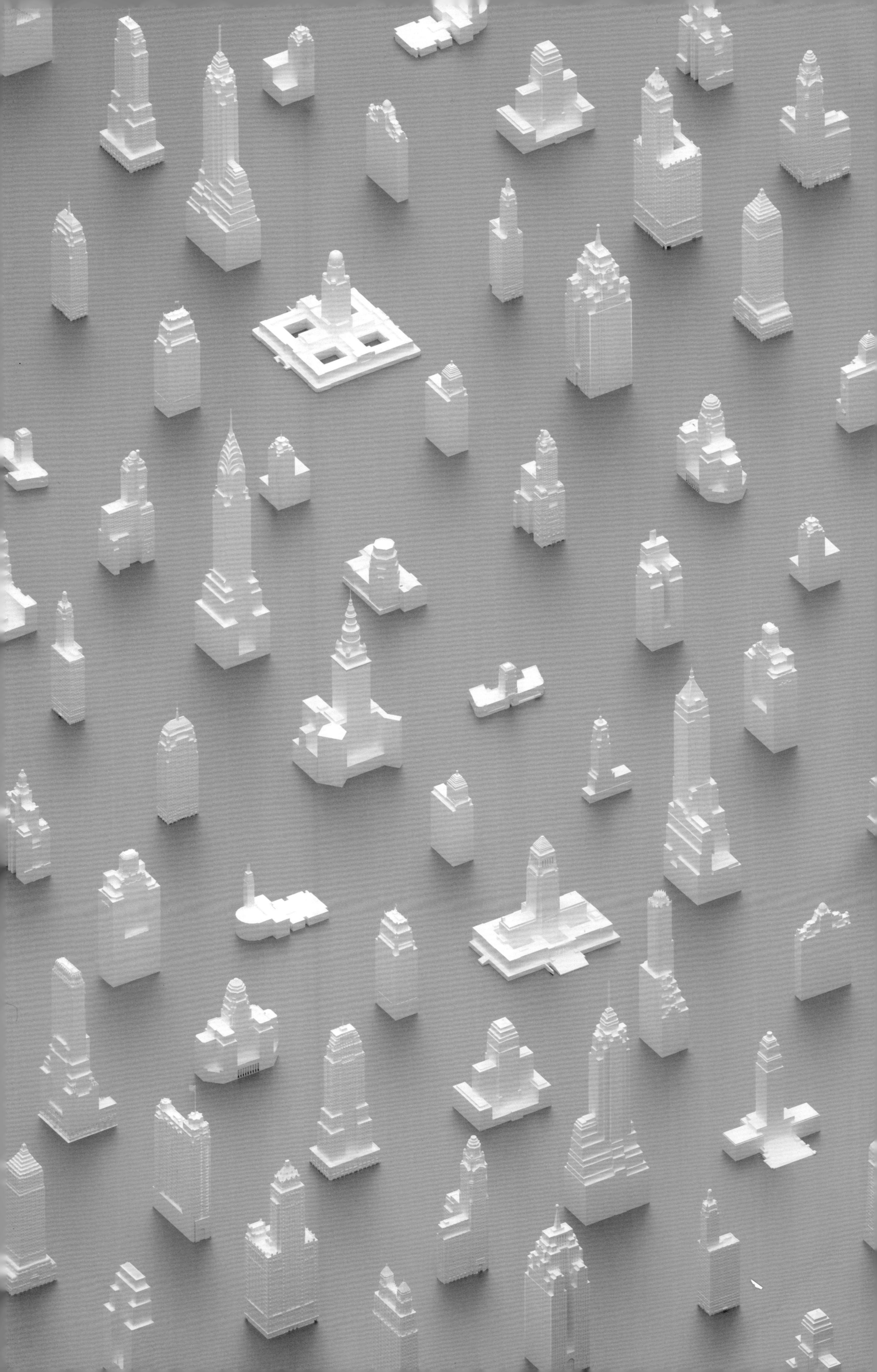

HIGHRISES

Art Deco

100 Spectacular Skyscrapers from the Roaring '20s to the Great Depression

Art by

Chris Hytha

Stories by

Mark Houser

“[A] skyscraper is at the same time a triumph of the machine and a tremendous emotional experience.”

- George Gershwin

To my parents for nurturing my passions from a young age -- Chris

To Diane, for her constant support and love -- Mark

First edition

Photography by **Chris Hytha**
Book design by **Chris Hytha**

To inquire about having **Mark Houser** as a speaker for your next conference or event, send an email to info@housertalks.com.

See the full collection at **HighrisesCollection.com**

ISBN: 979-8-9889537-0-8

Front cover image: Carbide & Carbon Building, Chicago
Table of Contents images: General Electric Building, New York City; Chicago Board of Trade; Los Angeles City Hall; Alabama Power Building, Birmingham

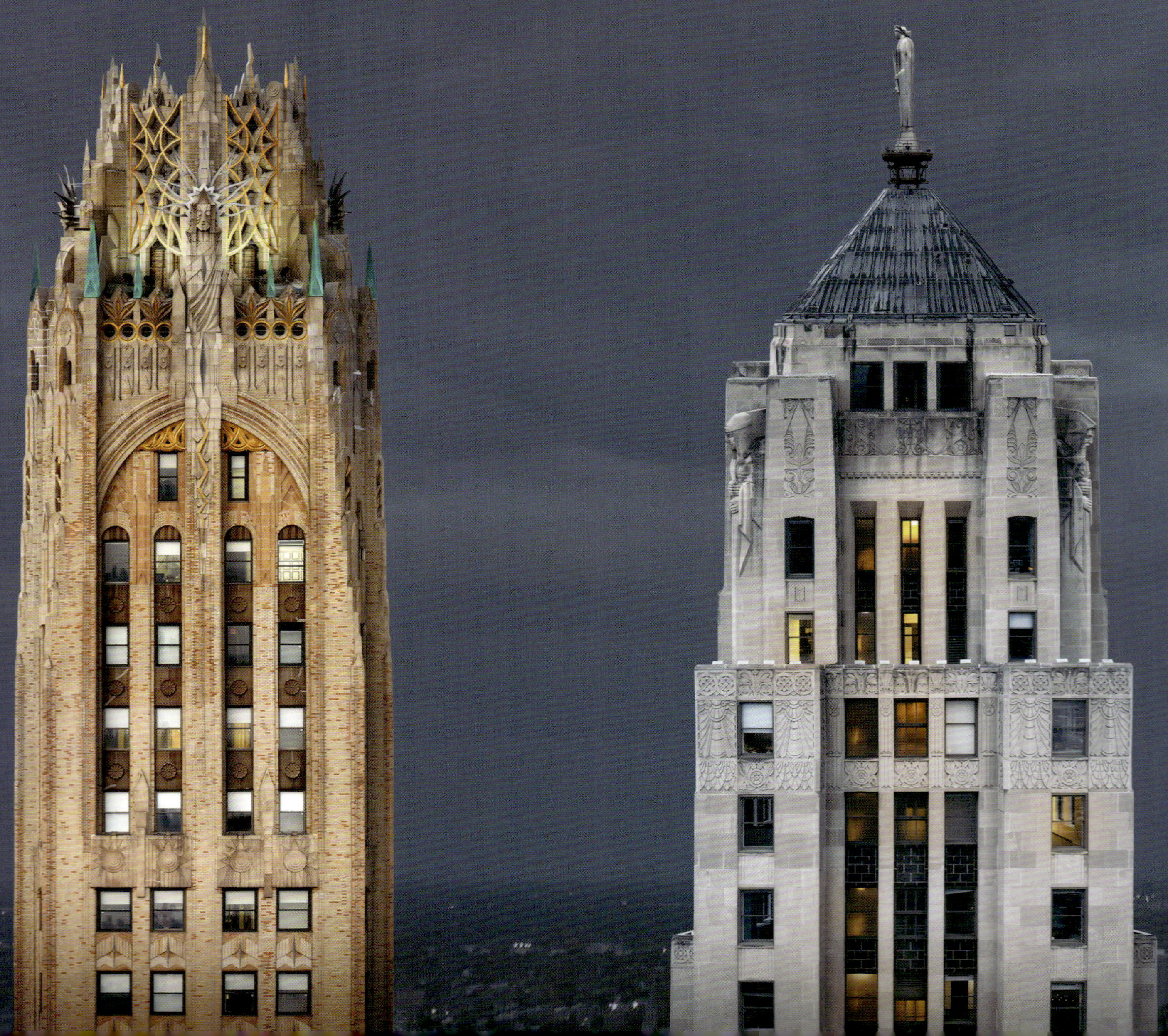

Table of Contents

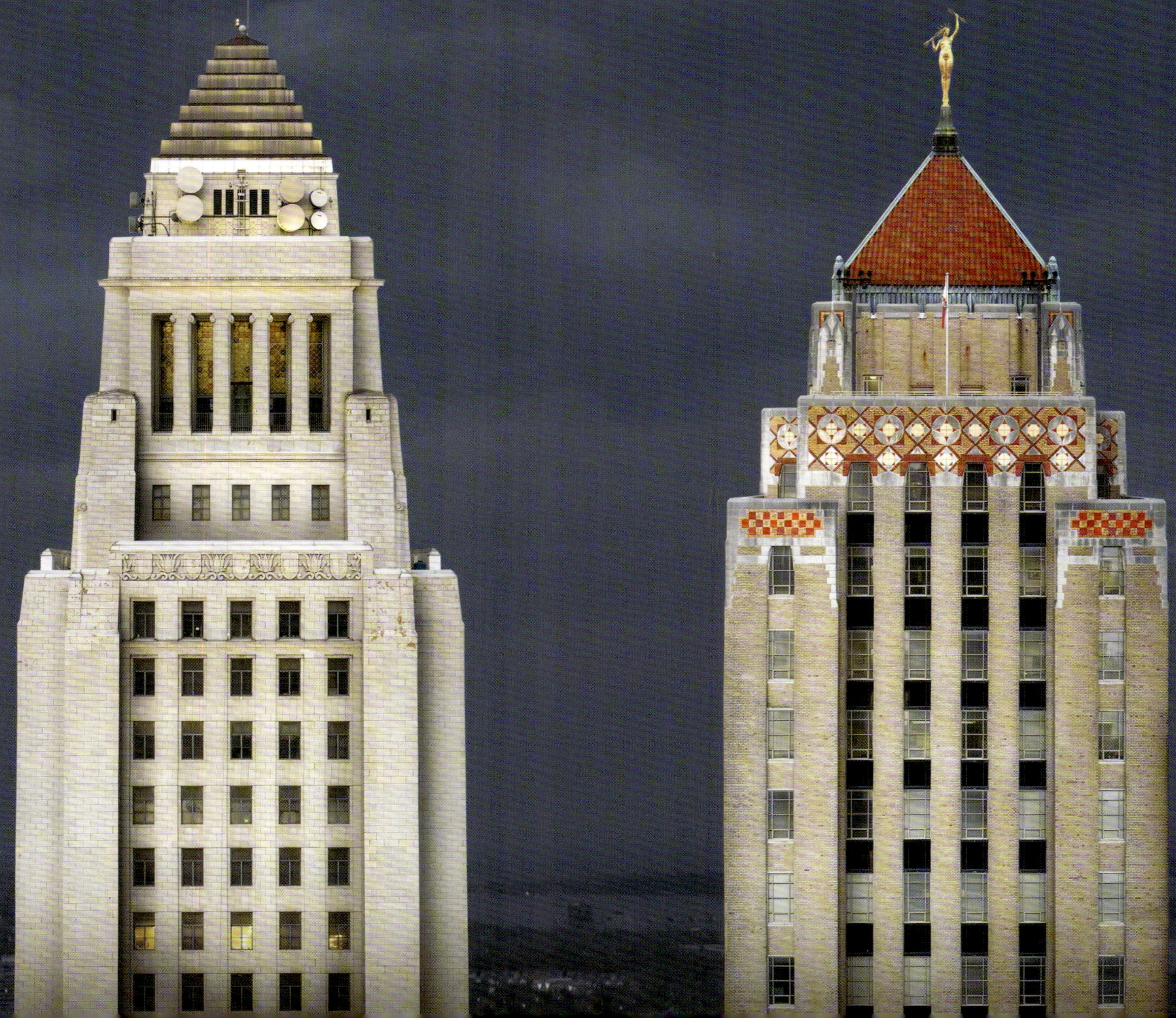

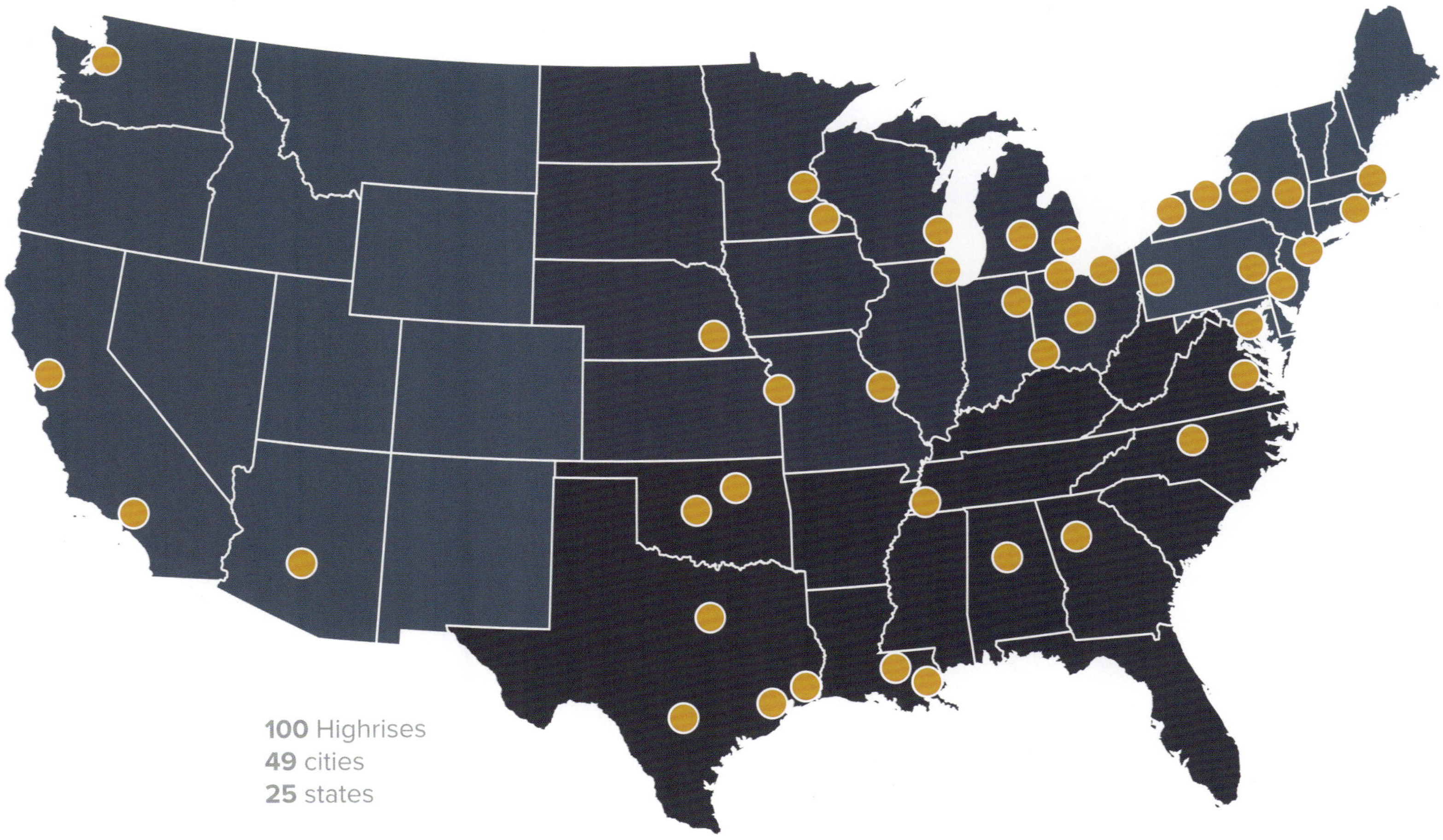

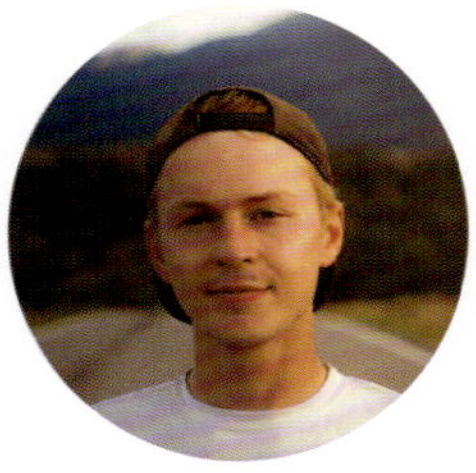

Chris Hytha

hythacg.com @hytha.cg

Chris is a designer and visual artist with a passion for photography and a degree in architecture from Drexel University. His early work focused on the creation of surreal scenes through Photoshop compositing and light painting. This evolved into collections studying the peculiarities of the built environment starting with the Rowhomes Project, which led to this study of historic skyscrapers.

"Reflecting on the past year and a half working on this project, I am most fascinated by how the ornamentation of these urban monuments communicates the context in which they are built. This is something we have lost in the uniform glass towers of the 21st century."

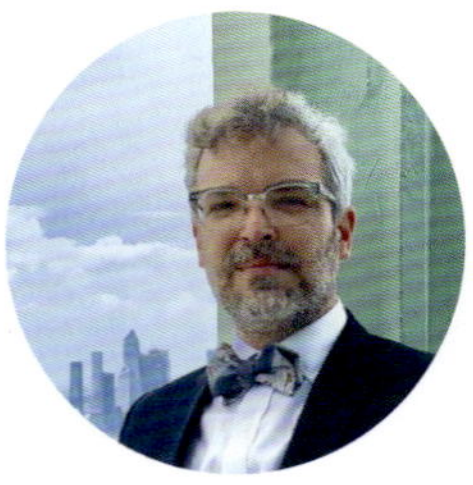

Mark Houser

housertalks.com

Mark is a Pittsburgh-based writer and professional speaker and the author of *MultiStories: 55 Antique Skyscrapers & the Business Tycoons Who Built Them*. A former investigative reporter and award-winning journalist, Mark has spoken to audiences from New York to California and appeared on CNN, FOX, NPR, and CuriosityStream. More than 1,000 people have taken his skyscraper tours.

"The people who commissioned these highrises and the architects who designed them left lasting legacies for their cities. Learning their personal stories makes each building more meaningful and provides insights about change and risk that still resonate with us today."

Introduction

America is where skyscrapers were born. The tall office tower — "a machine that makes the land pay," as the pioneering architect Cass Gilbert aptly put it — originated in Chicago and New York in the 1880s and spread to every large city in the United States within a few decades. Their steel frames were a major technological breakthrough that made these new tall buildings possible, but the girders supported walls that were rooted in the past. The first skyscrapers were cloaked in architectural motifs blending Classical and Renaissance ornamentation, a style known as Beaux-Arts after the French school where most prominent American architects were trained.

Then in the 1920s, something changed. Innovators began to break the old rules. They experimented with new shapes, colors, materials, and designs meant to celebrate the advent of a modern machine age. It was a wildly optimistic moment, one that was brought to a crashing halt by the Great Depression.

Highrises Art Deco is a collection of 100 of the best tall buildings from that brief period. Most of them will be unfamiliar to readers, not only because they are in cities that are not famous for skyscrapers, but because the images are created using technology that presents us with a view quite different from what we can see from the sidewalk.

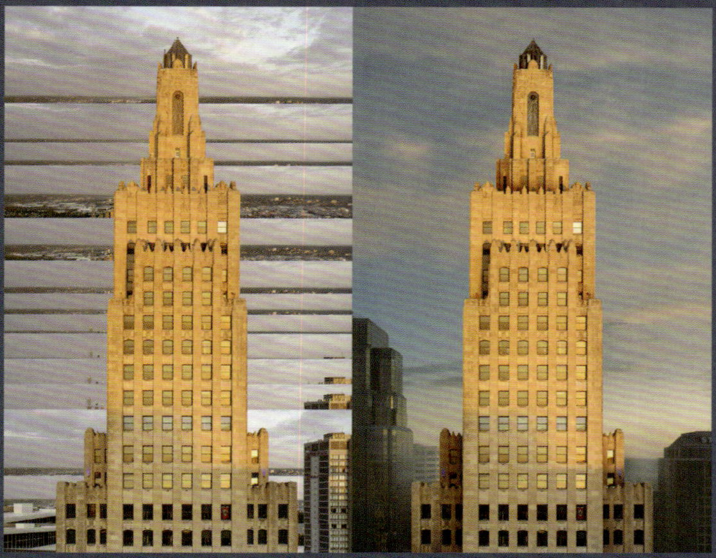

Each Highrises image is stitched together from more than a dozen photos taken at each floor level. A separate background is then composited in.

The Art

Rather than a single snapshot, each Highrises image is a composite made up of a series of photos taken by drone at each floor of the building, usually at sunrise or sunset. They are stitched together manually, eliminating perspective and creating a flattened scan similar to an orthographic architectural elevation drawing. A separate background image taken at the same location is composited into the frame. Lighting and shadow adjustments finish the visual with a subtle, rendering-like quality. Some minor creative liberties may be taken to enhance the presentation, such as removing modern rooftop equipment, but each image is a realistic photographic representation of the building.

The Research

Just as Highrises images would be impossible without current technology, the stories would be too. Each one begins with extensive research of online newspaper archives for coverage about the buildings and companies when they opened, as well as stories of the business leaders responsible for their construction. The internet also offers troves of journal articles, preservationist documents such as the National Register of Historic Places, and out-of-print business biographies to review. Recent media reporting and history and architecture blogs round out the picture, supplemented by the properties' own websites, interviews, and visits to the buildings.

Choosing the Buildings

Several criteria determined which buildings were selected for this book. First, they are exemplars of the style known as Art Deco or are otherwise significant skyscrapers that contributed to its development. Only buildings with a tall and narrow profile can fit the standard 2:3 aspect ratio of a Highrises composition. Permission was sought and granted by the Federal Aviation Administration for every drone flight in controlled airspace. Last but not least, the project prioritized skyscrapers beyond Chicago and New York to demonstrate the plethora of attractive and historic tall buildings in places most people would not think to look.

Highrises Collection

The buildings in this book are only half of the collection of historic tall buildings celebrated and profiled in the Highrises project, which has involved nearly two years of work and travel to dozens of cities. Many more images and stories can be found at HighrisesCollection.com.

What is Art Deco?

A 1925 Paris exhibition, the Exposition Internationale des Arts Décoratifs et Industriels Modernes, is the source of the term Art Deco. The show's displays of modern furnishings and designs accentuated trends favoring experimentation and bold expression of form and color then sweeping the worlds of art, fashion, design, and architecture.

Government regulation played a key role too. With skyscrapers turning Broadway into a gloomy canyon, New York passed a 1916 zoning code making new buildings step back gradually to let in more light and air. Other cities followed suit, and the setback shape quickly was seen as modern, preferred even where it was not mandated.

A widely promoted 1922 international contest sponsored by the Chicago Tribune to design its new headquarters awarded second prize to a setback skyscraper concept by Finnish architect Eliel Saarinen. Though his design was never built, it exerted a strong influence on the Jazz Age skyscrapers that followed.

Nobody called them Art Deco then; the term was not used until many decades later. Buildings that deviated from traditional styles were simply called "modern" — or "moderne" by the sophisticates. Other contemporary labels ranged from "zigzag" to "American Perpendicular Gothic." What they all shared was a sense of exuberance and optimism that defined the 1920s.

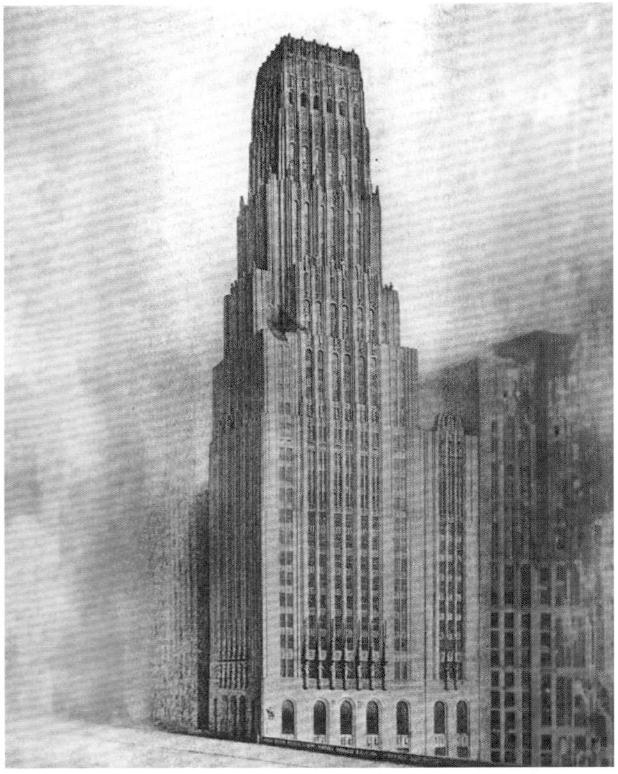

Eliel Saarinen's unbuilt Chicago Tribune design greatly influenced skyscraper construction.

Eagles

The patriotic symbol, often in a blocky modernist shape, expresses American pride in the skyscrapers defining the nation's cities.

Left to right: Buffalo City Hall (28), Fidelity Building (106), Times-Star Building (116), Washington Athletic Club (168)

Color

Many buildings of the era added a polychromatic pop to exteriors and interiors by using glazed terracotta tile in vivid hues.

Left to right: Nebraska State Capitol (112), Eastern Columbia Building (130), David Stott Building (94), Mayo Clinic (102)

Figures

Stylized representation of the human form used exaggerated and muscular lines, sometimes verging on the abstract.

Left to right: Chicago Board of Trade (72), Home Savings Bank Building (24), Times-Star Building (116), Nebraska State Capitol (112)

Spandrels

Decorative panels above and below window openings kept people's eyes trained on the vertical columns to emphasize height.

Left to right: First National Bank Building (104), Wilshire Professional Building (142), Bullock's Wilshire (132), AIU Citadel (122)

Reliefs

The setback shape of Art Deco skyscrapers recalled ziggurats and coincided with new interest in Mesopotamian and other ancient art.

Left to right: Medinah Athletic Club (76), Tower Building (42), United Office Building (34), Houston City Hall (202)

Clocks

A familiar feature of pre-skyscraper tall buildings, the town clock got an updated makeover with electric and neon lights.

Left to right: Central Terminal (30), Camden City Hall (44), Eastern Columbia Building (130), Houston City Hall (202)

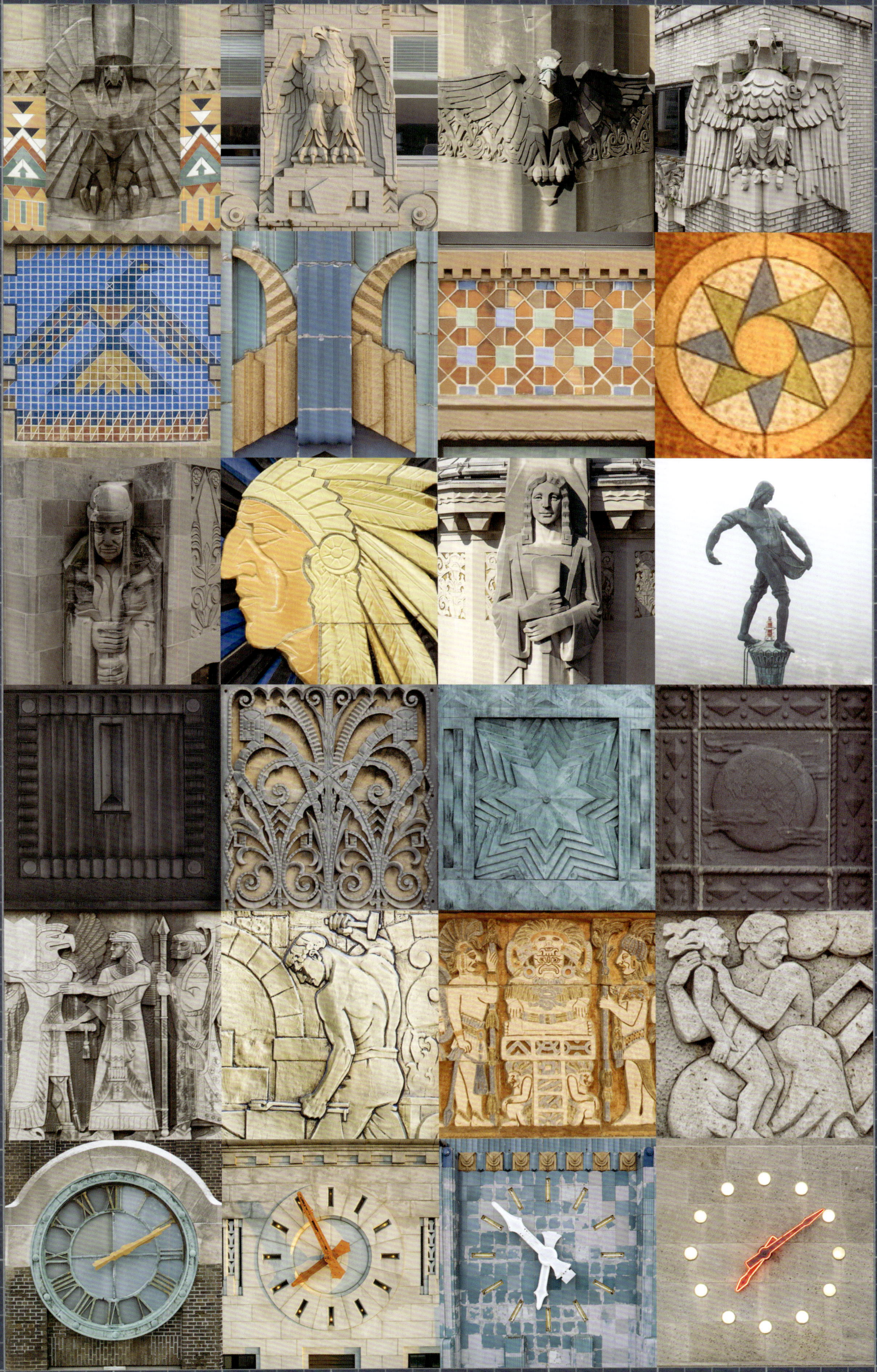

Numbers indicate how many buildings are featured in each city.

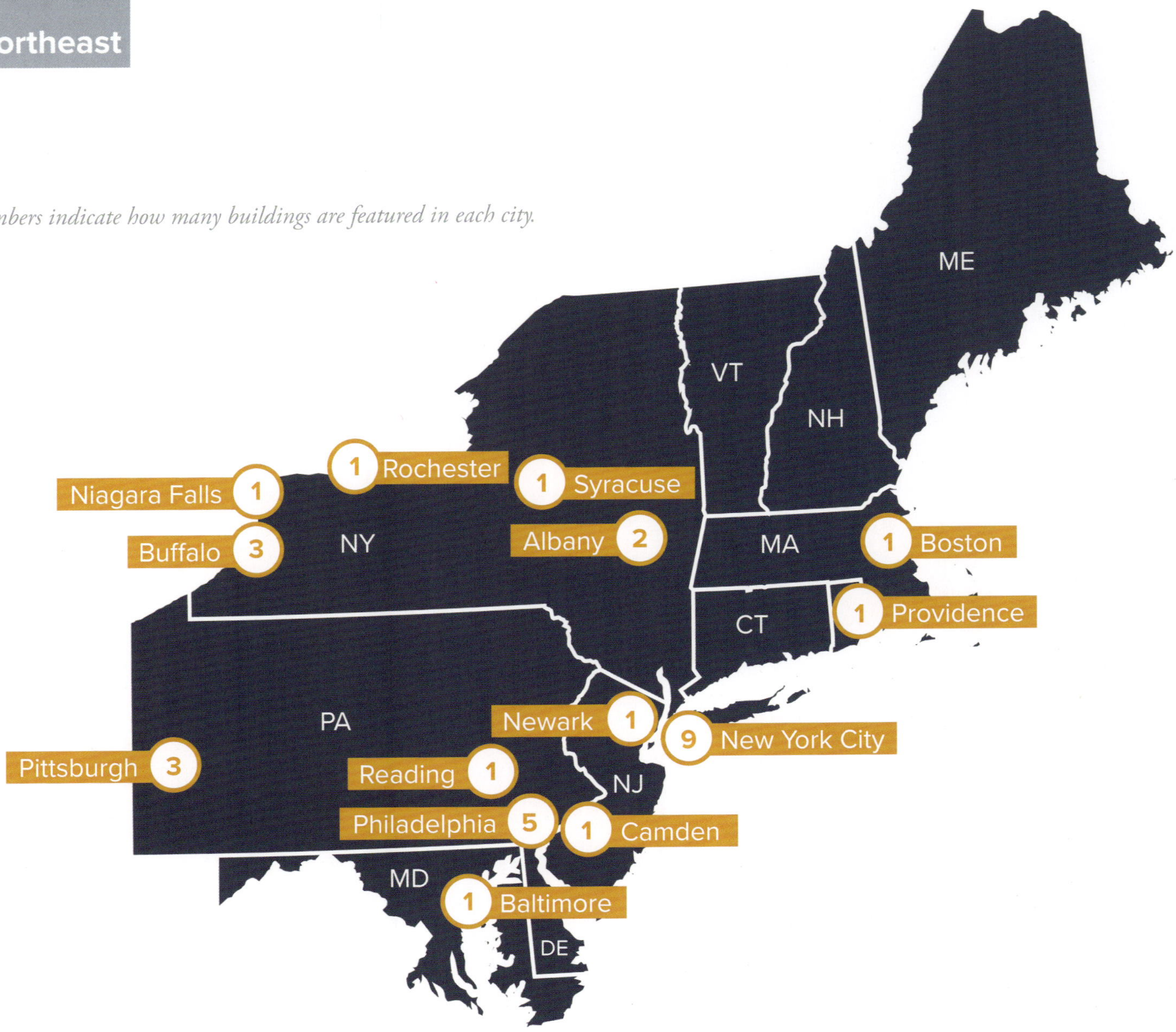

NORTHEAST

When the Chrysler Building surpassed the Eiffel Tower in 1930 to become the tallest structure on Earth, it was the first time a skyscraper claimed that distinction, rather than a church or monument. The honor, while historic, was fleeting. The Empire State Building seized supremacy the next year, aided by a 200-foot mast its builders implausibly claimed would be a hitching post for zeppelins.

Despite being usurped, the Chrysler Building with its sensational Art Deco spire remains a Big Apple icon nearly a century since its debut. Other Manhattan skyscrapers from its era may be overlooked by the passing throngs, but in rediscovering these landmarks, we can gain a sense of the awe they once inspired.

New York architects won commissions across the Northeast, and regional architects also made important contributions to their city skylines. Philadelphia was a hotbed of tower projects, though none dared to surpass the height of the William Penn statue crowning City Hall. In eastern seaboard cities from Baltimore to Boston, and in the manufacturing metropolises spread across western New York and down into Pittsburgh, skyscraper creators added their interpretations to the emerging canon of Art Deco.

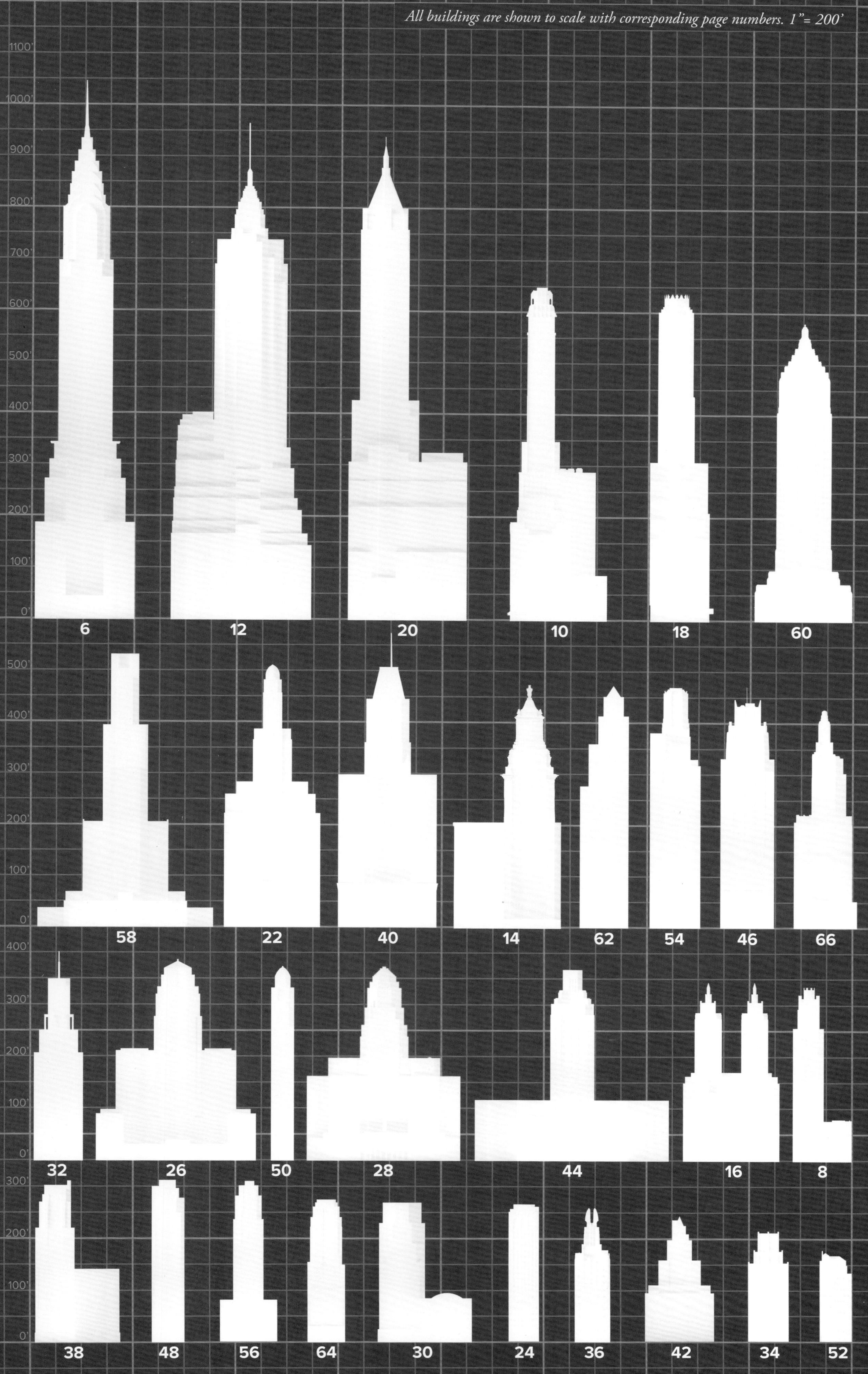

All buildings are shown to scale with corresponding page numbers. 1"= 200'
1100'
1000'
900'
800'
700'
600'
500'
400'
300'
200'
100'
0'
6
12
20
10
18
60
58
22
40
14
62
54
46
66
32
26
50
28
44
16
8
38
48
56
64
30
24
36
42
34
52

Chrysler Building

New York City, **NY**

Address .... **405 Lexington Ave.**
Opened **1930**
Height .... **1046'**
Stories **71**
Style .... **Art Deco**
Architect .... **William Van Alen**

As this and a competing skyscraper neared the finish of their race to the clouds in October 1929, headlines blared that the Manhattan Company Building (p. 20) would capture the title of world's tallest. But the Chrysler Building architect knew what reporters did not: Concealed inside his highrise's topmost stories was a 125-foot steel spire waiting to be hoisted up and bolted on.

Walt Chrysler was a railroad mechanic who rose to executive rank before switching to the nascent automobile industry. He oversaw production for General Motors, then started his own car company and began building a huge factory to compete against GM and Ford. Chrysler also acquired a stalled Midtown skyscraper project and told its designer to make it more eye-catching.

William Van Alen responded with eagle gargoyles, winged hood ornaments, and tire and hubcap patterns in the brickwork. He replaced a planned glass dome with gleaming stainless steel, and raised the spire like a middle finger toward his former partner, Manhattan Company Building architect Craig Severance, who had dumped Van Alen years earlier.

The red marble lobby features ceiling murals of an assembly line and the Chrysler Building itself, which was not universally admired. Influential critic Lewis Mumford savaged it for "meaningless voluptuousness" and expressed relief that the Great Depression would halt further displays of rich men's "barbarous egos."

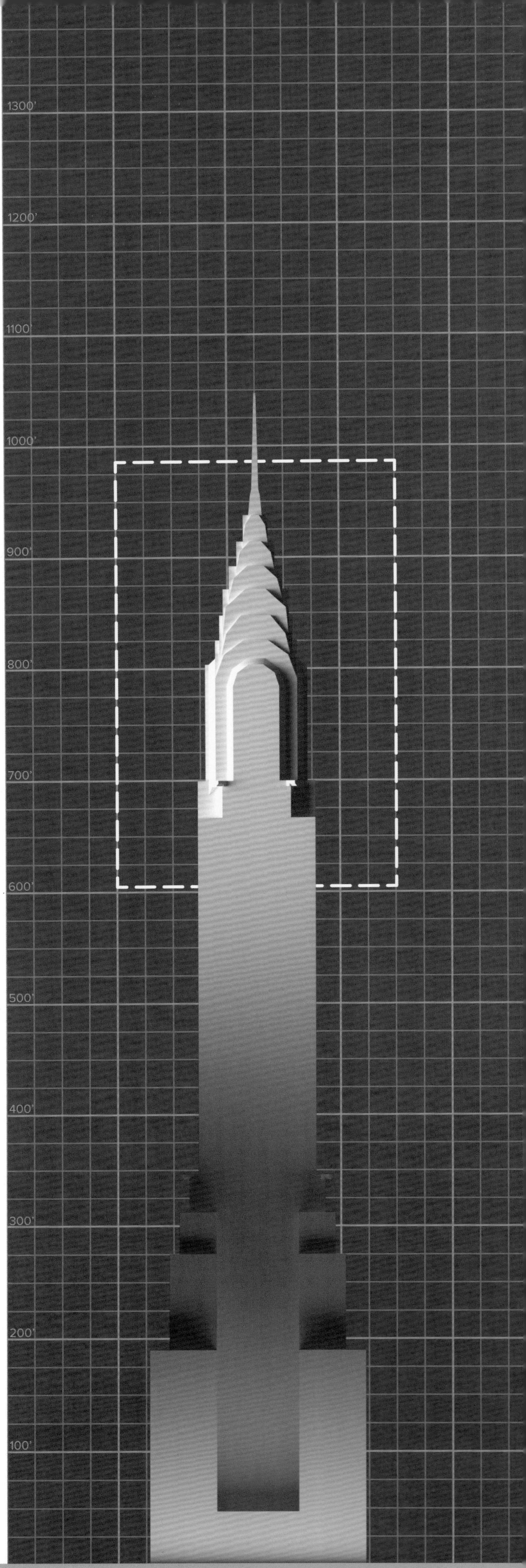

South Elevation *1" = 100'*

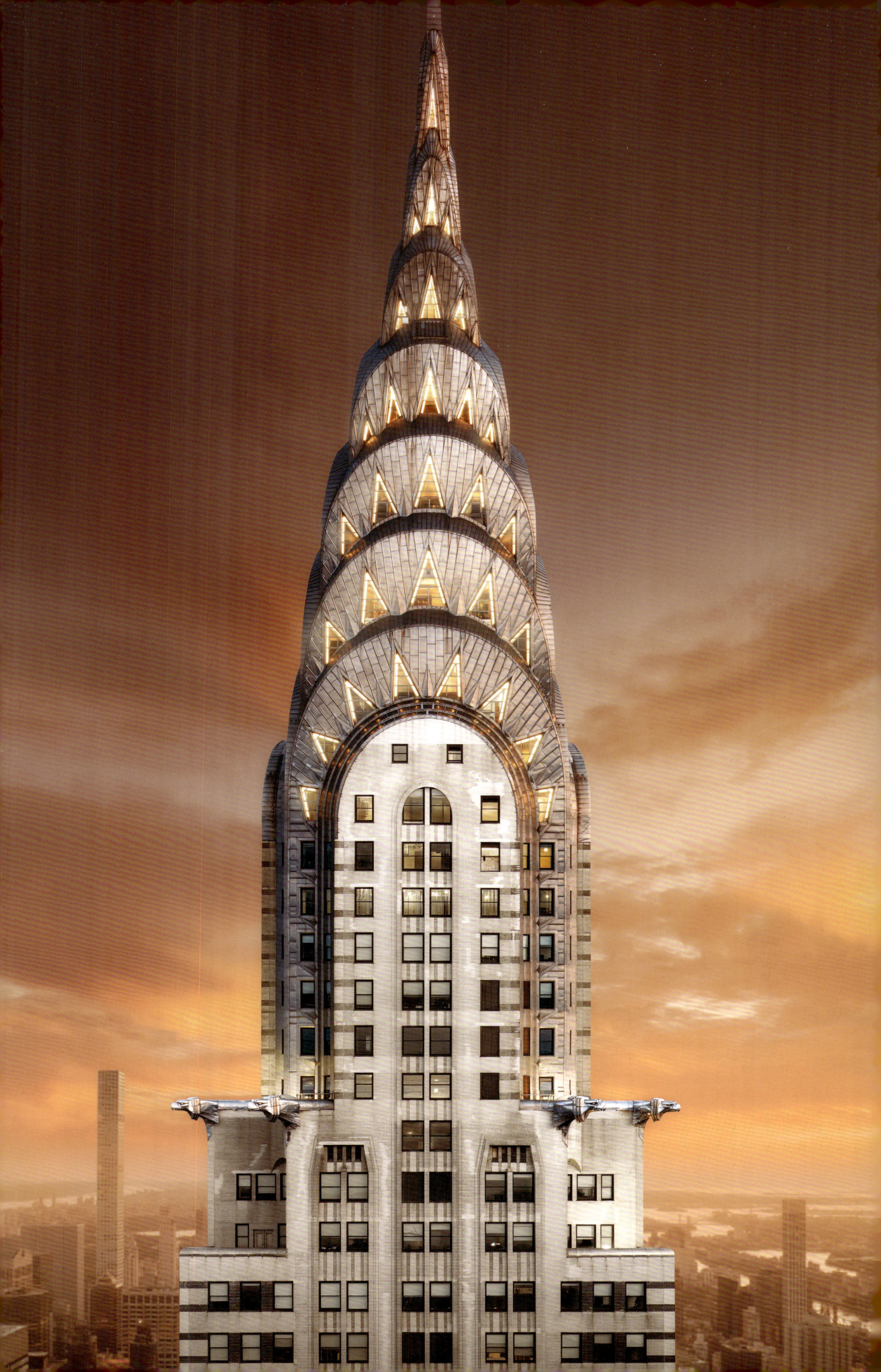

American Radiator
Building

New York City, **NY** — Bryant Park Hotel

Address	**40 W. 40th St.**
Opened	**1924**
Height	**338'**
Stories	**23**
Style	**Art Deco, Gothic**
Architect	**Raymond Hood**

Rising from obscurity with the winning entry in the 1922 Chicago Tribune skyscraper competition, Raymond Hood next created this radical black brick tower, which he said was inspired in part by the Eliel Saarinen design that took second prize.

To avoid the monotony of black window holes that he said made buildings look like waffles, Hood camouflaged the voids with a dark facade, then offset the gloom with gold accents. His modernized gloss on the more historic Gothic style used in the Tribune Tower helped to blaze a new trail for architecture a year before the Paris design expo that spawned the term "Art Deco."

People flocked to Bryant Park to inspect the remarkable highrise. The dean of architecture at Harvard deemed it magnificent and daring, though "open to the charge of vulgarity." Painter Georgia O'Keeffe portrayed it in one of her abstract canvases.

Hood praised American Radiator for backing his vision; he had designed radiator covers for the company before his rise to fame. Its president, Clarence Woolley, had cofounded a Detroit predecessor firm, and grew the home heating conglomerate through European expansion before merging with a maker of bathroom fixtures to become American Standard. The building is now a hotel, and its original radiator showroom in the basement is a cocktail lounge.

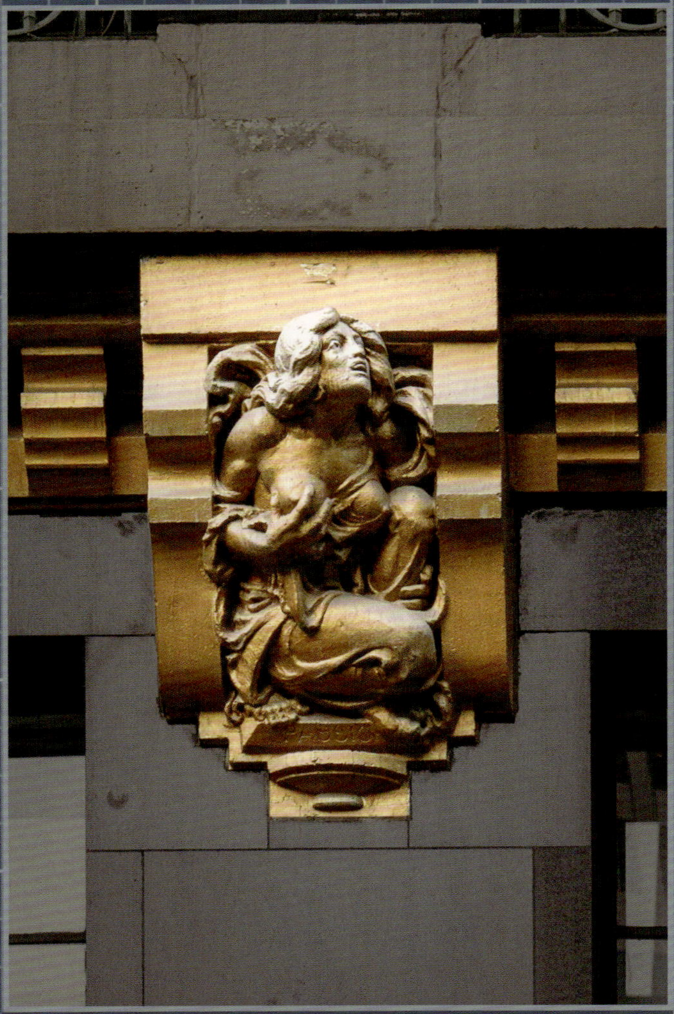

Exaggerated figures called grotesques decorate the corbels. This one is "Passion," hot as a radiator.

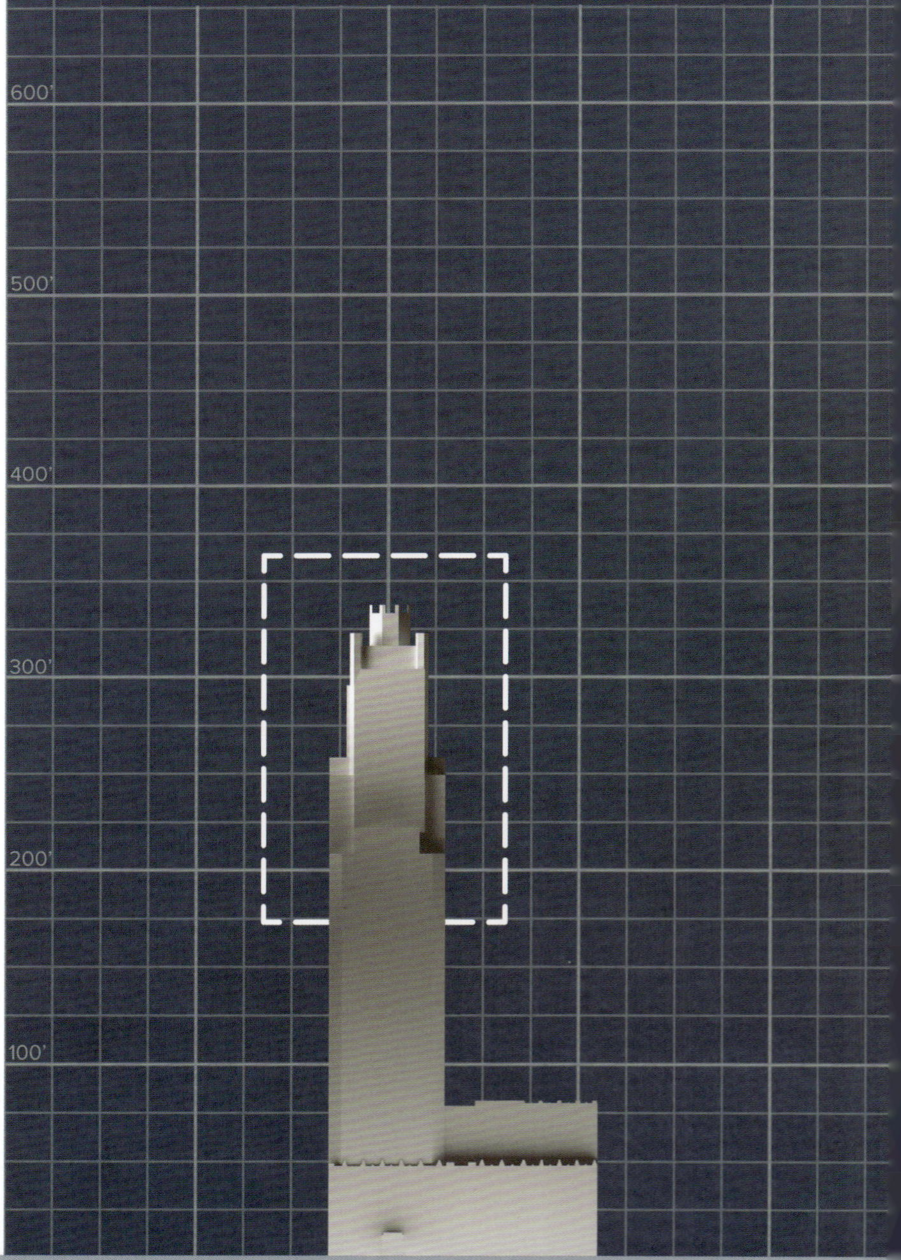

North Elevation *1" = 100'*

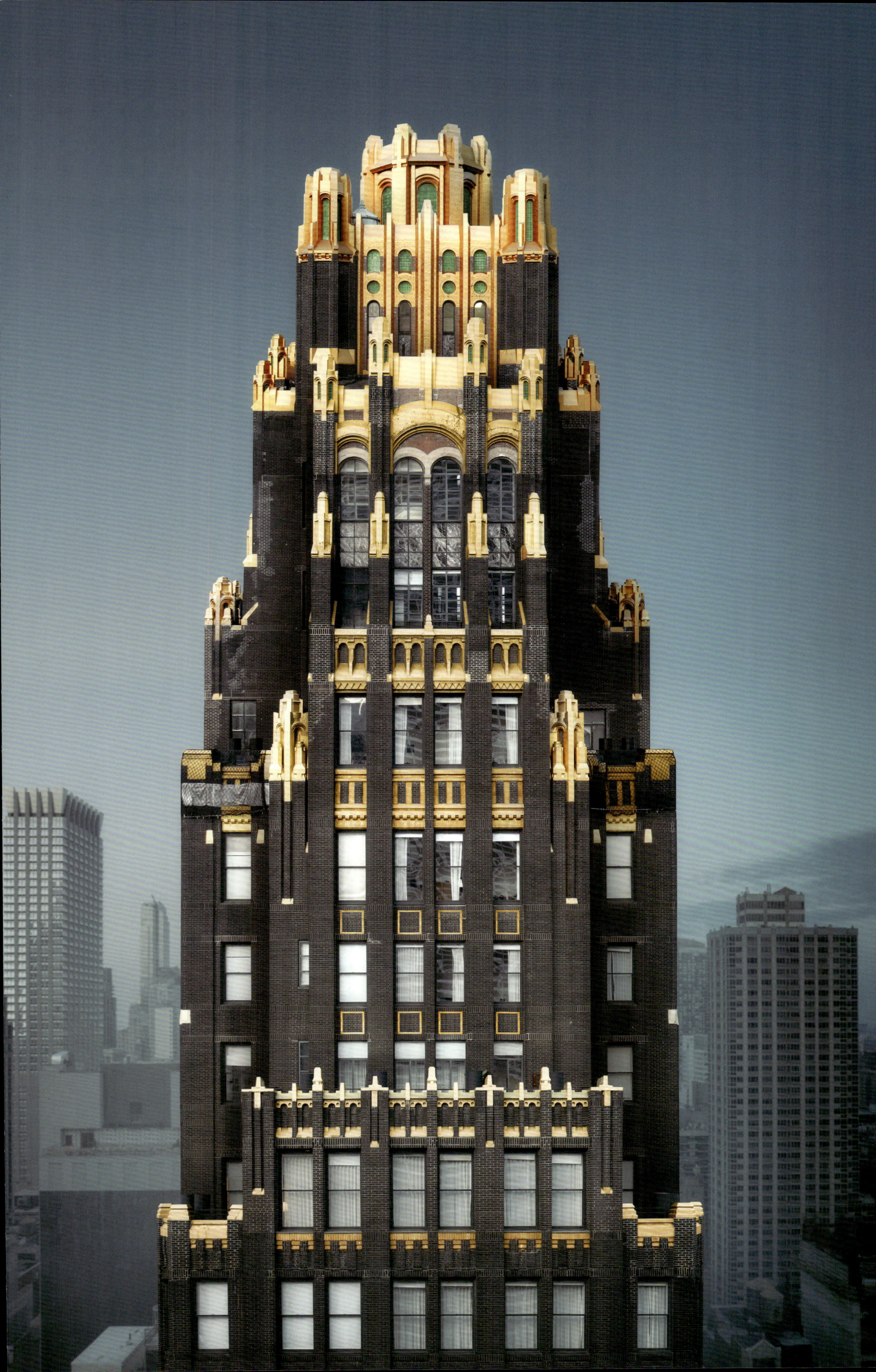

Chanin Building

New York City, **NY**

Address	**122 E. 42nd St.**
Opened	**1929**
Height	**649'**
Stories	**56**
Style	**Art Deco**
Architect	**Sloan & Robertson**

Unlike its neighbor, the Chrysler Building, this highrise displays its finest ornamentation where pedestrians can most easily see it. A wraparound bronze frieze at sidewalk level also makes a political statement, depicting an evolutionary procession of amoebas, sea creatures, and geese at a time when fundamentalists were battling to delete Darwinism from schoolbooks.

Born in Brooklyn, Irwin Chanin was the oldest child of Jewish immigrants who took their family back to Ukraine for a time before returning in his teen years. Earning an engineering degree at Cooper Union, Chanin went into business as a builder. Houses in Bensonhurst led to Brooklyn office buildings, then Manhattan theaters, including the 6,000-seat Roxy, and a mammoth hotel near Times Square.

Next came this, briefly the tallest skyscraper in Midtown. "There's no use going any higher unless you want to see the gates of paradise," announced Mayor Jimmy Walker at its dedication, although bigger projects were already underway.

Sculptor Rene Chambellan did the frieze, along with a handsome terracotta band of curling plants above it, plus bronze reliefs of striving men and hyperkinetic radiator grills in the entryways. From the headquarters atop his tower, Chanin designed two landmark apartments on Central Park West, the Majestic and Century, and showed up to work daily until his death at age 96.

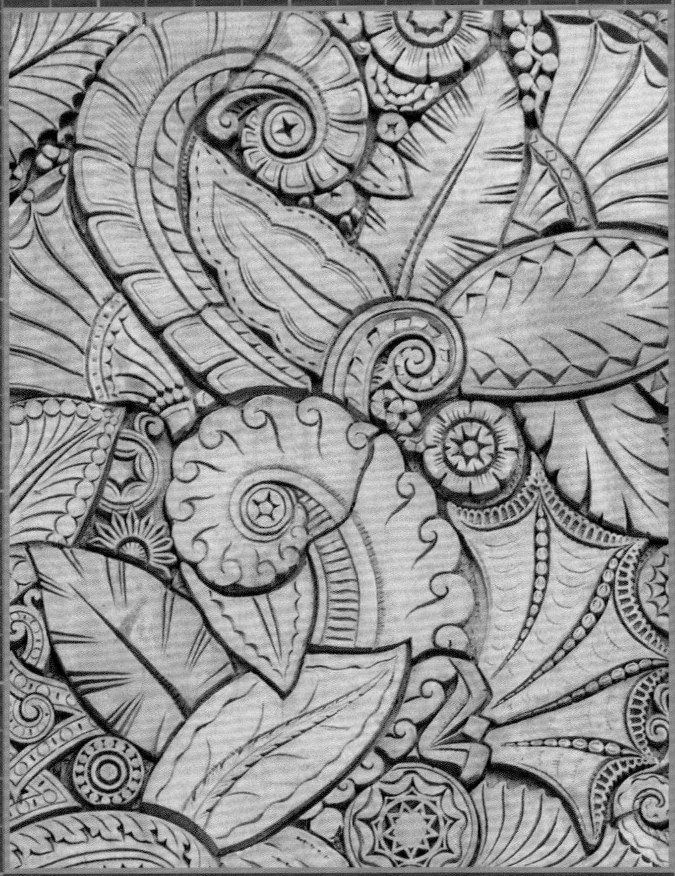

Ferns curl like ocean waves in the terracotta frieze.

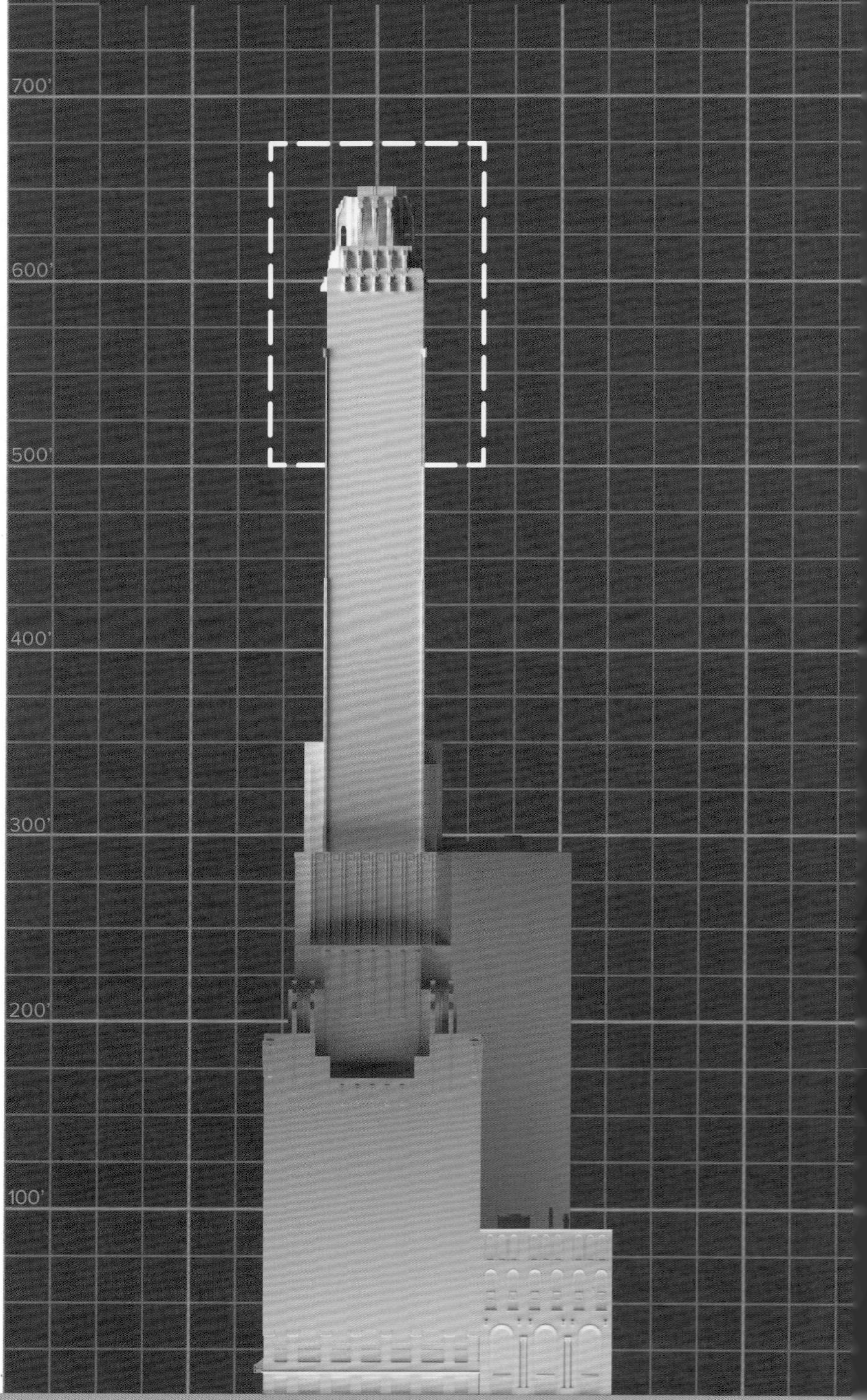

North Elevation *1" = 100'*

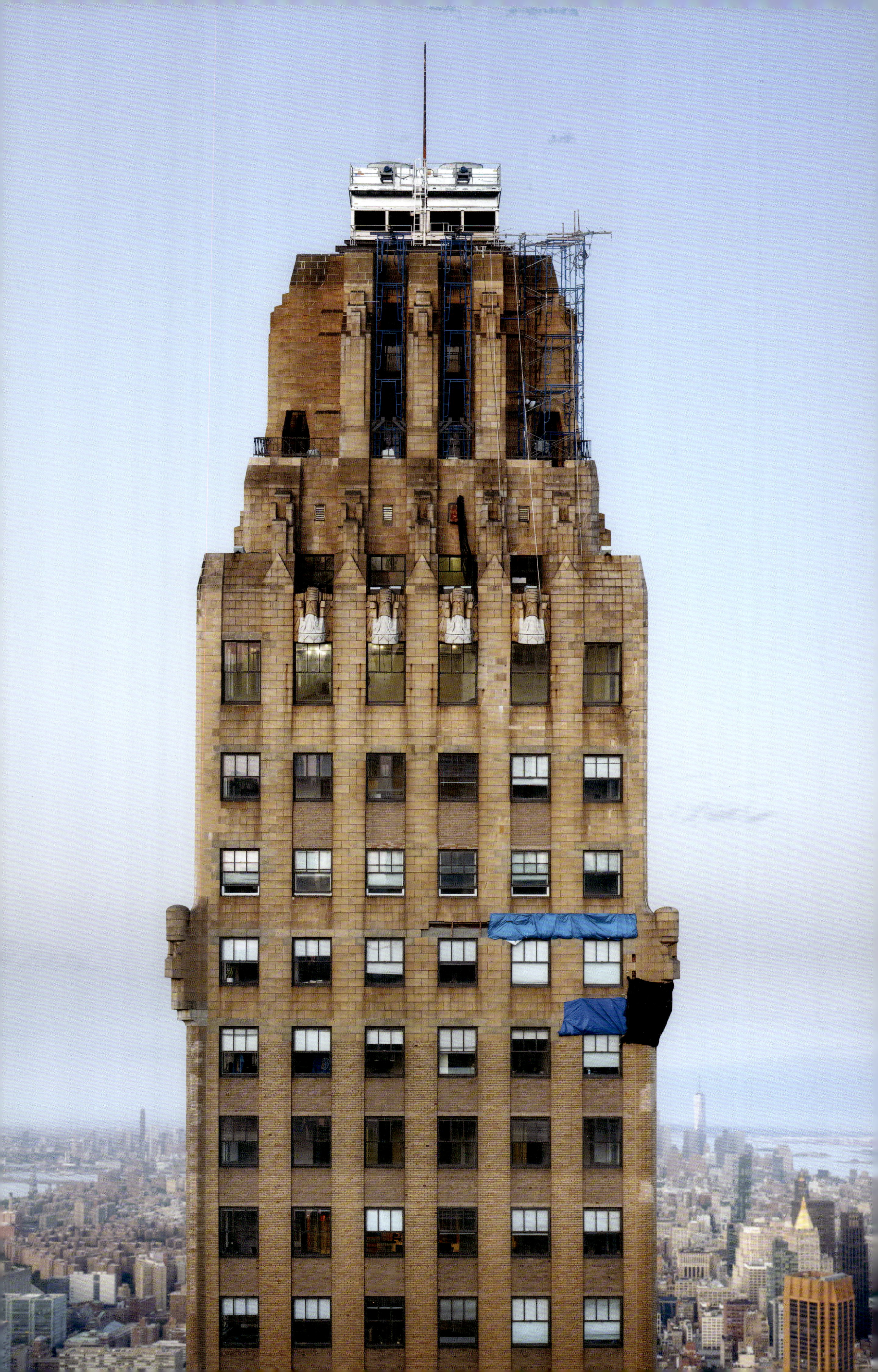

Cities Service
Building

New York City, **NY**

Address	**70 Pine St.**
Opened	**1932**
Height	**952’**
Stories	**66**
Style	**Art Deco**
Architect	**Holton & George**

Like a snowcapped mountain peak, this Financial District tower built for the company now known as Citgo has a shining white summit. Terraces where oil executives once conferred now furnish dizzying vistas to penthouse dwellers and patrons of an upscale cocktail lounge and restaurant.

Henry Doherty quit school at ten and worked at various Midwest utilities before launching Cities Service, a holding company that eventually controlled almost 200 oil, gas, power, light, and streetcar subsidiaries. A self-taught engineer with 150 patents, Doherty also devised a motorized bed for his penthouse that rolled out onto the balcony for fresh air.

Severe arthritis nearly forced him to retire in 1927, and the top two floors of his skyscraper, originally intended as a new apartment for him, instead became a boardroom and a public observatory. Rather than quit, the longtime bachelor got married and became a crusader for government regulation of oil drilling — which led to laws forcing his company to sell its public utility holdings and focus on petroleum.

Citgo left decades ago, though its triangle logo can be seen carved into the stone entrances of what is now a luxury apartment highrise. It can also be seen above sculpted aluminum elevator doors in a stunning earth-toned marble lobby .

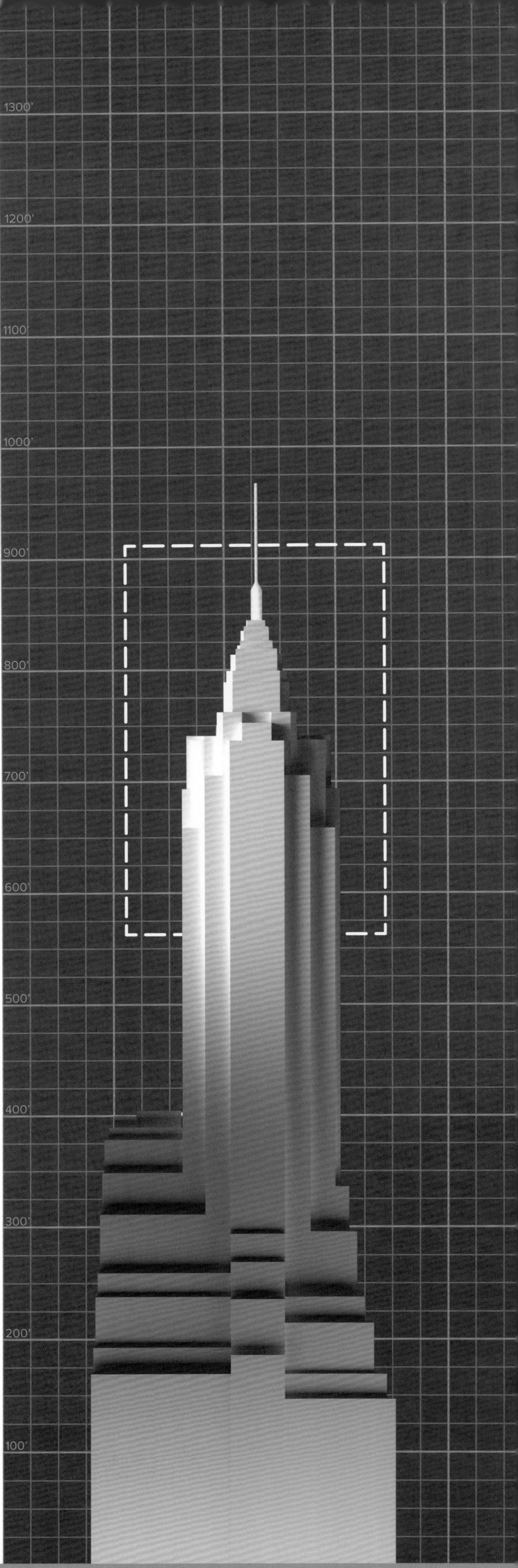

South Elevation *1" = 100'*

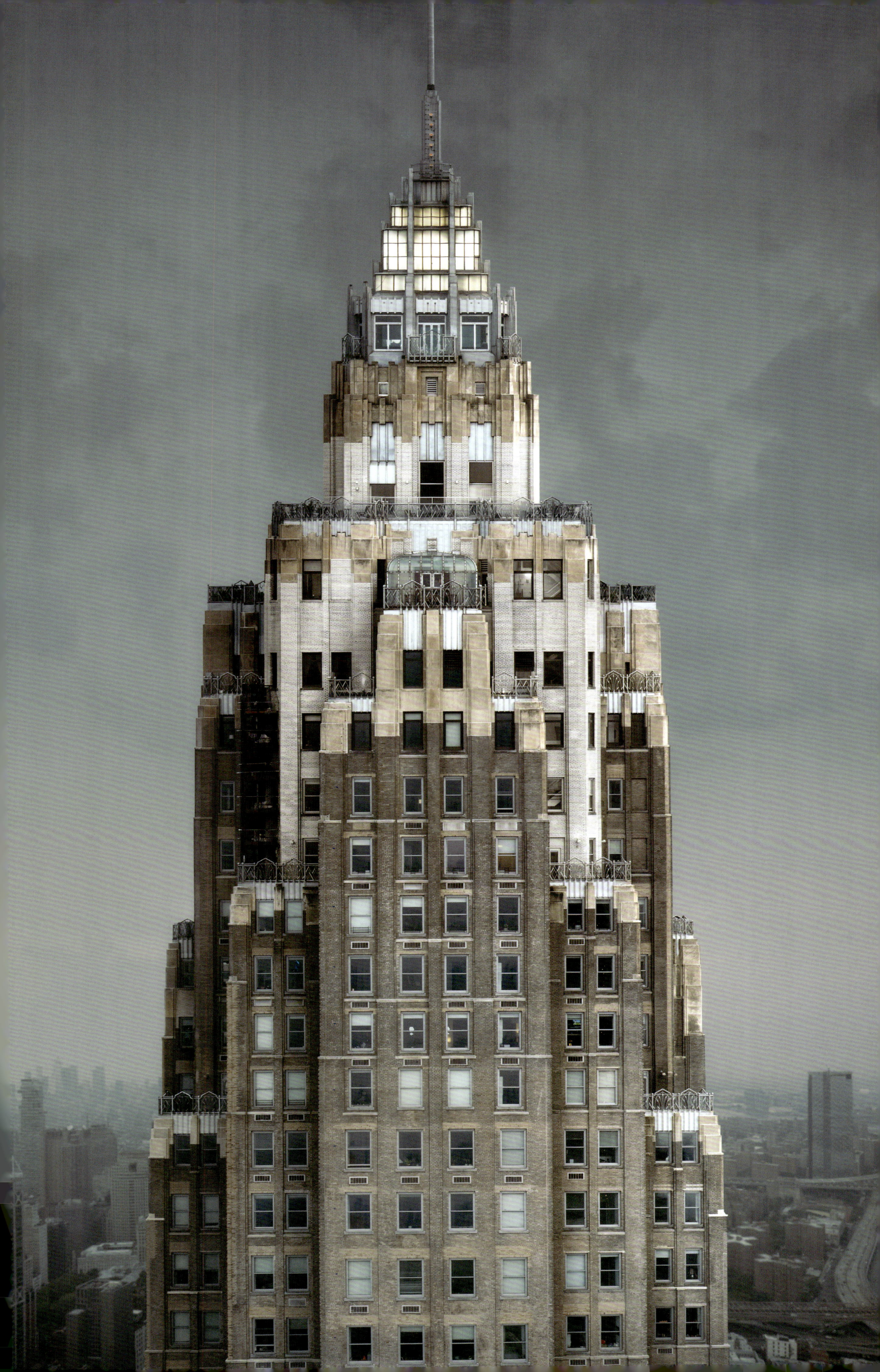

Consolidated
Edison Building

New York City, **NY**

Address	**4 Irving Pl.**
Opened	**1928**
Height	**478'**
Stories	**26**
Style	**Neoclassical**
Architect	**Warren & Wetmore**

A shining lantern beacon marks this highrise headquarters of New York's premier power company. Briefly known as the Consolidated Gas Building, it changed names in 1936 when the utility rebranded in favor of a subsidiary that had grown to dominate the revenue stream.

City lights were primarily fueled with coal gas in 1882, when the self-taught inventor Thomas Edison fired up his first electric power station on Pearl Street in Manhattan. Among its first 59 customers was the New York Times, which praised Edison's bulbs that did not flicker or smell and burned much cooler than gaslights. Edison's customer base ballooned, and Consolidated Gas bought his company in 1899 to harness the upstart rival.

This highrise was an expansion of adjoining headquarters built in 1914, which explains its matching throwback style. Stone-carved flaming urns on either side of the clocks memorialized 74 employees who died fighting in World War I. The company also developed gas masks for the army during the war, a fact noted at the dedication by president George Courtelyou, a former White House stenographer and secretary to three presidents who went on to hold cabinet posts for the commerce and treasury departments before taking the reins at the power company.

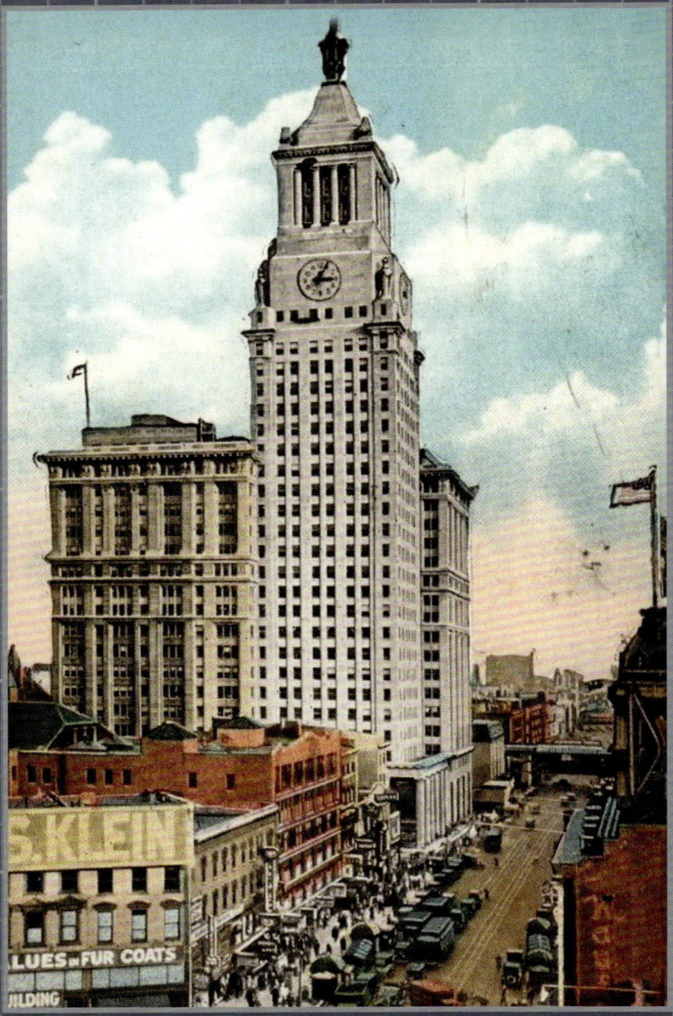

The tower was part of a major expansion of an earlier Consolidated Gas headquarters, pictured at left on this vintage postcard.

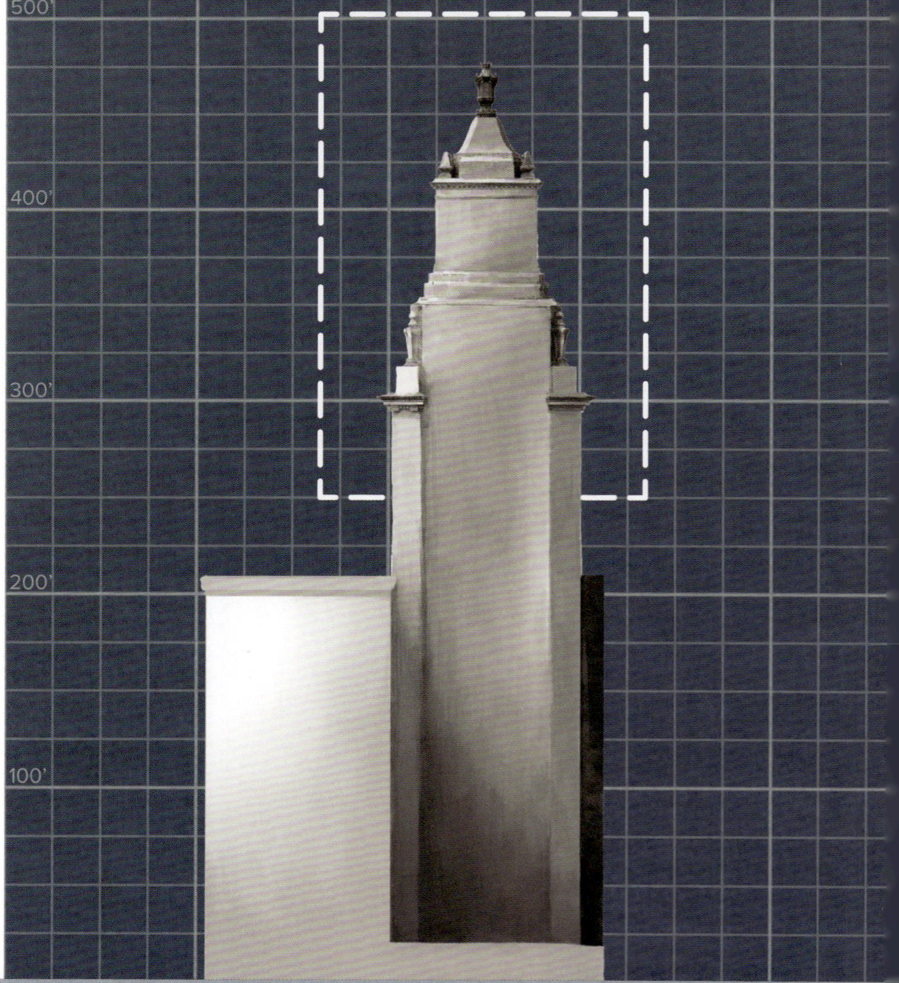

West Elevation *1" = 100'*

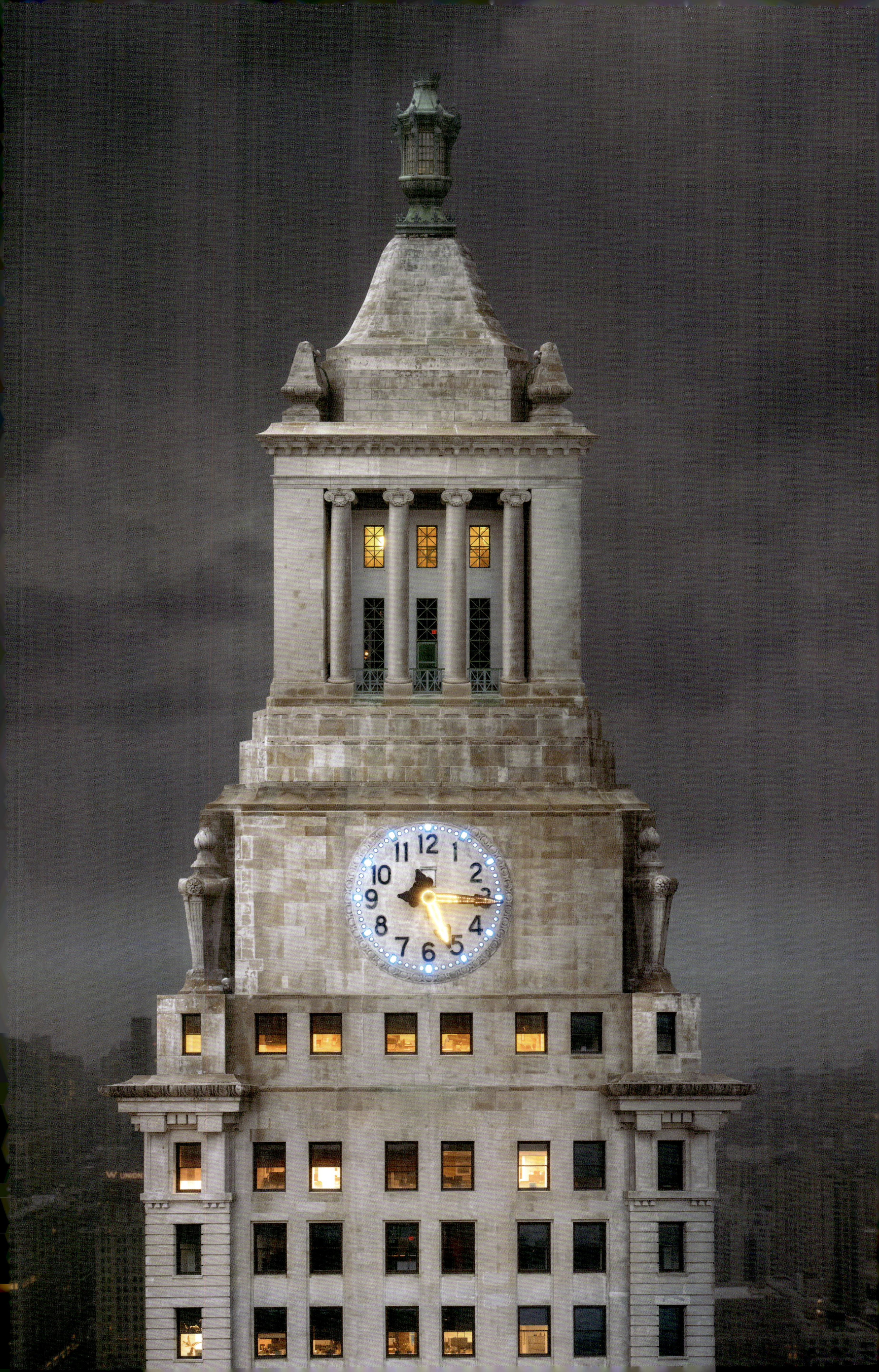

The Eldorado

New York City, **NY**

Address	**300 Central Park West**
Opened	**1931**
Height	**346'**
Stories	**34**
Style	**Art Deco**
Architect	**Margon & Holder**

Northernmost of four twin-towered apartments peering over the western edge of Central Park, the Eldorado makes a gorgeous reflection in the Jacqueline Kennedy Onassis Reservoir. Call it apt for a longtime abode of celebrities from Groucho to Bono to Marilyn Monroe, who once sang a sultry "Happy Birthday" to Jackie's husband.

A 1929 state law that permitted towers on multiple dwelling units triggered a burst of the doubled-up configuration, which yielded more windows for penthouses. The first was the San Remo, a Renaissance-style design by hotel architect Emery Roth. While that was underway, Roth was hired to consult on the Eldorado, which mimics the San Remo's shape but with a modern facade.

Louis Klosk, the project's Bronx-based developer, had his own architects create the Eldorado's Art Deco appearance. Construction commenced weeks after the stock market crashed, and Klosk lost the building a year later. Another pair of Art Deco twin tower apartments, the Majestic and Century, went up at the park's southern reaches before the Great Depression ended the trend.

The Eldorado became a co-op in 1982. Only one of its narrow tower tops — the southern one with the trees seen here — contains a penthouse apartment. The other holds a water tank.

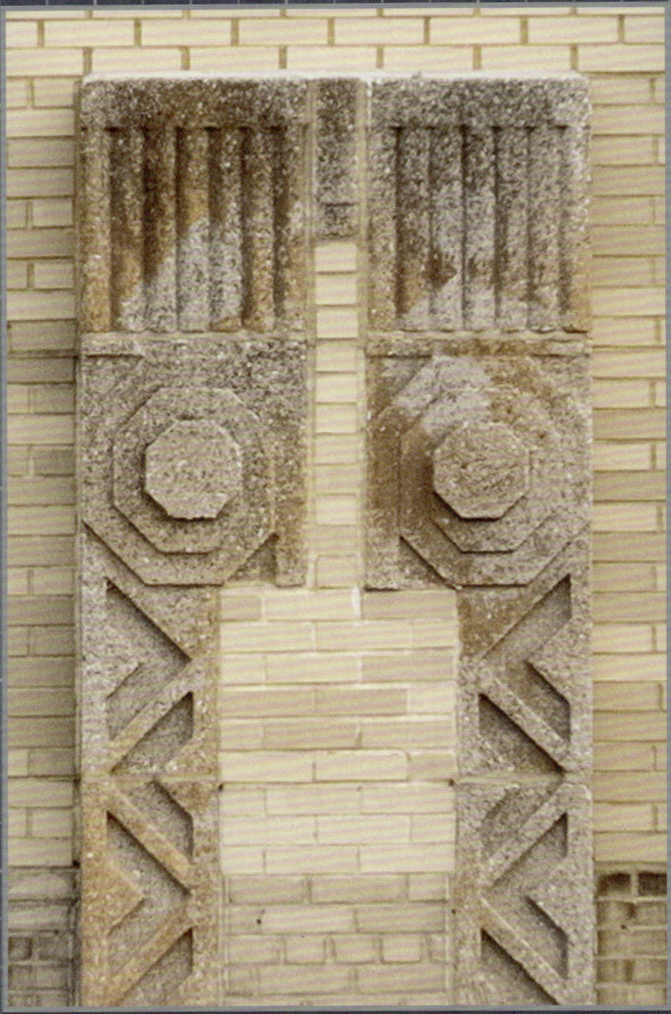

Chevrons and simple geometric shapes in the ornamental elements impart a modern look to the structure.

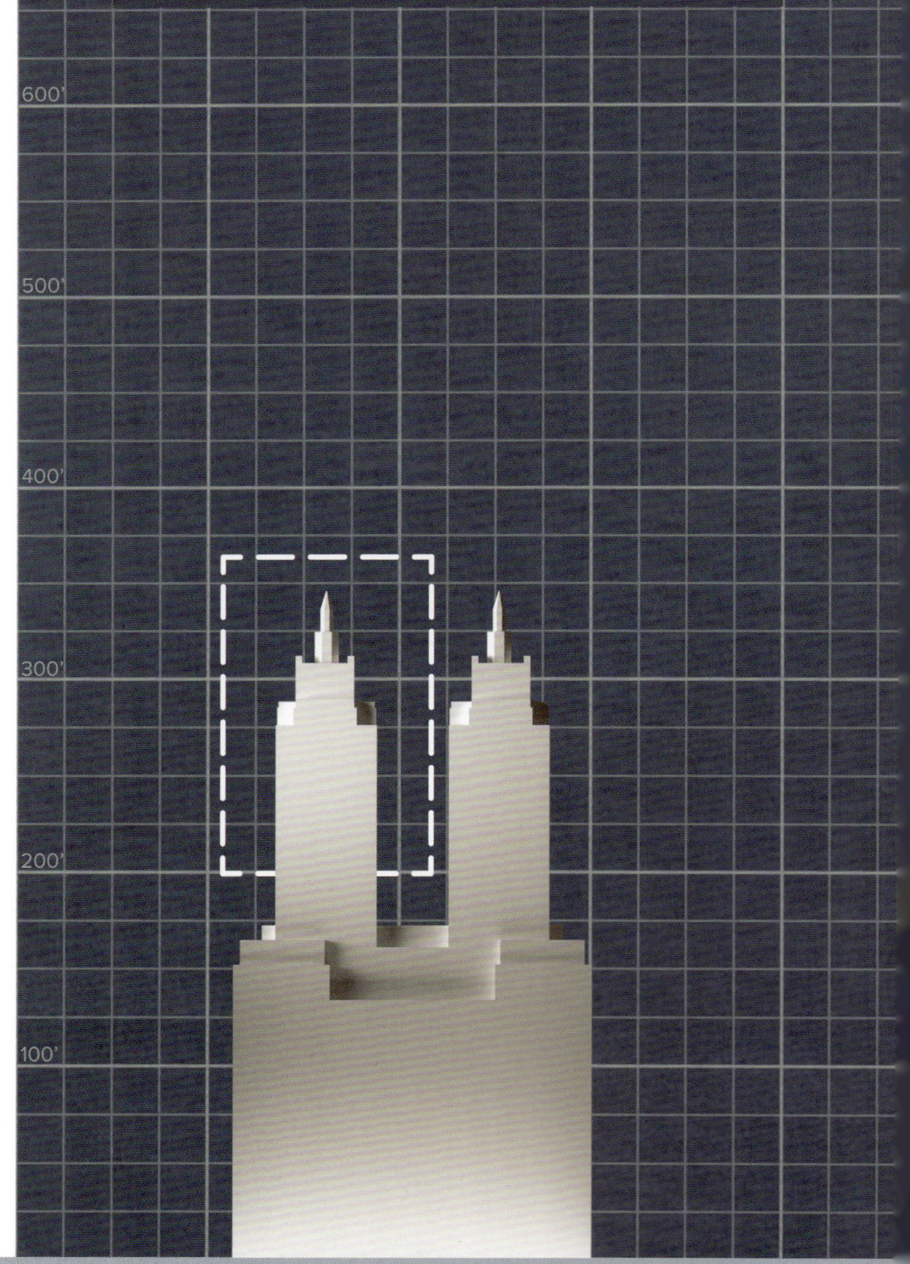

East Elevation *1" = 100'*

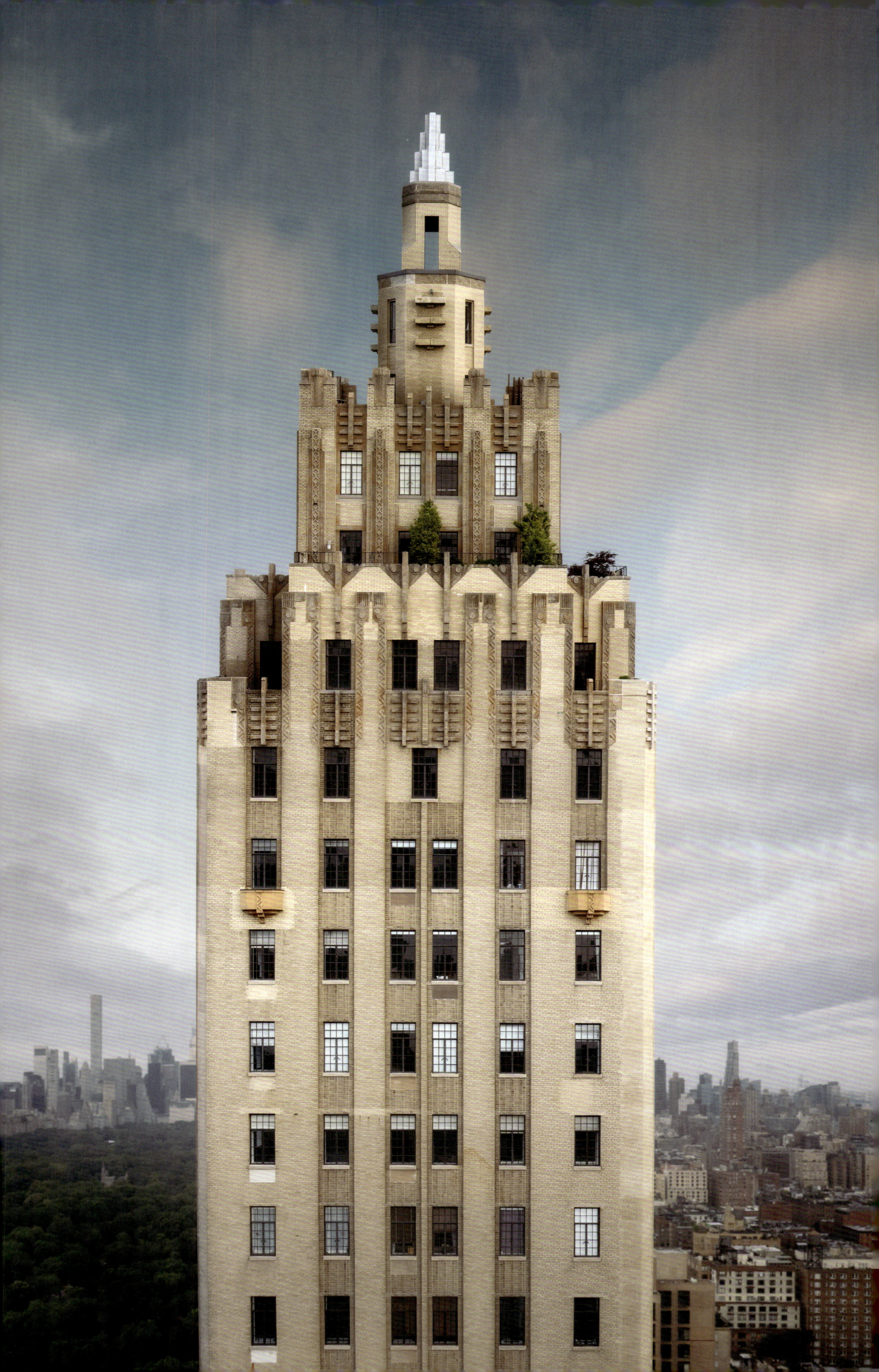

General Electric
Building

New York City, **NY**

Address	**570 Lexington Ave.**
Opened	**1931**
Height	**643'**
Stories	**50**
Style	**Art Deco**
Architect	**Cross & Cross**

Waves pulse from phantasmagoric figures representing the "spirit of radio" on the crown of this otherworldly highrise. It was originally commissioned by the Radio Corporation of America, but RCA transferred the still-unfinished building to its parent company after being wooed away to a planned development nearby called Radio City.

General Electric boss Owen Young created RCA after World War I, when the navy urged him to buy the American subsidiary of Marconi, a British firm dominating wireless transmission. The admirals had military concerns, since the technology was used chiefly for ship-to-shore communications. But the new company rapidly swung its core business to consumer radios and broadcasting, launching the NBC network.

Young was an attorney whom GE hired as its counsel in 1912 after he successfully represented utilities suing it. As chairman 20 years later, he was back in court, forced to sell RCA to settle a federal antitrust action. The newly independent radio company moved into 30 Rockefeller Plaza, which for 55 years was called the RCA Building — the name this highrise was meant to carry.

Soon after Young and GE moved into 570 Lexington, a short circuit in the service elevator lit a blaze that gutted company dining rooms on the upper two stories. Luckily, no one was injured; even the radio spirits survived.

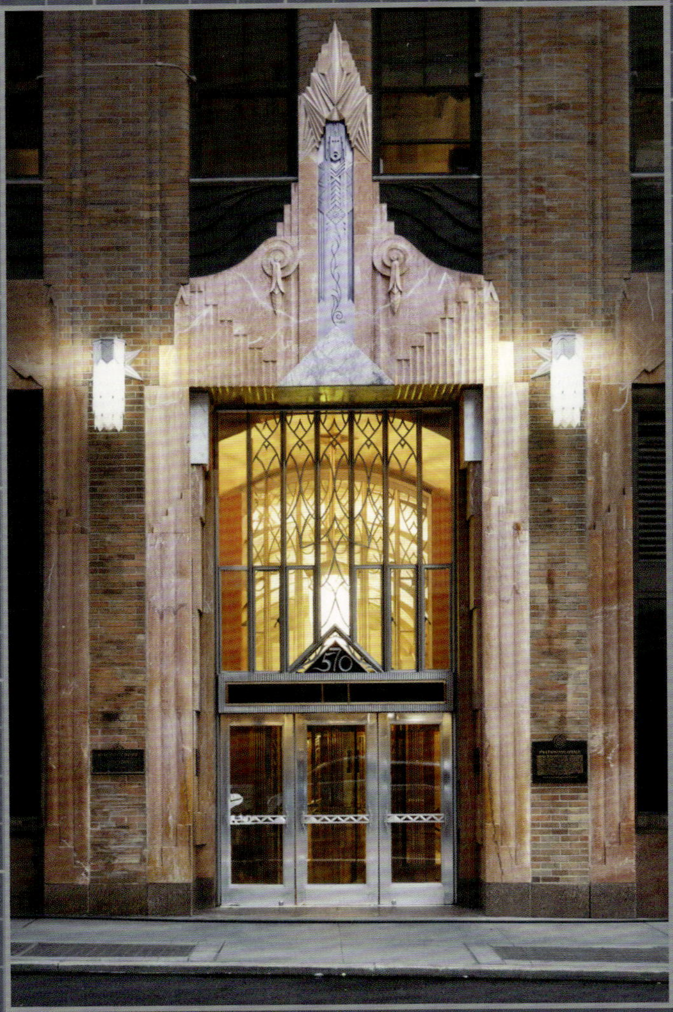

A "radio spirit" watches over the entrance.

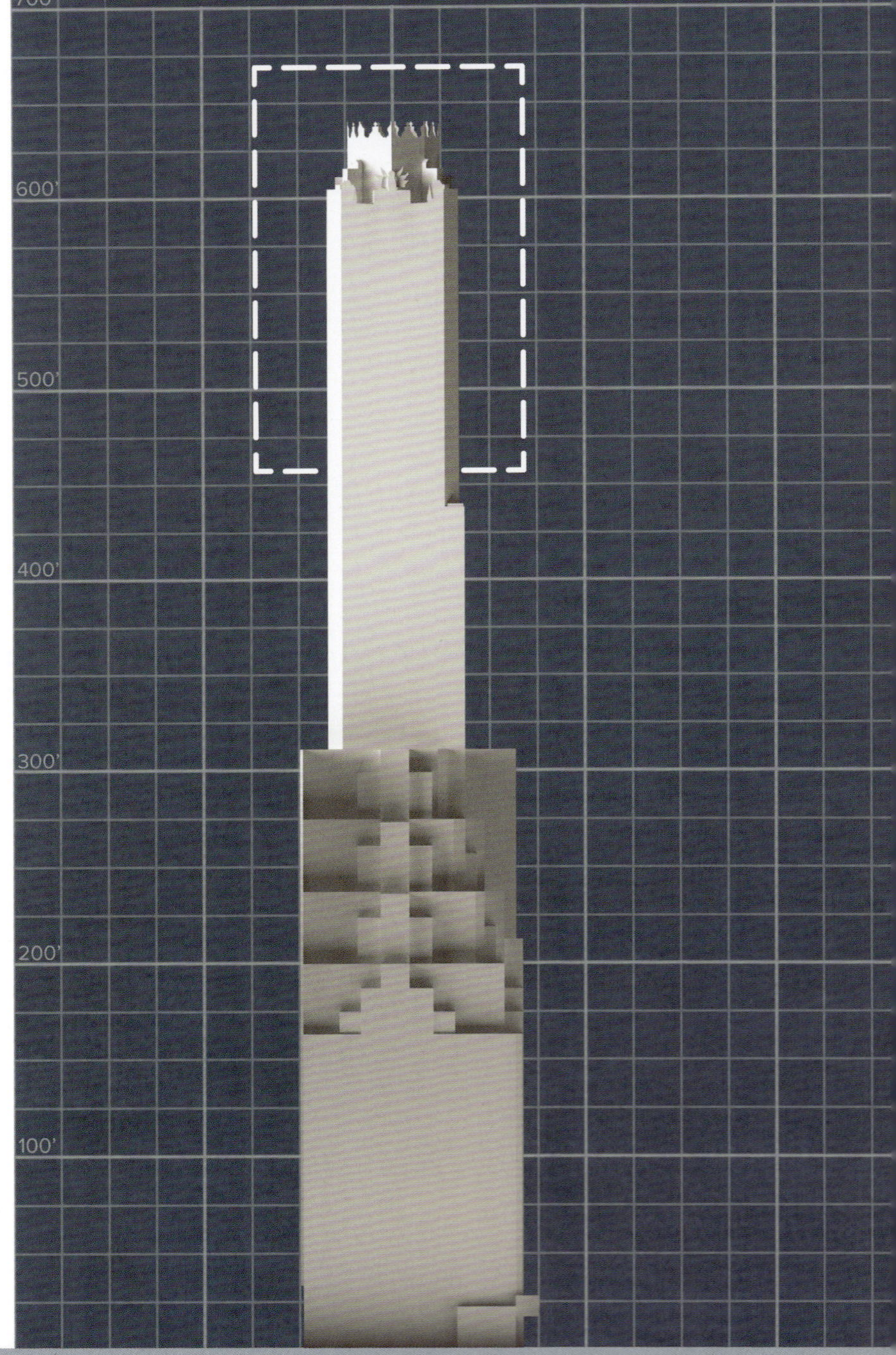

East Elevation *1" = 100'*

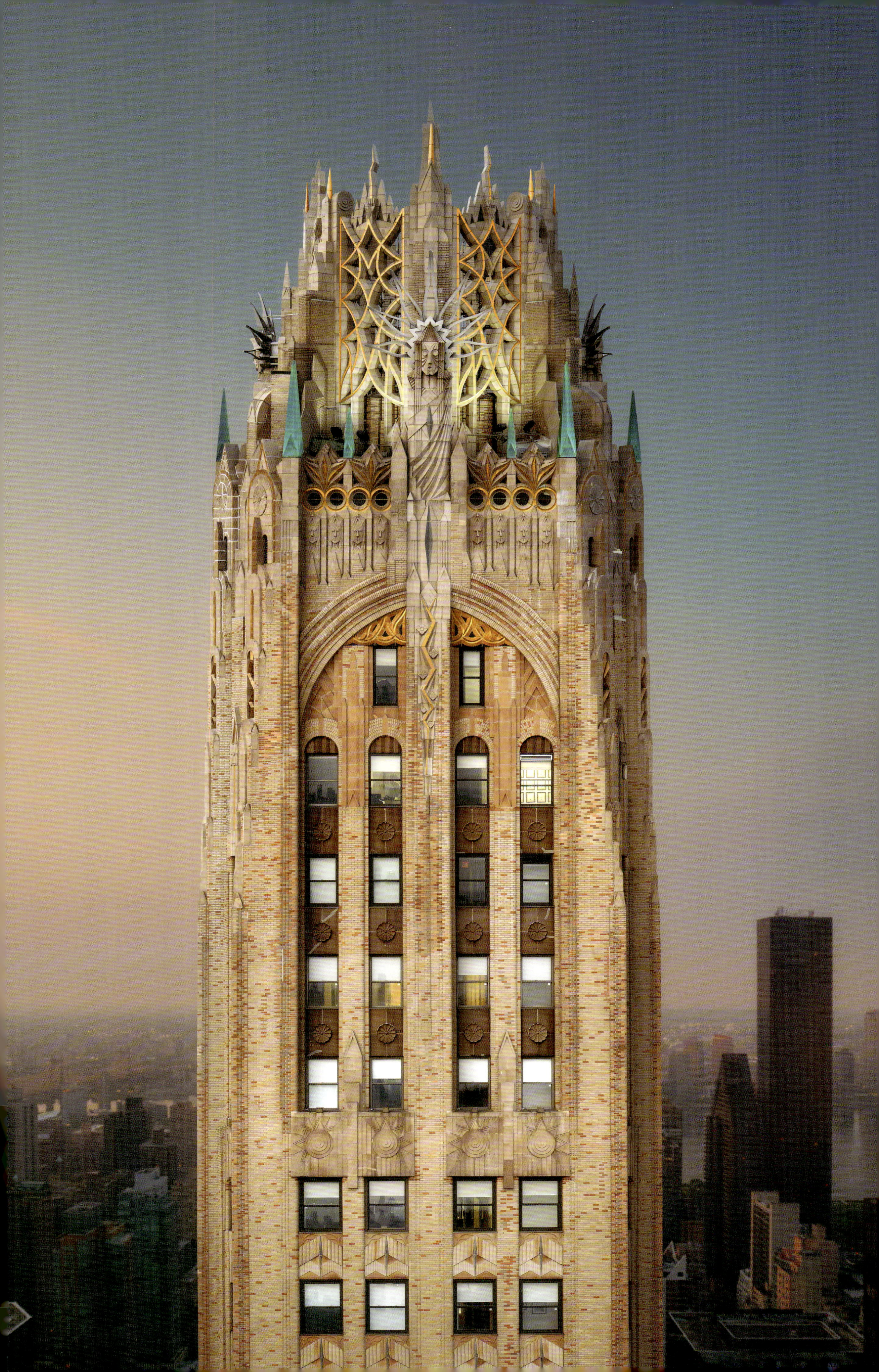

Manhattan
Company Building

New York City, **NY** — Trump Building

Address	**40 Wall St.**
Opened	**1930**
Height	**927'**
Stories	**71**
Style	**Gothic, Art Deco**
Architect	**Craig Severance**

To ensure they captured the title of the world's tallest skyscraper, the developers of this Wall Street highrise quietly added five extra stories, an observatory, and a 50-foot flagpole to the original plans during construction. But lead architect Craig Severance's bitter rival and former business partner, William Van Alen, stole the glory by cranking a spire out of the roof of his Chrysler Building (p. 6).

The Manhattan Company had its origin in similarly sneaky dealings. Aaron Burr chartered it in 1799 as an operation to supply clean drinking water, but included a clause allowing the company to use surplus capital however it wished. Thus Burr was able to open a bank, ending the monopoly of Alexander Hamilton's Bank of New York. Tensions escalated until Burr killed Hamilton in a duel five years later.

Lease income plummeted with the Depression, and when the original owners, investment banker George Ohrstrom and builder William Starrett, defaulted on the mortgage, their skyscraper was sold for less than they had paid for its elevators. The bank was absorbed by Chase, and its building was nearly vacant in 1995 when Donald Trump bought it and renamed it after himself in what his company calls "one of the great real estate deals of all time." The grand marble former banking hall is now a Duane Reade drugstore.

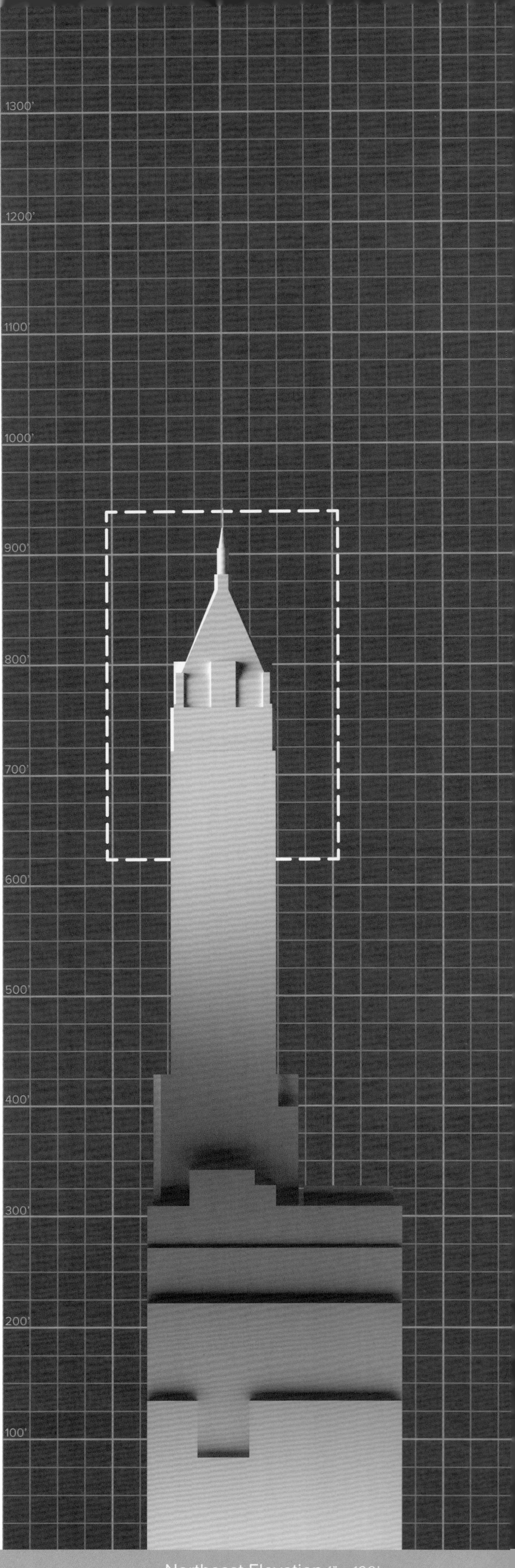

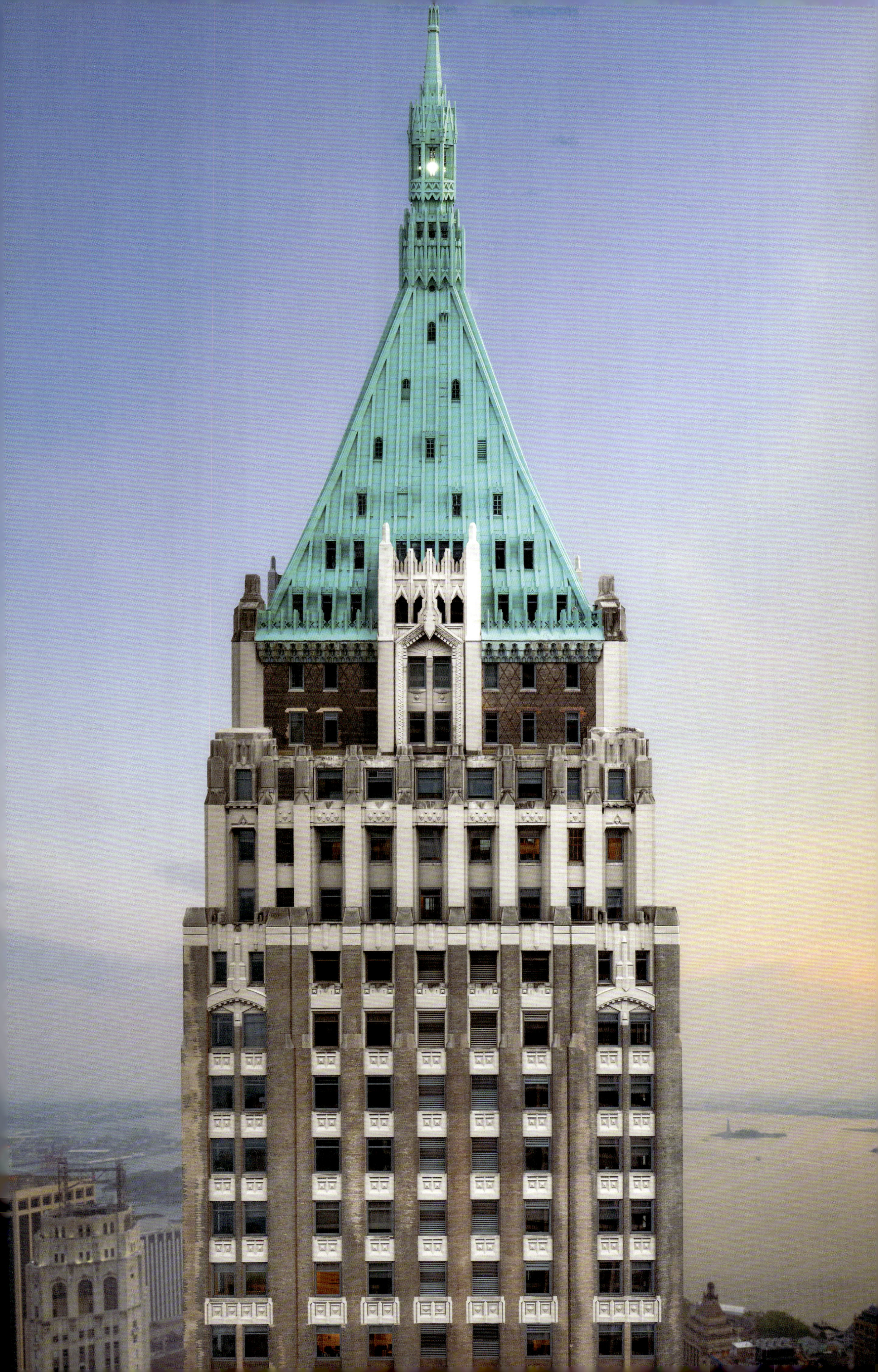

Williamsburgh
Savings Bank

New York City, **NY**

Address	**1 Hanson Pl.**
Opened	**1929**
Height	**512'**
Stories	**39**
Style	**Romanesque, Art Deco**
Architect	**Robert Helmer**

The institution that built this highrise was chartered in 1851, so it still has a final "h" that Williamsburg officially dropped the following year. Seven decades later, the savings bank was the country's fourth-largest and needed more space.

John Jewell, president during the tower's construction, had run his father's flour and feed business before helping him set up a small bank. That was absorbed by another institution, which in turn was swallowed up by Williamsburgh Savings.

Capped with a dome just like the bank's former location, this was long the tallest building in Brooklyn. Its vast banking hall is practically a basilica, with 60-foot ceilings, patterned marble floors, and an enormous glass mosaic map of the island's early Dutch settlements.

The teller who served the first customer gave 10-year-old Sonja Rosell a pencil as a souvenir for her $6 deposit, thinking her too young for the silver compact offered to women opening accounts. Another youthful admirer, Miles Morales or Spider-Man, calls this highrise his favorite hangout in *Across the Spider-Verse*. He must surely endorse the two cautionary carvings on the facade, which show a safecracker at work on one side and that same crook behind bars on the other. The vault is empty now, and the tower is a mix of condos, doctors, and dentists.

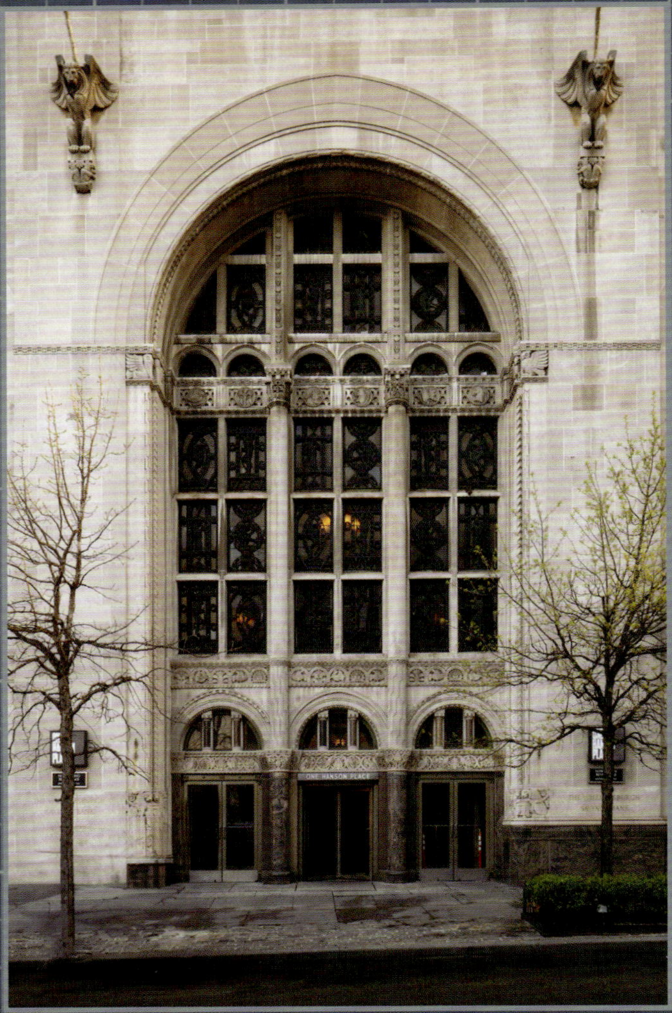

Polished granite and limestone columns anchor a Romanesque arch of carved stone and metal grillework.

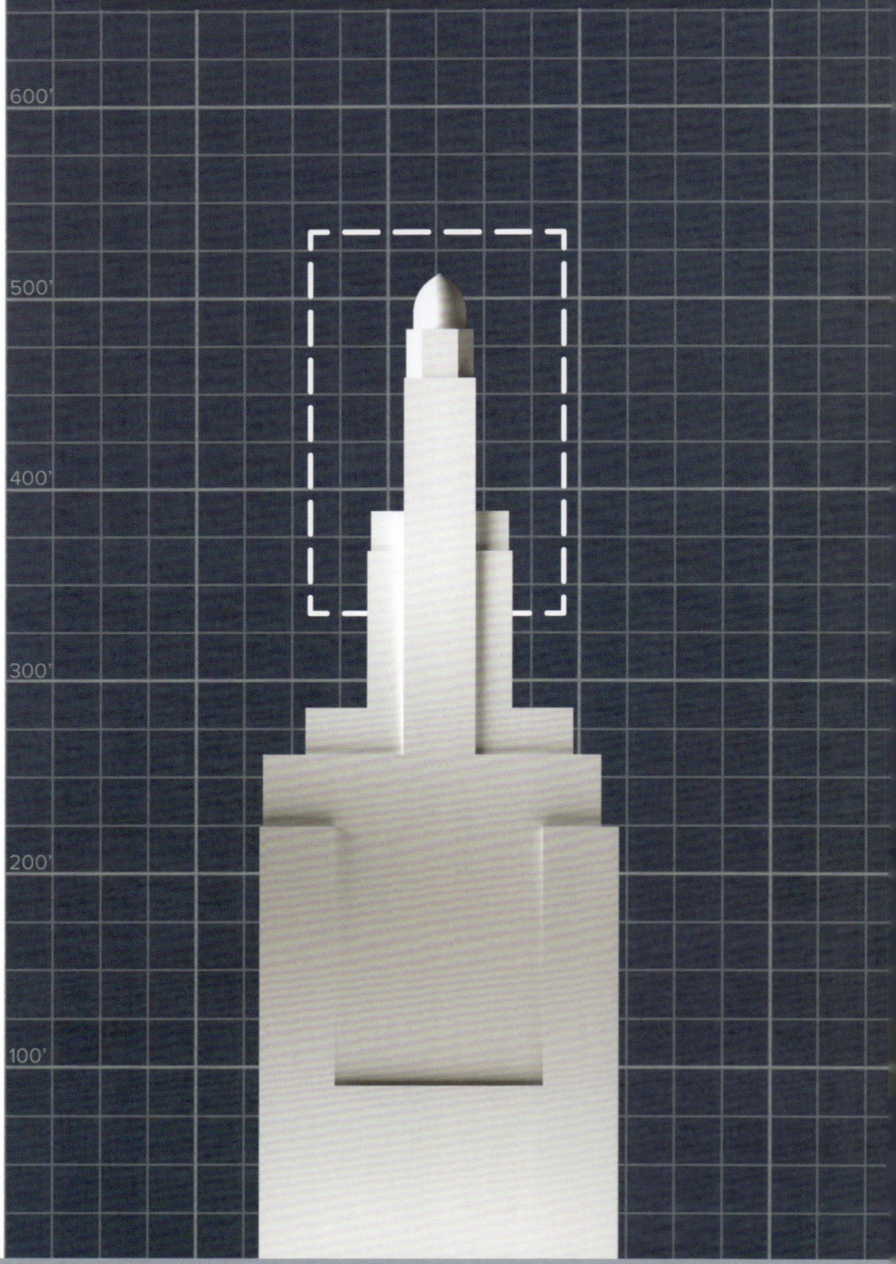

West Elevation *1" = 100'*

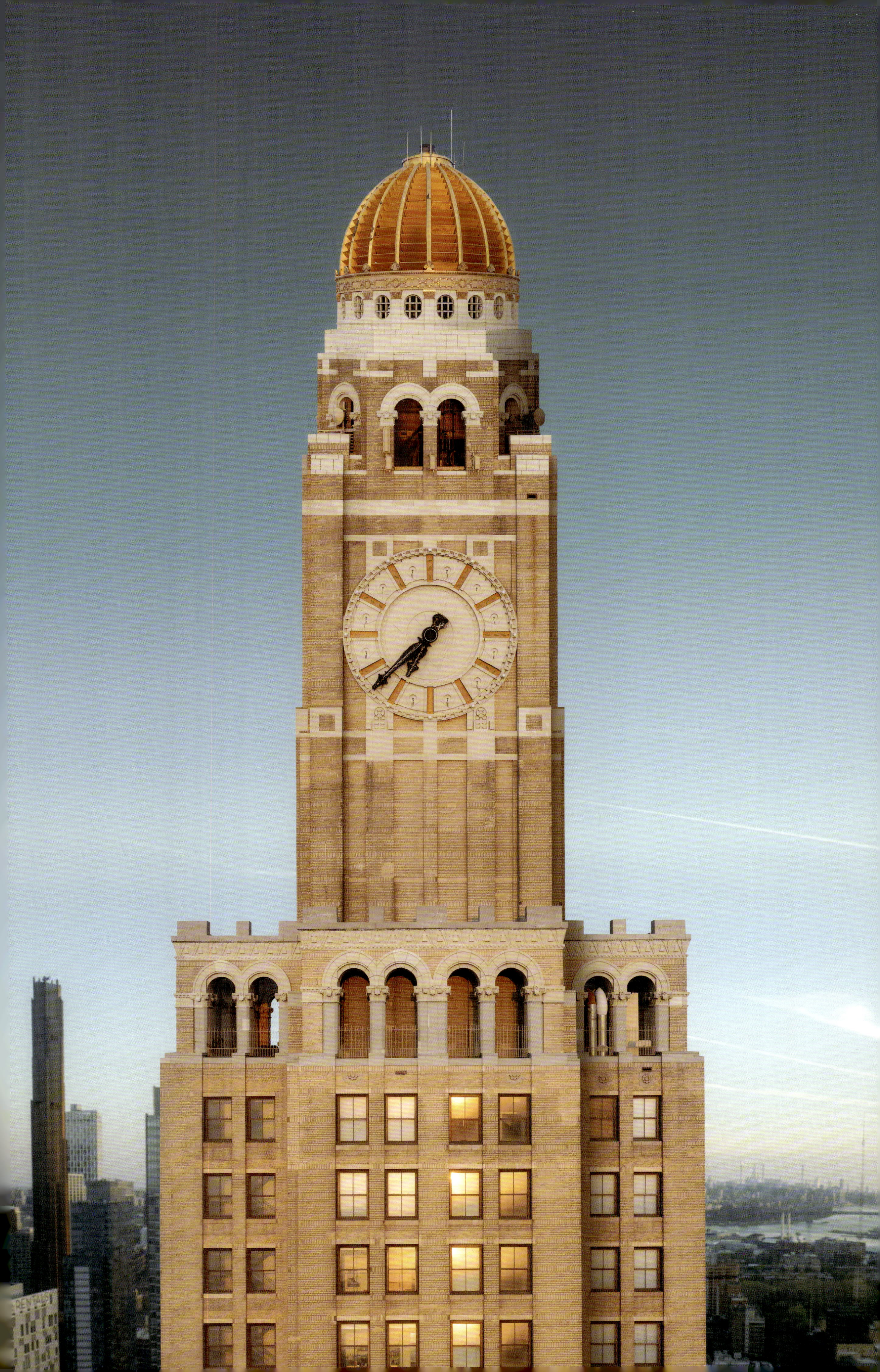
RENTALS

Home Savings Bank
Building

Albany, **NY**

Address	**11 N. Pearl St.**
Opened	**1927**
Height	**267’**
Stories	**19**
Style	**Art Deco**
Architect	**Dennison & Hirons**

Brightly painted glazed terracotta panels crowning this highrise show an early Dutch settler in a military helmet and a member of the Mohican tribe, which lived in the area when Europeans first arrived. Between and below them are stylized flowers and other decorations in deep blue, yellow, and ocher.

The panels are by Rene Chambellan, a leading Art Deco architectural sculptor. His work also embellishes the State Office Tower (p. 26) in town, as well as more famous skyscrapers including the American Radiator Building (p. 8) in Manhattan, Tribune Tower in Chicago (p. 80), and Buffalo City Hall (p. 28). The spiraling foliage motif repeats in carvings below on the granite base of the structure and on the ceiling inside the former banking hall, now used for wedding receptions and galas.

The financial institution that paid for this highrise boasted in ads that it was “Albany’s most beautiful savings bank.” An elegant scroll and wreath in low relief on the facade below the bank’s carved name commemorates its founding in 1871. Beneath that are additional profiles of the original residents of the region, interspersed with their noisy new neighbors.

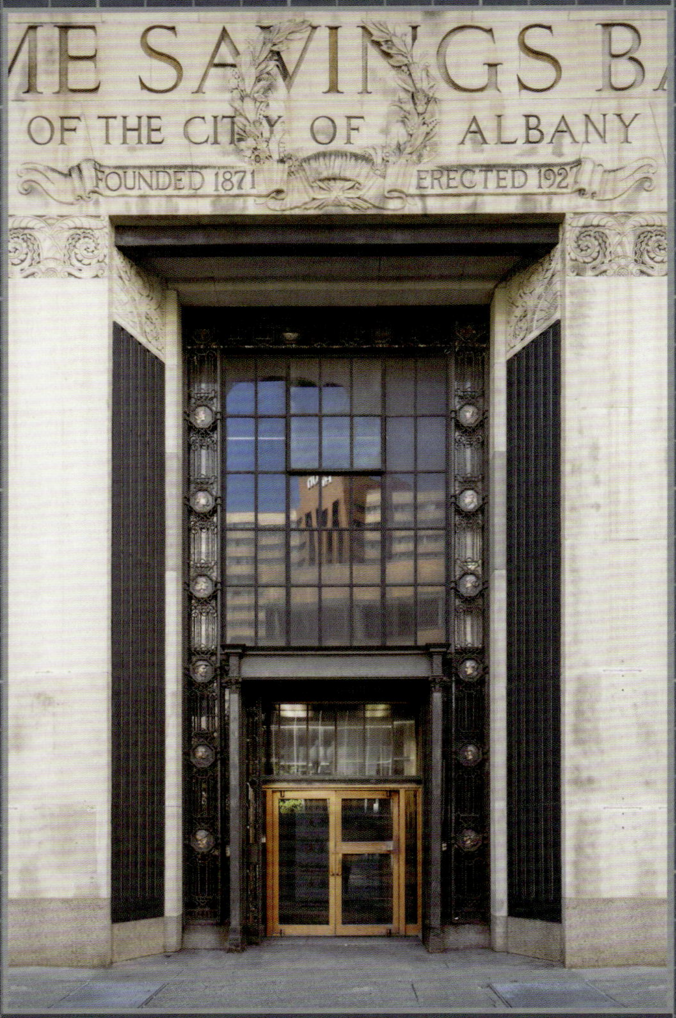

A delicate wreath in low relief superimposed over the bank name displays mastery in stone carving.

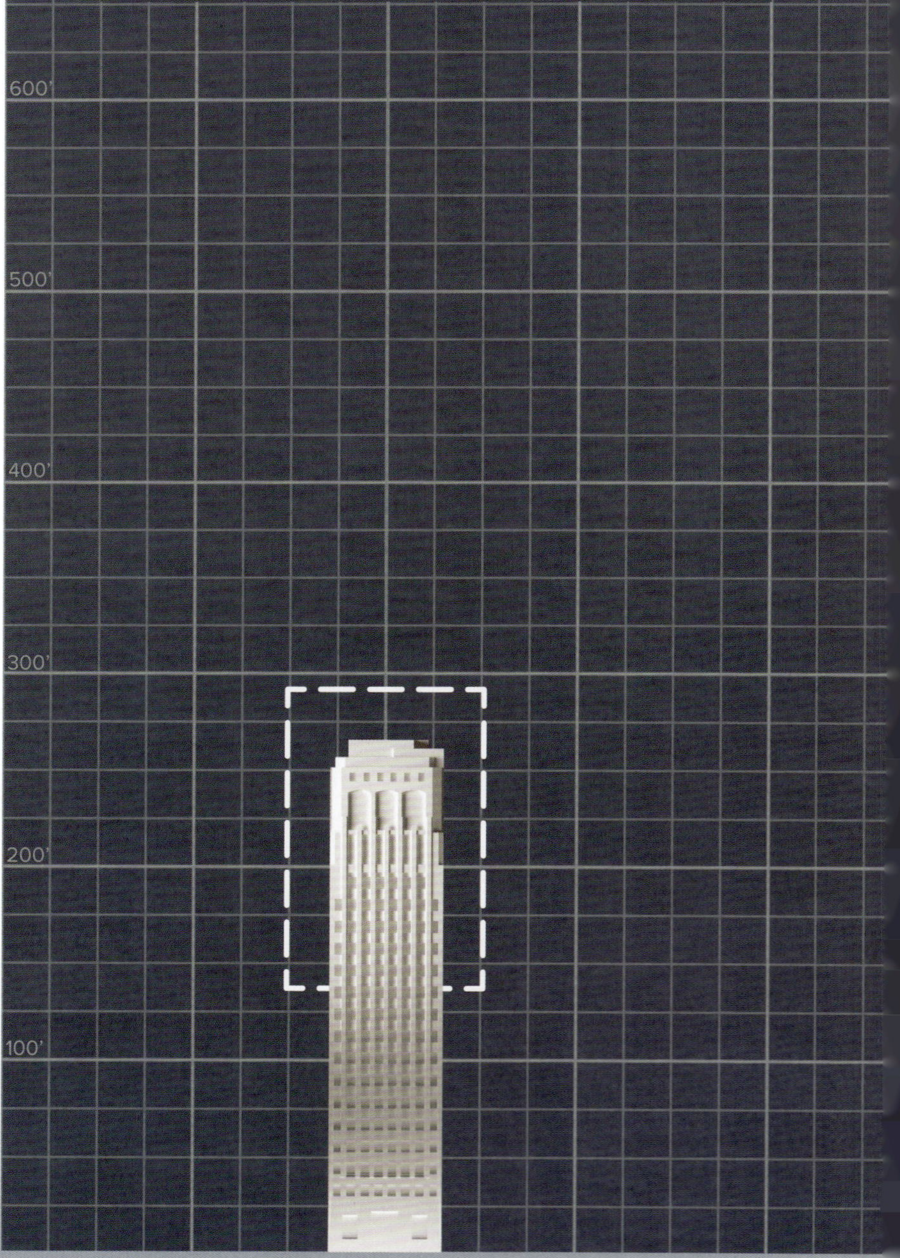

Northwest Elevation *1" = 100'*

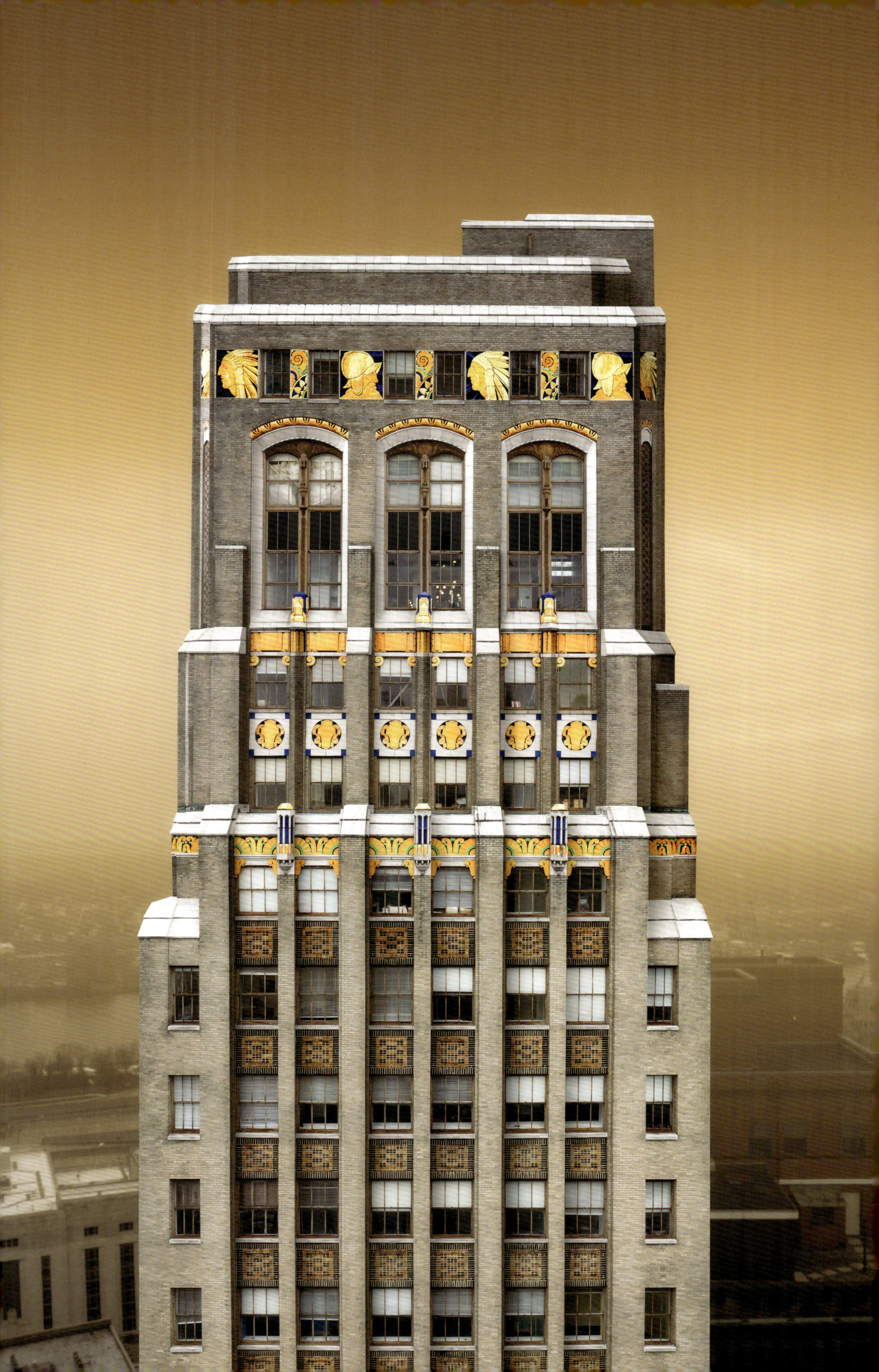

State Office
Building

Albany, **NY** | Alfred E. Smith Building

Address .... **80 S. Swan St.**
Opened **1930**
Height .... **388'**
Stories **32**
Style .... **Art Deco, Neoclassical**
Architect .... **Sullivan Jones**

Like many government jobs, this highrise was controversial before the first girder was hoisted. Opponents railed over the site and cost. The designer quit when his independent post of state architect was subsumed under the public works department.

But its champion, Al Smith, four-term governor of New York, pressed relentlessly for a tower to house Albany's scattered state workforce. Smith oversaw planning and even manned the steam shovel at the groundbreaking. Then, with construction underway, he ran for president against Herbert Hoover and lost in a landslide.

His gubernatorial successor, Franklin D. Roosevelt, won the White House four years later. Smith exited politics to head the corporation that raised the Empire State Building. Months after his death in 1945, legislators renamed the state office tower in Smith's honor. Today it stands above the State Capitol and Empire State Plaza like an Art Deco transition from the Gilded Age to the Space Age.

The lobby ceiling is painted with murals of important New Yorkers, and all 62 counties have their names carved into the facade. Ten important ones get a big font treatment — but not the neglected Bronx, small and nearly hidden on the side of the entrance.

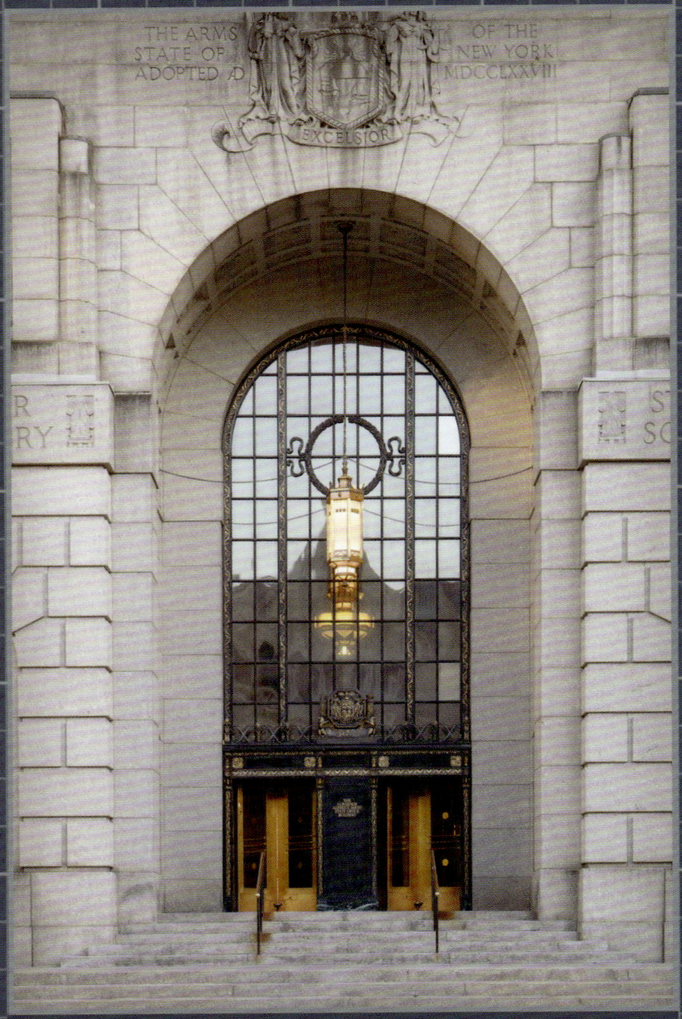

"Excelsior," the state motto above the door, means "Higher" and is apt for a state known for its skyscrapers.

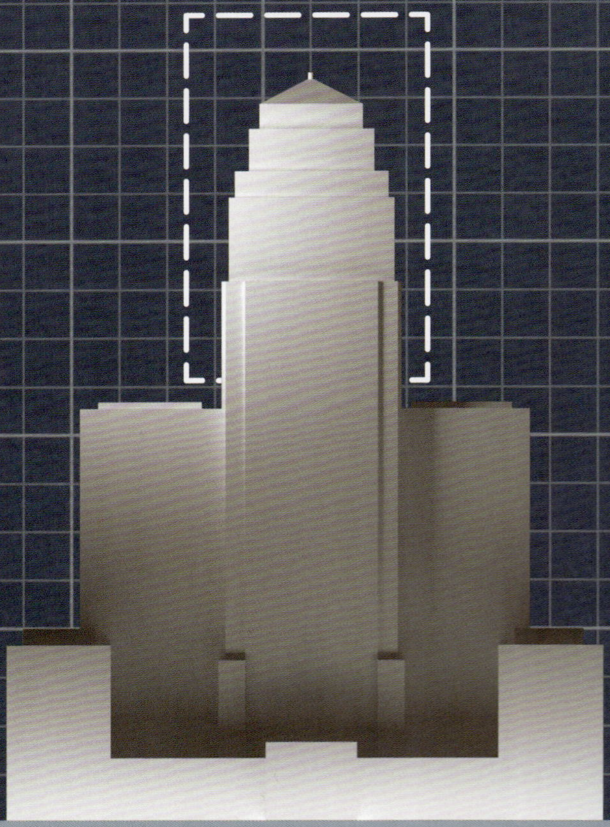

Southeast Elevation *1" = 100'*

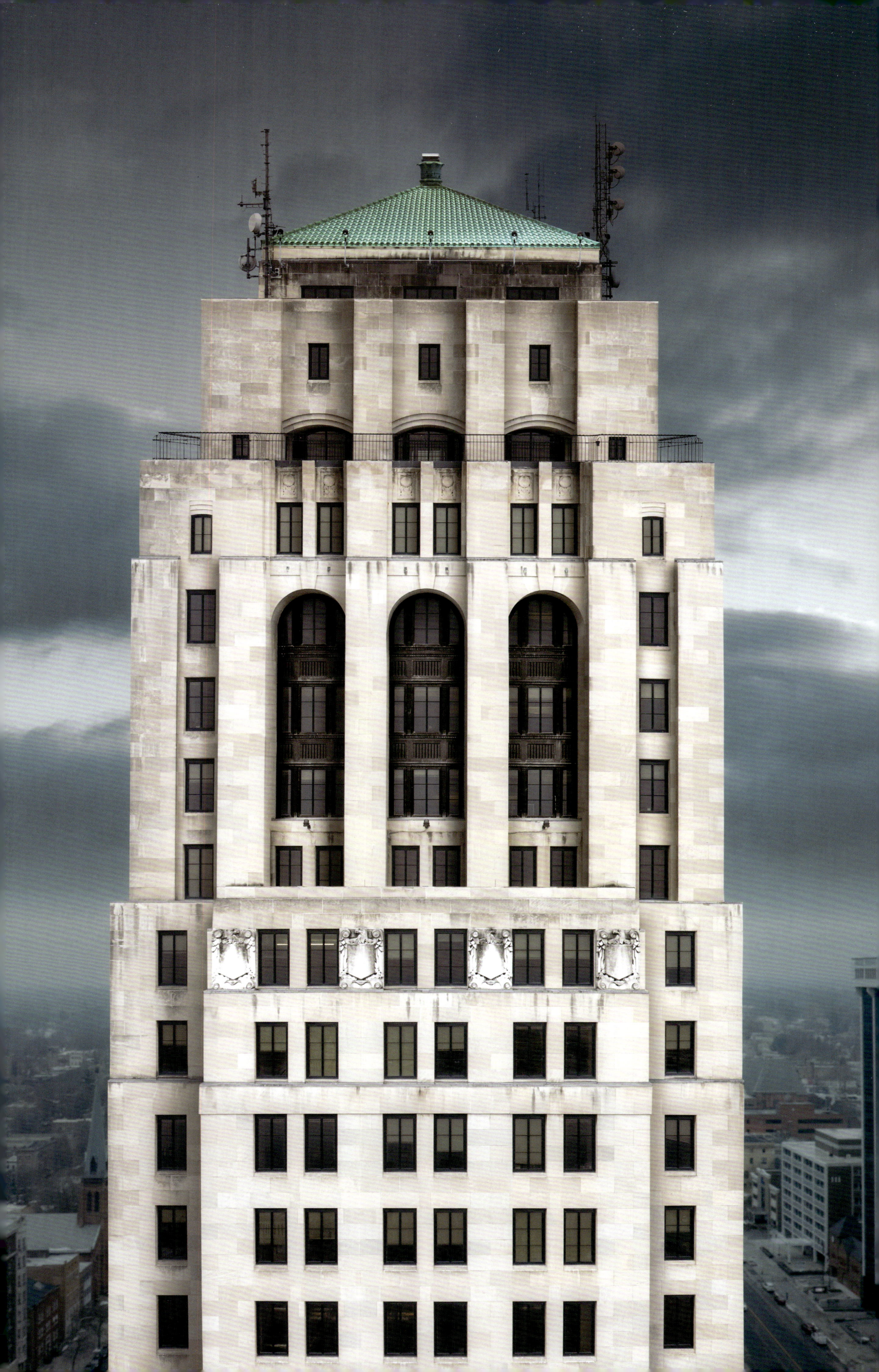

Buffalo City Hall

Buffalo, **NY**

Address	**65 Niagara Sq.**
Opened	**1931**
Height	**375'**
Stories	**28**
Style	**Art Deco**
Architect	**John Wade**

The city council of Buffalo made the best decision in its history in 1926 when it rejected its municipal architect's uninspiring plan for a new civic building. Instead they turned to John Wade, an opinionated local designer who produced one of the most spectacular Art Deco highrises ever constructed.

The elegantly stepped sandstone mass features stylized carvings and polychromatic terracotta in geometric Native American motifs. A frieze over the entrance depicts the city writing her future, surrounded by stevedores, ironworkers, and research chemists; the rear frieze showcases key historic episodes.

In the lobby are vivid, almost comic book murals of musclebound men and gleaming women by William de Leftwich Dodge, whose work also decorates the Library of Congress and the New York State Capitol. Buffalo's councilmen could not agree on which citizens to honor in their 13th floor chambers. So instead, identical busts represent various virtues, lit by a large stained glass skylight of the rising sun. Visitors to the free observatory on the top floor can take in the sprawling cityscape, Lake Erie, and distant Niagara Falls.

A park in front has an obelisk to President William McKinley, assassinated in Buffalo in 1901. Bronze statues of the two presidents who hailed from the city, Millard Fillmore and Grover Cleveland, are the site's sole concession to mediocrity.

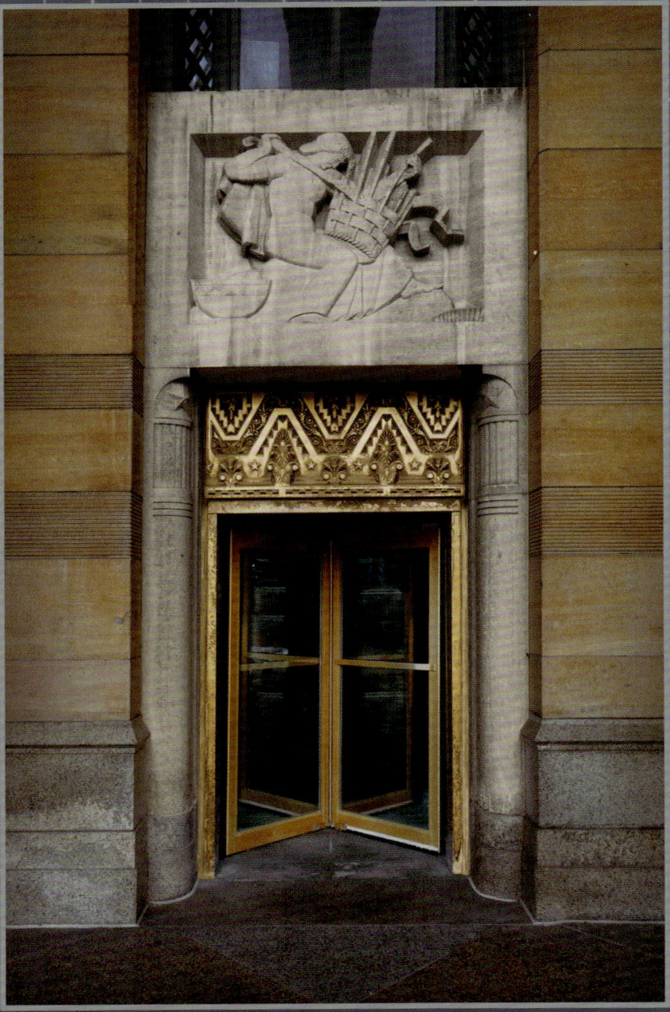

Extensive sculptures include this panel over the entrance showing a pioneer woman weaving a basket.

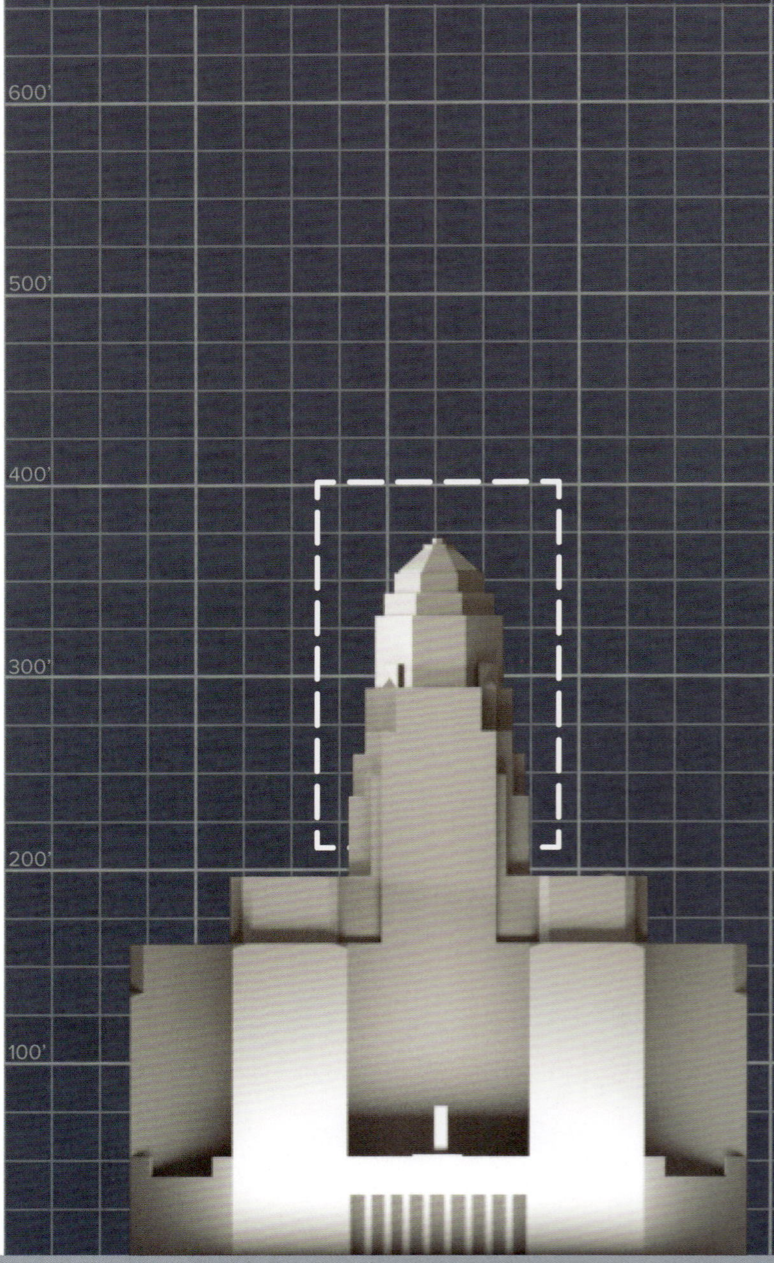

East Elevation *1" = 100'*

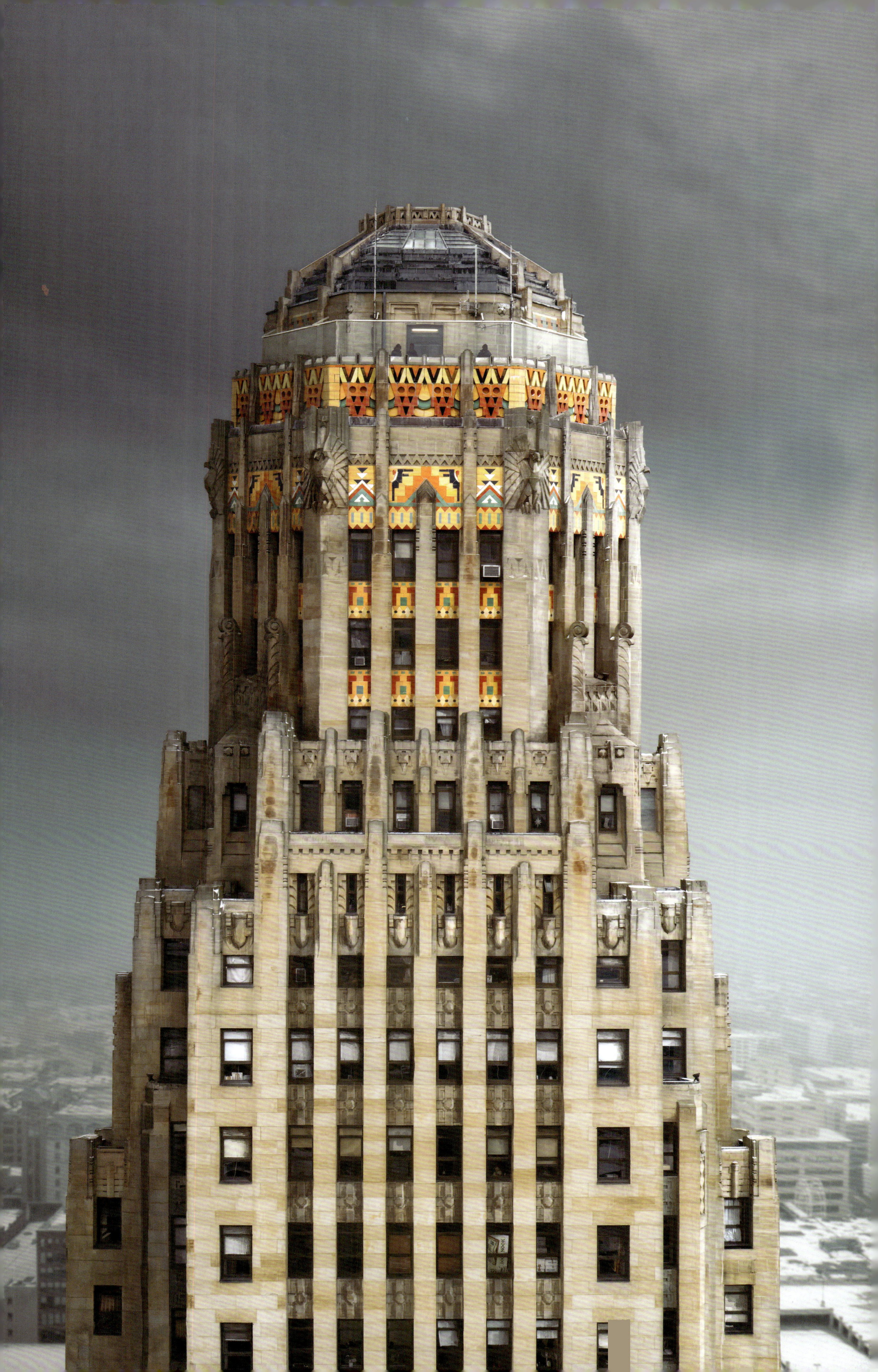

Central Terminal

Buffalo, **NY**

Address · · · · · · · · · · · · **495 Paderewski Dr.**
Opened · **1929**
Height · **271'**
Stories · **18**
Style · **Art Deco**
Architect · · · · · · · · · · **Fellheimer & Wagner**

By placing its new passenger terminal nearly three miles outside of downtown Buffalo, the New York Central Railroad demonstrated its optimism about the city's growth prospects. Unfortunately, that optimism proved to be unwarranted. Buffalo's urban core failed to expand here, and even if it had, the age of the automobile spelled the end of passenger rail.

The facility was designed to handle 200 trains and 10,000 people daily, with an attached office skyscraper whose lobby also served as the main entrance to the station. Alfred Fellheimer was a railway terminal expert and the lead architect of Grand Central Station in New York; his firm also designed Cincinnati's train station, considered an Art Deco masterpiece, at roughly the same time as this one.

The last train chugged out Buffalo station in 1979, and weeds now grow over its disused platforms. The property badly deteriorated under subsequent owners, a victim of weather, vandalism, and arson. Preservationists bought it in 1997 for one dollar plus back taxes. They restored the tower clocks and the main concourse, and recently released a master plan for renovating the rest of the abandoned complex.

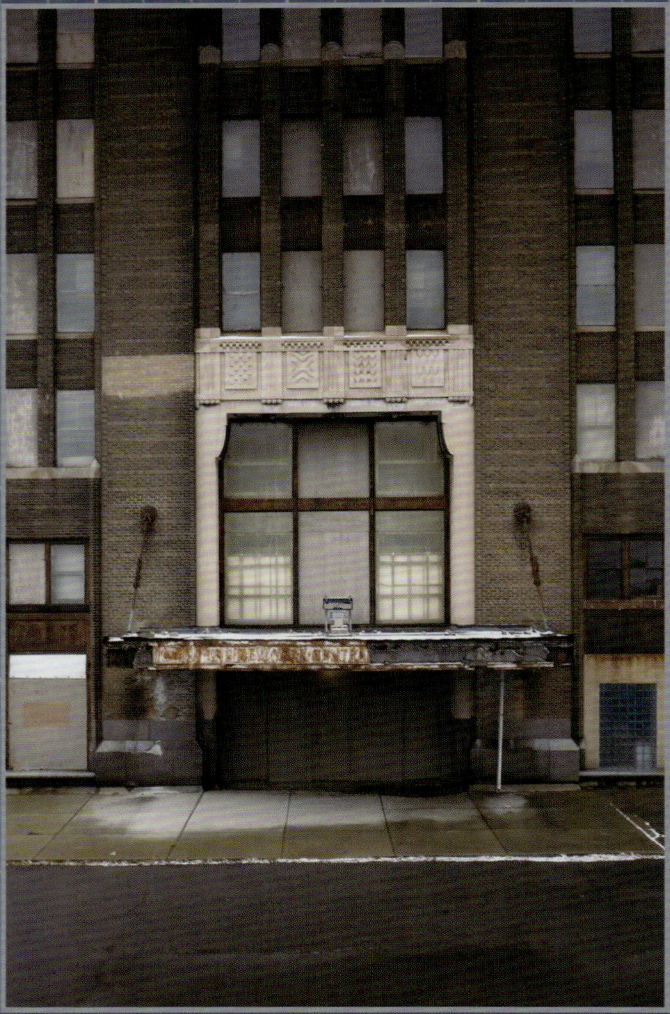

A rotting marquee testifies to the decades of neglect the property has suffered.

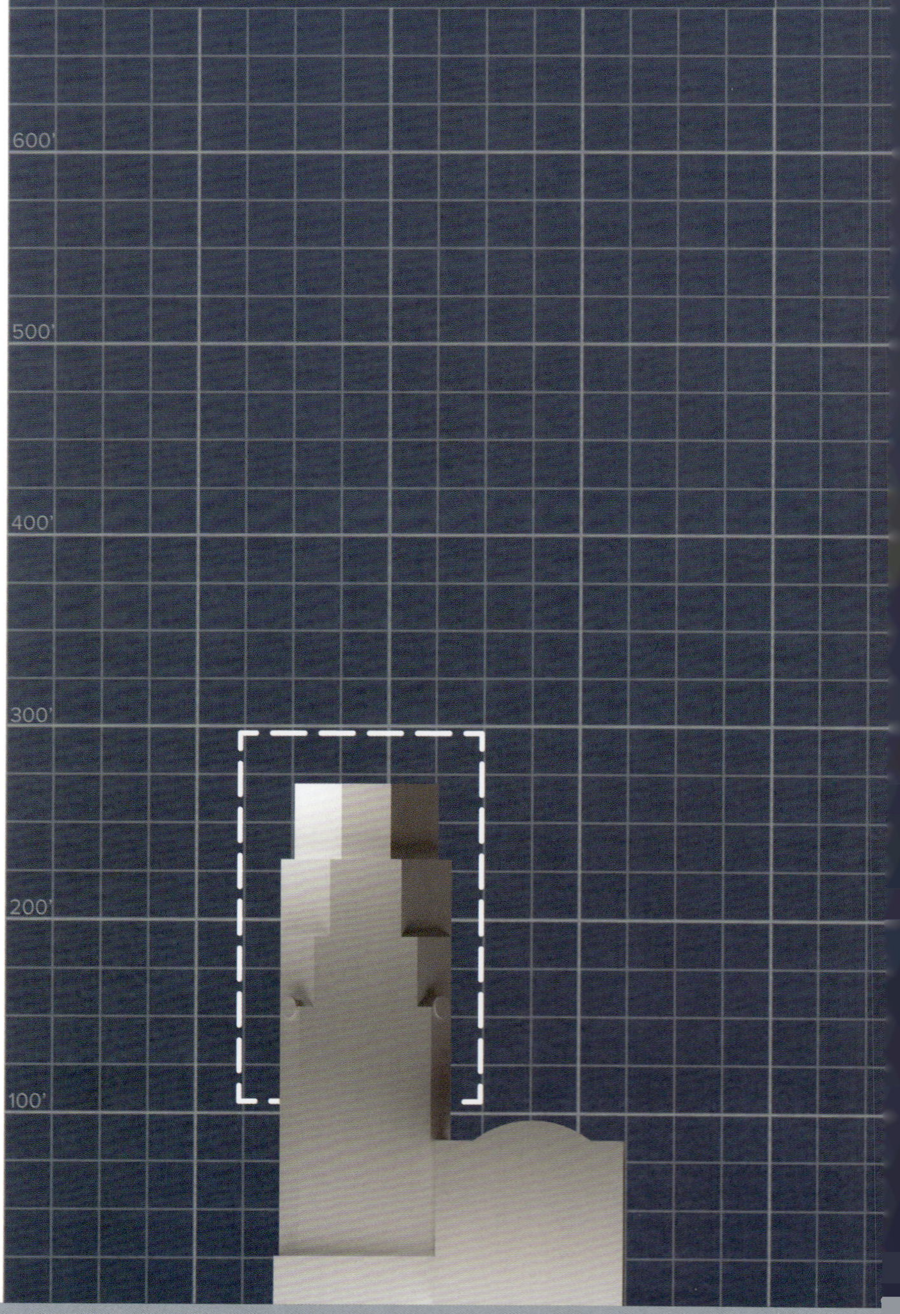

East Elevation *1" = 100'*

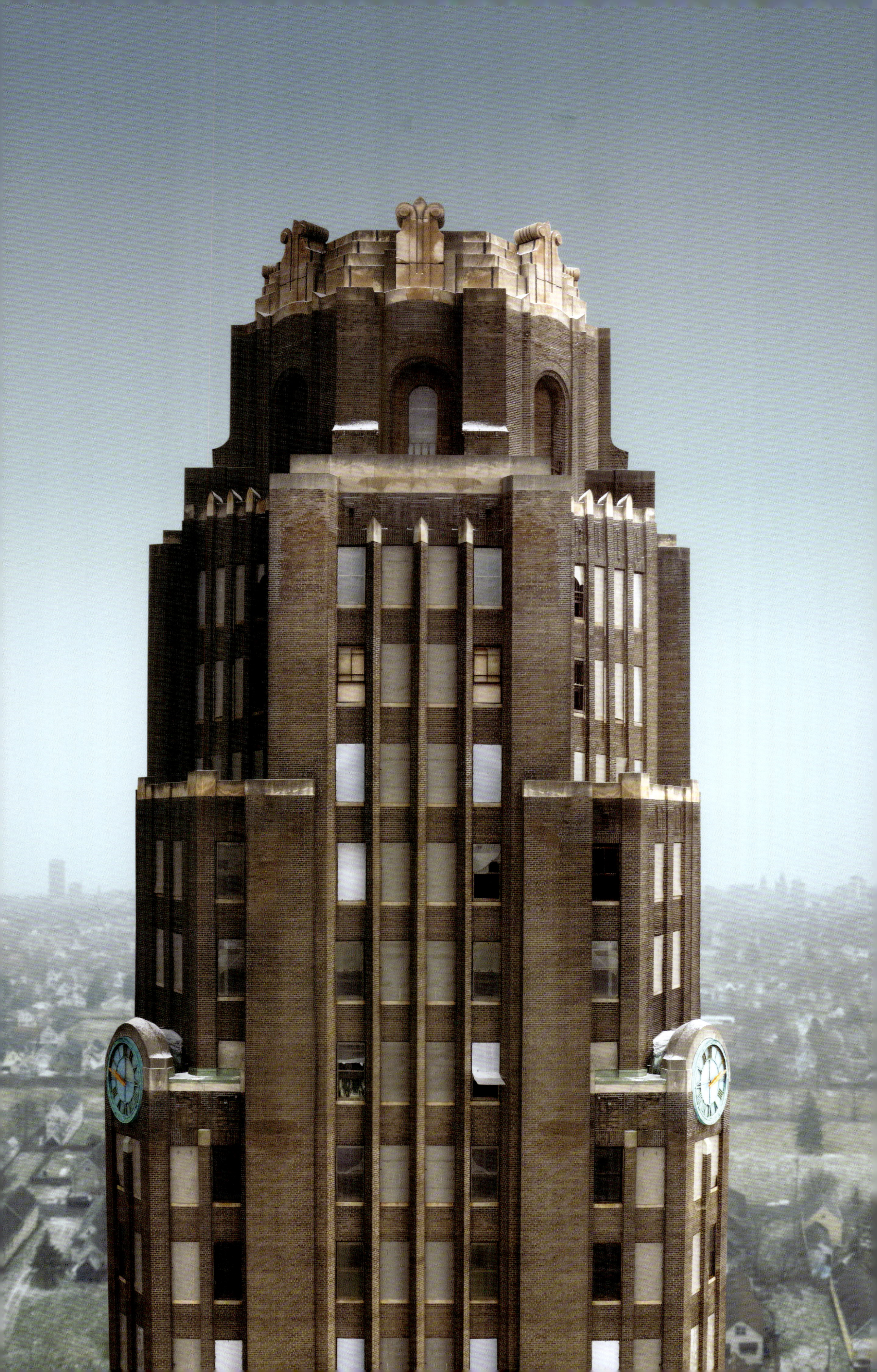

Rand Building

Buffalo, **NY**

Address	**14 Lafayette Sq.**
Opened	**1929**
Height	**405'**
Stories	**29**
Style	**Art Deco**
Architect	**Franklyn & William Kidd**

If the 40-foot spire atop the Rand Building was originally intended as a mooring mast for zeppelins, as is sometimes claimed, that plan never got off the ground. But searchlights and red neon made the spire a helpful beacon for airplanes in the days before radar, and it still blinks at night today.

It is a sobering tribute to the building's namesake, George Rand Sr., who died in a plane crash in England in 1919. Rand was president of Marine Trust, one of the state's largest banks. He was returning from Paris, where Rand had offered the French prime minister a large private sum to fund a new war memorial.

George Rand Jr. soon succeeded his father and oversaw planning of this new headquarters for the bank, which was the city's tallest skyscraper for more than 40 years. The 18th floor housed the studios of radio station WGR, whose call letters also commemorate George Rand.

This was the sole skyscraper designed by Franklyn and William Kidd, who immigrated with their parents from Scotland. Franklyn designed a mansion for the Rands in 1918, which helped him to land this commission.

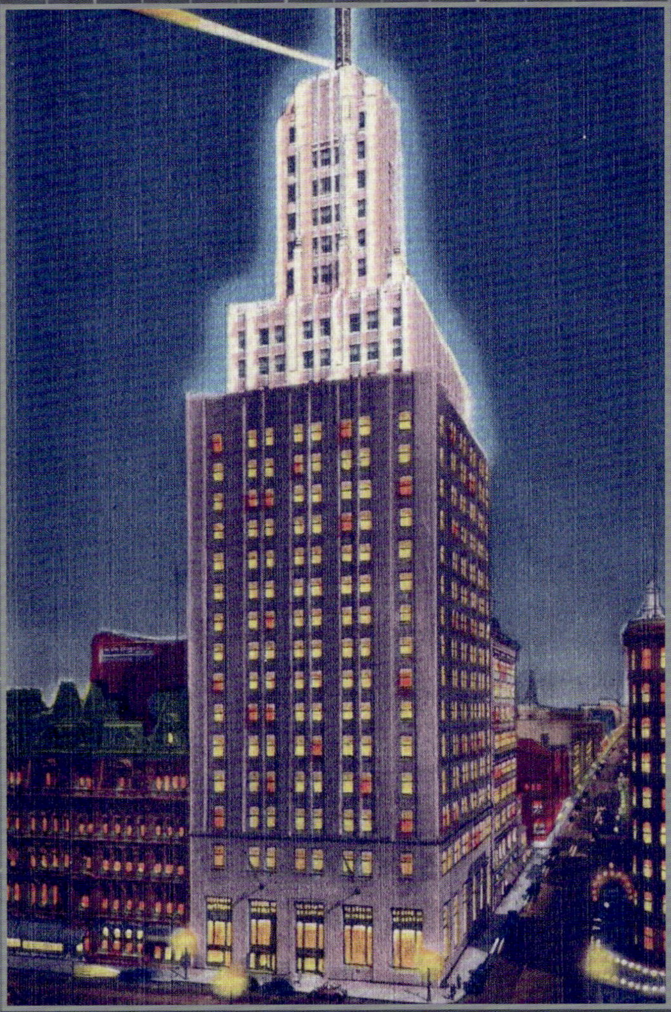

Art Deco highrises often used dramatic night lighting, as shown in this 1930 souvenir postcard.

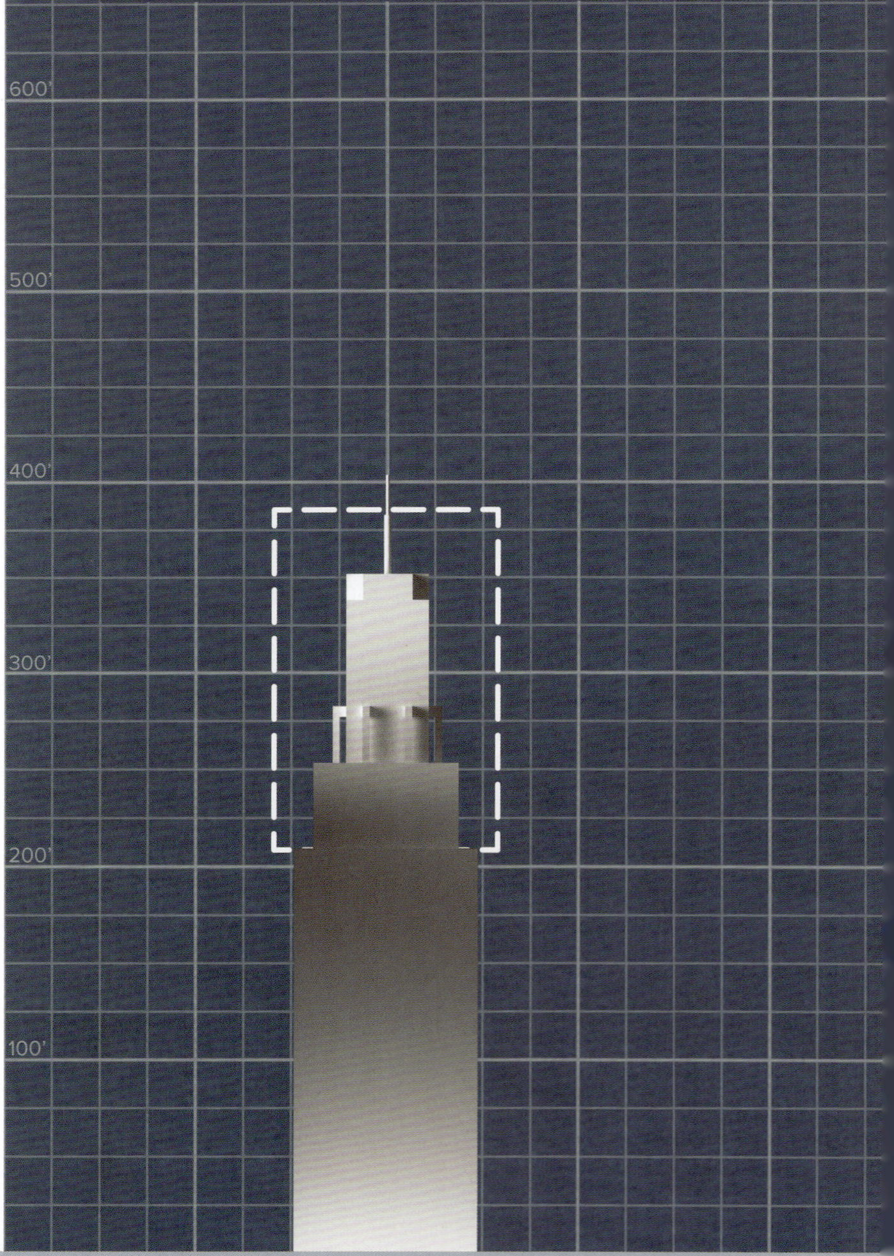

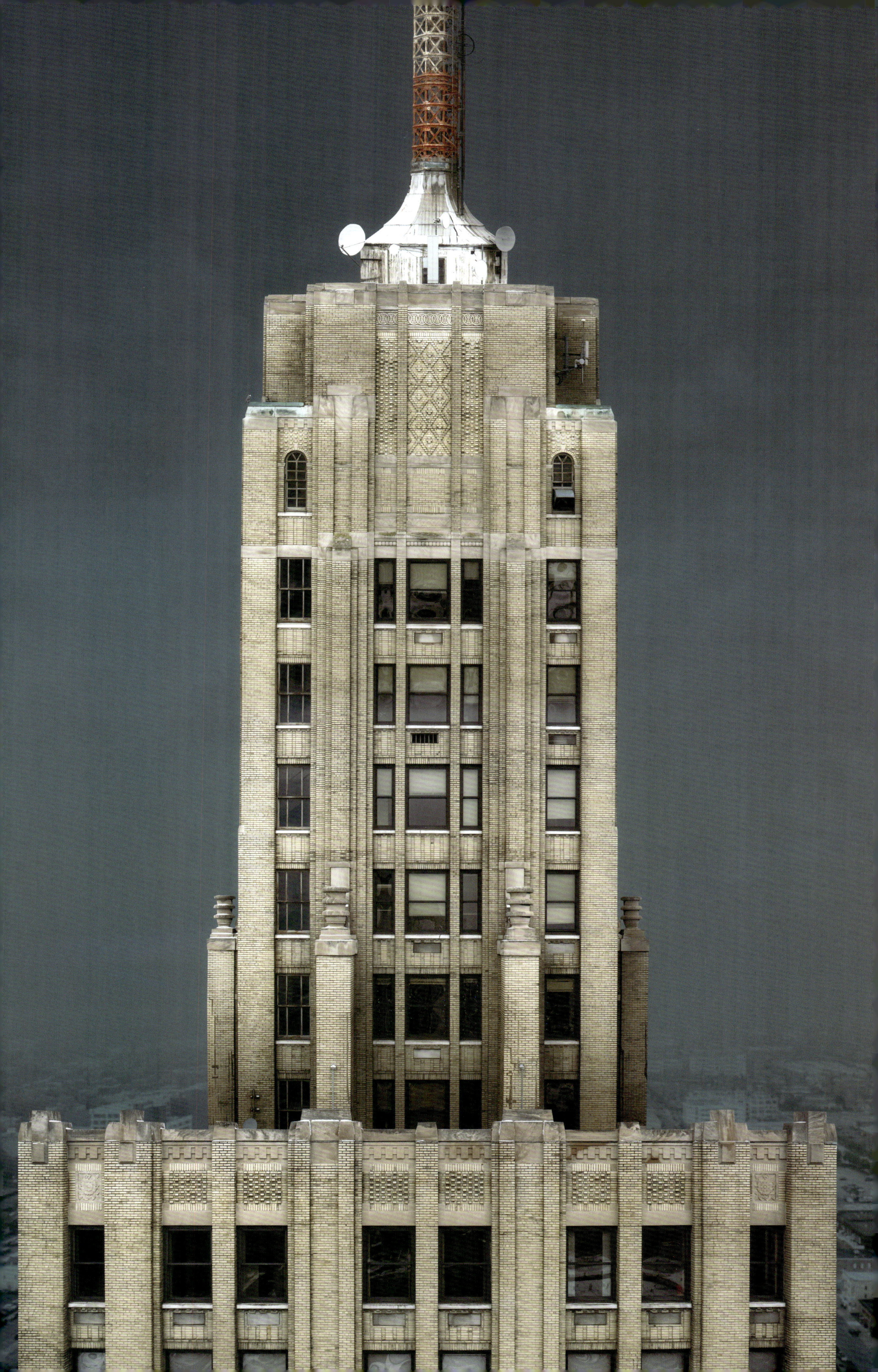

United Office
Building

Niagara Falls, **NY** — The Giacomo

Address ········ **222 First St.**
Opened ········ **1929**
Height ········ **217'**
Stories ········ **19**
Style ········ **Art Deco**
Architect ········ **James Johnson**

Art Deco took some interesting turns, including a brief fascination with Mayan motifs such as the painted friezes on this highrise. Buffalo architect James Johnson intended them to offset the stark verticality of what was the tallest skyscraper on the American side of Niagara Falls for almost 80 years.

It was constructed as the main headquarters of United Hotels, a luxury chain created by lawyer and entrepreneur Frank Dudley. Dudley helped to form several local ventures including a trolley company, an electric utility, and the city's first country club. He also developed the city's upscale Lewiston Heights neighborhood, where James Johnson designed a mansion for Dudley and his wife, Harriet.

United was one of the era's biggest hotel chains, with properties in the United States, Canada, and overseas. A flagship was the Niagara Hotel across the street, which has been vacant for several years. So was this highrise until it was renovated and reopened as a boutique hotel and apartment complex. The top story is now an observation room where guests can watch the river hurl itself over the escarpment to become the American Falls.

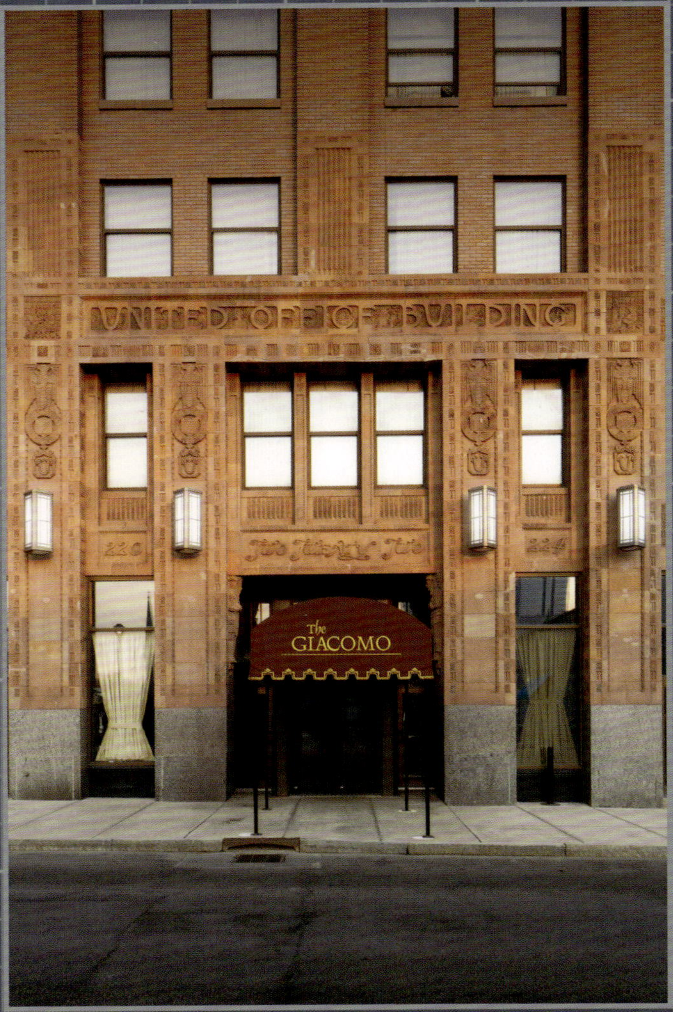

Fanciful and flowery terracotta script conveys an image of luxury the hotel chain wished to present.

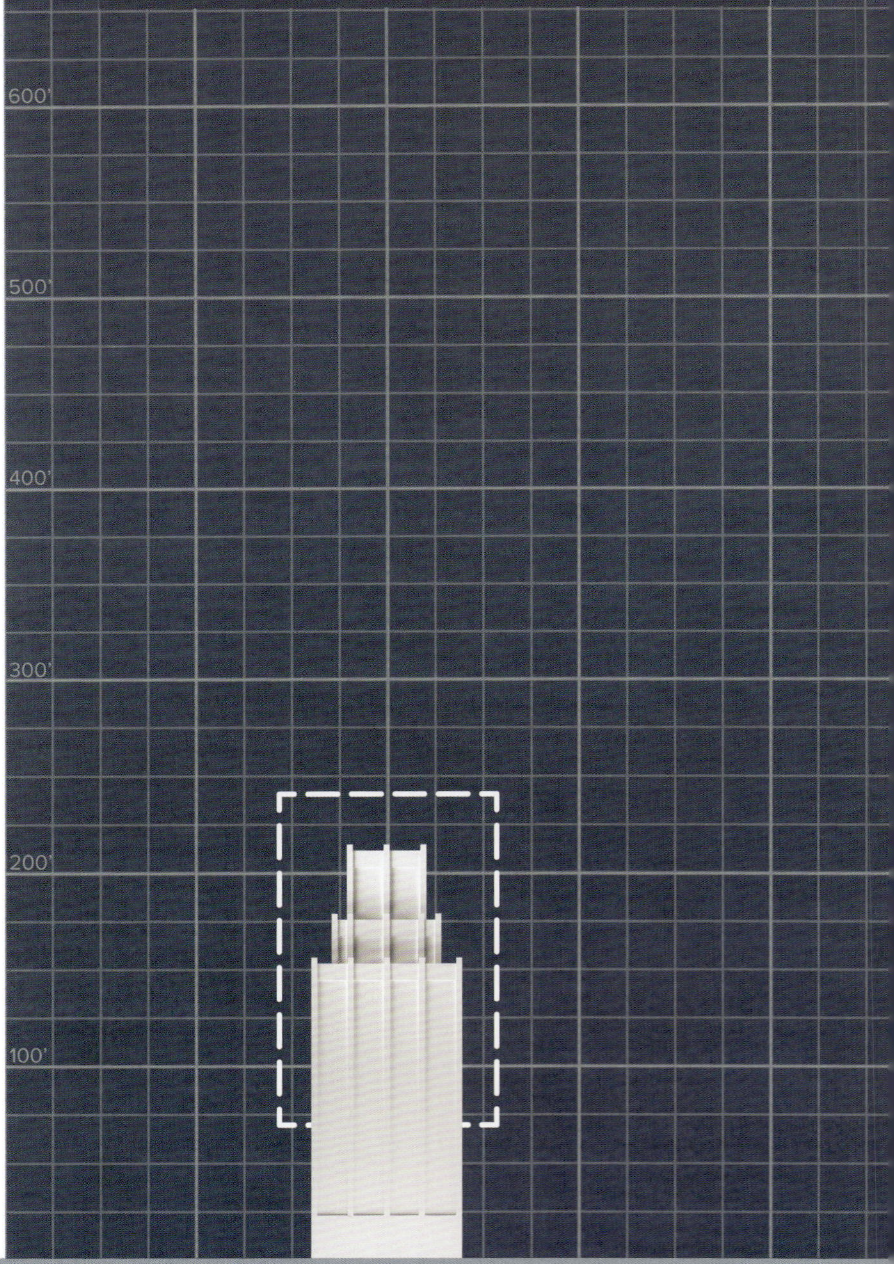

East Elevation *1" = 100'*

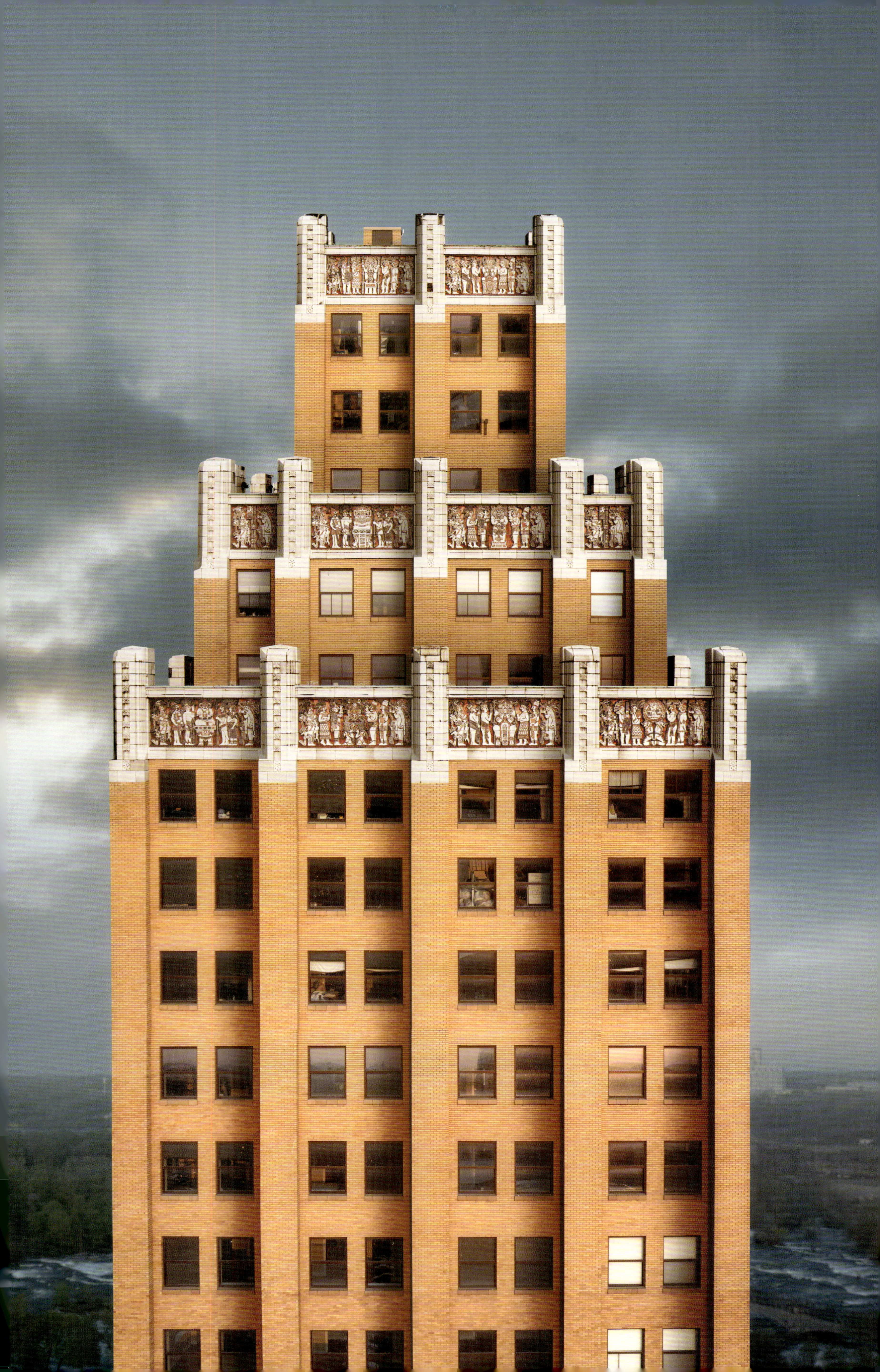

Genesee Valley
Trust Building

Rochester, **NY** Times Square Building

Address ············ **45 Exchange Blvd.**
Opened ························ **1930**
Height ························· **260'**
Stories ··························· **13**
Style ·························· **Art Deco**
Architect ················ **Ralph Walker**

Ever since its unveiling, "Wings of Progress," the bold 42-foot aluminum sculpture capping this bank highrise, has tempted residents of Rochester to speculate on its meaning. Some say it represents maple seedpods or bat wings, others say a screwdriver or an arrowhead shattered by the city's brutal winters.

Architect Ralph Walker, who helped to establish the canon for Art Deco skyscrapers with his Barclay-Vesey and Irving Trust buildings in Manhattan, said he wanted to convey a sense of flight and was inspired by seashells he found on the beach in Florida. Hailed by the American Institute of Architects in 1957 as "architect of the century," Walker later resigned from the organization over an ethics controversy. He committed suicide at the age of 83, rumor has it with a silver bullet he forged for himself.

The bank moved out after a 1955 merger, and the new owner redubbed this the Times Square Building after the former name of the intersection where it stands. A dramatic red marble lobby still features the original chandelier. Stylized bas-reliefs over the front windows by New York sculptor Leo Friedlander depict two Greek goddesses representing security and trust.

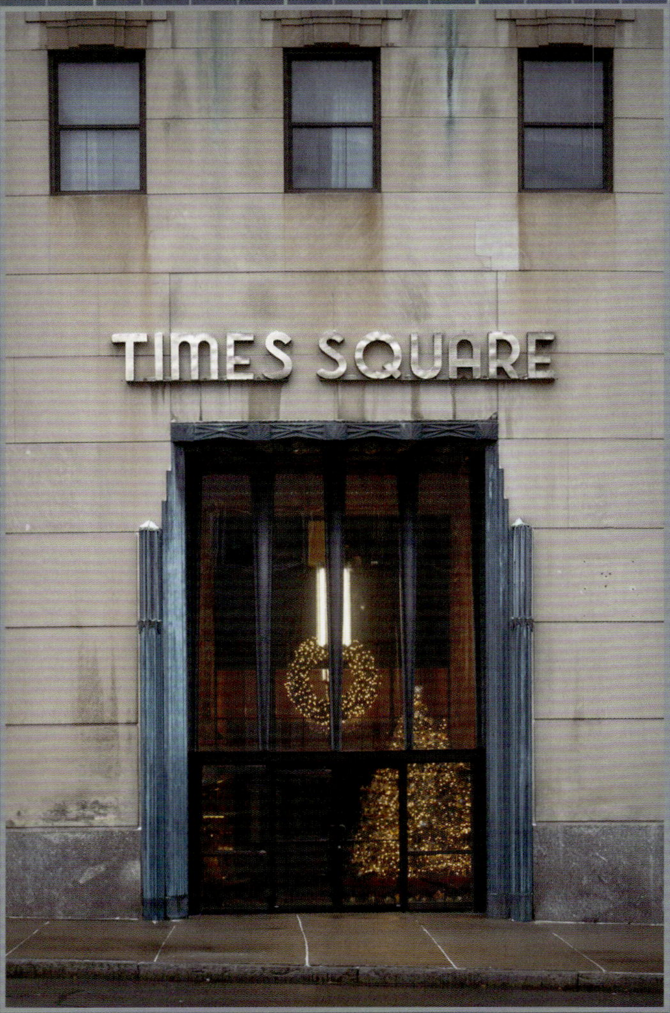

Simple metallic details on a stark stone facade are somewhat at odds with a sign that is not original.

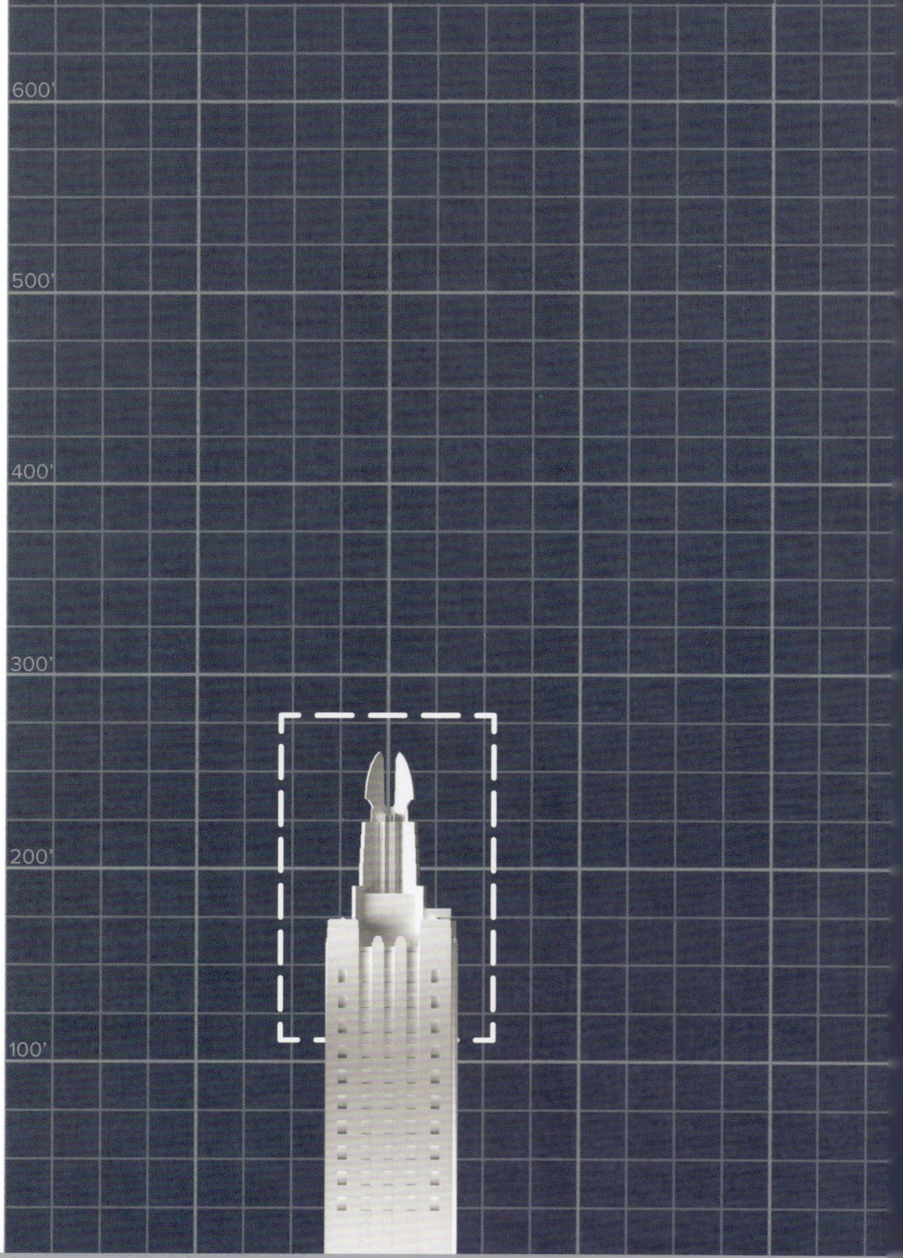

East Elevation *1" = 100'*

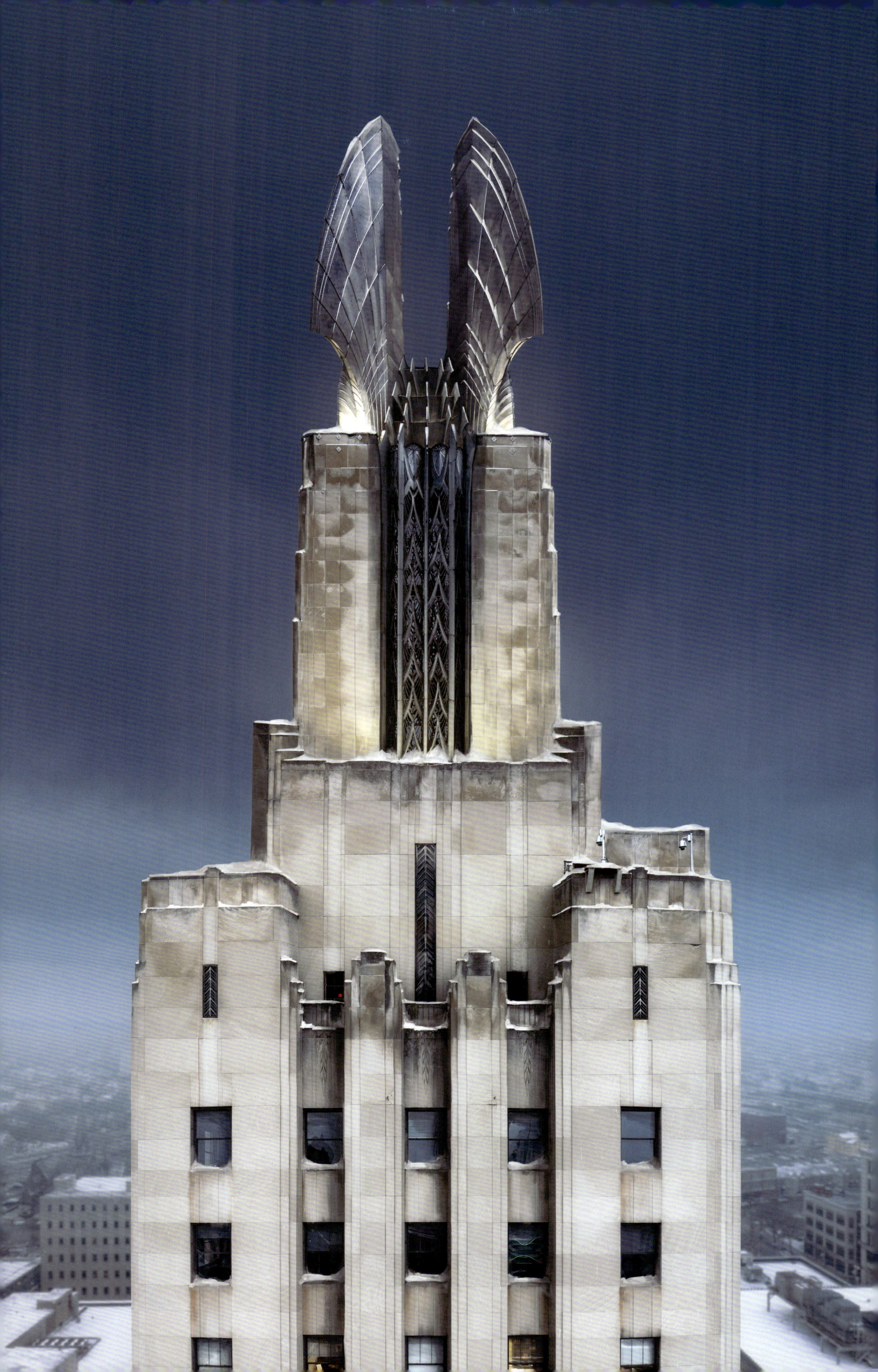

State Tower
Building

Syracuse, **NY**

Address ············· **109 S. Warren St.**
Opened ························· **1928**
Height ························· **315'**
Stories ···························· **21**
Style ························ **Art Deco**
Architect ········ **Thompson & Churchill**

"Harmony without dullness" is how architect Henry Churchill summarized this office highrise, still the tallest building in central New York. Besides its bold terracotta accent panels, the bricks get lighter the higher they go, adding an illusion of sunlight even on gloomy days. Inside, the elevator lobby is a panoply of geometric designs.

Built for New York developer Albert Meyer, the tower was the fruit of a creative if short-lived partnership between Churchill and Stuart Thompson. In their home base of Manhattan, their Lowell Hotel still has a lush pink tiled entrance, and their Bauhaus-style glass box loft was one of very few American buildings included in a 1932 Museum of Modern Art exhibition that defined the International Style, which would supplant Art Deco.

The skyscraper stands on the site of a prior office block destroyed in a 1923 fire that killed three people and triggered a new city requirement for sprinklers. A 1962 gas explosion was strong enough to buckle the State Tower Building's basement walls, but fortunately caused only a few injuries. The property has undergone recent renovations and now has apartments in its upper floors.

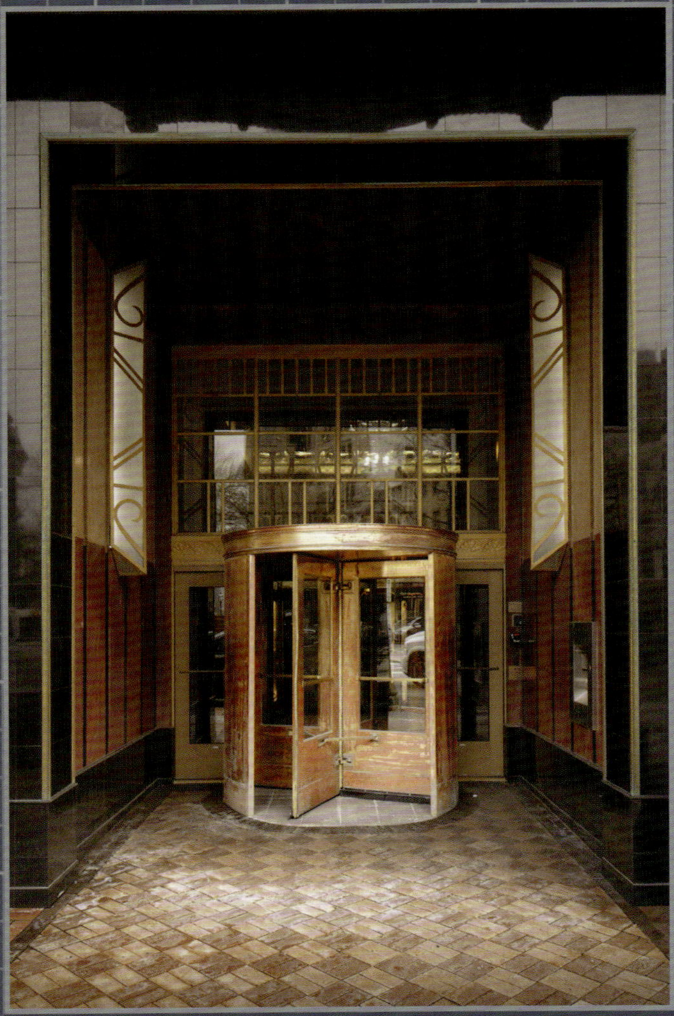

Major restoration work repaired the original entrance and lobby, adding a revolving door.

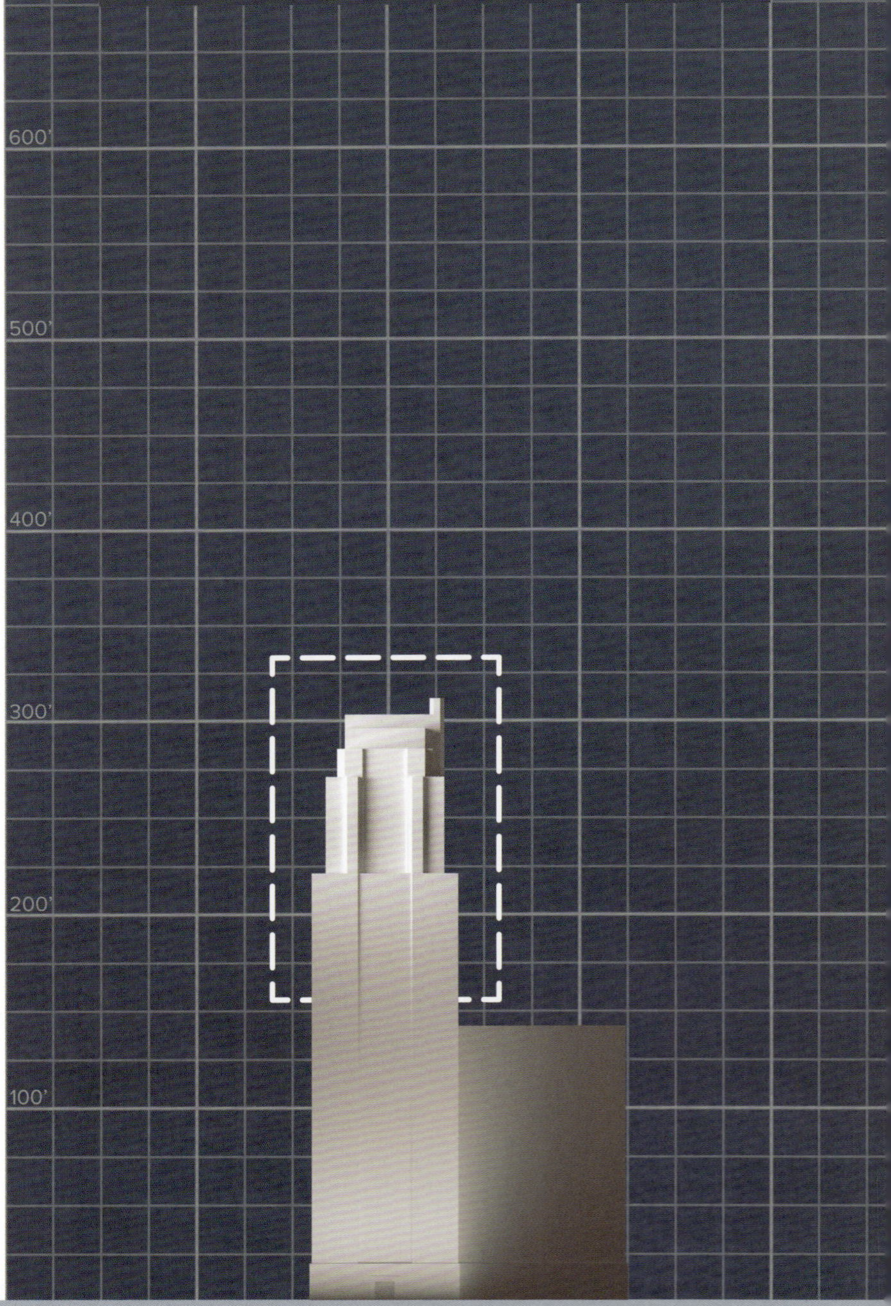

West Elevation *1" = 100'*

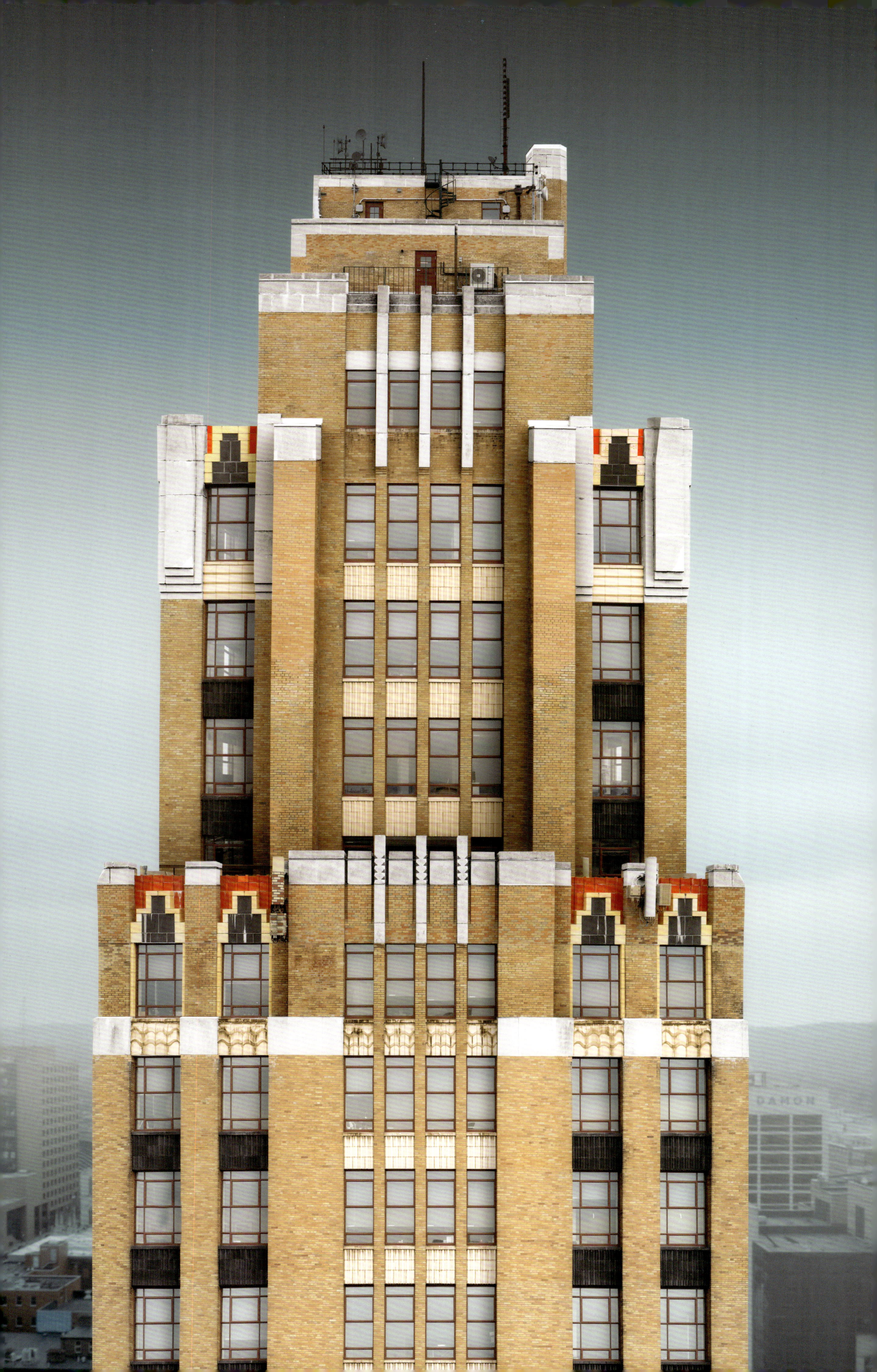
DANON

Baltimore Trust
Building

Baltimore, **MD** Bank of America Building

Address	**10 Light St.**
Opened	**1929**
Height	**509'**
Stories	**34**
Style	**Art Deco, Gothic**
Architect	**Taylor & Fisher, Smith & May**

The exuberant exterior of Baltimore's only Art Deco skyscraper features cresting ocean waves and crabs to go with its gargoyles. Its interior is equally breathtaking, with multicolored marble columns supporting the painted beamed ceiling and four large murals depicting the city in each century of its existence.

Alas, the lovely hand-wrought iron gates by master blacksmith Samuel Yellin now bar the public from the former banking hall, which has been repurposed as a gym. Its spectacular mosaic floor by the acclaimed muralist Hildreth Meière — creator of Radio City Music Hall's signature sculptures and the remarkable mosaics of the Nebraska State Capitol (p. 112) — is covered with mats to protect it.

Once the state's biggest financial institution, Baltimore Trust did not survive a 1933 banking panic. Now a residential highrise, the building has changed hands and names repeatedly. Its most colorful owner, West Virginia millionaire and political gadfly Raymond J. Funkhouser, renamed it the O'Sullivan building in 1942 after a company he owned that made rubber shoe heels. He also kicked an upscale barbershop out of the top floor so he could put his penthouse there.

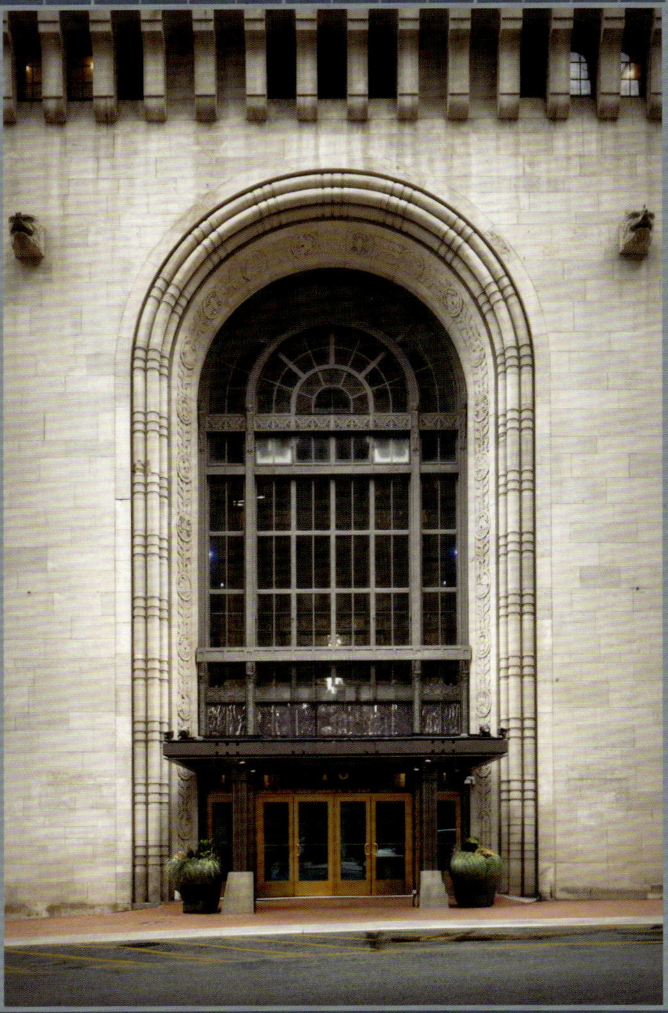

The tall arched main entrance opens to a staircase into a massive and ornate banking hall.

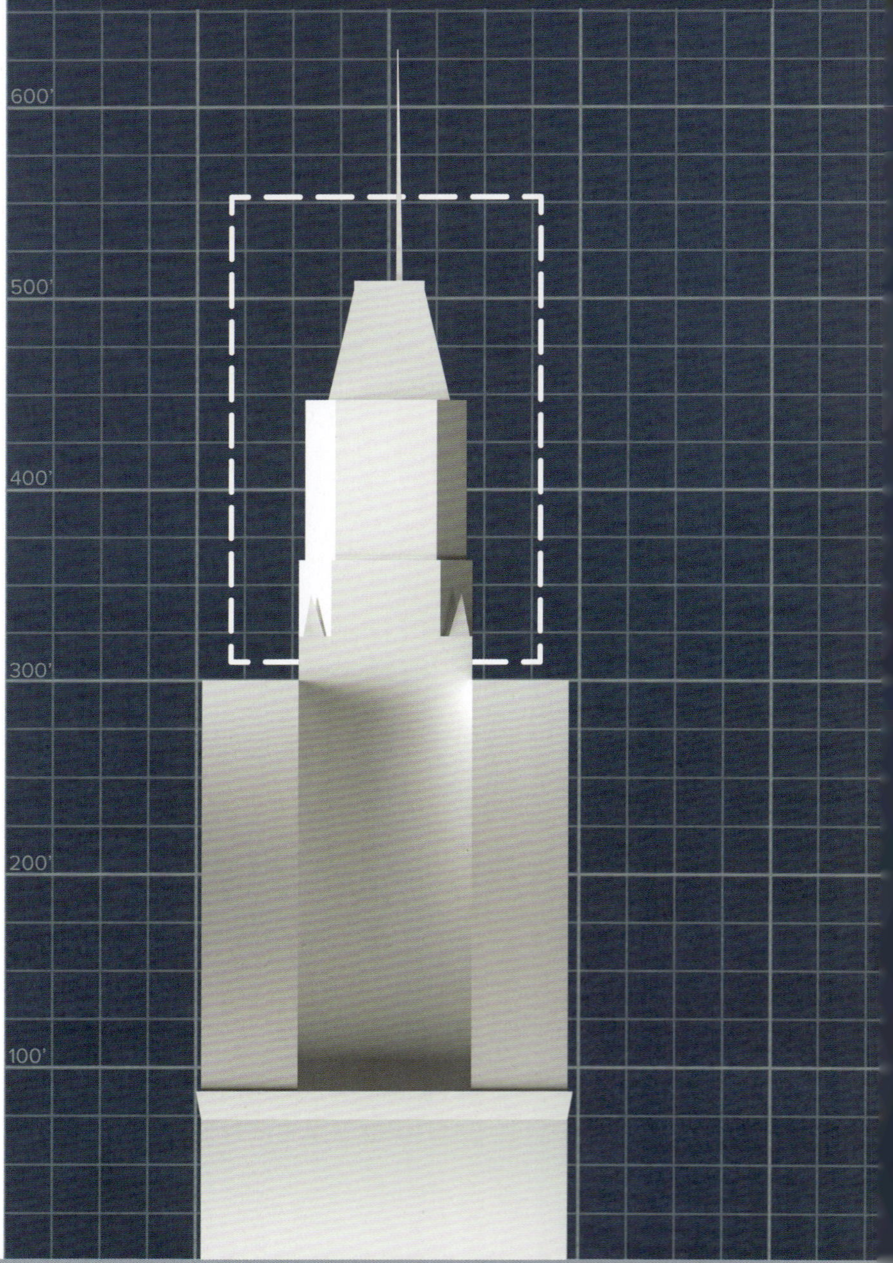

East Elevation *1" = 100'*

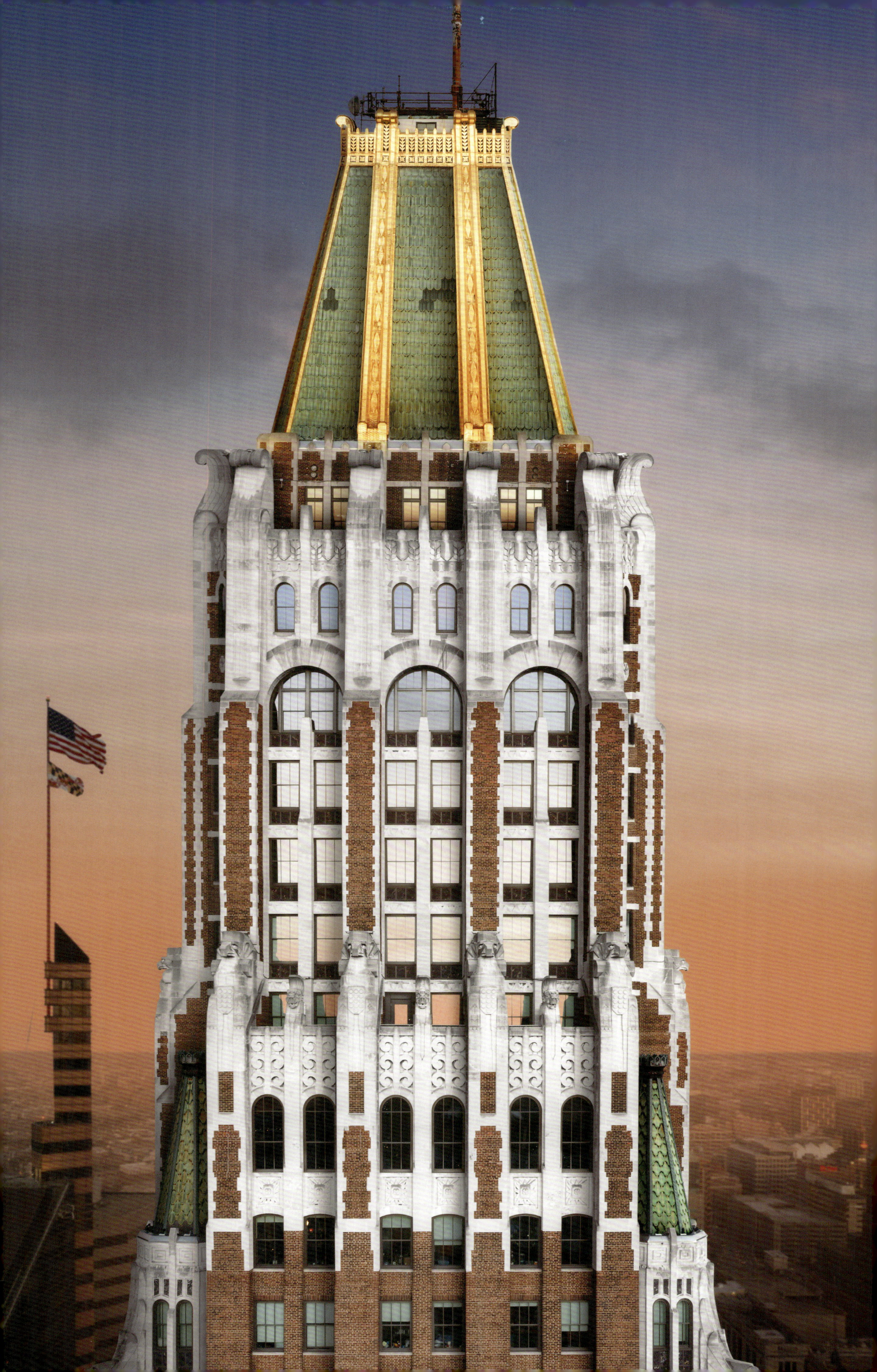

Tower Building

Boston, **MA** 75-101 Federal Street

Address .... **111 Franklin St.**
Opened **1930**
Height .... **245'**
Stories **21**
Style .... **Art Deco**
Architect .... **Thomas James**

The wedding cake shape of this and other Deco-era American highrises was due to zoning rules requiring floors above a certain height to step back, letting more sunlight down to the street. Such limits clearly could not quash this building's exuberance, with its terracotta floral panels stretching to the roofline.

Nearer to the sidewalk, stylized bronze bas-reliefs display acts of labor and technological prowess by burly men who are mostly shirtless and occasionally pants-less. Mythical heroic figures join the cast over the main entrance on Franklin Street. A well-preserved honey and ebony marble lobby shows off additional craftsmanship and metalwork.

The highrise was financed by a consortium led by Louis Abrons, a New York builder whose family immigrated from present-day Belarus when he was a boy. One lead investor was stockbroker Charles Hayden, who made a fortune in copper mining, then built public planetariums in Boston and New York that still bear his name.

Originally called the Tower Building, this was more commonly referred to by its ground floor tenants Second National Bank and later State Street Trust. In 1985 the building became part of 75-101 Federal Street when it was fused to a taller office tower erected next door after Boston finally relaxed its height limits.

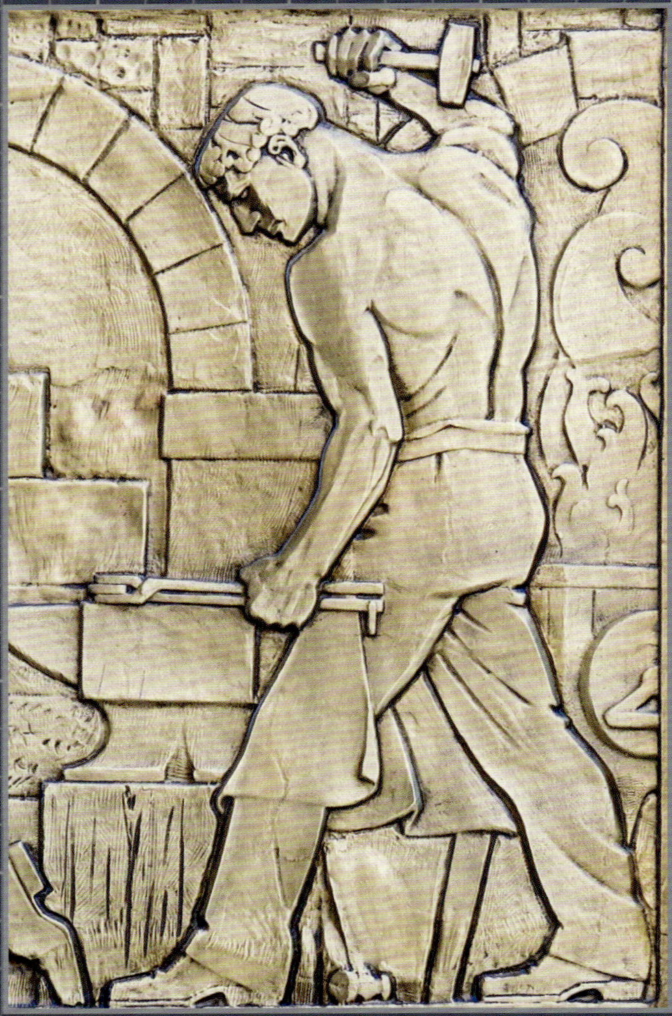

A mighty laborer hammers at his forge in this detail from one of the bronze frieze panels.

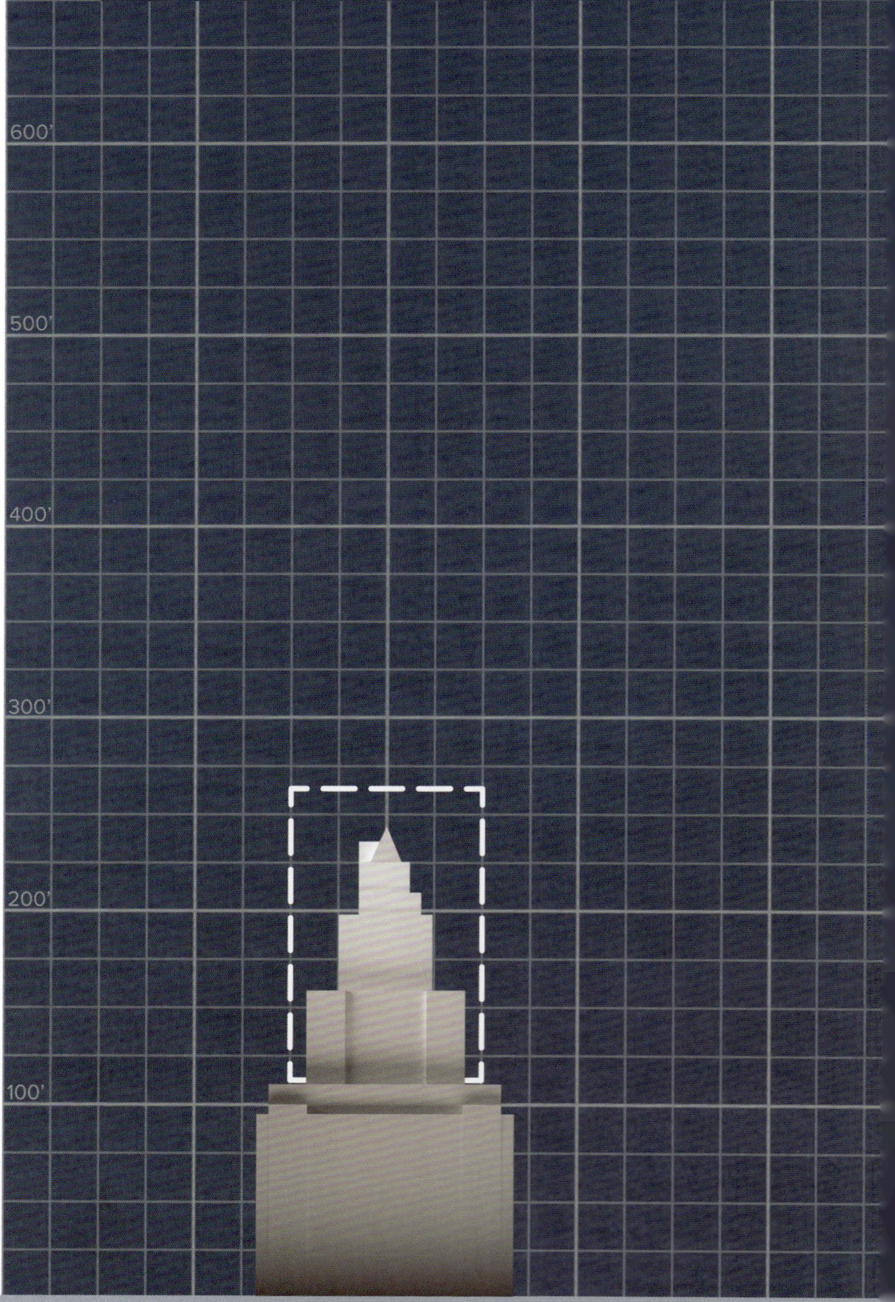

East Elevation *1" = 100'*

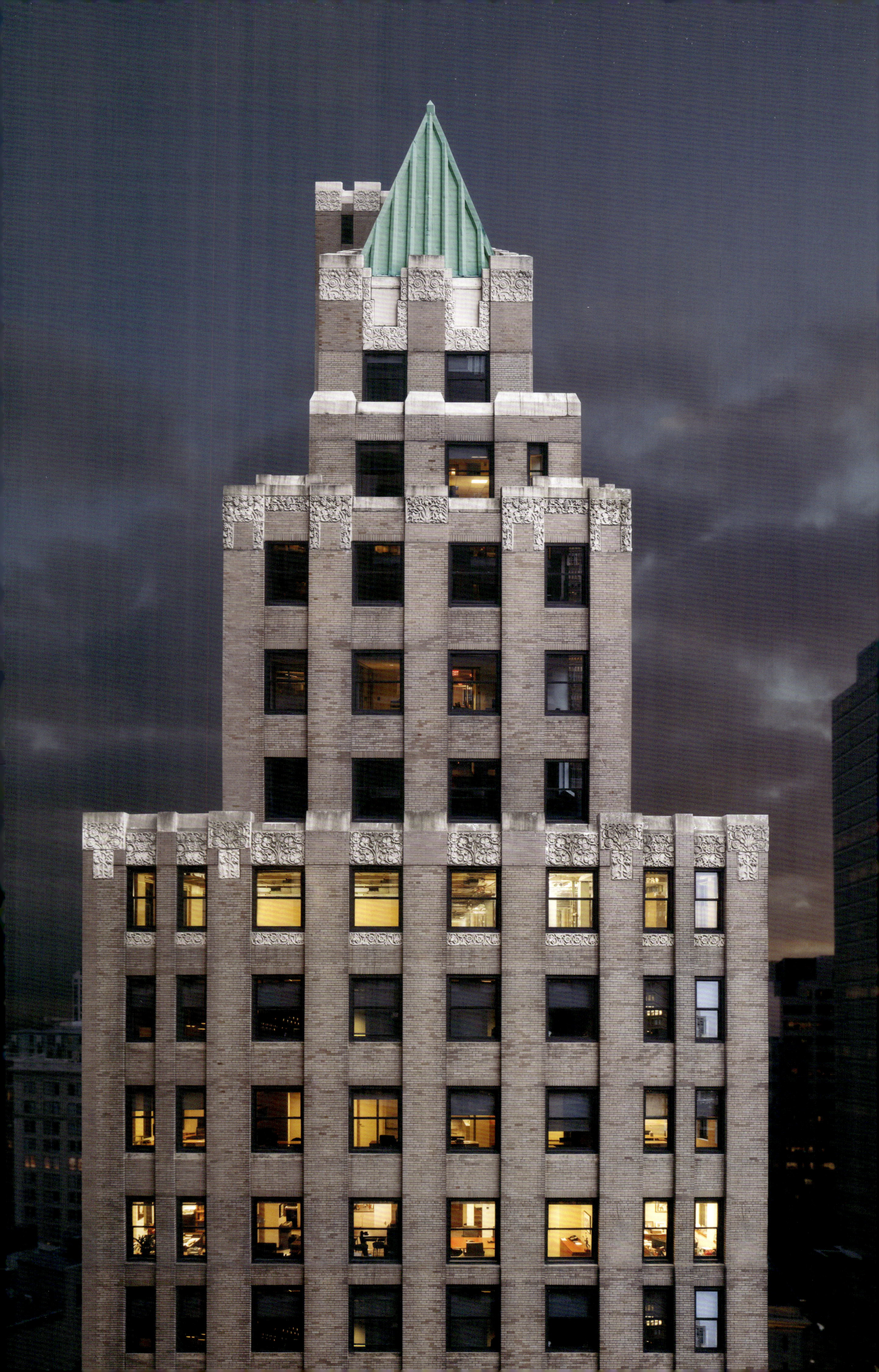

Camden City Hall

Camden, **NJ**

Address .... **520 Market St.**
Opened **1931**
Height .... **371'**
Stories **18**
Style .... **Art Deco, Neoclassical**
Architect .... **Edwards & Green**

When a one-ton weight in Camden's old city hall clock tower crashed down in 1929, narrowly missing four commissioners and three secretaries, officials congratulated themselves for having already started construction of a replacement.

To emphasize that Camden was the home of RCA Victor, a leader in sound recording and radio, the new clock tower housed a "synthetic tone producer" that mimicked the chime of Big Ben. Loudspeakers mounted to the tower blasted loud enough to be heard two miles away, causing floors to vibrate inside the building.

It was all meant as a bold statement to put Camden on the map. A line by poet and longtime Camden resident Walt Whitman carved into the granite exterior gives a sense of the spirit of the project: "In a dream I saw a city invincible."

But a year after the opening and further into the Great Depression, more than 3,000 angry taxpayers crowded into the building for hearings about wasteful government spending exemplified by the new municipal edifice. Frederick von Nieda, a former councilman and future mayor, announced to cheers: "Camden bought a high hat and a diamond ring when it needed a pair of shoes and pants." Subsequent efforts to sell the building have never come to fruition.

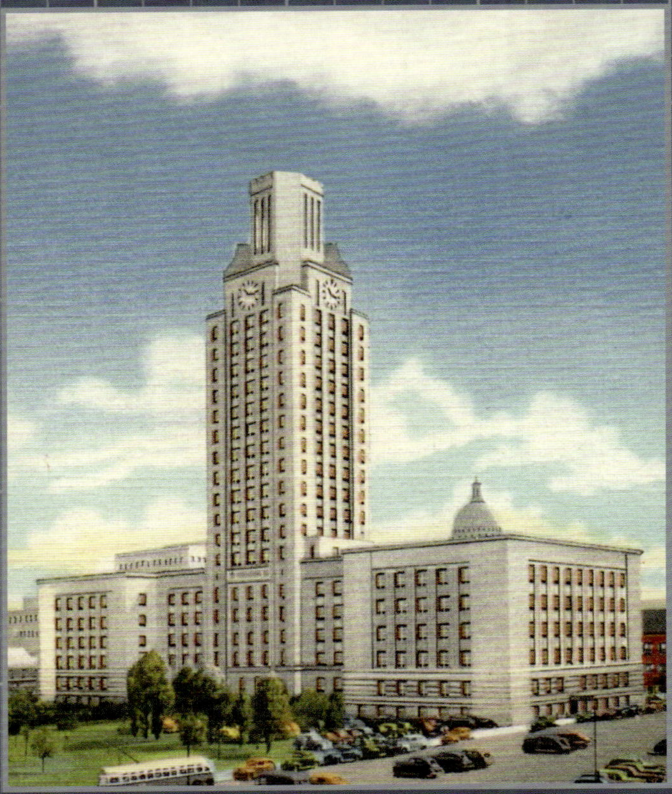

A vintage postcard shows the city hall tower and the dome of the courthouse, which was torn down in 1954.

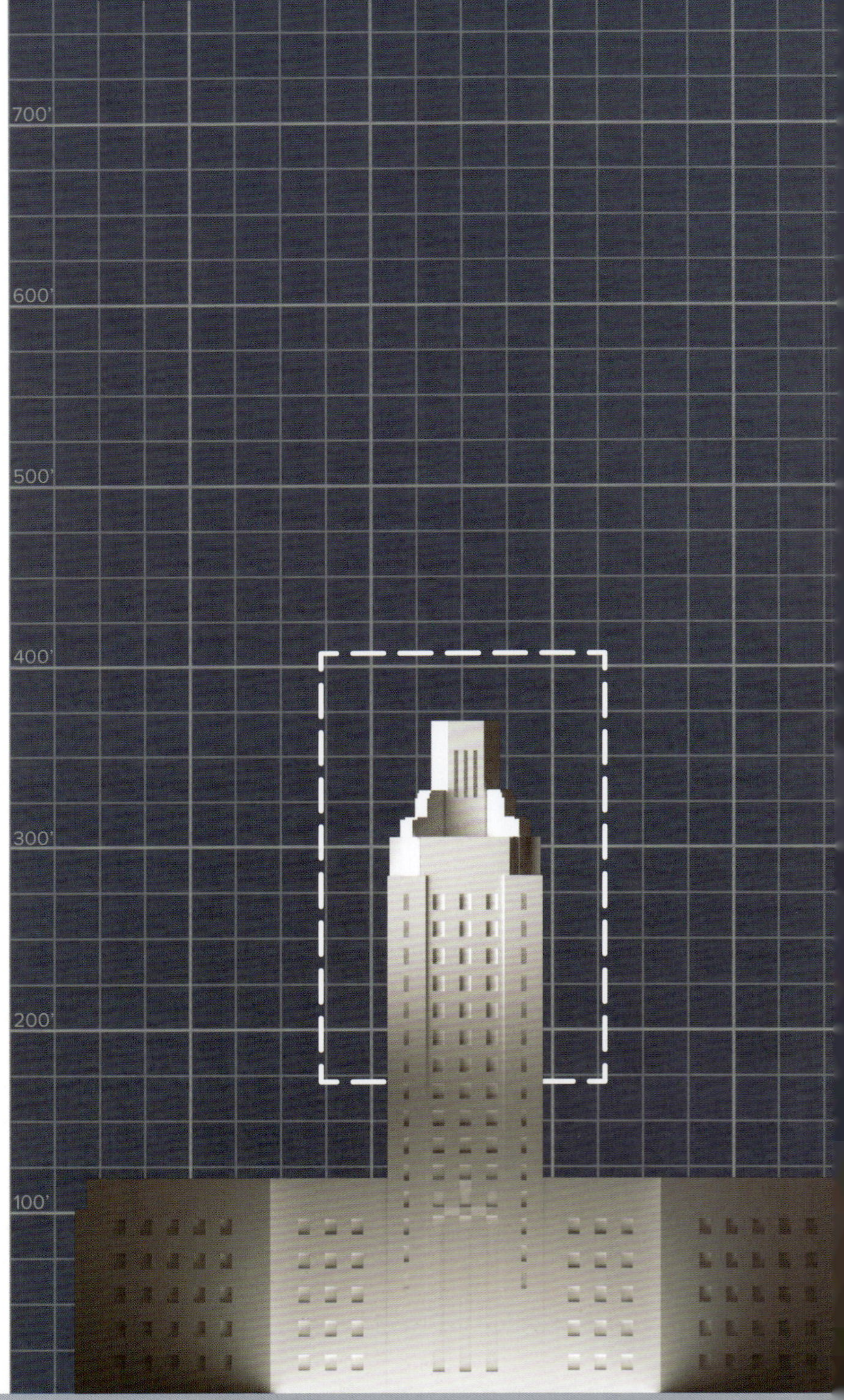

West Elevation *1" = 100'*

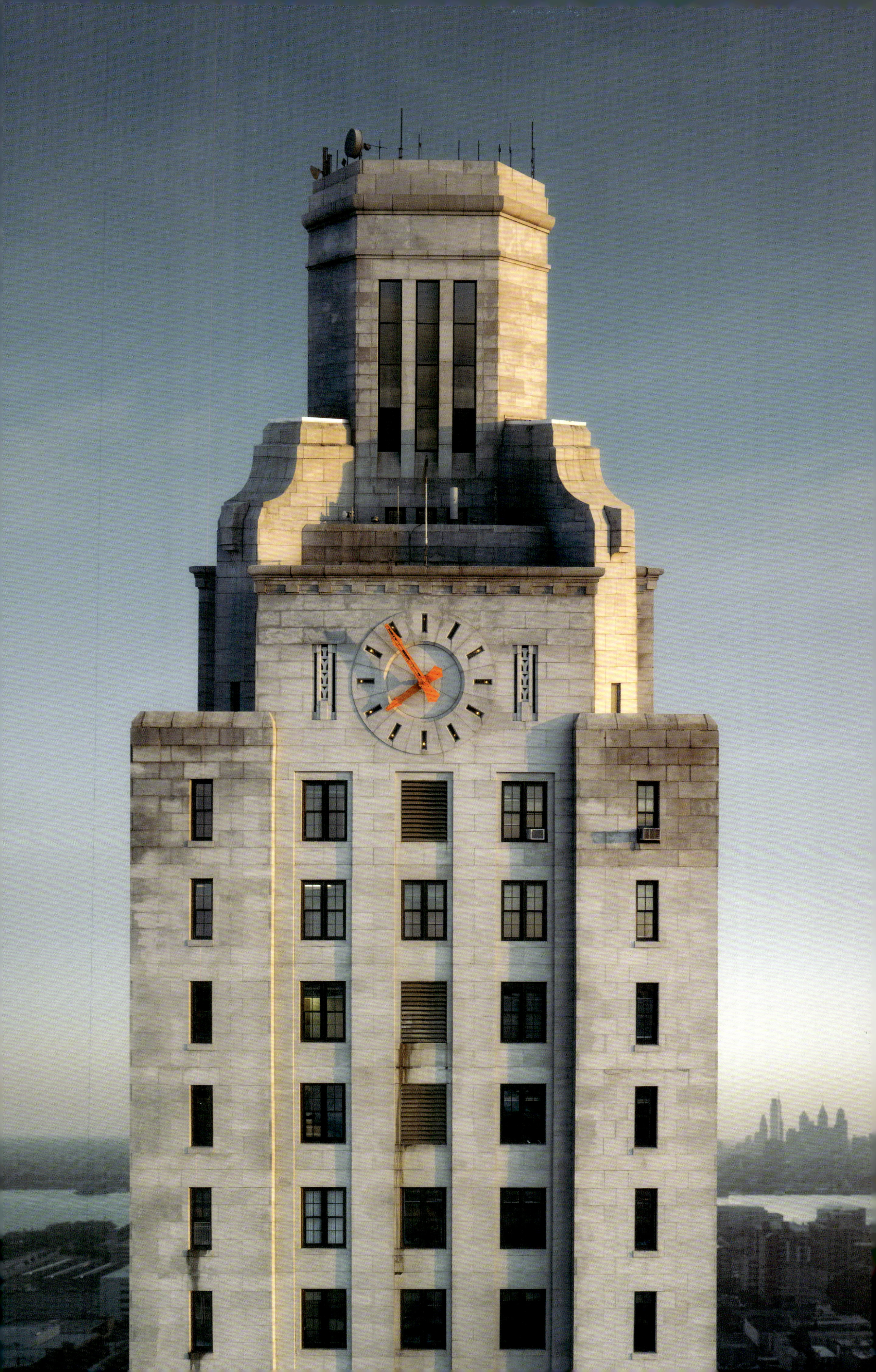

Lefcourt-Newark
Building

Newark, **NJ**

Address	**1180 Raymond Blvd.**
Opened	**1930**
Height	**448'**
Stories	**35**
Style	**Art Deco**
Architect	**Frank Grad**

For a brief moment, this Newark highrise was a bauble in the empire of Abraham Lefcourt, a bombastic real estate titan who slapped his name on Midtown skyscrapers long before the world ever heard of Donald Trump.

Born Abraham Lefkowitz, Lefcourt came to the Lower East Side with his Russian Jewish family in 1882. He made money in garment wholesaling, then put it into commercial lofts and offices. Through shrewd deals and luck, Lefcourt built a Manhattan skyscraper portfolio worth $125 million, and started boasting he would put up the world's tallest one next. But the death in 1930 of his 17-year-old son two months before this highrise opened sent Lefcourt reeling, and the stock market collapse wiped him out. He died of a heart attack two years later.

Another immigrant, Frank Grad, designed Lefcourt's handsome Newark tower with its elegant details and opulent black marble and bronze entrances. Grad's two sons joined him in the business, which steadily grew into New Jersey's biggest architectural firm.

The tower, known for most of its existence as the Raymond Commerce Building, was vacant for nearly two decades before 2006, when it reopened as a luxury apartment complex. As its namesake knew, real estate can be unpredictable.

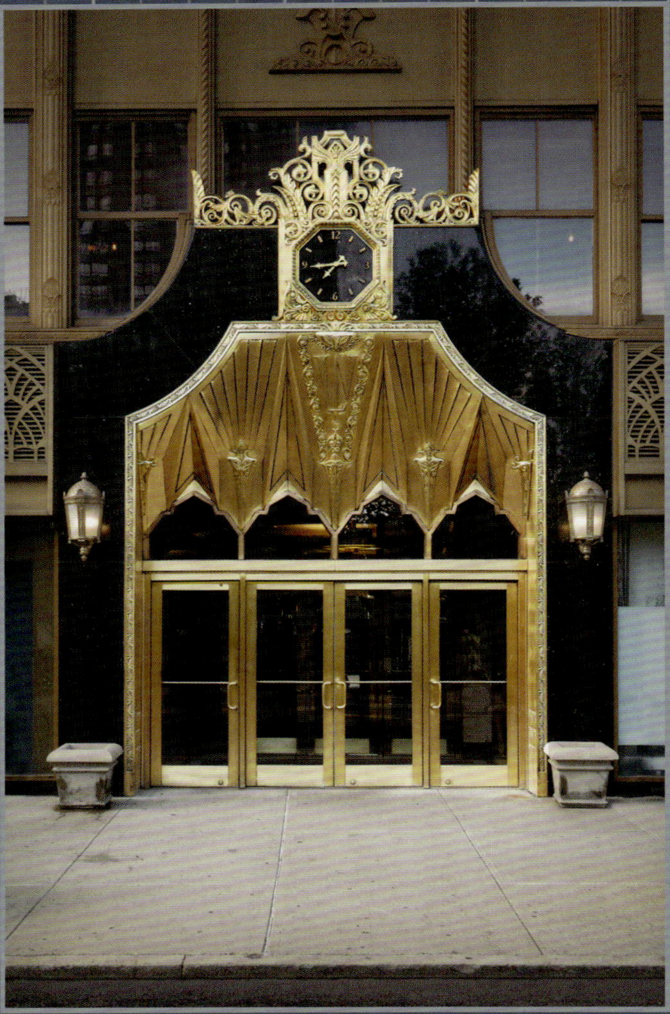

Below an ornate clock, sculpted bronze panels pull back like curtains from the ebony granite frame.

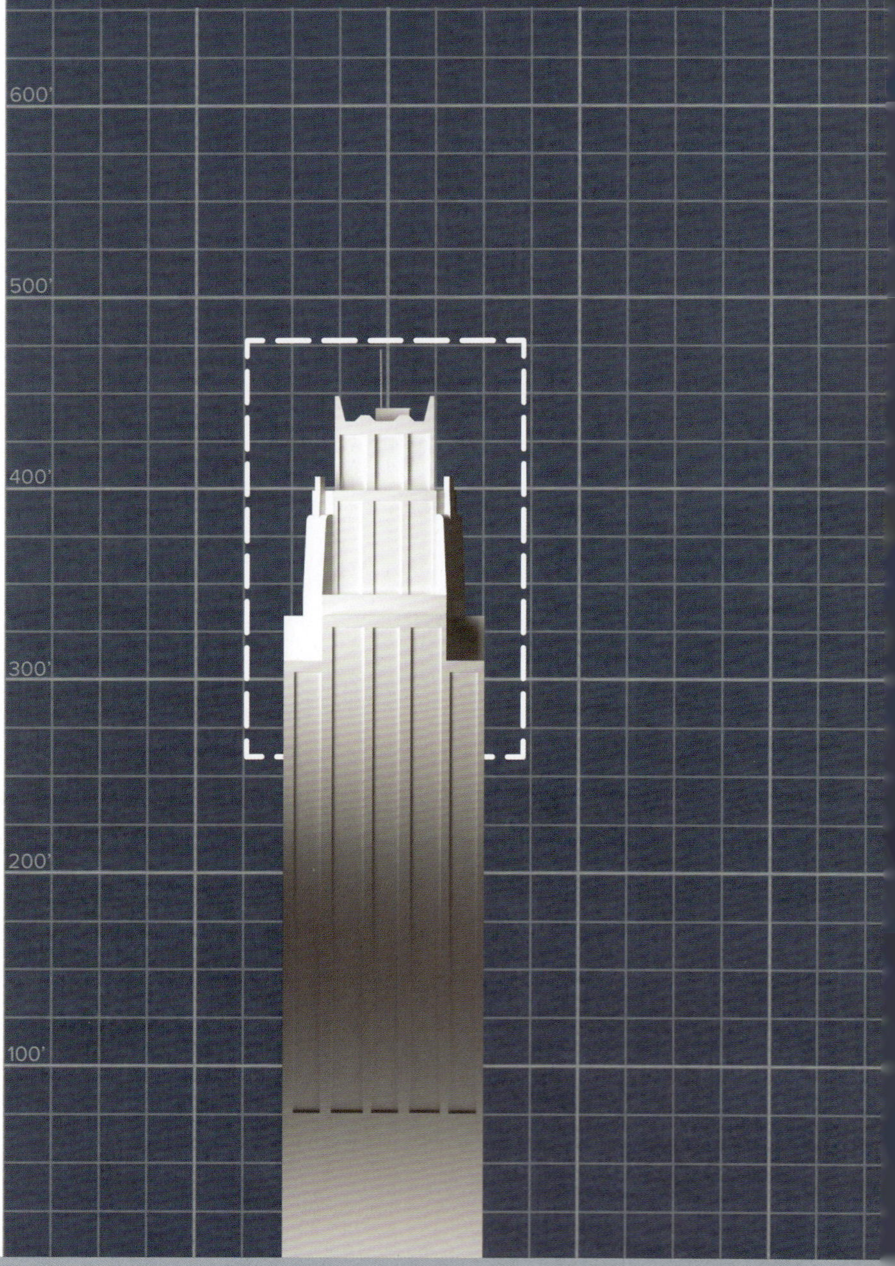

West Elevation 1" = 100'

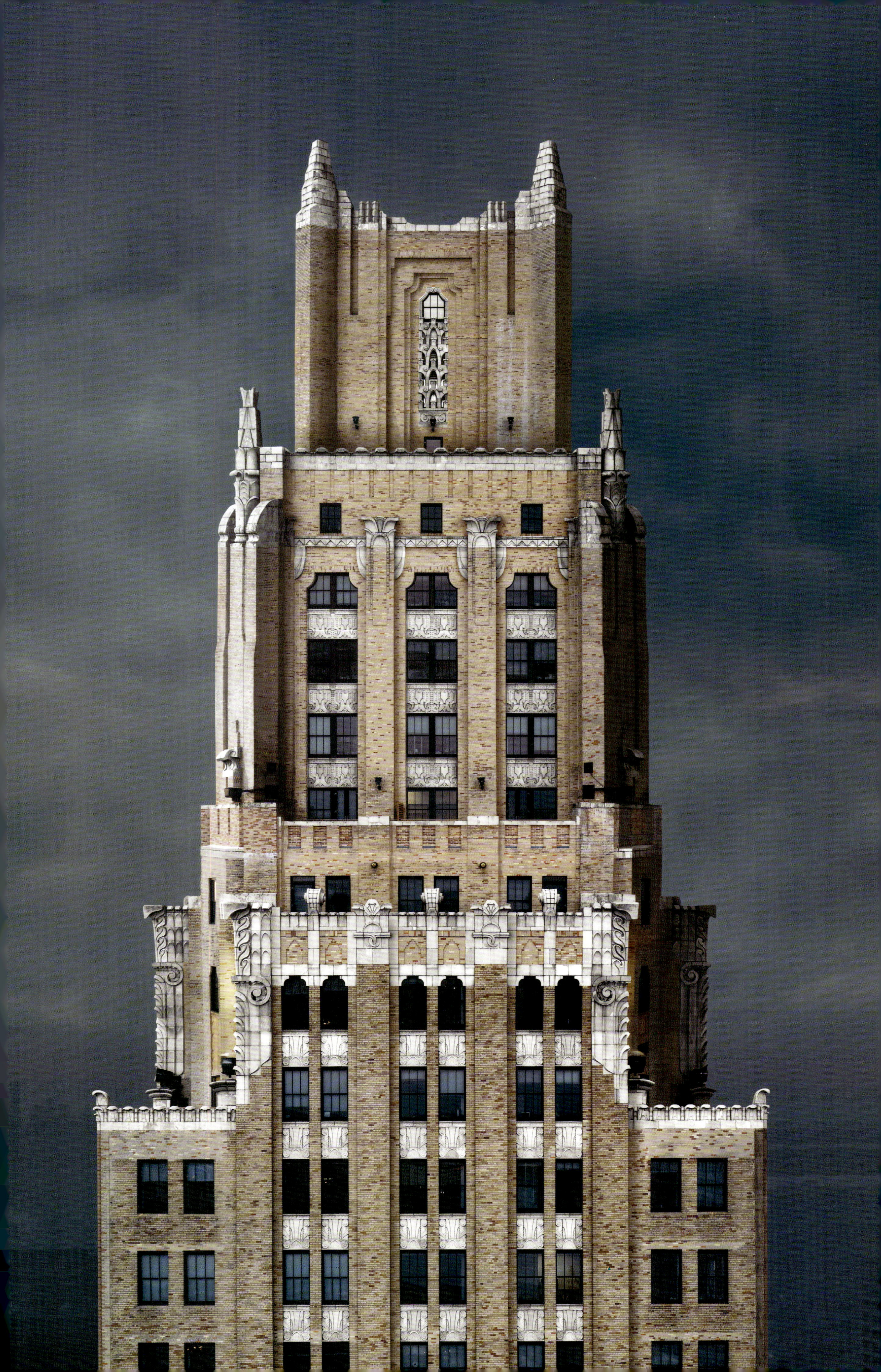

Architects Building

Philadelphia, **PA** Hotel Palomar

Address	**117 S. 17th St.**
Opened	**1930**
Height	**313'**
Stories	**24**
Style	**Art Deco**
Architect	**Rankin, Johnson, Abel et al.**

As the name implies, this tower provided offices for architects. It also was designed by them, as 20 firms participated in a committee headed by John Hall Rankin, respected dean of the field and former president of the local chapter of the American Institute of Architects.

Shortly after the building opened, the AIA held a public exhibition showcasing the work of several members who now occupied offices upstairs. Paul Cret, for instance, displayed photos of his Rodin Museum on the Benjamin Franklin Parkway, recently dedicated and containing one of the most extensive collections of the Paris sculptor's work. The AIA relocated in 2008, but its library on the top floor has been preserved as it once appeared.

The building, now a hotel, has a sleek Art Deco exterior with handsome bronze panels and patterned brickwork testifying that the architects knew what they were doing. Best of all is the historic second floor elevator lobby, which combines vibrant tilework and carved wood with a dramatically coffered plaster ceiling and Welsh quarry tile floor.

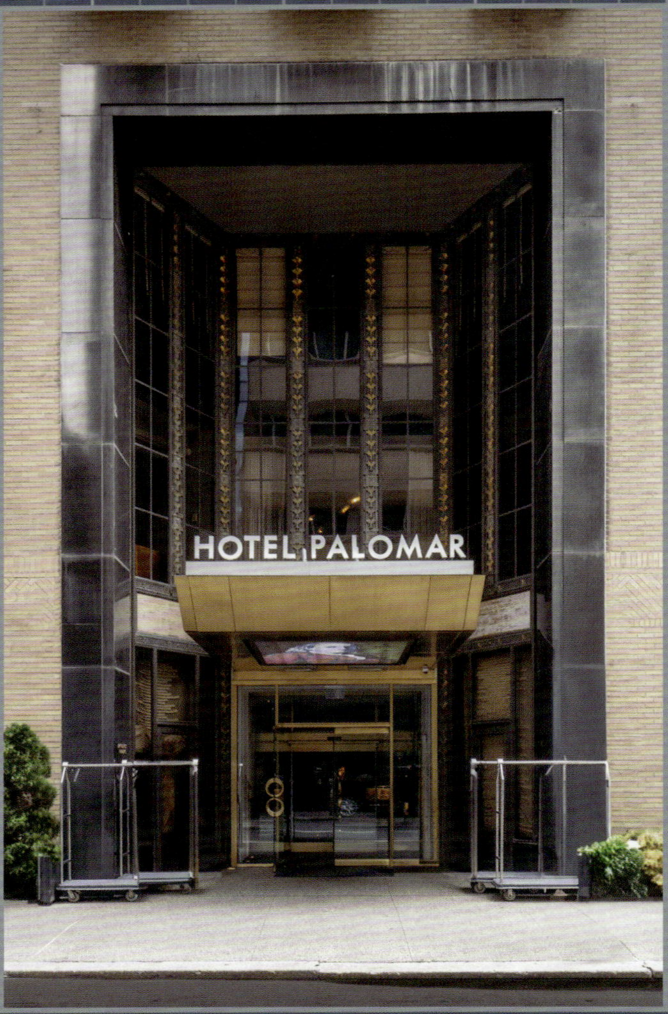

The hotel marquee is new, but the rest of the elegant two-and-a-half story entrance remains as it was at its opening.

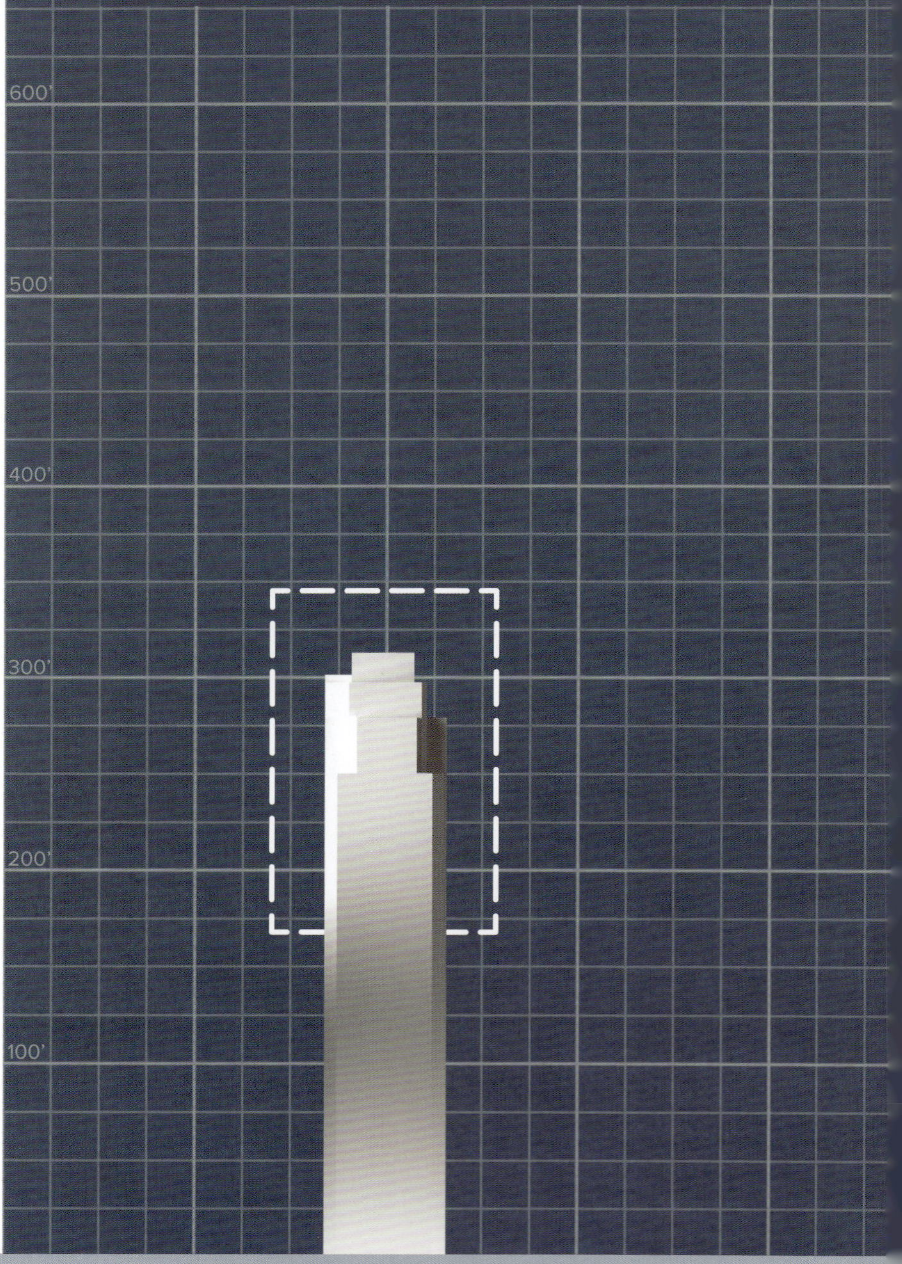

West Elevation *1" = 100'*

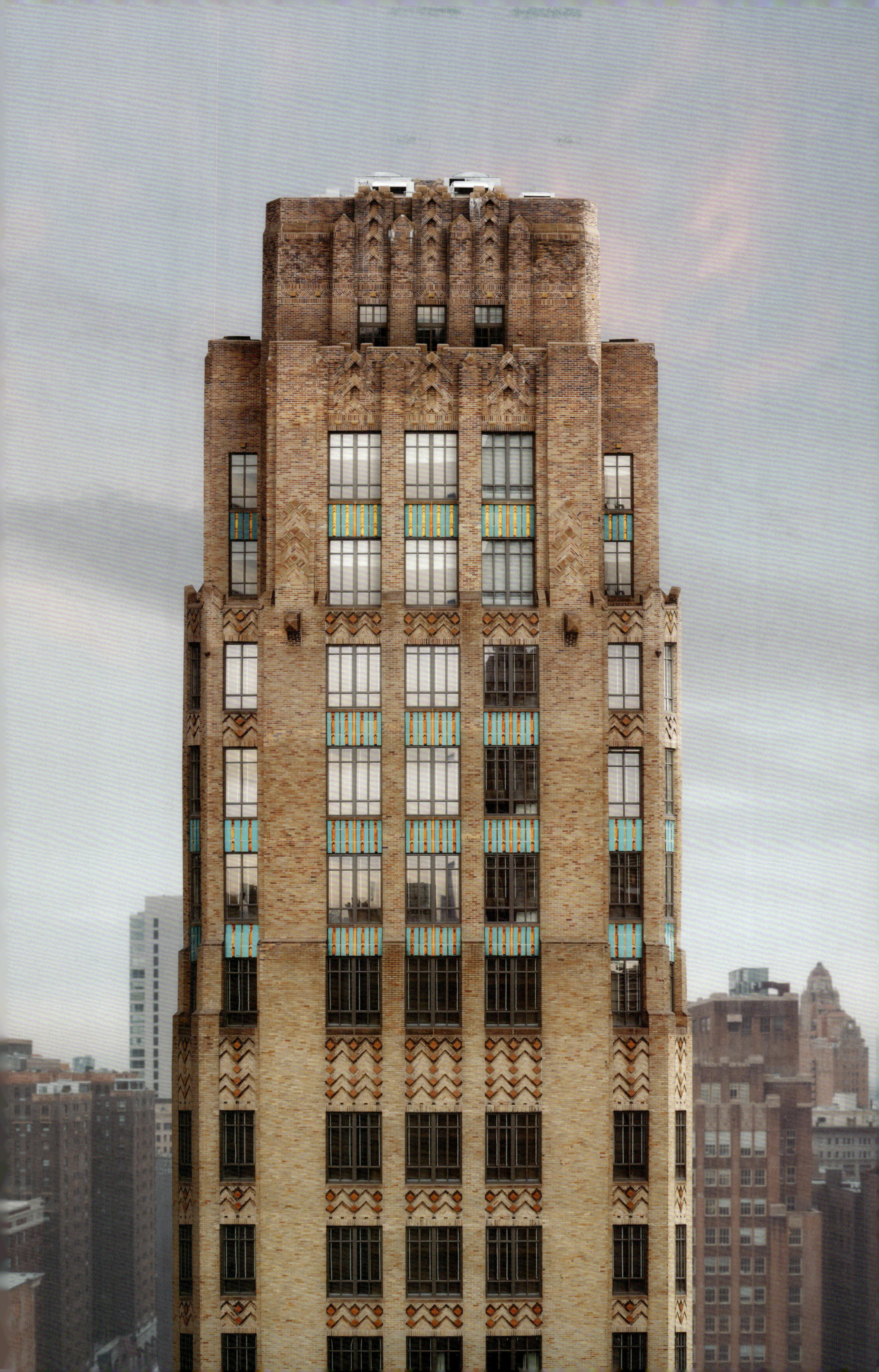

The Drake

Philadelphia, **PA**

Address	**1512 Spruce St.**
Opened	**1929**
Height	**375'**
Stories	**30**
Style	**Art Deco, Spanish Baroque**
Architect	**Ritter & Shay**

The contours of this slab skyscraper are Art Deco, but slathered on top is an icing of terracotta and tiled rooftops and gazebos seemingly transplanted from Seville or Southern California. Developers named the luxury residential highrise for a celebrated English privateer who looted goodly sums of Spanish booty while claiming the Pacific coast for Queen Elizabeth I.

Architects Ritter & Shay also designed Market Street National Bank, a cousin to the Drake that features ornamentation more strictly Deco though no less exuberant. With 300 apartments and a cluster of penthouses, the Drake touted true high society city living.

In the 1970s, owners Stanton and Robert Miller ran high stakes bingo games in the ballroom five nights a week — allegedly for charity, in reality for their pockets. Unlike Sir Francis Drake, the Millers wound up sentenced to prison for their ill-gotten gains, and the property suffered through bankruptcy and other ignominies until its eventual renovation.

The two-story penthouse on top affords breathtaking views from its twin patios, but not from the red-roofed dome, which just hides a water tank.

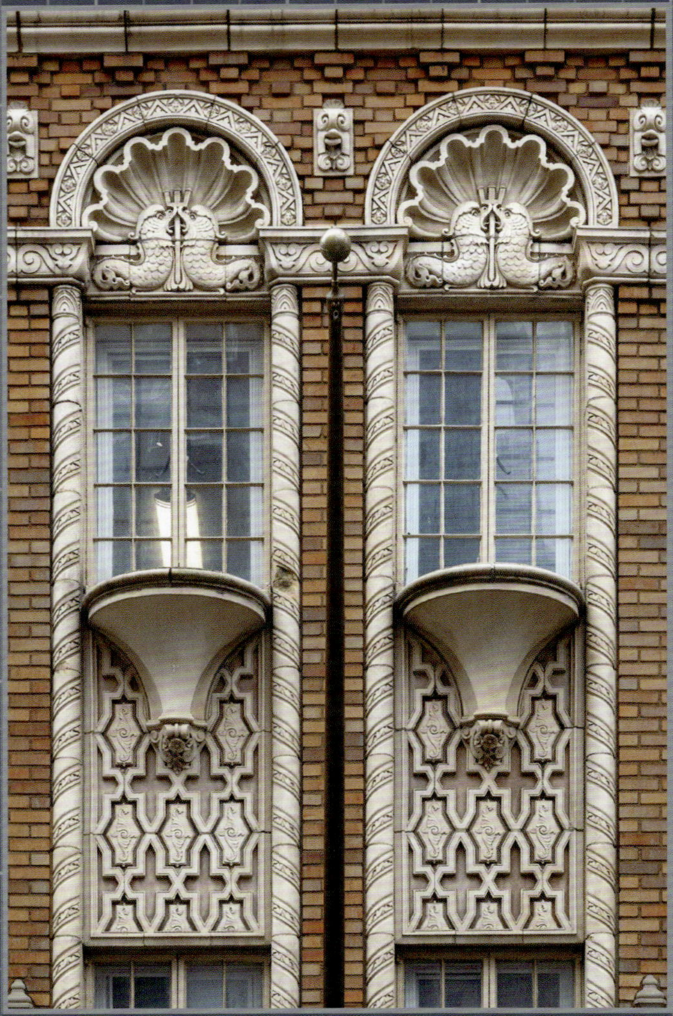

A pair of medieval dolphins flanking a trident within a scalloped shell convey a seafaring theme for the building's namesake.

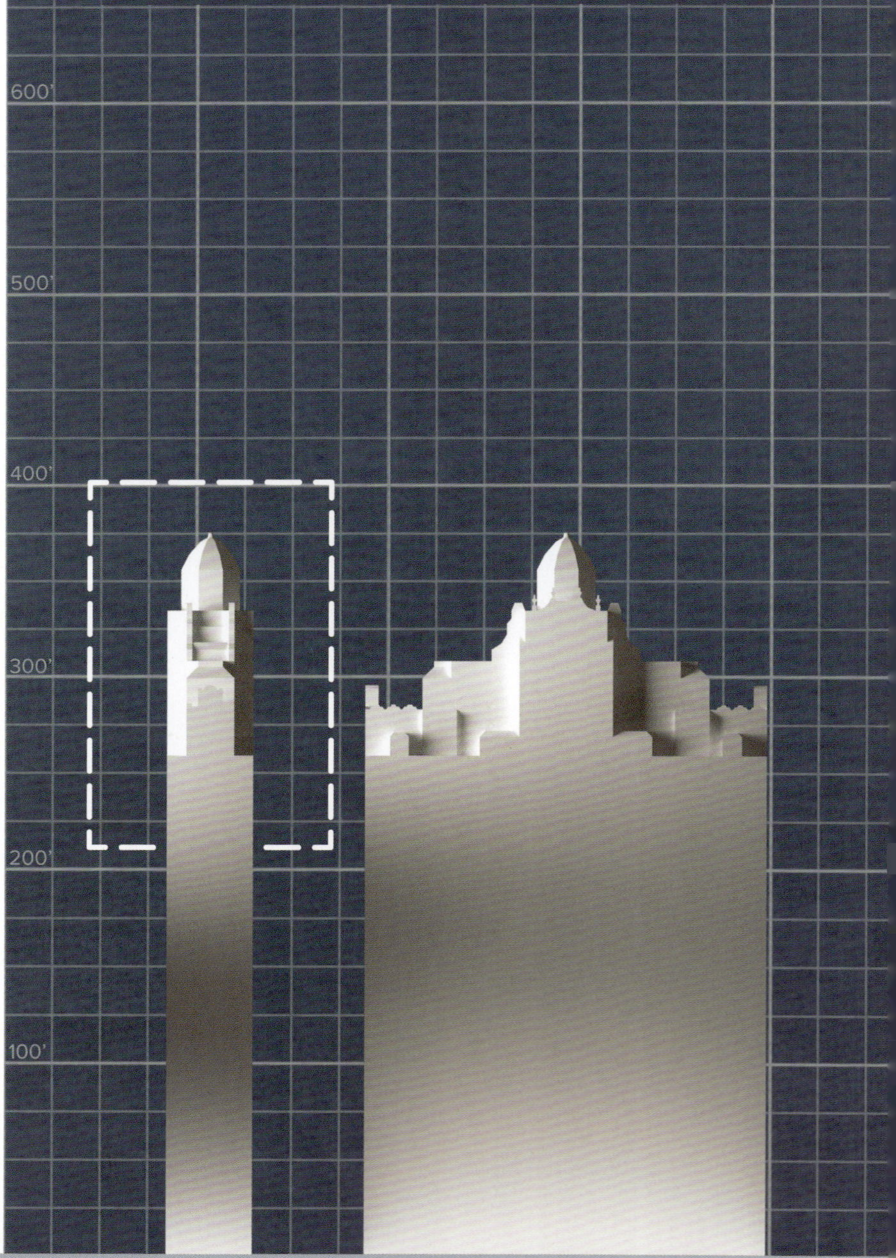

South Elevation East Elevation *1" = 100'*

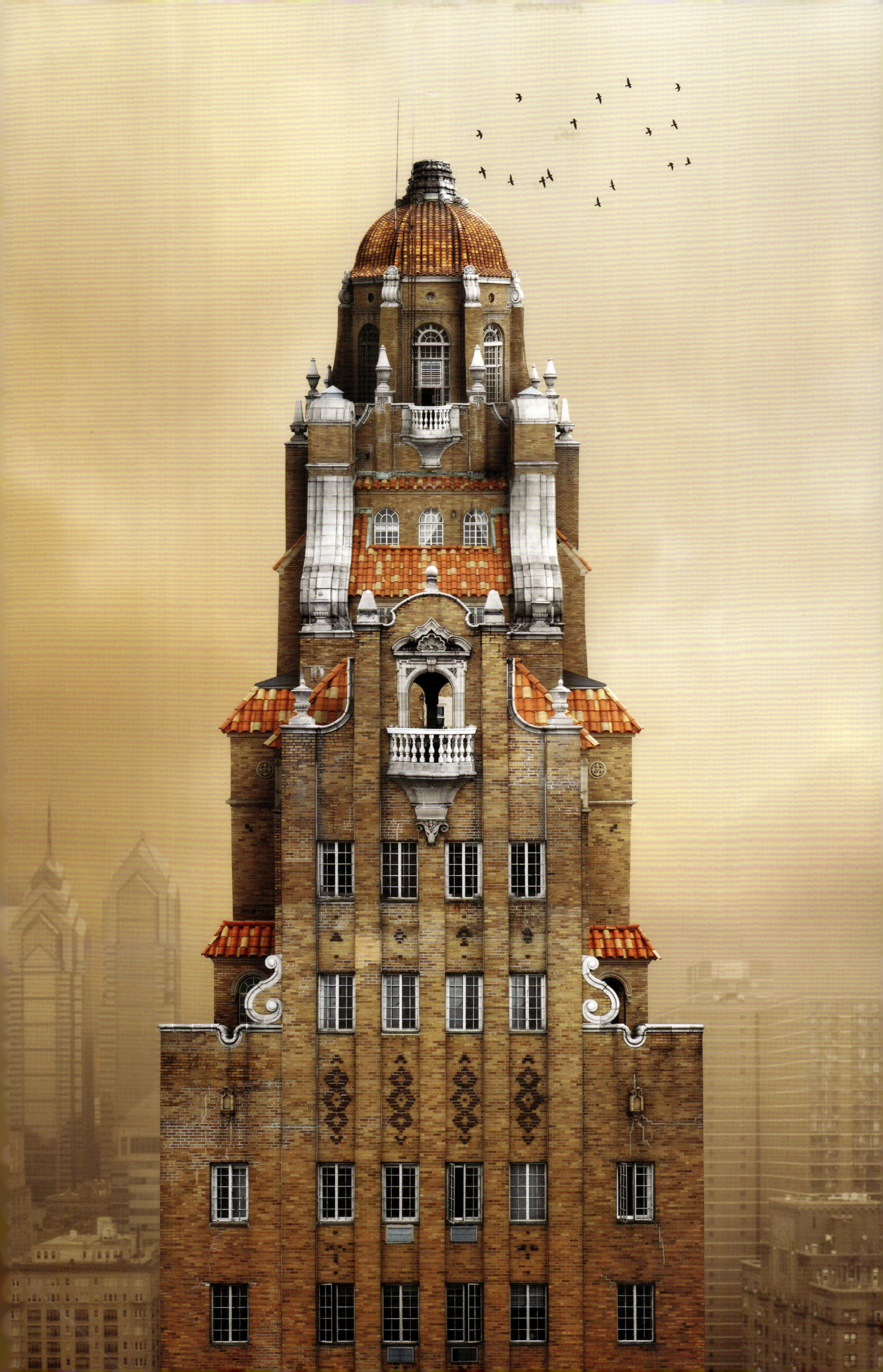

Beury Building

Philadelphia, **PA**

Address	**3701 N. Broad St.**
Opened	**1926**
Height	**178'**
Stories	**14**
Style	**Art Deco**
Architect	**William Lee**

The founders of the National Bank of North Philadelphia, which opened in 1920, chose as their first president the attorney Charles Beury, a graduate of Princeton and Harvard Law. The financial institution's rapid success led to construction of Uptown's first skyscraper, which was initially called the National Bank of North Philadelphia Building.

Beury, meanwhile, had new presidential obligations. An influential trustee at nearby Temple University, he was picked for the executive job following the death of the institution's founder. Refocused on the university, Beury remained the bank's chairman until it was acquired by Bankers Trust Company in 1930. The successors renamed the building after him in September, then three months later became the first large Philadelphia bank to fail in the Great Depression.

Beury guided Temple's steady growth in his 15 years as president, and a building on campus also bears his name. His once-stylish Art Deco tower on Broad Street long stood abandoned, crumbling, and infamously adorned by a pair of graffiti artists who proudly tagged it with their noms-de-can: "Forever" and "Boner." After decades of neglect, it is being renovated into a hotel.

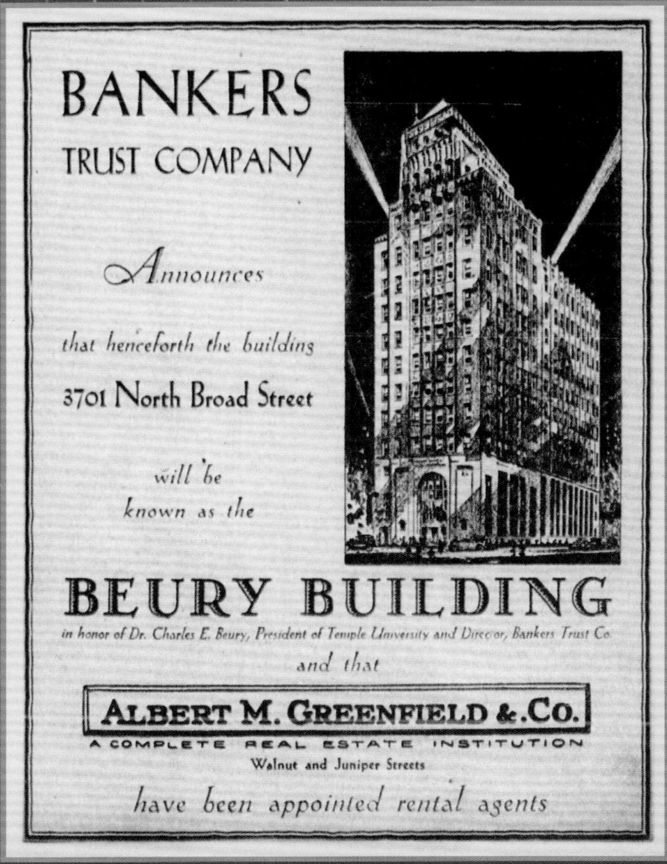

BANKERS TRUST COMPANY

Announces that henceforth the building 3701 North Broad Street will be known as the

BEURY BUILDING

in honor of Dr. Charles E. Beury, President of Temple University and Director, Bankers Trust Co.

and that

ALBERT M. GREENFIELD & CO.

A COMPLETE REAL ESTATE INSTITUTION

Walnut and Juniper Streets

have been appointed rental agents

An announcement from 1930 when the building was renamed after the bank's former chairman.

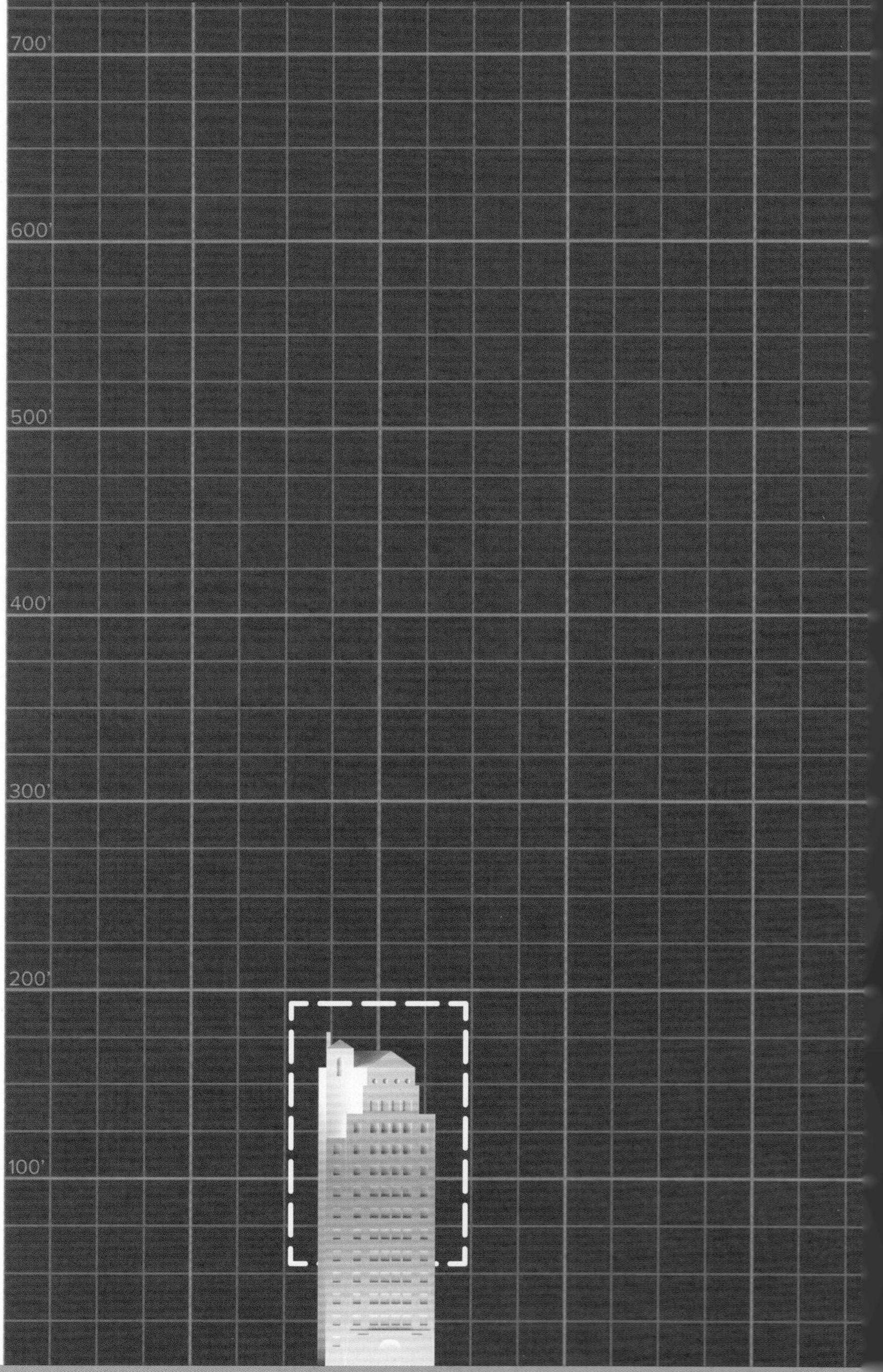

West Elevation *1" = 100'*

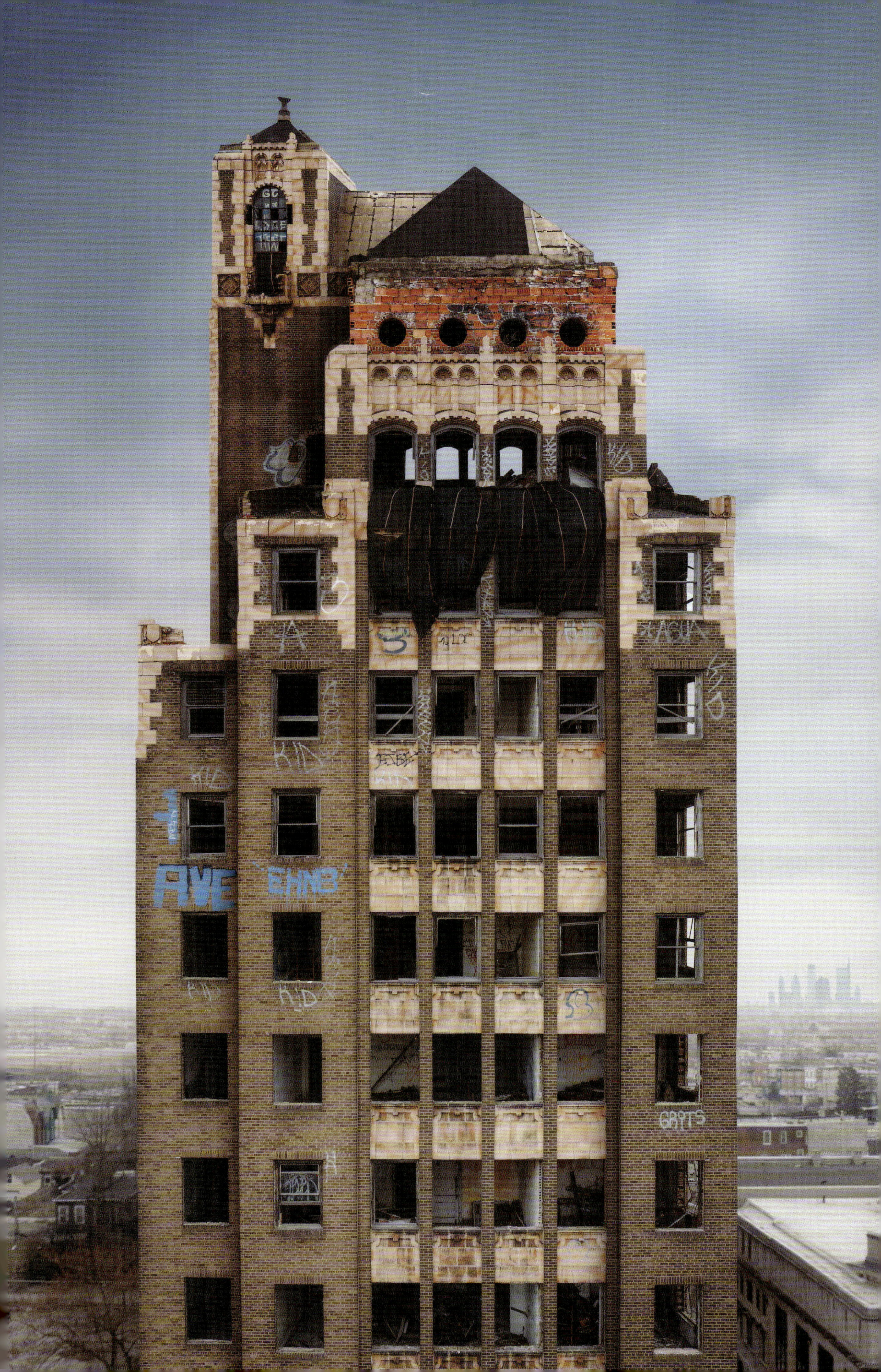
AVE
EHNB
GRITS

Lincoln-Liberty
Building

Philadelphia, **PA**

Address	**1 S. Broad St**
Opened	**1932**
Height	**472'**
Stories	**25**
Style	**Art Deco**
Architect	**John T. Windrim**

While Wanamaker's is famed for its enormous pipe organ, this granite highrise built to hold a much-expanded men's department for the store next door is known for the hourly tolls of its gigantic bell.

The 17-ton Founder's Bell was commissioned in memory of John Wanamaker, who considered becoming a Presbyterian minister before finding success as a retail clothing merchant. The bell first rang from a tower on his great department store, but was soon relocated to the belfry of this skyscraper, the first seven floors of which purveyed a tasteful array of tailored suits, fashionable overcoats, hunting costumes and sporting goods for the discerning gentleman.

A pair of much-admired 1890s skyscrapers had to be torn down to make way for the new construction, so its original appellation name-checked them both in order to assuage any hard feelings.

After Philadelphia National Bank bought the tower, four sets of its illuminated initials "PNB" perched atop the belfry for nearly 60 years. They were finally removed by cargo helicopter in 2014 from the building now known as One South Broad, and one huge "B" was rehung in the lobby.

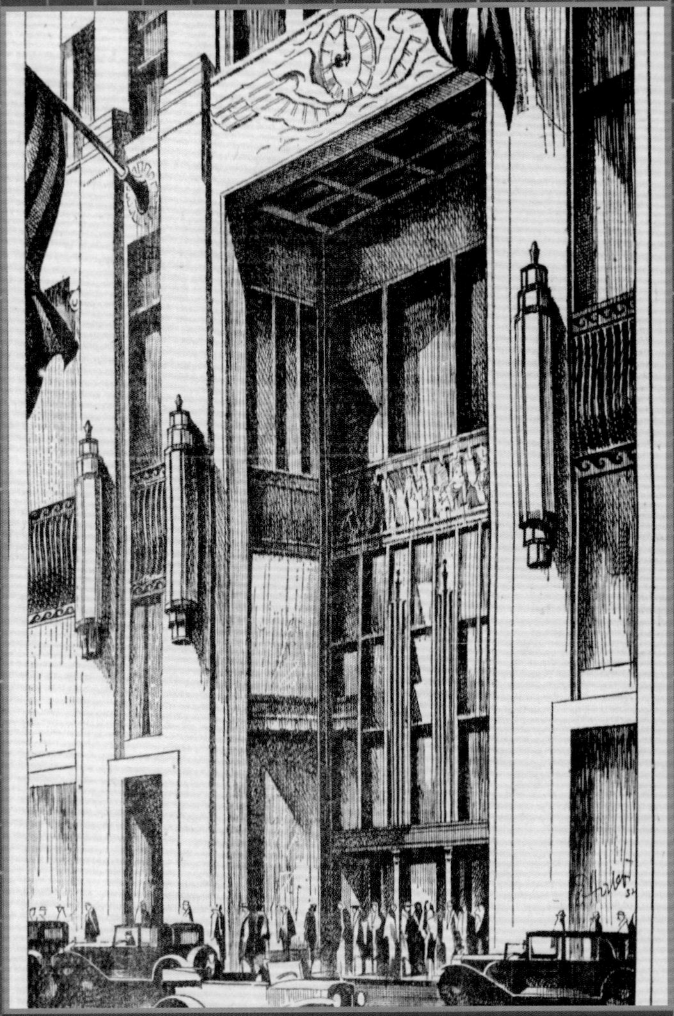

A 1932 illustration from the Wanamaker's store opening shows the entrance before it was remodeled.

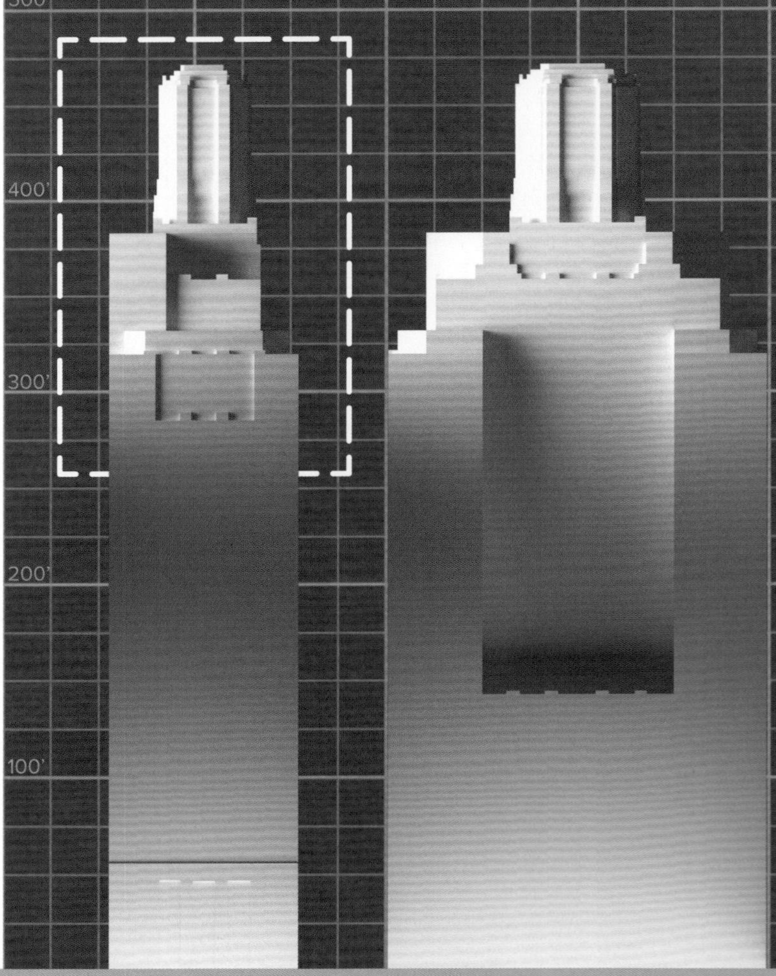

South Elevation

West Elevation 1" = 100'

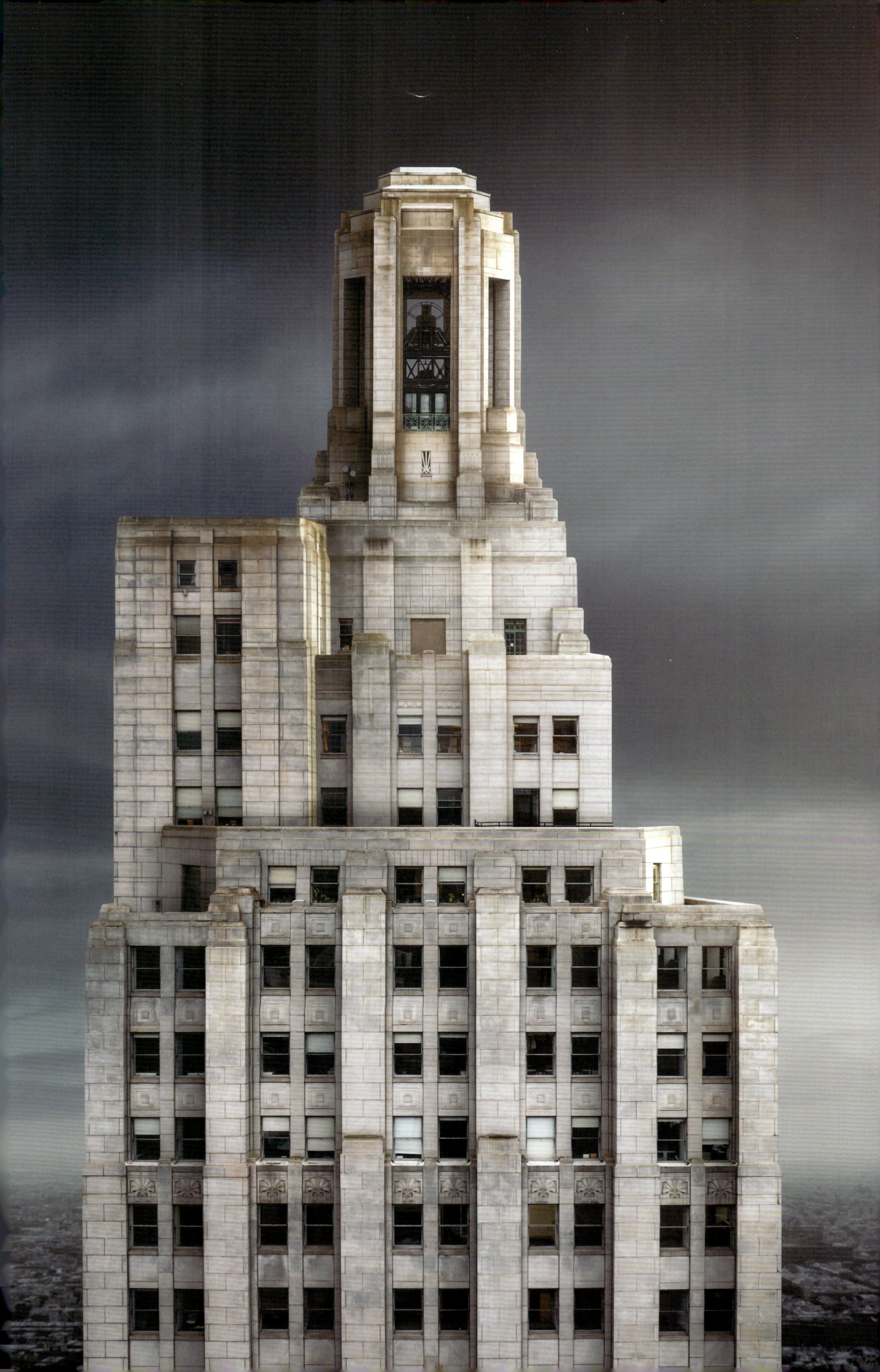

1616 Walnut

Philadelphia, **PA** Icon

Address	**1616 Walnut St.**
Opened	**1930**
Height	**309'**
Stories	**25**
Style	**Art Deco**
Architect	**Tilden, Register & Pepper**

One of several skyscrapers built by real estate developer Joseph Greenberg, this has a garage occupying most of the first five floors. Ads when it opened promised "Park your car under your desk!" Office tenants included investment brokers, insurance firms, the Philadelphia Grand Opera, and the local office for Cunard White Star ocean liners.

The powerfully wealthy but publicity-shy Pew family took the penthouse as their pied-à-terre, since it was conveniently located next door to the headquarters of their family business, Sun Oil Company, also known as Sunoco.

Philadelphia architects Tilden, Register & Pepper won an award for their design at the 12th International Buildings Congress in Budapest, Hungary. Their spectacular Art Deco lobby features a ceiling of contoured geometric patterns, futuristic chandeliers, mottled tan marble walls, a patterned terrazzo floor, and elegant aluminum trim and elevator doors.

The building served as the home of Temple University Center City from the 1970s until 2001. Now it contains luxury apartments, and residents have access to the Pews' former rooftop sundeck.

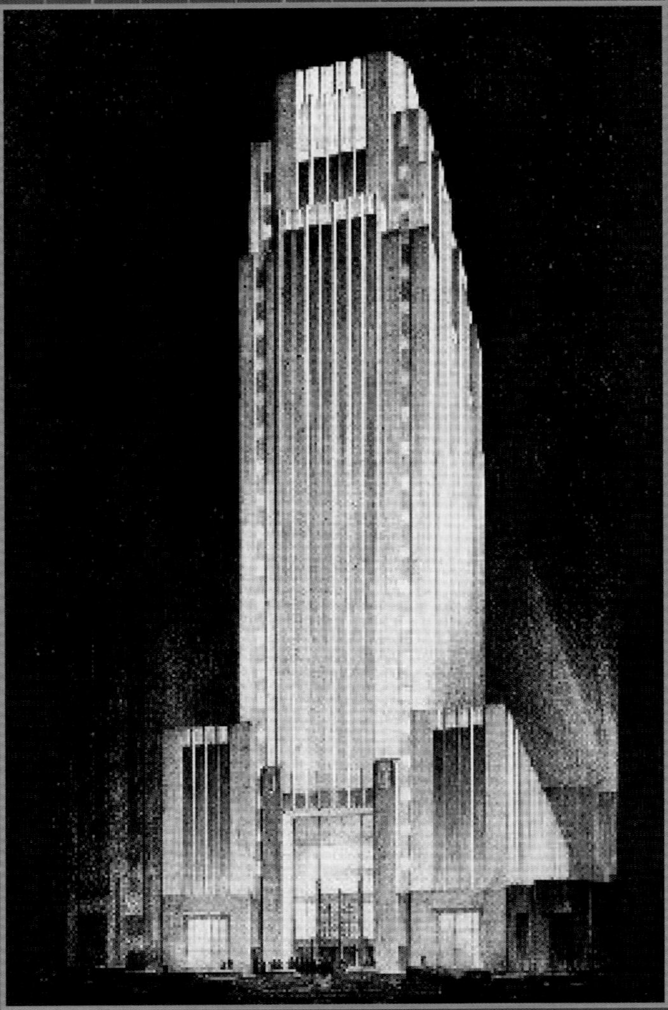

Dramatic lighting emphasizes an award-winning Art Deco design in this original architectural drawing.

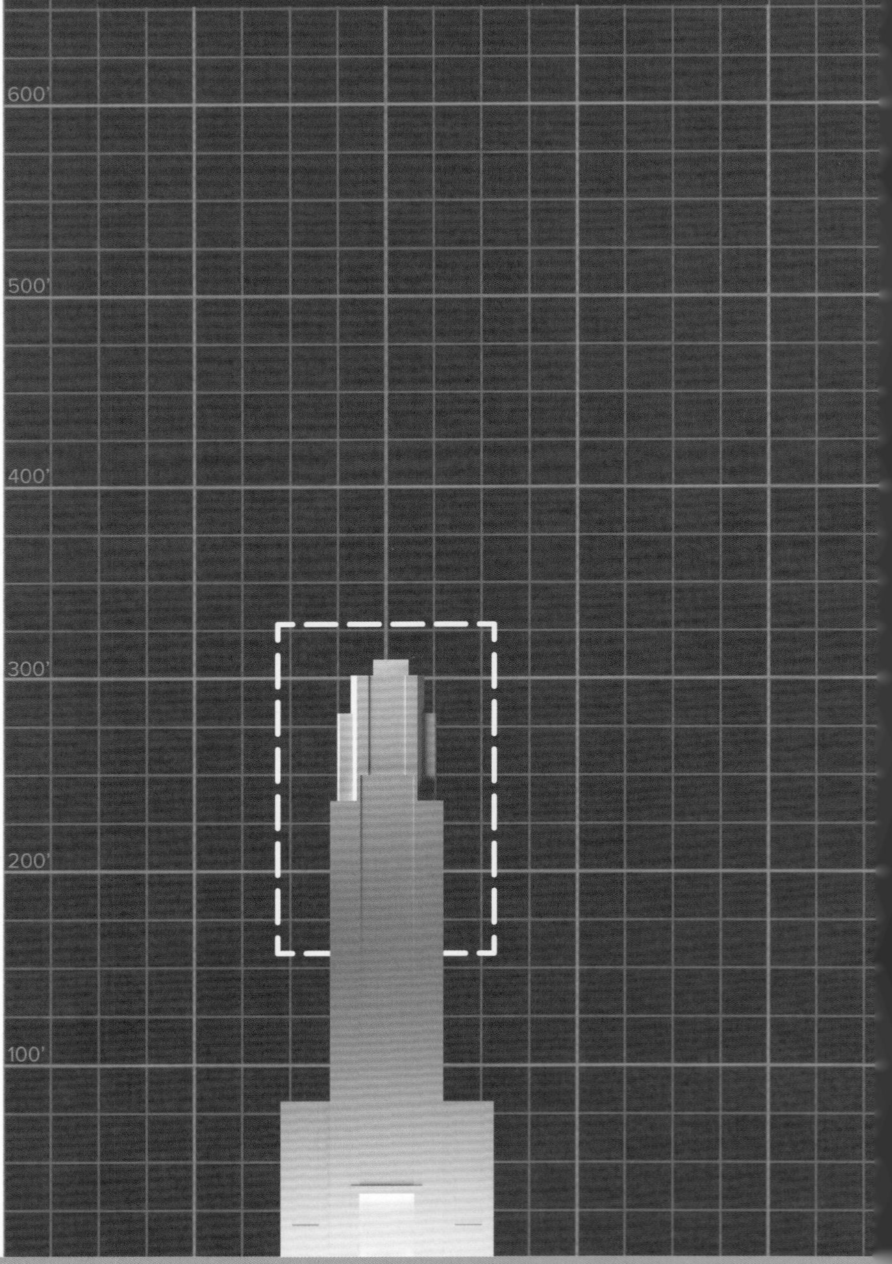

East Elevation *1" = 100'*

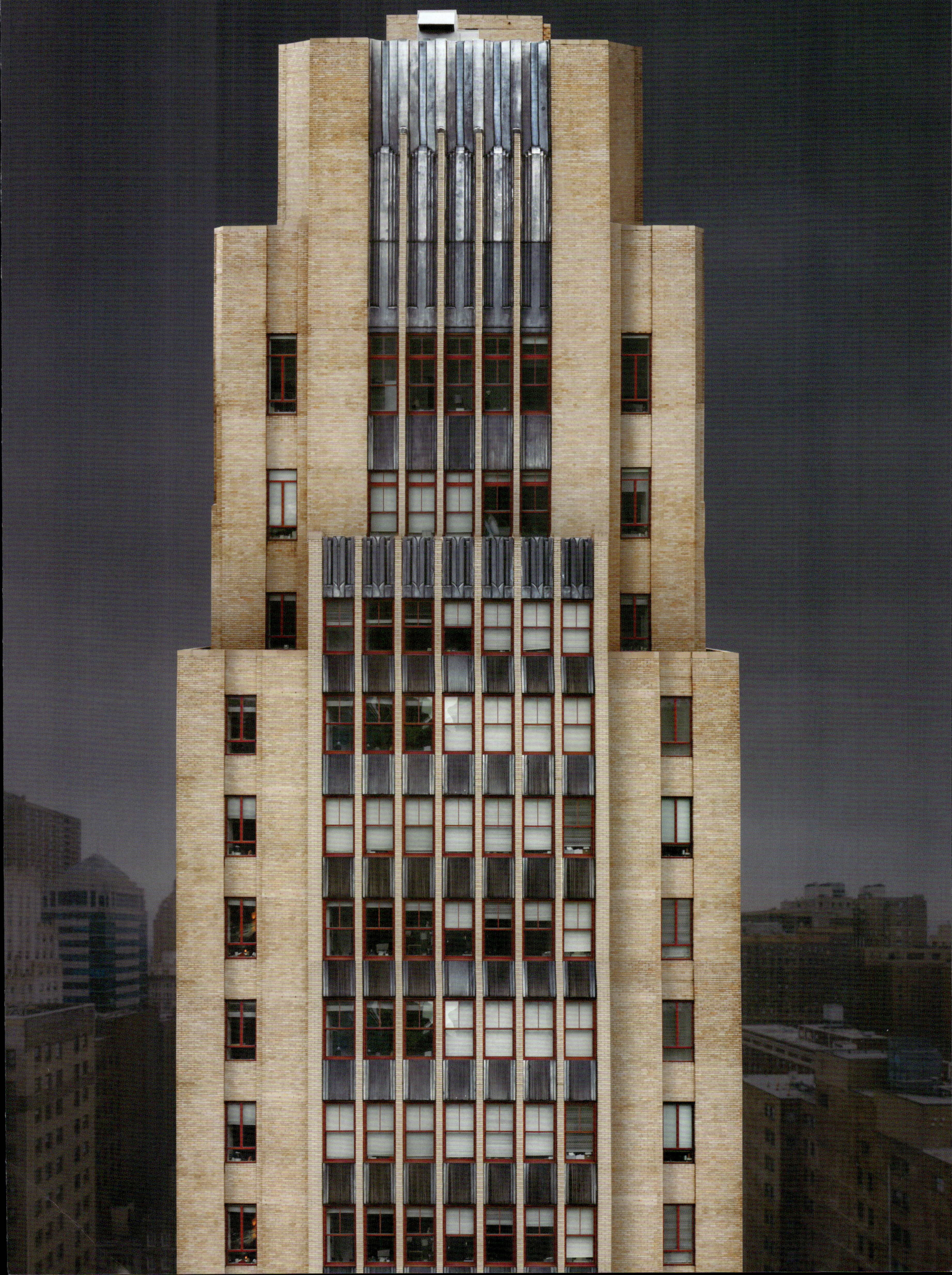

Cathedral of Learning

Pittsburgh, **PA**

Address	**4200 Fifth Ave.**
Opened	**1937**
Height	**535'**
Stories	**40**
Style	**Art Deco, Gothic**
Architect	**Charles Klauder**

When John Bowman became chancellor of the University of Pittsburgh in 1921, he proposed a bold plan for his growing institution: a college skyscraper. Philadelphia architect Charles Klauder, renowned for his campus buildings at Princeton and Cornell, designed the tower as a blend of Art Deco and his signature Collegiate Gothic style.

Ground was broken in 1926, and the first classes were held in the building in 1931, though the Great Depression delayed completion of the dramatic four-story Commons Room for six more years.

The 40-story limestone highrise was the tallest educational building in the world until Moscow State University surpassed it in 1953. The university subsequently boasted having the tallest such building "in the free world," until the Cathedral of Learning was supplanted by school skyscrapers in Japan and Spain.

At the time of construction, surveys showed that one of every three Pitt students was the child of an immigrant. To honor that heritage, the university invited Pittsburgh's various ethnic organizations to design and fund 18 Nationality Rooms representing the mother countries. Students taking classes in the rooms, which now number 31, quickly learn to expect occasional interruptions by curious visitors peeking in the doorways.

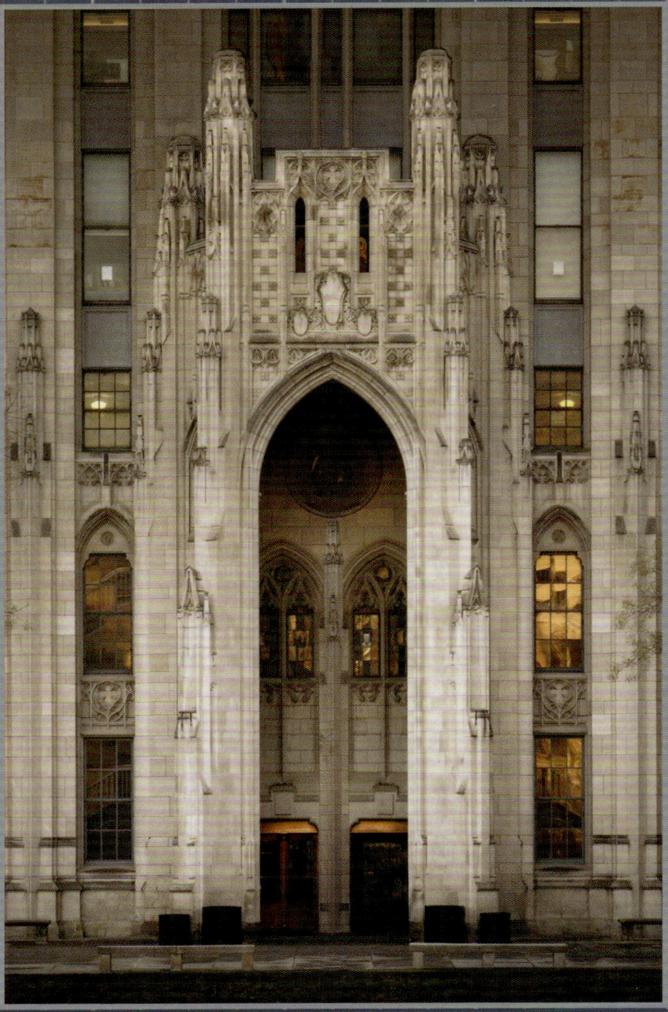

An elaborately carved Gothic portal nearly five stories high aptly conveys the cathedral theme.

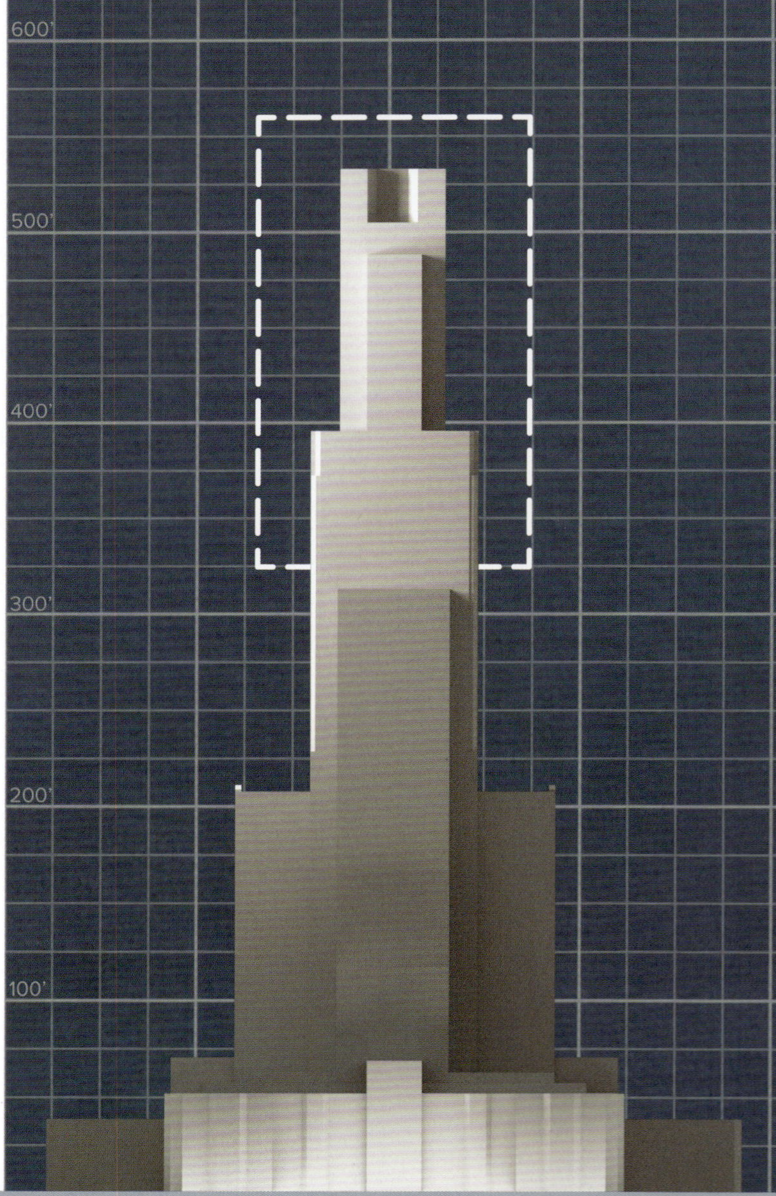

Southwest Elevation *1" = 100'*

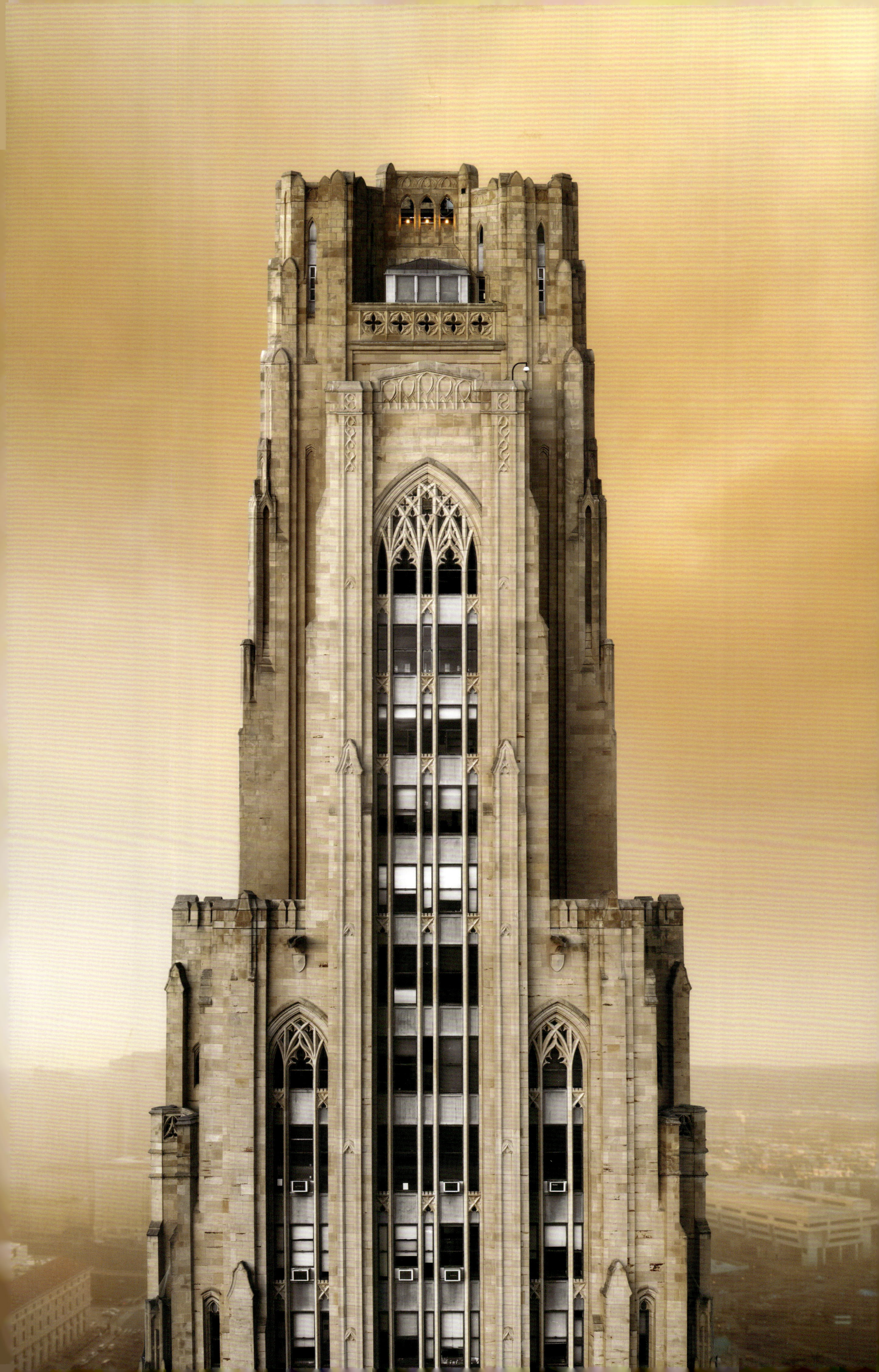

Gulf Tower

Pittsburgh, **PA**

Address	**707 Grant St.**
Opened	**1932**
Height	**582’**
Stories	**38**
Style	**Art Deco**
Architect	**Trowbridge & Livingston**

As this headquarters for Gulf Oil was rising up to dominate the city skyline, the stature of the local banking magnate behind it was plunging just as dramatically. Andrew Mellon, who formed Gulf from his investments in the Spindletop oilfield in Texas, served three Republican presidents as secretary of the treasury. But the Great Depression cost him his cabinet post and reputation, turning him into a pariah.

Forced to resign amid accusations of enriching his personal portfolio while steering the economy into meltdown, the cashiered financier faced embarrassing public investigations and trial for tax fraud in the final years of his life. Still the old tycoon donated his priceless collection of paintings to the country and paid to build the National Gallery of Art to hold them.

The stepped pyramid capping this highrise is a blockier version of a roof design the architects used for a Wall Street bank tower. The weather beacon on top originally shone with an orange or blue light to indicate fair or foul weather ahead. That signal was later supplanted by neon lights on the roof and is now achieved with multicolor LED displays, although the value is surely more aesthetic than meteorological.

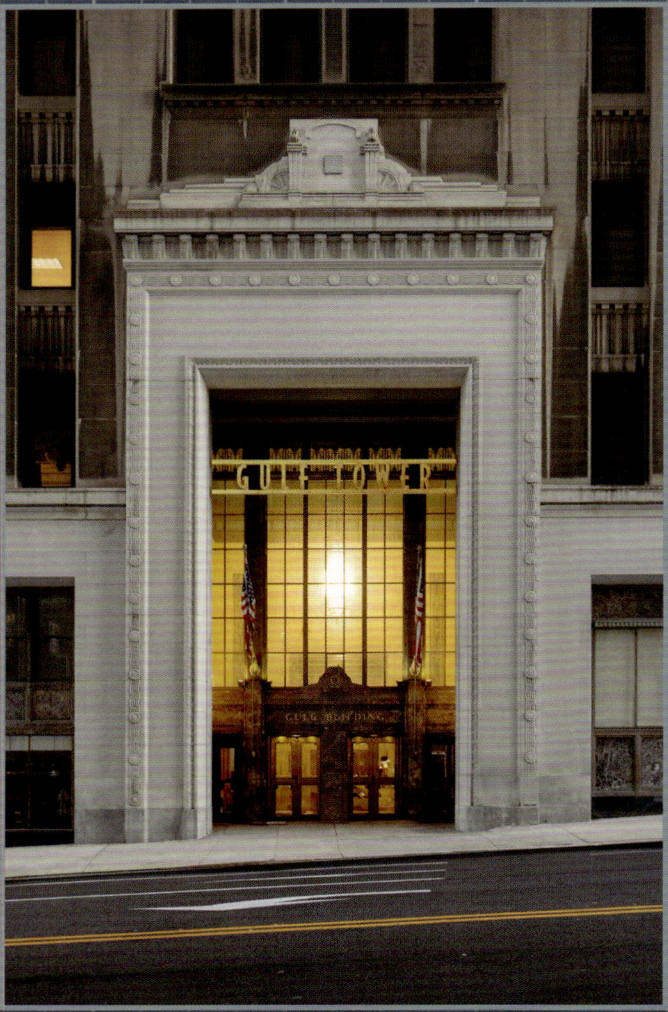

Art Deco elements of this tower are restrained to match the taste of a conservative industrial financier.

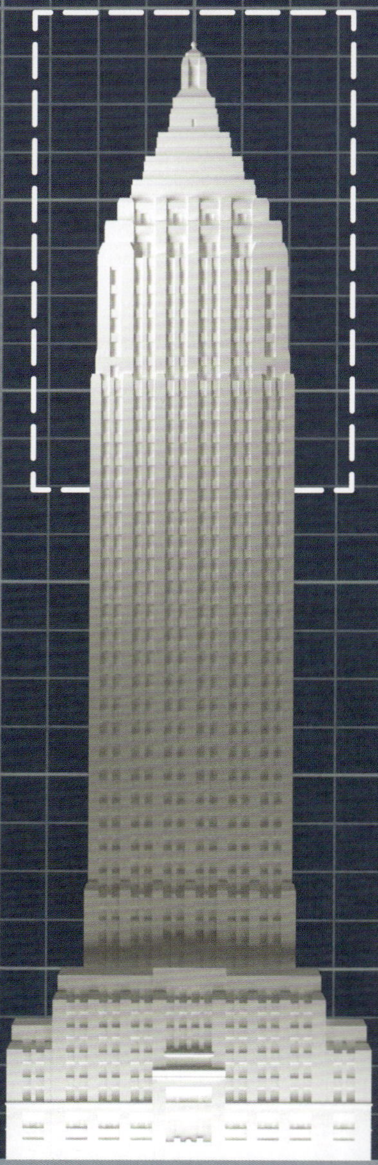

South Elevation *1" = 100'*

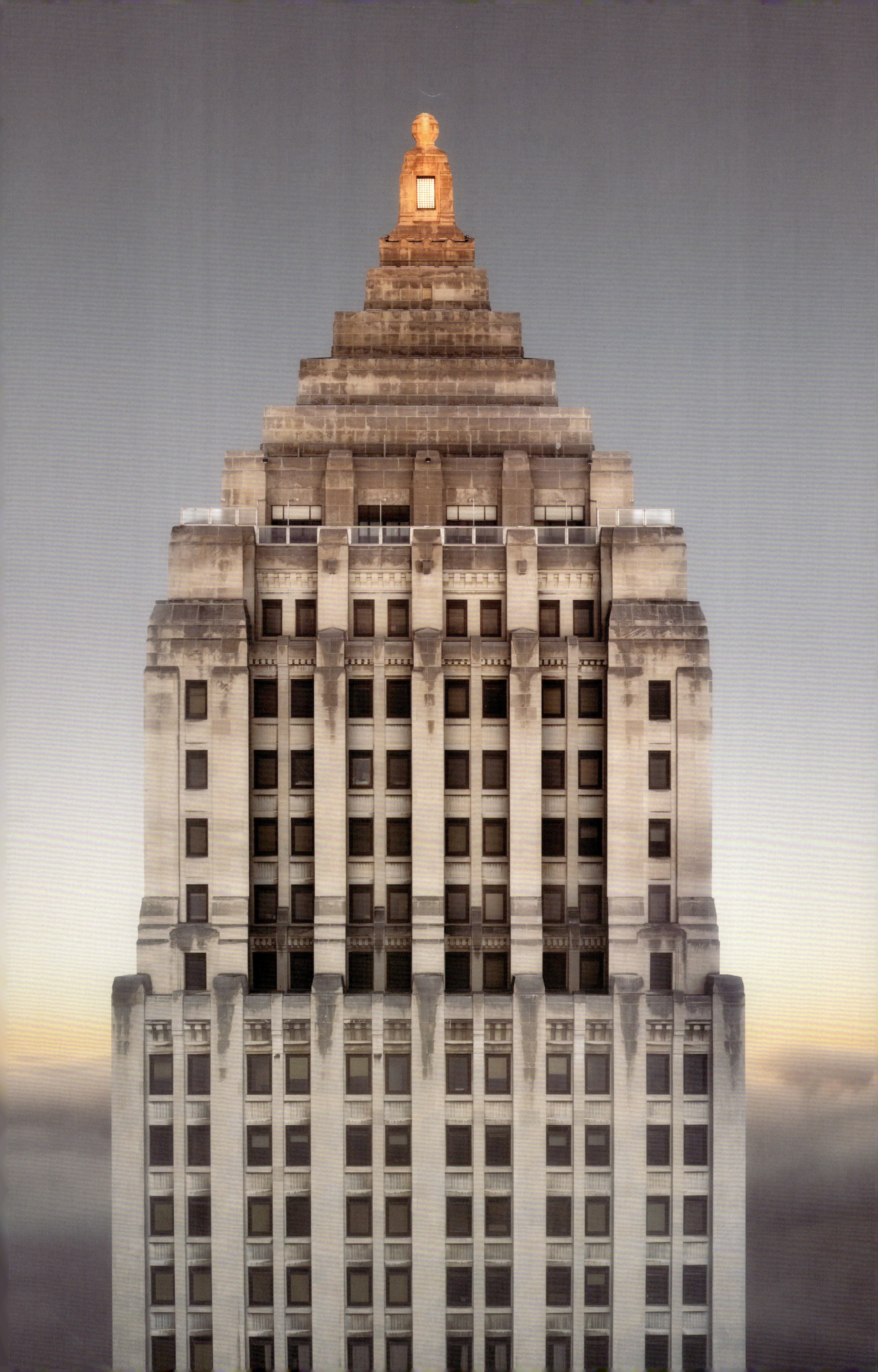

Koppers Building

Pittsburgh, **PA**

Address ·············· **436 Seventh Ave.**
Opened ························ **1929**
Height ························ **475'**
Stories ························ **32**
Style ······················· **Art Deco**
Architect ··········· **Graham, Anderson, Probst & White**

Heinrich Koppers of Germany developed an efficient industrial oven for producing coke, the essential fuel for iron and steel furnaces, while also capturing gas and tar byproducts for other uses. That interested U.S. Steel, so Koppers formed a Chicago company in 1907 to supply the American steel industry.

Financier Andrew Mellon soon acquired a controlling stake and moved the company to Pittsburgh. The founder's remaining minority stake, amounting to one-third of the company, was seized by the government during World War I as enemy property and sold to Mellon and his business partners.

Graham, Anderson, Probst & White designed the company's Art Deco headquarters with a polished granite and limestone exterior and a chateau-style roof made of – what else – copper. It was briefly the city's tallest skyscraper until overshadowed by the Gulf Building across the street, the headquarters of another company in the Mellon portfolio.

Koppers grew into a sprawling industrial conglomerate until a 1988 British hostile takeover led to the sale of several divisions. Managers bought the chemicals business, which is still based in the skyscraper. The building's three-story marble lobby with bronze accents has been extensively restored.

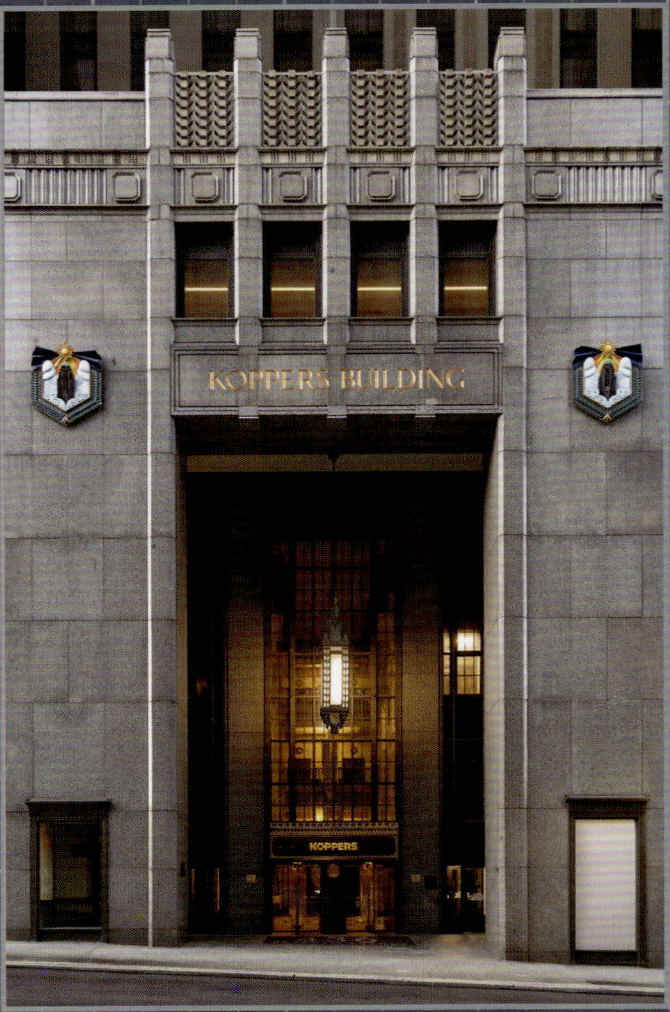

Vibrant medallions offset the gray and show the sun beaming down on the building as it pierces the clouds.

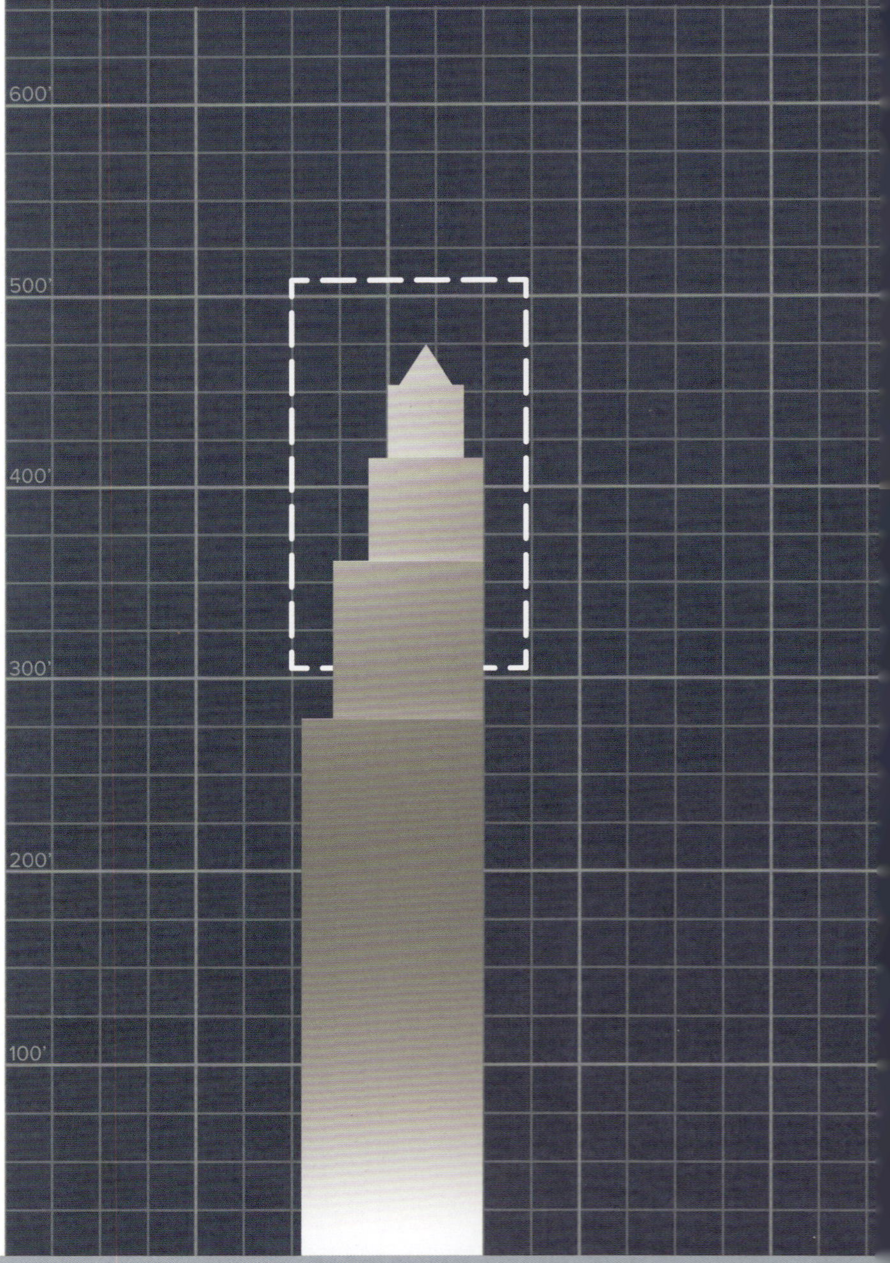

West Elevation *1" = 100'*

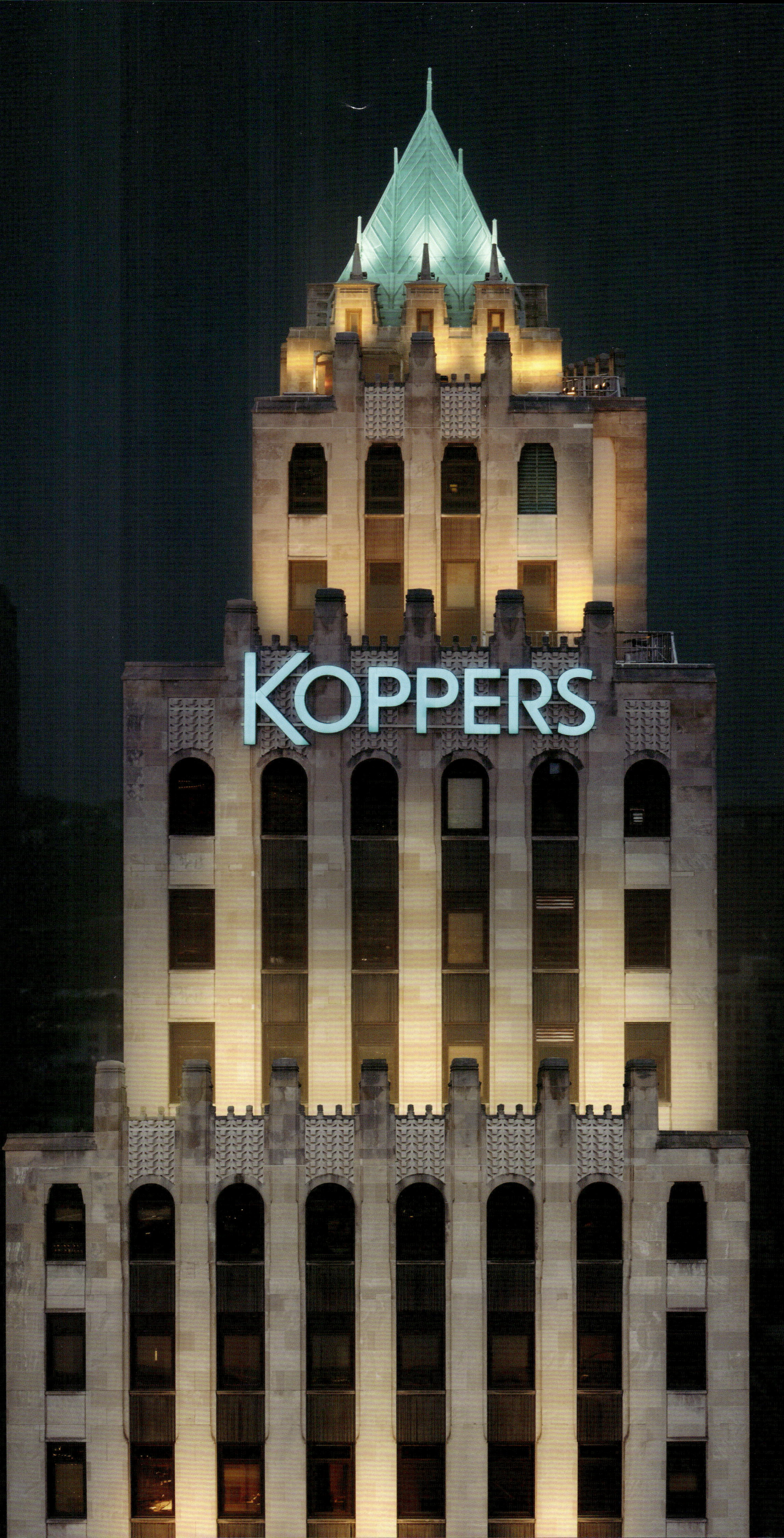
KOPPERS

Berks County
Courthouse

Reading, **PA**

Address	**605 Court St.**
Opened	**1932**
Height	**275'**
Stories	**18**
Style	**Art Deco, Renaissance**
Architect	**Miles Dechant**

To celebrate the opening of their new skyscraper courthouse, the judges of Berks County reinstated the practice of wearing judicial robes while serving on the bench. The tradition had fallen by the wayside, but robes seemed an appropriate degree of formality for the fancy new courtrooms on the fifth and seventh floors.

Even more striking was the lobby, which is beautifully preserved in contrasting ocher and black marble with hammered bronze elevator doors and an Italian Renaissance painted beam ceiling. Hanging above the guard desk is an original stained glass light globe of the Earth, while above the side entrance is a shield inscribed "Justitia et Lux," Latin for justice and light.

Miles Dechant, the local architect picked for the job, nevertheless was assailed for supposedly cutting corners. His rooftop soars with four great eagles, but county commissioners had to squabble with Dechant to supply additional promised rows of decorative lion heads. Critics alleged he used imitation gold leaf but charged for the real thing.

County offices expanded to a Postmodern highrise next door in 1991. But court is still in session in Reading's granite and limestone tower.

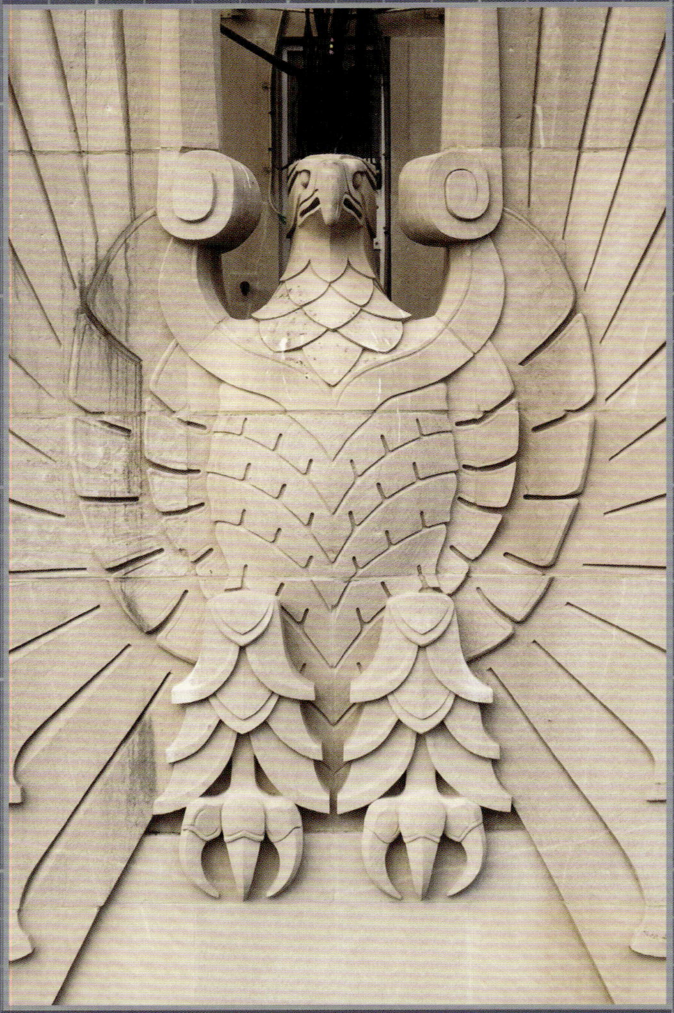

Heavily stylized stone birds perched at the rooftop show Art Deco creativity.

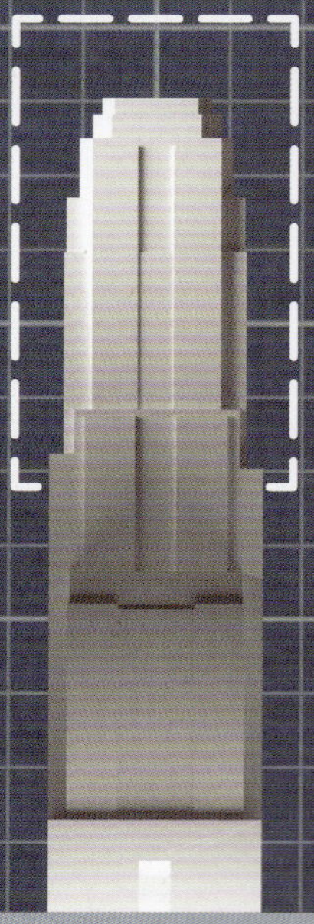

West Elevation *1" = 100'*

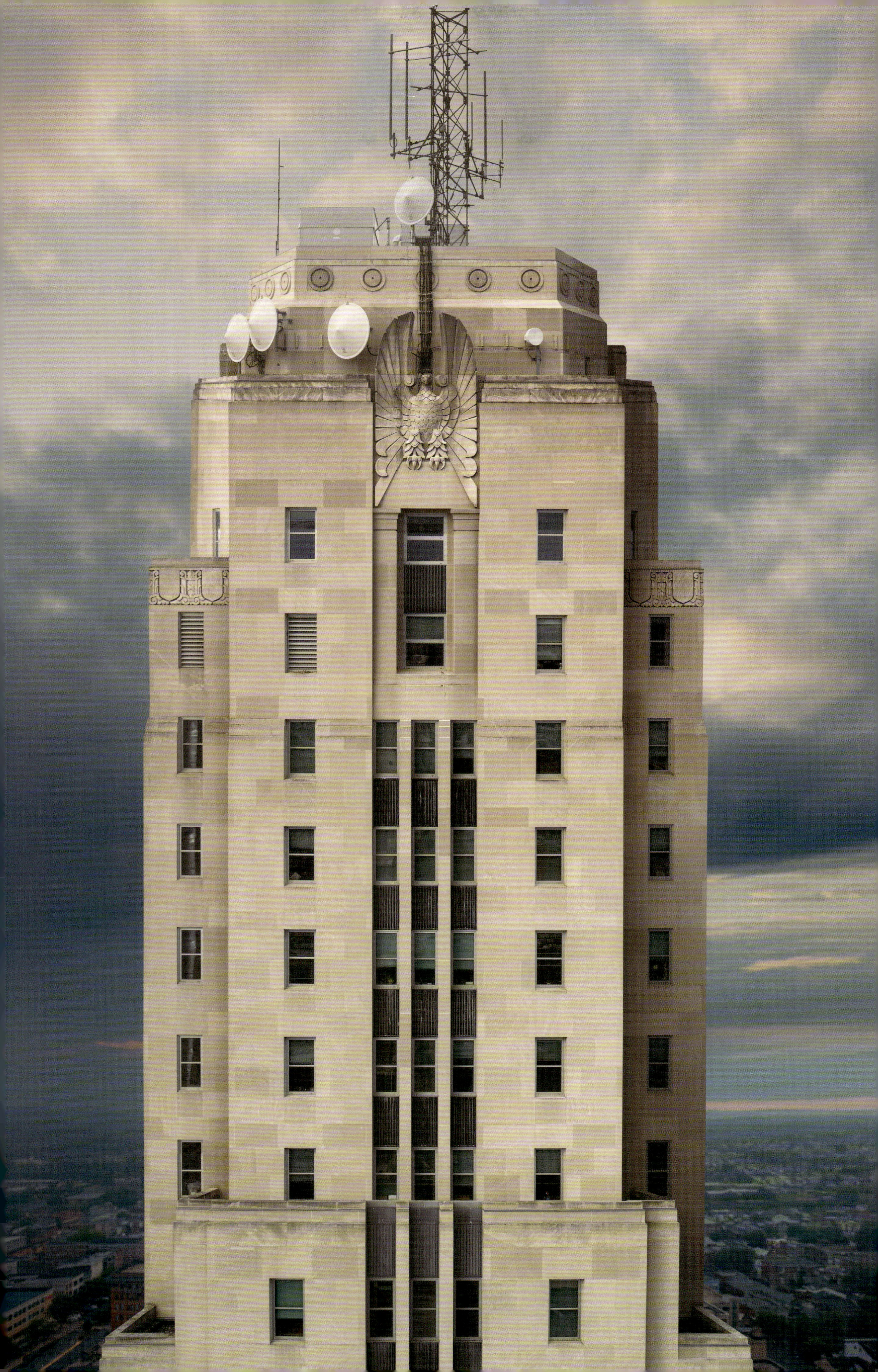

Industrial Trust
Building

Providence, **RI** — Superman Building

Address	**111 Westminster St.**
Opened	**1928**
Height	**428'**
Stories	**26**
Style	**Art Deco**
Architect	**Walker & Gillette**

Long known as the "Superman building" for its supposed resemblance to the Daily Planet, this long-vacant highrise is still the tallest building in Rhode Island. The green lantern at its tip could serve as a lighthouse for Narragansett Bay. Four stone eagles above it once glared at Boston and the mansions of Newport, but when one of their heads broke off and plummeted to the ground, the other three were decapitated for safety.

Industrial Trust was founded in 1886 by Samuel Colt, a former Rhode Island attorney general and nephew and namesake of the famed pistol maker. He did not live to see construction of this new headquarters, which features stone friezes of Providence's founding on one side and the birth of the city's industries on the other.

The great banking hall is well preserved, with tall black marble columns lining either side. But it has been unused since 2013, when successor Bank of America became the last tenant to depart, leaving the building vacant. The threat of demolition spurred action, and in 2022 the owners announced a government-subsidized plan to convert the building into 285 rental apartments.

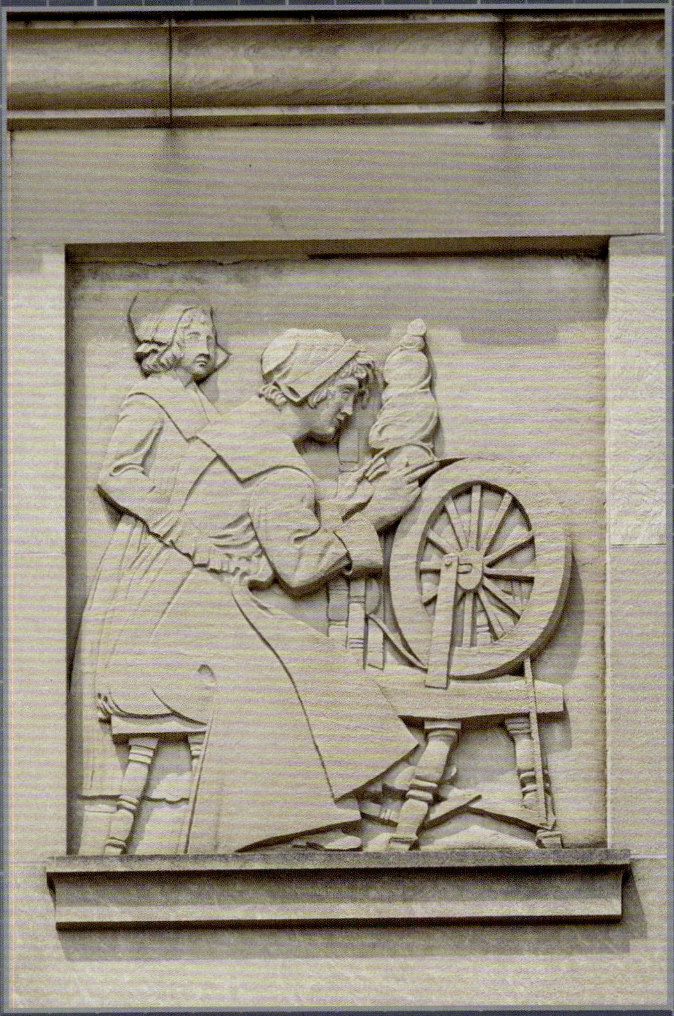

Scenes of labor and industry include this panel of a mother and daughter at a spinning wheel.

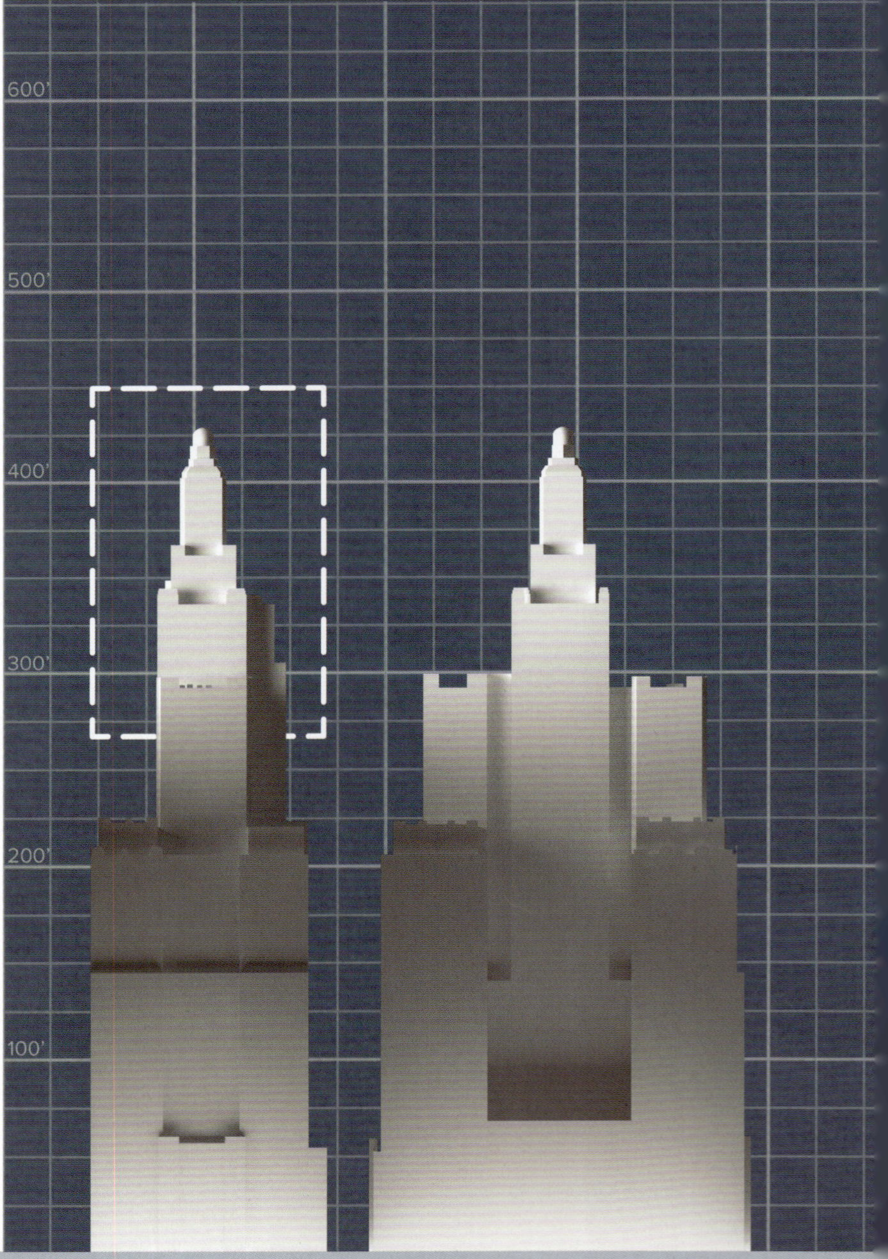

South Elevation — West Elevation 1" = 100'

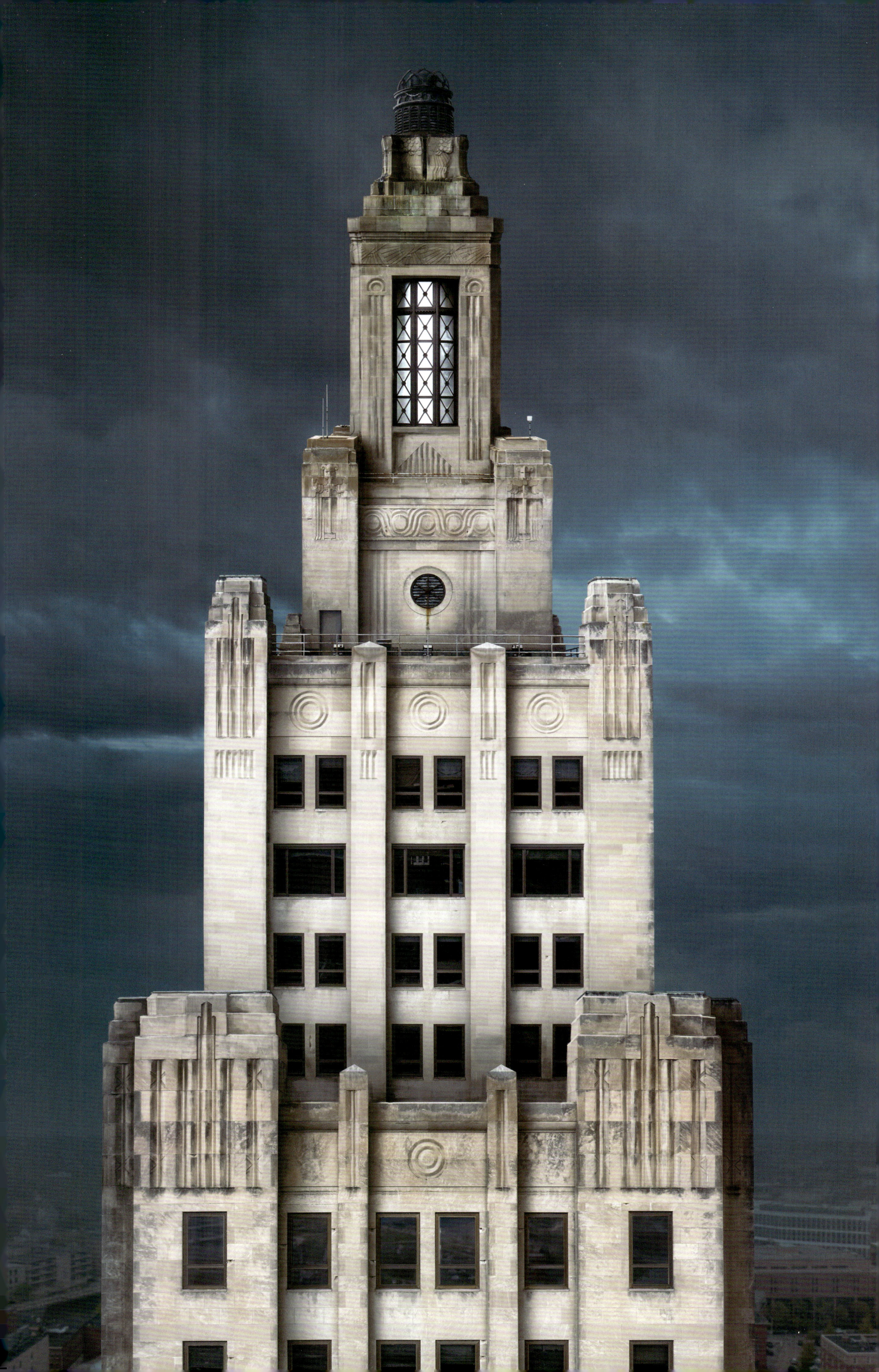

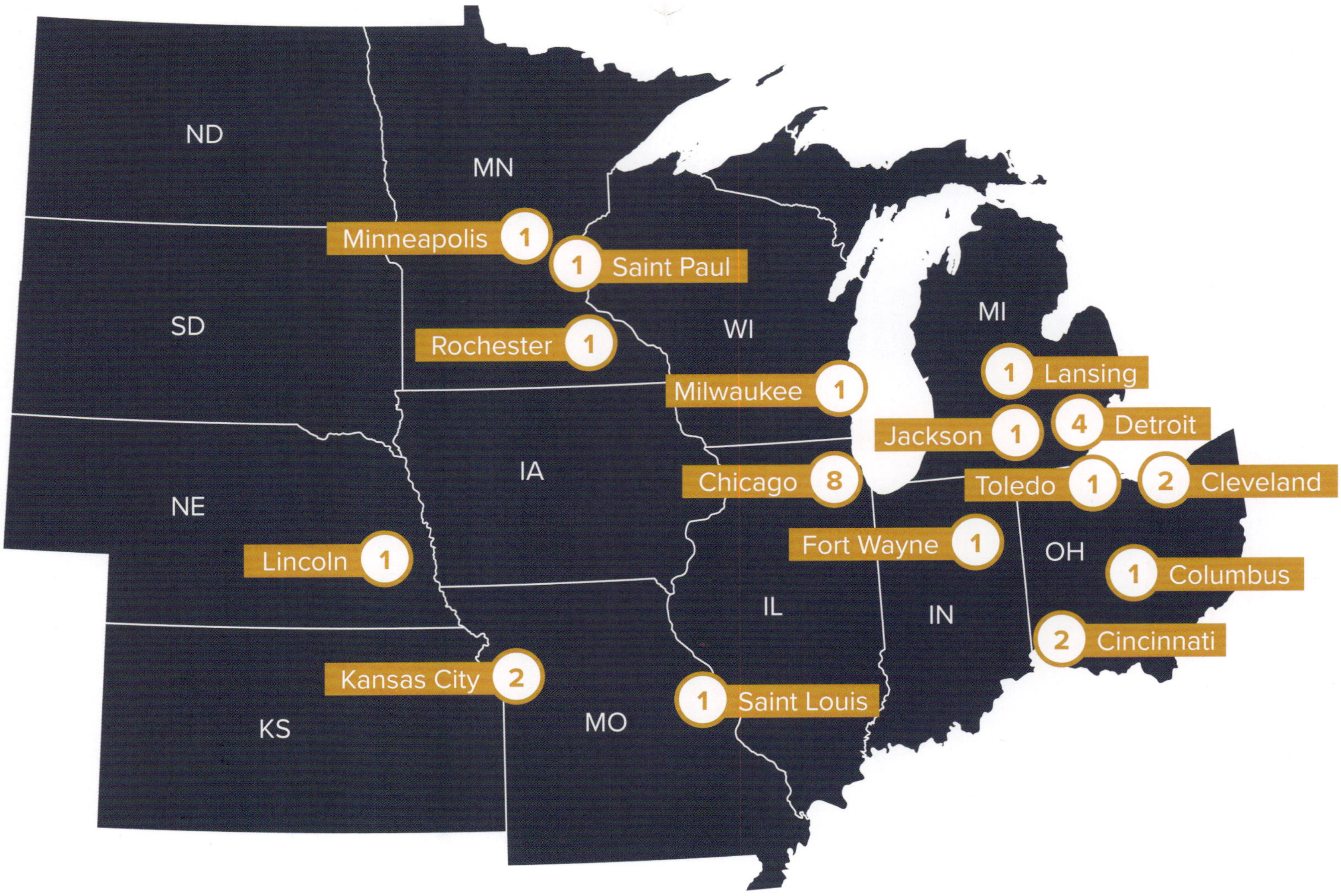

Numbers indicate how many buildings are featured in each city.

MIDWEST

Chicago is widely regarded as the birthplace of the skyscraper. Even those who dispute the claim — the debate hinges on height, number of floors, steel framework, elevators, and more — readily concede that the city played a pioneering role in developing technologies that made tall office buildings possible. A 1922 Chicago Tribune contest to design the world's most beautiful building fueled public interest in new concepts and trends in architecture. While the paper picked a Gothic design, it soon saw modern neighbors rising up and down Michigan Avenue.

From the Great Lakes to the Great Plains, cities teemed with creative approaches to the tall building challenge. Detroit produced a pair of Art Deco classics: the sensational Guardian and exquisite Fisher buildings. Iconic highrises in Cincinnati and Kansas City also flashed the very latest in fashionable exteriors. And it was Cleveland, not Chicago, that held the title of tallest skyscraper outside New York for decades, with its Terminal Tower.

One groundbreaking structure, the nation's first skyscraper state capitol, arose in a Midwestern locale few would have anticipated: Nebraska. Its design by New York architect Bertrand Goodhue emerged from an architectural competition too, one that preceded the Tribune's by two years and also left a powerful imprint.

All buildings are shown to scale with corresponding page numbers. 1"= 200'

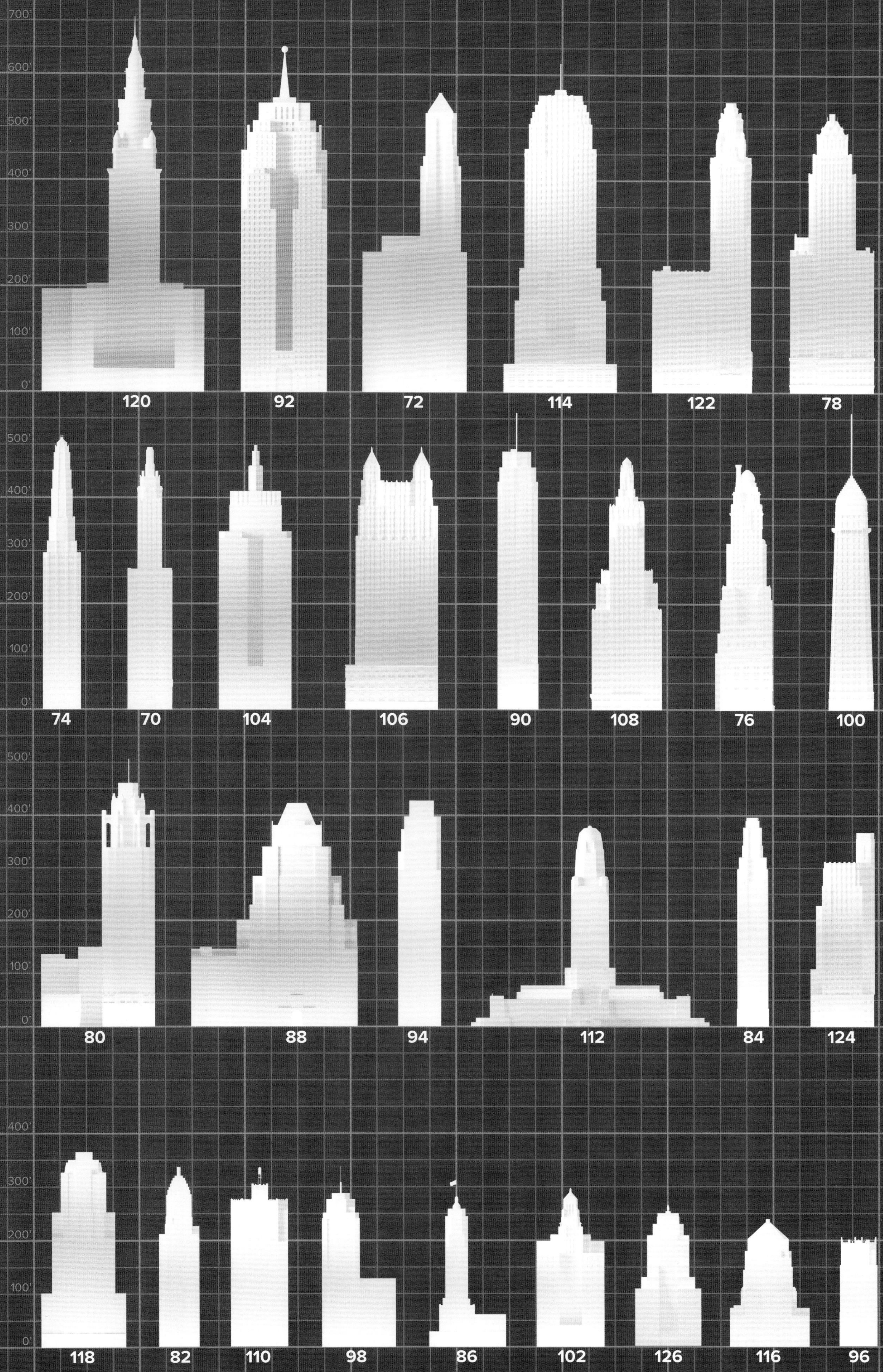

Carbide & Carbon
Building

Chicago, **IL** — Pendry Hotel

Address	**230 N. Michigan Ave.**
Opened	**1929**
Height	**503'**
Stories	**38**
Style	**Art Deco**
Architect	**Burnham Bros.**

The golden spire rising from this earthy green tower often invites comparisons to a champagne bottle. It also resembles the glaring flame of an acetylene torch, an essential tool for welding steel for skyscrapers — and also the product line manufactured by the original anchor tenant of this highrise.

Union Carbide and Carbon, a New York-based chemicals conglomerate, owned several companies involved in acetylene, which burns brighter and hotter than other gases. Oxweld Acetylene, a Chicago subsidiary, produced industrial welding and cutting tools fueled by acetylene and compressed oxygen. The company took ten floors initially and eventually purchased the building, but its parent got the naming rights.

The designers took over the firm founded by their late father, Daniel Burnham, the famous Chicago architect whose scores of early highrise designs include the Flatiron Building in Manhattan. He might well have been pleased with his sons' imaginative creation, the first building in Chicago to use colored terracotta cladding.

It was converted into a hotel in 2004, and its lofty entryway and marble elevator lobby are extensively restored. A 24th floor rooftop cocktail lounge allows guests to contemplate the tower's shiny tip from a closer vantage, the better to admire how sunlight glints on its gold leaf highlights.

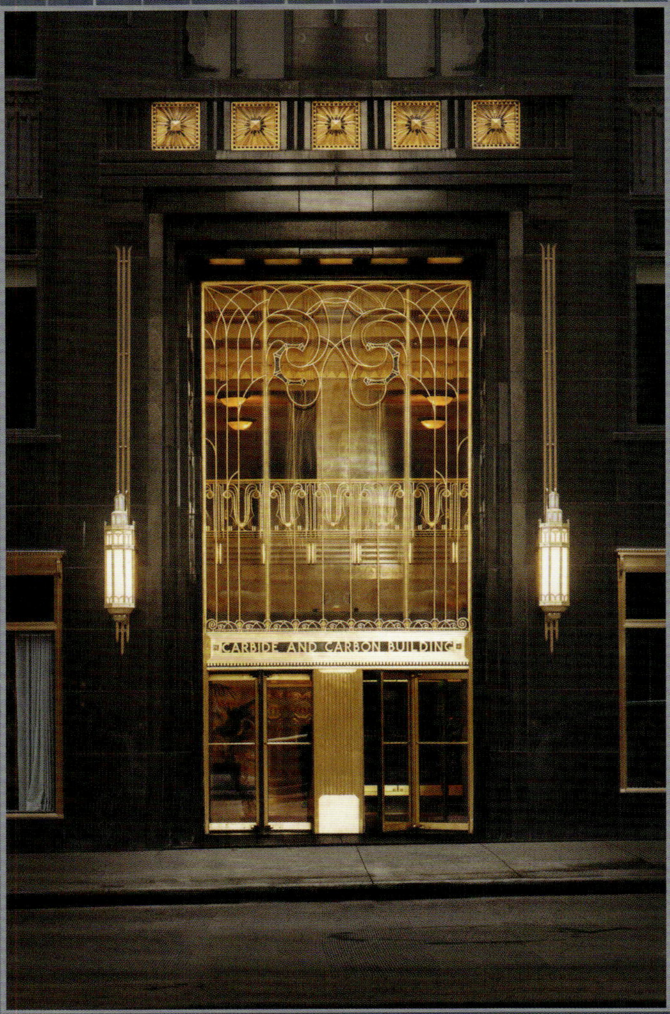

Curving brass grillework in the large entry window culminates in two facing "C"s from the company name.

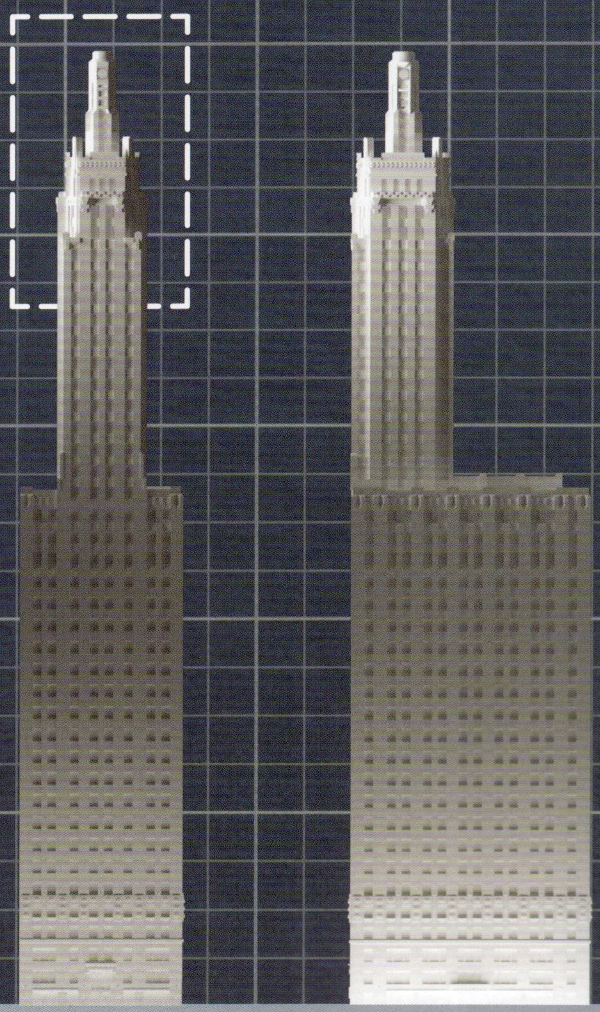
East Elevation   North Elevation 1" = 100'

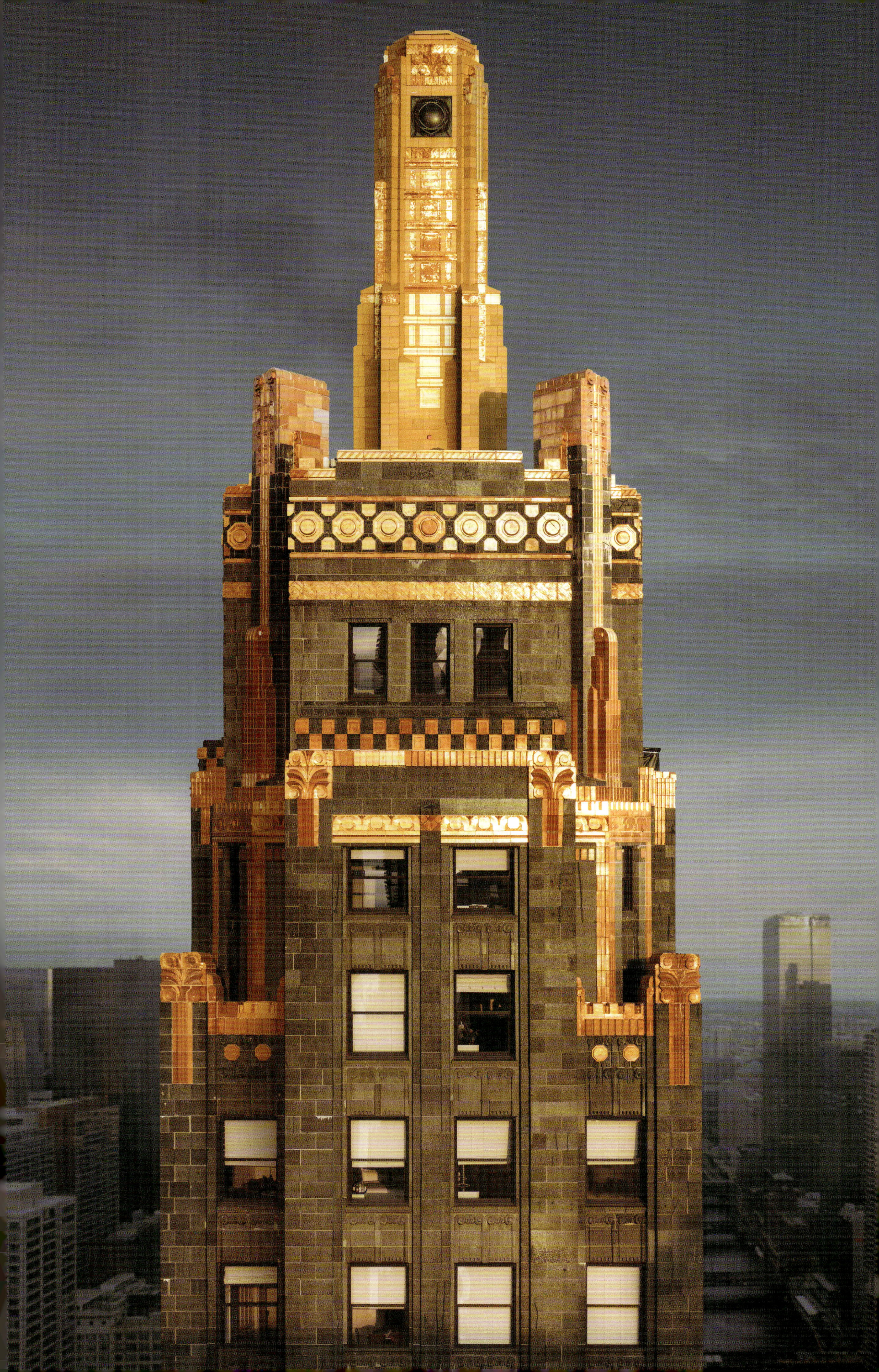

Chicago Board of Trade

Chicago, **IL**

Address ·········· **141 W. Jackson Blvd.**
Opened ························ **1930**
Height ························ **605'**
Stories ························ **44**
Style ························ **Art Deco**
Architect ·············· **Holabird & Root**

When the world's largest commodities exchange was also Chicago's tallest skyscraper, tourists flocked to observatory windows that once lined the base of its roof. More thrills awaited in the cavernous main trading hall, where they could watch traders in the chaotic pits shout and signal their buy and sell orders for bushels of corn, wheat, and soybeans.

The exchange was founded in 1848 by grain brokers and dealers to bring stability and standardization to unruly markets. Initially meant to establish prices for immediate sales, the exchange soon introduced futures contracts for hedging and speculating on where prices would be in months to come.

Carved figures on the limestone exterior recall the ancient farmers who first cultivated grains. Above them perches 33-foot-tall Ceres, a faceless, modernist version of the Roman harvest deity. Two more iterations of her are below: a classical statue from the former exchange now in a courtyard, and a huge mural that once hung in the trading hall and is now in an atrium, depicting an athletic goddess sowing seeds while topless.

The rooftop deck closed in 1971 and the pits are gone too, replaced by computer trading. But the skylit lobby still feels futuristic, lined by blocky black marble columns inlaid with metal strips and third-floor balconies perched on rippling cascades of buff stone.

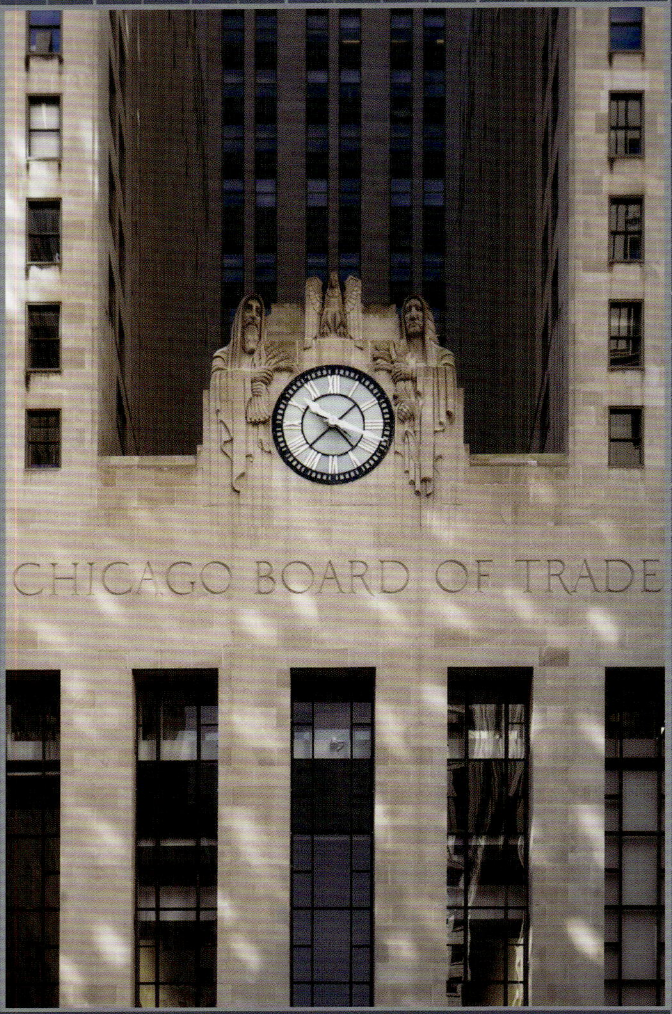

An ancient Babylonian with wheat and Native American with corn are carved near the clock and the roof.

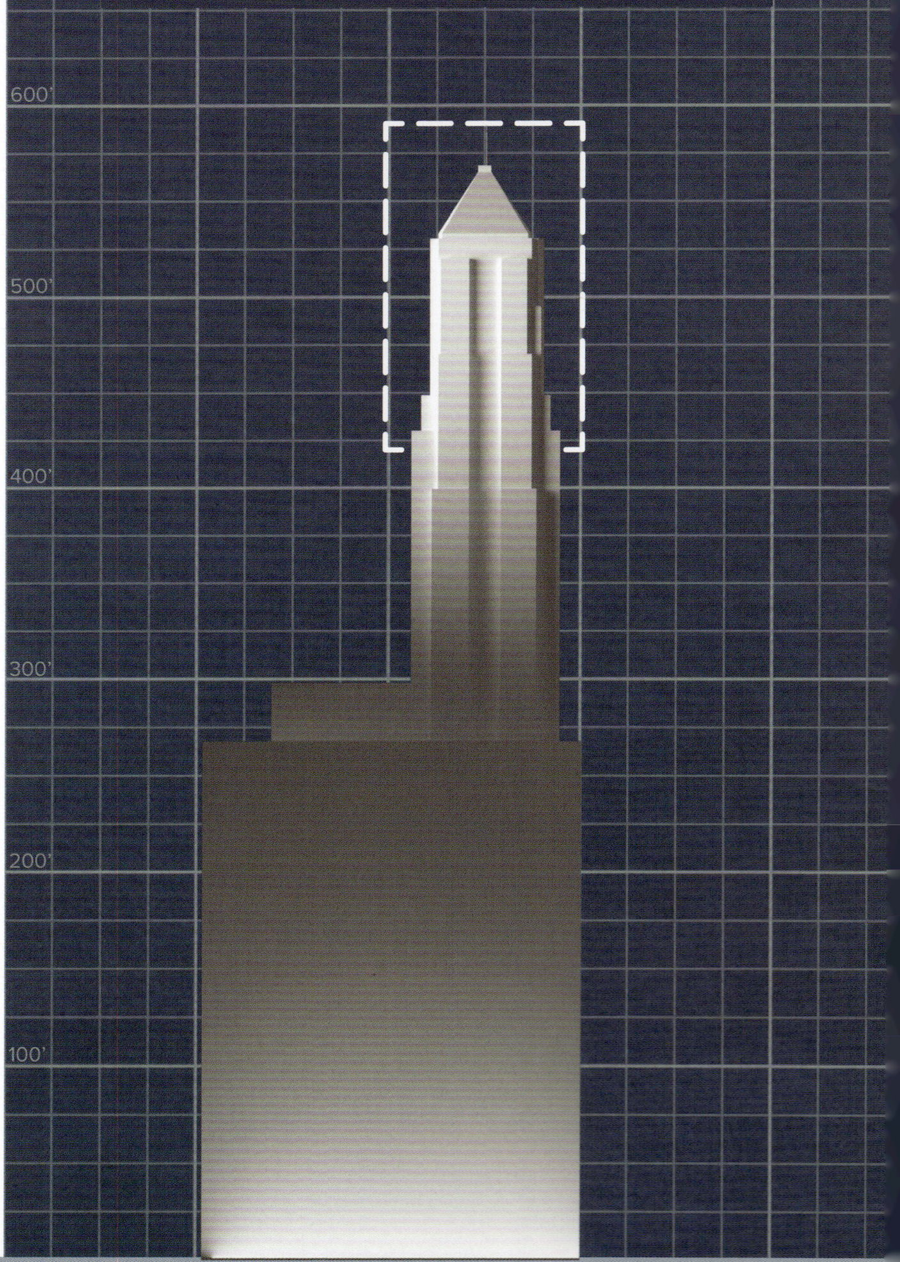

West Elevation *1" = 100'*

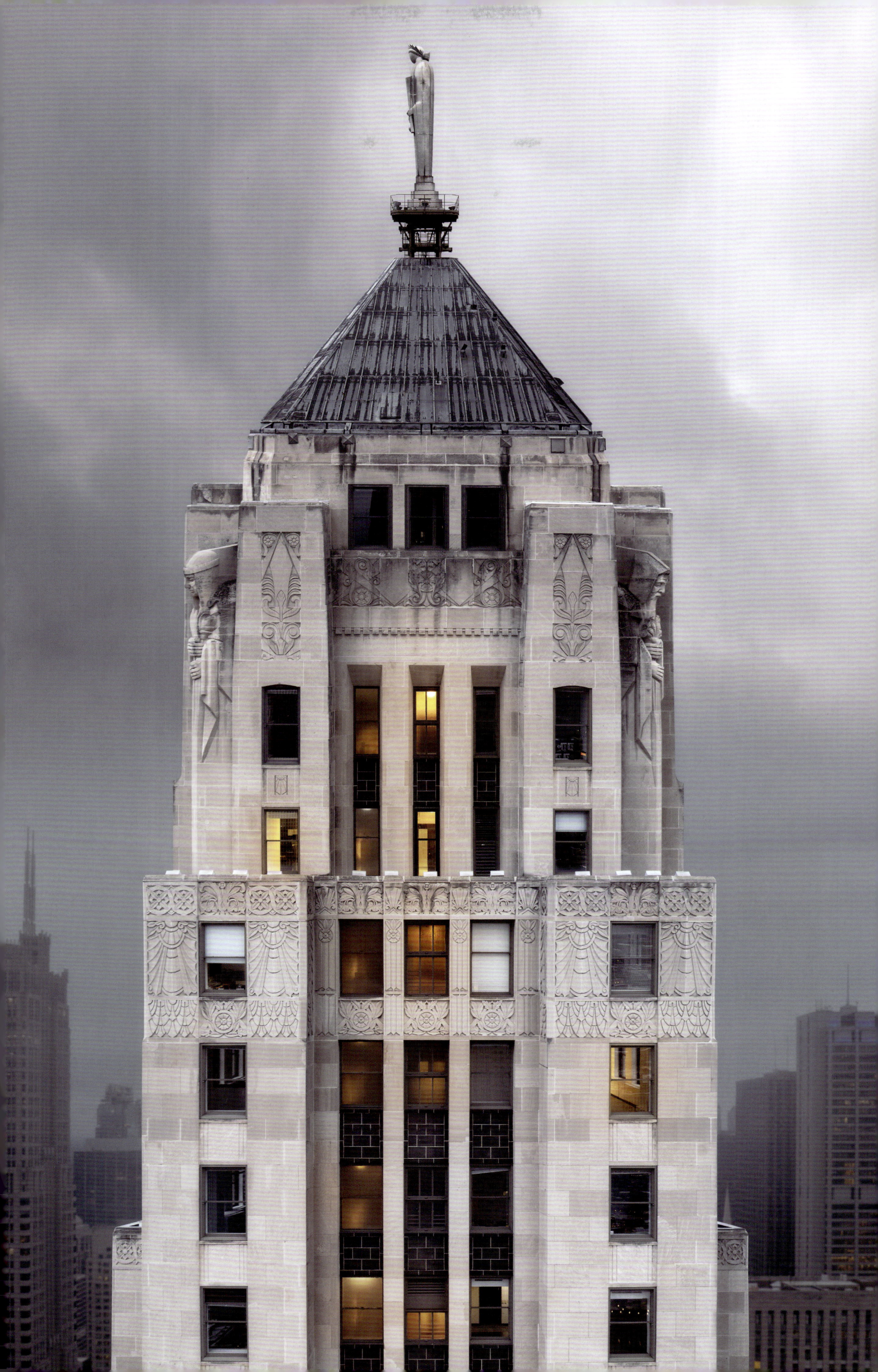

Mather Tower

Chicago, **IL** River Hotel

Address	**75 E. Wacker Dr.**
Opened	**1927**
Height	**519'**
Stories	**41**
Style	**Gothic, Art Deco**
Architect	**Herbert Riddle**

Thirty years after Chicago curtailed its skyscrapers with a strict height limit, a 1923 zoning ordinance let towers exceed the 264-foot cutoff as long as they occupied no more than a quarter of the lot. This telescoped highrise took advantage, soon welcoming sightseers to the city's highest observation platform. Under the original plans, visitors could have waved to other sightseers on a twin tower about 100 feet away, but the second on Michigan Avenue never got past the drawing board.

Owner Alonzo Mather, from the same family as Puritan preacher Cotton Mather, built a company that manufactured and leased railcars for transporting livestock. The well-traveled tycoon also proposed building a bridge across the Niagara River from Buffalo to Canada, with turbines suspended in the surging current underneath to supply electrical power. Permitting delays dissuaded Mather, but a bridge was eventually constructed there, flanked by a Canadian park named after him.

Once prized by artists, ad agencies, and design studios for its abundant natural light, the tower is now a hotel, and its marble lobby staircase gleams almost as brightly as the new cupola. Weather and wind made the original structurally unsound, so it was removed in 2000 and a replacement was plunked on via helicopter.

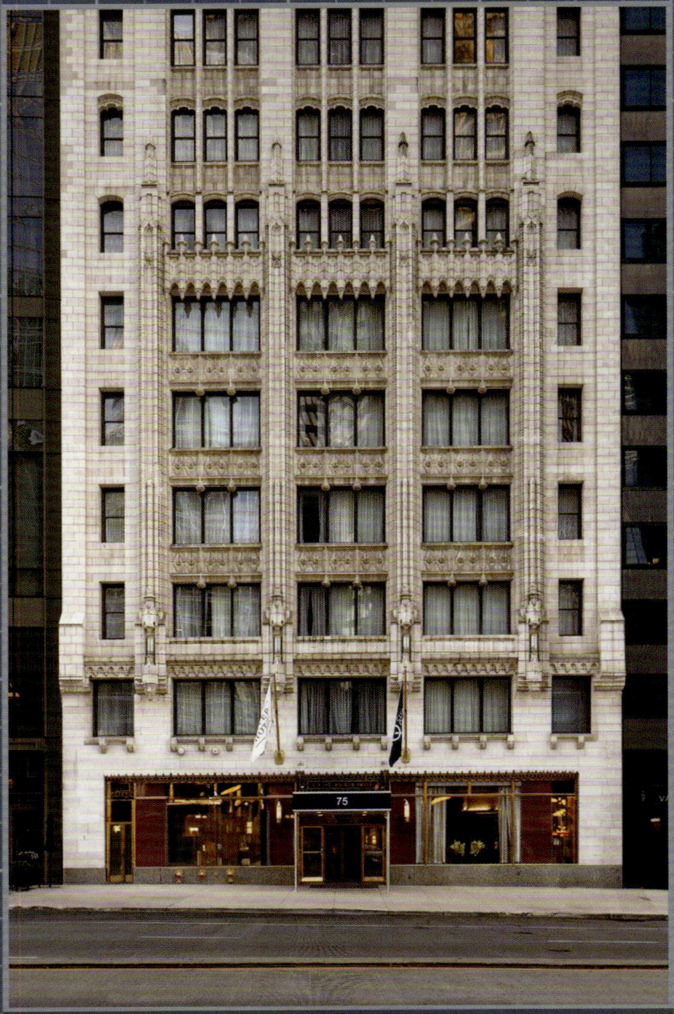

Terracotta Gothic details convey verticality and were a popular skyscraper motif a decade before Art Deco.

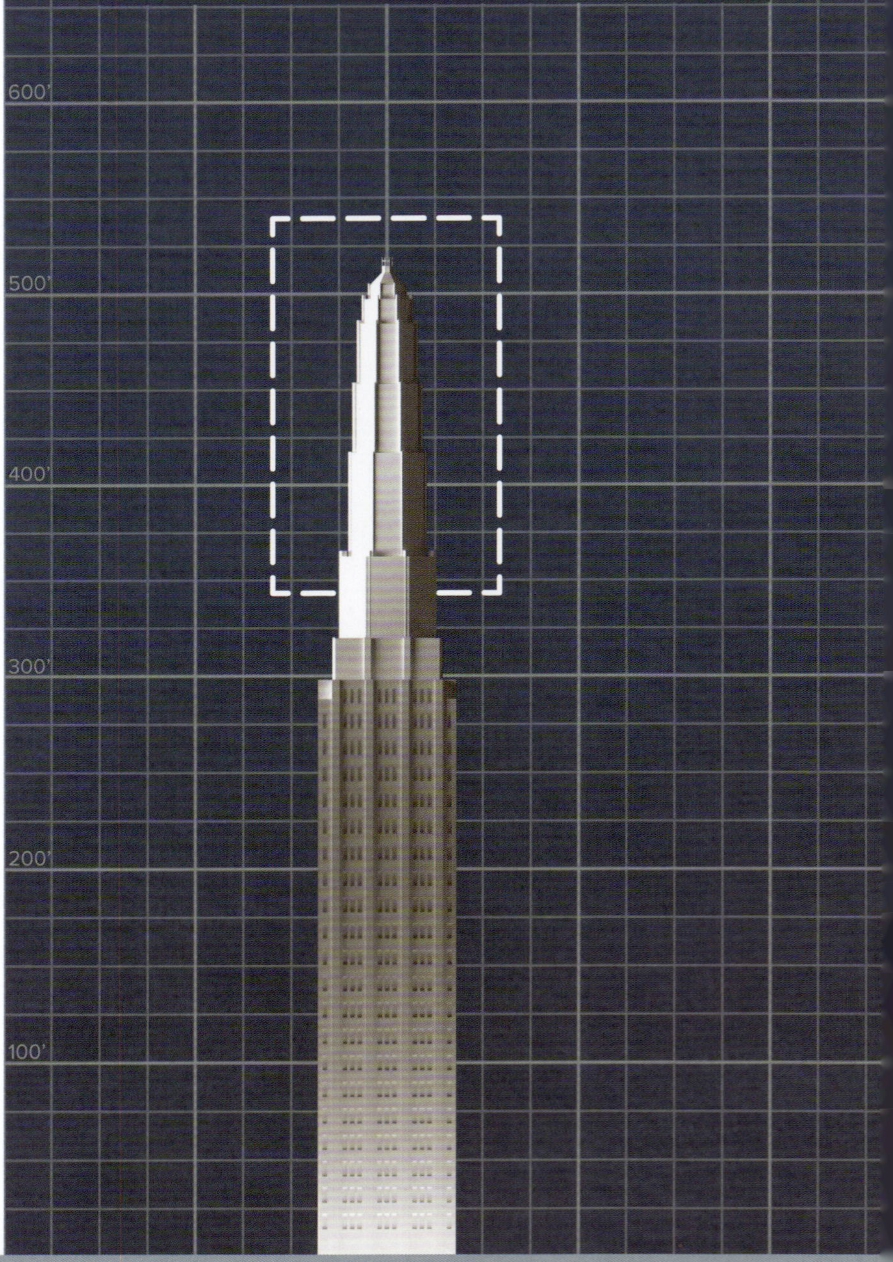

West Elevation 1" = 100'

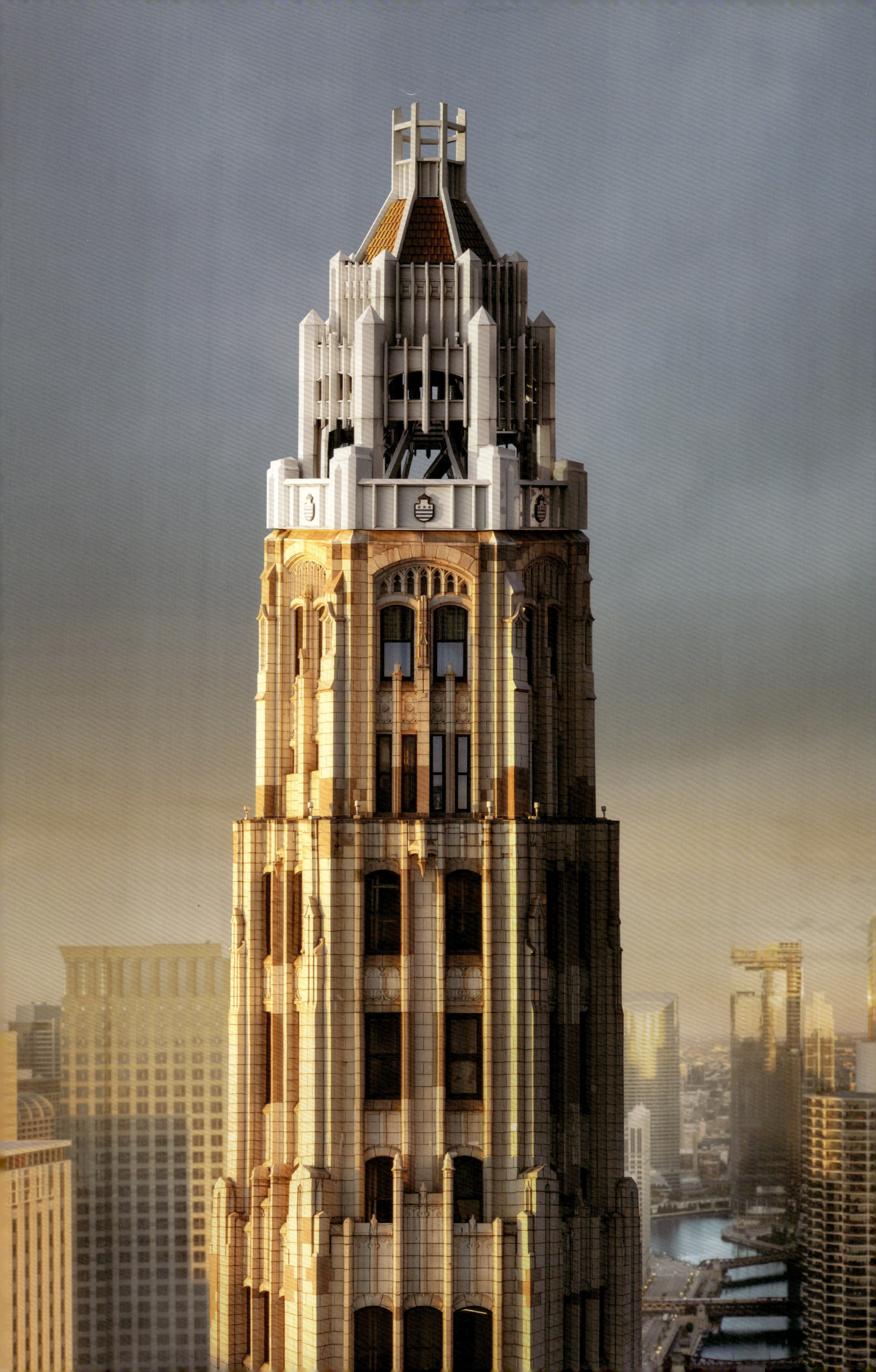

Medinah Athletic
Club

Chicago, **IL** — Hotel InterContinental

Address	**505 N. Michigan Ave.**
Opened	**1929**
Height	**471'**
Stories	**42**
Style	**Art Deco, Moorish**
Architect	**Walter Ahlschlager**

Like the red fezzes Shriners wear at parades, the Moorish dome and minaret capping this highrise are all part of the fraternal organization's Middle Eastern theme. Built to provide recreation facilities, banquet space, and 440 guest rooms for Chicago's largest masonic group, the eclectic skyscraper has been a hotel for most of its existence.

A Shriners children's hospital in Oak Park and country club in DuPage County were both underway in 1925 when plans for this building, three blocks from the Medinah Shrine on Wabash Avenue, were announced. Mayor "Big Bill" Thompson broke ground two years later with the club tower's president, Thomas Houston, an insurance man who headed Thompson's civil service commission. In 1931, Houston was named imperial potentate of all Shriners in America; two months later, he was bounced from the presidency of his athletic club, which had defaulted on its loans and eventually filed for bankruptcy.

The tower first was remodeled into a hotel in 1944. After a series of owners, it underwent extensive restoration and reopened as the Hotel InterContinental in 1990. Lavishly decorated inside and out, the building especially leans into its stonemasonry heritage. Three Mesopotamian-inspired friezes wrap around the building and depict scenes in the construction of a great temple.

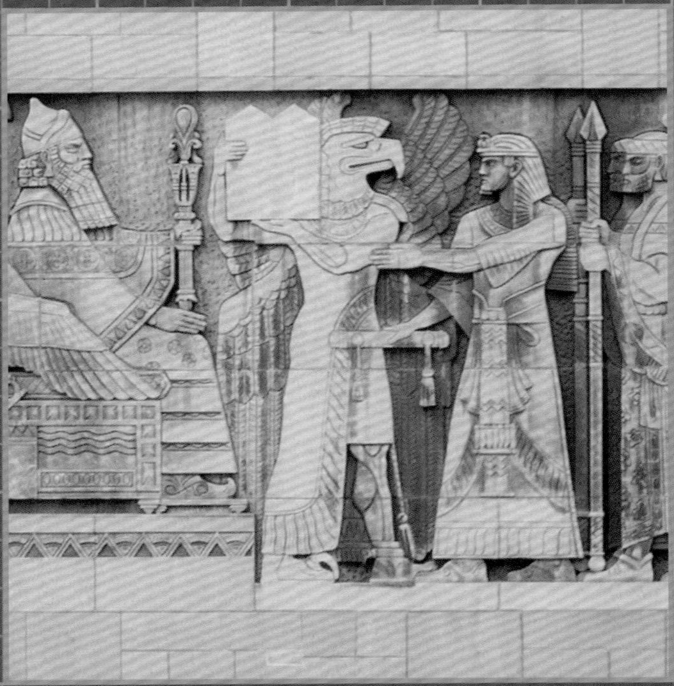

Frieze detail shows the architect presenting a scroll with his plans for a temple to the ruler on the throne.

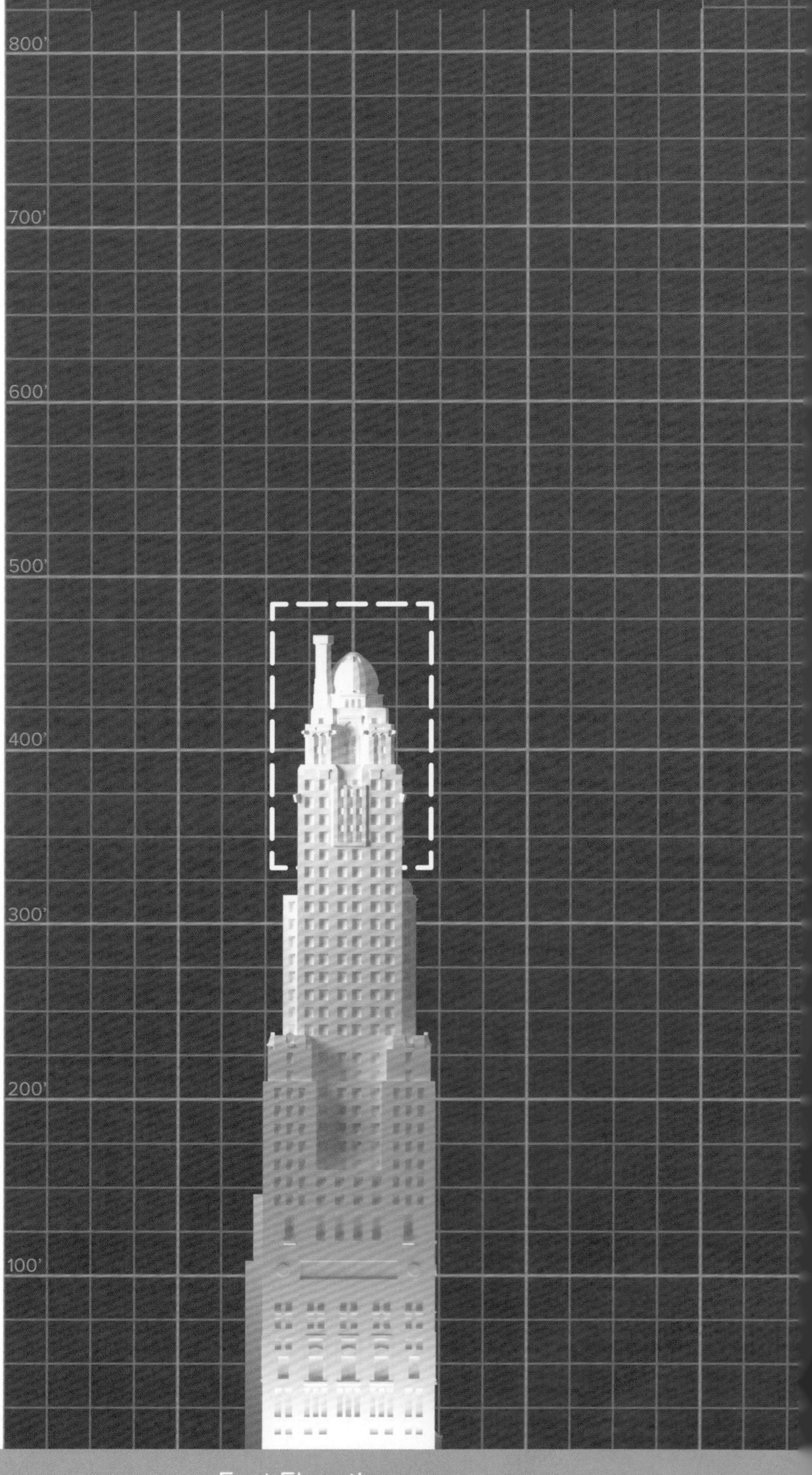

East Elevation *1" = 100'*

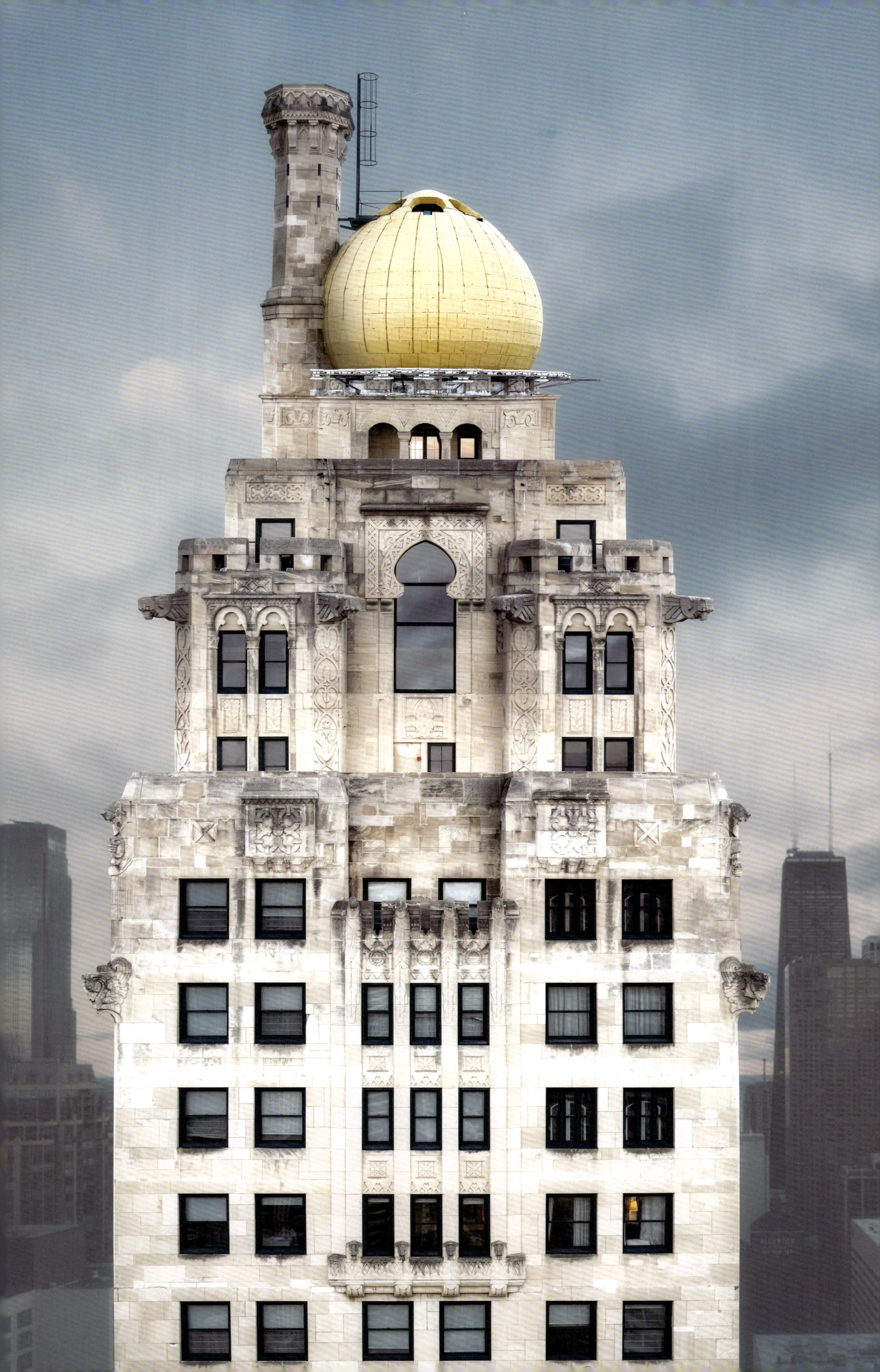

Pittsfield
Building

Chicago, **IL**

Address	**55 E. Washington St.**
Opened	**1927**
Height	**557'**
Stories	**40**
Style	**Gothic, Art Deco**
Architect	**Graham, Anderson, Probst & White**

Named for the Massachusetts town where department store king Marshall Field learned the dry goods trade, this highrise was built by Field's fabulously rich grandson and sole heir to the estate. Relaxed zoning height restrictions spurred a spate of tower construction in the 1920s, and this was for a time the city's tallest skyscraper, besting the Chicago Temple by a single foot.

Field actually flopped in his first job clerking at his hometown general store. A second attempt at a Pittsfield dry goods store went so well that he was offered a partnership. Spurning it, Field lit out for Chicago and built his retail empire. Its flagship store stands a block away from this building, which housed doctors and dentists for most of its existence. The tower was later given to the city's natural history museum, which Field had also established, though museum trustees eventually sold it.

In 1992, the Chicago River burst into an underground tunnel network linking old buildings in the Loop, including the Pittsfield. More than 20 feet of water flooded its basement, forcing a temporary evacuation.

A residential conversion is partially complete, but has been plagued by delays and legal wrangles. The marble lobby, with its deeply coffered painted ceiling and elegant bronzework, connects to an airy five-story shopping arcade.

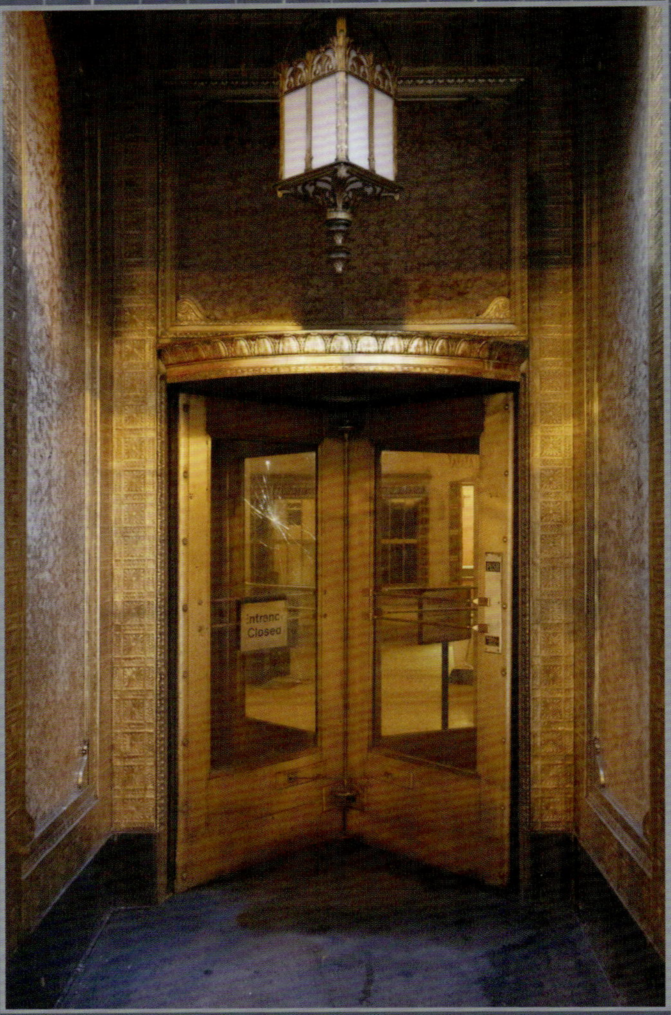

Mottled pink polished granite with bronze trim frames a revolving door with an egg and dart crown.

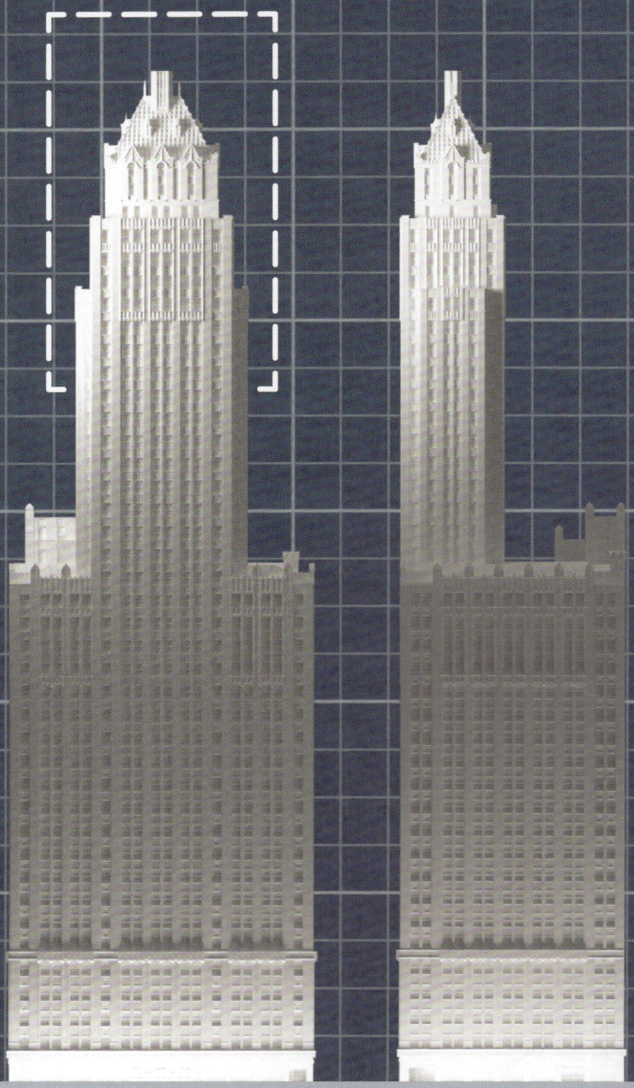

North Elevation West Elevation *1" = 100'*

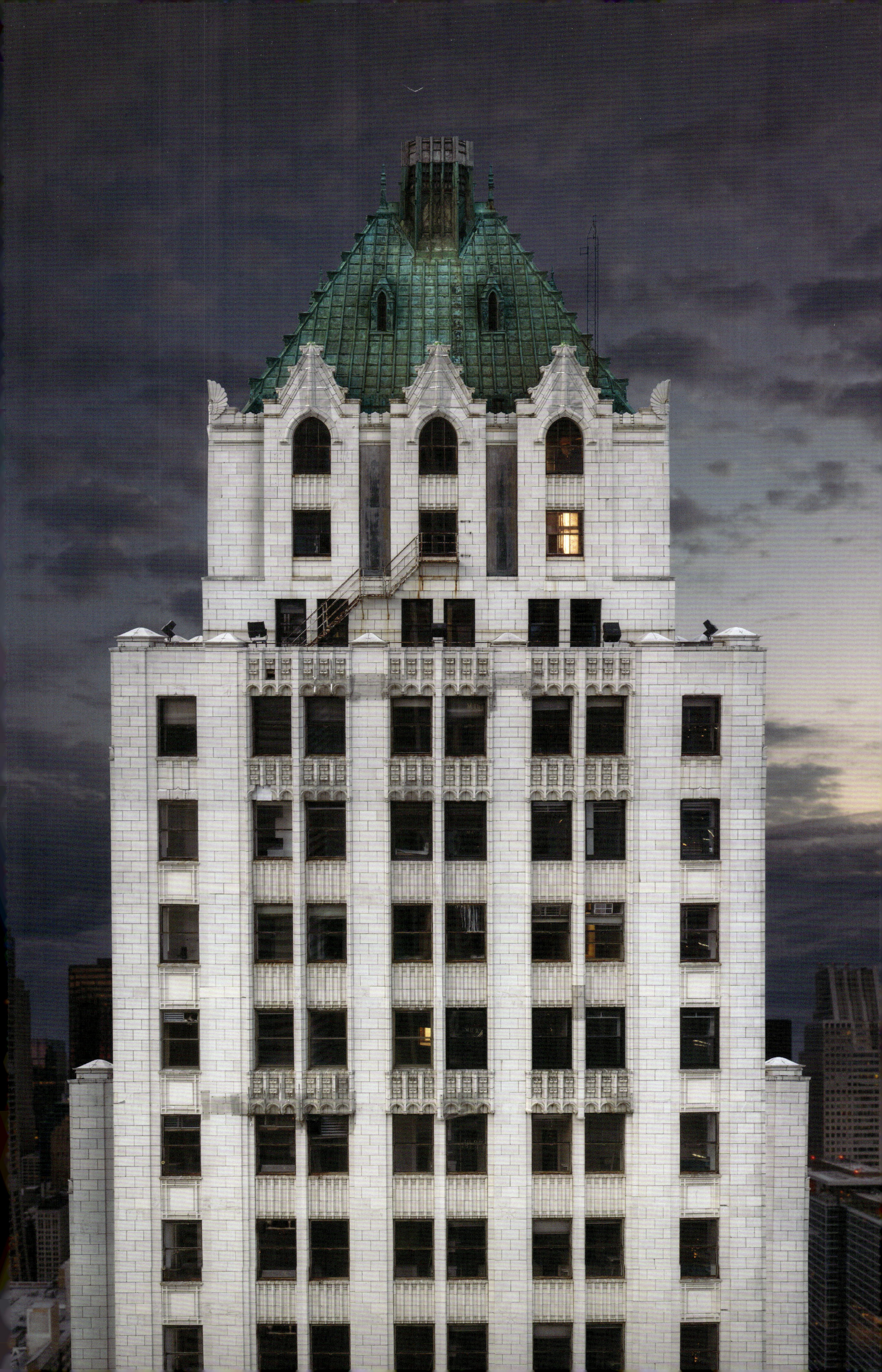

Tribune Tower

Chicago, **IL**

Address	**435 N. Michigan Ave.**
Opened	**1925**
Height	**463'**
Stories	**34**
Style	**Gothic**
Architect	**Howells & Hood**

Sprung from an international architecture competition promoted by the self-proclaimed "World's Greatest Newspaper," this highrise is one of the most influential skyscrapers ever constructed. That importance is not primarily due to its Rouen Cathedral-inspired design, but rather to the more than 260 contest entries that poured in from architects around the globe eager for publicity and the $100,000 prize.

Conceived by editor, publisher, and publicity pro Robert McCormick, the Chicago Tribune contest marked the public debut of several novel architectural concepts. Many felt that it missed the obvious winner, a stepped vertical massing by Finnish architect Eliel Saarinen that earned second place. Though never built, his design became a template for the waves of Art Deco skyscrapers soon to come.

After city planners widened Michigan Avenue and bridged the Chicago River, stretching the thoroughfare northward, Tribune Tower became the second highrise to go up outside the Loop after the Wrigley Building, its neighbor across the street. The tower served as the newspaper's headquarters for nearly a century and was converted into luxury apartments in 2018.

Visitors in the grand lobby are surrounded by quotes from McCormick and others about the value of a free press. But an inscription on the marble floor more aptly summarizes the Tribune Tower's lasting contribution: "When we build, let us think that we build forever."

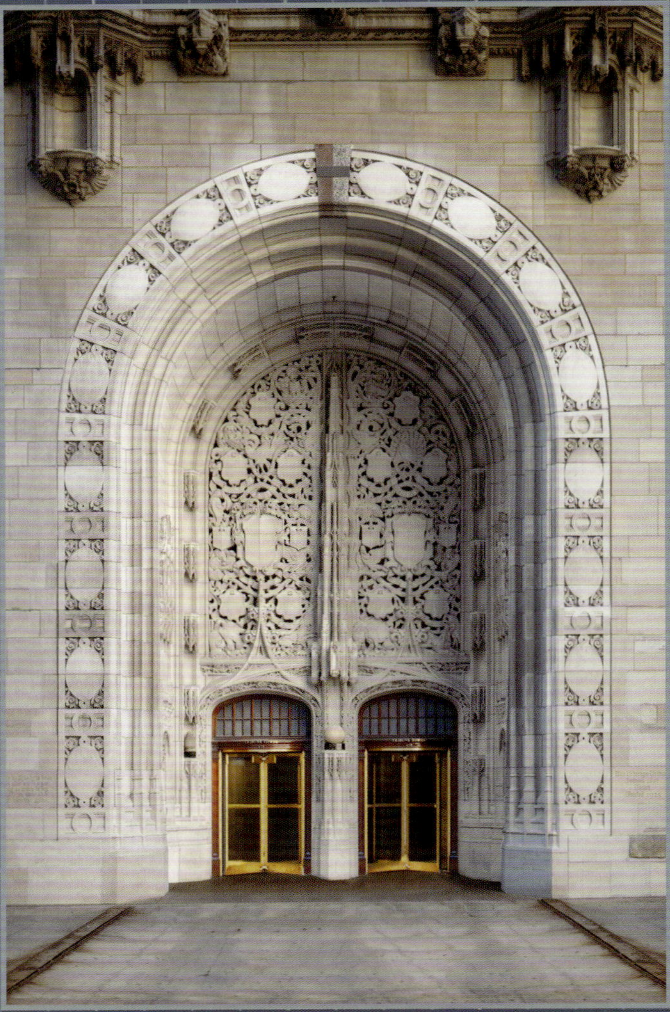

An elaborate stone screen over the entrance by Rene Chambellan has scenes from Aesop's fables.

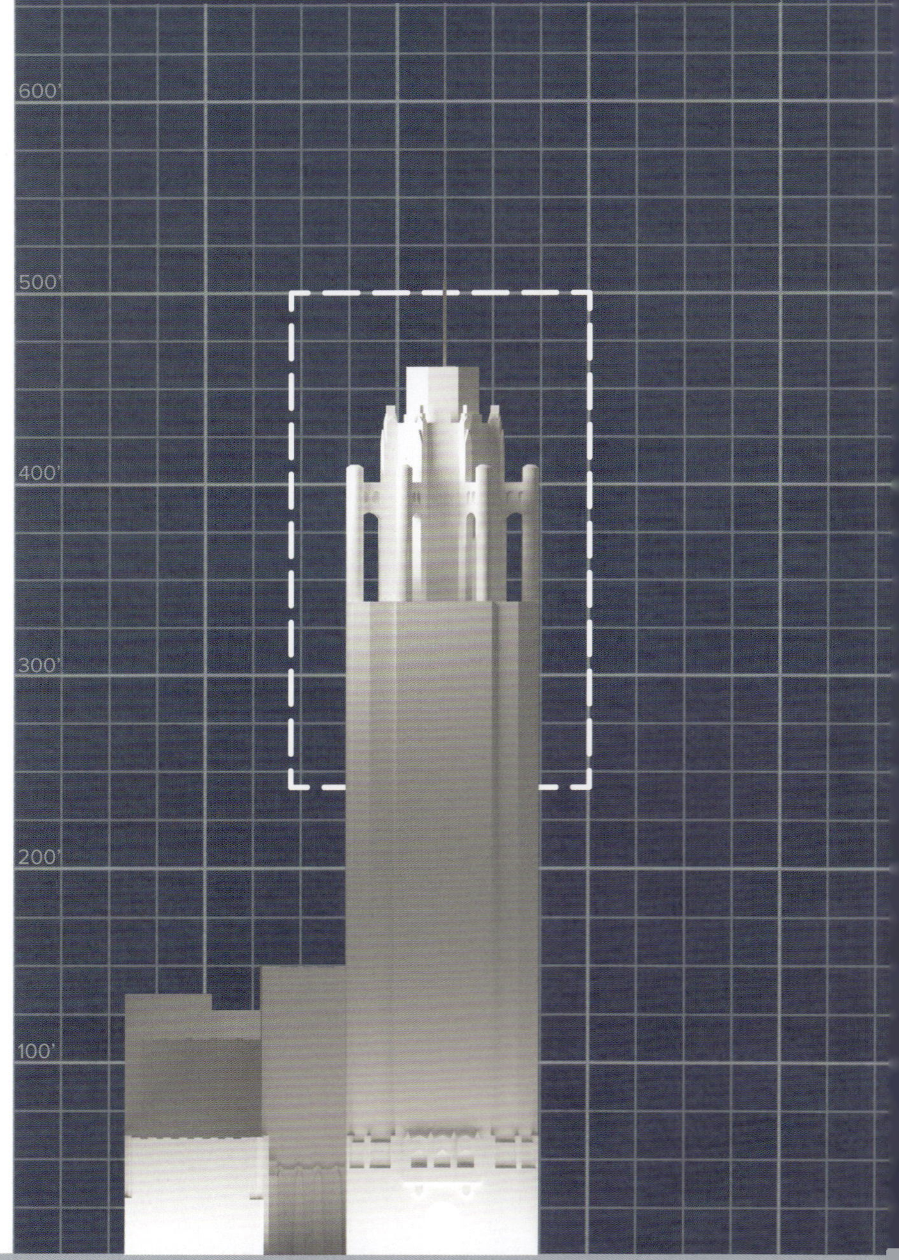

West Elevation *1" = 100'*

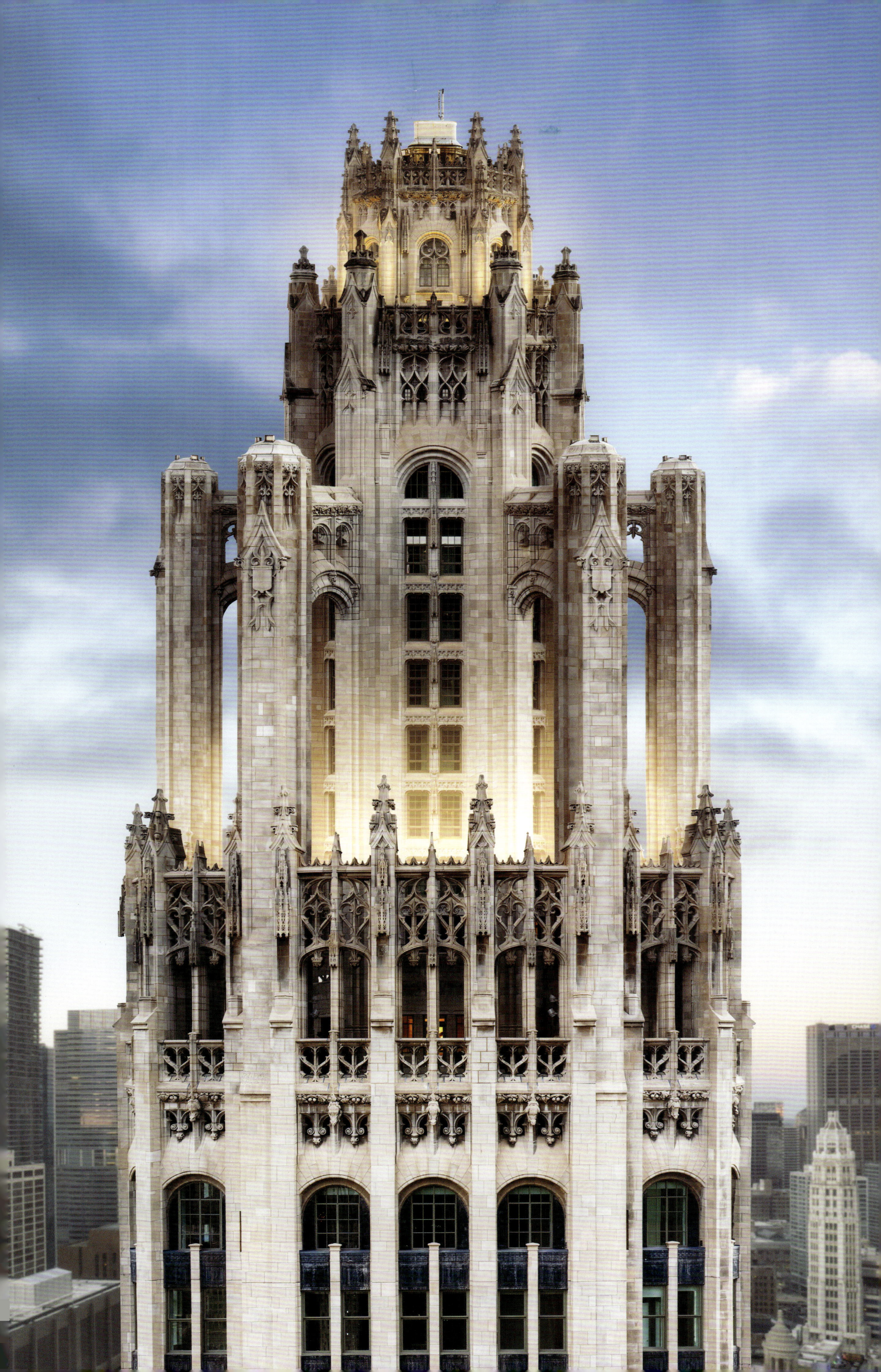

Trustees System
Service Building

Chicago, **IL** | Century Tower

Address ·············· **182 W. Lake St.**
Opened ······················ **1930**
Height ························ **336'**
Stories ························· **28**
Style ···················· **Art Deco**
Architect ··········· **Thielbar & Fugard**

Raised "El" tracks wrap around this highrise, which makes viewing the facade tricky. It's a pity, because the entrance is splendid, surrounded with limestone relief panels of the history of commerce by Chicago artist Gwen Lux and an exquisite cut lead grille overhead with silhouettes of farmers, riveters, lumberjacks, and other laborers.

Inside, two more Lux panels flanking a red marble main staircase reveal the rationale of the consumer mortgage bank that built this tower. One shows a workingman cradling a miniature house, with the legend "Life prospers the thrifty." On the other side, a balding, shoeless figure glares ruefully above the legend "Life punishes the thriftless."

Life prospered and punished John Corcoran, who founded Trustees System Service in Birmingham, Alabama, to offer mortgages to working people. He grew it to 24 branches, relocated to Chicago, and commissioned this tower, but the bank failed in the Depression a few years later. Corcoran and five other company officials, including his brother, were accused of deceiving investors. The case was thrown out on a technicality, and prosecutors dropped the issue since the Corcorans had lost their own money in the crash too. The longtime office building is now fully residential.

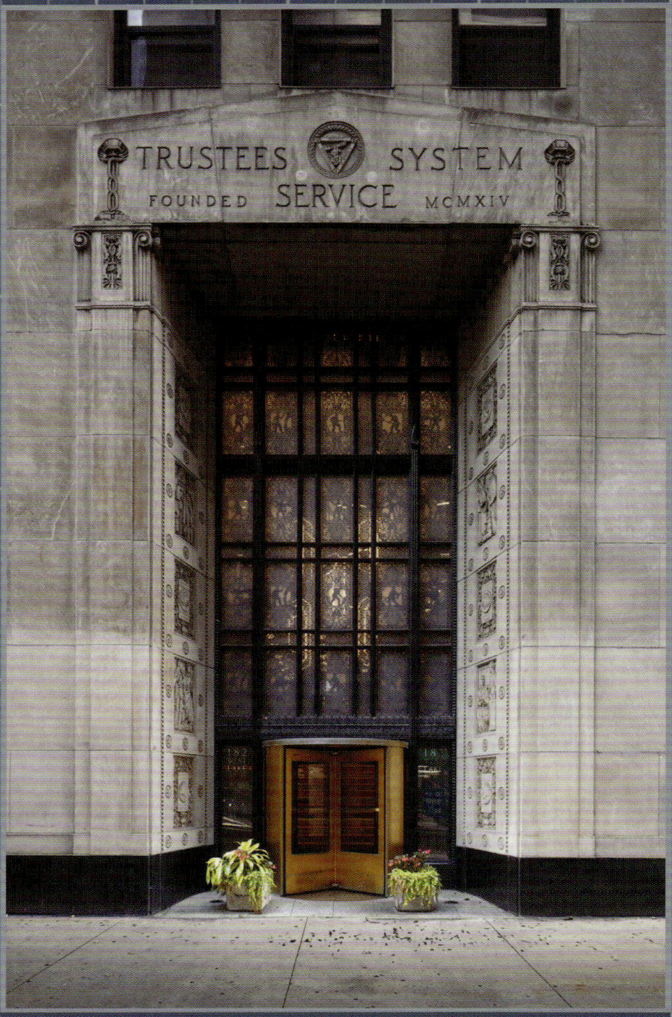

Carved scenes of commerce begin with figures bartering for animal hides and end with a stock ticker.

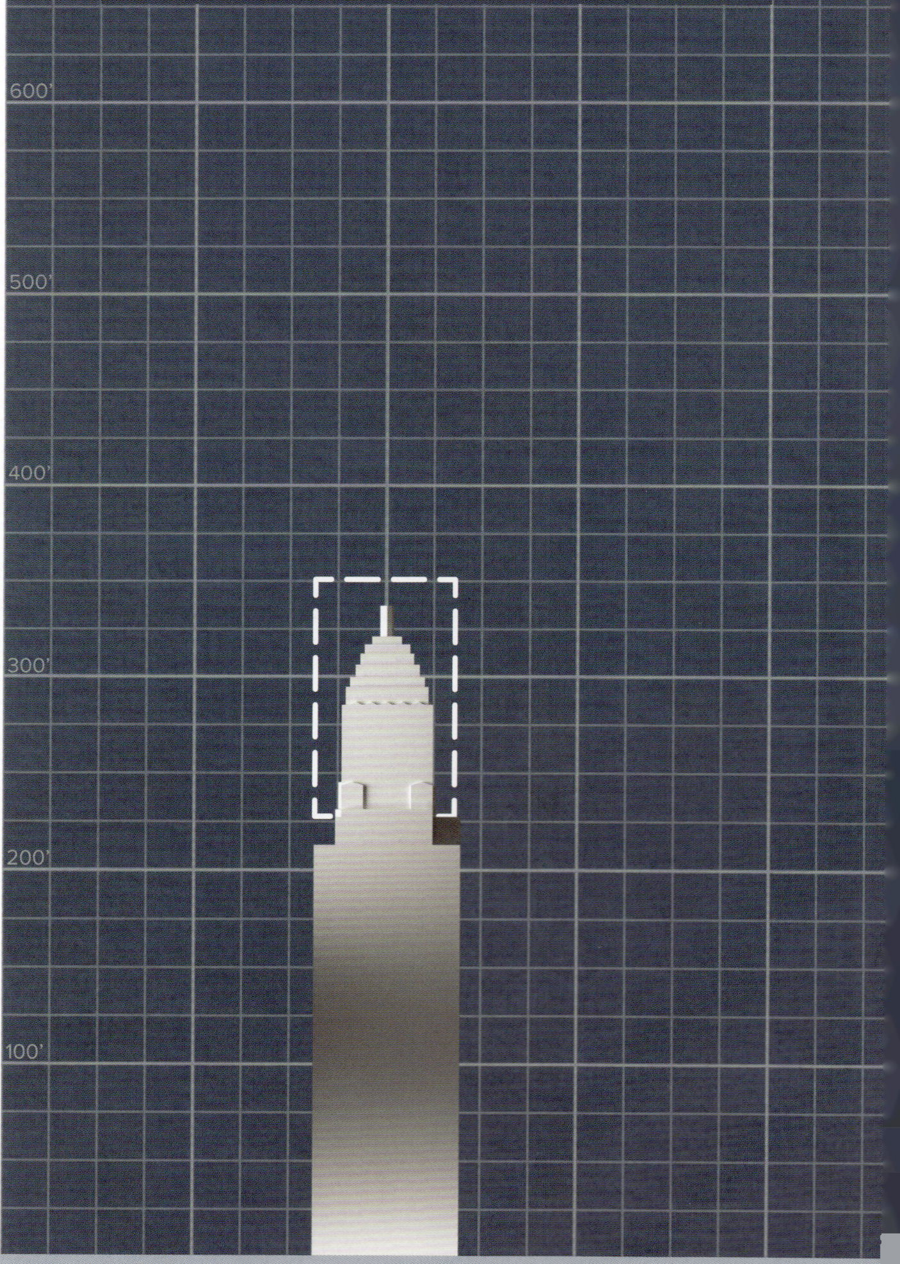

South Elevation *1" = 100'*

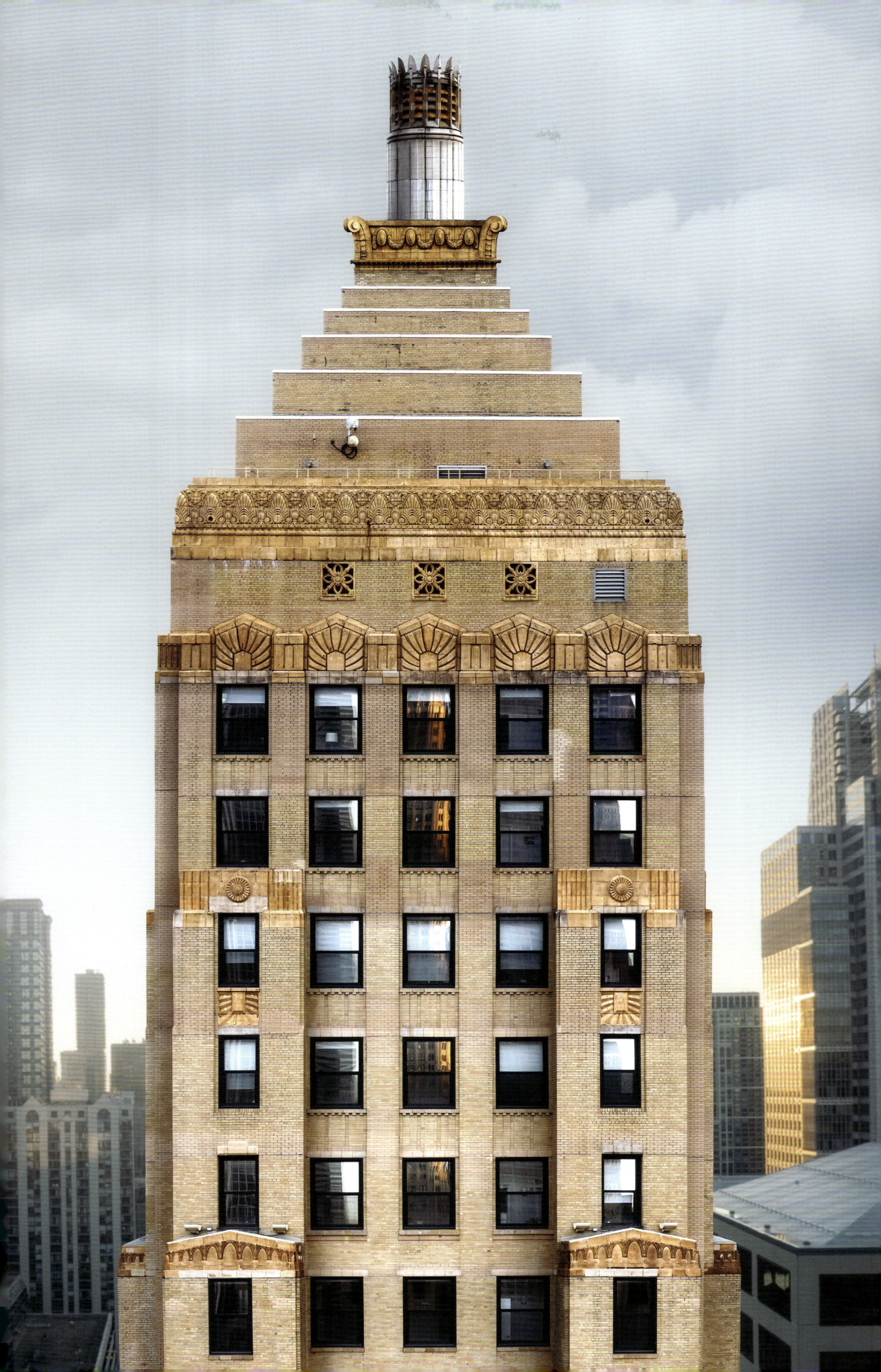

333 North Michigan

Chicago, **IL**

Address ·········· **333 N. Michigan Ave.**
Opened ···························· **1928**
Height ····························· **396'**
Stories ································ **34**
Style ························ **Art Deco**
Architect ················ **Holabird & Root**

The sons of two of Chicago's most celebrated architects designed this highrise at the spot where Michigan Avenue bridges the Chicago River. The mostly ramrod-straight thoroughfare deviates slightly from its course there, a fortunate jitter that makes the stylish landmark visible the full length of the Magnificent Mile.

John Root and William Holabird were responsible for some of the first skyscrapers ever built. Their sons, both named John, were also part owners of this slender slab just 60 feet wide, and their firm occupied offices near the top. The building was inspired by Eliel Saarinen's second-place entry in the Tribune Tower contest, the younger Root acknowledged.

It stands on the former site of Fort Dearborn, and the developers considered historic names before deciding "333" was more mellifluous. Instead, history is expressed through life-size frieze panels of pioneers, settlers, and Native Americans carved in the limestone between the windows on the fifth story.

Nowadays the public is welcome for drinks at the once-private Tavern Club on the 25th and 26th floors. In 1933 the establishment hosted a tremendous beer bash as the long-awaited end of Prohibition finally hove into view. Two months later, in a more sobering moment, attorneys for the building filed for bankruptcy.

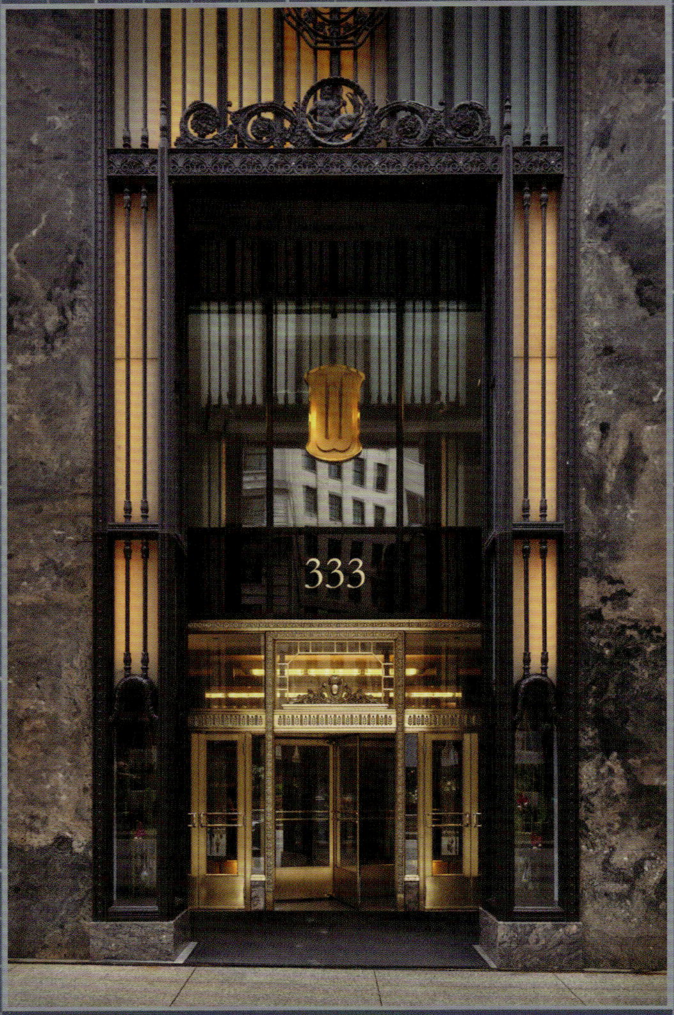

A severe 1960s remodel was reversed a decade ago to restore the entrance to its historic appearance.

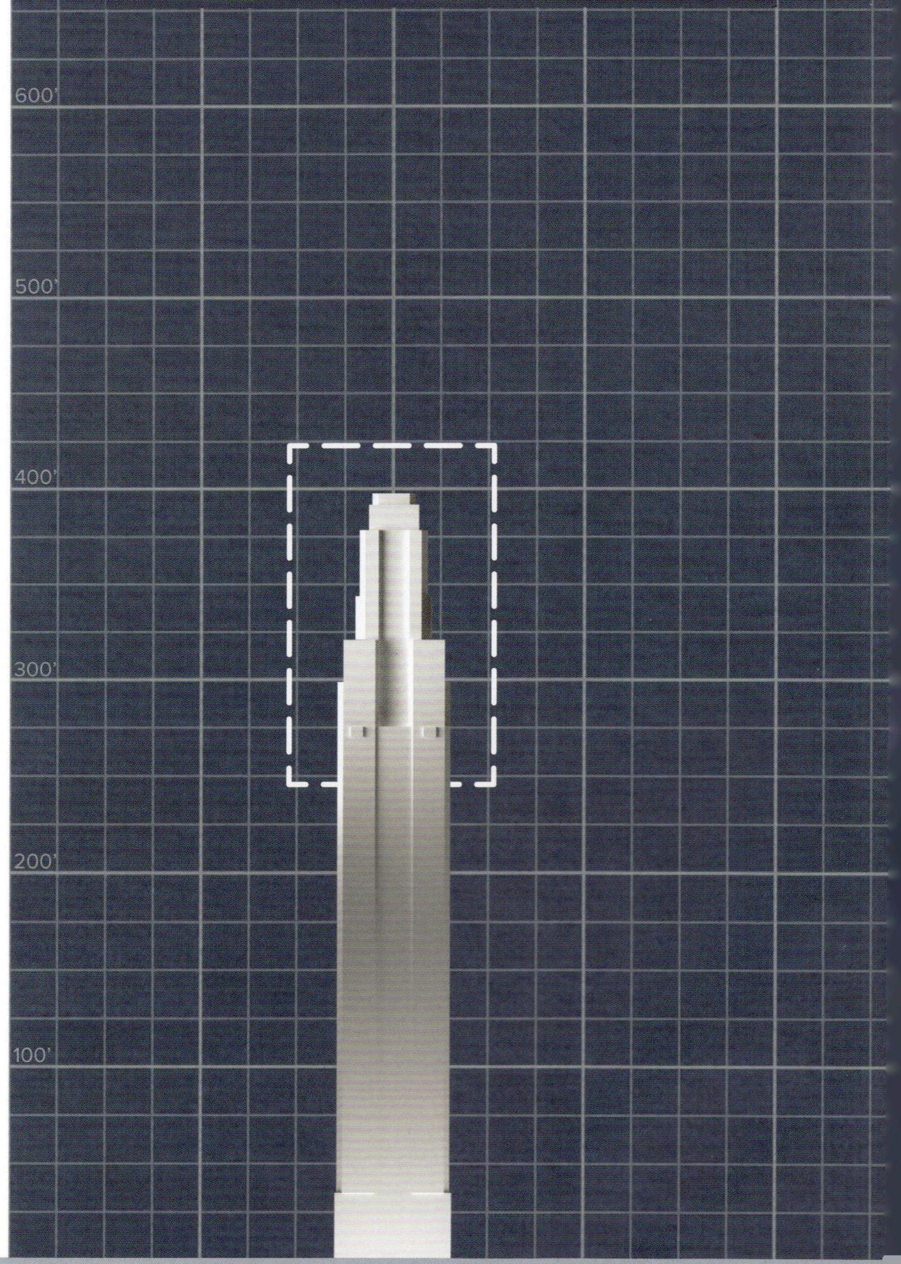

North Elevation *1" = 100'*

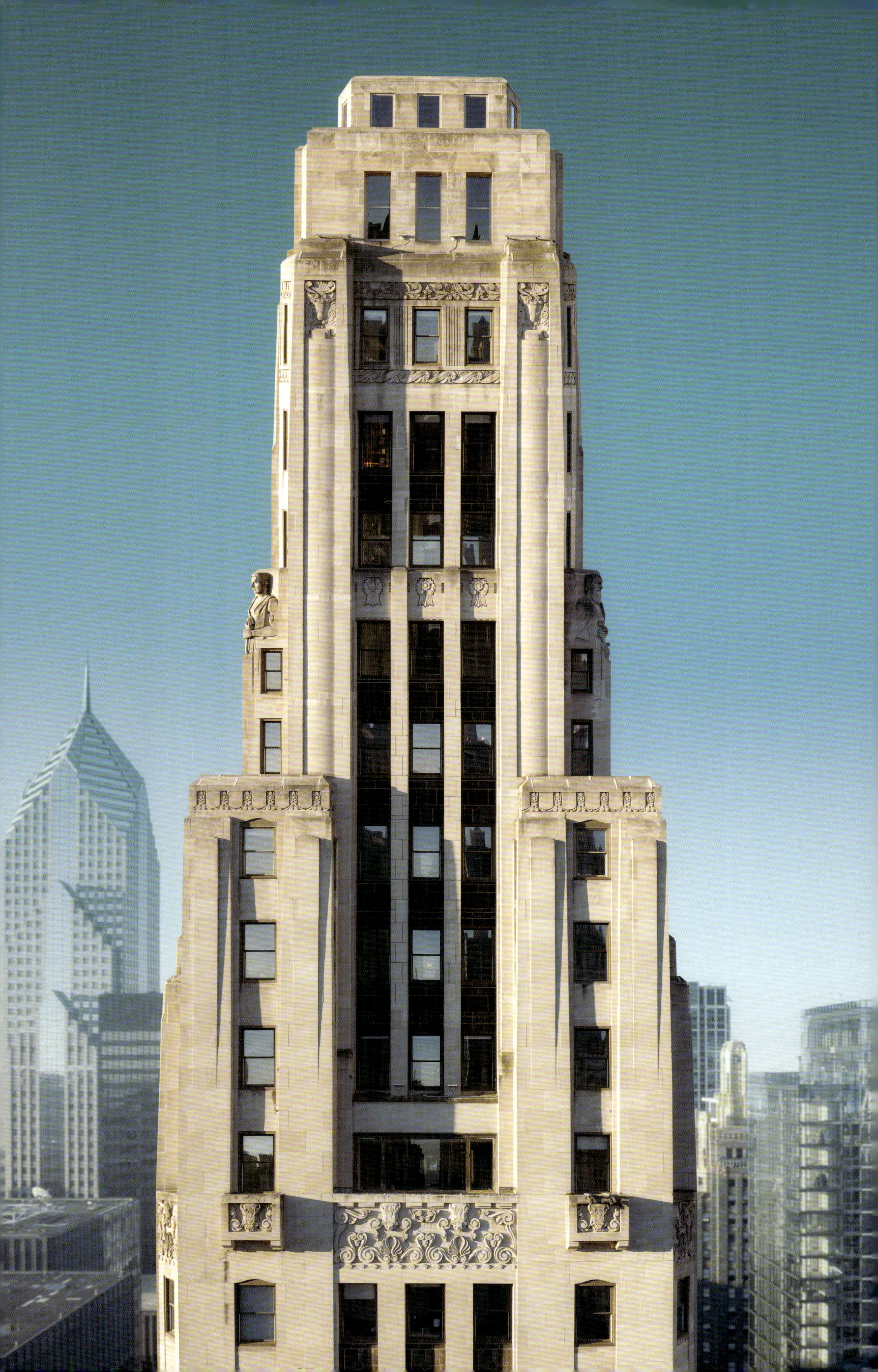

Lincoln Tower

Fort Wayne, **IN**

Address	**116 E. Berry St.**
Opened	**1930**
Height	**285'**
Stories	**22**
Style	**Art Deco**
Architect	**Alvin Strauss**

Although he came to fame as a lawyer and politician in Illinois, Abraham Lincoln grew up in Indiana. That was reason enough for the German-American National Bank of Fort Wayne to give itself a patriotic rebrand as Lincoln National Bank during World War I.

German immigrant Charles Buesching was president of the bank when it built this skyscraper, then Indiana's tallest building. He started as a teenage messenger boy shortly after the institution opened its doors in 1905. Clientele included skilled German hosiery workers who came to Fort Wayne to work in its sock factory, Wayne Knitting Mills.

The president of that business, Samuel Foster, founded the bank. He was already rich thanks to another clothes factory in town, one he had built to capitalize on a fashion craze for shirtwaists. The button-down blouses were for boys originally, but around 1890 they suddenly became a must-have for every lady.

Painted tiles decorate this highrise like embroidery on a sleeve. Its spectacular banking hall is appointed with brightly colored murals of a man attired only in a loincloth and a woman who seems to have forgotten her shirtwaist in the dresser.

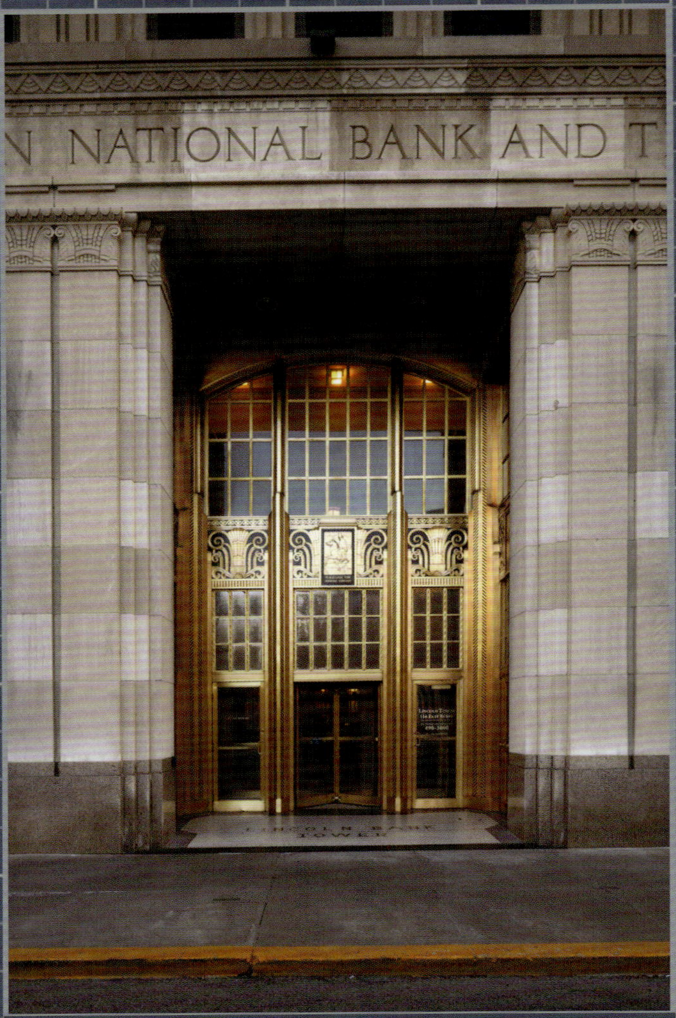

Abraham Lincoln travels the judicial circuit on horseback in a scene from his lawyer days in the doorway.

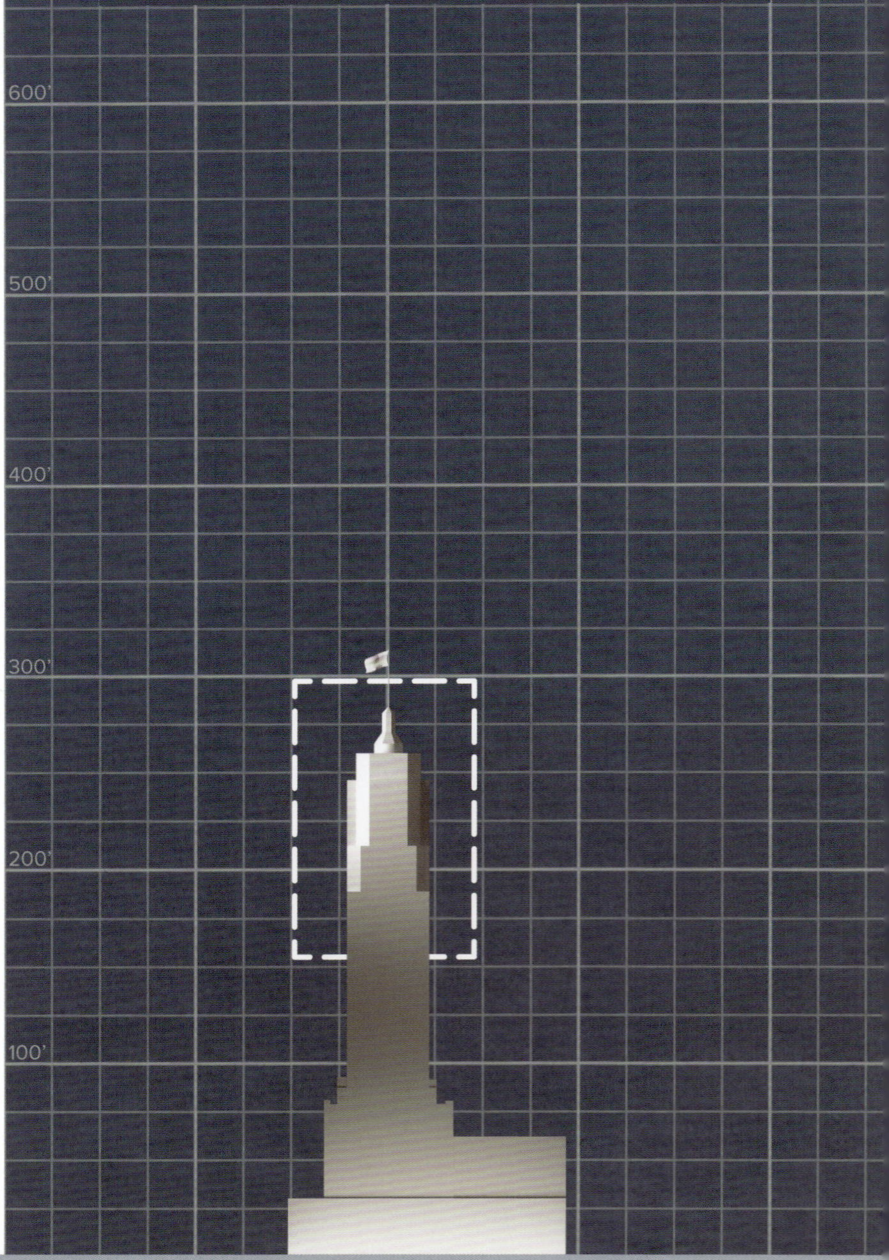

North Elevation *1" = 100'*

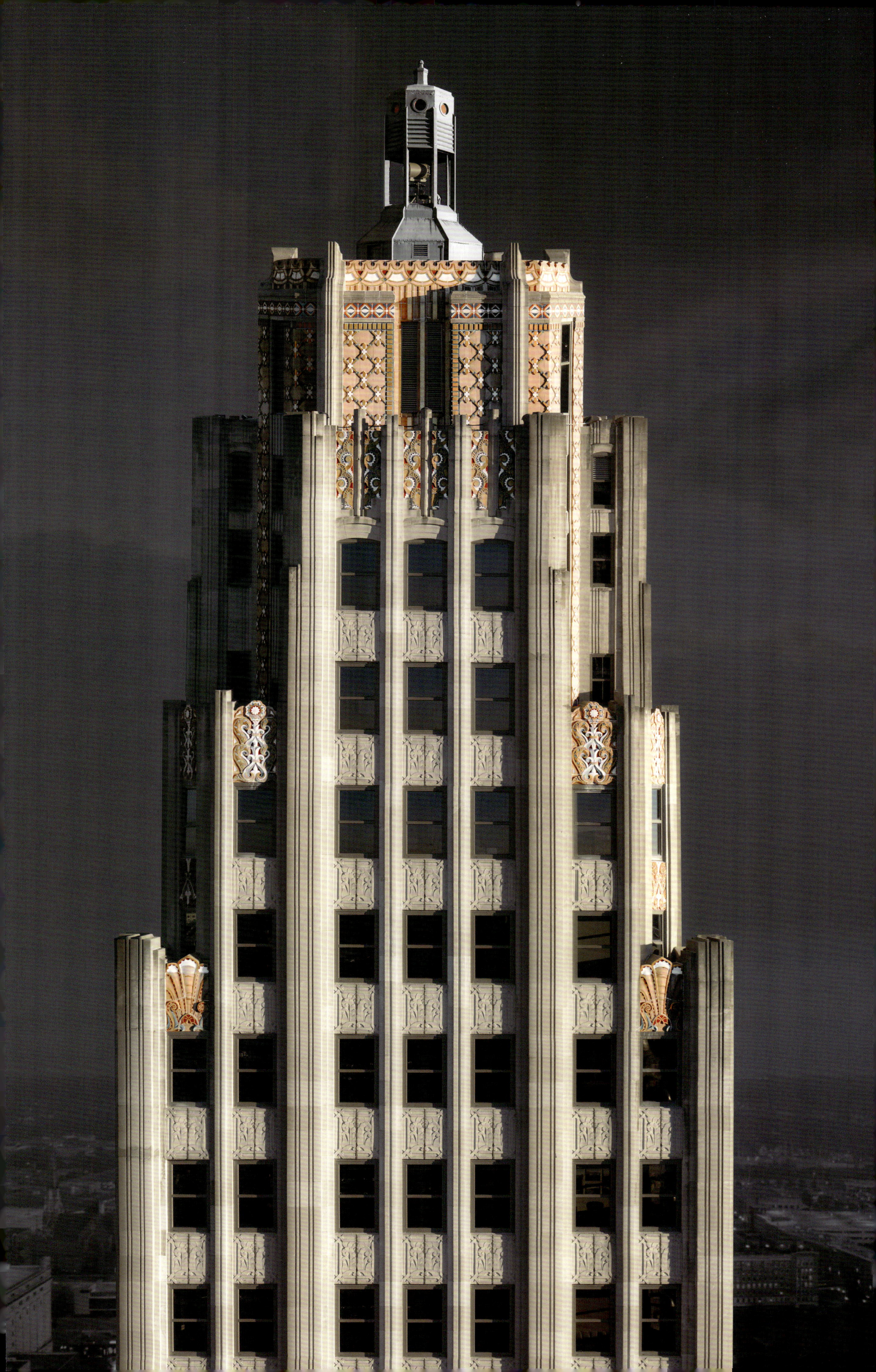

Fisher Building

Detroit, **MI**

Address ·········· **3011 W. Grand Blvd.**
Opened ·········· **1928**
Height ·········· **441'**
Stories ·········· **28**
Style ·········· **Art Deco**
Architect ·········· **Albert Kahn**

Money was no object for the Fisher brothers, the auto tycoons who ordered this opulent edifice enveloped inside and out with marble. It is Albert Kahn's most spectacular creation, if not his most consequential — his no-nonsense car factories inspired the next movement in architecture, the International Style.

Kahn, who came to Detroit as a boy with his German Jewish family, showed early promise with his house designs before landing a 1902 commission for a Packard plant. The reinforced concrete structure, well lit by floor-to-ceiling windows, led to a Model T factory job from Henry Ford, and Kahn quickly became known as a master of industrial design.

The Fisher brothers manufactured wooden car bodies for some of the first automobiles, and got their big break in 1910 when Cadillac ordered 150. In 1926 their factories — including one by Kahn — rolled out a million, and General Motors bought the business. When oldest brother Fred Fisher broke ground on this highrise the next year, it was meant to be the first of three towers on the block, but the Great Depression intervened.

Tour groups still goggle in awe at the frescoes, chandeliers, marble, and mosaics in the breathtaking three-story arcade. Traveling Broadway shows perform at the theater, which was originally decorated as a Mayan temple.

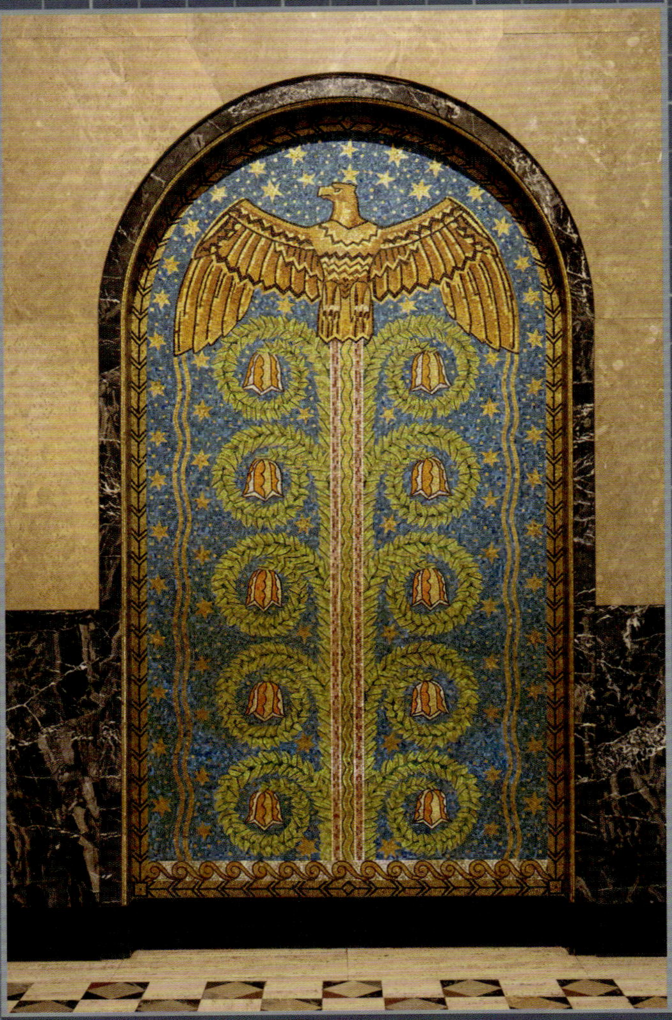

Hungarian artist Géza Maróti created the vivid mosaics and ceiling fresco with eagles as a main theme.

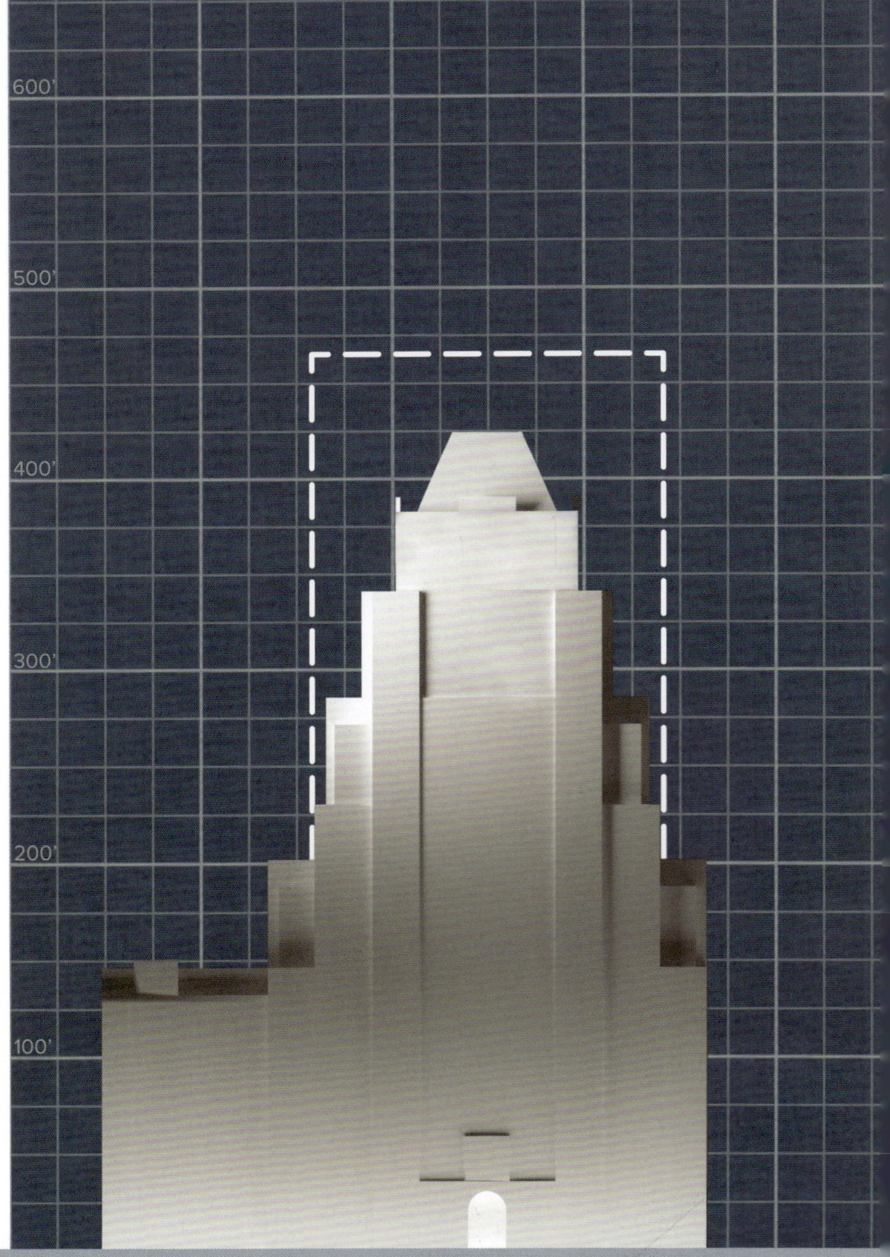

South Elevation *1" = 100'*

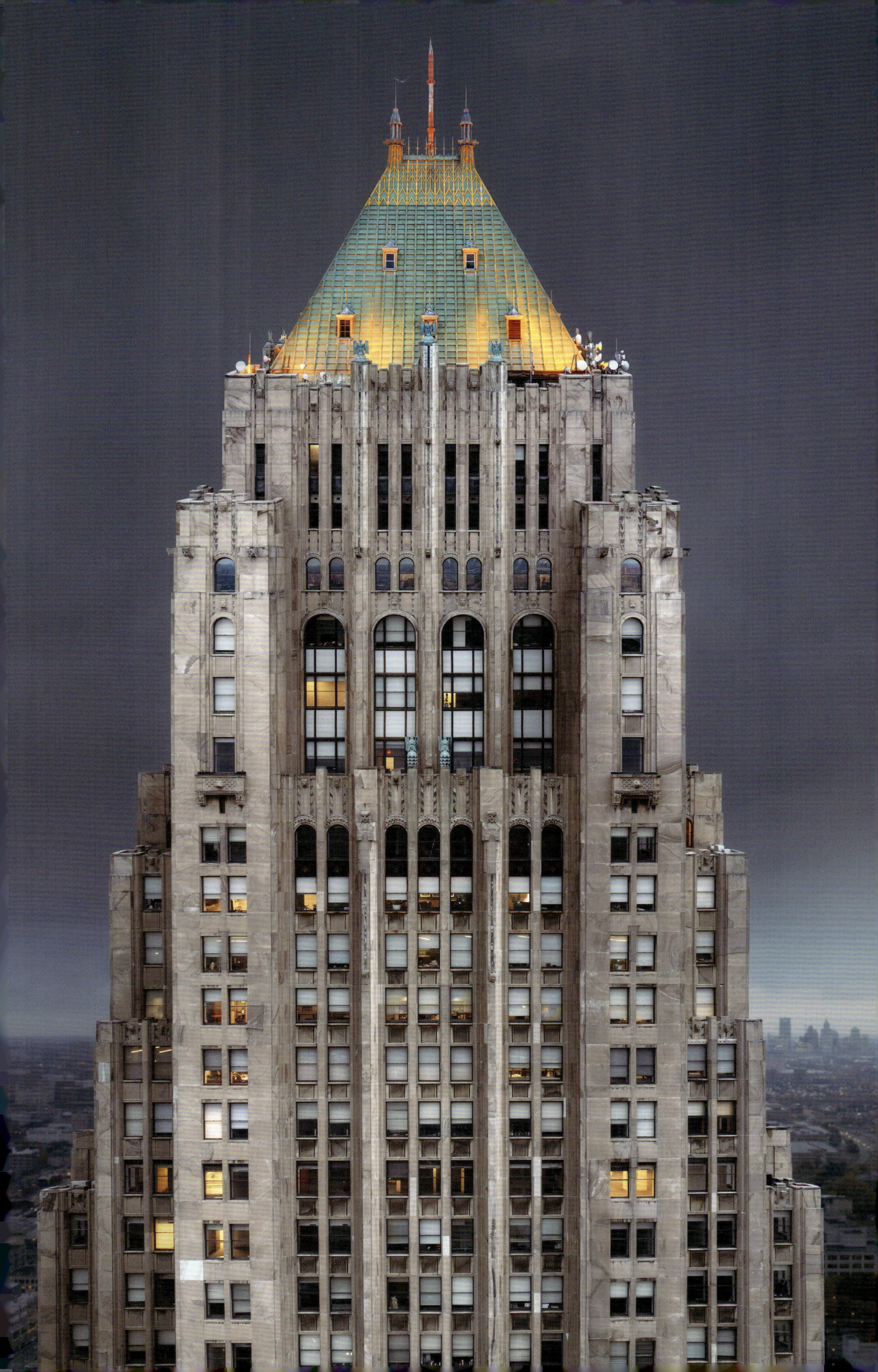

Guardian
Building

Detroit, **MI**

Address	**500 Griswold St.**
Opened	**1929**
Height	**496'**
Stories	**40**
Style	**Art Deco**
Architect	**Wirt Rowland**

Vivid tile patterns play across the orange brick of this highrise, a technicolor tower hailed at its dedication as a "vertical rainbow" for the bold use of color inside and out. The inspiration came to architect Wirt Rowland on a trip to Barcelona, where he admired the Sagrada Familia and other polychromatically iconoclastic edifices by Antoni Gaudí.

Rowland lived a block from Detroit's Pewabic Pottery, and asked its founder, Mary Chase Stratton, to decorate this building's concave half-dome entryway. Her design of an aviator appears to spring from a Navajo blanket, flanked by figures resembling 8-bit space Aztecs. The dazzling elevator lobby and banking hall they guard are a scarcely controlled riot for the optic nerve, a throne room for the Queen of Legos.

That Rowland persuaded a trust company to let him try out his ideas on their new building testifies to his lofty reputation among the city's corporate elite. The skyscraper opened as the Union Trust Building, but its name changed within a year after merger with the Guardian Group, and the institution went into receivership soon after. The army put a production command center here during World War II, and today the Guardian is America's most fantastic county office building.

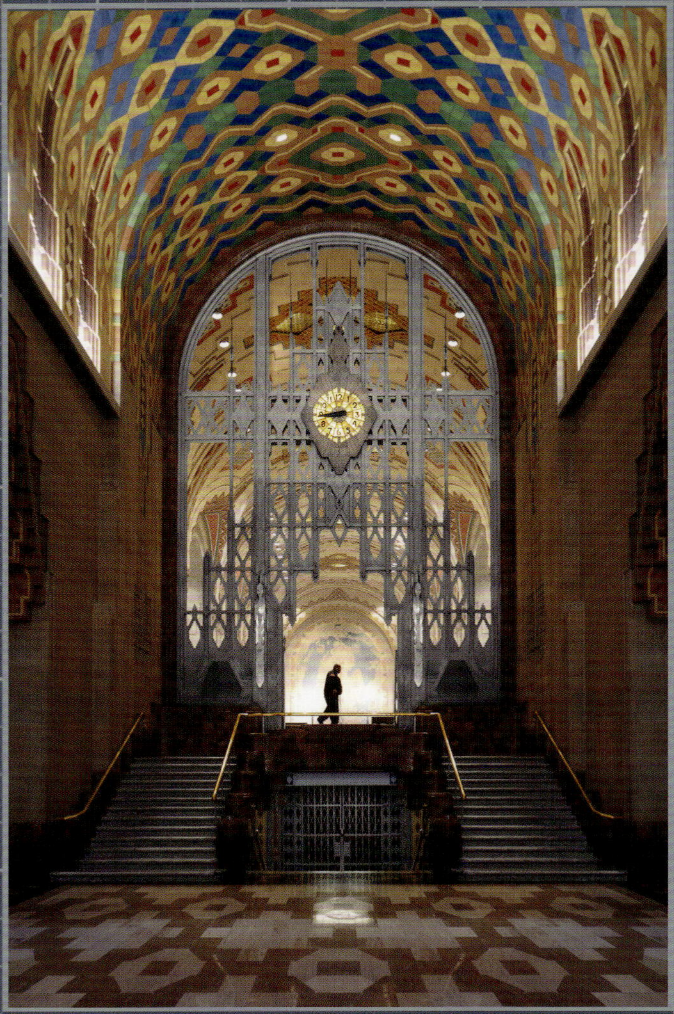

Exuberant colors in the barrel-vaulted lobby pop against a gray metal screen with a Tiffany glass clock.

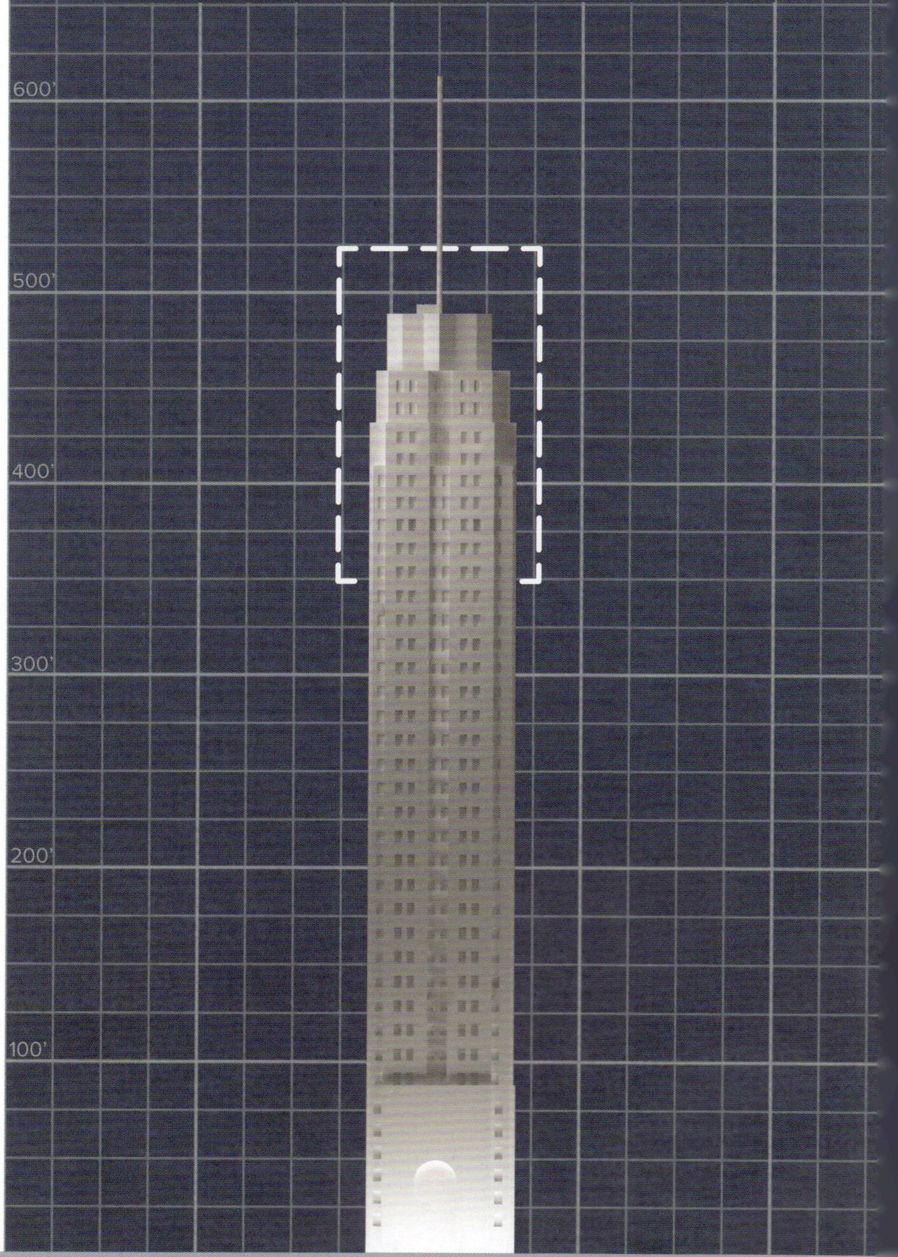

North Elevation *1" = 100'*

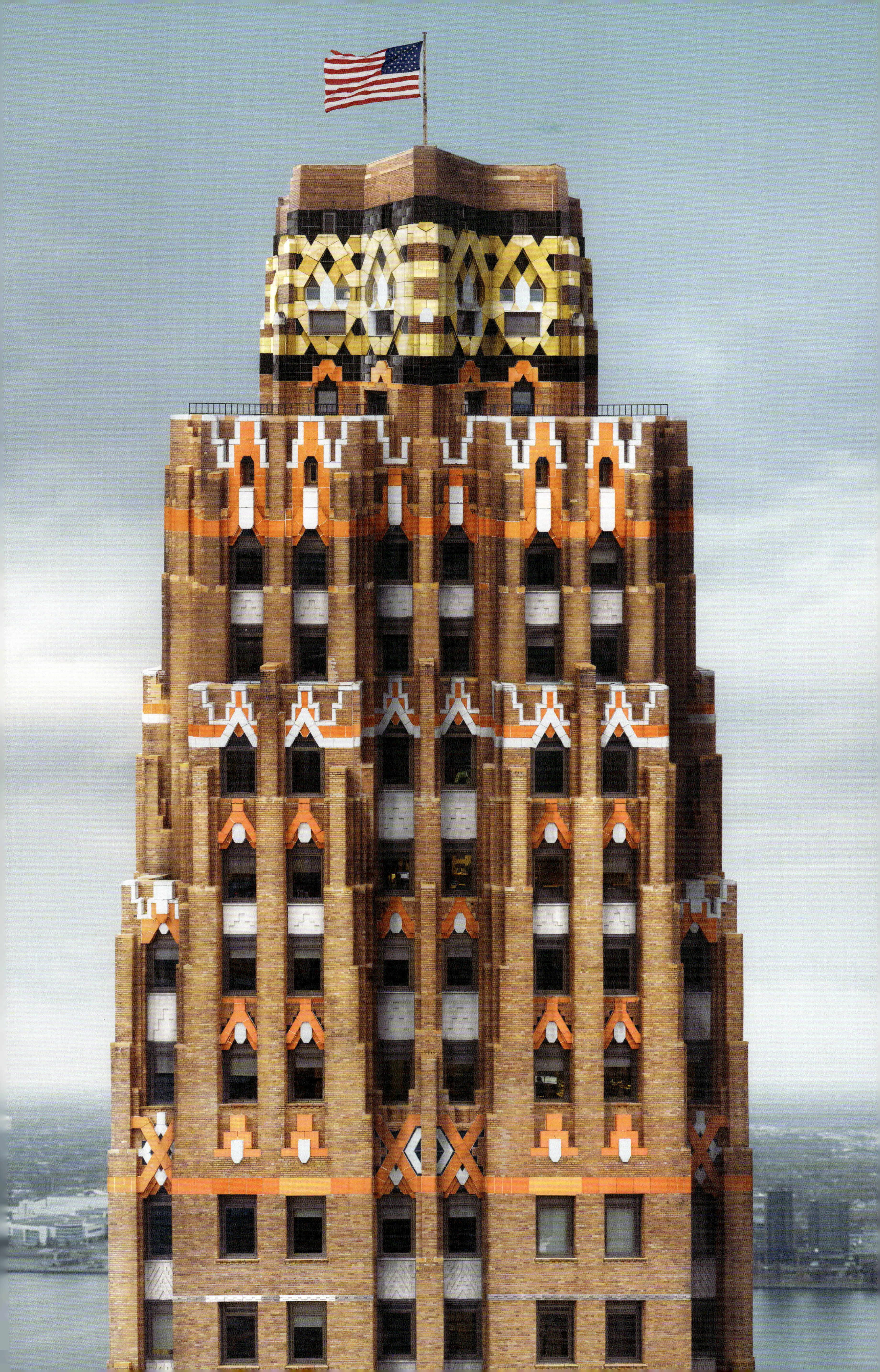

Penobscot
Building

Detroit, **MI**

Address • • • • • • • • • • • • • • **645 Griswold St.**
Opened • **1928**
Height • **654'**
Stories • **47**
Style • **Art Deco**
Architect • • • • • • • • • • • • • • • **Wirt Rowland**

This highrise is the last and tallest of three interconnected Penobscot Buildings that demonstrate the rapid advance of early skyscraper technology, as well as a ballooning family fortune. All are named for the Maine river where Simon Murphy first learned the lumber trade before moving to Detroit in 1866 to harvest the vast Michigan pine forests.

Murphy's timberlands would stretch to Wisconsin and eventually the West Coast, his assets multiplying with iron ore mineral rights under the trees and and oil beneath a southern California ranch. His son, William, became the lead investor and financial manager of Henry Ford's first and second car companies in 1899 and 1901, and when that contentious partnership dissolved, the younger Murphy founded Cadillac. Both men wound up rich enough for hard feelings to dissipate, and the first tenant to move into the new Penobscot was Ford's consumer finance division.

The building's main banking hall initially housed the Guardian Group, a local bank and trust company that merged in 1929 with a competitor opening its own Wirt Rowland-designed Art Deco skyscraper a block away. The illuminated orb at the Penobscot's pinnacle — the knob on the 'Nob — was the highest point in Detroit for nearly 50 years.

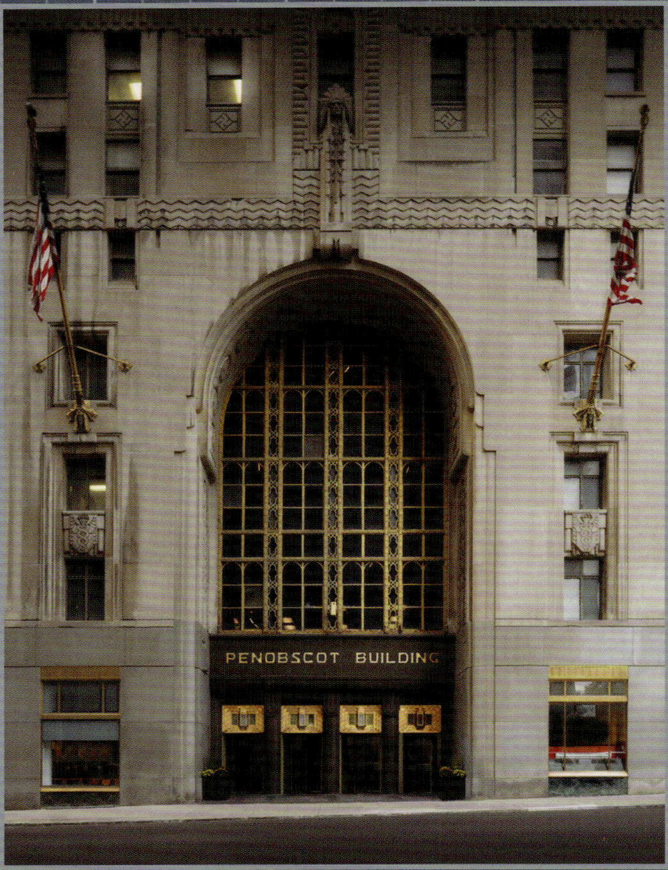

Corrado Parducci sculpted Native American figures for this building and the nearby Buhl and Guardian buildings.

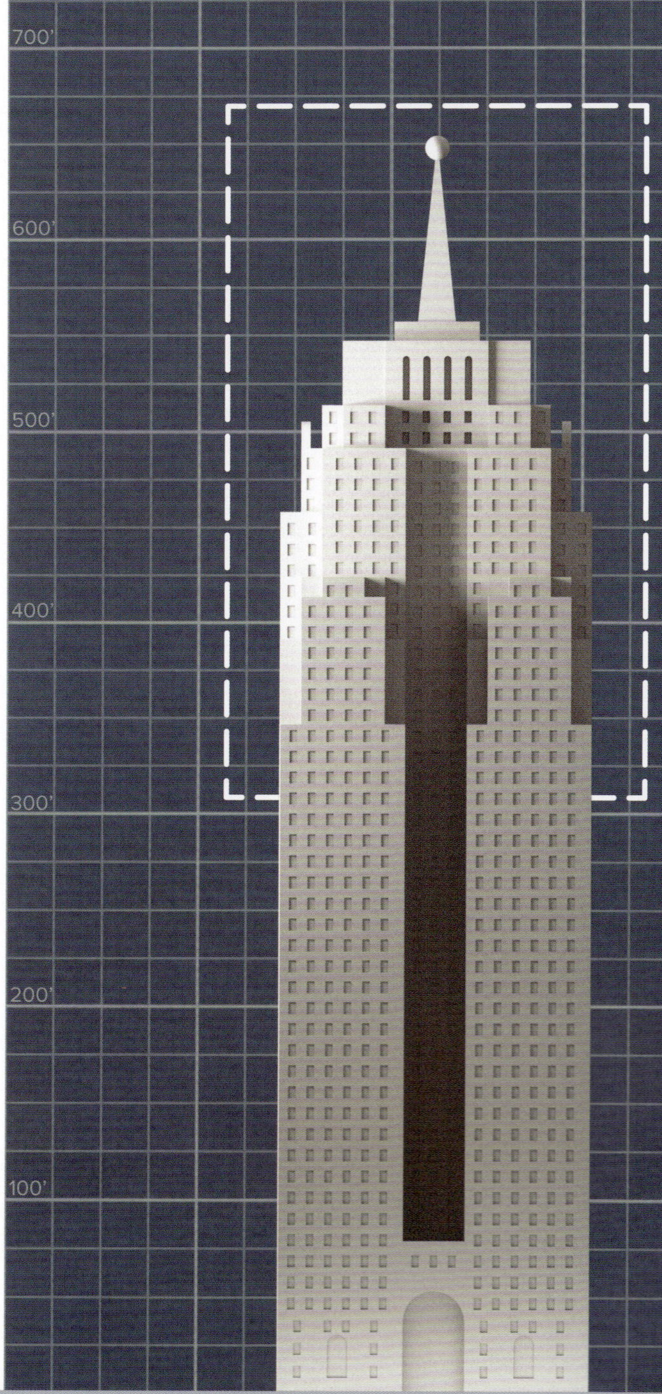

East Elevation *1" = 100'*

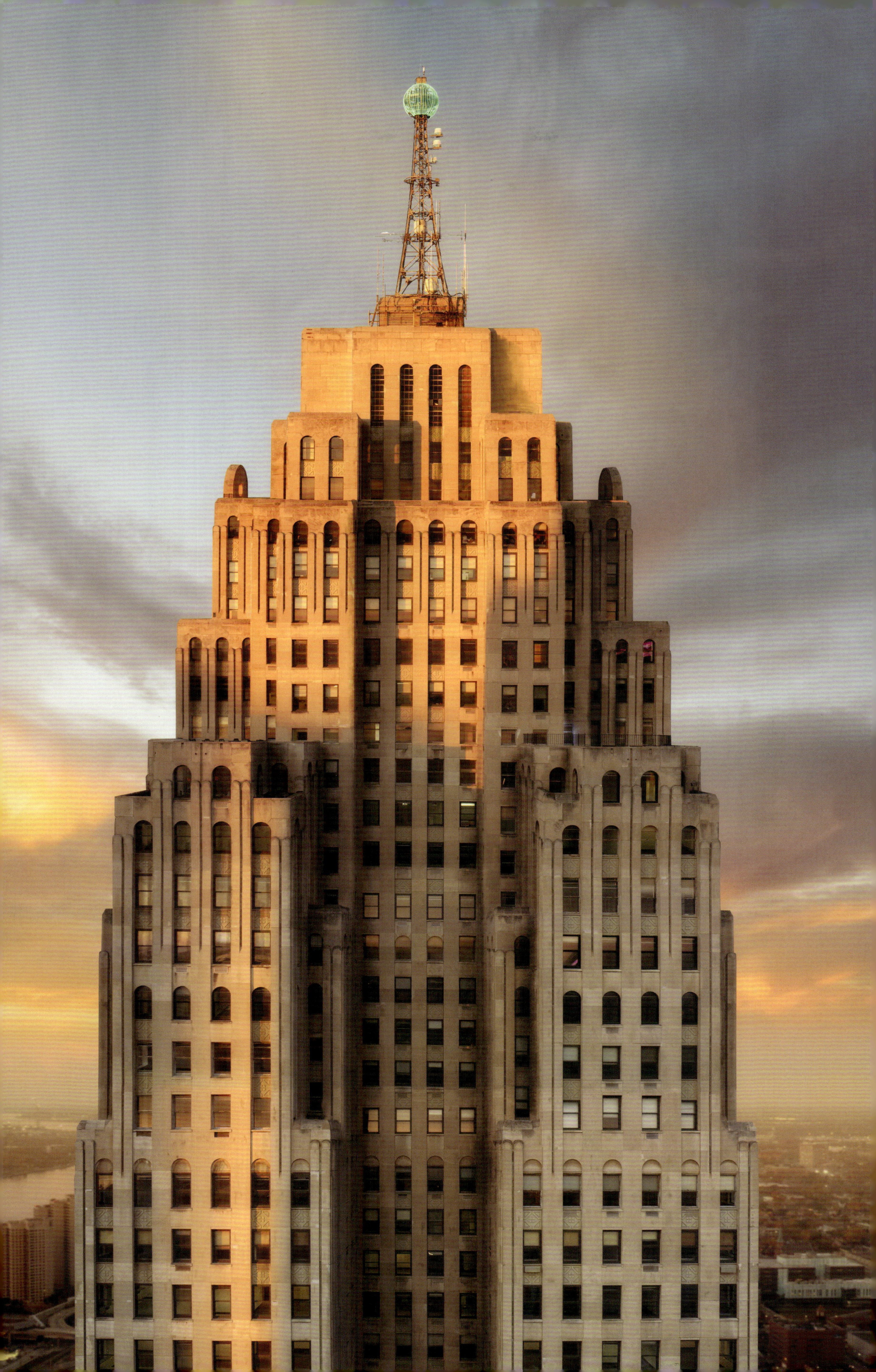

David Stott
Building

Detroit, **MI**

Address	**1150 Griswold St.**
Opened	**1929**
Height	**437’**
Stories	**35**
Style	**Art Deco**
Architect	**John Donaldson**

Opened two months after the unveiling of the stunning Guardian Building three blocks down the street, this highrise did not get the same publicity for its orange bricks and brightly colored tile accents. But it is a handsome specimen of Art Deco nonetheless.

The building’s namesake was 13 when he sailed from England to work on his uncle’s farm near Detroit. After Stott had his own farm, he built a small milling operation. Over the years, that expanded into a sprawling complex four miles outside the city center that was the state’s largest flour mill. Stott left his seven children a fortune, and they built this skyscraper in tribute to him, though that quickly soured into an inheritance squabble and lawsuit.

Architect John Donaldson also immigrated to Detroit as a child, albeit under less trying circumstances than Stott. His Scottish parents could afford to send their son to study in Munich and Paris. His career had a rocky start — his first business partner killed himself — but Donaldson married the young man’s widow and enjoyed a long and successful career designing numerous houses and churches as well as the first two versions of the Penobscot Building.

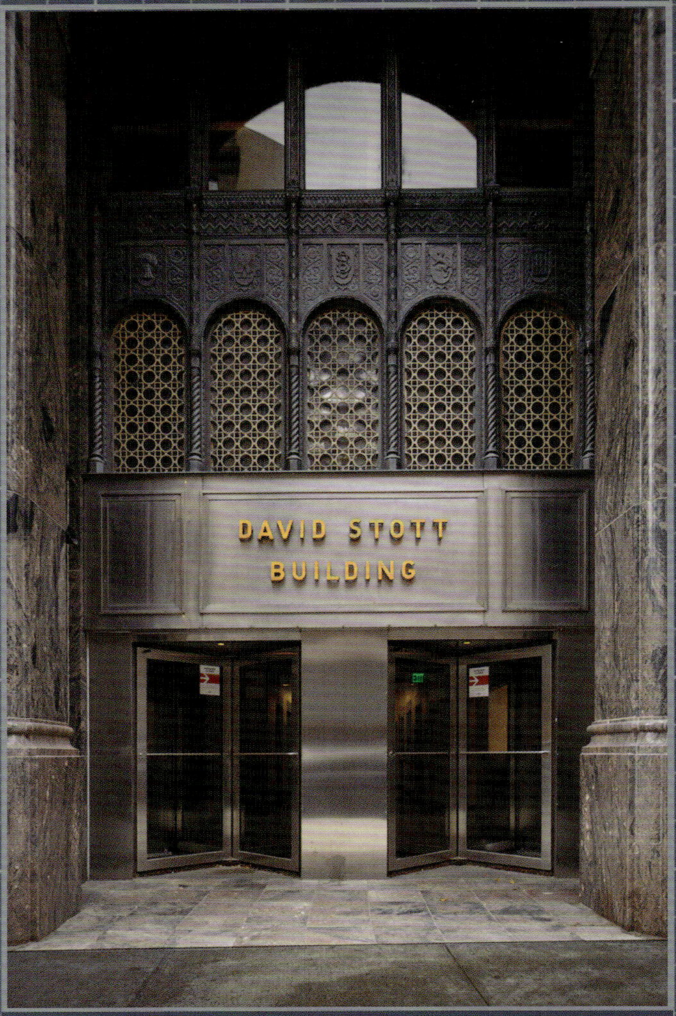

Remodeling has significantly altered the original entrance, though part of it still survives.

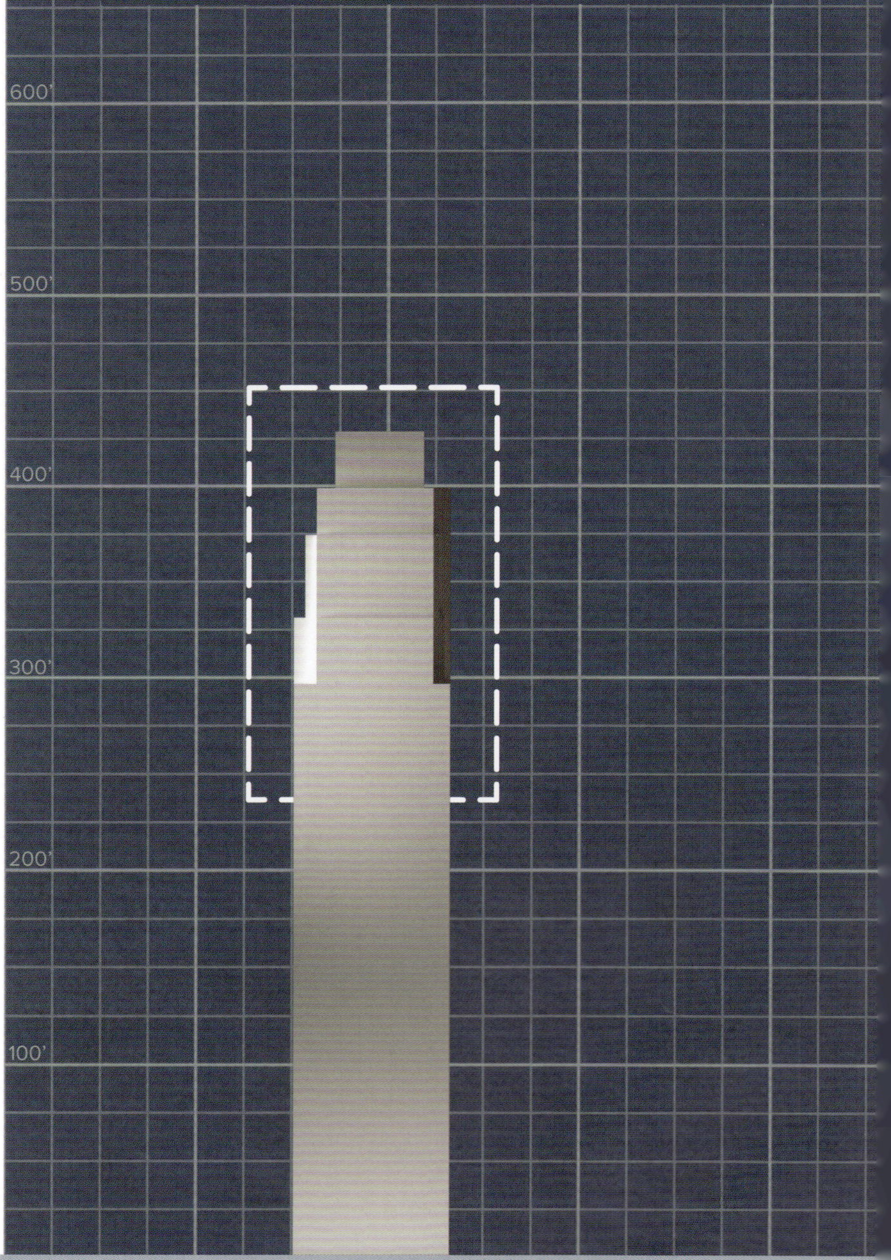

West Elevation *1" = 100'*

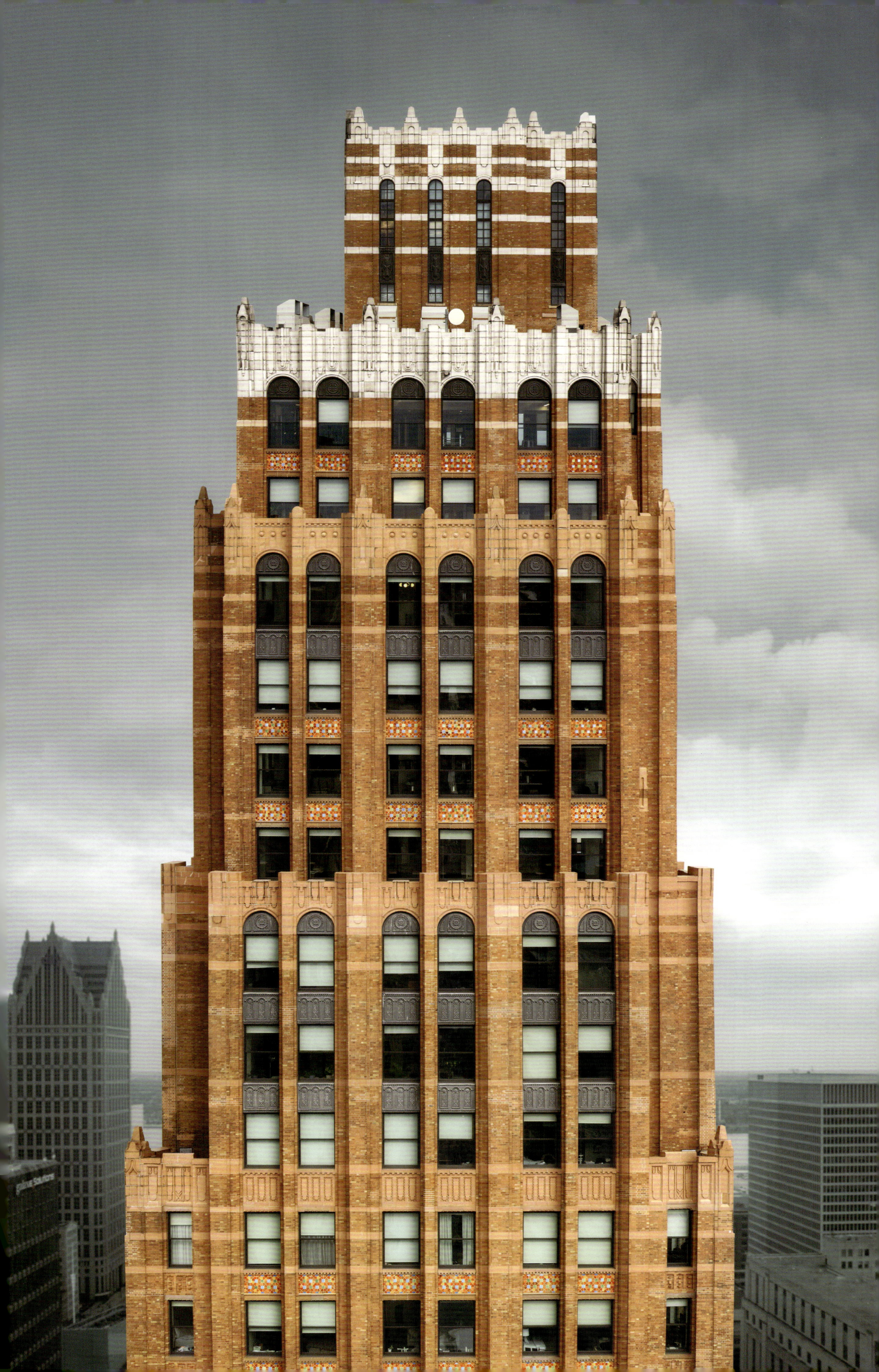

Union & Peoples
National Bank

Jackson, **MI** Jackson County Tower

Address **120 W. Michigan Ave.**
Opened **1930**
Height **190'**
Stories **15**
Style **Art Deco, Renaissance**
Architect **Albert Kahn**

The president of the bank that ordered this highrise had an ulterior motive. When it became the tallest building in town, it surpassed a tower just down the street named after his older brother.

Wiley Reynolds was first in line to take over the bank his father founded, but instead started a factory in 1899 to make cushion springs for buggies, and soon, automobiles. He succeeded in this and further ventures, from plastics to real estate, and commissioned the 14-story Reynolds Building, the tallest thing in Jackson.

Meanwhile, Herbert Reynolds, two years Wiley's junior, succeeded their father at the bank in 1903. When his bank's tower topped his brother's, Herbert was able to gloat for two years until the bank failed; he was forced into early retirement and died in 1939. Wiley's plant prospered and expanded to supply military contracts during World War II; he died in 1948 aboard his yacht in Florida.

The county occupies the building, and has restored the former banking hall's intricate barrel-vaulted ceiling and arched stained glass windows modeled after ones in a Florentine palazzo. The parks department rents the space for weddings and other events.

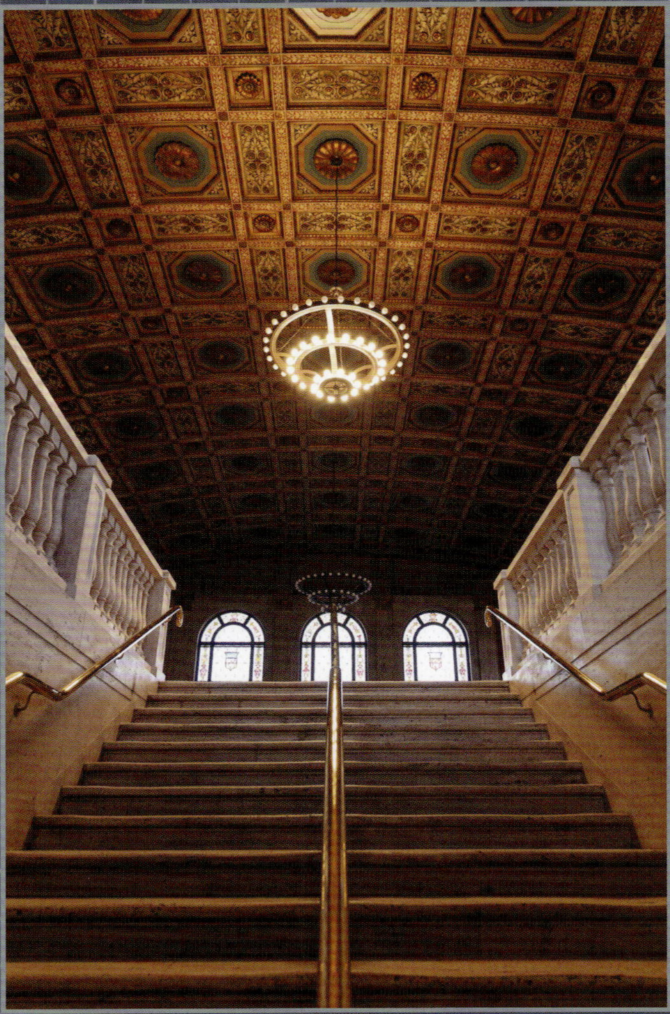

Restored painted and coffered ceilings in the former banking hall, now rented as an event space.

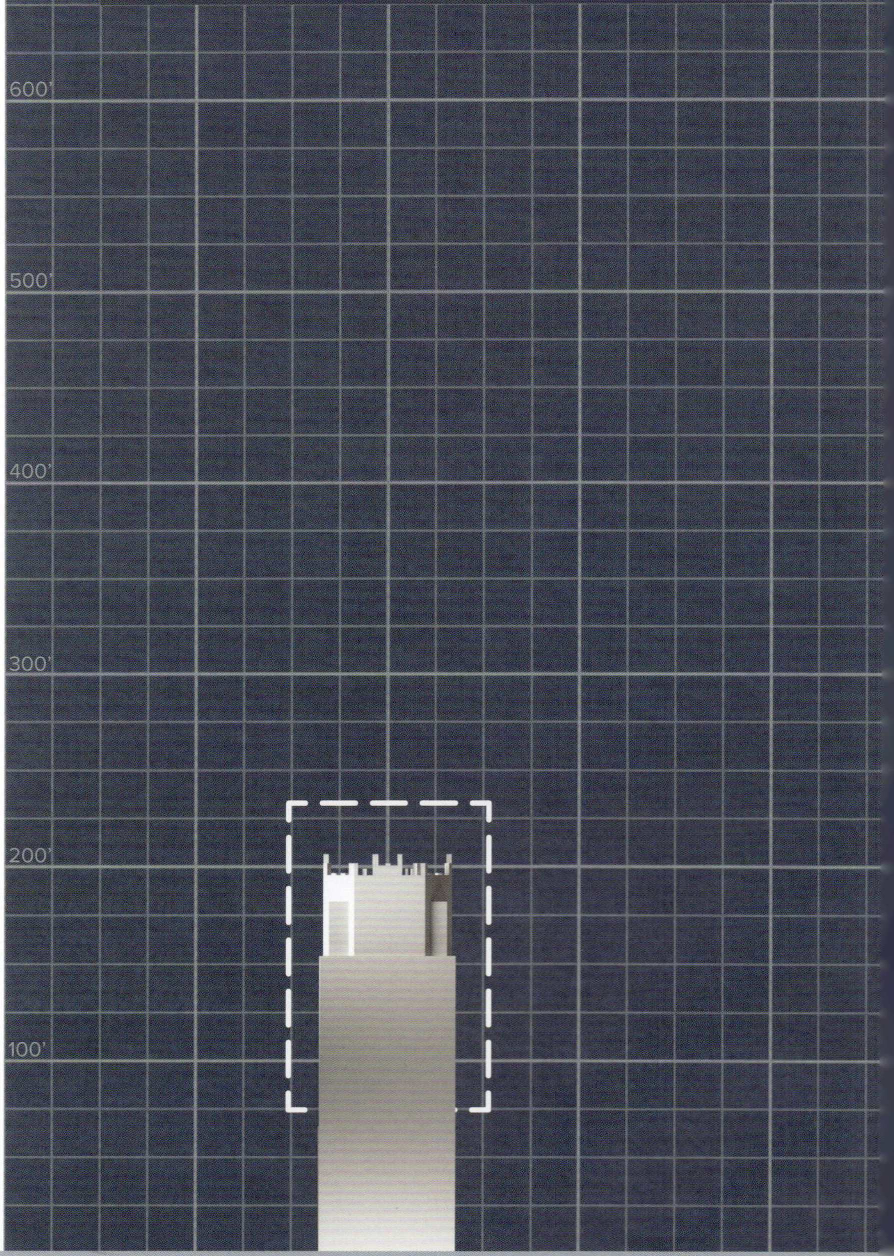

South Elevation *1" = 100'*

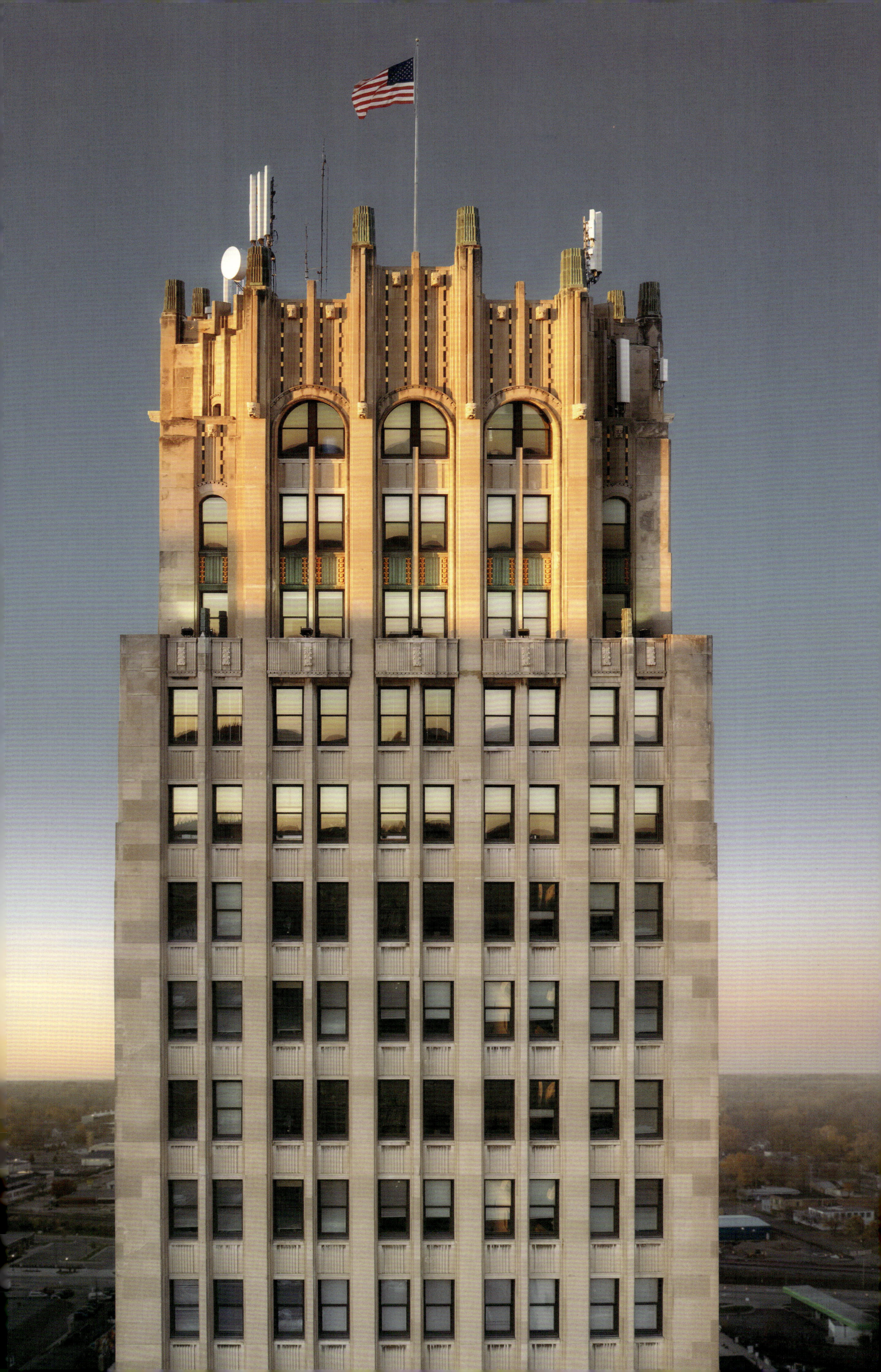

Olds Tower

Lansing, **MI** — Boji Tower

Address	**124 W. Allegan St.**
Opened	**1931**
Height	**297'**
Stories	**23**
Style	**Art Deco**
Architect	**Hopkins & Dentz**

The auto pioneer who created America's first mass-produced car built this highrise across the street from the Michigan state capitol. An electric carillon on top used to play "In My Merry Oldsmobile," a tune that delighted Ransom Olds.

The first primitive "horseless carriages" Olds invented ran on steam power to hawk the engines his factory manufactured. He also experimented with battery-powered cars, but ultimately decided a gasoline engine worked best. Thousands of the first Oldsmobile were sold starting in 1901. Their creator touted the environmental and safety benefits of automobiles versus horses, which stank up city streets and were sometimes prone to bolting.

Olds left his company in an ownership dispute and launched a second automaker. Its popular light truck, the REO Speed Wagon, gave its name to a popular light rock band. Olds also founded a bank that was in the base of this tower briefly until it folded in the Great Depression.

A successor bank, Michigan National, bought the building after Olds died and renamed the tower after itself. When that bank was absorbed in a merger, the building was again renamed for its owners: Louie Boji, a developer who immigrated from Iraq in 1968, and his son and business partner Ron.

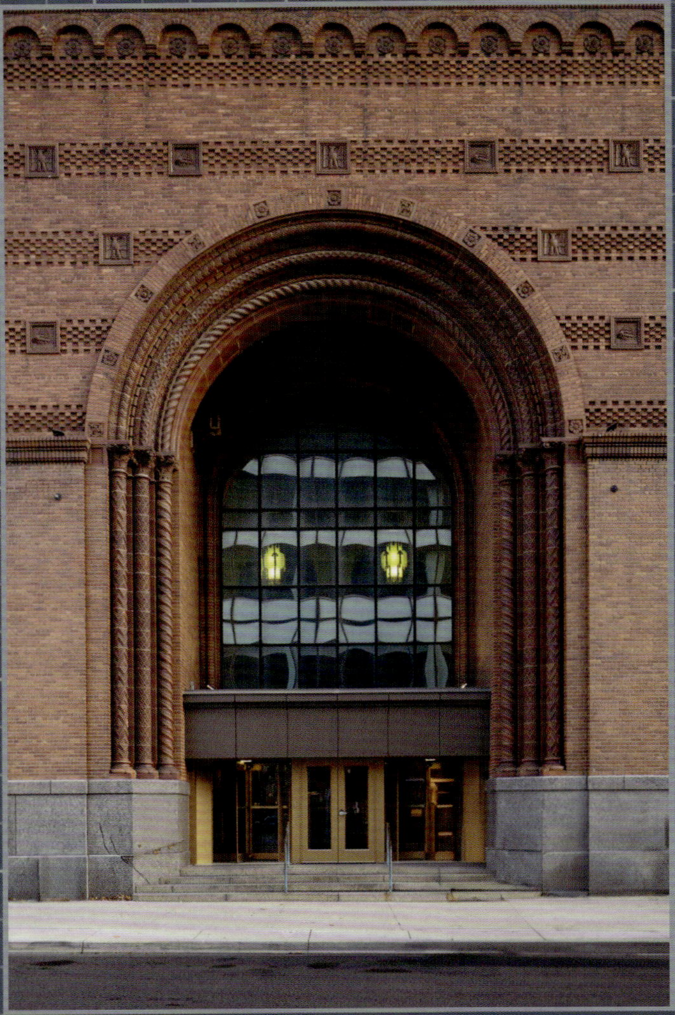

Red brick and terracotta offer a twist on intricate Renaissance-style archways usually done in stone.

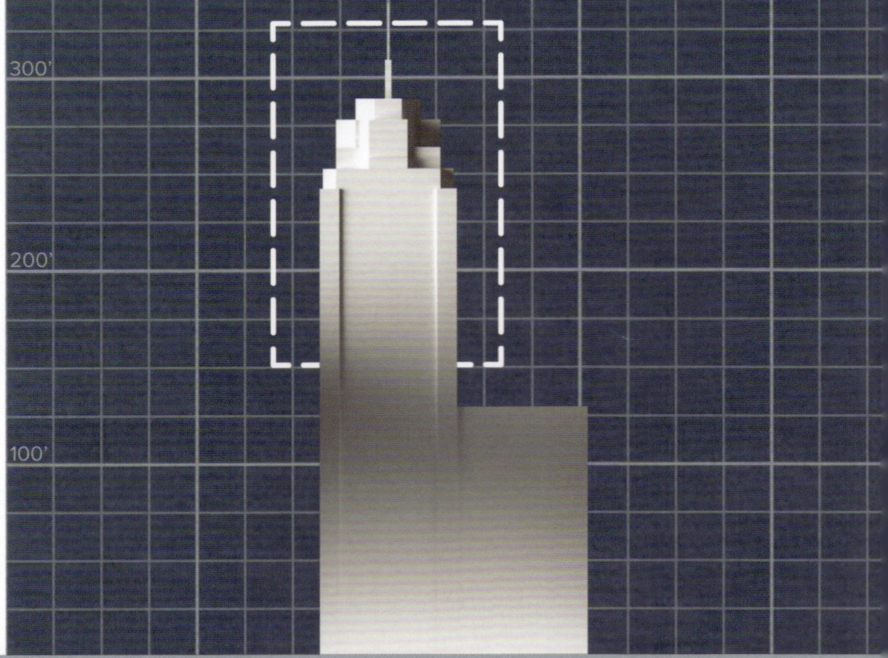

South Elevation *1" = 100'*

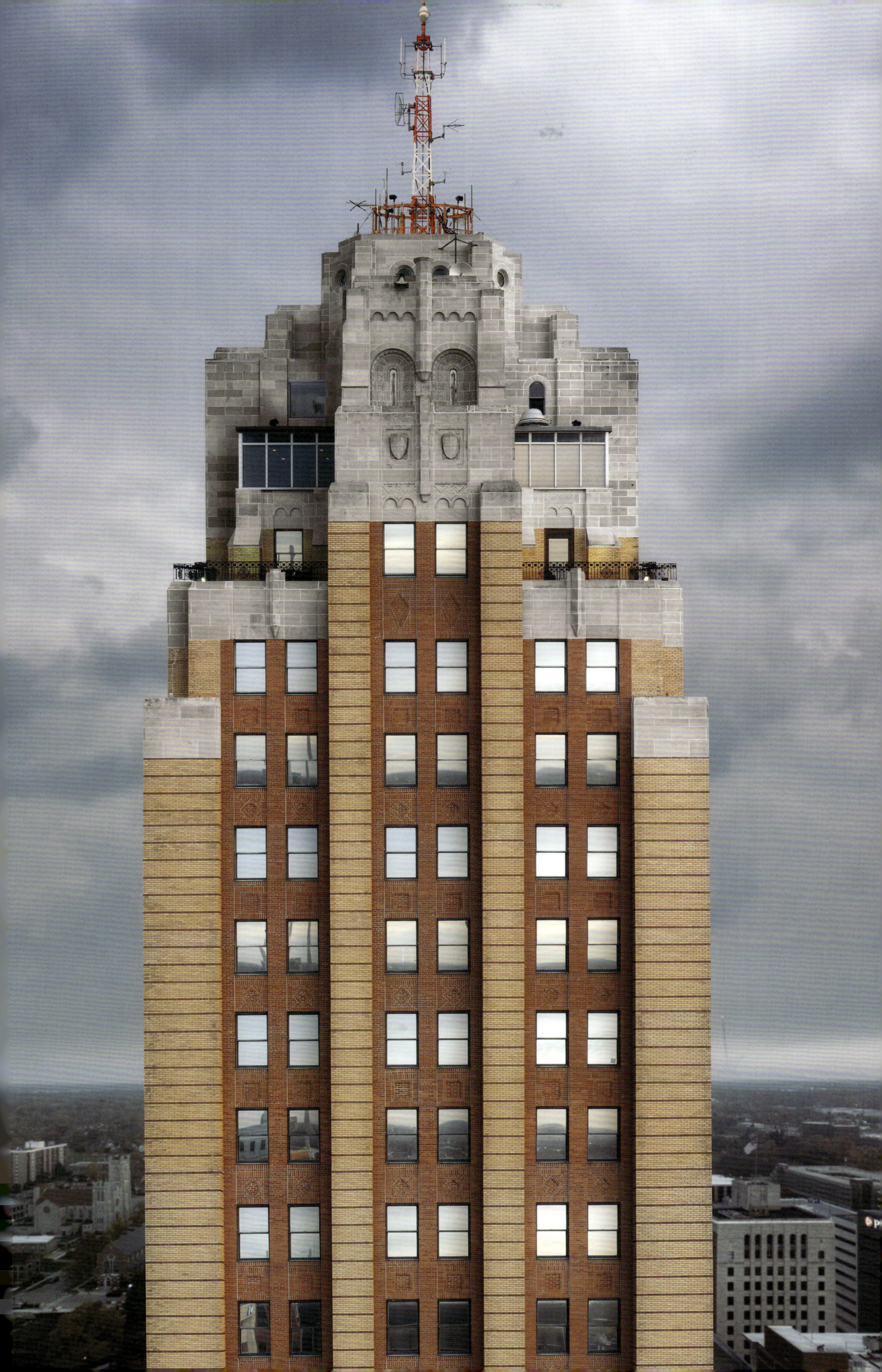

Foshay Tower

Minneapolis, **MN** W Hotel

Address ·········· **821 S. Marquette Ave.**
Opened ·········· **1929**
Height ·········· **447'**
Stories ·········· **30**
Style ·········· **Art Deco**
Architect ·········· **Leon Arnal**

This office obelisk was intended as the Washington Monument of the Midwest. So said Wilbur Foshay, who apparently saw no issue with emblazoning his name in lights on a purported presidential memorial. It was one of many dubious claims made by Foshay, who went to prison four years after this highrise opened.

An eastern transplant who briefly managed a Kansas power company, Foshay relocated to Minneapolis and built a portfolio of small utilities, paying a fraction up front and financing the rest by issuing shares for sale to the public. As his paper empire ballooned to 30 states, he commissioned the tower and financed a blowout three-day dedication gala headlined by John Philip Sousa.

Two months later, the market crashed, investors were stuck with worthless stock, and the company went into receivership. Foshay was convicted of mail fraud and served three years in Leavenworth, until a letter-writing campaign by his supporters prompted a commutation from Franklin D. Roosevelt.

The failed businessman then brought his creative energies to Colorado, where he ran a promotional campaign claiming the mountain streams were so cold that the trout grew fur. Visitors to the tower, now a swanky hotel, can have cocktails in a mahogany-paneled lounge that was once, if only briefly, Foshay's office.

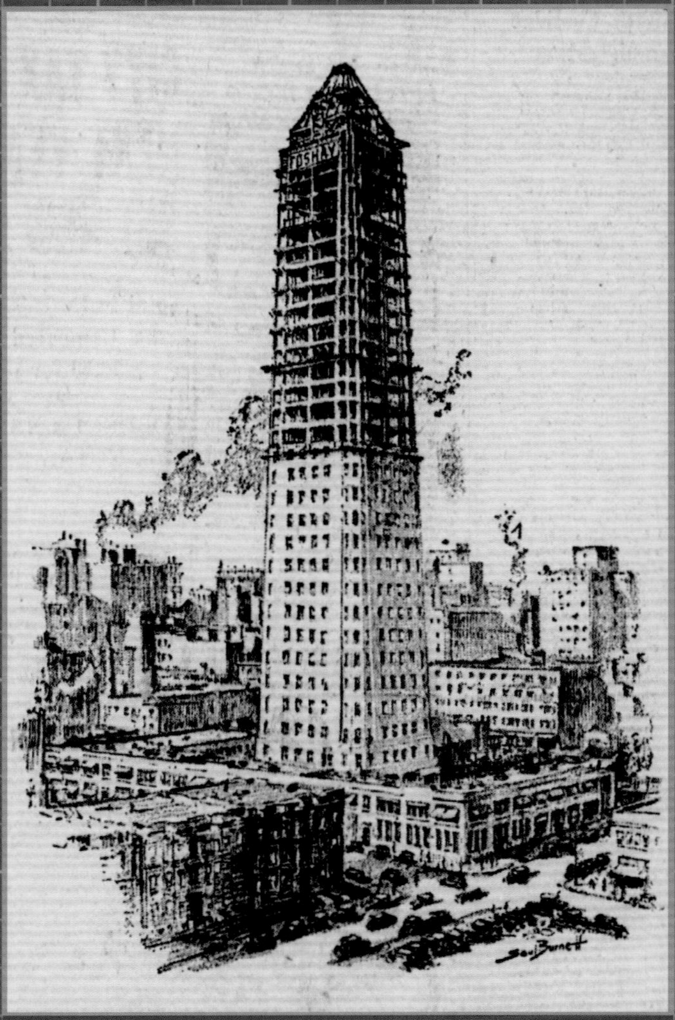

A 1929 illustration of construction shows the steel framework that supports skyscrapers.

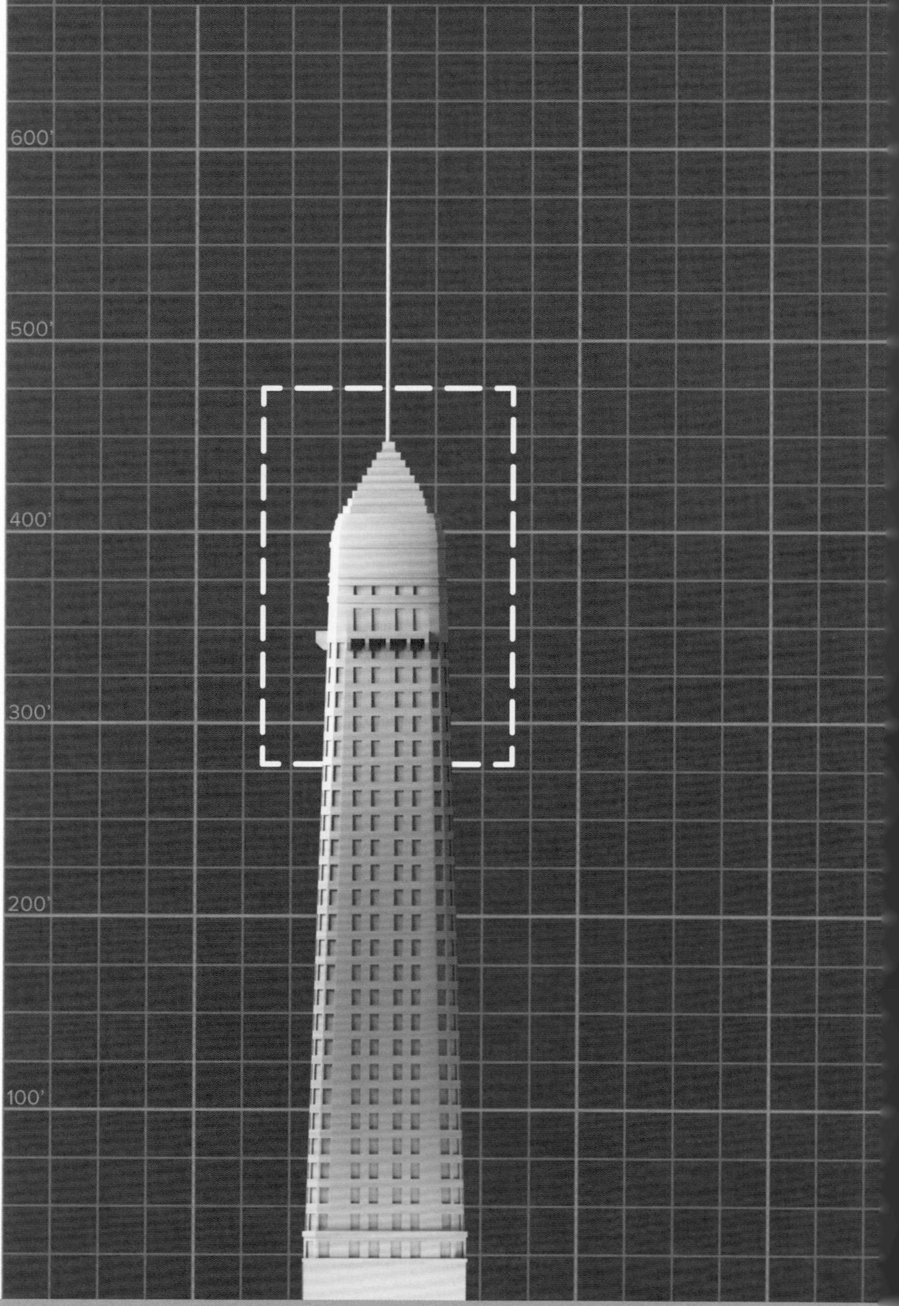

South Elevation *1" = 100'*

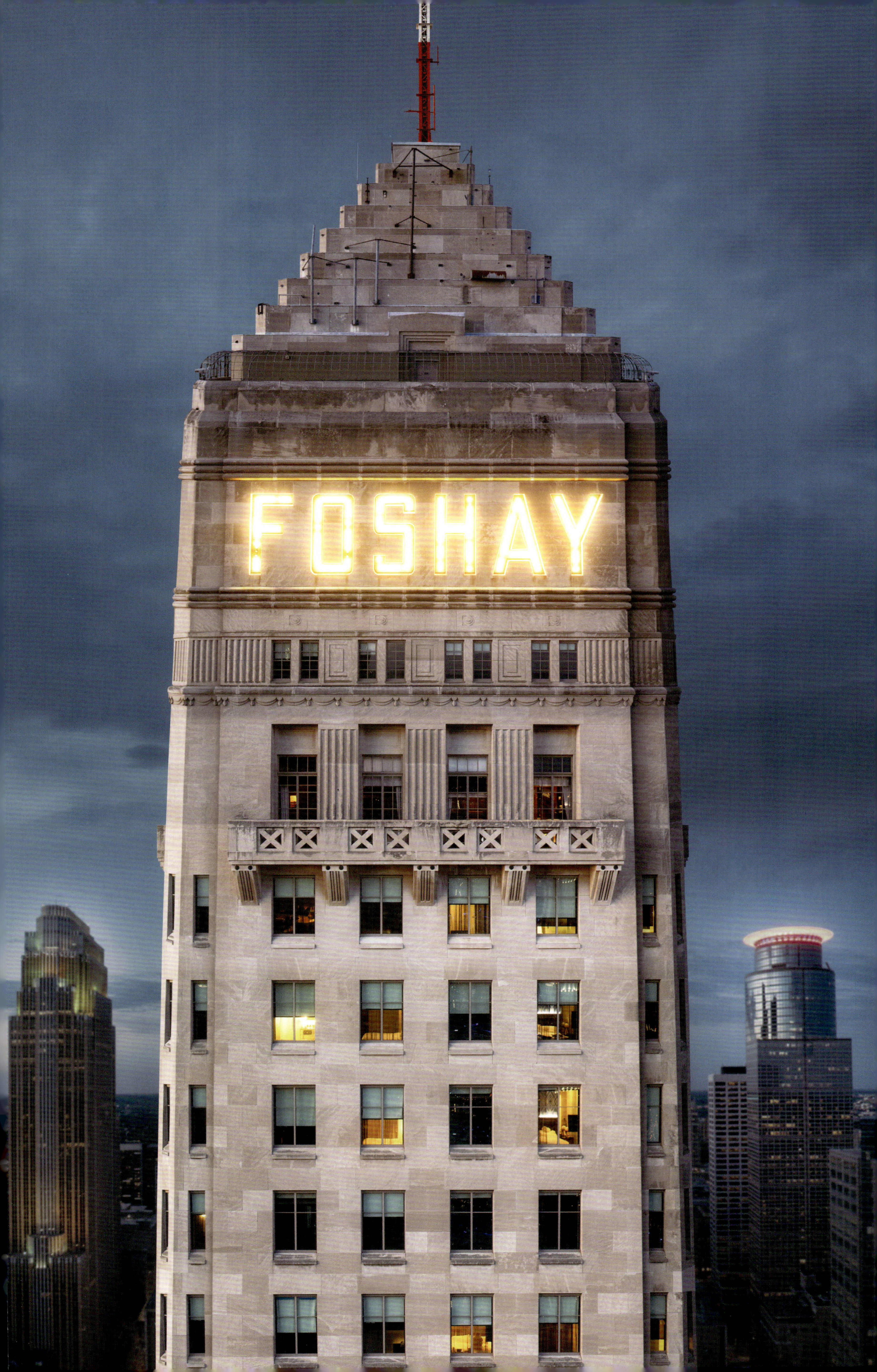
FOSHAY

Mayo Clinic

Rochester, **MN** Plummer Building

Address	**200 First St. SW**
Opened	**1928**
Height	**298'**
Stories	**15**
Style	**Art Deco, Renaissance**
Architect	**Thomas Ellerbe**

Terracotta nurses survey the prairie from this highrise, revealing its medical mission and paying tribute to the women essential to its success. That includes Edith Graham, the clinic's first professional nurse and wife of Dr. Charles Mayo, who with his brother, Will, oversaw this tower for their family's storied institution.

Their father, William, arrived in town as a government physician to examine Union recruits for the Civil War. Later, when a tornado devastated Rochester in 1883, Mayo cared for victims with the aid of Franciscan nuns. The sisters went on to build a hospital that the doctor and his two sons staffed.

The practice quickly outgrew its first facility, prompting construction of this colorful addition. Great bronze doors open to a flamboyant lobby and oil painting of the brothers, whose offices upstairs are preserved as a museum. A carilloneur — the clinic's fourth since construction — plays daily concerts on the tower bells.

In 1954 the building was named after Dr. Henry Plummer, a thyroid specialist who designed several innovative features of the structure, including an instrument sterilization system. On the facade, a sculpted stone relief portrays Plummer poring over a blueprint. A similar tile commemorating the actual architect, Thomas Ellerbe, was never mounted.

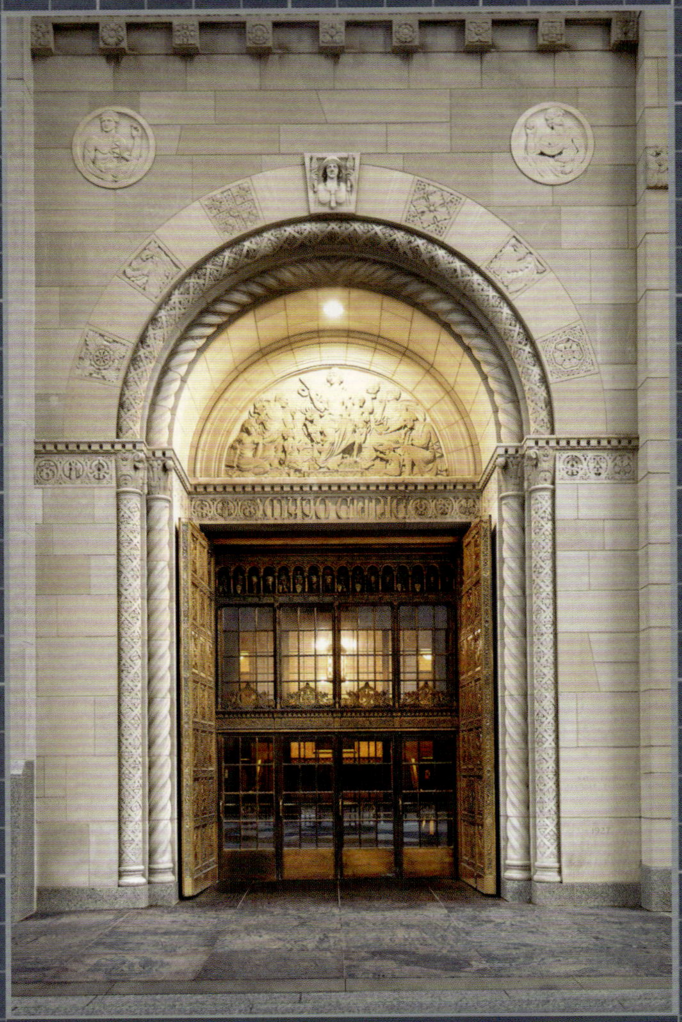

The elaborate entrance has ornamental bronze doors that are closed only for ceremonial occasions.

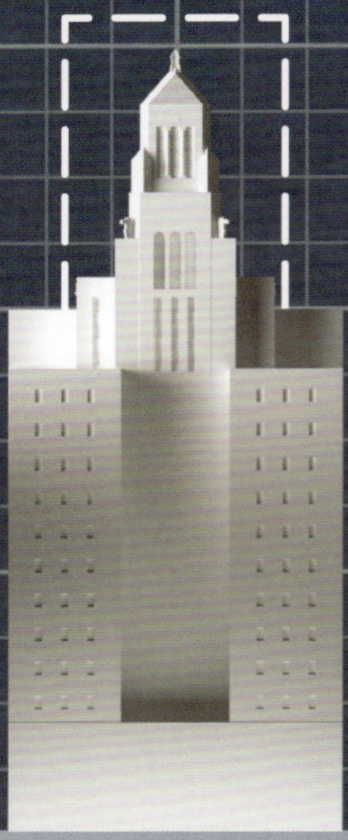

West Elevation *1" = 100'*

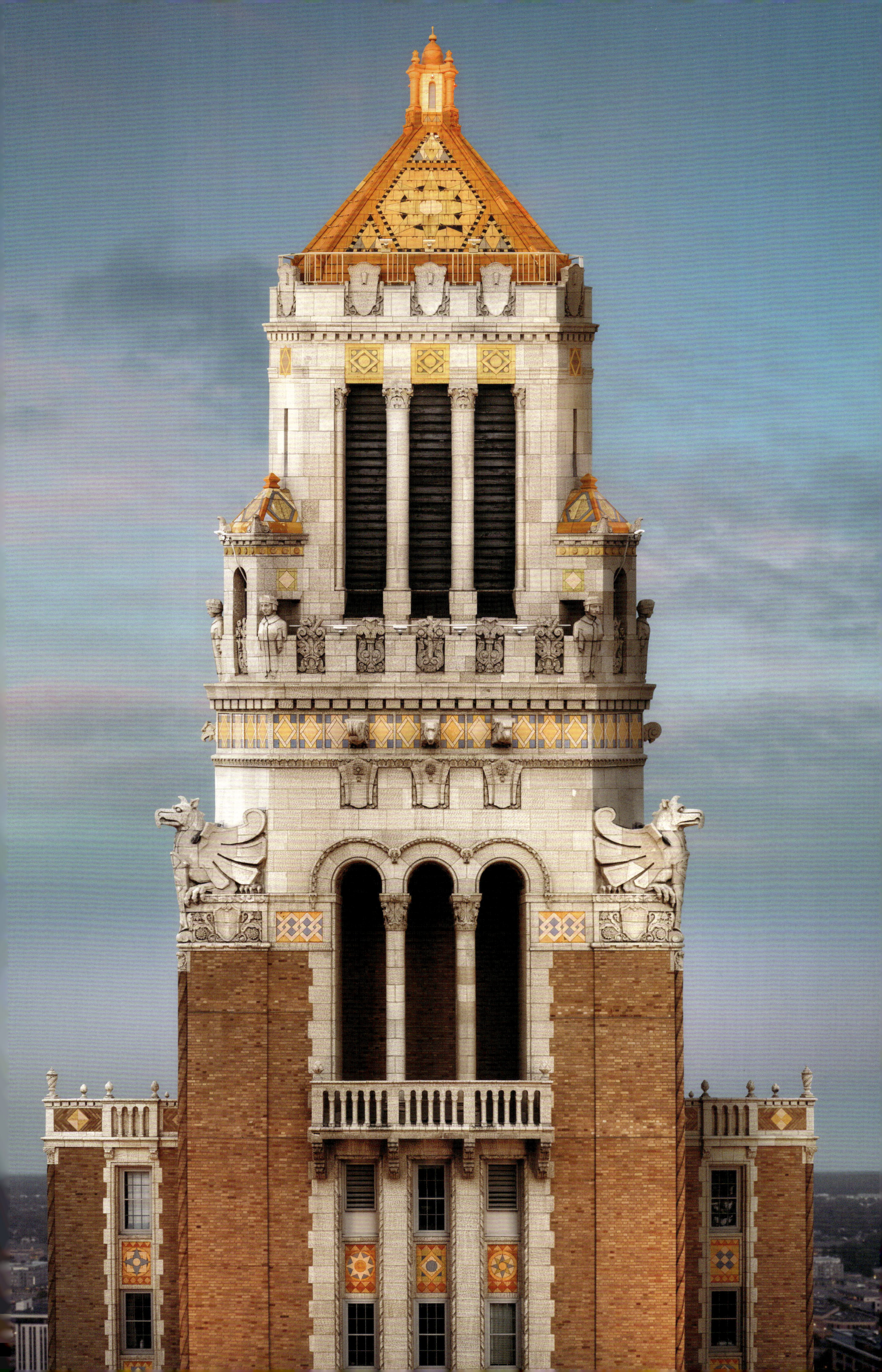

First National Bank
Building

Saint Paul, **MN**

Address ············· **332 Minnesota St.**
Opened ························· **1931**
Height ························· **402'**
Stories ···························· **31**
Style ······················· **Art Deco**
Architect ··········· **Graham, Anderson, Probst & White**

The three-sided, 50-foot illuminated logo on the roof has been out of date since the financial firm it refers to changed its name to U.S. Bancorp in a 1997 merger. Its irrelevance only heightened when the company moved out a few years later. But St. Paul maintains the iconic sign, presumably to inform Minneapolis where the older, smaller twin city sees itself in the pecking order.

This skyscraper originated in an earlier merger, when First National Bank of St. Paul joined forces with next-door neighbor Merchants National, the first bank to build a highrise on the block. A skybridge connecting the 17th floor of the new tower to the 16th of the old curiously rises instead of descending, due to differing story heights. Louis Hill, chairman of First National, wrangled the deal through deft family diplomacy; his father, Great Northern Railroad tycoon James Hill, had bought the bank in 1912 and left his eight children each an equal share.

News coverage at the dedication noted a basement shooting range where the private security guards could practice "the manly art of bank defense." It also marveled that every one of the uniformed women operating the elevators was exactly 5'1" tall.

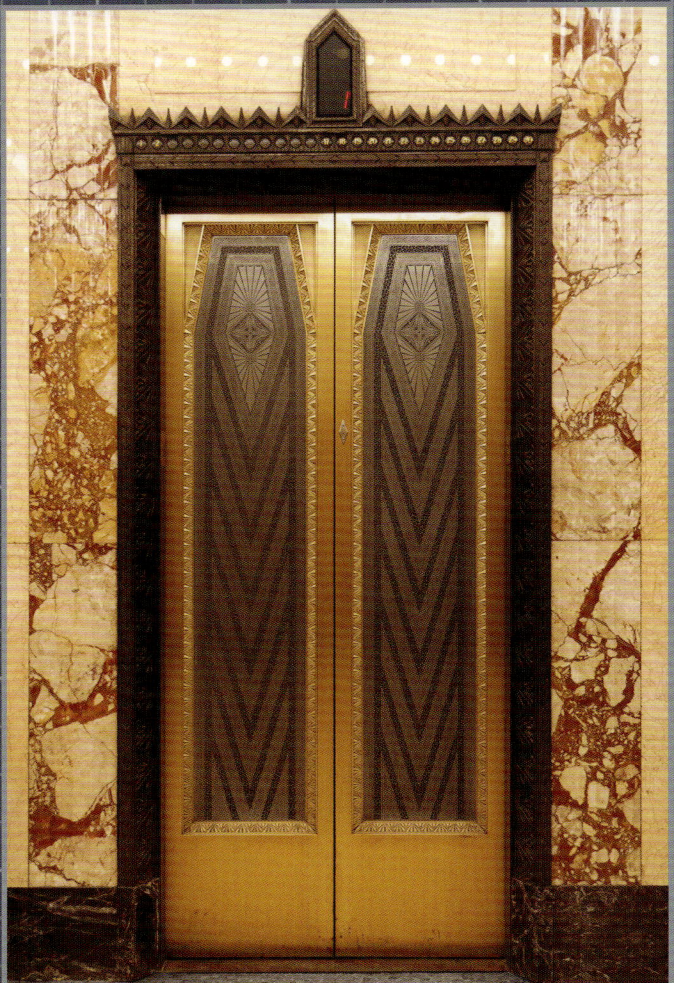

Cast iron frames surround two-tone bronze elevator doors with engraved steel panels.

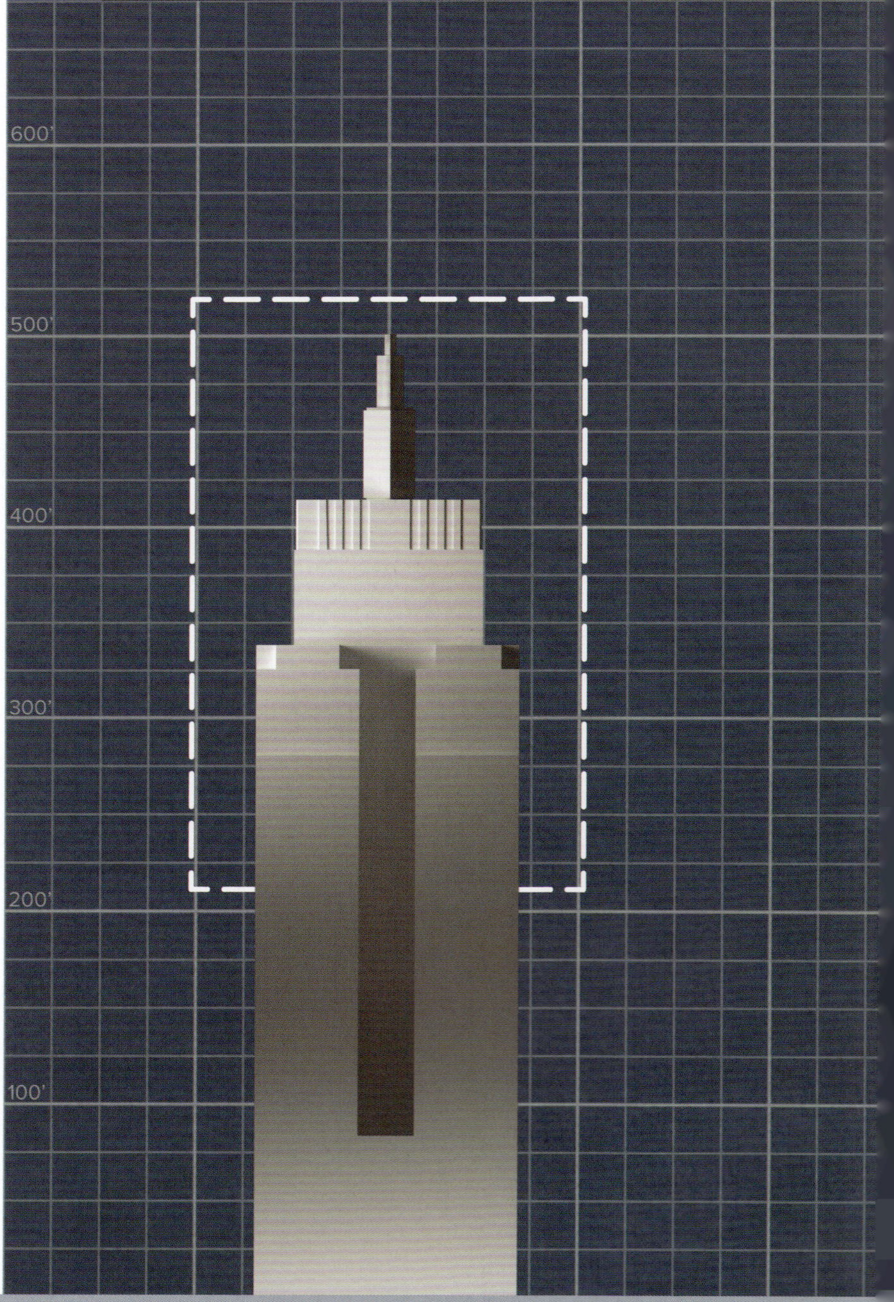

South Elevation *1" = 100'*

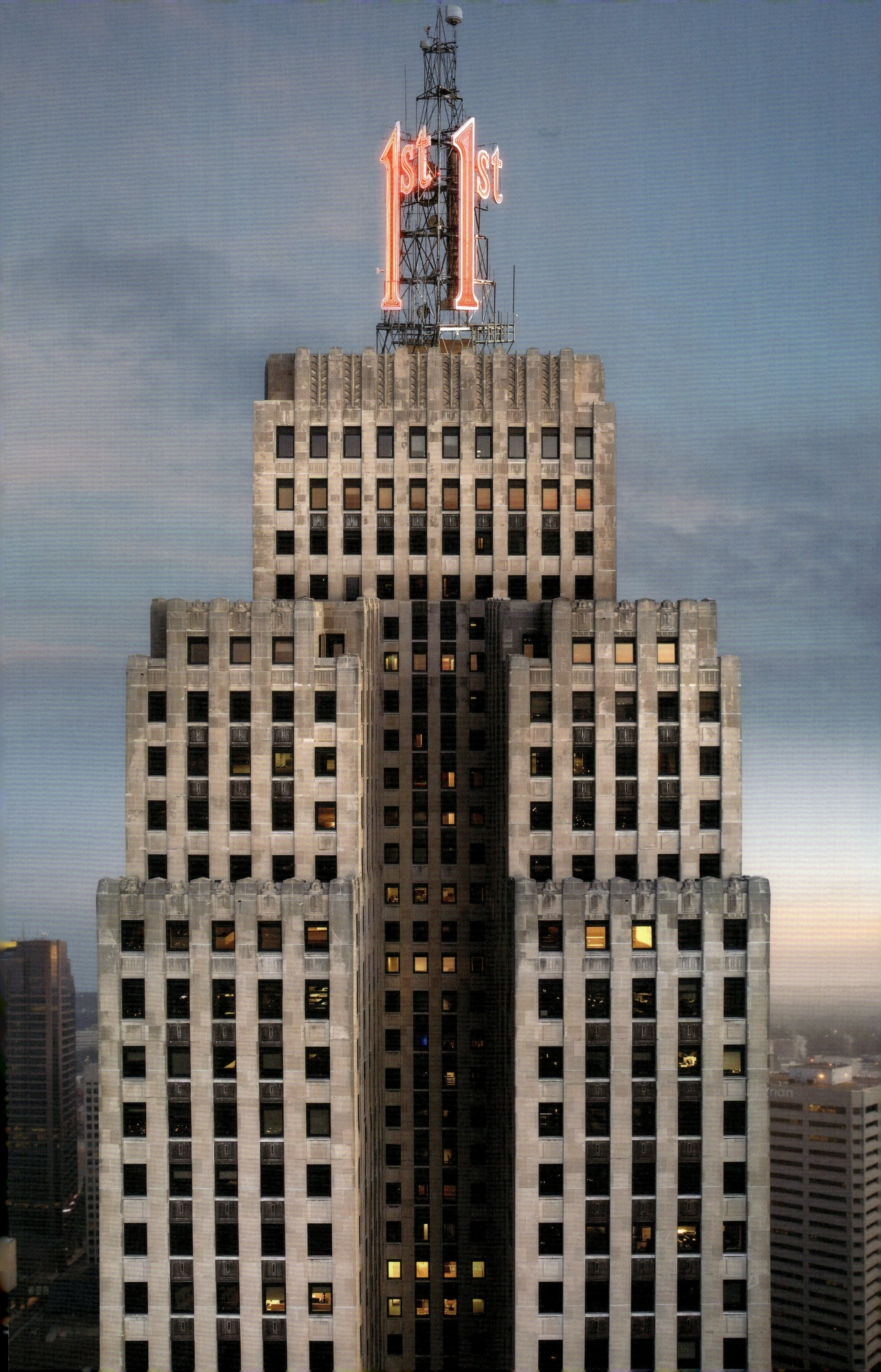
1st
1st

Fidelity Building

Kansas City, **MO**

Address	**909 Walnut St.**
Opened	**1932**
Height	**454'**
Stories	**35**
Style	**Art Deco, Renaissance**
Architect	**Hoit, Price & Barnes**

When the federal reserve system was created in 1914, Kansas City was chosen for a reserve bank, and its financial sector reaped the rewards. That ultimately was no help for the bank whose name is carved into the limestone of this towering slab.

"I'd rather be a lawyer than a banker any day," said the president of Fidelity National Bank & Trust, Henry Flower, in a 1930 interview as construction got underway on a new headquarters. Flower had practiced law in town for 15 years before a New York financier persuaded him to charter Fidelity in 1899.

The bank resided in the old main post office for three decades, leading to the slogan "Under the Old Town Clock." When that was razed for this highrise, the four clock faces were removed, refurbished, and reinstalled on pointed towers at either end. But a year after opening, Fidelity was in liquidation amid rumors that construction costs had helped speed its demise.

In a complete reversal, the government then moved into the old bank building, which was a federal office complex for many decades. It is now residential, with large windows in place of the clocks, removed more than 50 years ago.

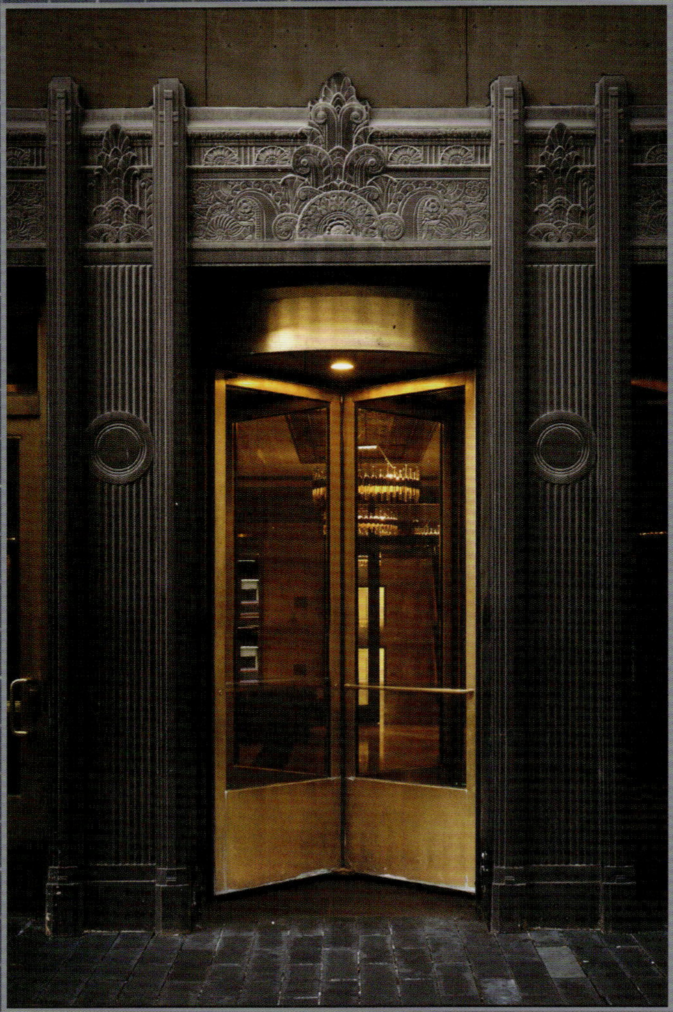

Painted metal fluted pilasters surround the elevator lobby entrance topped with Art Deco organic forms.

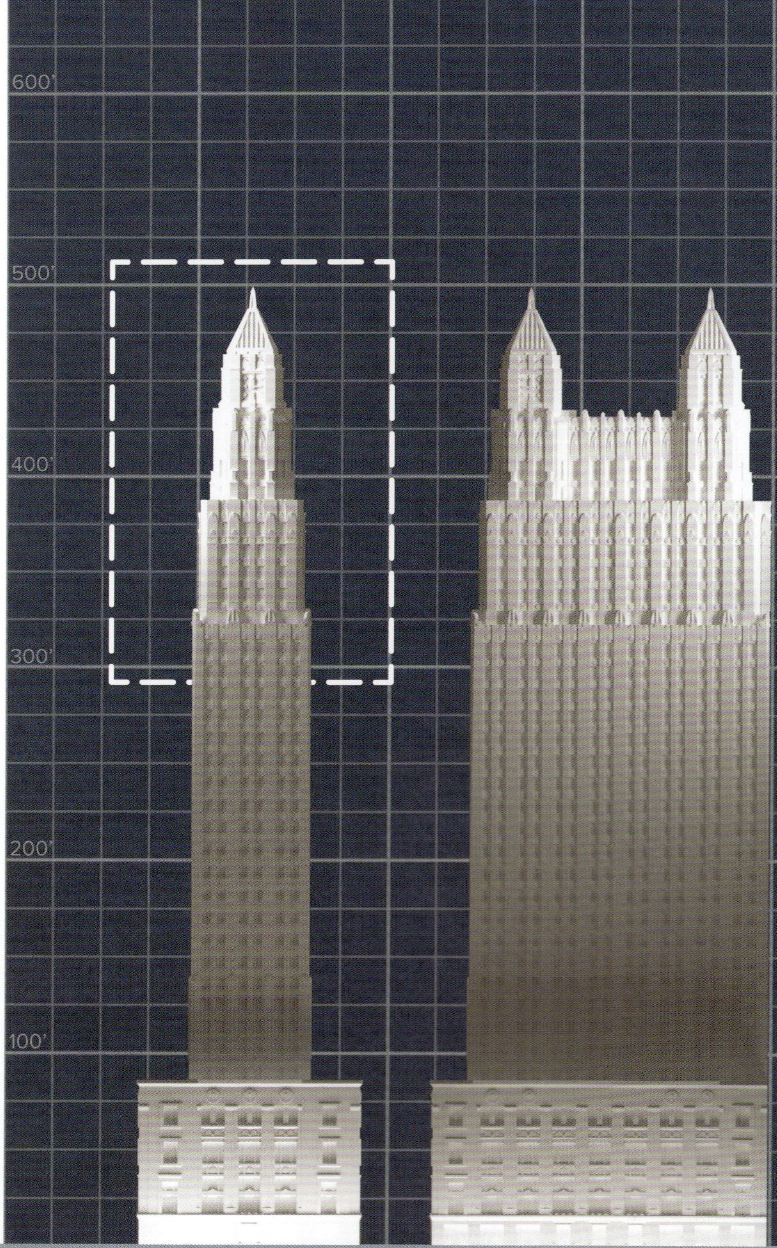

North Elevation West Elevation 1" = 100'

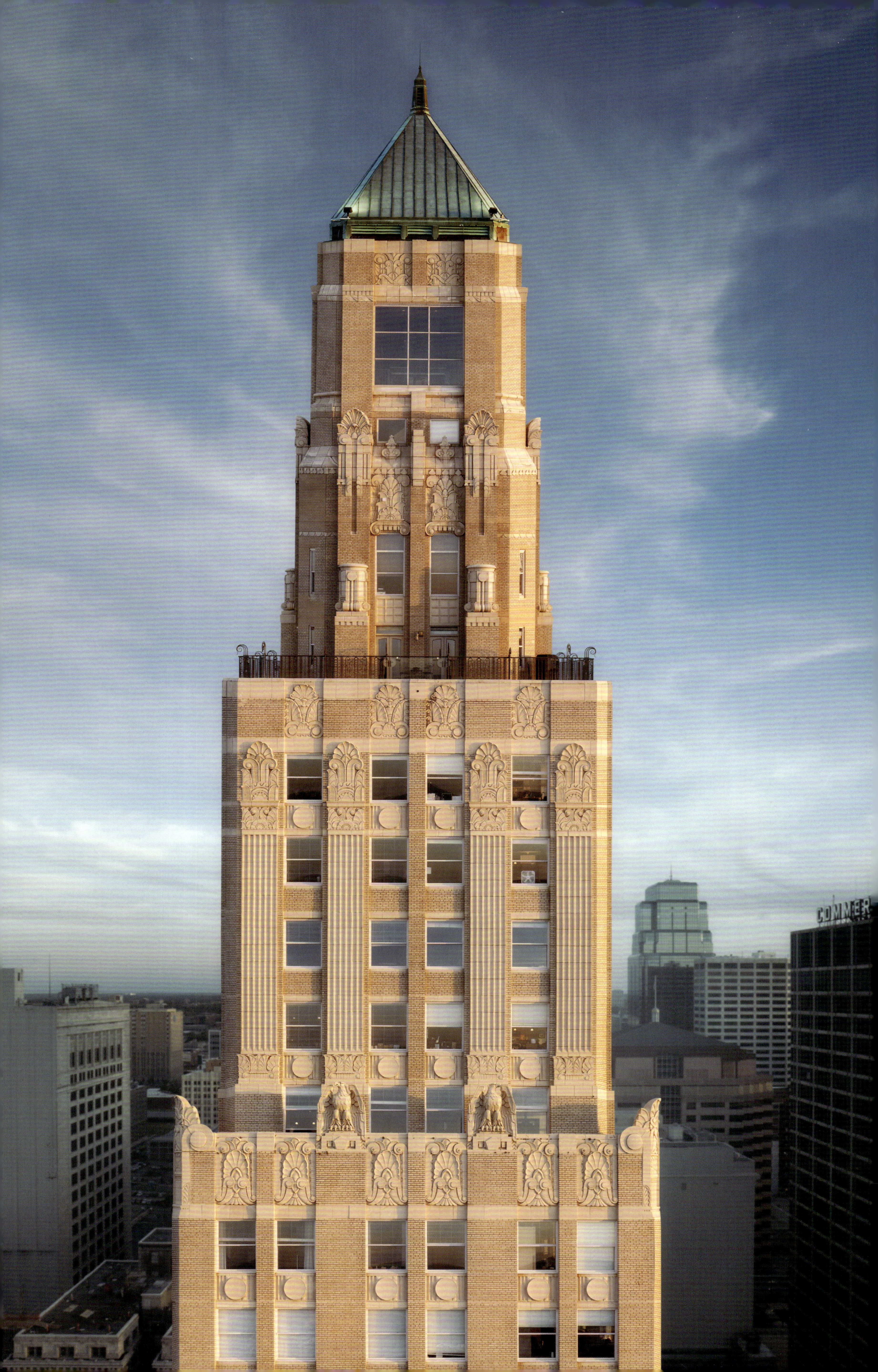
COMMER

Power & Light
Building

Kansas City, **MO**

Address	**1330 Baltimore Ave.**
Opened	**1931**
Height	**481’**
Stories	**32**
Style	**Art Deco**
Architect	**Hoit, Price & Barnes**

Once the tallest building west of the Mississippi, this iconic skyscraper with its sunburst beacon lights the Kansas City skyline and lends its name to the Power & Light District, the city’s entertainment quarter.

The main entrance is a study in stone and terracotta drama, with another shining sun etched over the doorway and ornamental panels portraying power and light that beams from stylized palm fronds. An elegant cast iron balcony at the fourth floor repeats the sunburst motif.

After earning his engineering degree in 1884 from Iowa State, Joseph Porter took a job as an electrician at a power plant in Des Moines associated with Thomas Edison’s young company. Before the decade was out, Porter had been promoted to Edison’s headquarters in New York. The successful executive was weighing early retirement in 1917 when he was asked to help a foundering Kansas City utility. That kept him busy for another two decades.

Porter’s power company initially occupied nearly the entire tower. It finally moved out in 1991, and the building has been converted to luxury apartments. The marble lobby and mezzanine are brilliantly preserved and now used as an event space.

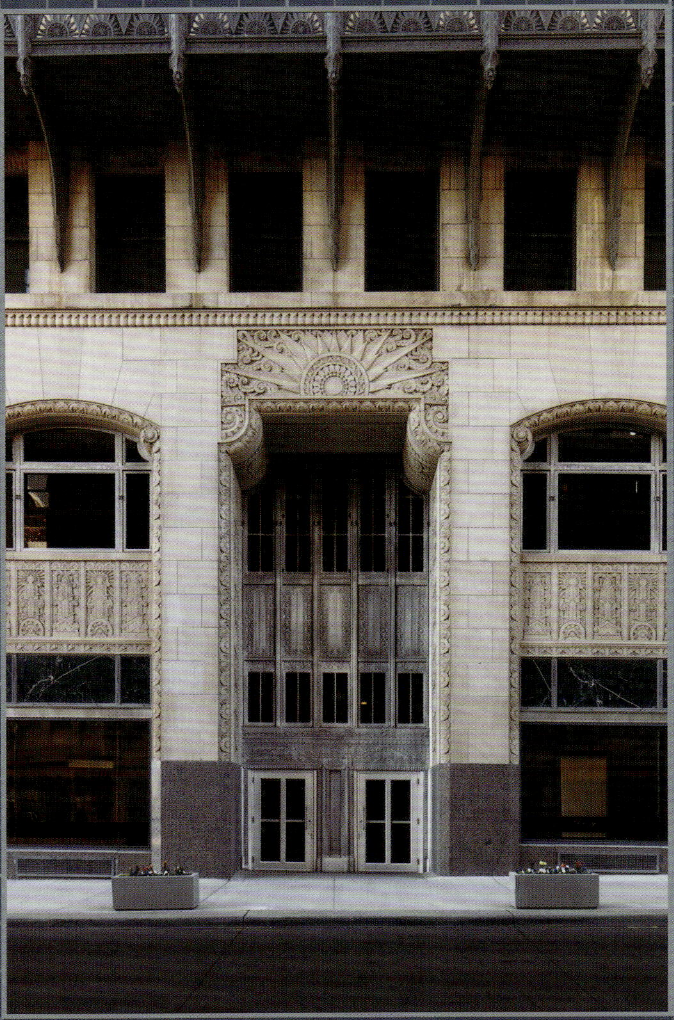

A carved sunburst shooting out lightning bolts vividly dramatizes the role of the electric utility.

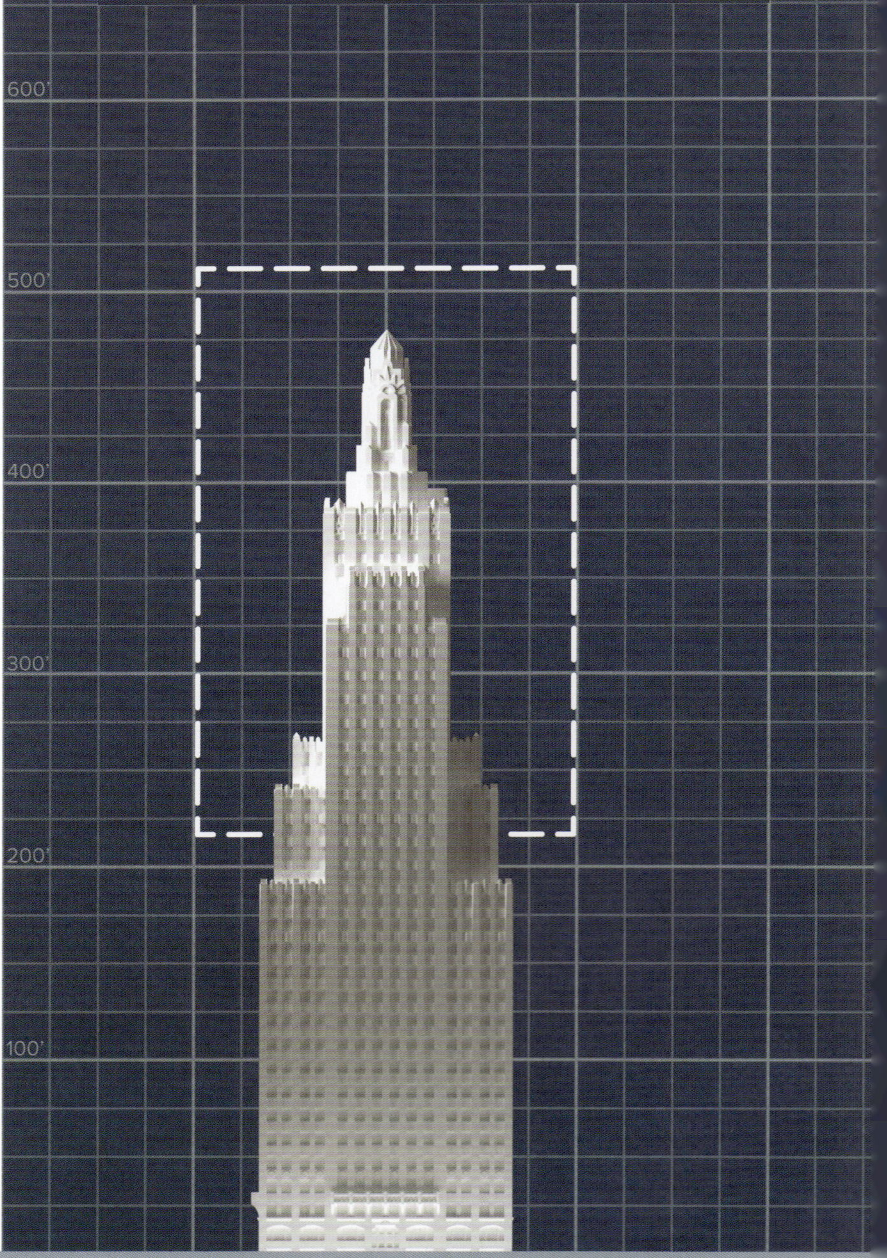

East Elevation *1" = 100'*

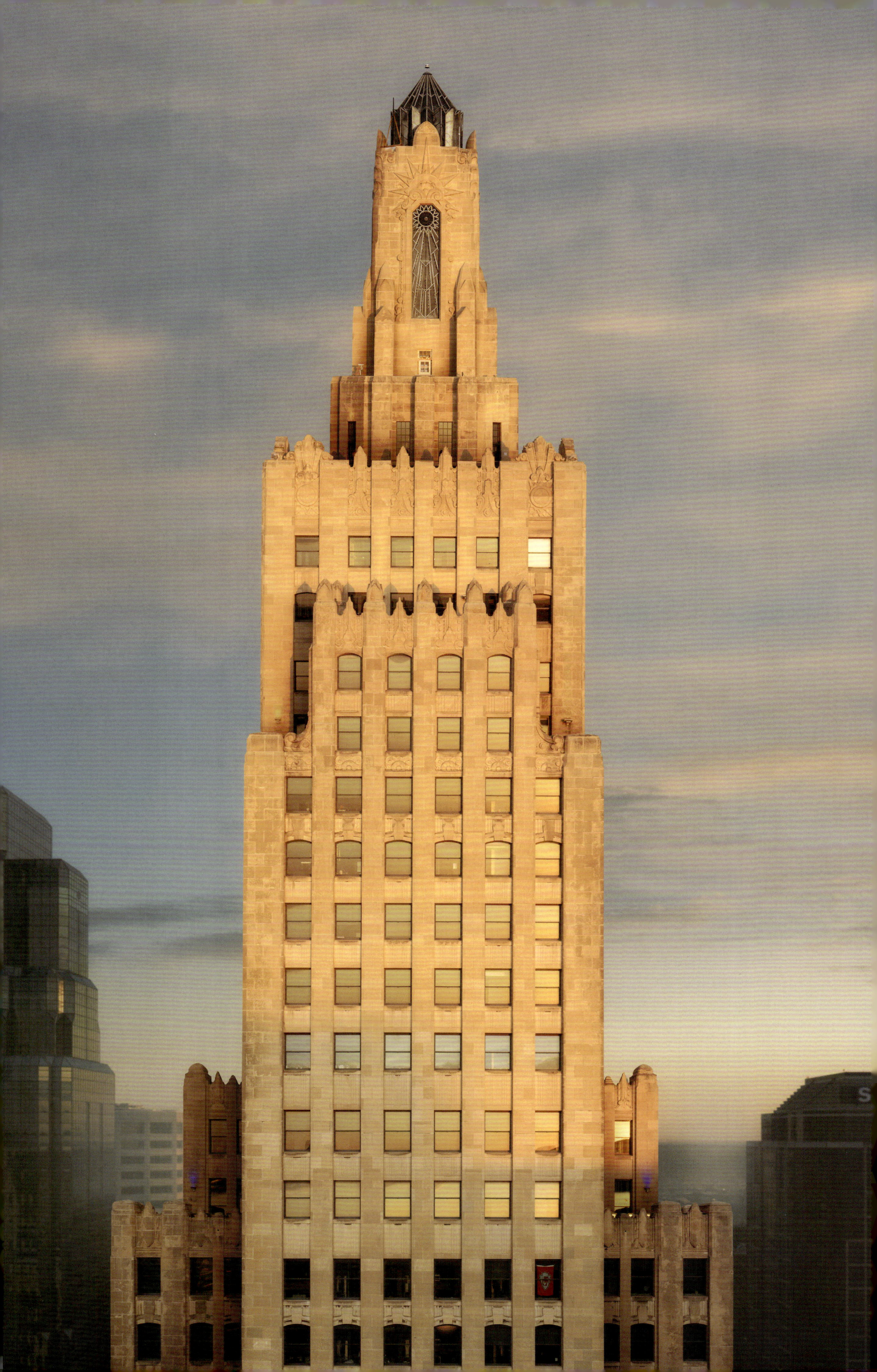

Continental Life
Building

Saint Louis, **MO**

Address	**3615 Olive St.**
Opened	**1930**
Height	**286'**
Stories	**23**
Style	**Art Deco**
Architect	**William Ittner**

College students from nearby St. Louis University rent apartments in this highrise named for an ill-fated insurance company. Older alumni may recall illicit parties in the tower, which stood vacant for decades while its hallways collected empty beer cans and fraternity graffiti.

Continental Army soldiers and their wives sculpted on terracotta piers symbolize the eponymous firm whose president, Ed Mays, started out as a bank clerk in the Arkansas Ozarks. He soon ran that institution, invested in zinc and copper mines and a factory making barrel staves, and eventually moved to St. Louis for bigger opportunities.

Besides the insurance firm, Mays was also president of a local bank, Grand National, and commissioned this skyscraper in the city's theater district to house both. To economize, he had the bank's vault door unhinged and moved to its new location here. But robbers found out, and broke into the weakly guarded old vault before its contents were transferred.

Mays paid a ransom to get back most of the loot, but he still lost the bank in the Depression, along with the insurance company and his luxurious two-story penthouse atop this building. He returned dejectedly to Arkansas and resumed the less panic-prone barrel stave business.

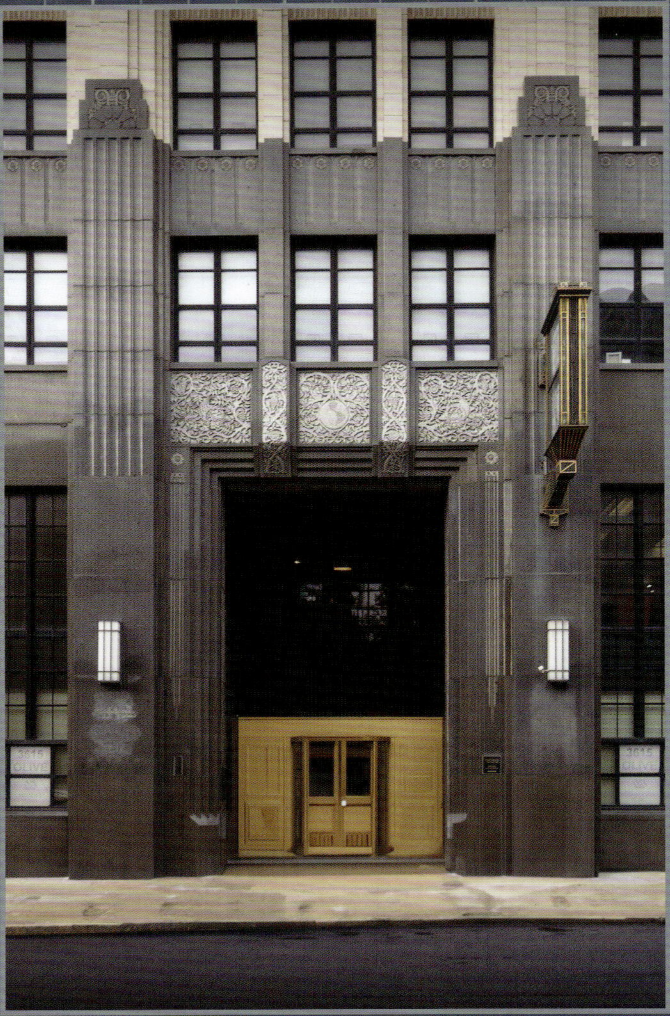

Carved grapevines and a globe add a complex counterpoint to the austere gray granite base.

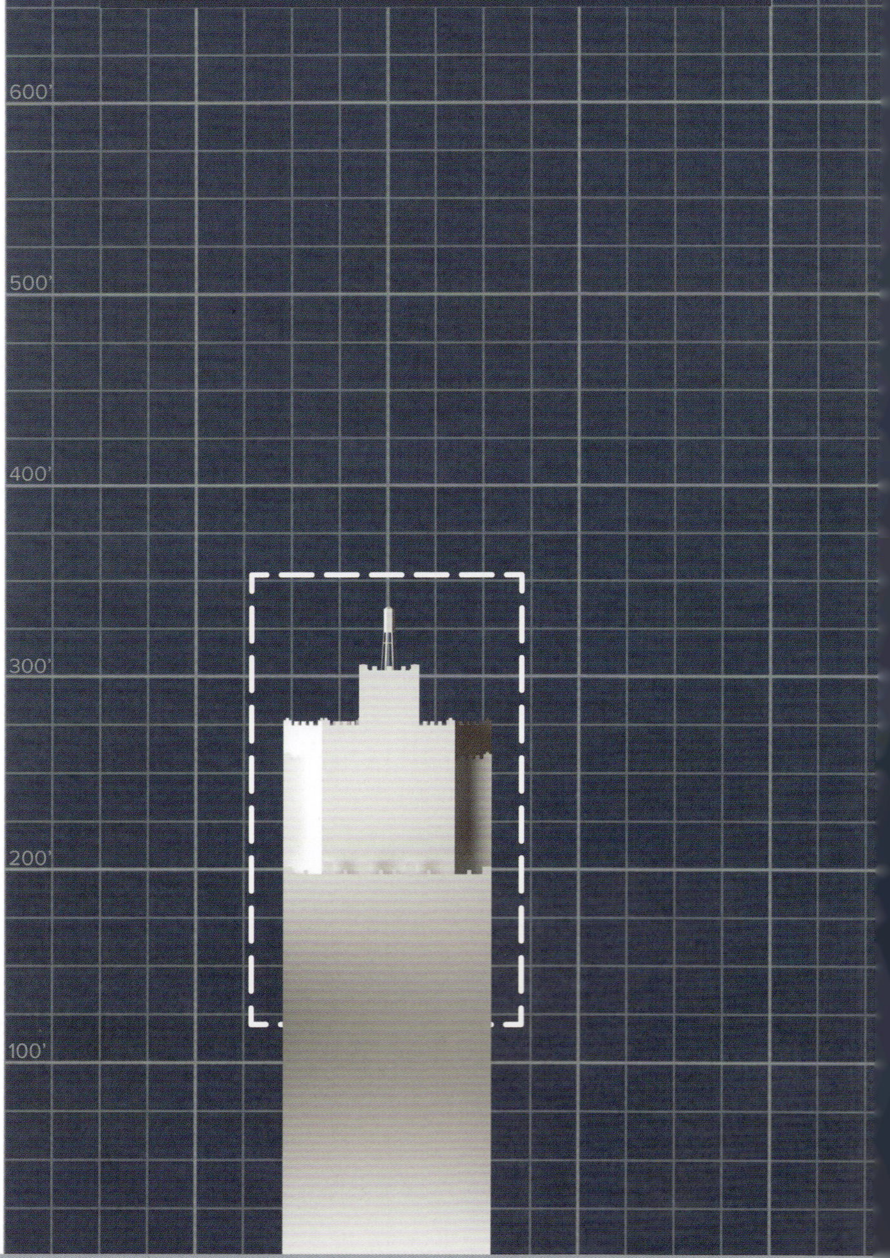

Southwest Elevation *1" = 100'*

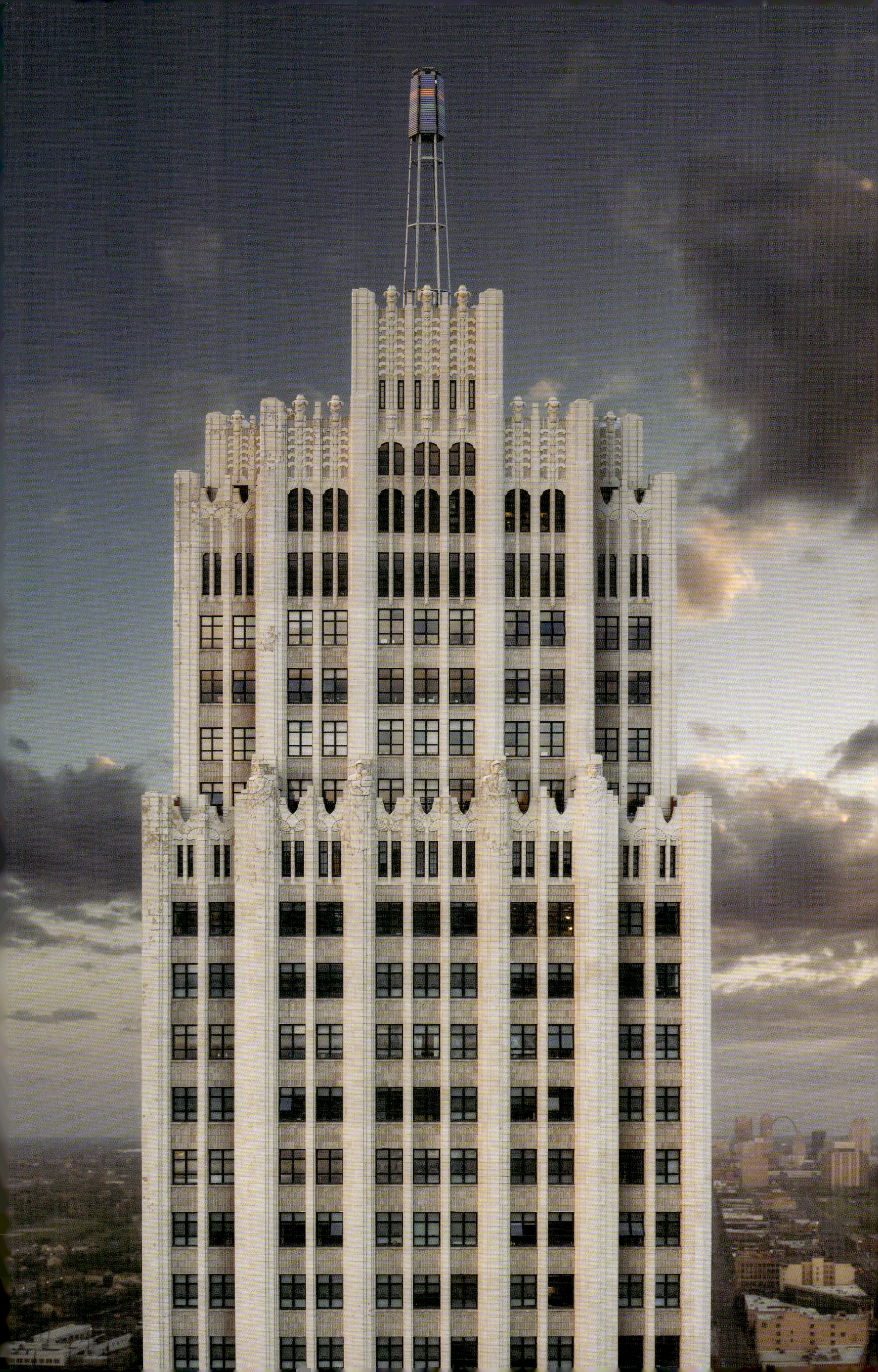

Nebraska
State Capitol

Lincoln, **NE**

Address	**1445 K St.**
Opened	**1932**
Height	**398'**
Stories	**14**
Style	**Art Deco**
Architect	**Bertram Goodhue**

Sweeping aside cookie cutter temple templates, Nebraska raised America's first state capitol skyscraper. Their proto-Deco tower on the plains inspired Roaring '20s architects to reimagine how tall buildings ought to look.

Bertram Goodhue had no formal training as an architect, yet his talents as a draftsman landed his firm numerous prestigious jobs, particularly Gothic cathedrals. Going solo in 1914, Goodhue branched into other historic styles, but his winning entry in a 1920 competition for the new Nebraska seat of government "makes no pretense of belonging to any period of the past," he said — it was "of the here and now, and naught else."

Colorful thunderbirds beneath the gold dome pay tribute to Native Americans, as do numerous symbolic decorations in the spectacular interior halls. But a plaque in the top floor memorial chapel also reveals that more Nebraskans were awarded the Medal of Honor for service in the Indian Wars than for any other conflict.

Powerful sculptures by Lee Lawrie, including the 19-foot "Sower" on the dome, and scintillating mosaics overhead and underfoot by Hildreth Meière won both artists many more commissions, including Rockefeller Center. But Goodhue never saw his tower, which took a decade to construct; he died of a heart attack in 1924 at the age of 55.

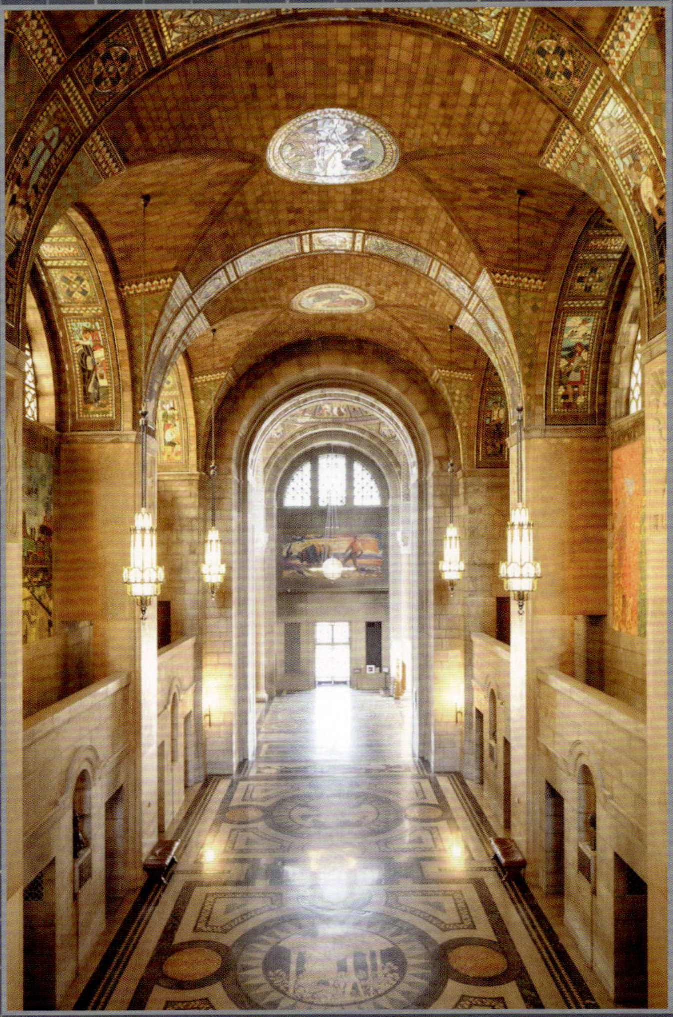

Ceiling mosaics depict virtuous citizens, while the floor represents evolution with dinosaurs and a trilobite.

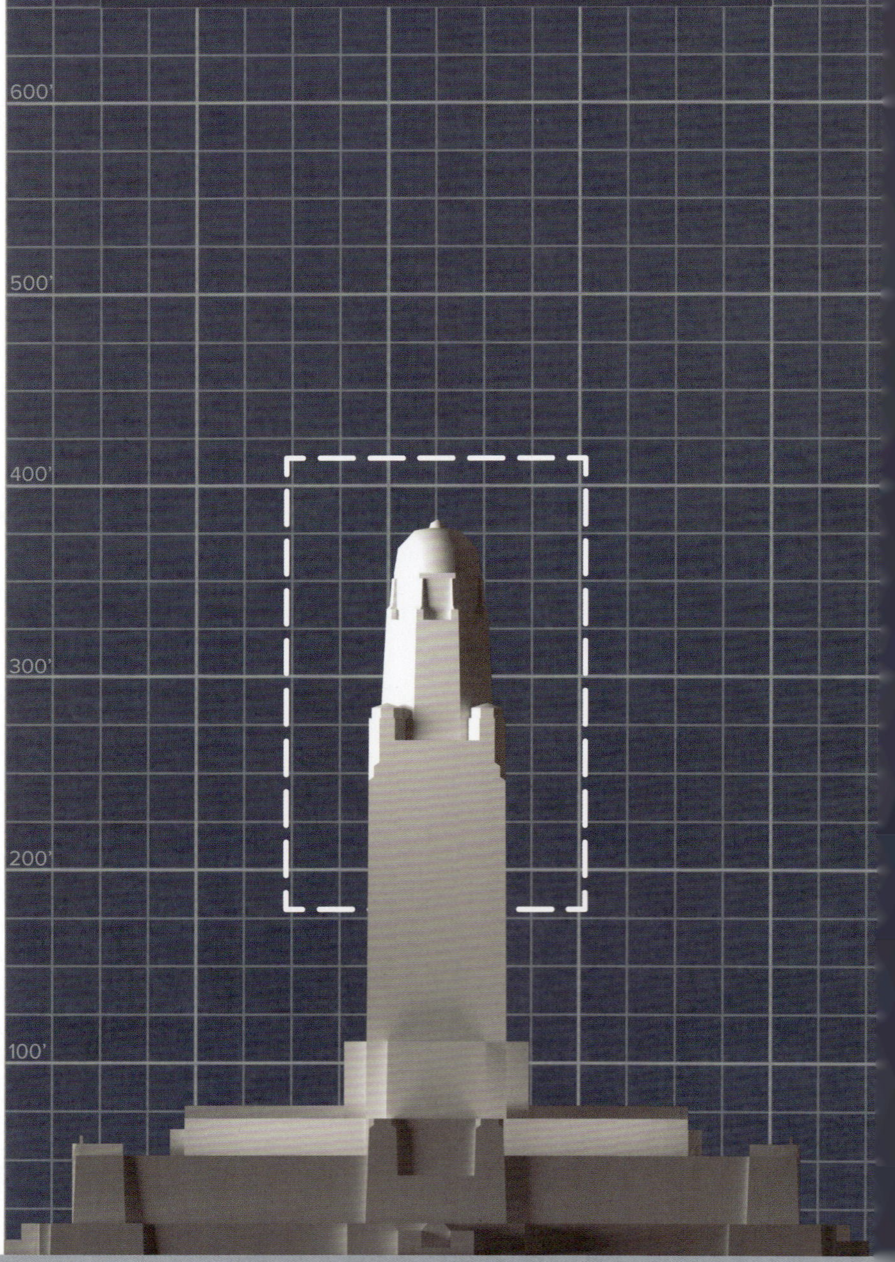

South Elevation *1" = 100'*

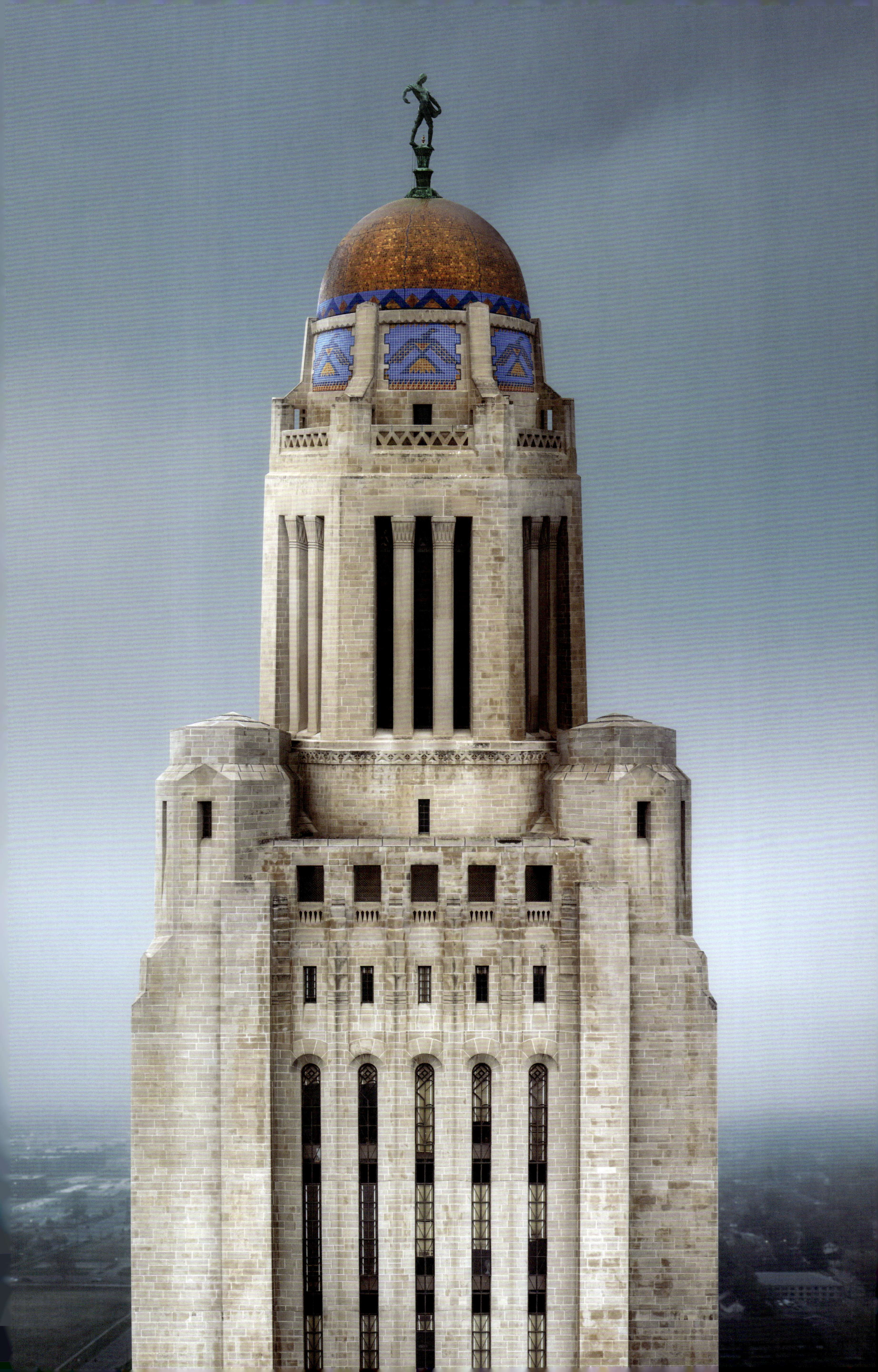

Carew Tower

Cincinnati, **OH**

Address	**441 Vine St.**
Opened	**1930**
Height	**574'**
Stories	**48**
Style	**Art Deco**
Architect	**Walter Ahlschlager**

Generations of sightseers flocked to the rooftop observatory on this pinnacle of Art Deco design until its recent closure. The highrise takes its name from the popular proprietor of a department store that formerly filled five floors at street level.

Joseph Carew established the city's first Mabley & Carew emporium in 1877. He opened a bigger one in 1889 and built a handsome office block across the street a year later, all facing the "Genius of Water," a monumental bronze fountain and downtown gathering place. For the office construction, Carew demolished a so-called "nasty corner" of saloons and rundown storefronts, winning him much admiration and praise.

Developer Jack Emery was only 31 when he announced plans to replace the deceased Carew's Victorian office block with this soaring skyscraper and two more attached: a luxury hotel and a parking garage. The family empire had been founded by Emery's grandfather, who followed the lead of two other Cincinnati entrepreneurs, William Procter and James Gamble, by manufacturing candles out of fat from meatpacking plants that once earned Cincinnati the sobriquet "Porkopolis."

Long abandoned by Mabley & Carew and a successor store, the office tower is undergoing conversion into residential units.

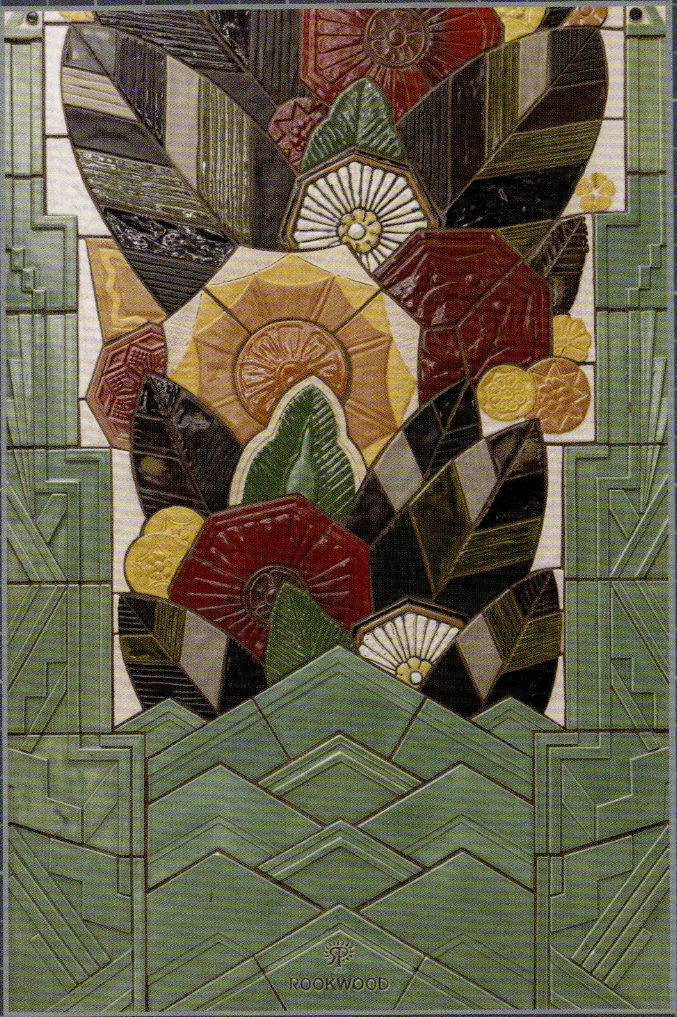

Tiles by Rookwood Pottery adorn the arcade. The Cincinnati firm also made tiles for the New York subway.

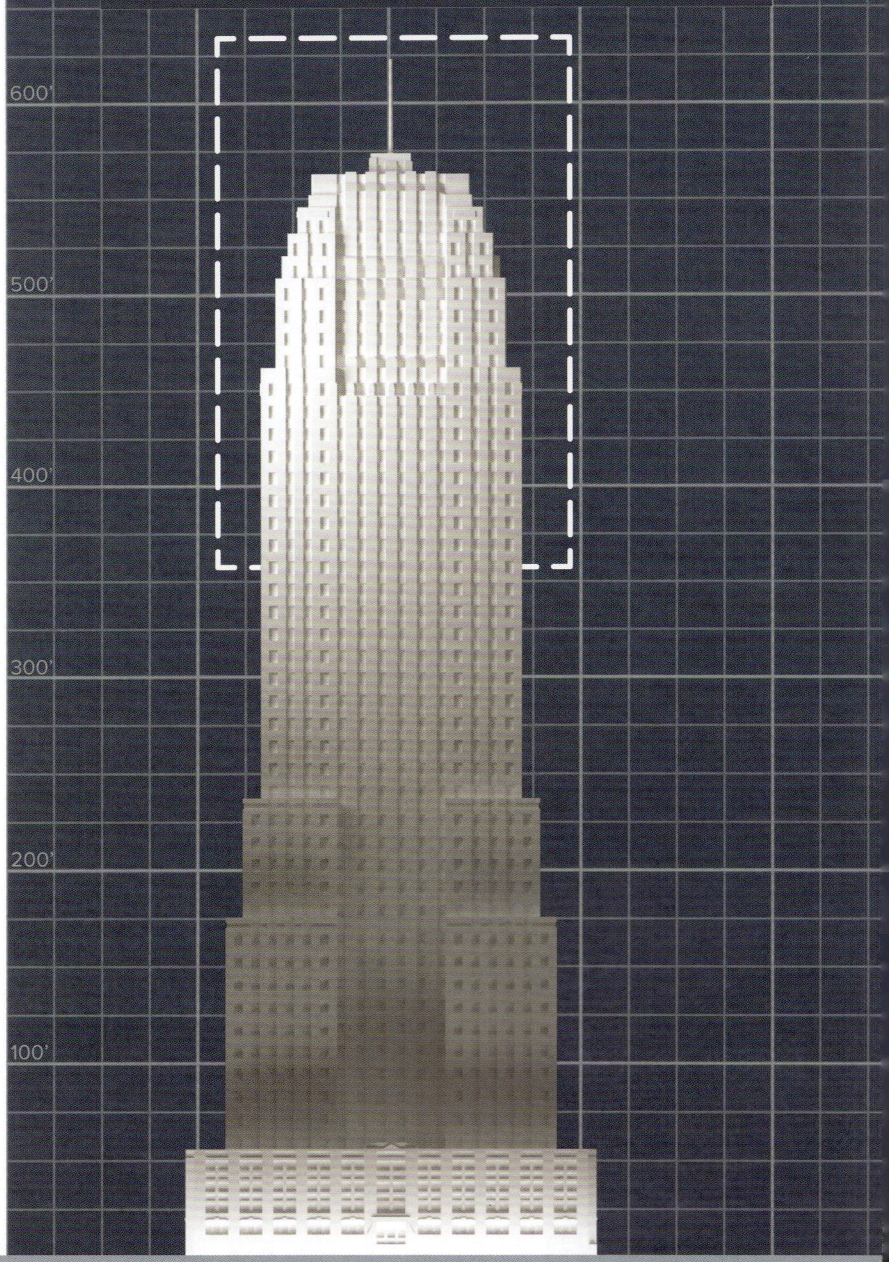

East Elevation *1" = 100'*

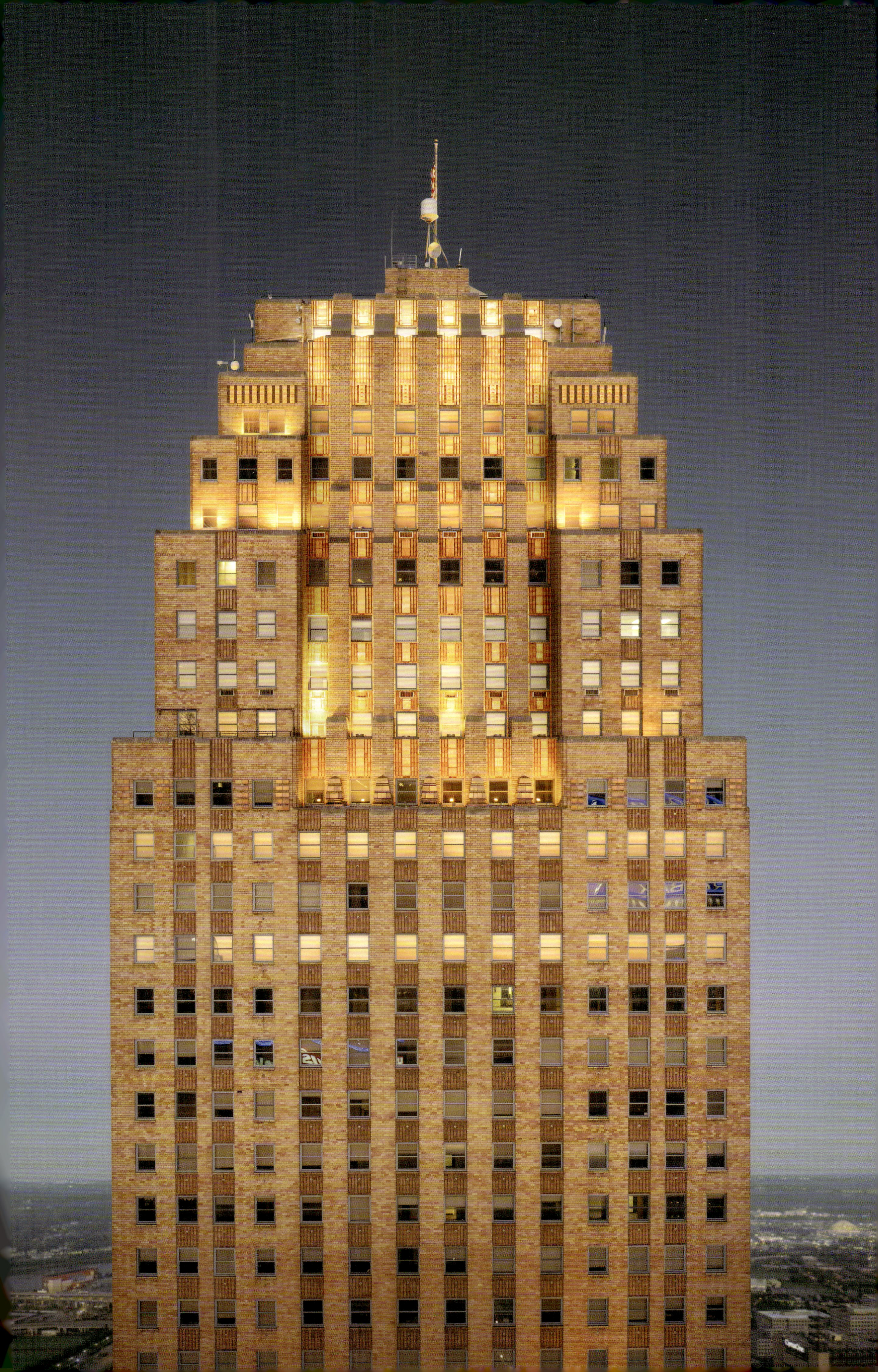

Times-Star
Building

Cincinnati, **OH**

Address ················ **800 Broadway**
Opened ························· **1933**
Height ························· **239’**
Stories ·························· **15**
Style ············ **Art Deco, Renaissance**
Architect ········ **H. Eldridge Hannaford**

A quartet of figures arrayed along the roofline represent the values of the newspaper this highrise housed: Truth, Patriotism, Progress, and Speed. Its stone exterior is carved with reliefs of key figures in the history of printing, a theme repeated in the ornamental entryway grille.

Though he served brief terms in the state house and Congress, Charles Taft preferred to exercise political muscle as editor-in-chief of the newspaper he founded in 1880. Among the causes it promoted was the election of the publisher’s younger half-brother, William Howard Taft. Like the famously fat president who went from the White House to the Supreme Court, this building switched careers and is now used by the county judiciary.

Its sturdy frame was poured by the company that built the world’s first reinforced concrete skyscraper in 1903 in Cincinnati. A plaque crediting Samuel Hannaford & Sons for the design is a humble nod by the project’s true architect to his grandfather, who designed city hall but was long gone by the time this went up.

Charles and Anna Taft also did not live to see this building completed; both are memorialized on bronze plaques in its elegant Art Deco lobby. Their former mansion, now an art museum, is a 10-minute walk away.

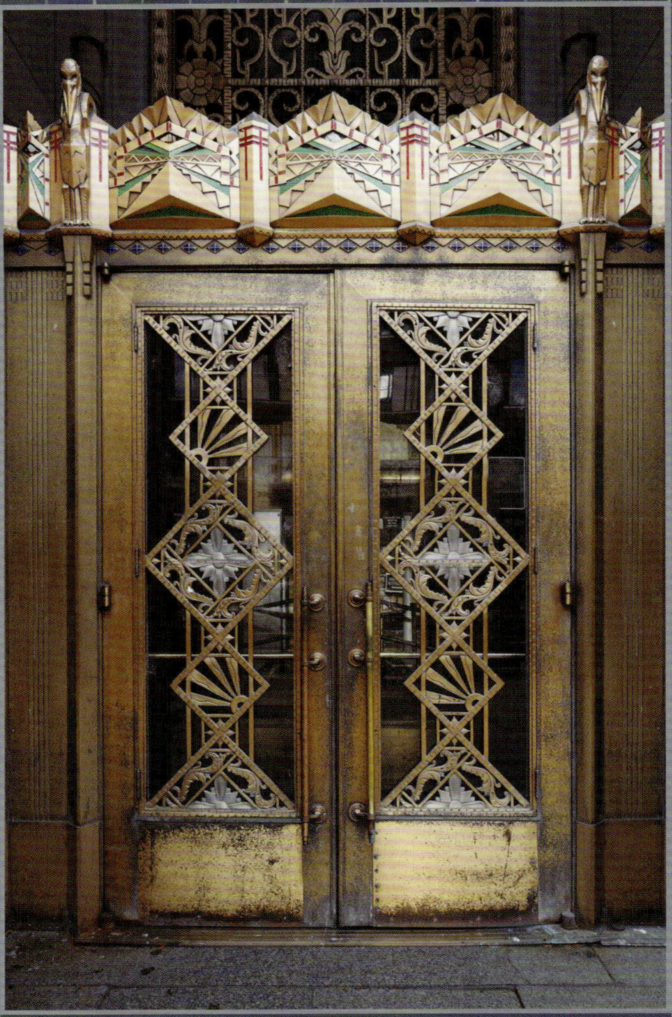

Bronze entrance doors with aluminum highlights meld zigzag patterns with curved and flowing elements.

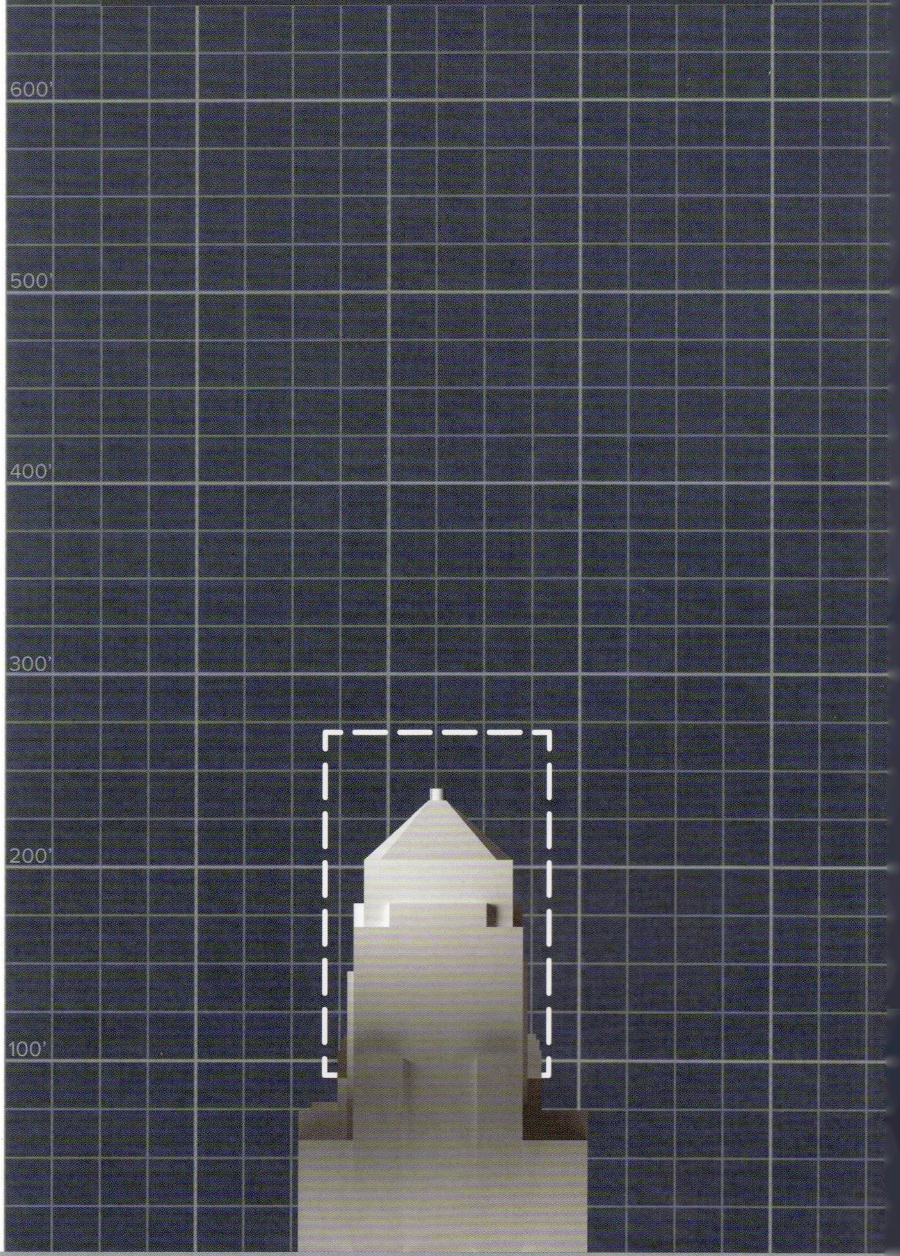

West Elevation *1" = 100'*

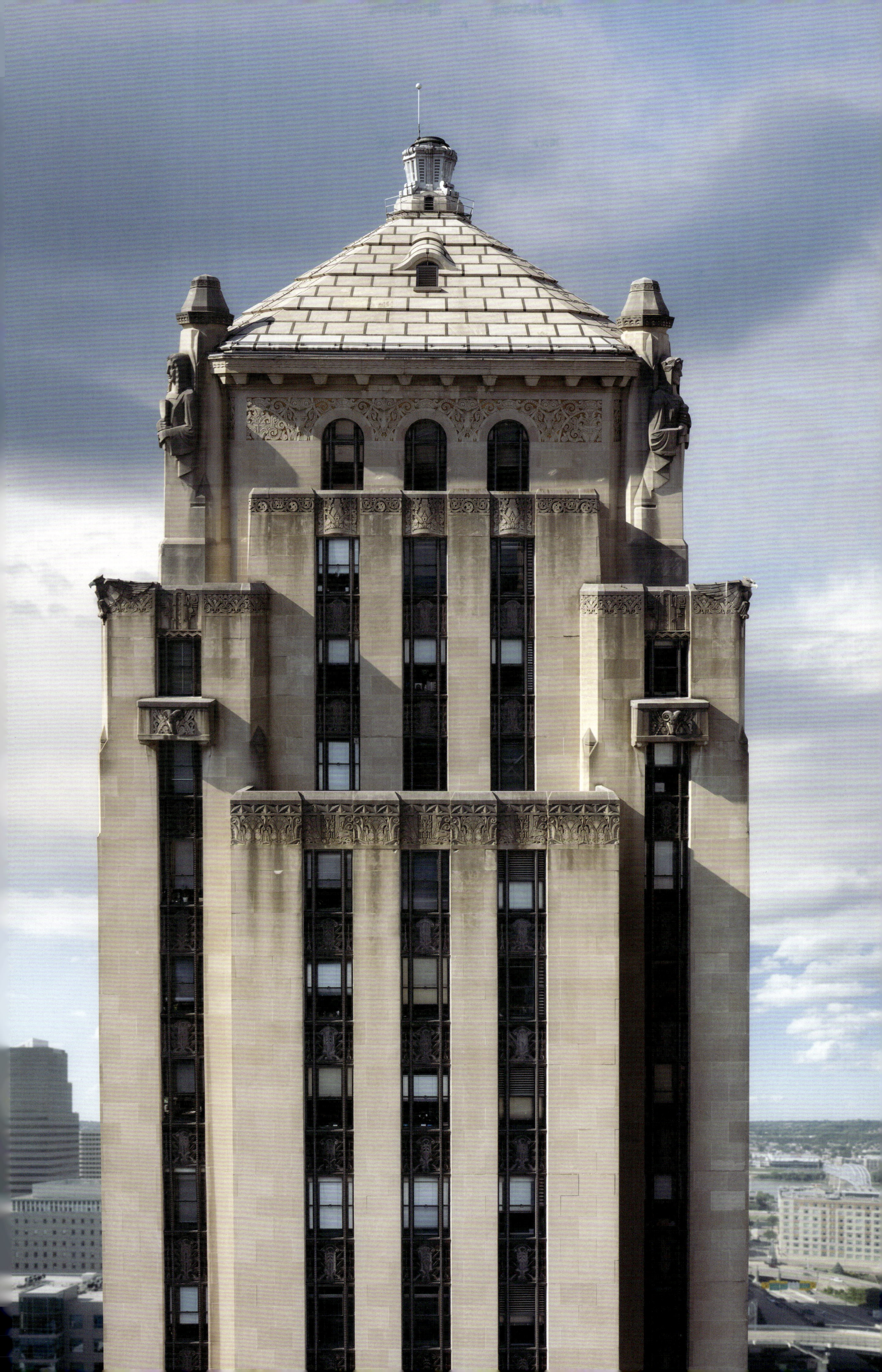

Ohio Bell
Building

Cleveland, **OH**

Address	**750 Huron Rd.**
Opened	**1927**
Height	**365'**
Stories	**23**
Style	**Art Deco**
Architect	**Hubbell & Benes**

Baseball fans who come to see the Guardians, the local team recently renamed after Art Deco statues on a nearby Cuyahoga River bridge, have a clear view of the city's other important structure in the signature style of the era: this skyscraper looming over the left field bleachers.

The new headquarters for Ohio Bell and parent company American Telephone & Telegraph was a heavyweight. Besides offices, it was engineered to support multiple floors of heavy automatic telephone switching equipment, which replaced the human operators who had connected calls by hand until then. Ohio Bell reassured the public that its "girls" would all be offered new jobs. Their former workplace, a Victorian era office block with a crenelated castle tower, was torn down to make room for the huge Terminal Tower complex.

That highrise would soon dominate the Cleveland skyline. But for a few fleeting months, the city's first Art Deco skyscraper — or as one of the local architects responsible dubbed it, "American Perpendicular Gothic" — was the tallest building in town. Although the company built a new headquarters closer to the lakefront in 1983, this skyscraper continues to house telephone equipment.

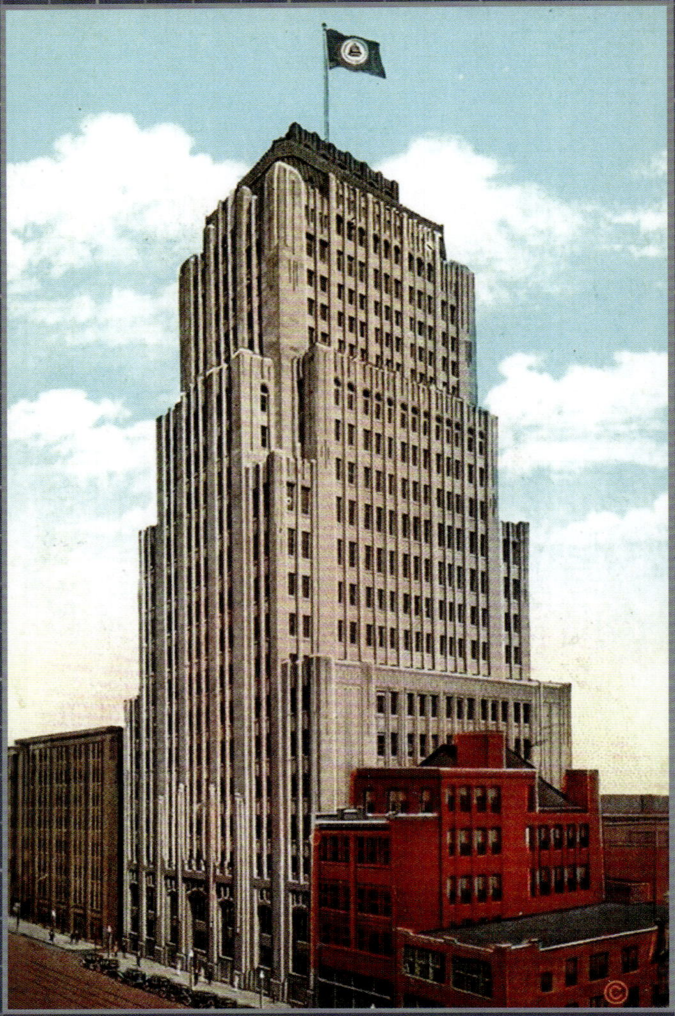

An oversized flag with the Bell Telephone logo flies above the building in this vintage postcard.

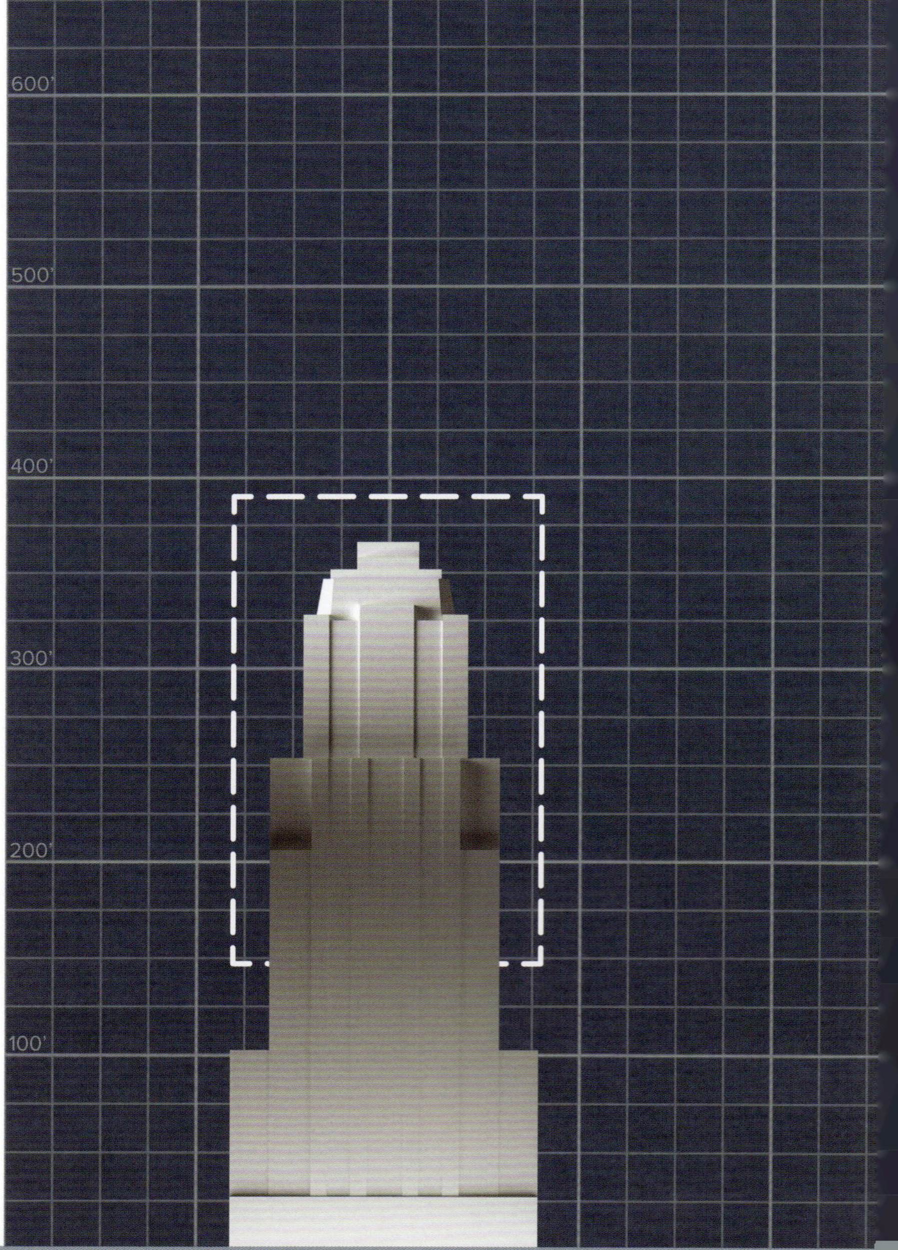

North Elevation *1" = 100'*

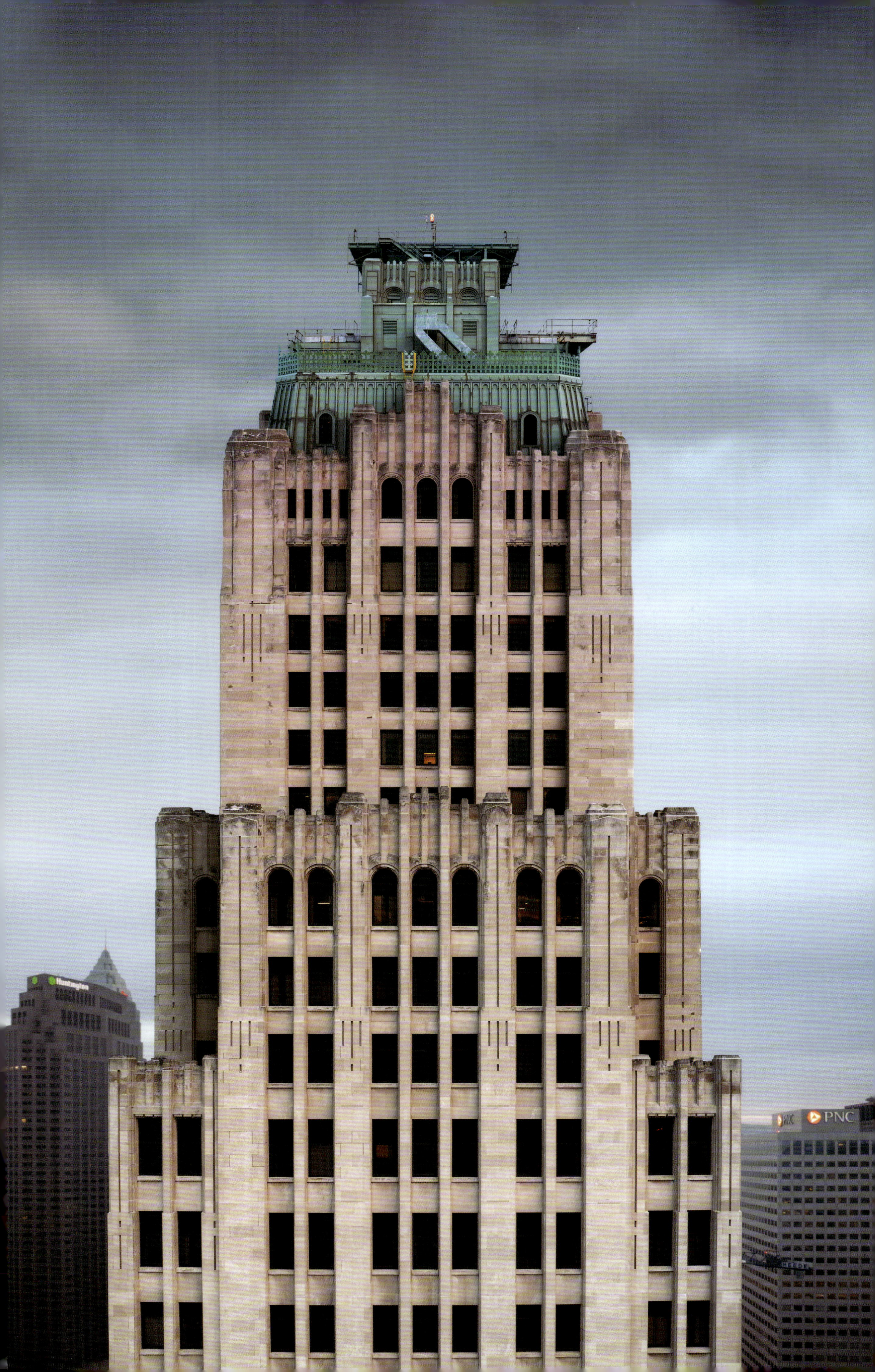
Huntington
PNC

Terminal Tower

Cleveland, **OH**

Address .... **50 Public Sq.**
Opened **1928**
Height .... **708'**
Stories **52**
Style .... **Neoclassical**
Architect .... **Graham, Anderson, Probst & White**

This highrise named for the centralized urban transit hub it straddles stood as the tallest skyscraper outside Manhattan for decades. Ironically, the immense project was the product of two unmarried brothers so shy they skipped the dedication ceremony and listened to it on the radio.

Oris and Mantis Van Sweringen first found success developing a suburb they dubbed Shaker Heights. Next they bought land downtown and began to connect it to their development via a commuter rail line. Initial plans for a downtown hotel metastasized to a massive office complex, department store, and central underground passenger rail terminal. But suburbanites preferred to drive their own cars rather than take trains, and the Van Sweringens lost control of their sprawling railroad holdings in the Great Depression.

The terminal was remodeled into a shopping mall and the department store is now a casino, but the hotel is still operating. The tower, converted to apartments in 2019, still has its gargantuan vaulted lobby and waiting room, and an oak-paneled library and dining room where the brothers once had their daily lunch with senior staff is preserved. From the observation deck on the 42nd floor, it is possible to pick out the distant rising patch of green that is Shaker Heights.

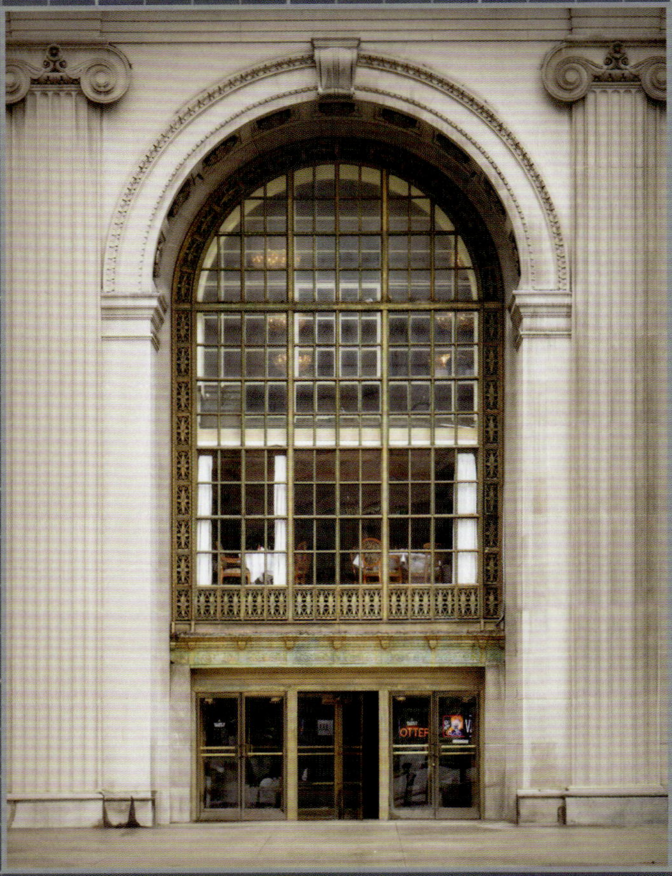

Classical pilasters at the mammoth entry arch embody a conservative design built to enormous scale.

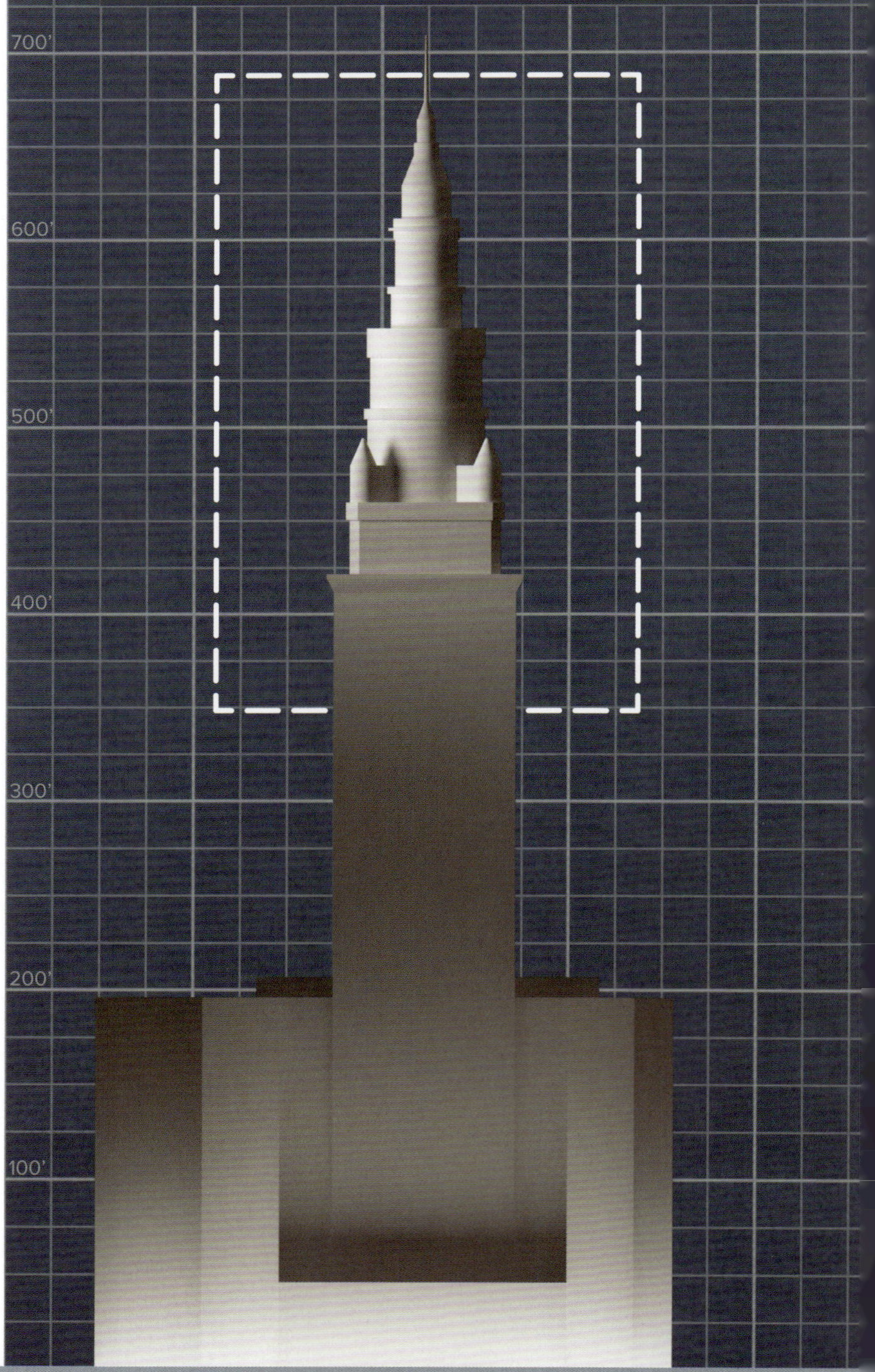

South Elevation *1" = 100'*

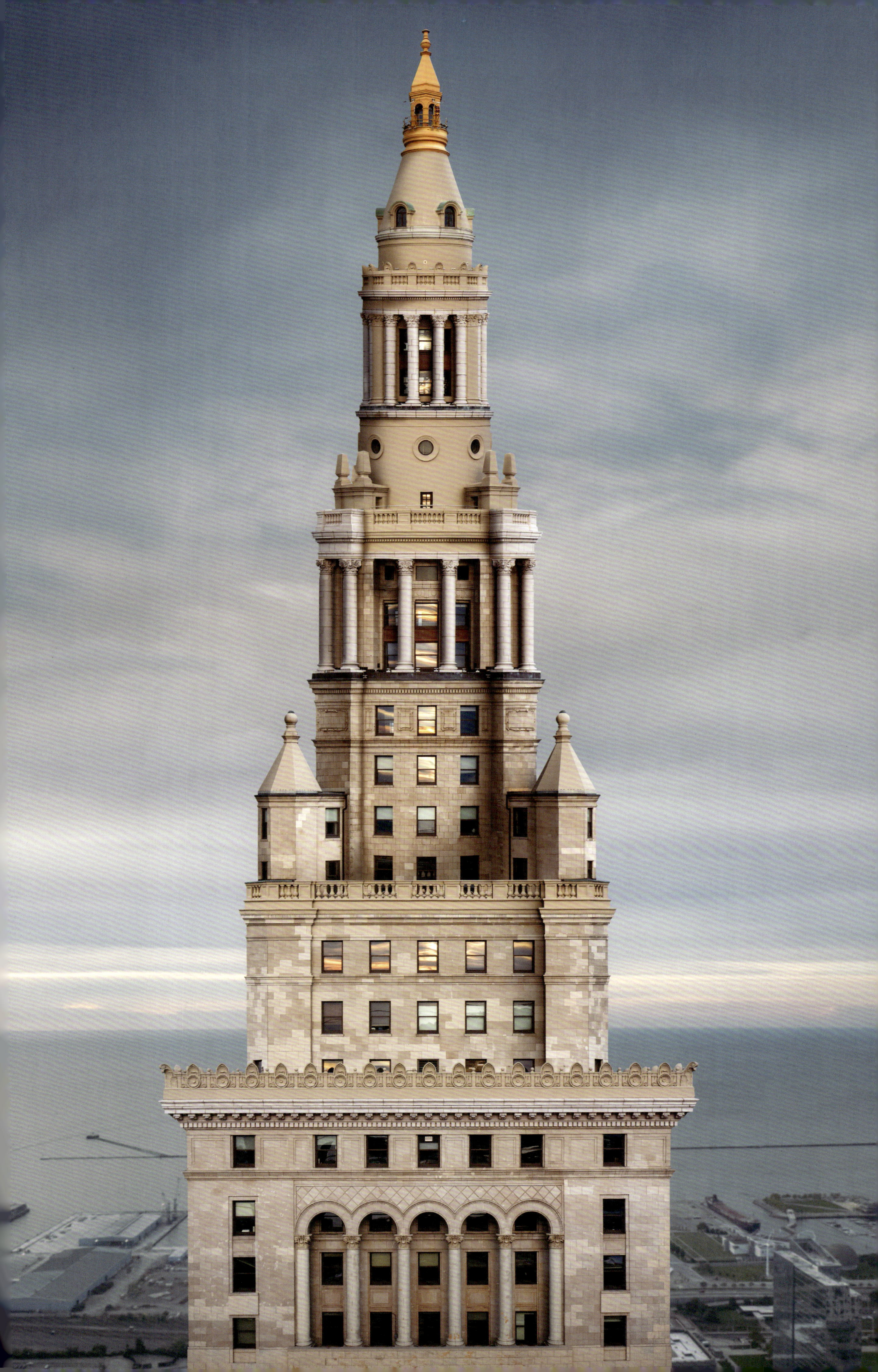

AIU Citadel

Columbus, **OH** LeVeque Tower

Address	**50 W. Broad St.**
Opened	**1927**
Height	**555'**
Stories	**47**
Style	**Art Deco**
Architect	**C. Howard Crane**

Eight terracotta guardian angels symbolize the protective role of the insurance company that built this allegorical fortress. Their blank scrolls denote a future yet to be written — one which would turn out to be truncated and tragic for American Insurance Union and its highrise's subsequent owners.

AIU founder John Lentz, an attorney and former congressman, spun his company's initials into the slogan "American Ideals Uppermost." Rapid growth of his business led Lentz to erect a headquarters identical in height to the Washington Monument. Cost overruns, and then the Depression, doomed AIU. Lentz died in 1931; a day after his funeral, lightning blasted off a piece of the building. Crumbling terracotta eventually forced the removal of four large eagles and four other statuary groups, and left the rooftop cherubs headless.

Investors Leslie LeVeque and John Lincoln bought the building in 1946, but LeVeque, who owned an airplane parts factory, and his wife were killed when their plane crashed into a New Hampshire mountain two months later. Their son, Fred, also died in a private plane crash in 1975.

The renovated highrise is now a mix of hotel and residential units. Its marble lobby is festooned with colorful murals and has elaborate original bronze elevator doors marked Health, Happiness, and Prosperity.

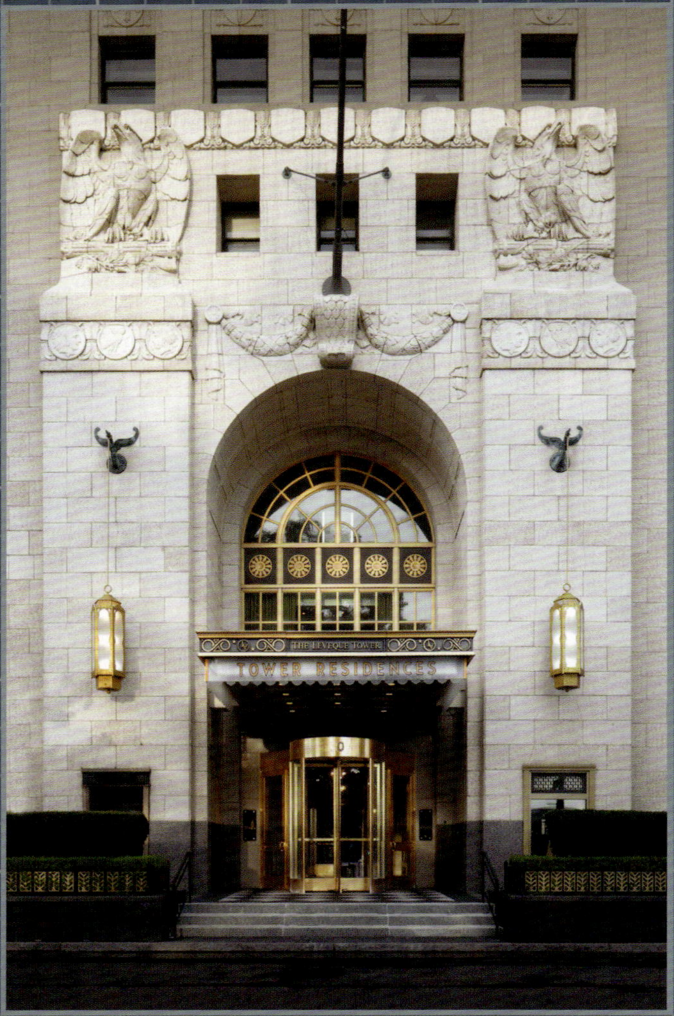

The entranceway is richly ornamented with terracotta sculpture that continues to the top of the tower.

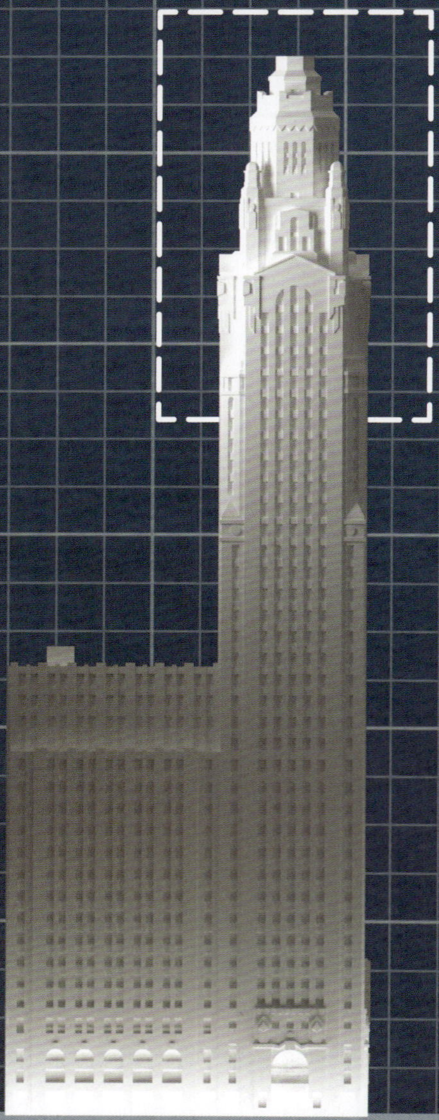

West Elevation *1" = 100'*

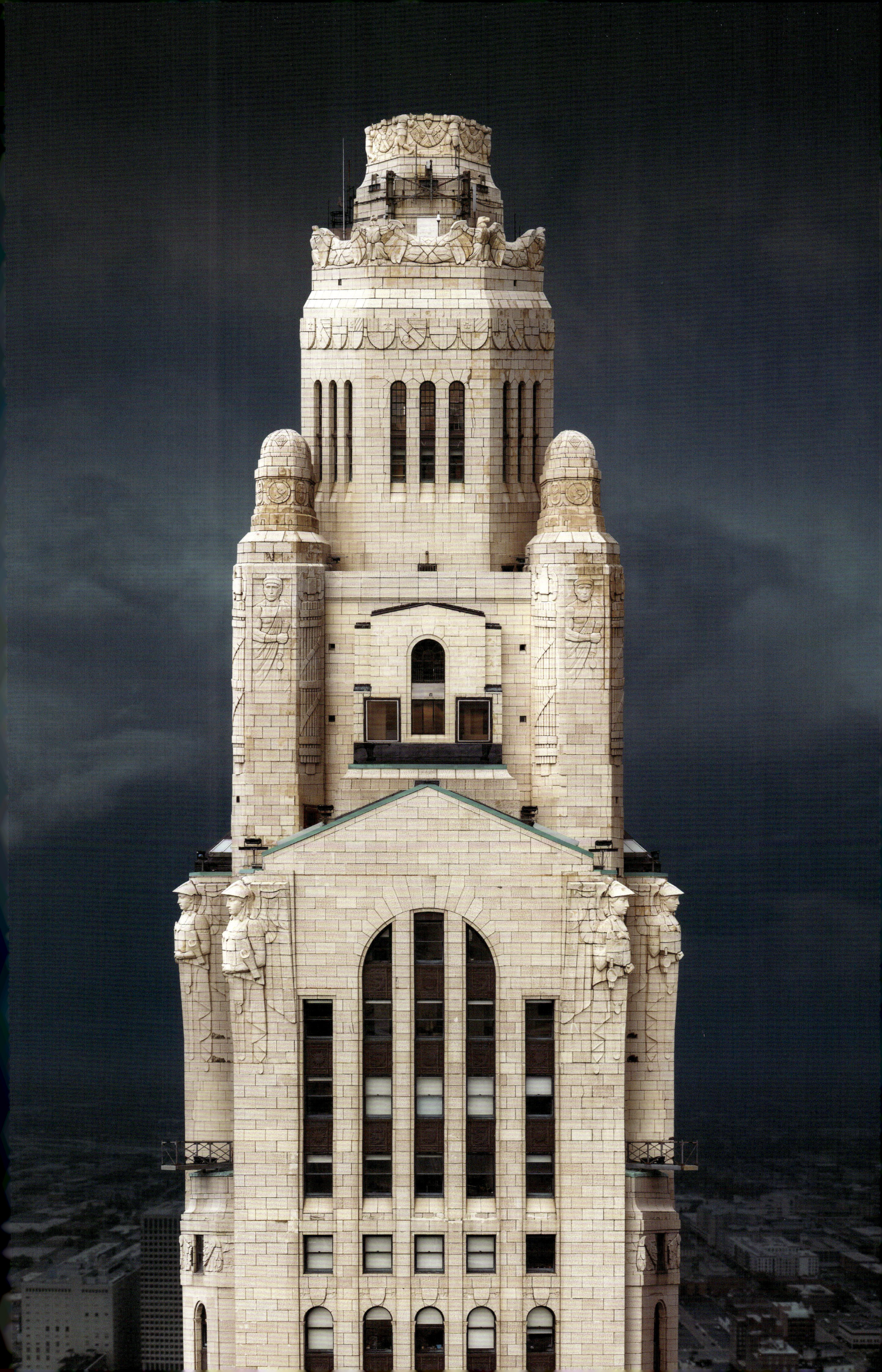

Ohio Bank
Building

Toledo, **OH**

Address ············· **405 Madison Ave.**
Opened ························· **1930**
Height ···························· **368'**
Stories ······························ **23**
Style ························ **Art Deco**
Architect ··· **Mills, Rhines, Bellman & Nordhoff**

Four different banks have called this highrise home, so its original name seems appropriate to this day, but the financial institution that built it went out of business after less than a year of occupancy. Ohio Savings Bank & Trust, the biggest financial institution in the city, was one of six Toledo banks to fail in a 1931 panic.

For almost 50 years, this asymmetrical edifice in the Lake Erie port known as "Glass City" was the headquarters of a major manufacturer of bottles, Owens-Illinois Glass. Bottles were a better business than banks in the Great Depression after Prohibition was repealed in 1933, letting producers broaden their product lines from milk bottles to beer and liquor.

Founder Michael Owens made a fortune after inventing the world's first fully automated glass bottle making machine in 1903. His company maintained its focus on innovation; the year it moved to this location, it began working with another glass company in New York on an insulation product, fiberglass, they produced through their joint venture Owens Corning.

Deco gargoyles stud the facade, while two figures in relief flank the arched entrance, one carrying a beehive for industry, the other a gear for technology.

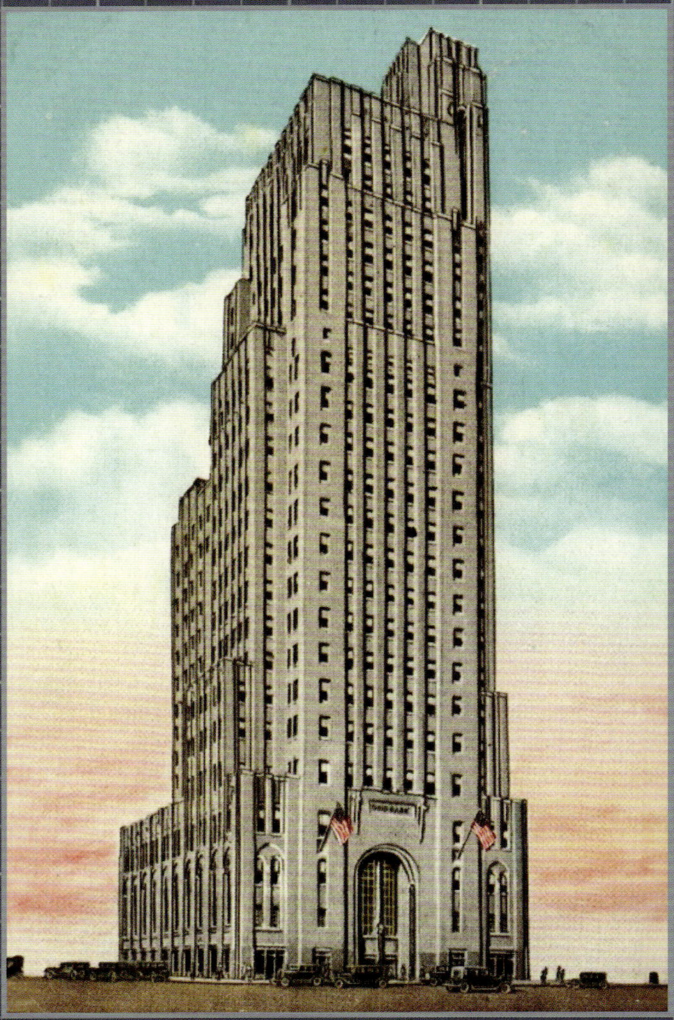

This vintage souvenir postcard conveniently erases the neighbors to highlight the angular profile of the building.

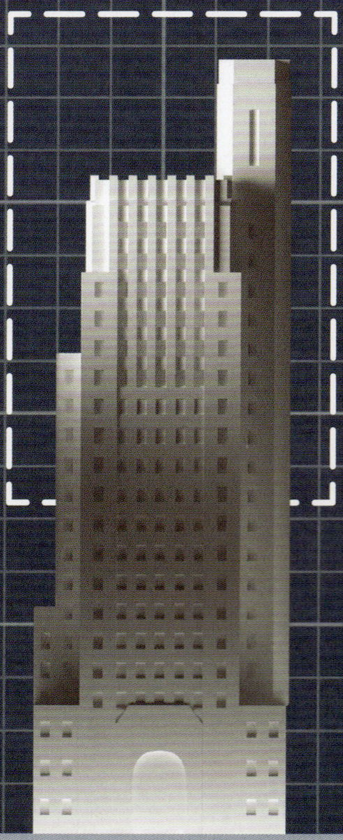

North Facade *1" = 100'*

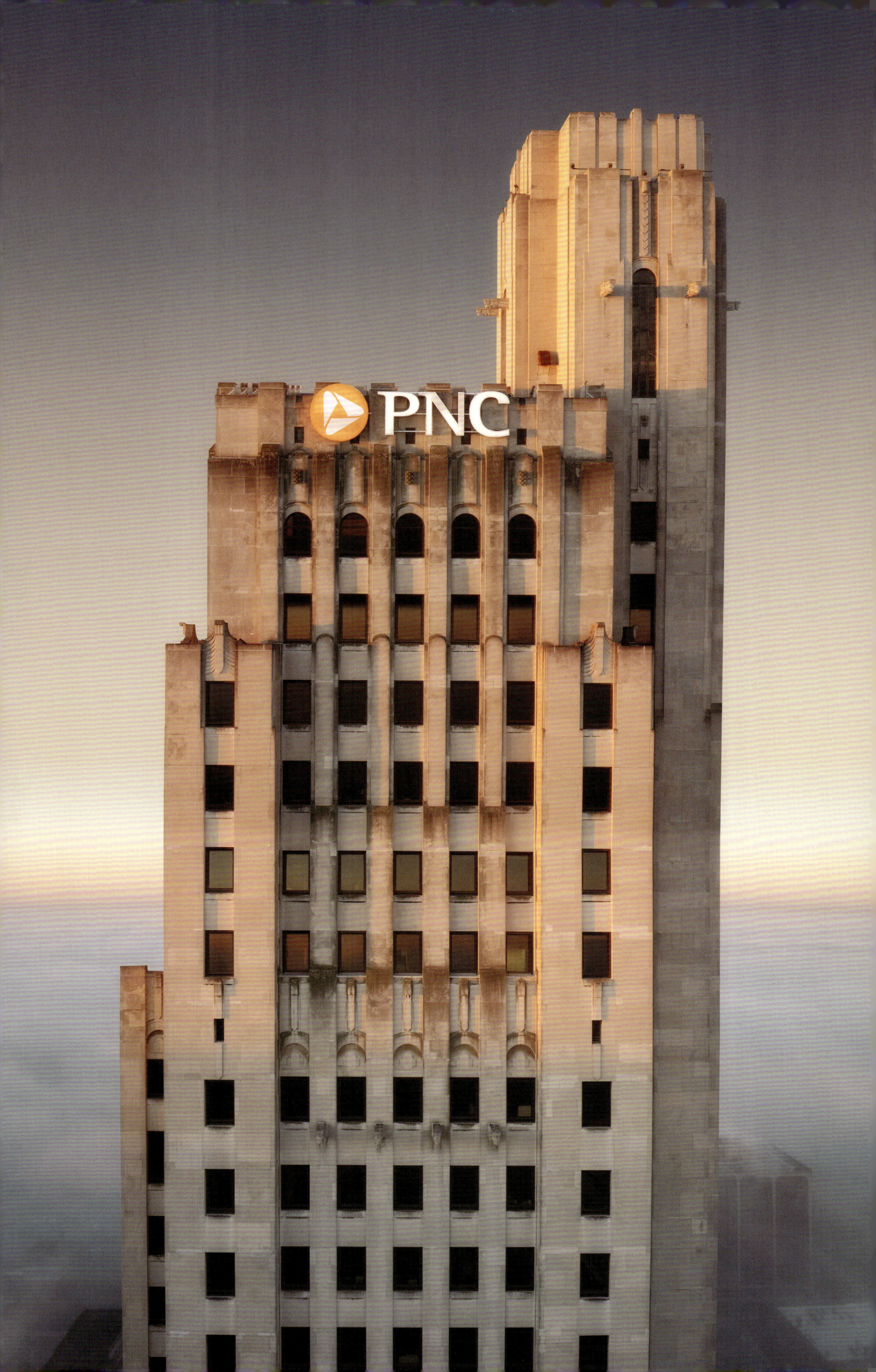
PNC

Milwaukee Gas Light
Building

Milwaukee, **WI**

Address	**626 E. Washington Ave.**
Opened	**1930**
Height	**250'**
Stories	**20**
Style	**Art Deco**
Architect	**Eschweiler & Eschweiler**

Prohibition complicated construction of this highrise. Agents raided a small hotel on its planned footprint on the eve of demolition and found booze in the kitchen. So a federal judge padlocked the grill, and excavators had to leave the room propped on pilings for a year while they tore down everything around it to dig the foundation.

The flame beacon on the roof, while not original, signals the building's main purpose as utility offices and showrooms for gas appliances. The gas was not the natural kind, but rather manufactured by cooking coal. This was done at a large plant on the city's west side designed by local architect Alexander Eschweiler, who also designed iconic gas stations in the shape of Japanese pagodas. His three sons joined his firm just in time for this skyscraper project.

A large bronze sunburst over the entrance, destroyed in an earlier remodeling, has been replaced and complements other Mayan-inspired elements. The exterior lightens as it rises, and it is not Wisconsin's famed dairy output but the pale yellow local bricks at the top that are the source of the Milwaukee moniker "Cream City."

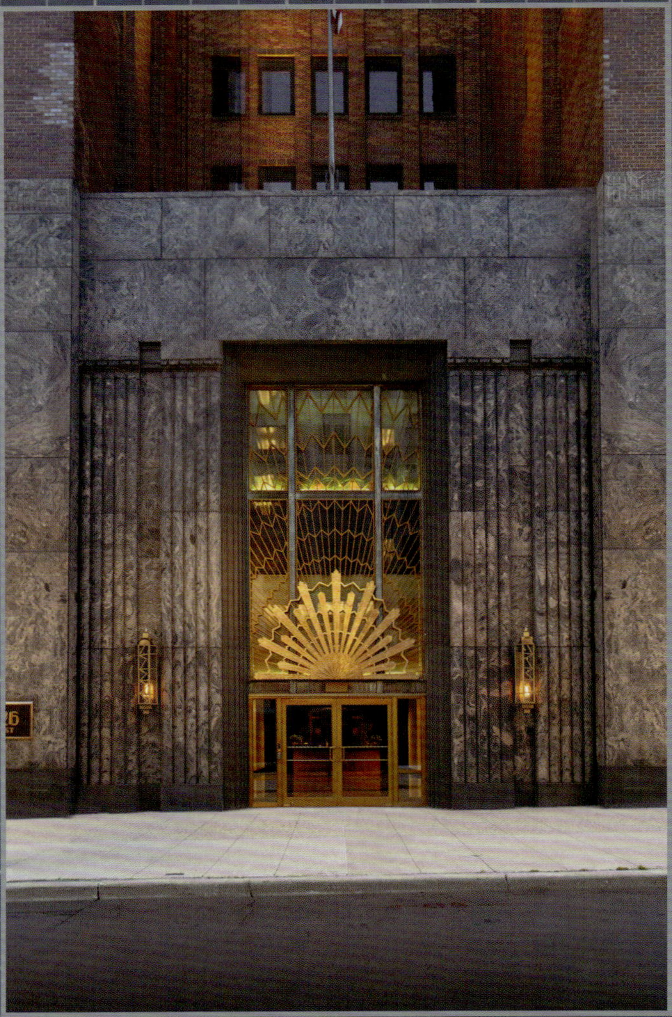

The bronze sunburst was recreated in 2003 by a local sculptor from the original architectural drawings.

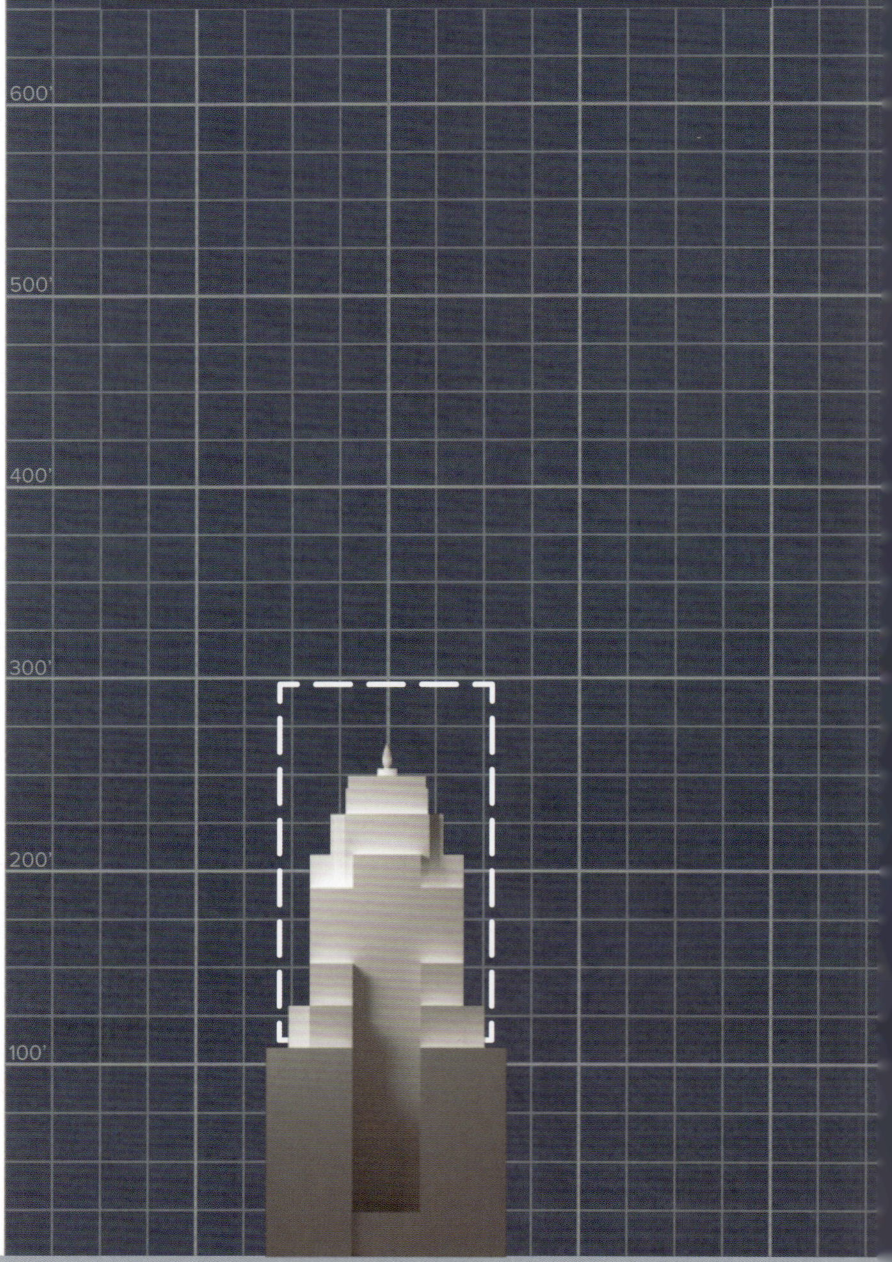

South Elevation *1" = 100'*

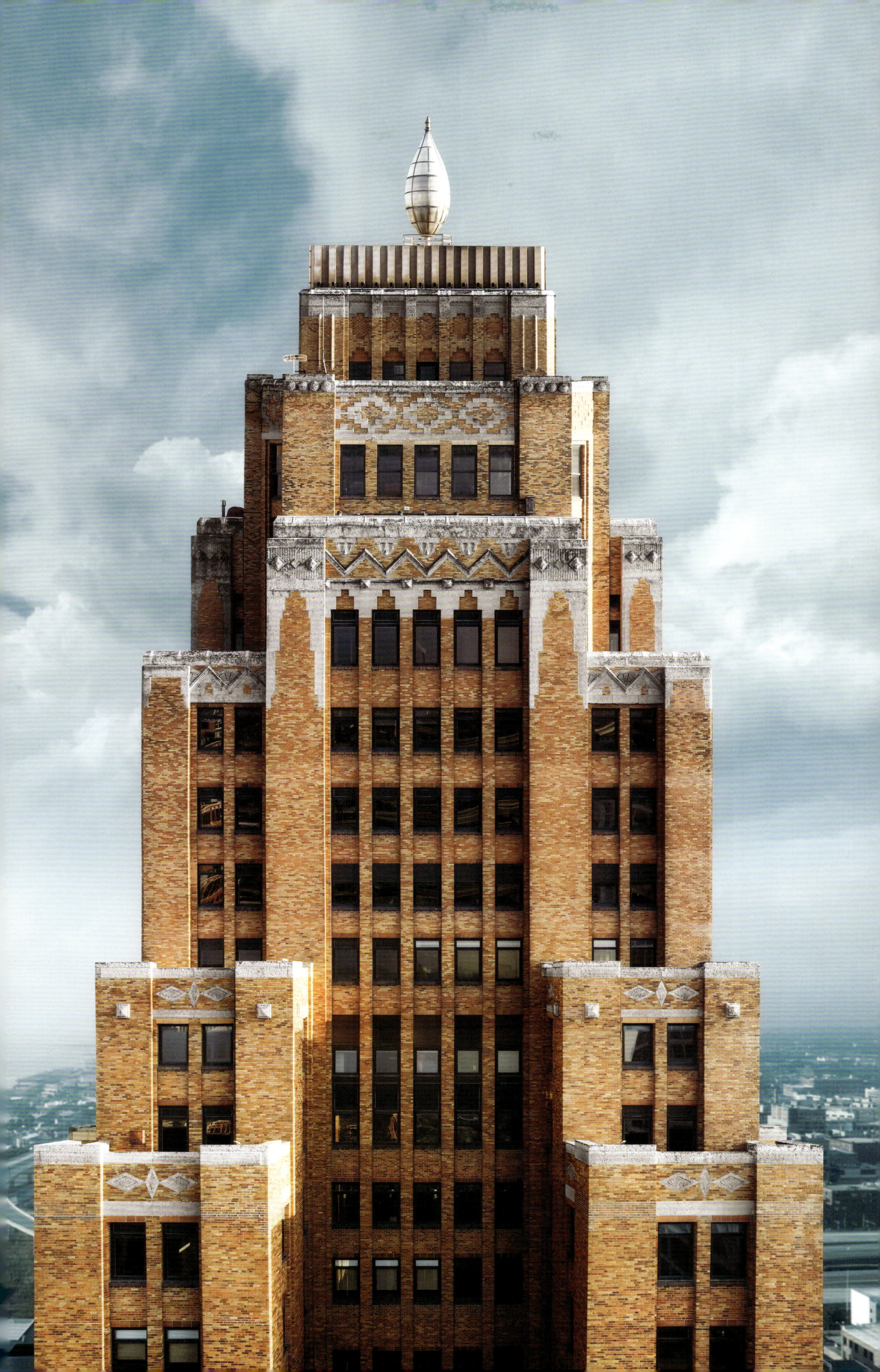

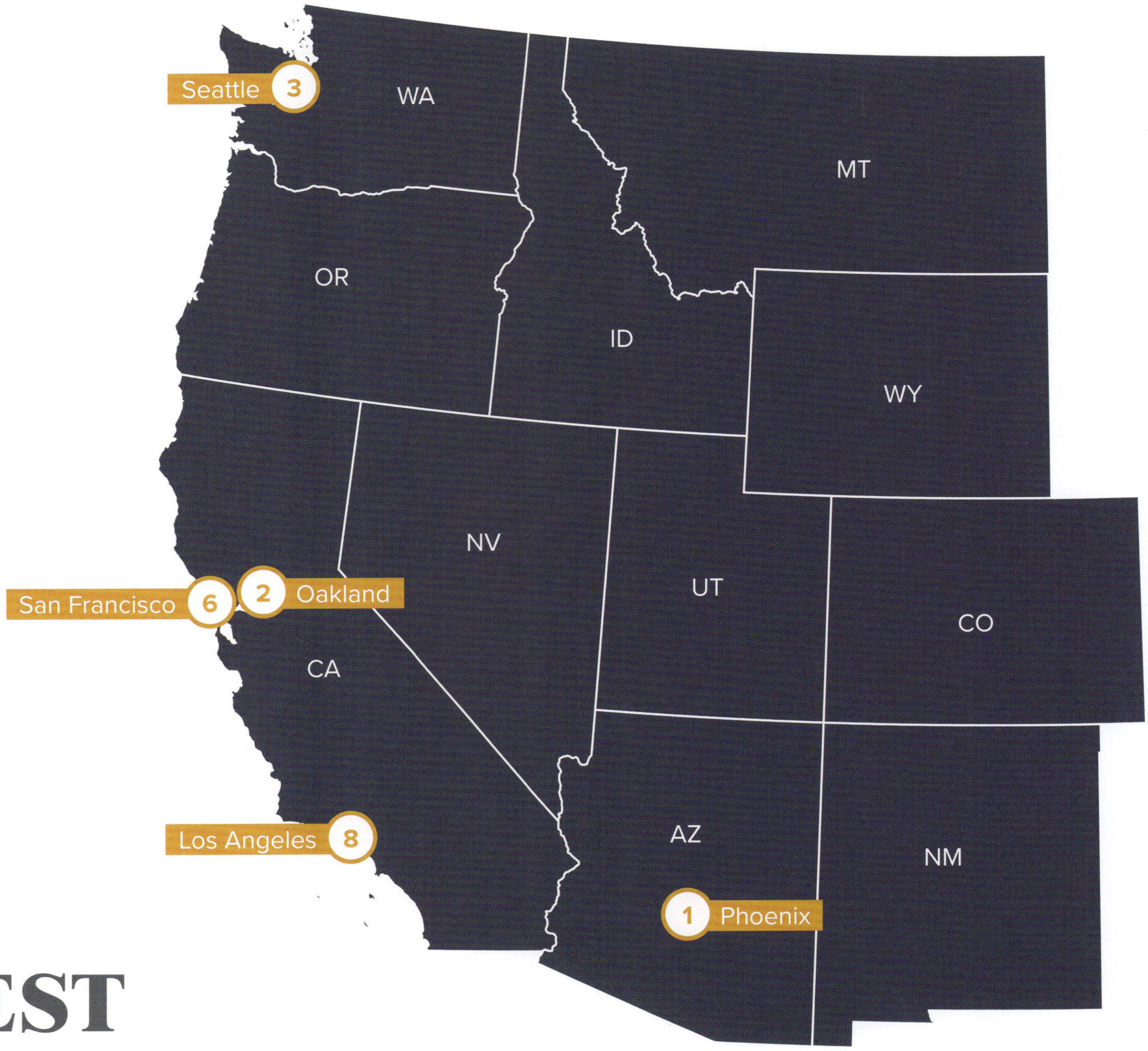

WEST

Sunny skies and scenic vistas that lured the motion picture industry to Hollywood a century ago also attracted throngs of new residents and businesses, and in 1920 Los Angeles became California's most populous city. Building height restrictions meant City Hall towered over everything else until the late 1960s, so architects found creative ways to bend the rules, extending ornamental towers beyond the strictly enforced roofline height to punch up the vertical.

L.A.'s neighbor to the north was under no such limitations. As the first great city of the West Coast, San Francisco already boasted a spectacular collection of classic skyscrapers, including several that survived the devastating 1906 earthquake and fire. Many more arose during the Roaring '20s, and they helped to develop a new stylistic vocabulary for tall buildings while cementing a tradition of daring architecture that continues to the present.

Yet the tallest skyscraper in the West in those days was not in California, but Seattle. The Smith Tower of 1914 held that distinction for nearly five decades, and its Jazz Age successors were marvels in their own right.

Numbers indicate how many buildings are featured in each city.

All building outlines are shown to scale. 1"= 200'

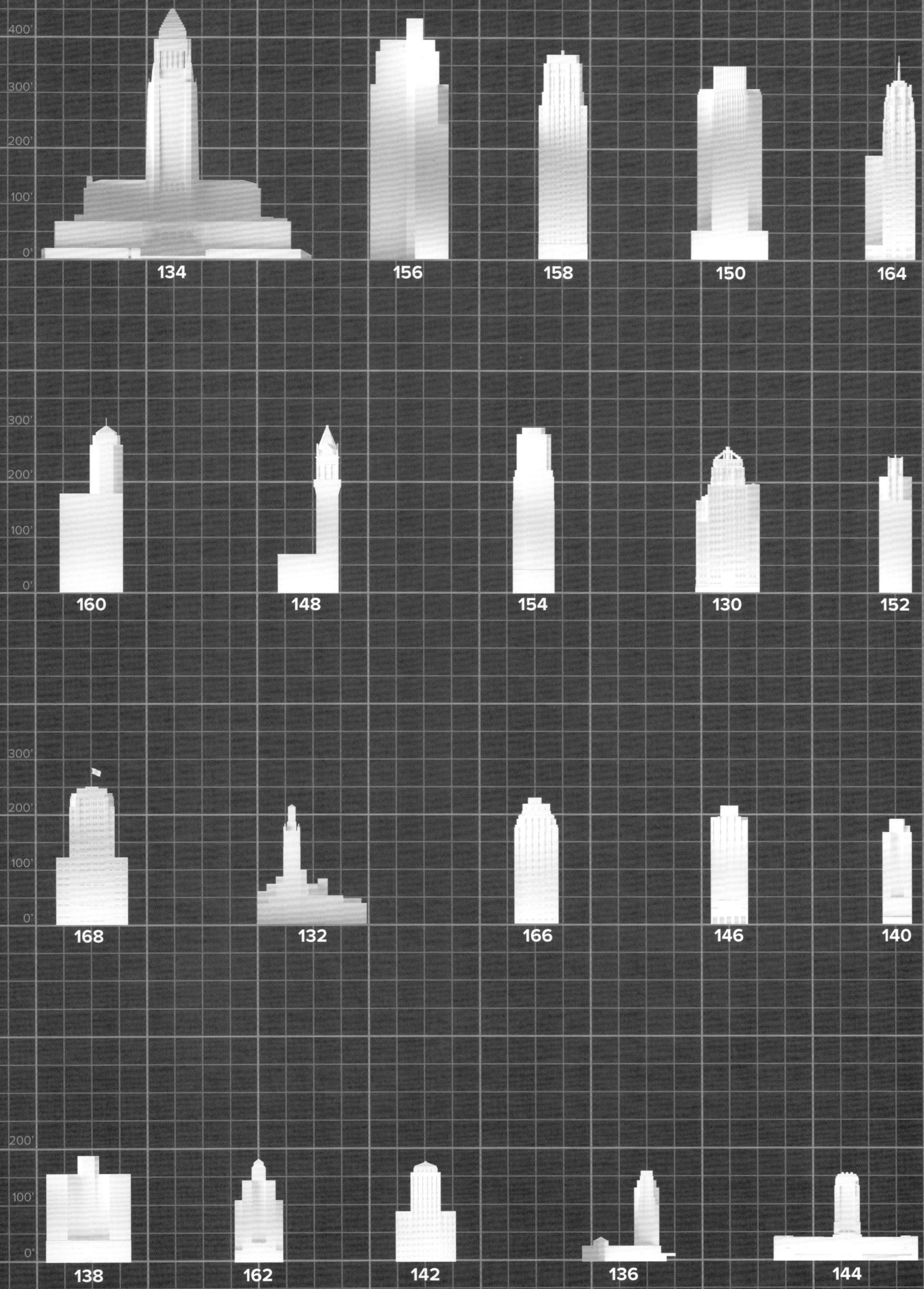

Eastern Columbia
Building

Los Angeles, **CA**

Address	**849 S. Broadway**
Opened	**1930**
Height	**264'**
Stories	**14**
Style	**Art Deco**
Architect	**Claud Beelman**

Turquoise, gold, and cerulean blue glazed terracotta tiles sheath this Art Deco landmark that was originally a department store — actually, two department stores under one roof. The four clock faces held special significance for Adolph Sieroty, a Jewish immigrant who got his start in L.A. retail when he opened a clock shop.

Bolstered by Sieroty's willingness to sell on credit, the business grew into Eastern Outfitting, a California chain of furniture and housewares stores. A retail clothing business, Columbia Outfitting, prospered too, and in 1930 Sieroty put both into this flagship store.

Entering through the three-story vestibule under a Mayan-inspired sunburst design in gold leaf and glazed tiles, visitors could stroll past displays for Columbia men's and women's outfits on the left and Eastern home furnishings on the right. Up above, beneath the clock, a model bungalow showhome stood in the rooftop garden. Fashion shows filled the 700-seat auditorium on the 12th floor.

The retail business closed in 1957, and Sieroty's son Julian converted the tower to office space. Now it has been renovated as a condominium with 147 residential units. Swimmers in the rooftop pool never have to wonder what time it is.

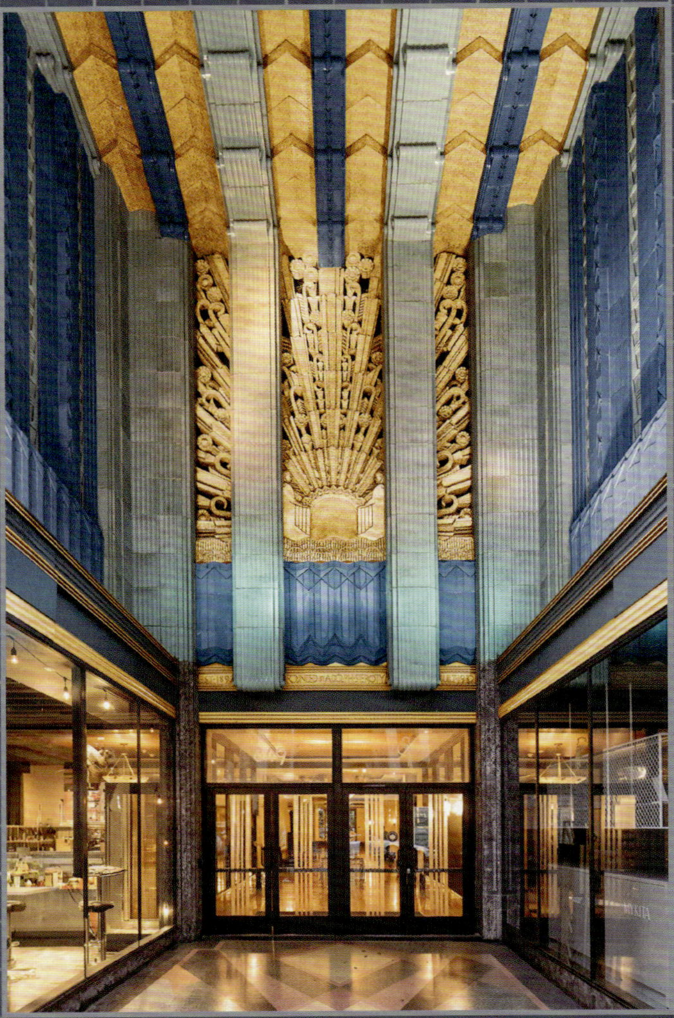

Southern California's famous sunny skies and endless blue ocean vistas are captured here in terracotta.

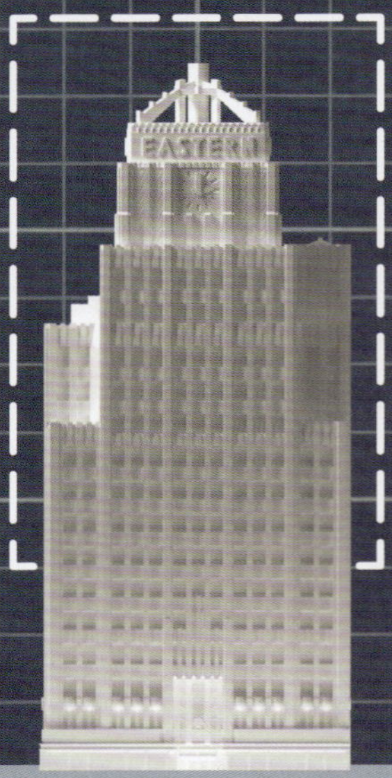

East Elevation *1" = 100'*

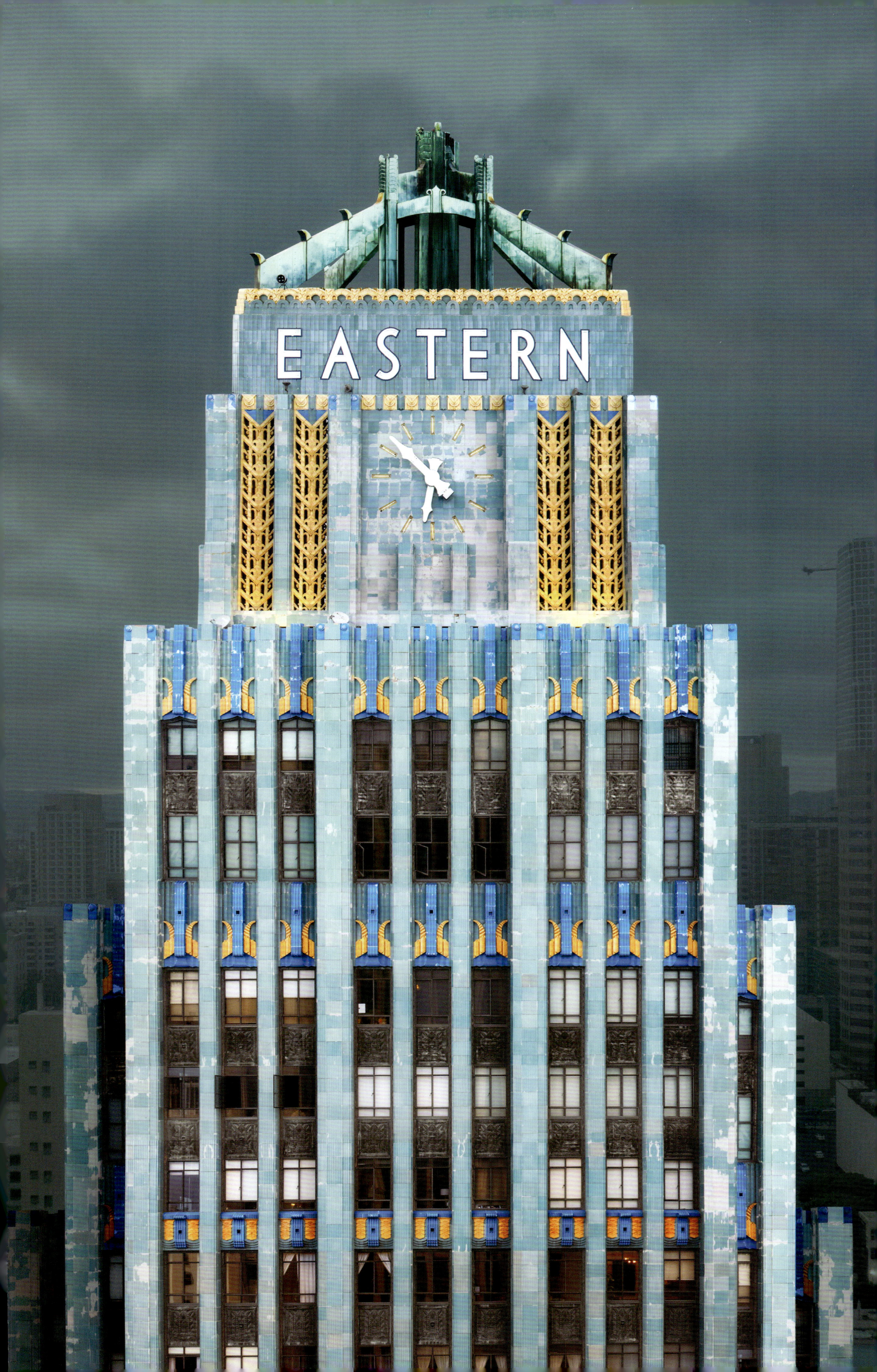
EASTERN

Bullock's Wilshire

Los Angeles, **CA** Southwestern Law School

Address	**3050 Wilshire Blvd.**
Opened	**1929**
Height	**241'**
Stories	**5**
Style	**Art Deco**
Architect	**John & Donald Parkinson**

Its copper-clad ornamental tower gleams "like a jewel of jade upon the breast of a Titan goddess," gushed one Los Angeles Times reviewer at the opening of this suburban retail temple. "It's almost sacrilege to call it a store," her colleague averred.

The five-story flagship was a grand gallery of modern design, displaying ladies' merchandise next to sophisticated murals, eye-catching clocks, and elevators straight out of a Kandinsky painting. Shoppers left their cars with a uniformed valet under a mural-adorned porte cochère to step into a sleek, pink marble hall redolent of perfume samples.

Store founder John Bullock drove a delivery wagon in his native Ontario before coming to Los Angeles alone as a teenager. He worked in a downtown department store and won over its owner, who encouraged Bullock to open his first store in 1907. Its success led to this establishment closer to Hollywood and other tony neighborhoods.

Later absorbed by Macy's, this Art Deco landmark closed in 1993 during the New York firm's bankruptcy. Southwestern Law School bought out the lease and extensively restored the property. It now houses faculty offices, a law library in the former sportswear department, and a mock courtroom where well-to-do women once shopped for purses and accessories.

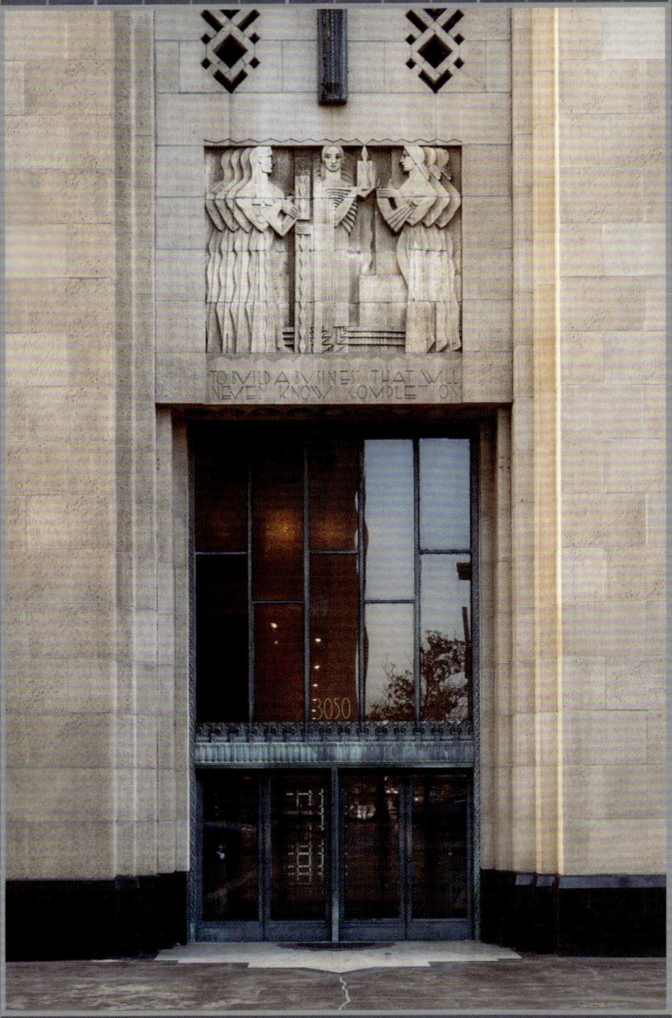

Local artist George Stanley sculpted this relief and also the statue for the Oscars, first awarded in 1929.

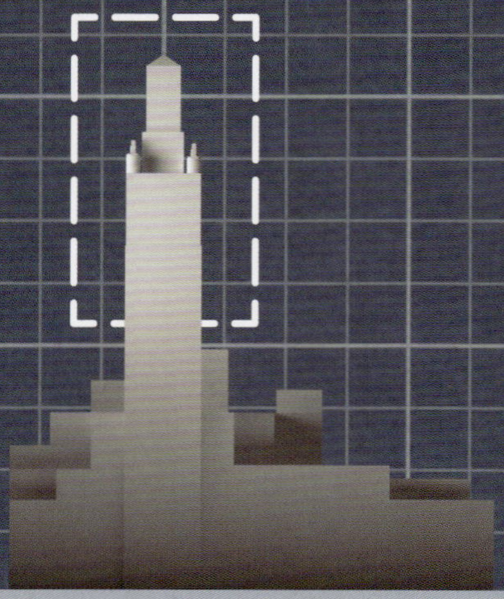

North Elevation 1" = 100'

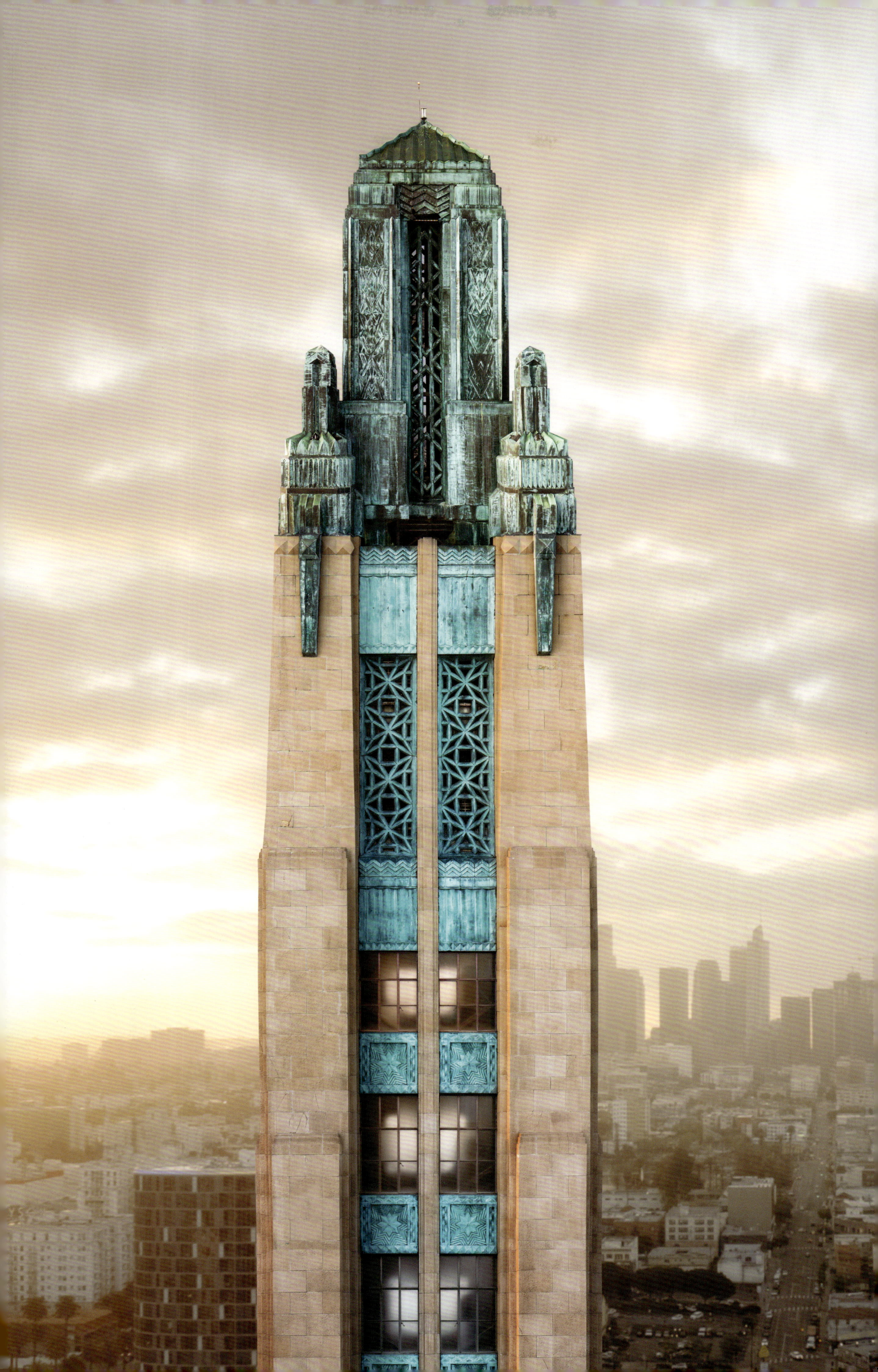

Los Angeles
City Hall

Los Angeles, **CA**

Address	**200 N. Spring St.**
Opened	**1928**
Height	**454'**
Stories	**28**
Style	**Neoclassical, Art Deco**
Architect	**John Parkinson**

As dazzling as a movie star's bleached smile, this glazed terracotta highrise towered over every other building in Los Angeles for more than 30 years. Its commanding position was due to a citywide height limit — one from which government buildings were exempt.

Designer John Parkinson had drawn up Los Angeles's first skyscraper, the 1904 Braly Building, four blocks down Spring Street. While that 175-foot tower was under construction, Parkinson was picked for a blue ribbon panel on proposed height restrictions. Its recommendations led to a 150-foot limit imposed for half a century, ensuring that the California sunshine beamed bright even downtown, in contrast to the shadowy skyscraper canyons of the east.

An English immigrant, Parkinson built fences in Winnipeg and stairs in Minneapolis before his first architectural commission, a bank extension in Napa. He moved on to design schools and commercial buildings in Seattle before settling in Los Angeles, where he enjoyed an enormously prolific career, completing in excess of 200 commissions, of which more than 50 still stand.

Offsetting the stark exterior is a soaring, arched third-floor rotunda rich with colorful tile mosaics and inlaid marble flooring. The observation deck is open to the public and displays portraits of every mayor since L.A.'s founding.

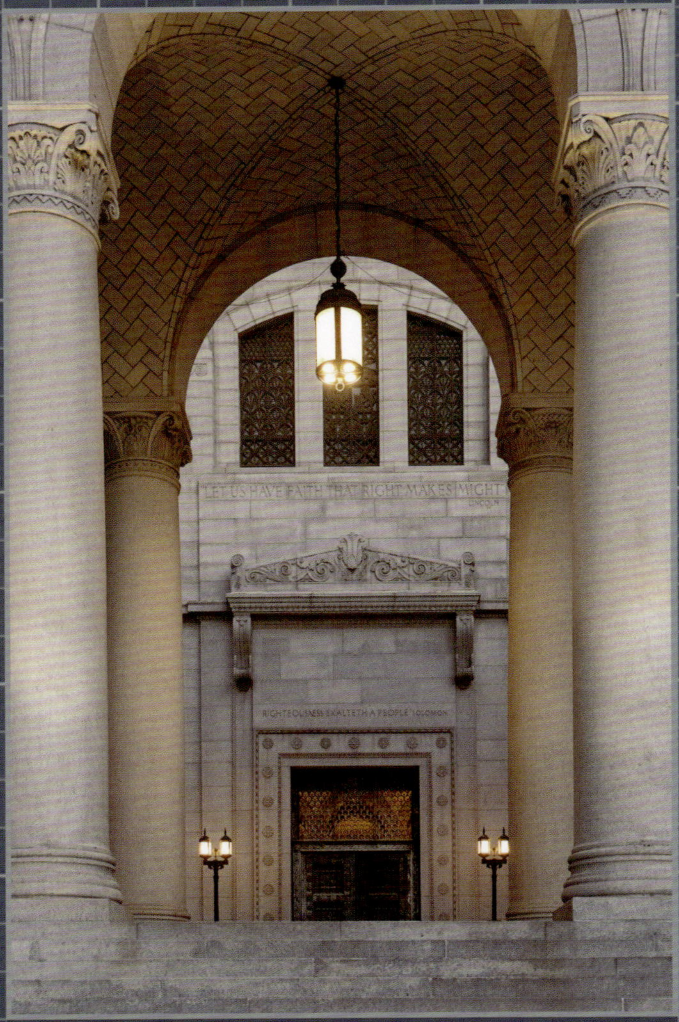

An arcade leads to the forecourt, with engraved quotations from Abraham Lincoln and King Solomon.

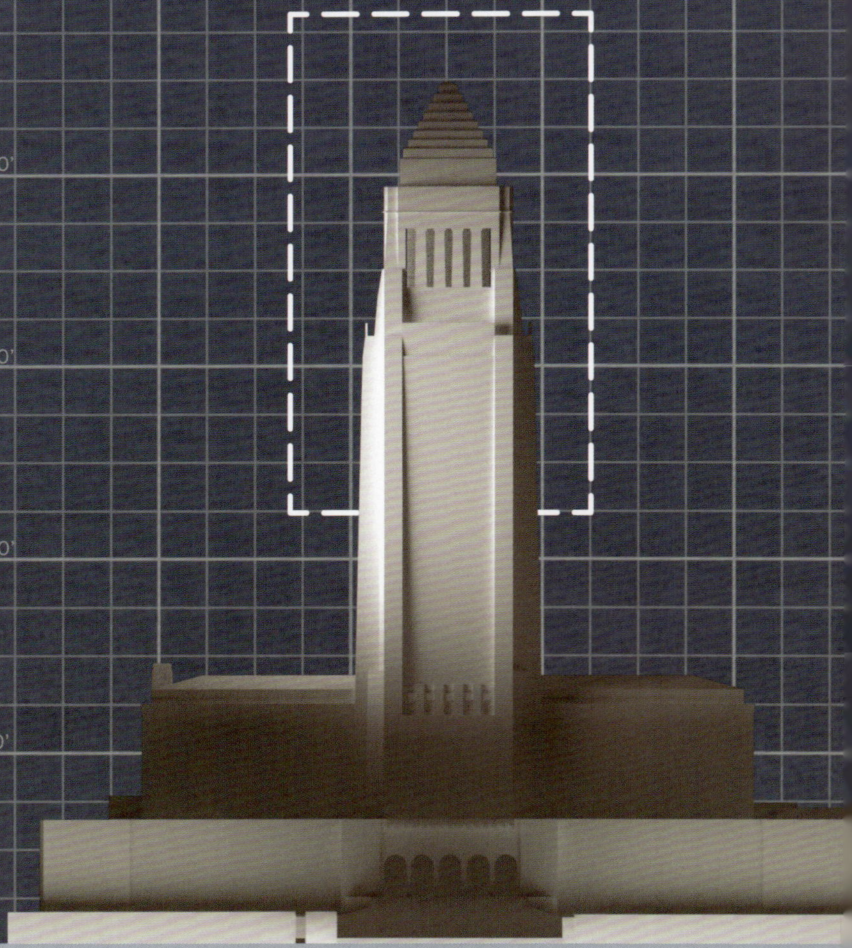

West Elevation *1" = 100'*

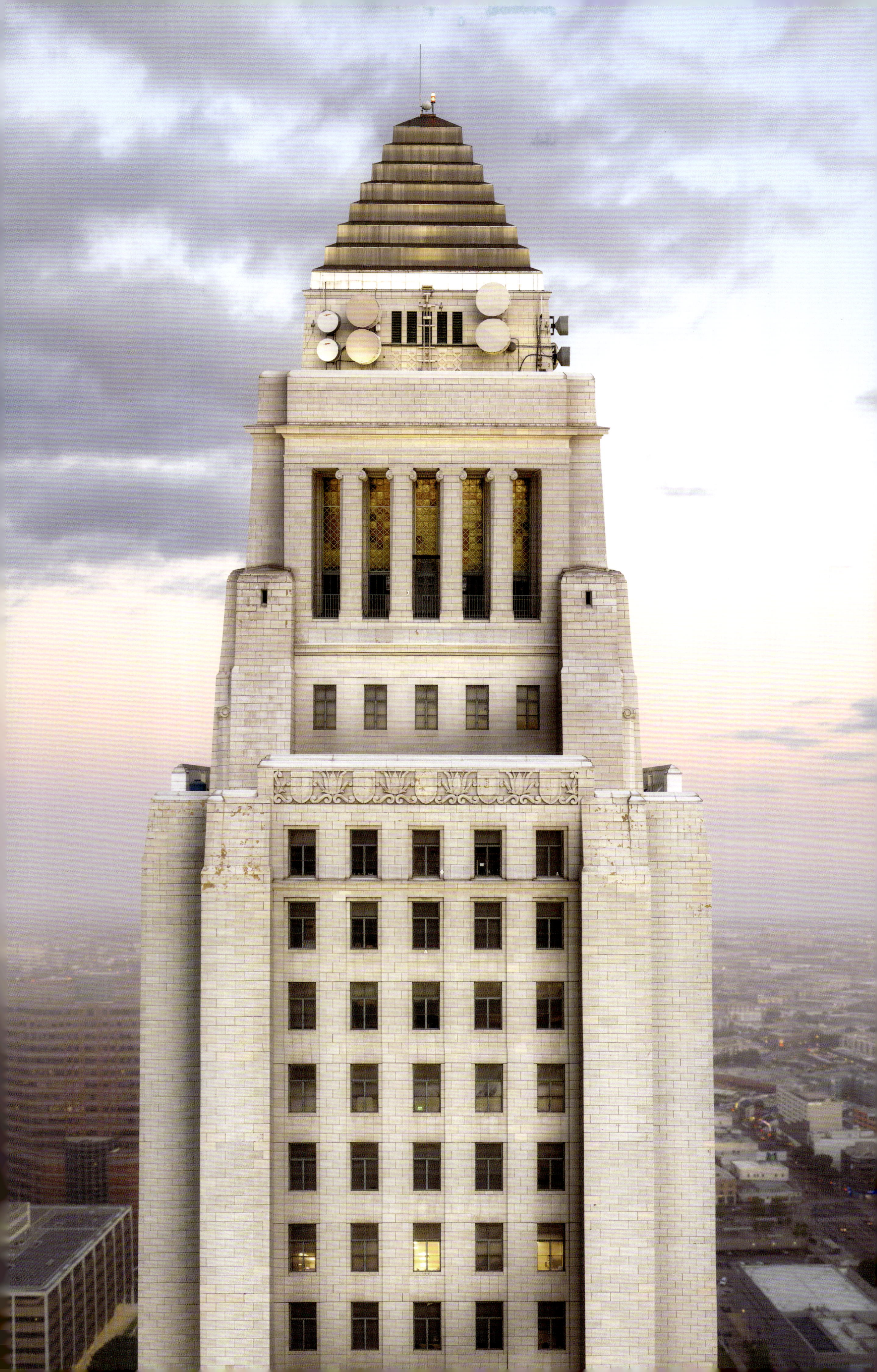

Pellissier Building

Los Angeles, **CA** Wiltern Theater

Address ··········· **3780 Wilshire Blvd.**
Opened ························ **1932**
Height ····························· **162'**
Stories ···························· **12**
Style ·························· **Art Deco**
Architect ··············· **Stiles Clements**

Towering above a fabulous Art Deco movie palace marquee that shields a bank of carved mahogany entrance doors, this highrise won a reprieve from the wrecking ball in 1980 and became an early success story for Los Angeles preservationists.

Its namesake, Germain Pellissier, was a French immigrant sheep rancher in the formerly agricultural district, and his flocks were renowned for their fine merino wool. His grandson Henry de Roulet developed this building on a subdivided parcel of the old family ranch, at the busy intersection of Wilshire and Western — combined in the Wiltern Theater name.

Film mogul Jack Warner personally attended the opening night gala for this, the first Warner Brothers cinema in the city's developing western reaches. But poor box office returns prompted the studio to drop its lease not long afterward, and the auditorium hosted a popular Sunday self-help preacher until arrangements were made to bring movies back under new management.

Thoroughly restored with energy efficient technology, the revitalized performance venue has a colorful period lobby and an auditorium dominated by a ceiling sunburst design from which seven stylized skyscrapers sprout. Step into the elevator from the multihued marble tower lobby and you will see the logo of former tenant Desilu Productions, the husband-and-wife team that created "I Love Lucy."

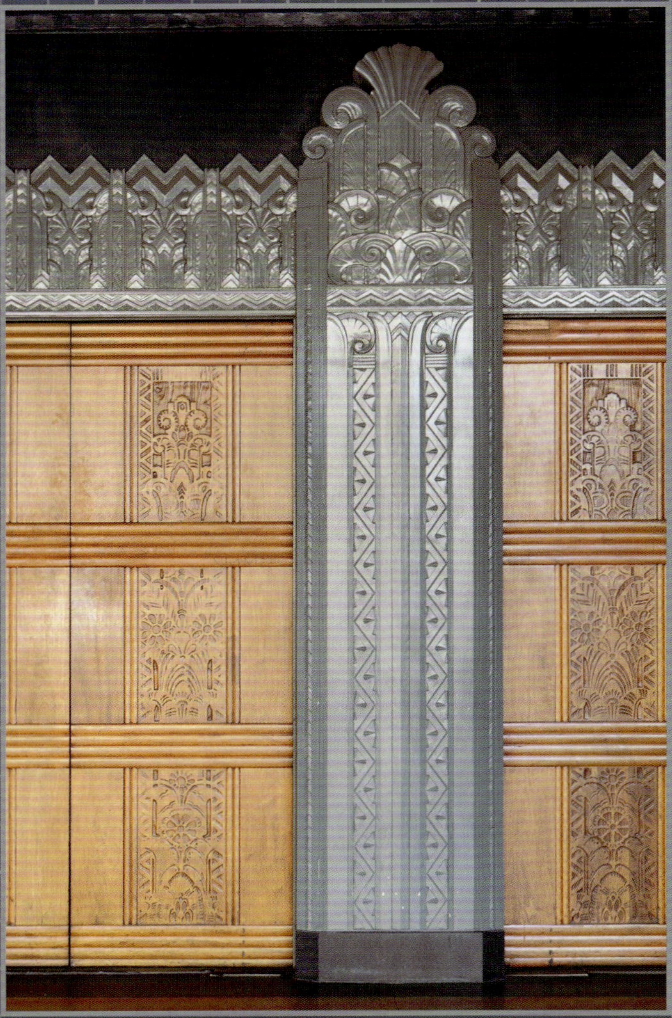

Original carved mahogany doors under the marquee have withstood the test of time.

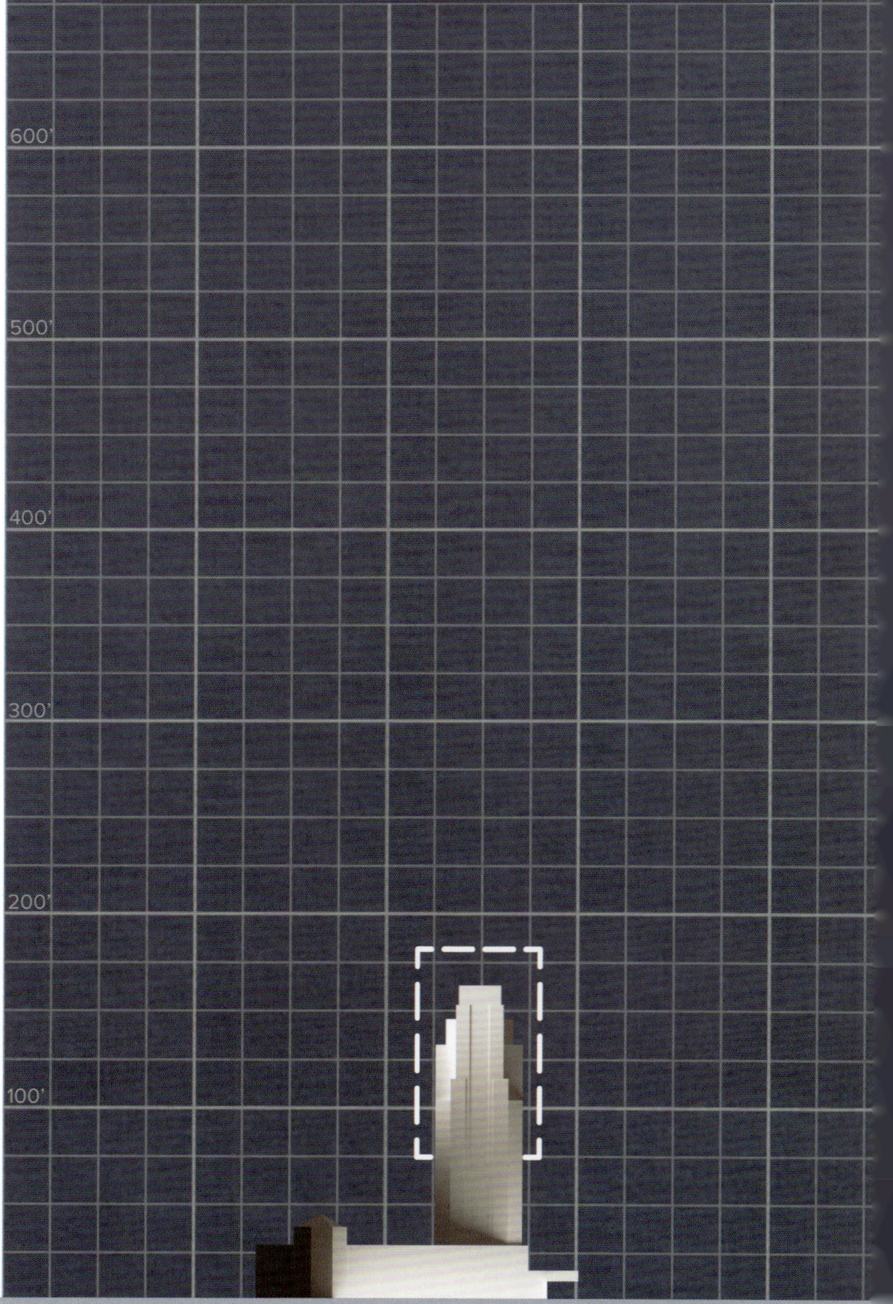

Northeast Elevation *1" = 100'*

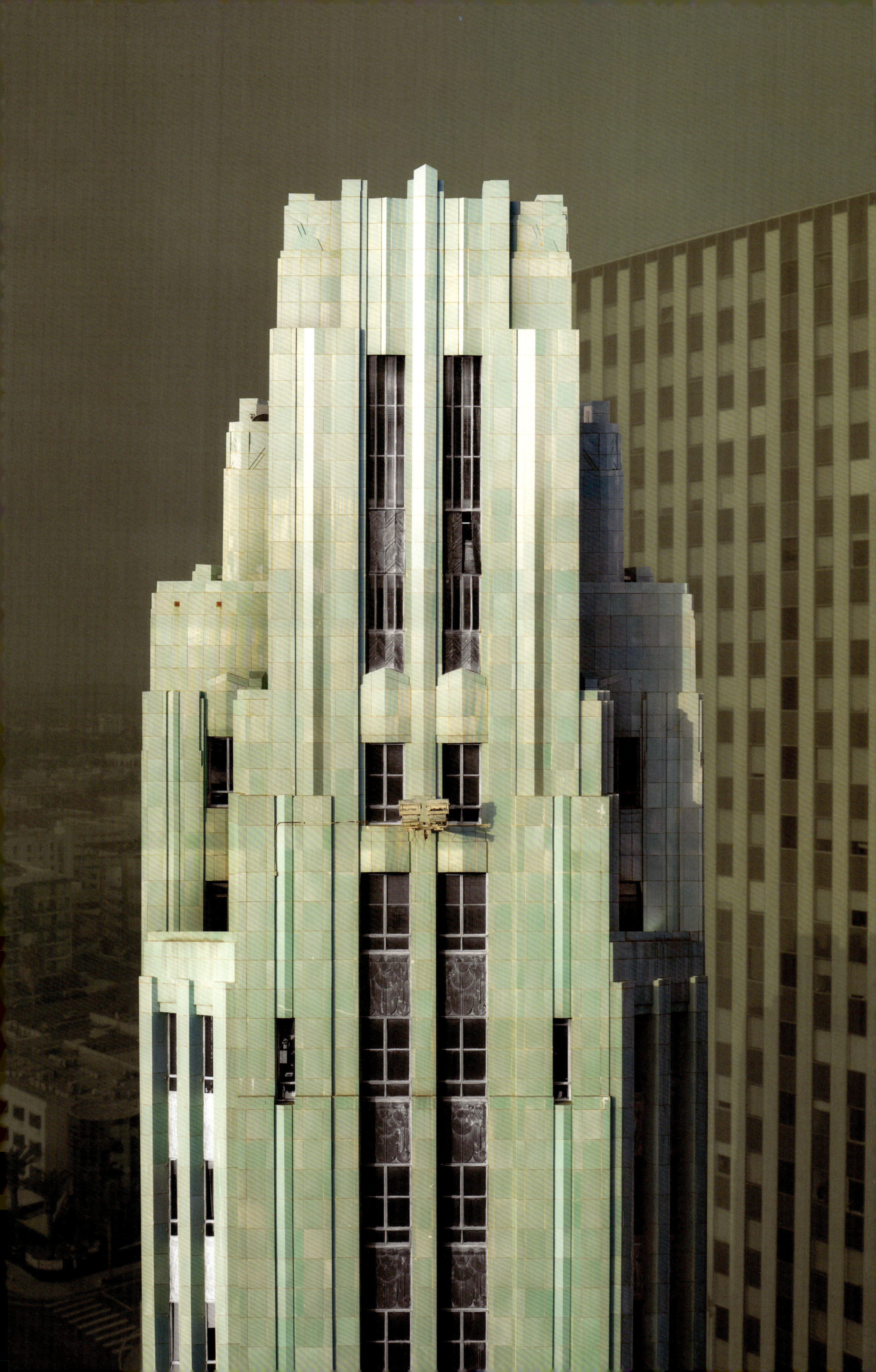

Garfield Building

Los Angeles, **CA**

Address	**403 W. Eighth St**
Opened	**1929**
Height	**191'**
Stories	**13**
Style	**Renaissance, Art Deco**
Architect	**Claud Beelman**

This speculative venture in commercial real estate for Sun Realty was one of a half dozen properties the developer named after Republican presidents. It has survived repeated financial false starts and long vacancies; the entry doors beneath its elegant wrought iron canopy have been barred for more than 30 years.

Soon after opening, the building was the scene of front-page news. An attorney there presented a $78,500 settlement check to his client, a Japanese immigrant widow, from the account of Lois Pantages, convicted of manslaughter after killing the woman's husband in a drunk driving crash. The next day, the convicted woman's husband, theater maven Alexander Pantages, was sentenced to prison for sexually assaulting a young dancer. Yet the power couple would each see their convictions overturned, leading many to conclude that justice was for sale in California.

One person with few doubts on that score was the widow's attorney, former city council president William Bonelli, who used his fee to settle debts from a failed mayoral campaign. Bonelli then won a seat on the state assembly, and soon used his influence in Sacramento to trade liquor licenses for bribes. When exposed, the corrupt politico fled to Mexico and stayed there the rest of his life.

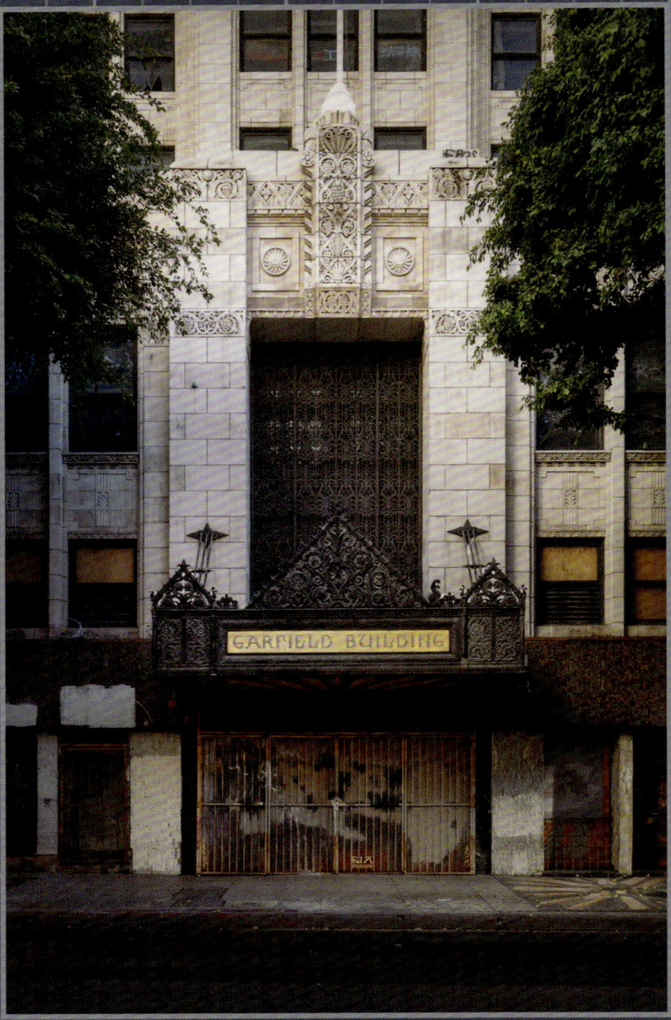

The iron canopy, a replica of the original, extends the patterns of the grillework and terracotta.

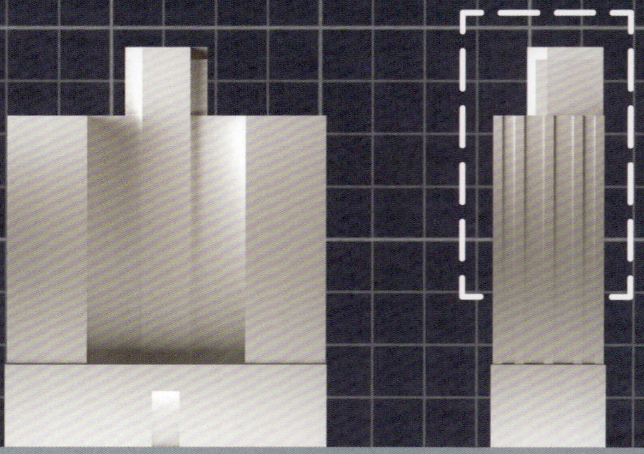

Southwest Elevation Southeast Elevation *1" = 100'*

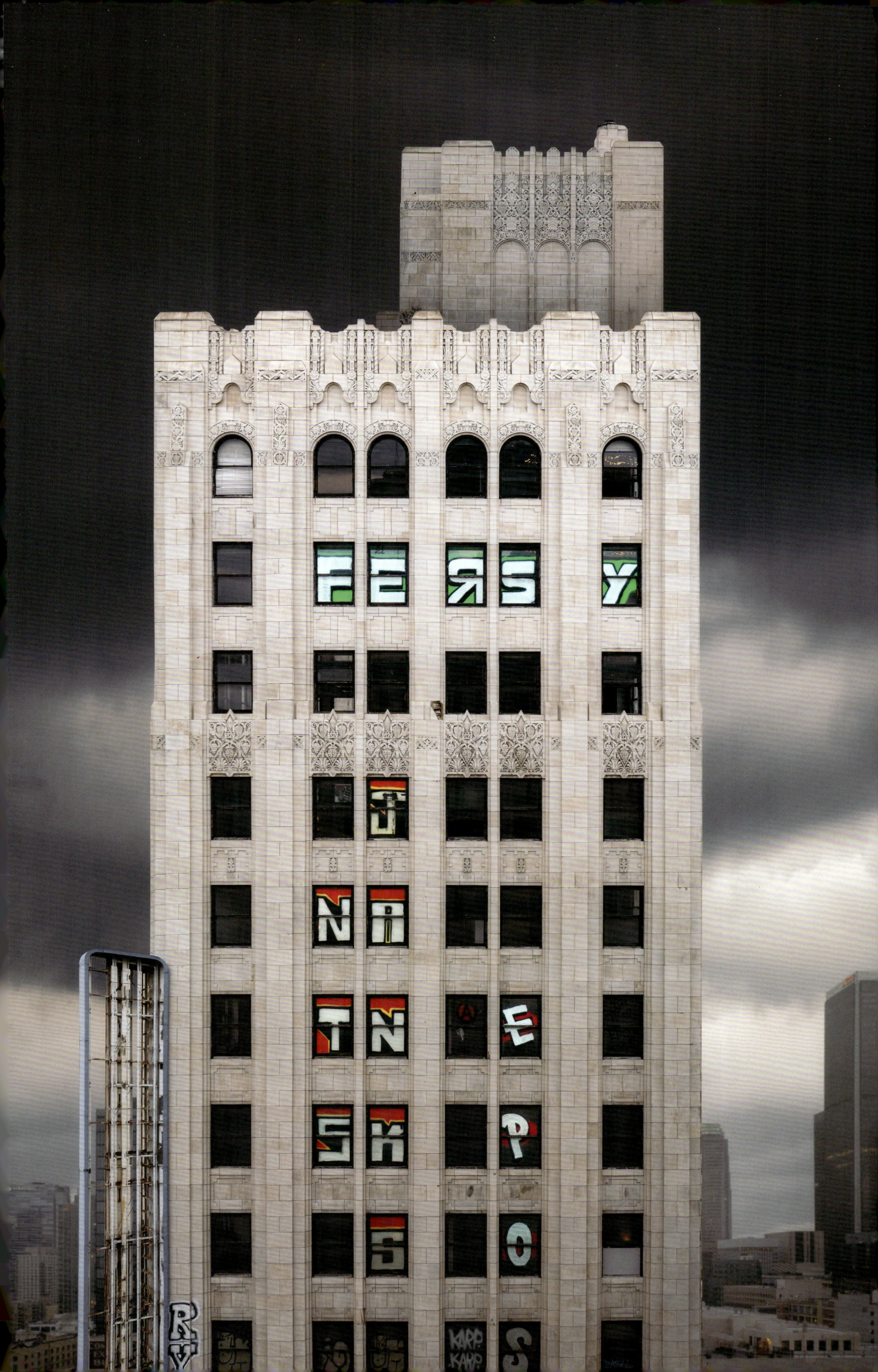

Sun Realty
Building

Los Angeles, **CA** L.A. Jewelry Center

Address ········ **629 S. Hill St.**
Opened ········ **1931**
Height ········ **191'**
Stories ········ **13**
Style ········ **Art Deco**
Architect ········ **Claud Beelman**

If the aqua green tile skin of this highrise seems to come from the same palette as the electric blue Eastern Columbia Building, it is because both Art Deco classics are products of the same architect, one with an uncanny ability to adapt to the times.

Claud Beelman first worked with tints as a painter in his dad's Ohio carriage shop. As an architect in Los Angeles, Beelman employed virtually every popular commercial style over the decades, from Beaux-Arts to International. Active into his 70s, Beelman got to design the first L.A. skyscraper to rise after voters in 1958 repealed the city's height limit: an 18-story bank slab sheathed in aluminum panels.

He was a favorite architect of Sun Realty, which began as the property arm of Sun Drug, a pharmacy chain with locations in office buildings it also owned. In 1924 the president, a Polish immigrant and former tailor named Isidor Eisner, sold the drugstores to a bigger competitor but held onto the office buildings and erected more, including this one, hoping to capitalize on sky-high downtown rental rates.

When rents plunged in the Depression, Sun Realty folded. Its gem of a headquarters has been a retail jewelry exchange since 1978.

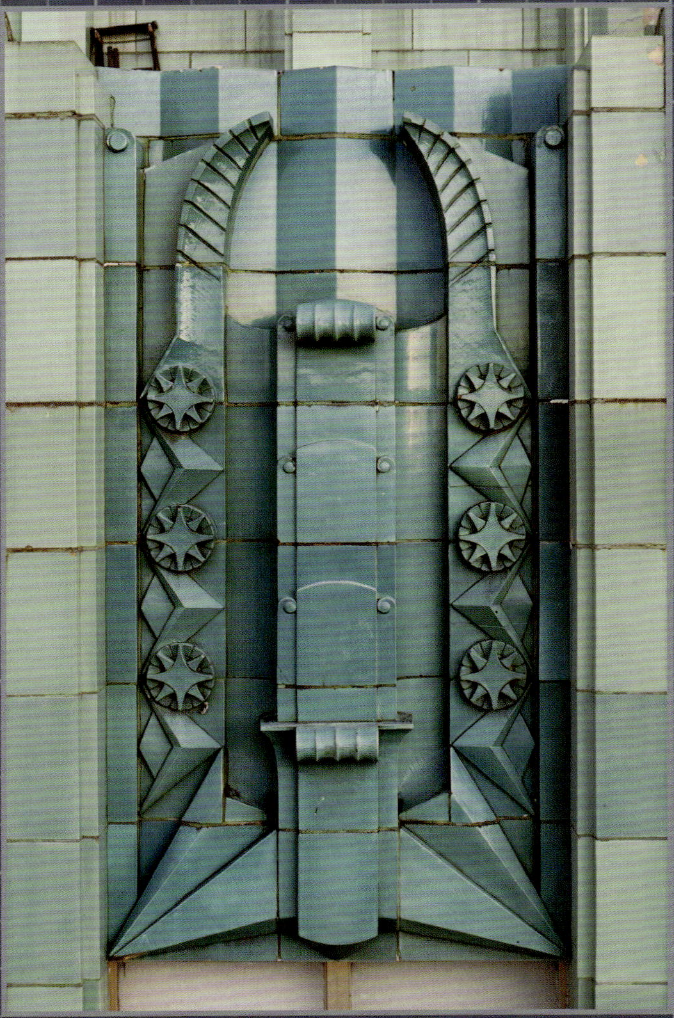

The abstract sculptures look like lobsters, but the ones with big claws live in the Atlantic Ocean, not the Pacific.

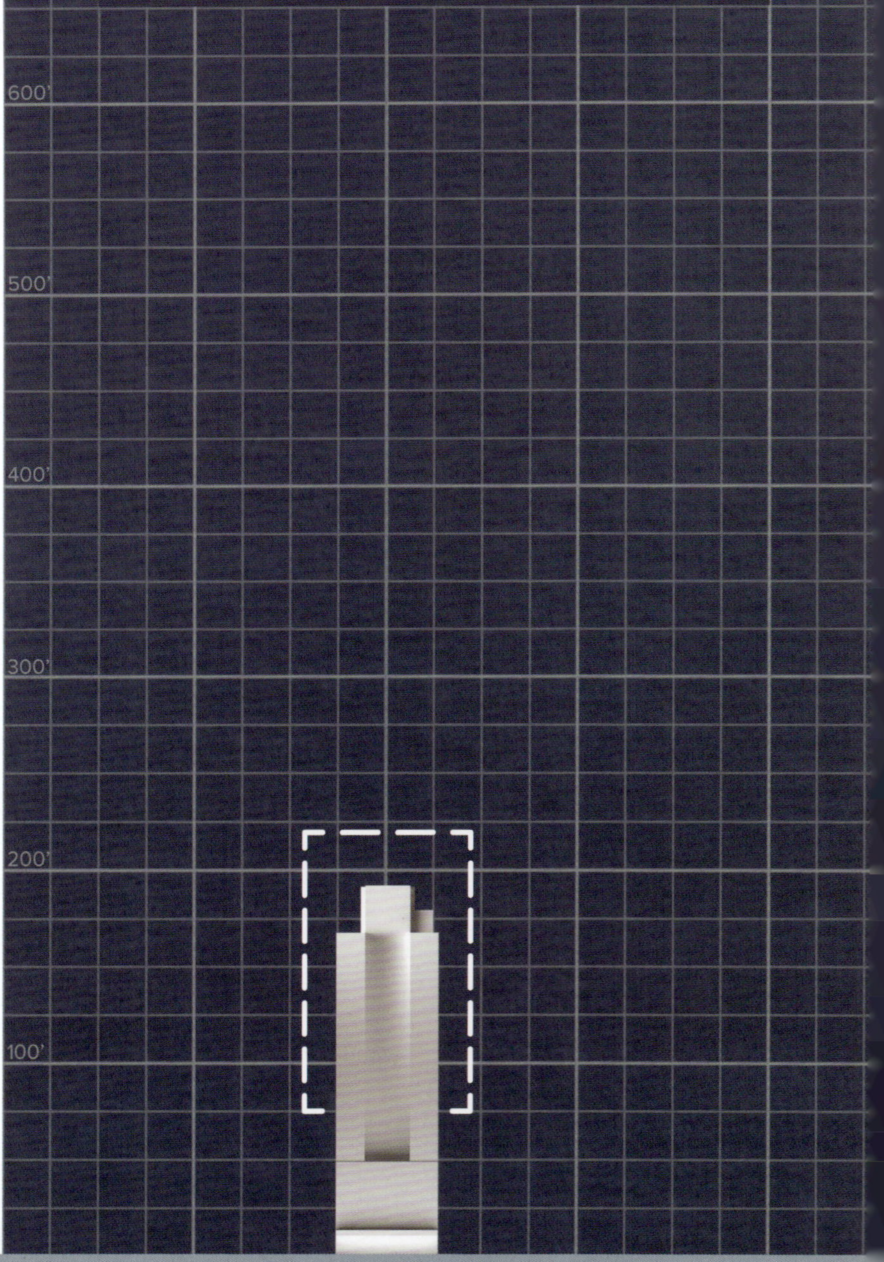

Southeast Elevation *1" = 100'*

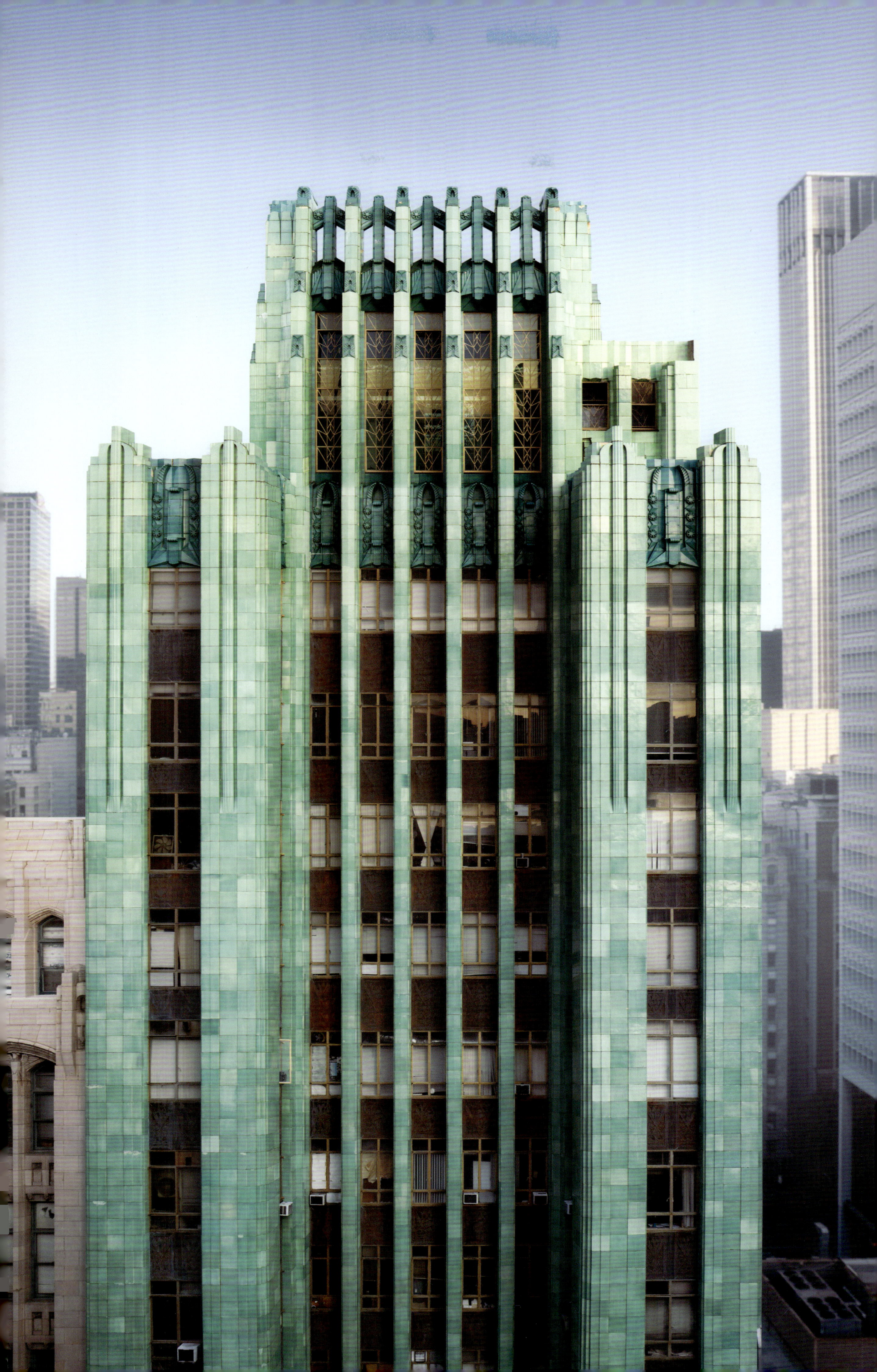

Wilshire Professional
Building

Los Angeles, **CA**

Address ············ **3875 Wilshire Blvd.**
Opened ························· **1929**
Height ···························· **181'**
Stories ···························· **13**
Style ······················· **Art Deco**
Architect ················ **Arthur Harvey**

This highrise in the showy Art Deco style known as Zigzag Moderne was constructed for real estate developer Preston Wright to house offices for doctors and dentists. The contractors who poured its concrete form also installed a terrazzo sidewalk in front that remains today.

Gaylord Wilshire, namesake of the building and the boulevard, was a land developer and an ardent socialist. The son of a rich Cincinnati banker, Wilshire purchased 35 acres of farmland west of what is now MacArthur Park and offered to give the city a strip down the middle as long as the road was named after him and permitted no train tracks or heavy trucks.

Wilshire ran as a socialist for Congress three times — and for the British Parliament once while married to a Welsh woman — but was unsuccessful each time. He also founded a magazine, "The Challenge," and a quack medical company, Ionaco, that made an electric plug-in belt Wilshire claimed could cure cancer, tuberculosis, arthritis, and a host of other ailments by magnetizing the iron in its wearer's blood.

The building has been vacant for years and is tagged with graffiti. Its owner, one of Koreatown's biggest landlords, is building an eight-story apartment complex behind it.

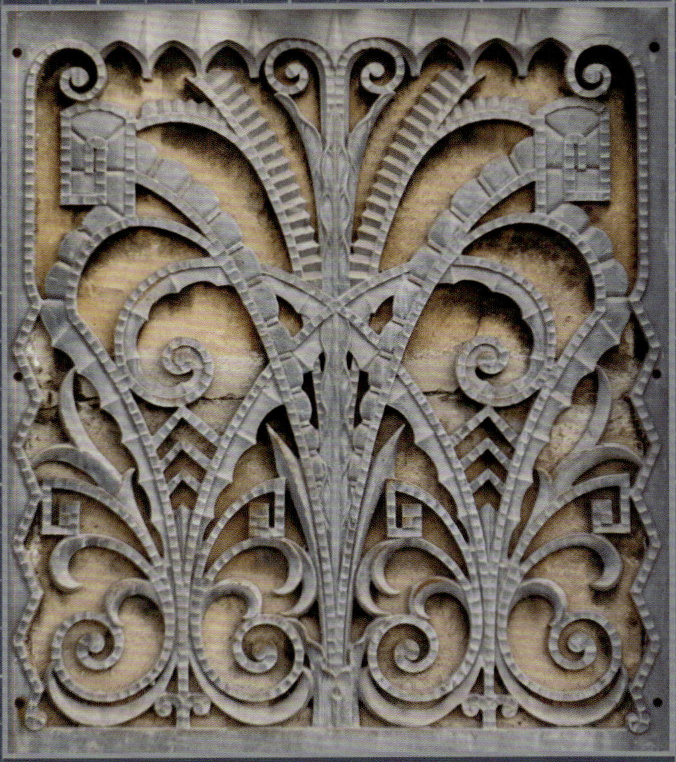

Floral designs on the metal spandrel panels complement the flowing forms that accent the exterior.

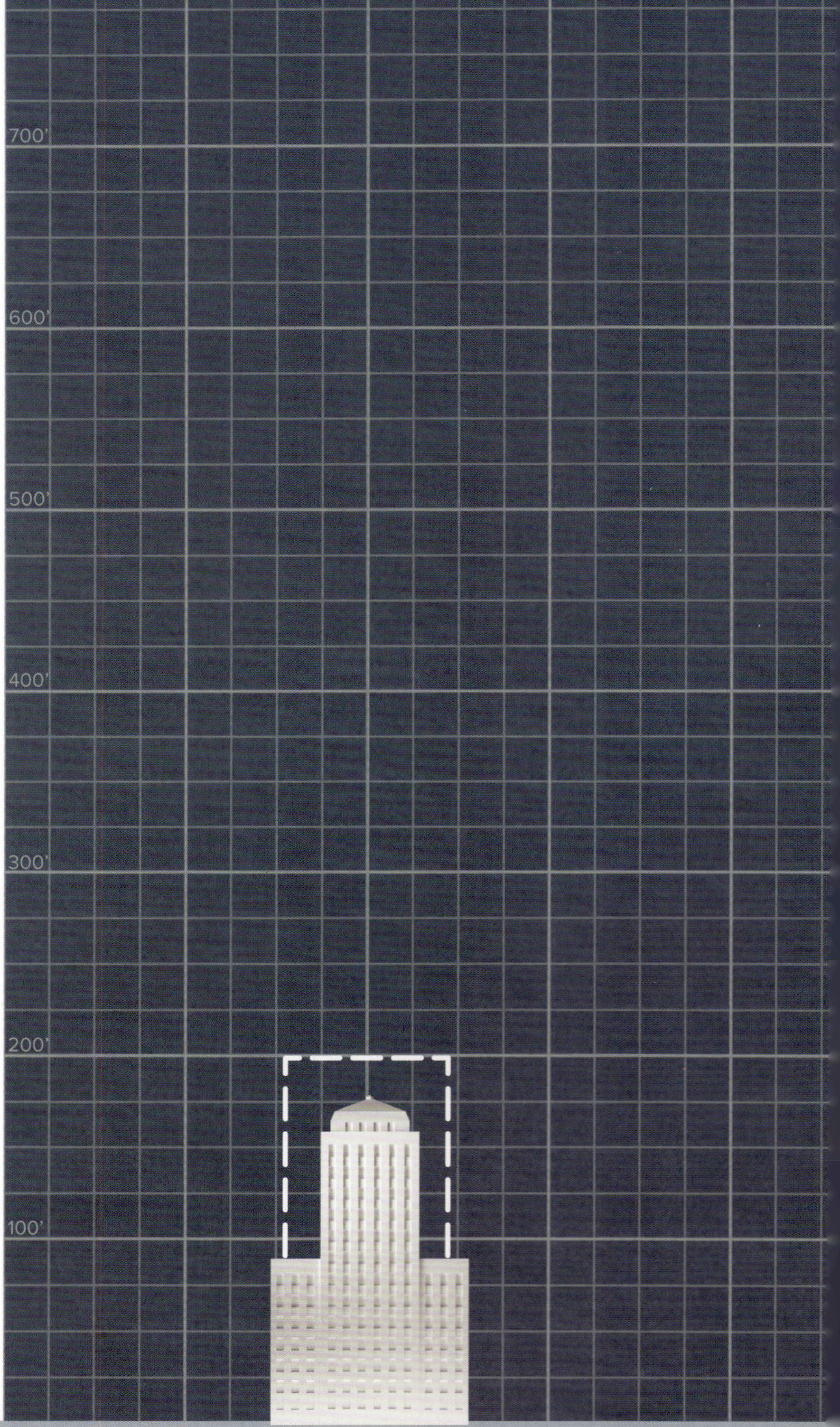

East Elevation *1" = 100'*

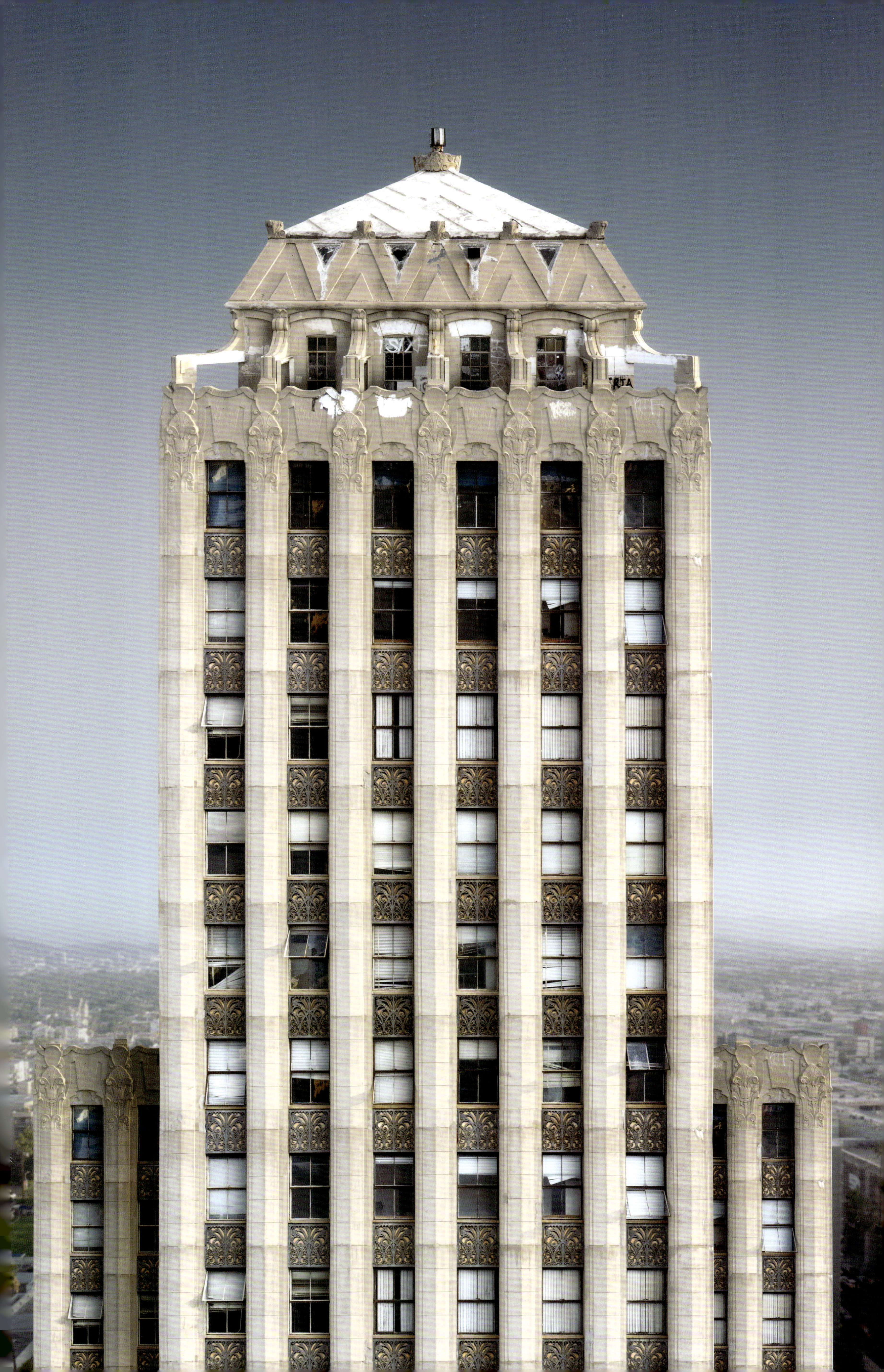

Wilshire Tower

Los Angeles, **CA** Desmond Tower

Address ·········· **5514 Wilshire Blvd.**
Opened ·························· **1929**
Height ··························· **160'**
Stories ····························· **11**
Style ······················· **Art Deco**
Architect ·········· **Gilbert Underwood**

This tower is barely half the height of the spire on the Wilshire Grand, L.A.'s tallest skyscraper. Yet it is historic nonetheless, as the first highrise on the Miracle Mile stretch of Wilshire Boulevard. By luring two department stores five miles from the city center to a site within whiffing distance of the La Brea Tar Pits, Wilshire Tower heralded the age of the automobile.

The future thoroughfare was a dirt road flanked by oil wells in 1921, when developer A.W. Wood bought 18 roadside acres. By decade's end, more than 70,000 cars a day motored past his new block-long complex, and more than a few turned to take advantage of its ample rear parking lot. This was the first highrise for architect Gilbert Underwood, who had earned notice with his national park lodges at Yosemite, Yellowstone, and Bryce Canyon.

Despite anchor stores Desmond's and Silverwoods closing long ago, their rooftop signs remain landmarks in their own right. The tower escaped demolition in the 1980s and recently has been in the midst of extensive renovation. A bronze bust honoring Wood, the prescient developer, stands five blocks west of this building, his signature triumph.

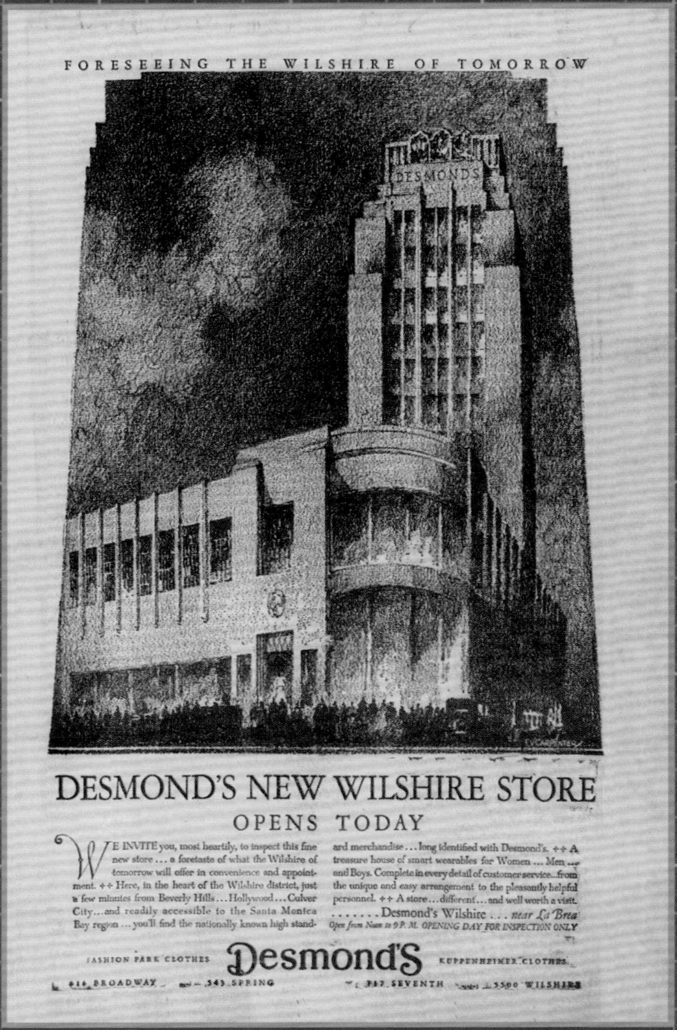

When it opened, this was the fourth Desmond's in the city and the first outside the downtown area.

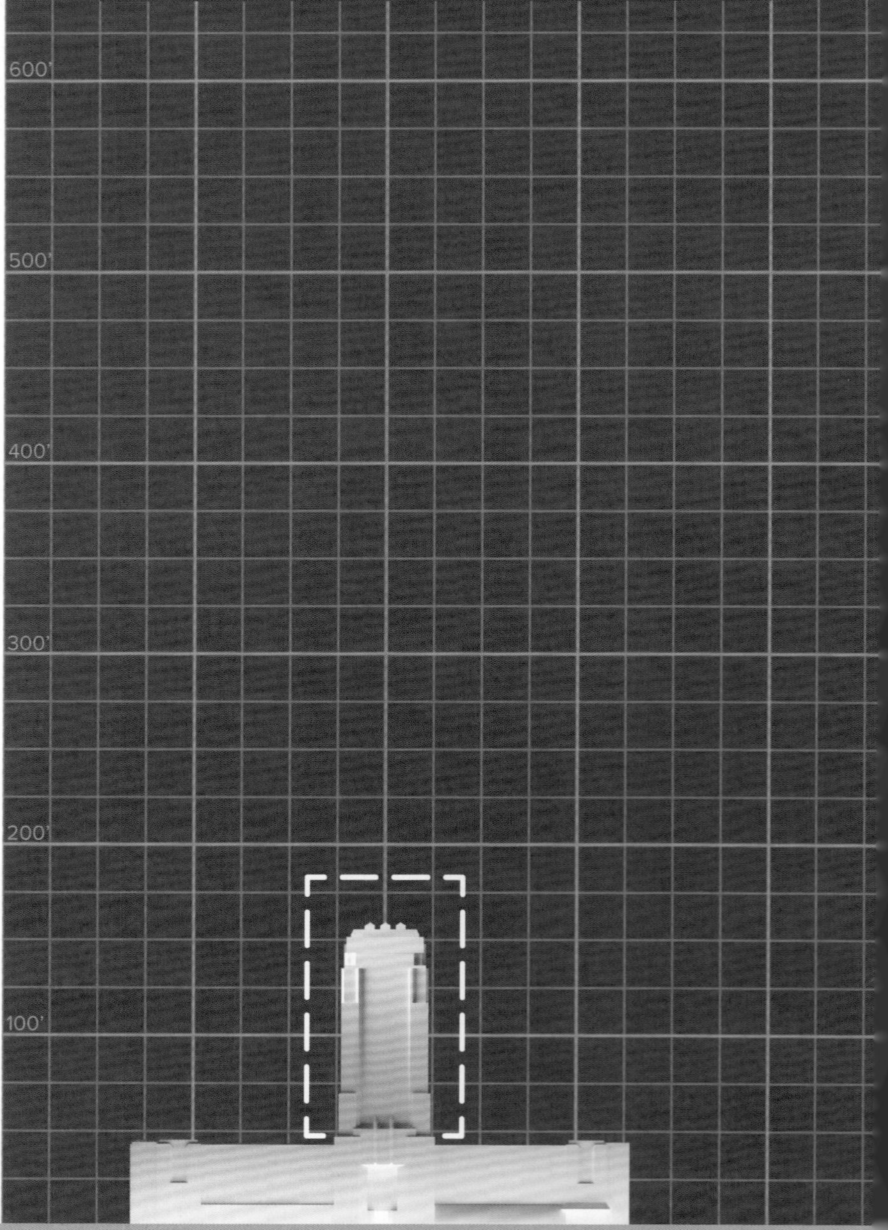

North Elevation *1" = 100'*

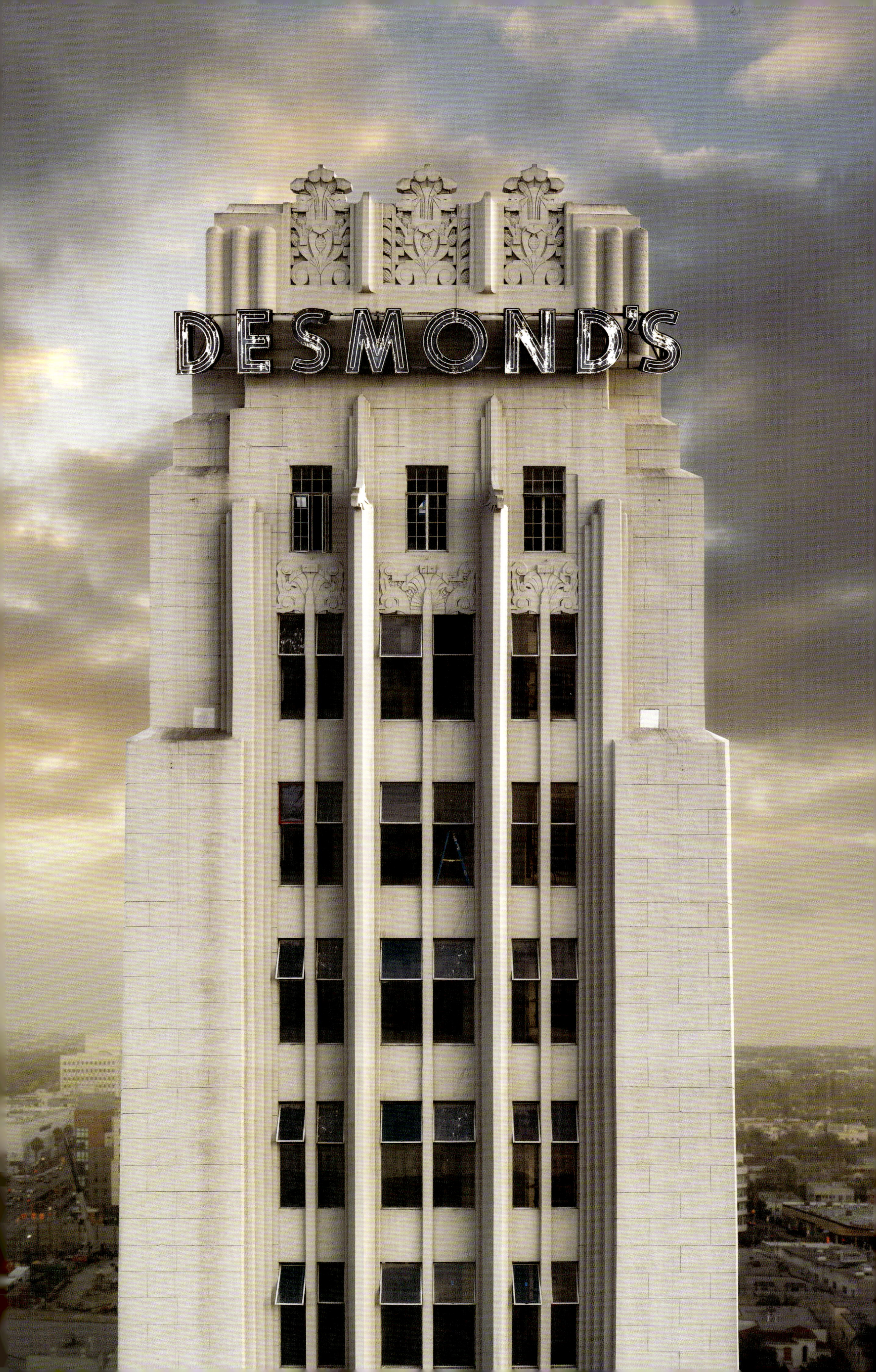
DESMOND'S

Financial Center
Building

Oakland, **CA**

Address ········ **405 14th St.**
Opened ········ **1929**
Height ········ **215'**
Stories ········ **16**
Style ········ **Art Deco, Renaissance**
Architect ········ **Reed & Corlett**

Oakland attorney Harrison Robinson and two business partners built this tower for investment and insurance firms. Robinson played an active civic role, heading a committee that established a public health clinic in 1921 in memory of Ethel Moore, a leading social worker and activist. He then became president of the Oakland Chamber of Commerce, which would later lease the third floor of Harrison's highrise.

Perhaps most consequentially, he personally lobbied Herbert Hoover to provide federal funds to build the Bay Bridge. Harrison headed the bridge's finance committee during its construction and served as the master of ceremonies in 1936 for its dedication, when the governor, instead of cutting a ribbon, severed a golden chain with an acetylene torch.

Terracotta trim at the base features eagles, shields emblazoned with "FCB," and a pair of rams glowering over the entryway. The modern massing and lines of the exterior transition to wrought-iron railings and a bronze decorative motif of Romans in profile in the two-story marble lobby. Architects Walter Reed and William Corlett would more fully commit to Art Deco in their next project, a ziggurat-like Palo Alto hospital known as Hoover Pavilion.

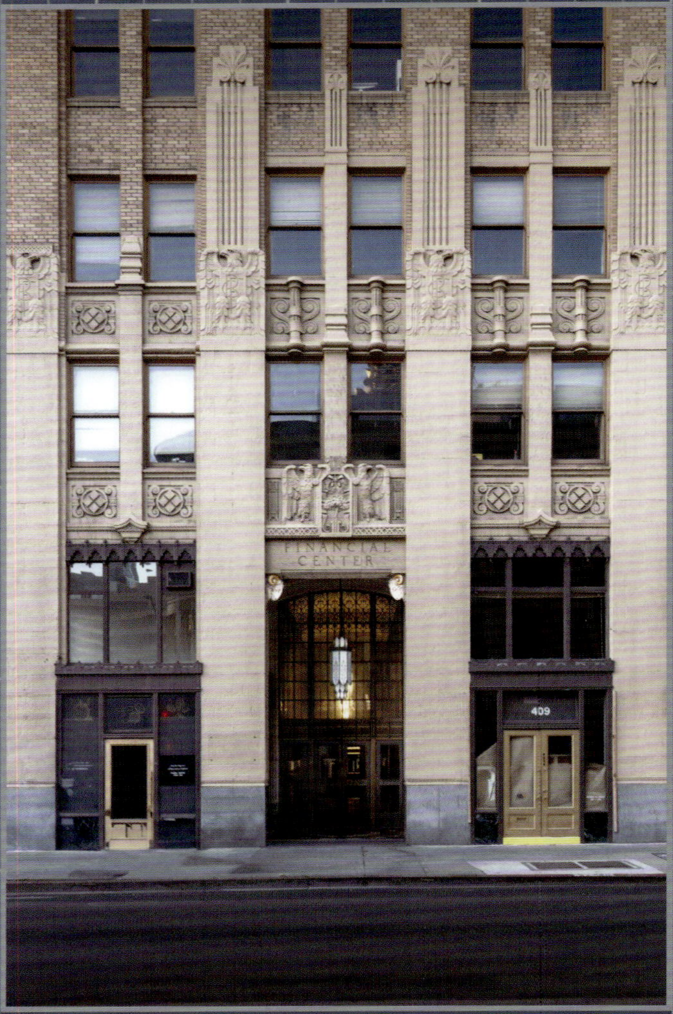

A gray granite base and black iron shopfronts create an interplay with creamy terracotta and tan bricks.

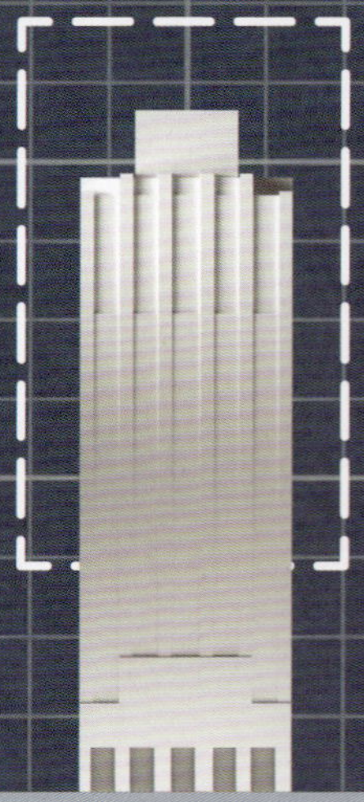

North Elevation *1" = 100'*

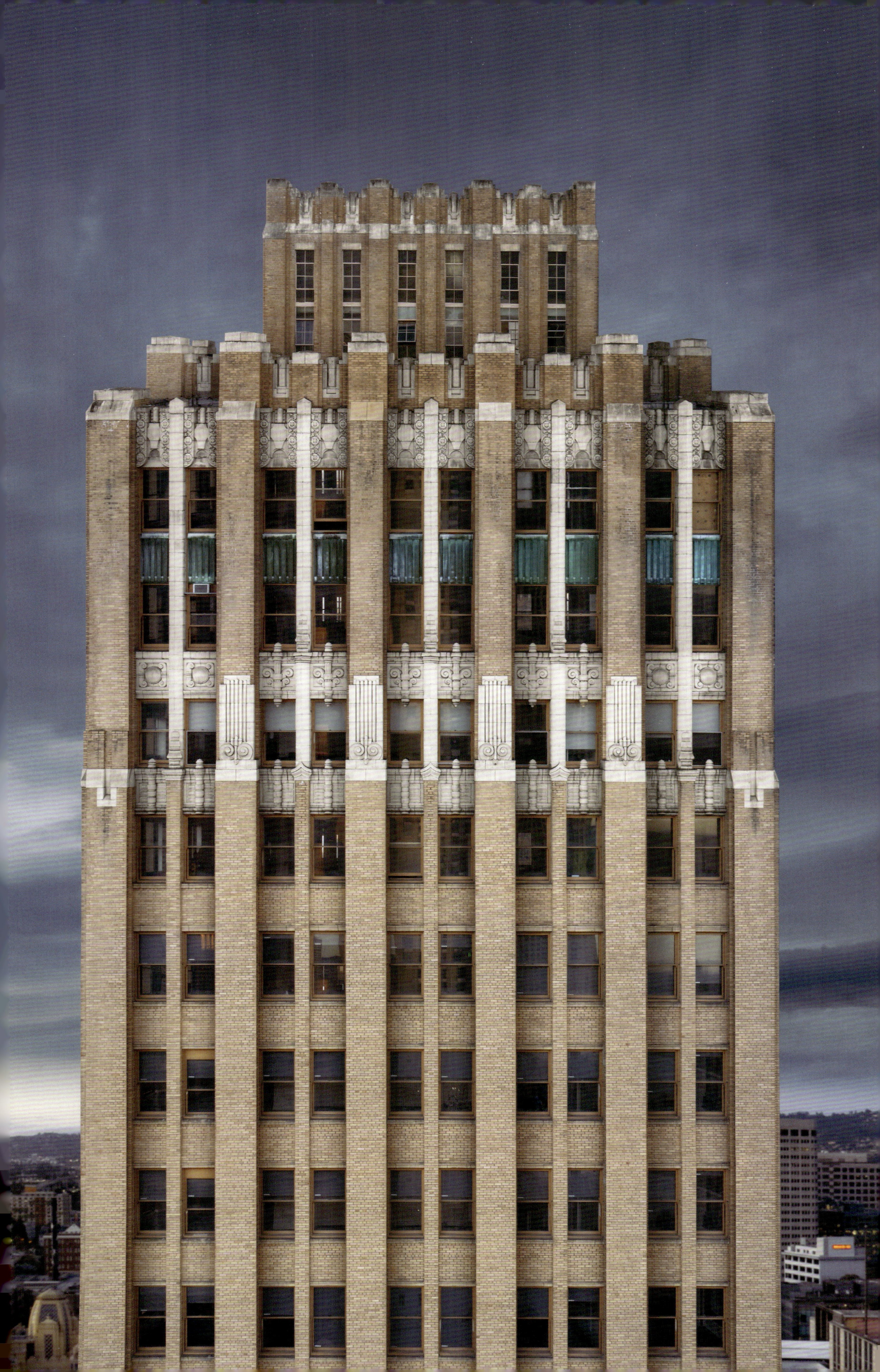

Tribune Tower

Oakland, **CA**

Address	**409 Thirteenth St.**
Opened	**1923**
Height	**305'**
Stories	**20**
Style	**Renaissance**
Architect	**Edward Foulkes**

The newspaper it advertises ceased to exist, but this campanile-style tower encircled in electric orange neon remains a treasured element of the Oakland skyline. Its former owners were politicians who both turned to publishing after their reach for higher office exceeded their grasp.

Alameda native Joseph Knowland, son of a prosperous lumber merchant, served six terms as a Republican congressman, then bought the Oakland Tribune after losing a race for senator. He relocated the paper to a six-story furniture company showroom in 1918, added the tower five years later, and began grooming his son, William, for bigger things.

The younger Knowland got as far as senate majority leader, but flopped in an ill-advised run for governor in 1958. Succeeding his father as publisher, Knowland became increasingly burdened by gambling debts. In 1974, two days after commemorating the newspaper's 100th anniversary, he shot himself.

The elevator goes to the 20th floor, where radio station KLX once had its studios behind the clock. Up two flights of unfinished stairs is the workshop of neon light caretaker and renegade artist John Law, one of the founders of Burning Man.

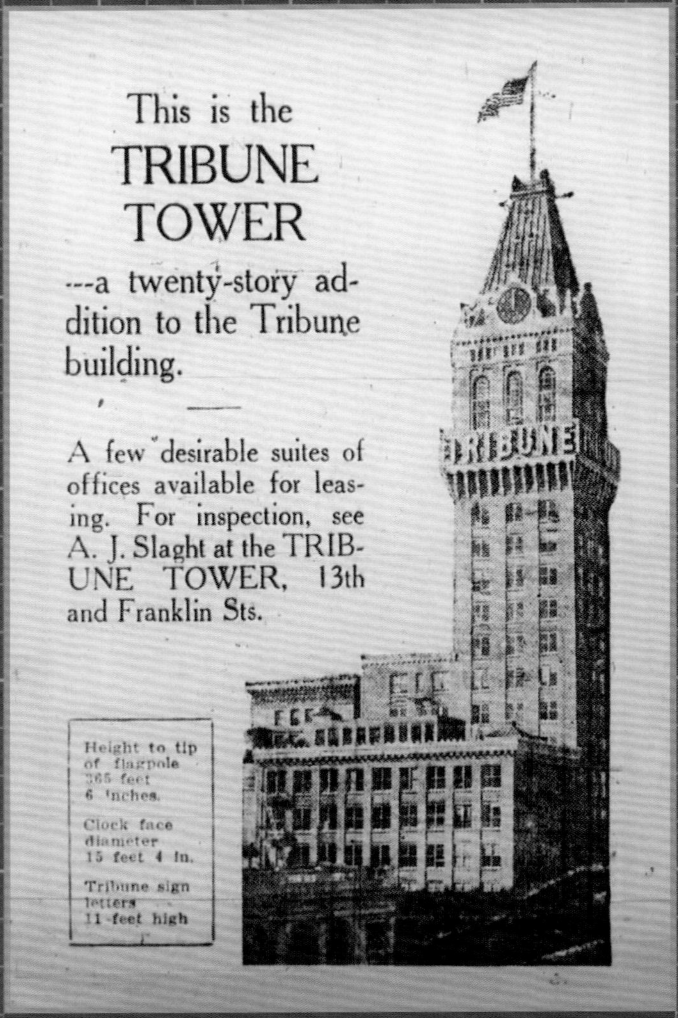

The sign, shown in this 1923 ad, was one of the first uses of commercial neon lighting in the United States.

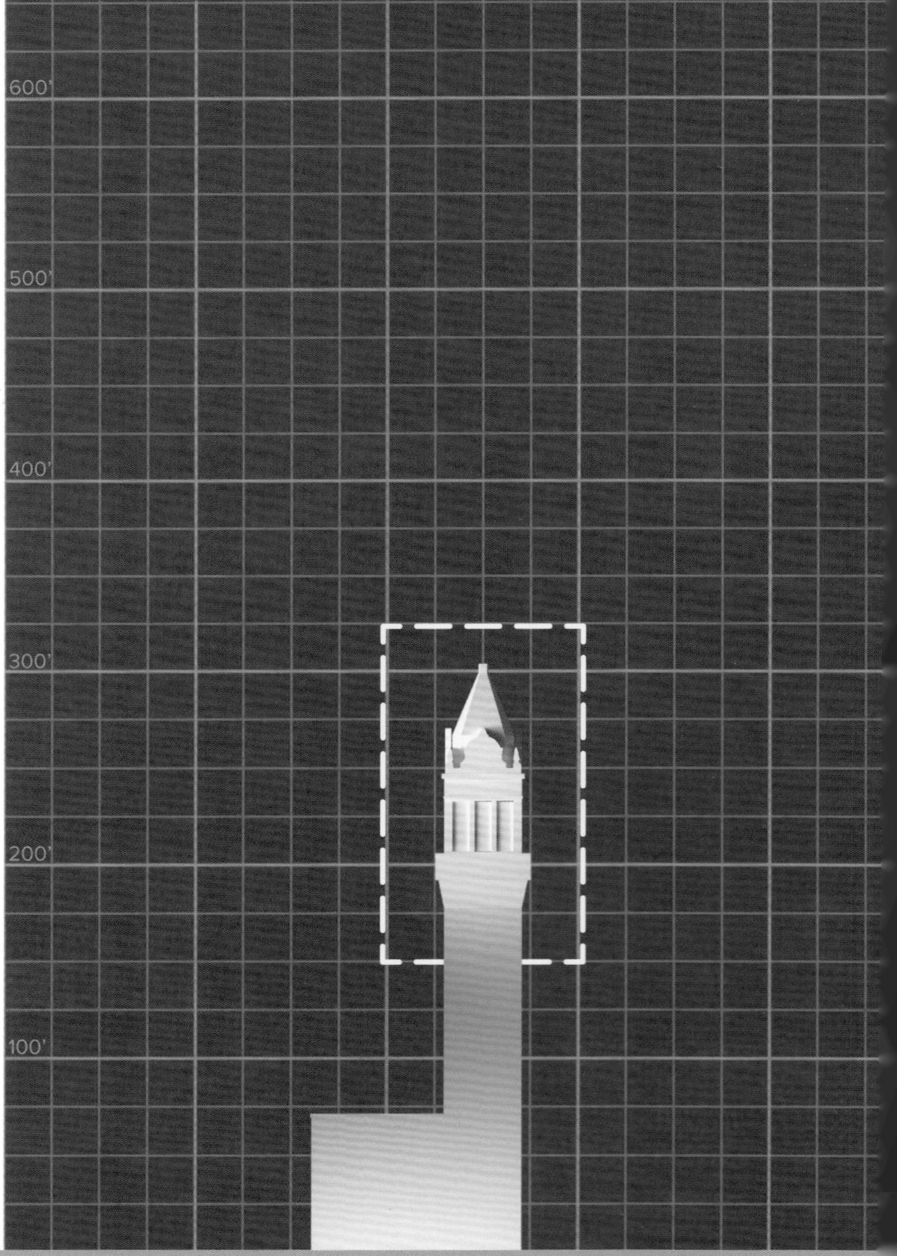

North Elevation 1" = 100'

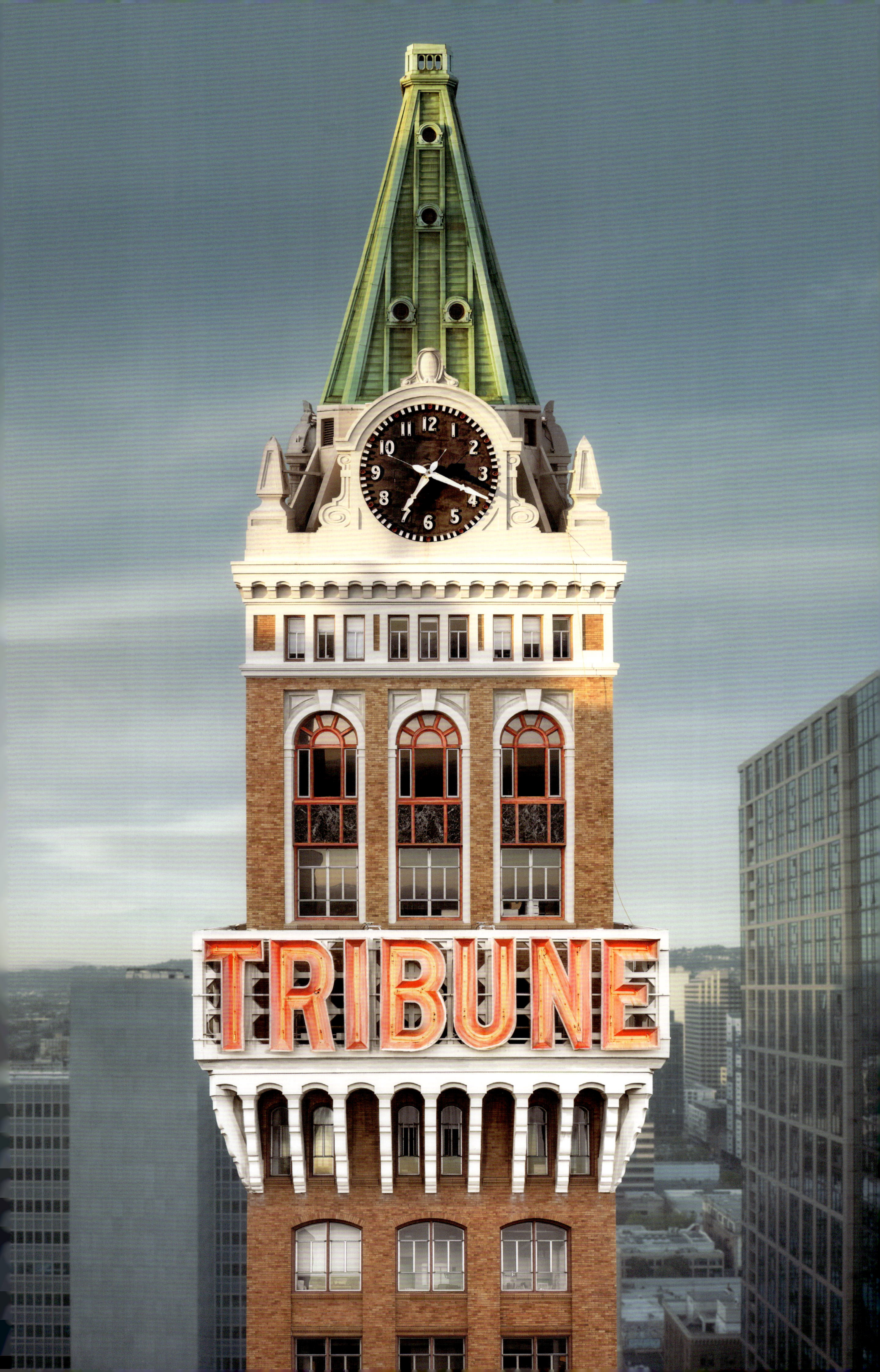
TRIBUNE

450 Sutter

San Francisco, **CA**

Address	**450 Sutter St.**
Opened	**1929**
Height	**350'**
Stories	**26**
Style	**Art Deco**
Architect	**Miller & Pflueger**

Bold Mayan decorative motifs and a strikingly unique silhouette make this building a singular specimen of Art Deco's outer limits.

Timothy Pflueger designed it for a dentist, Dr. Francis Morgan, who dabbled in real estate and wanted another medical and dental complex like one he had opened in Los Angeles. The T-shaped tower he got has a lobby so dazzlingly ornamented in burgundy marble, cast aluminum elevators, and gilded reverse-ziggurat ceiling and light fixtures that patients exiting might wonder if their anesthesia has truly worn off.

After this project, Pflueger's affinity for the avant-garde led him to lure muralist Diego Rivera to San Francisco for several commissions, including a series of giant concrete panels for the World's Fair on Treasure Island in 1940. Rivera rewarded his patron by portraying the architect and two of his skyscrapers — this one and Pacific Telephone & Telegraph (p. 156) — on the panels. Pflueger's theatricality also made him a natural at designing movie palaces and luxe hotel lounges.

One noteworthy physician who practiced at 450 Sutter was Dr. Harry Benjamin, a pioneering sexologist. Benjamin was among the first to offer hormonal treatment and surgical referrals to patients wishing to change gender, and he wrote a groundbreaking 1966 medical textbook, *The Transsexual Phenomenon.*

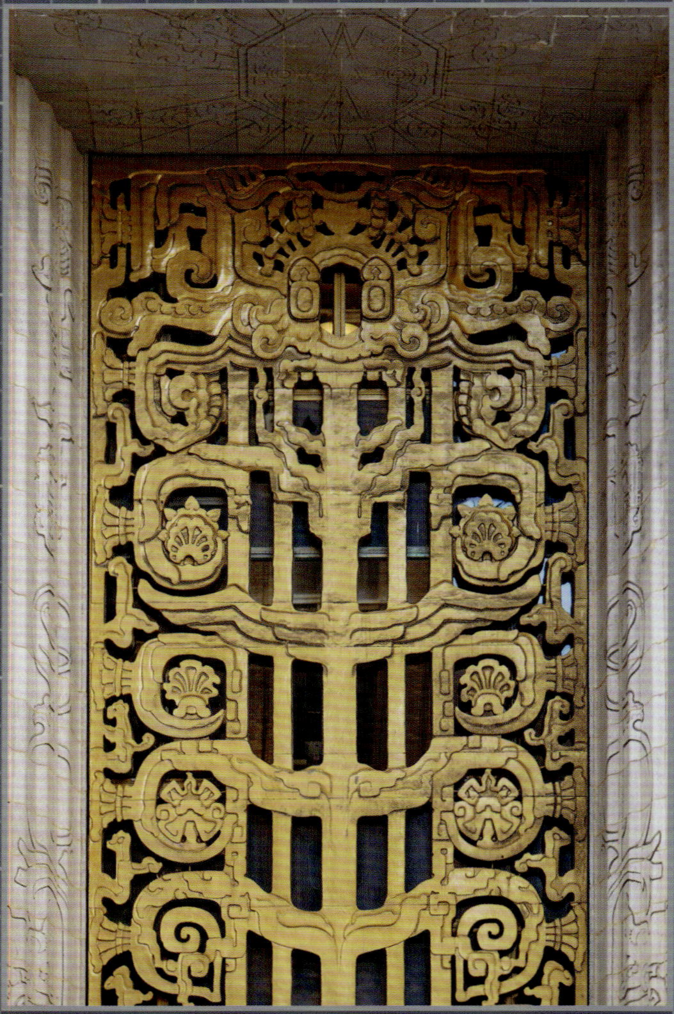

Mayan themes had a heyday in the 1920s as architects sought inspiration beyond European tradition.

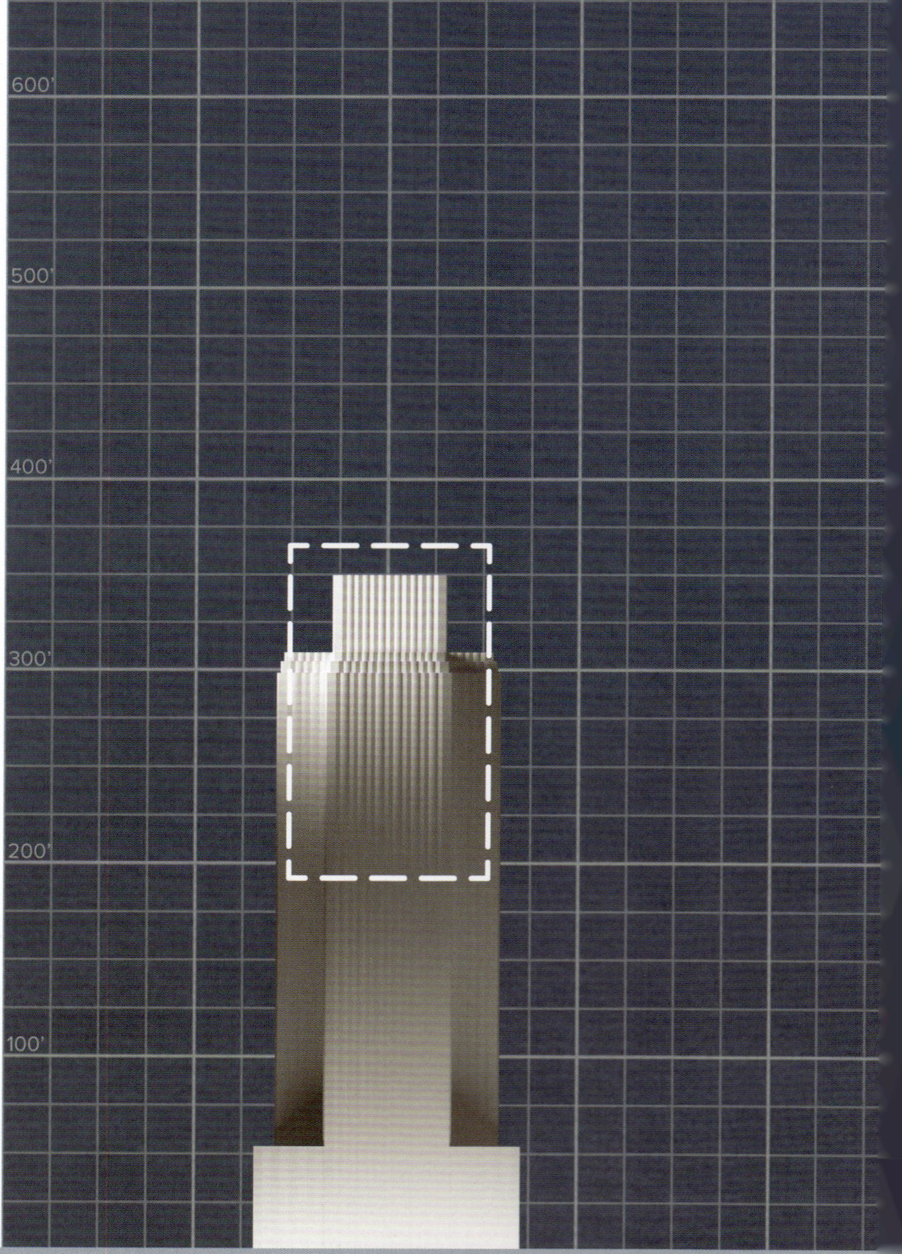

South Elevation *1" = 100'*

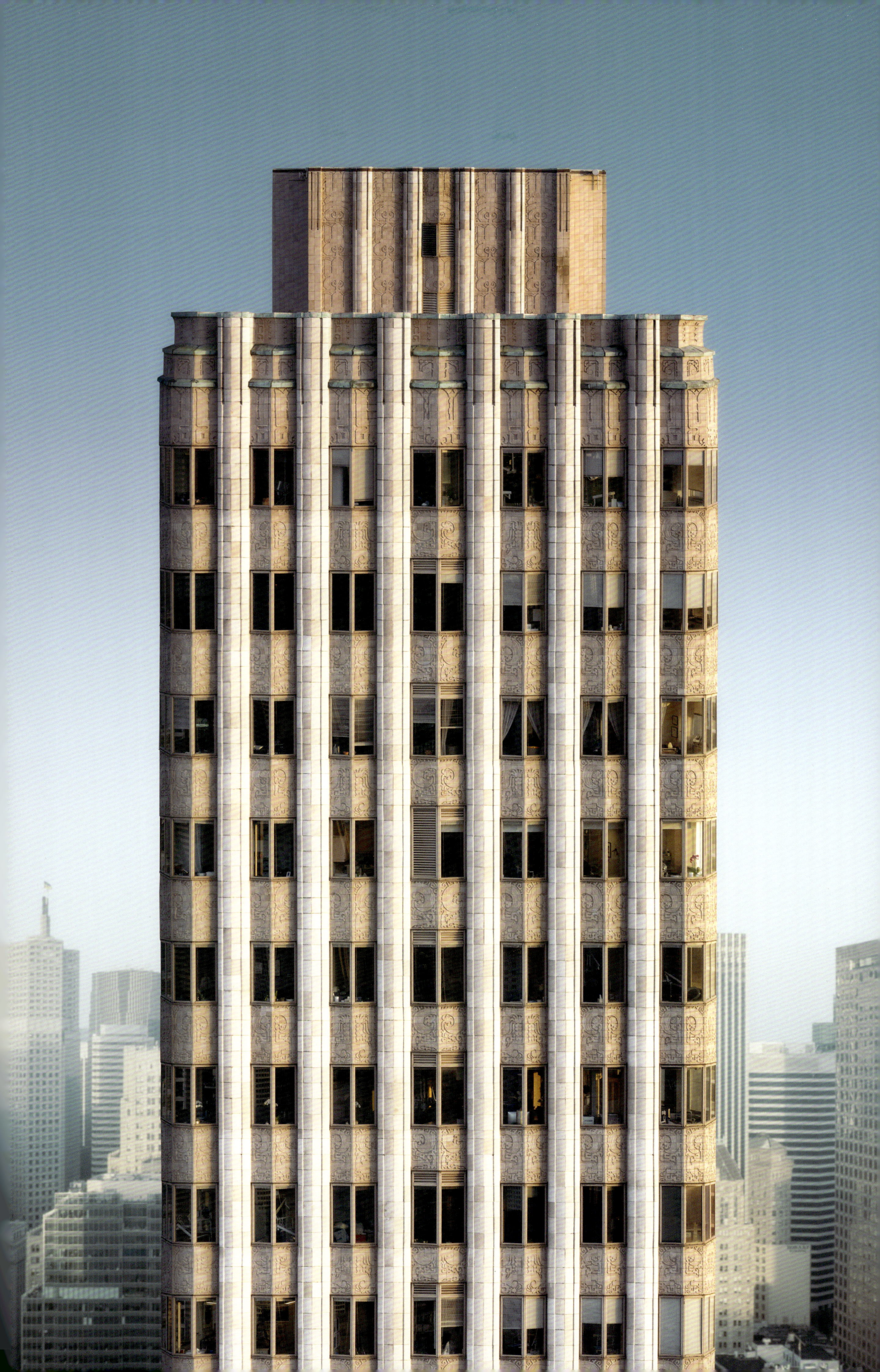

The Bellaire

San Francisco, **CA**

Address	**1101 Green St.**
Opened	**1930**
Height	**252'**
Stories	**20**
Style	**Art Deco, Spanish Baroque**
Architect	**Herman Baumann**

Commanding views from the top floors of this Russian Hill highrise "will probably never be obstructed," the San Francisco Examiner claimed when construction began. The boast has mostly held up, with exceptions for a couple tall neighbors and the modern towers downtown blocking a few vantages towards Oakland.

Opening his architectural practice a year before the 1906 earthquake, Herman Baumann found plenty of work. He specialized in apartments; this one, like his Gaylord Hotel in Nob Hill, places Spanish flourishes onto a stark white Deco form. The Bellaire was built for Guy Hardison, a Santa Paula citrus rancher whose father had come west from the Pennsylvania oilfields to try drilling along the Santa Clara River and struck it rich, co-founding Union Oil.

Another oil baron's son, Peter Getty, once lived in the penthouse. He sold it to his friend and business partner, then-mayor Gavin Newsom, who enjoyed the views only for a few years before moving out to begin an eventually successful quest for the governorship. Other residents who climb to the windswept roof deck for its panoramas can see the Pacific and the farthest reaches of San Francisco Bay, with the aforementioned exceptions.

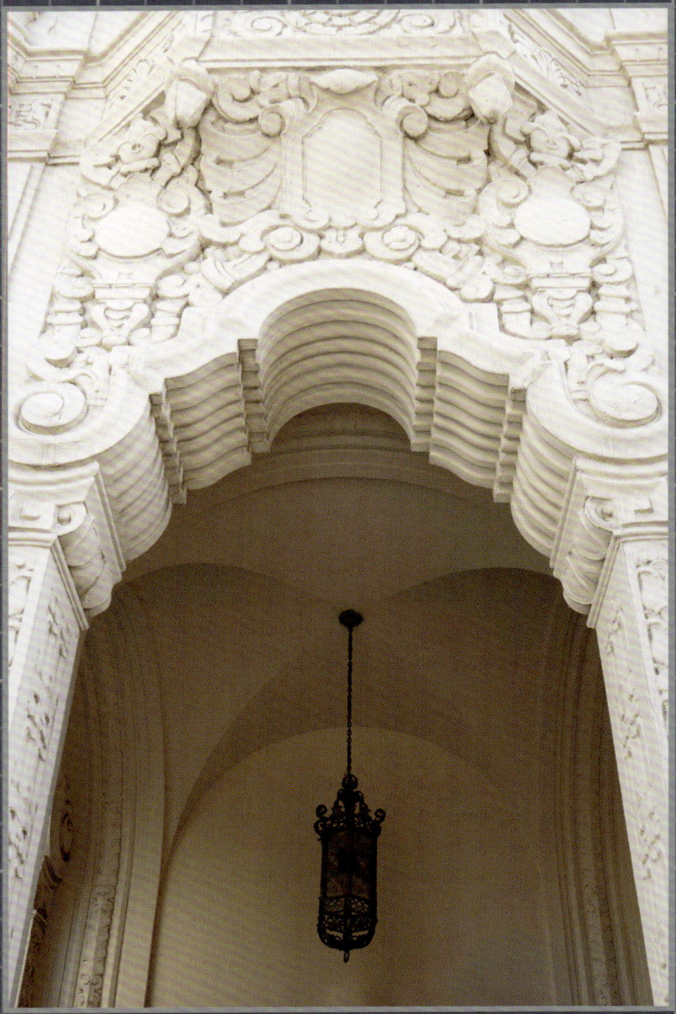

The most extravagant sculptural elements are reserved for the ground floor, with smooth walls above.

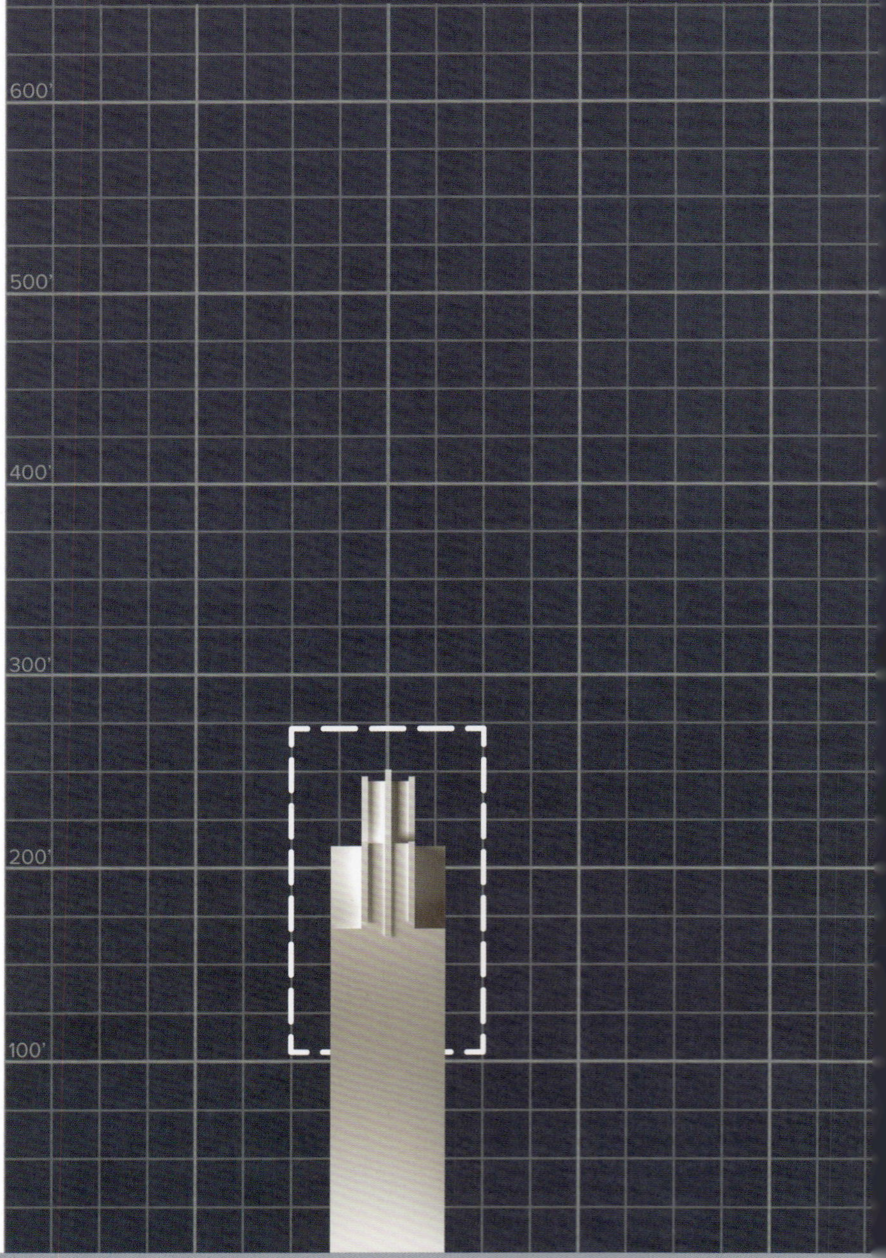

South Elevation *1" = 100'*

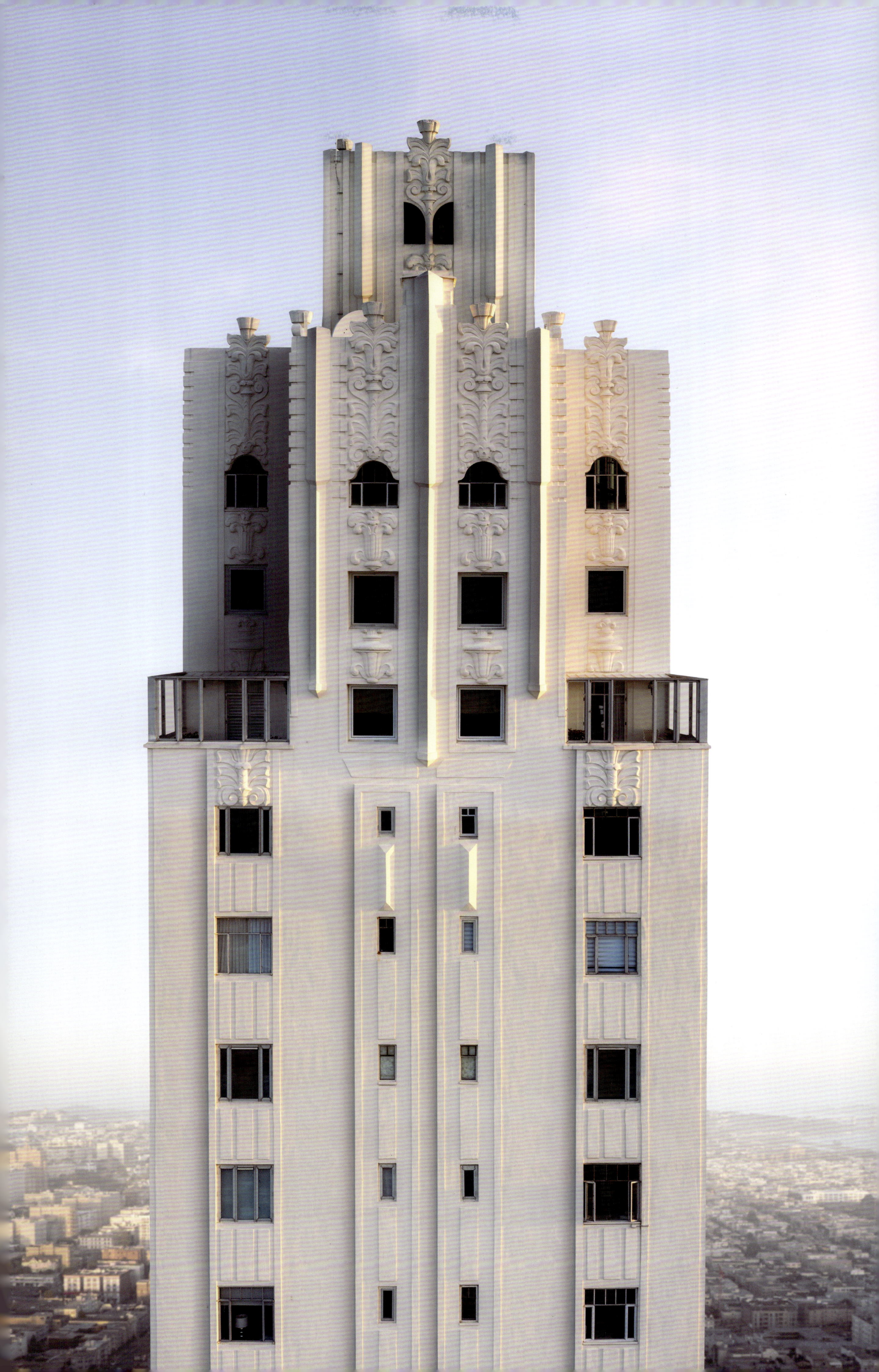

Central Tower

San Francisco, **CA** Claus Spreckels Building

Address	**703 Market St.**
Opened	**1897**
Height	**299'**
Stories	**21**
Style	**Art Deco**
Architect	**Reid Brothers, Albert Roller**

Once the city's most famous skyscraper, this highrise was rendered unrecognizable by a 1938 Art Deco redesign that replaced its baroque dome with a new six-story top. A lobby display of bronze doorknobs emblazoned with "CS" are the only clue to its former identity as the Claus Spreckels Building.

The German immigrant ran a grocery store and a brewery before opening a sugar refinery. With relentless focus, Spreckels built an empire of cane plantations in Hawaii, beet fields in California, factories, ships, and railroads to supply West Coast tables with sugar.

When the San Francisco Chronicle alleged stock fraud, Spreckels's outraged son Adolph burst into its newsroom and shot the editor, Michael de Young. The victim survived, the assailant got away with a temporary insanity plea, and the rivalry intensified. Spreckels bought the San Francisco Call and built it a new headquarters overshadowing the Chronicle building across the street.

The Call's tower rode out the 1906 earthquake intact but gutted by fire. It was restored and the presses rolled again, but Spreckels's oldest son, John, preferred San Diego and eventually sold the paper to Michael de Young. Adolph and his wife, Alma, avenged the family honor by building an art museum to dwarf de Young's, but he parried with an expansion; today cooler heads have combined the two institutions.

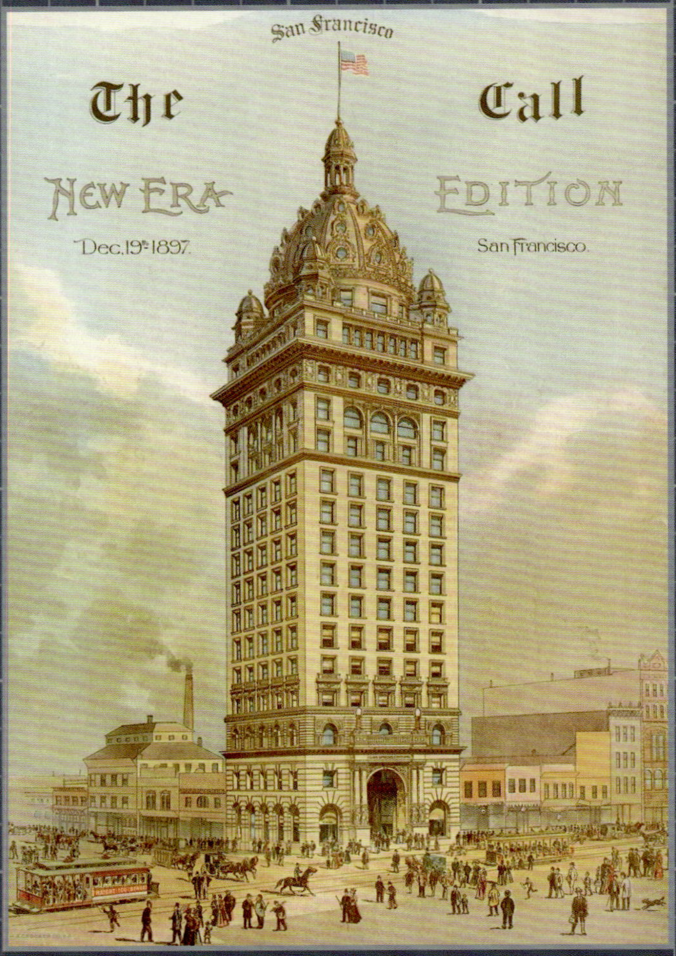

An 1897 engraving from the San Francisco Call shows the tower's original dome, which held a private club.

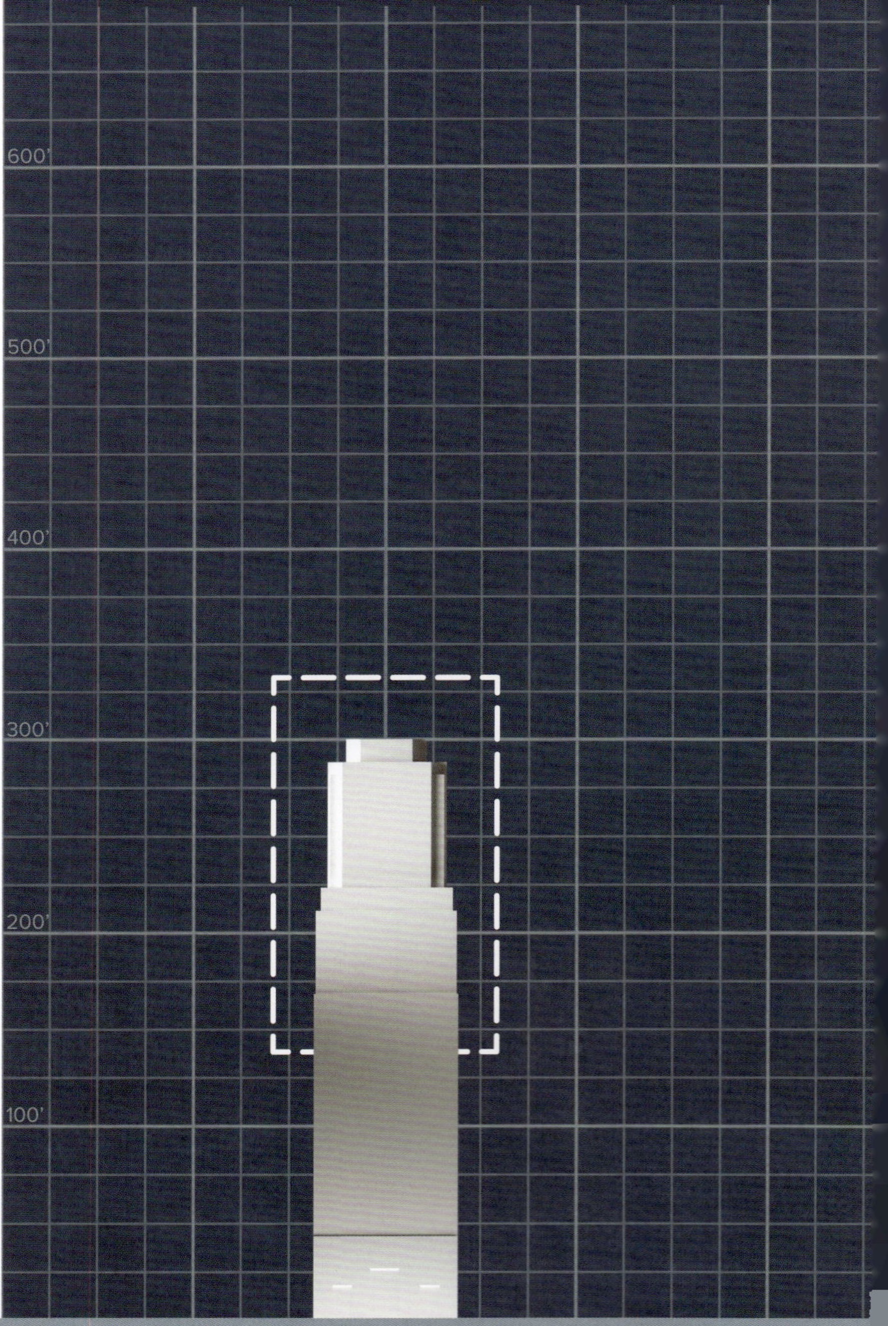

Northwest Elevation *1" = 100'*

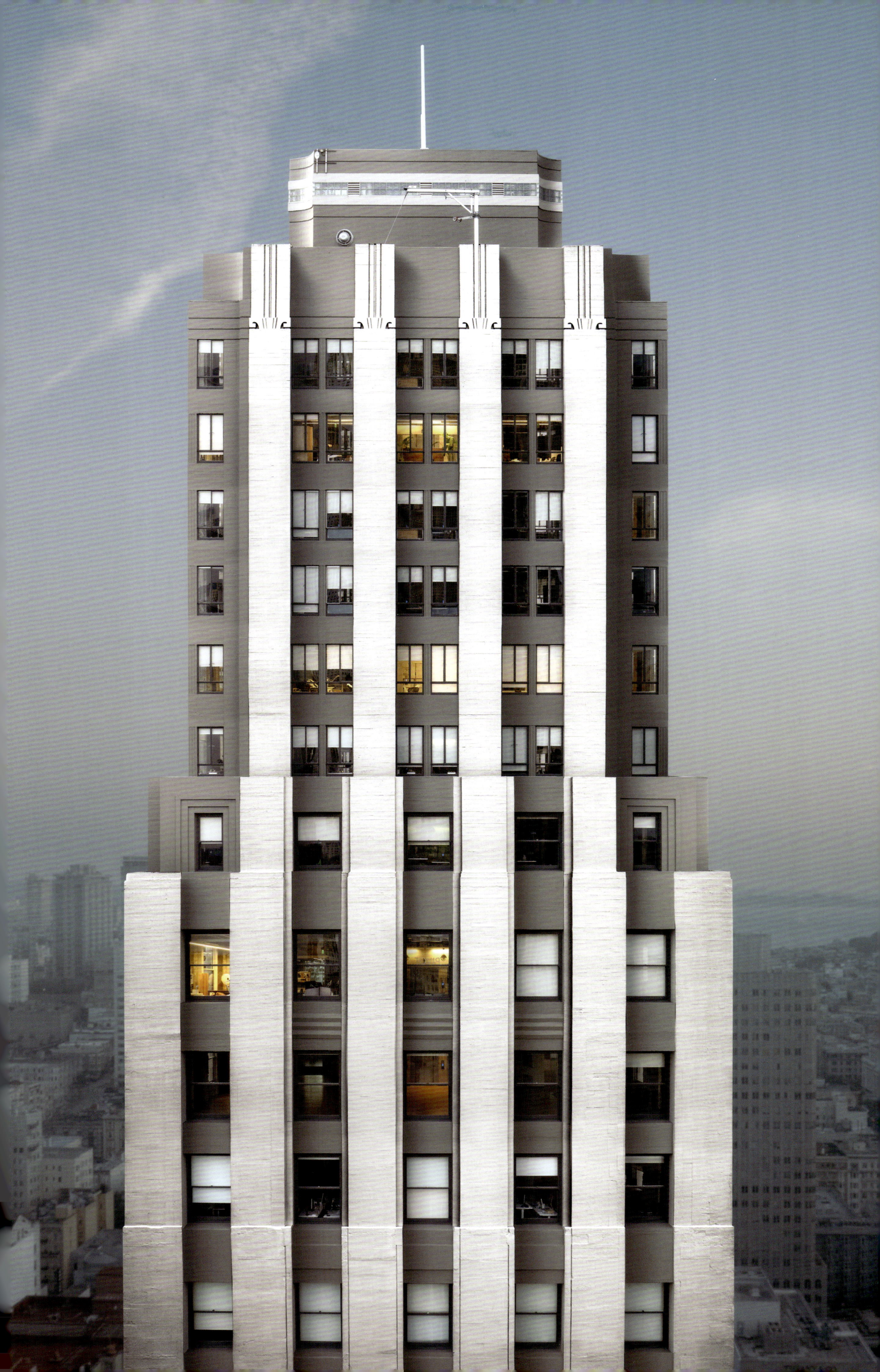

Pacific Telephone
& Telegraph Building

San Francisco, **CA**

Address	**140 New Montgomery St.**
Opened	**1925**
Height	**435'**
Stories	**26**
Style	**Art Deco**
Architect	**Miller & Pflueger**

The craggy granite peaks of the Sierra Nevadas were the inspiration for the young architect who designed this as his first skyscraper, though its gray walls are terracotta, not stone. Despite a lack of formal training, Timothy Pflueger rose rapidly from apprentice draftsman to junior partner at his mentor's firm before the pair won this commission. It was briefly the city's tallest highrise until the Russ Building surpassed it by mere inches.

A newspaper poet dubbed the new phone company headquarters "a shimmery, gleaming monument to Talk!" For George McFarlane, president of Pacific Telephone & Telegraph, the California subsidiary of AT&T, fawning poetry was far preferable to the ugly headlines his company had endured in its rocky recent history. Besides labor unrest and recurring strikes by its linemen and operators, Pacific was the main culprit in a 1906 city hall bribery scandal that got the mayor's right-hand man sentenced to 14 years in San Quentin.

Now the headquarters of numerous high-tech companies, the building stood vacant for several years after the phone company left. Luckily, Pflueger's spectacular lobby has survived in nearly pristine condition, with its black mottled marble walls, lacquered multicolor trim, and orange ceiling embossed with Chinese animal prints.

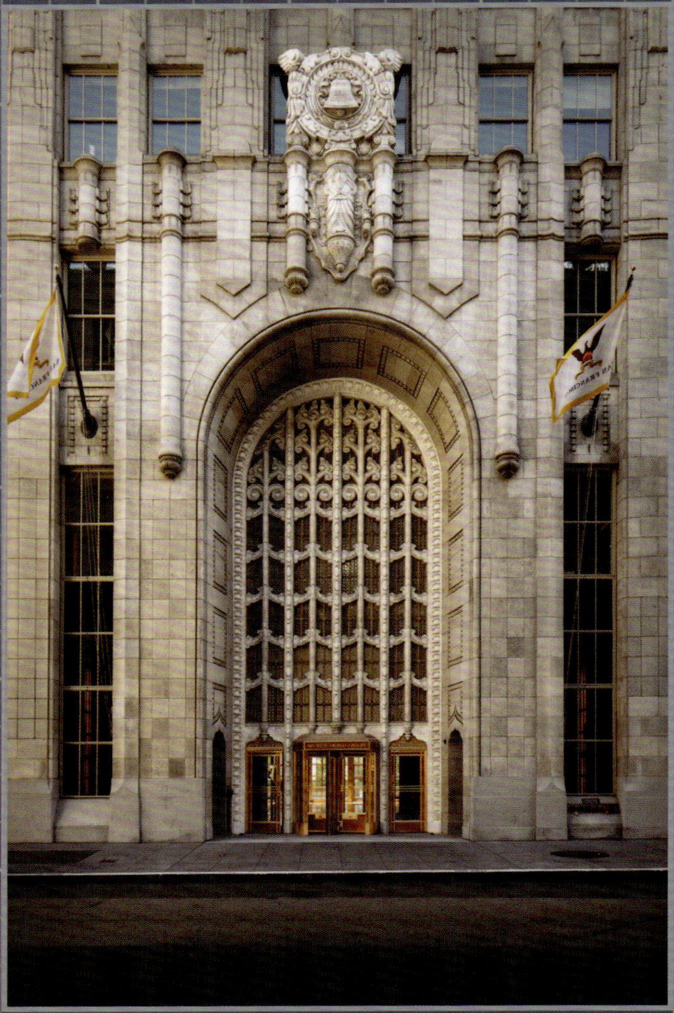

While the terracotta is a uniform gray, unusual shapes in the multistory grille add a mark of individuality.

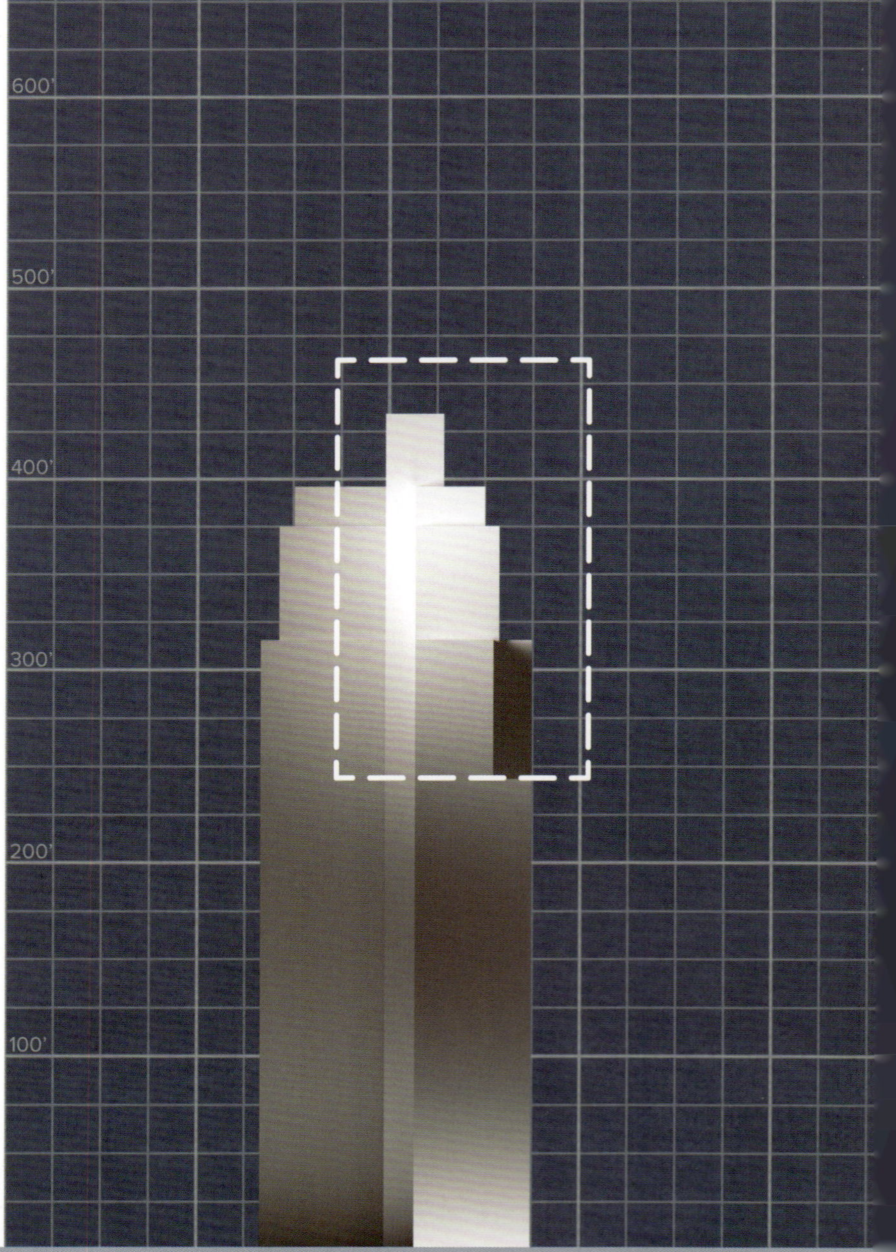

Southeast Elevation *1" = 100'*

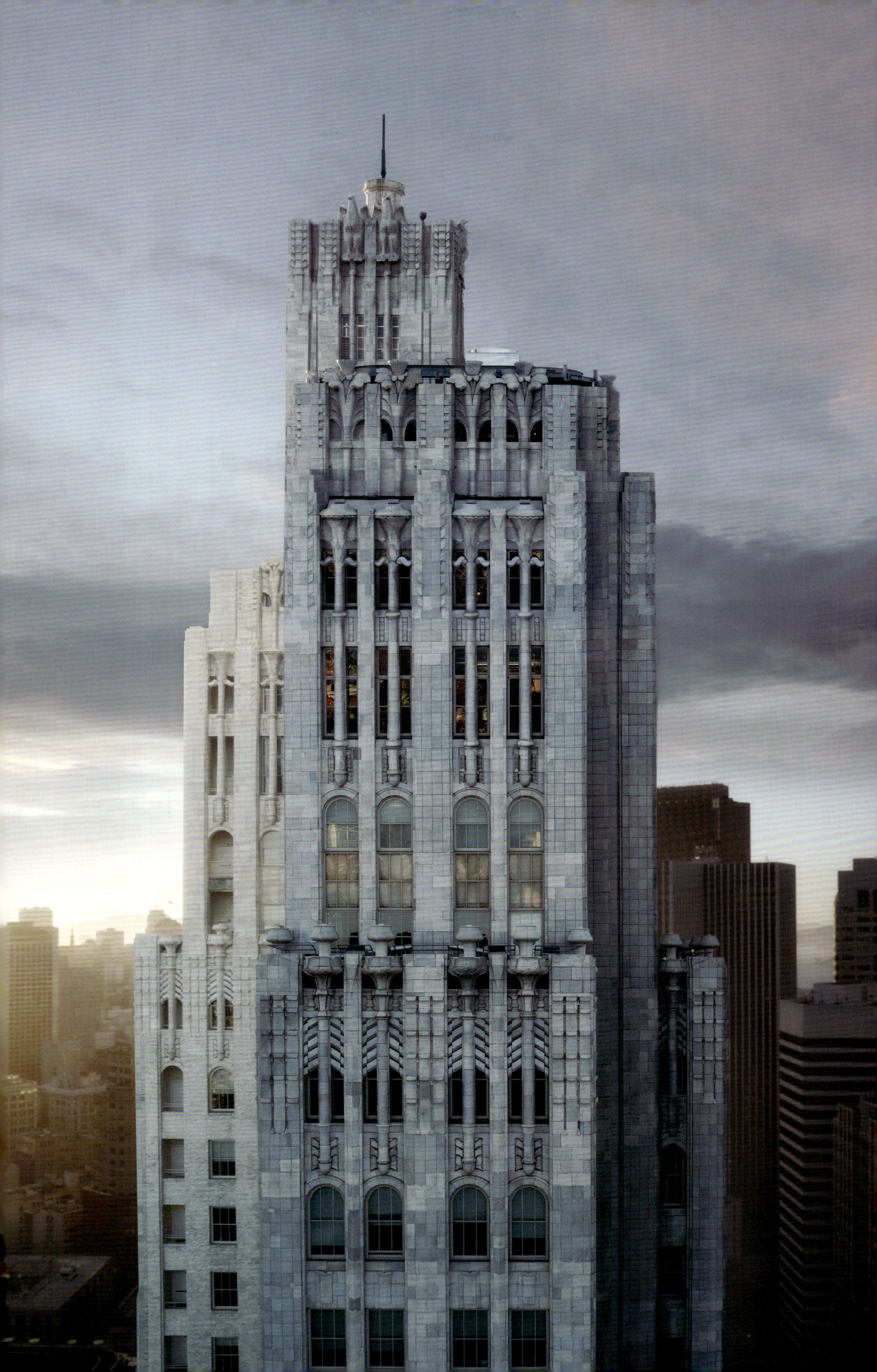

Shell Building

San Francisco, **CA**

Address	**100 Bush St.**
Opened	**1930**
Height	**378'**
Stories	**28**
Style	**Art Deco**
Architect	**George Kelham**

With this terracotta tower emblazoned inside and out with the company's signature mollusk, Royal Dutch Shell proclaimed its determination to challenge Standard Oil for control of the California oilfields. Each contestant was controlled by one of the world's richest families: Rothschilds vs. Rockefellers.

Only three years after opening an office in the United States, the British-Dutch conglomerate built a refinery in 1915 at Martinez, on the tidal estuary emptying into San Francisco Bay. Shell's geologists fanned out across the state seeking petroleum to fill their tankers, each ship christened with the names of various shells — Murex, Cowrie, Conch, Clam — to honor the founder's father, a London seashell merchant. In 1921 Shell hit a massive gusher at Signal Hill near Long Beach, and soon California was producing a quarter of the world's oil.

When Standard moved into a new skyscraper the following year, Shell temporarily leased their rivals' former offices just across Bush Street. Next the European upstarts hired George Kelham — the same architect responsible for the Standard Oil Building — to design them a taller headquarters a block away. Eventually, with their West Coast wells sucked dry, Shell and Standard successor Chevron packed up and moved to Texas. Now new tenants occupy George Kelham's battling Bush Street highrises.

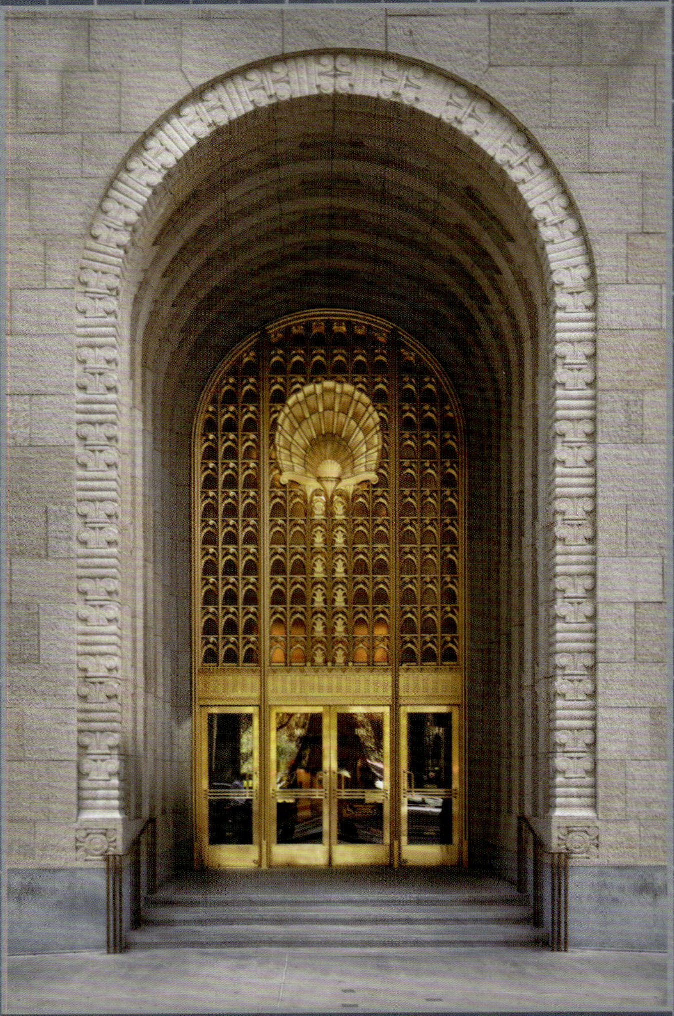

The textured terracotta archway encloses a bronze grille that is surmounted by what else — a shell.

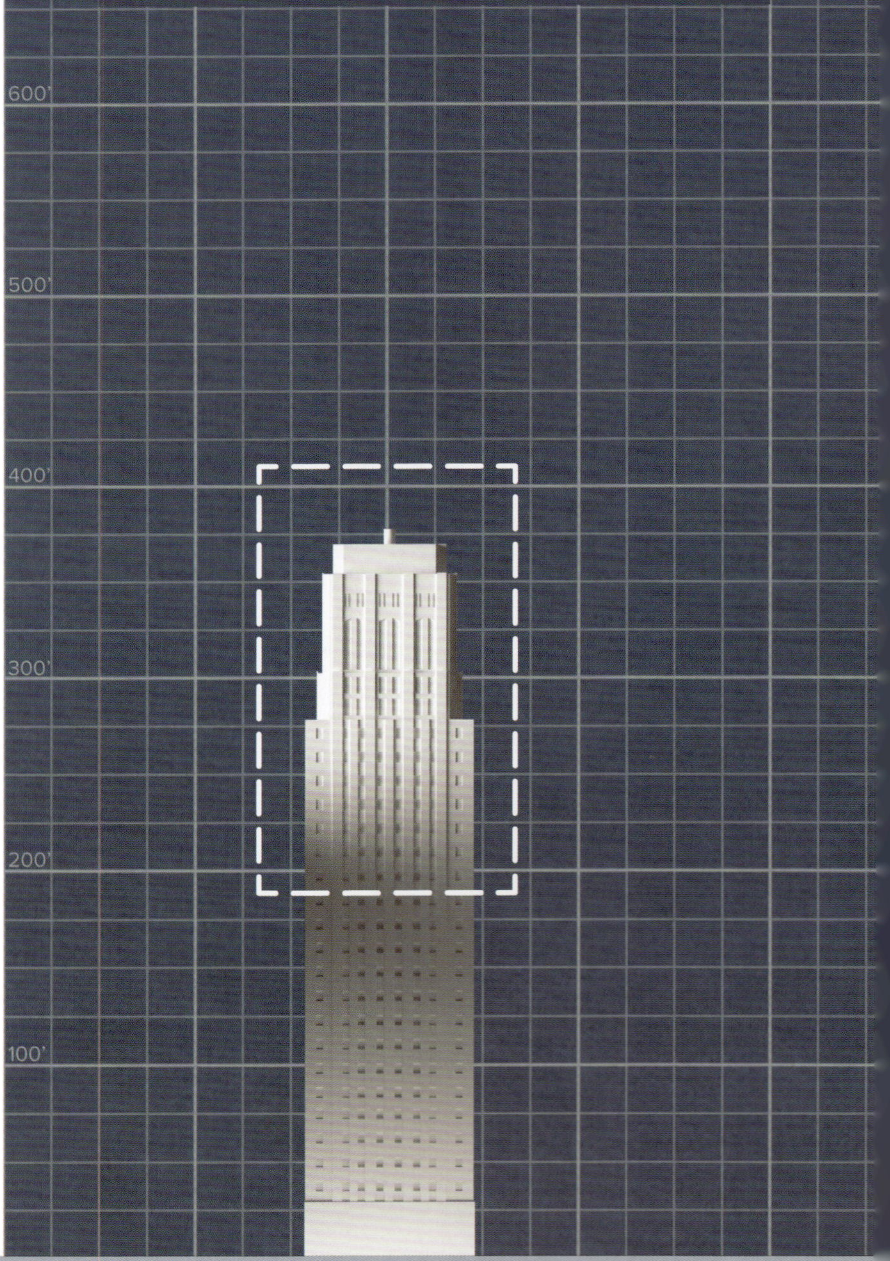

South Elevation *1" = 100'*

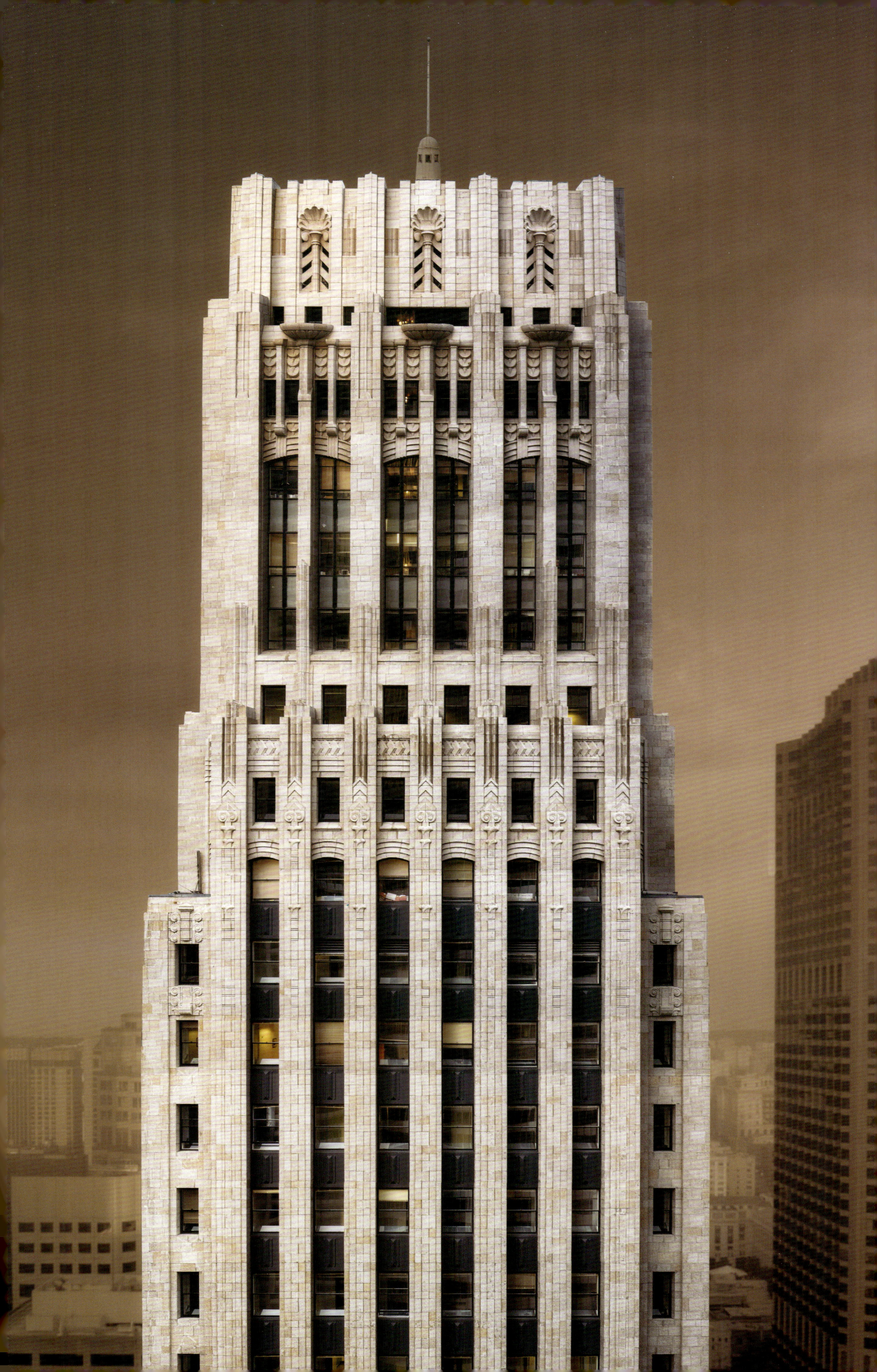

Sir Francis Drake
Hotel

San Francisco, **CA** — Beacon Grand

Address	**450 Powell St.**
Opened	**1928**
Height	**315'**
Stories	**21**
Style	**Art Deco, Renaissance**
Architect	**Weeks & Day**

While the legendary English navigator is believed to have landed in California during his 16th century circumnavigation of the globe, his Golden Hind never sailed through the Golden Gate. Still, Drake's name was affixed to one of San Francisco's swankiest hotels for nearly a century, until a long Covid shutdown resulted in new owners and a new name.

The Drake's Beefeater doorman was once the city's most photographed resident. Other folks in fancy costumes performed a long-running Sunday drag brunch in the top-floor Starlight Room. But the most astonishing transformation belonged to the hotel itself. One night in 1954 while high on peyote, Allen Ginsberg saw the facade melt into "the robot skullface of Moloch." The vision inspired his Beat poem "Howl," which Ginsberg penned in the Drake's coffee shop.

The highrise was built for Fort Worth hotelier Leon Huckins, who sold it in 1938 to another Texan, Conrad Hilton, then just beginning to expand his hospitality chain outside the Lone Star State. Charles Weeks, the architect, died months before the Drake opened. Engineer William Day had years left; he built Treasure Island in the bay for San Francisco's 1939 World's Fair. One of its most heralded exhibits was a brass plate allegedly left by Drake himself on California's shores, though it was later proven to be a forgery.

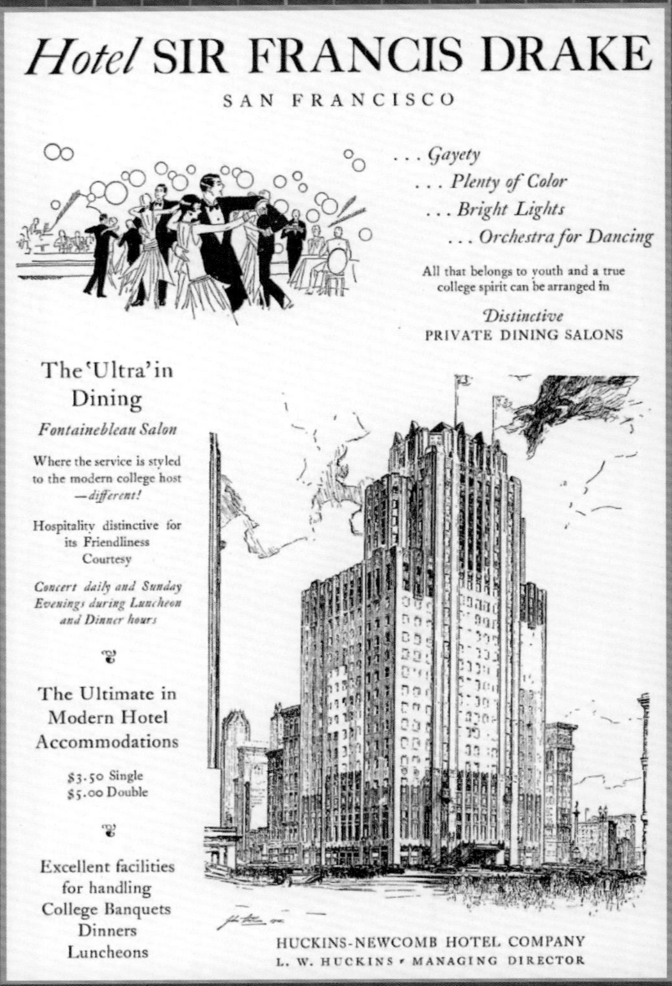

A 1920s hotel ad stresses its bright lights and colors in a bid for banquet business from the college crowd.

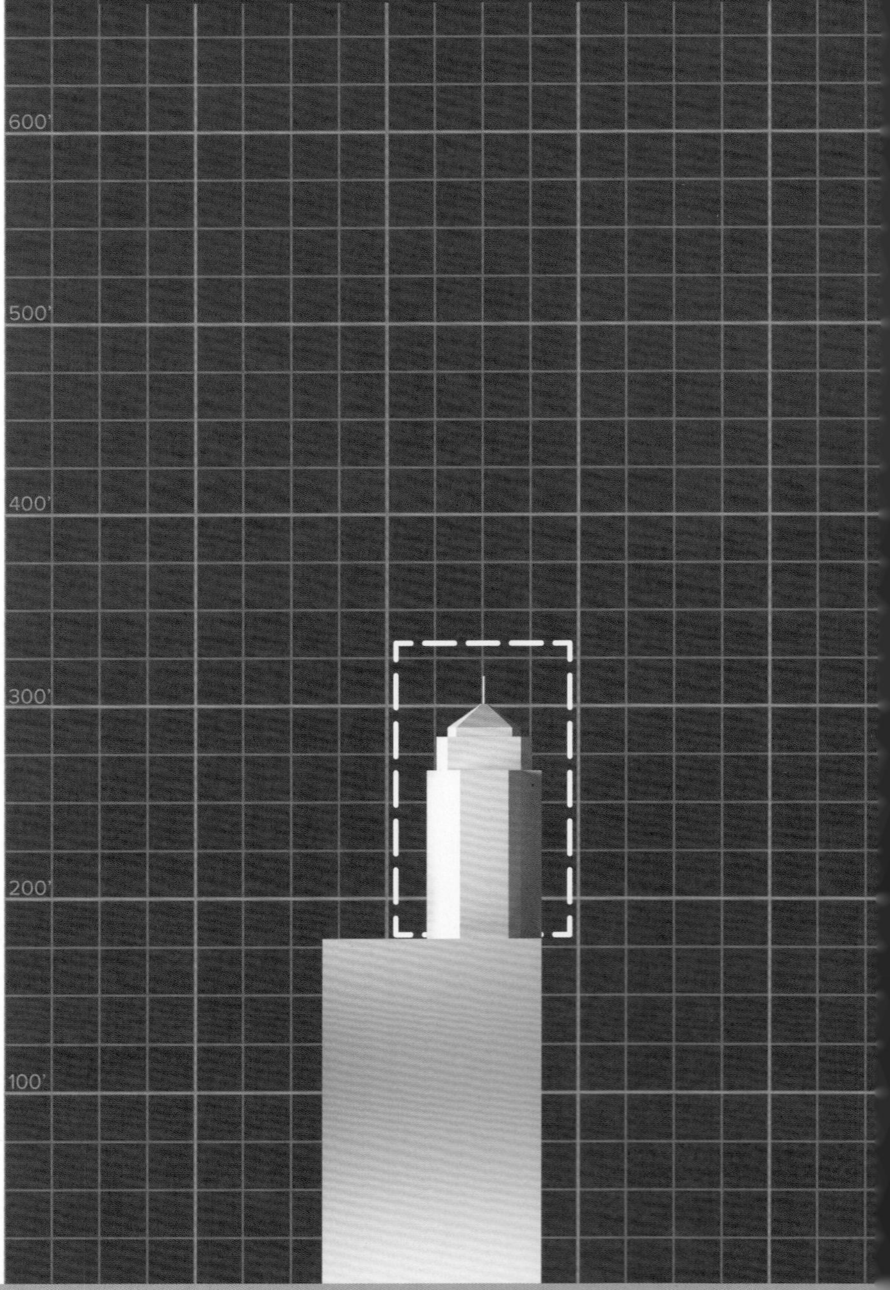

North Elevation 1" = 100'

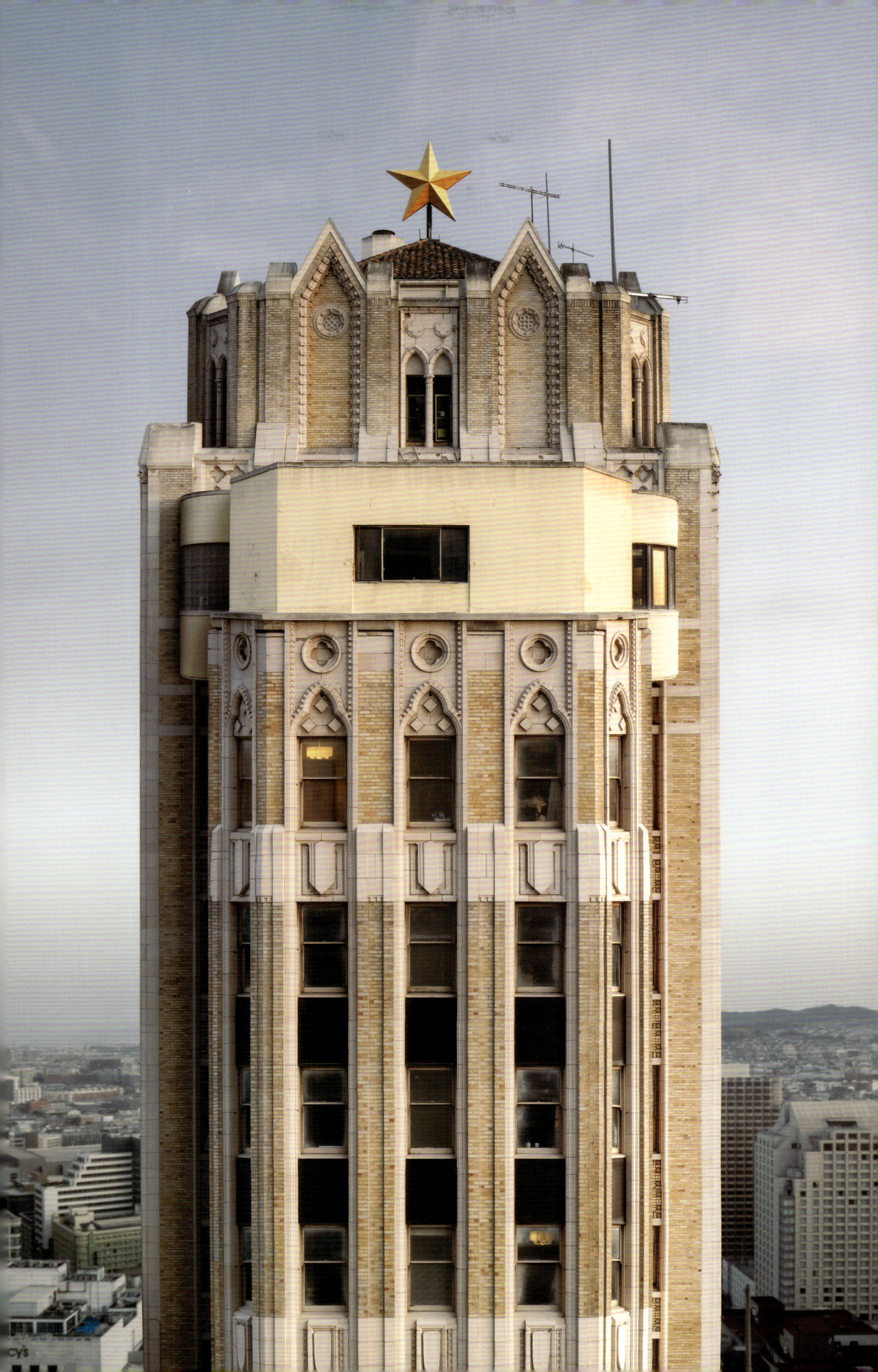

Luhrs Tower

Phoenix, **AZ**

Address	**45 W. Jefferson St.**
Opened	**1930**
Height	**185'**
Stories	**14**
Style	**Art Deco , Renaissance**
Architect	**Henry Trost**

Sharing the same block with the state's first skyscraper, this highrise was built six years after it by the same family on the grounds of their original homestead. Georg and Gretchen Luhrs, German immigrants who opened a hotel in Phoenix decades before Arizona won its statehood, also claimed to own the city's first bathtub.

Both attended the groundbreaking of this tower, though Georg did not make it to the opening. Their youngest son, George Jr., ran the tower and the 10-story Luhrs Building, which had a private men's club on its top four floors. At one time the complex also housed both the state Prohibition headquarters and a front company for mafia-controlled bookmakers. The latter operation was run by mobster Gus Greenbaum, who would go on to manage two Las Vegas hotels before getting whacked along with his wife in their Phoenix home in 1958.

Henry Trost of El Paso designed both highrises for the Luhrs family, but the architect's second effort is far more original and modern in appearance. It turned out so well that Trost successfully proposed a near duplicate, with slightly altered ornamentation and an extra floor, for a banker back in El Paso months after work began on this structure.

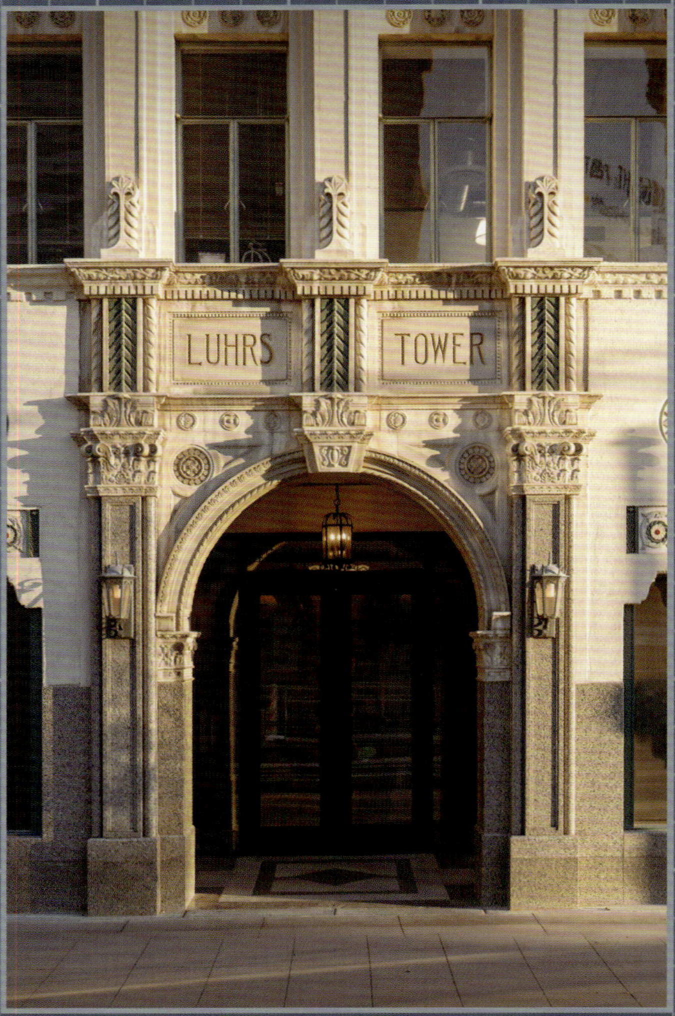

Apart from the granite and carved stone entrance, the rest of the exterior is ornamental concrete stucco.

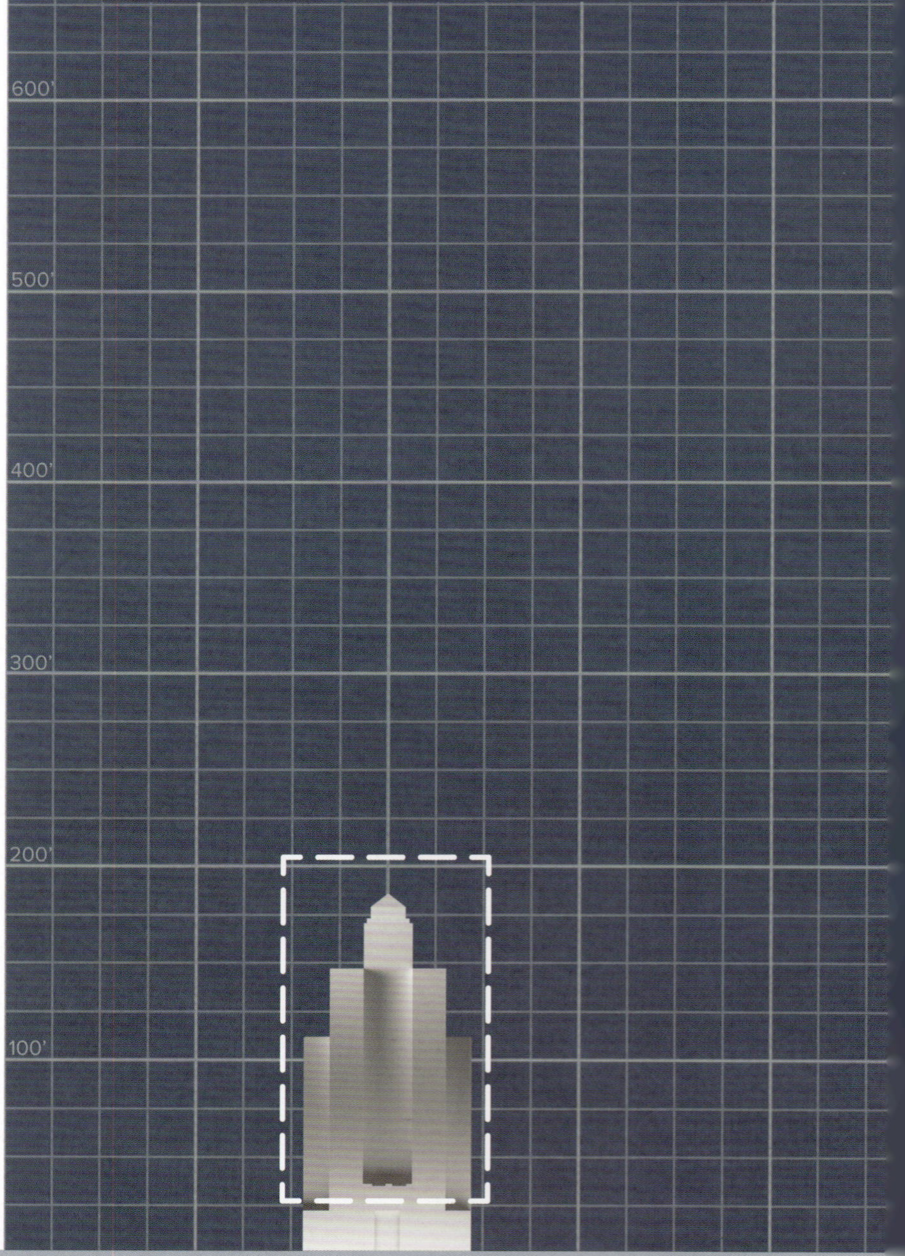

North Elevation 1" = 100'

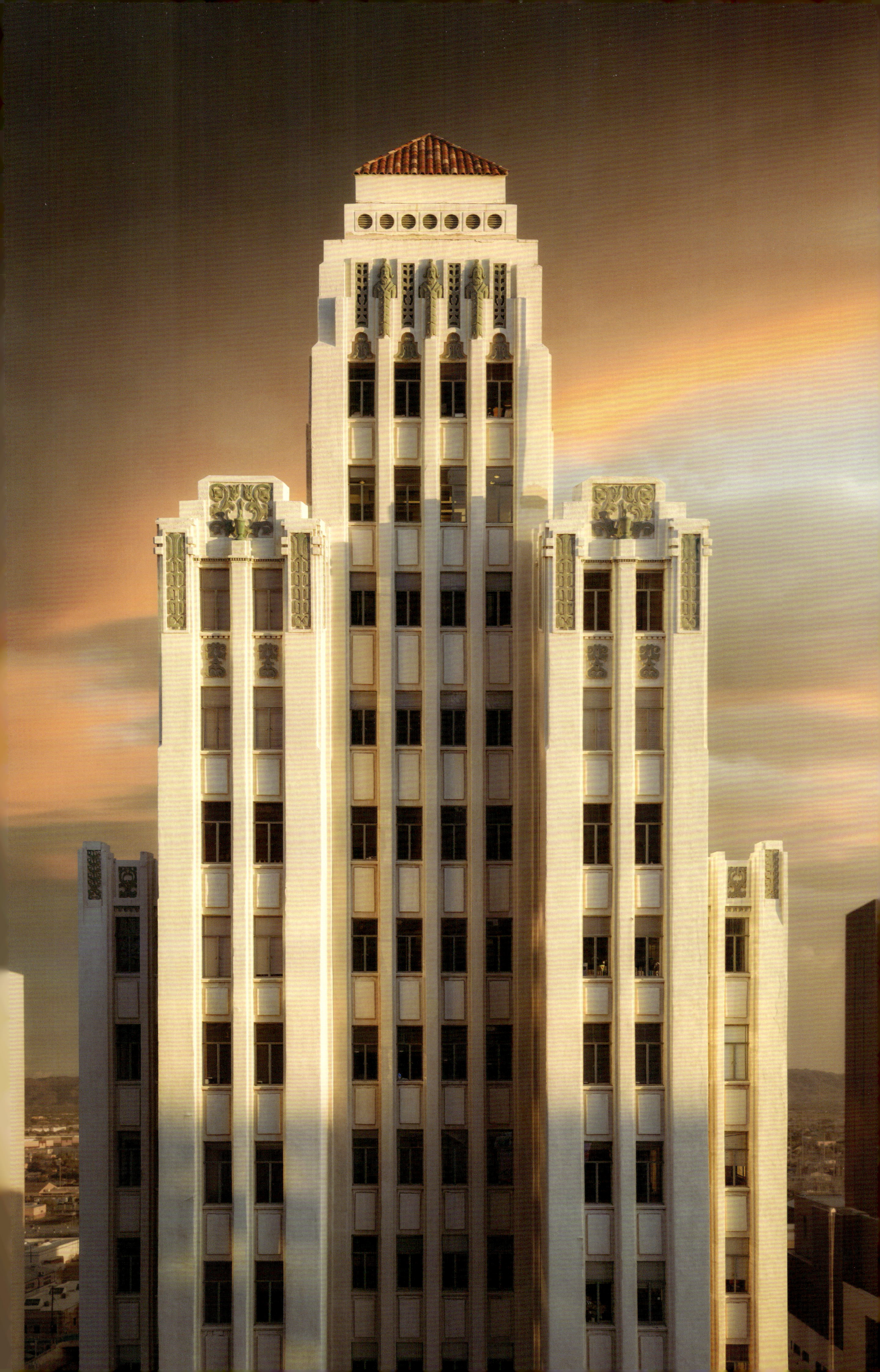

Northern Life
Tower

Seattle, **WA** — Seattle Tower

Address	**1218 Third Ave.**
Opened	**1929**
Height	**327’**
Stories	**27**
Style	**Art Deco**
Architect	**Abraham Albertson**

Conceived as an Art Deco mountain, this highrise once dominated the city skyline. Its roof is capped by tapered spires meant to resemble evergreens, while its dark gray marble lobby, brightened by a gold leaf ceiling, feels like an elegant cave. Spelunk to the end to find a bronze map of the Pacific and a plaque with the founders of the insurance company that erected the building.

Ohio brothers Tasso and David Morgan came to Oregon in 1887 and started an insurance business, relocating to Seattle in 1906. They bundled health and accident policies with life insurance, a novel combination that won them many customers. Innovations persisted, including a “souvenir tower policy” commemorating this skyscraper’s dedication that offered a triple payout if the holder died in a car crash.

Now known as Seattle Tower, the building stands on the original site of the University of Washington, which relocated in 1895 but continues to lucratively lease its large lot, called the Metropolitan Tract. Architect Abraham Albertson came to Seattle in 1907 to supervise construction of a Beaux-Arts office and retail complex on the sprawling tract, including the Cobb Building, the earlier development’s sole survivor, just across what is still called University Street.

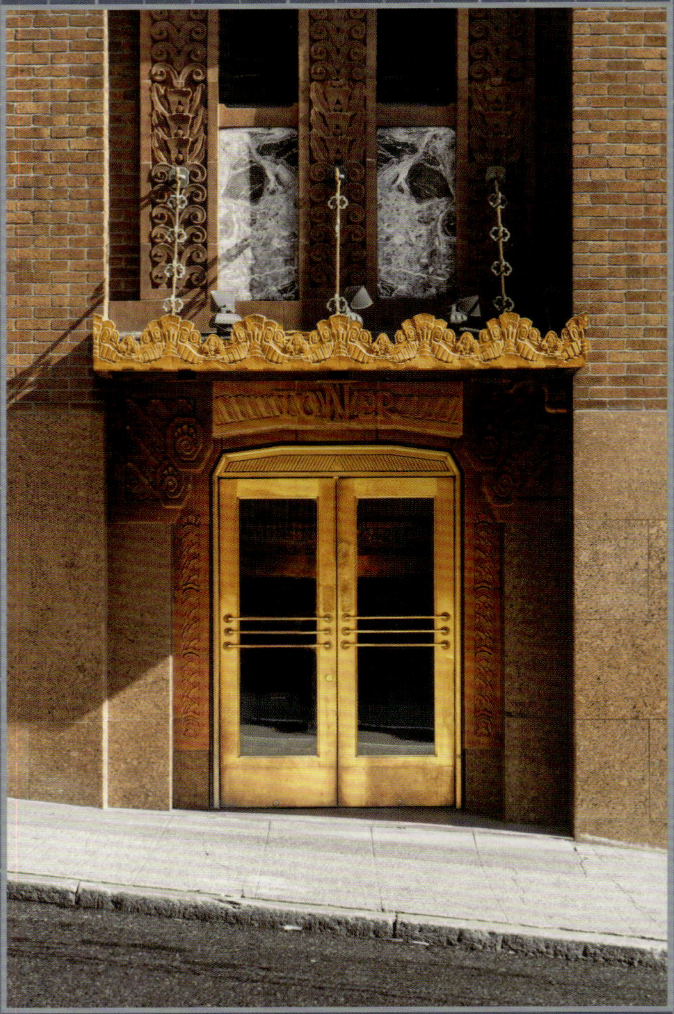

A steep Seattle sidewalk climbs past the side entrance, with brown terracotta and marble panels over the marquee.

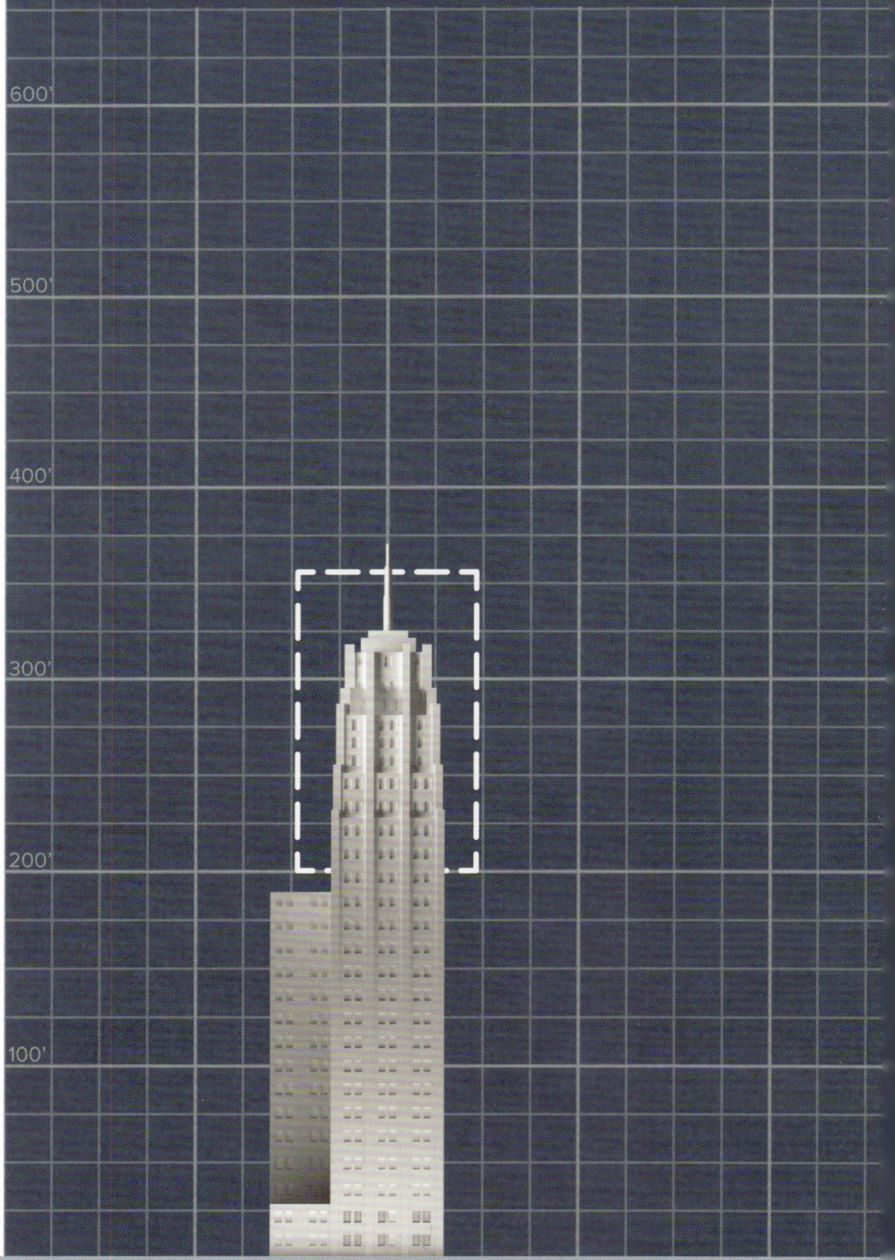

Southwest Elevation *1" = 100'*

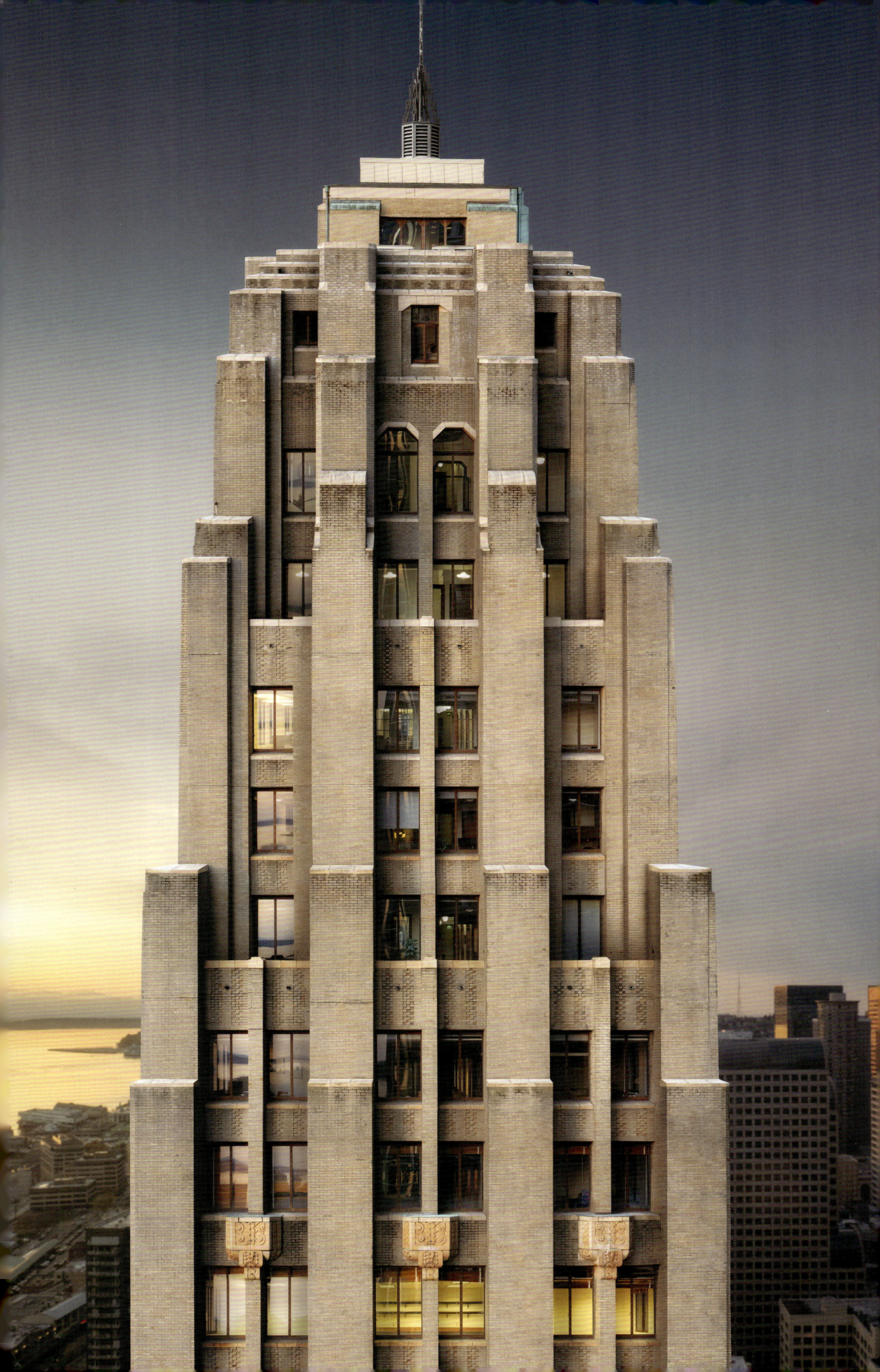

Hotel Roosevelt

Seattle, **WA** — Hotel Theodore

Address	**1531 Seventh Ave.**
Opened	**1930**
Height	**229'**
Stories	**19**
Style	**Art Deco**
Architect	**John Graham Sr.**

This highrise is one of countless hotels named for America's youngest president. Theodore Roosevelt visited Seattle in 1903 in a ceremonial flotilla, his bully pulpit bluster set at full wattage. The chief executive assured the welcoming crowd that their neighbor Alaska would eventually surpass the Scandinavian peninsula in population — a feat that would have required 7 million more Alaskans then, or 15 million now.

Seattle semi-Scandinavian Severt Thurston, an Icelandic immigrant, headed Western Hotels, the regional chain that opened the Roosevelt in 1930. Steady growth over the following decades led to a name change, first to Western International, then the abbreviated Westin. Thurston's successor, Edward Carlson, also organized the 1962 Seattle World's Fair and inspired its centerpiece, the Space Needle.

That futuristic tower was the creation of architect John Graham, whose father designed this hotel. The senior Graham was prolific; the hotel was one of two Art Deco towers he contributed to Seattle's skyline in 1930, along with the Exchange Building.

Now the boutique Hotel Theodore, the property features avant-garde lobby art and displays curated from the Museum of History and Industry. The bold decor mirrors the spirit of the original hotel, which when it opened had a coffee shop painted with scenes of life on other planets.

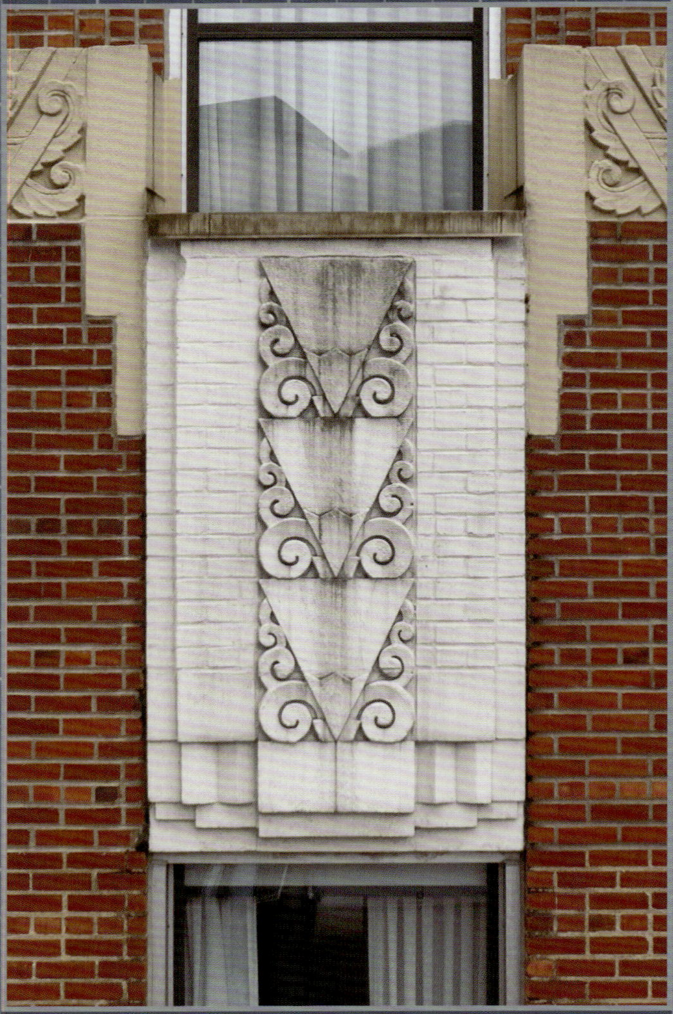

Curling spiral shapes and triangles, two quintessential Art Deco shapes, combine in this highlight.

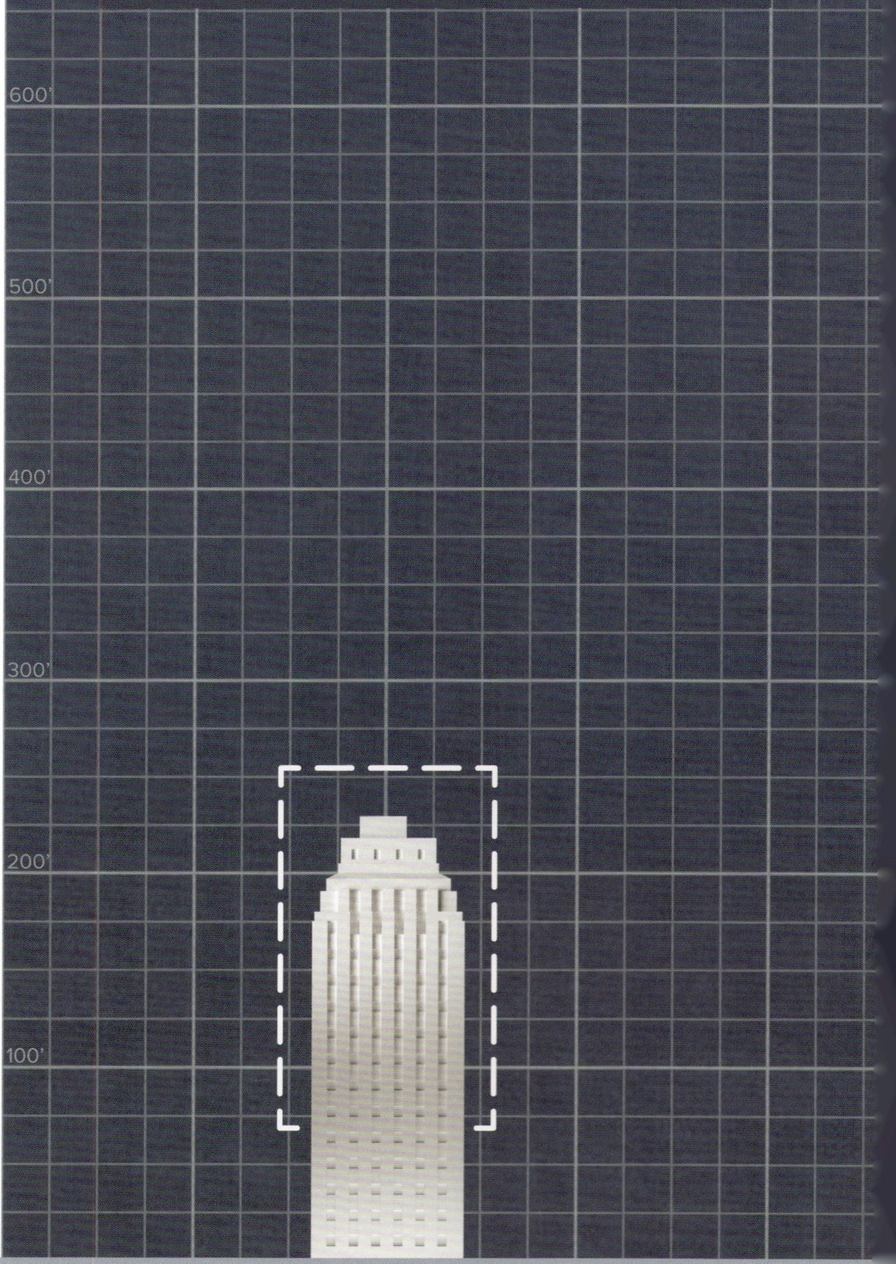

Northwest Elevation *1" = 100'*

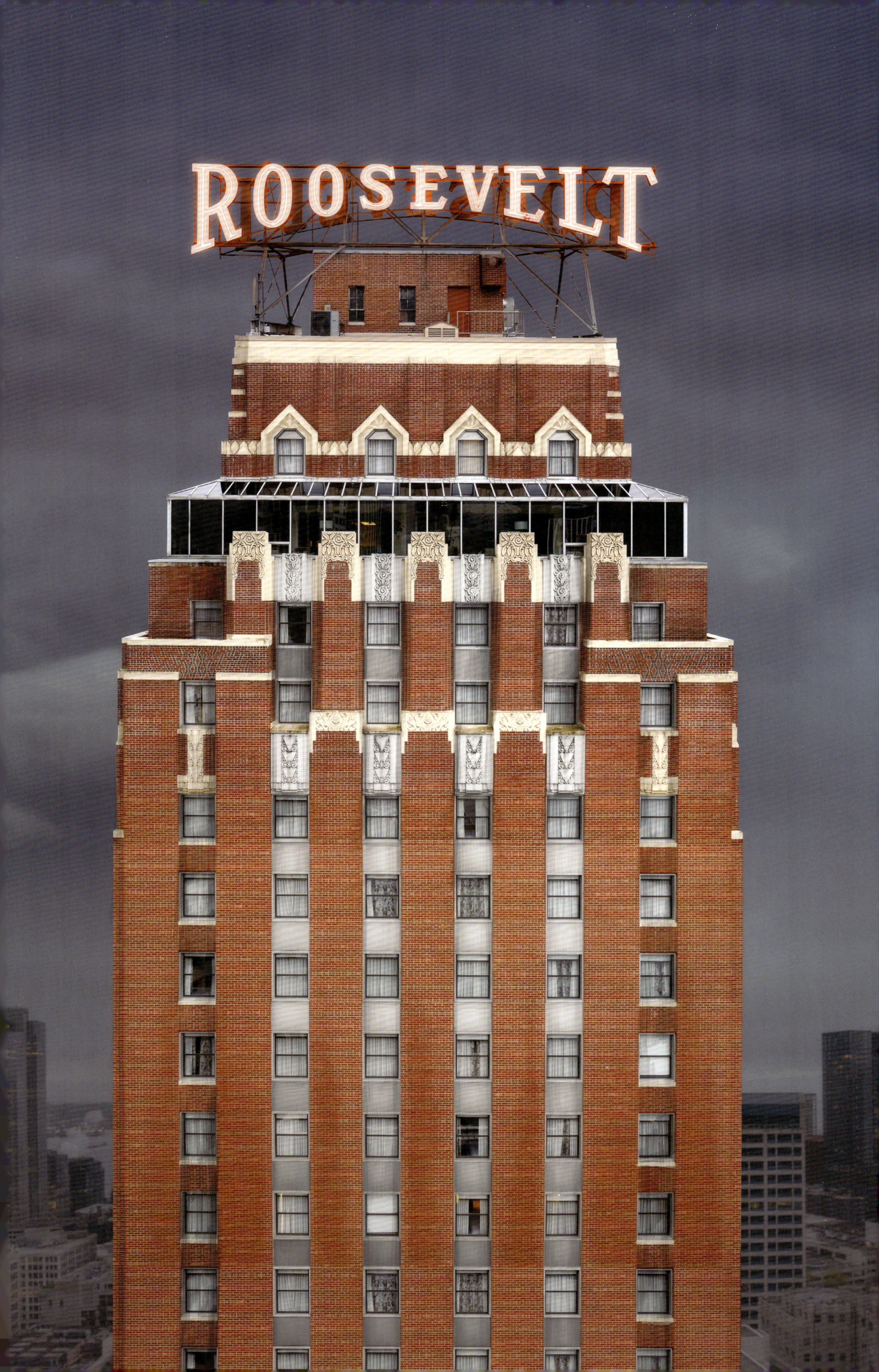
ROOSEVELT

Washington Athletic Club

Seattle, **WA**

Address	**1325 Sixth Ave.**
Opened	**1930**
Height	**250'**
Stories	**21**
Style	**Art Deco**
Architect	**Sherwood Ford**

The original promoter of this sports skyscraper skedaddled under scrutiny for questionable real estate dealings. The financier who stepped in after him to finish the job later went to prison for financial misdeeds. Neither man was as noteworthy as the local high school girl who trained in the Washington Athletic Club's sixth-floor swimming pool.

Members invited Helene Madison and her coach to join them even before the doors of their new highrise opened. In a brief but unprecedented career, Madison became the only athlete in history to hold every world record in a sport — 16 record women's freestyle times from 100 meters to a mile — and capped that achievement by winning three gold medals at the 1932 Olympics.

The pool is now named after her, and a plaque at sidewalk level honors another important woman in the club's history: Hannah Newman, the prior owner of the parcel. Her husband diplomatically had it cast to balance out a statue he commissioned in Alaska to honor another woman, a long-lost love he met during the Klondike gold rush.

The club's winged logo features prominently in the sculpted terracotta facade. Preserved elements inside include etched elevator doors and the original club library.

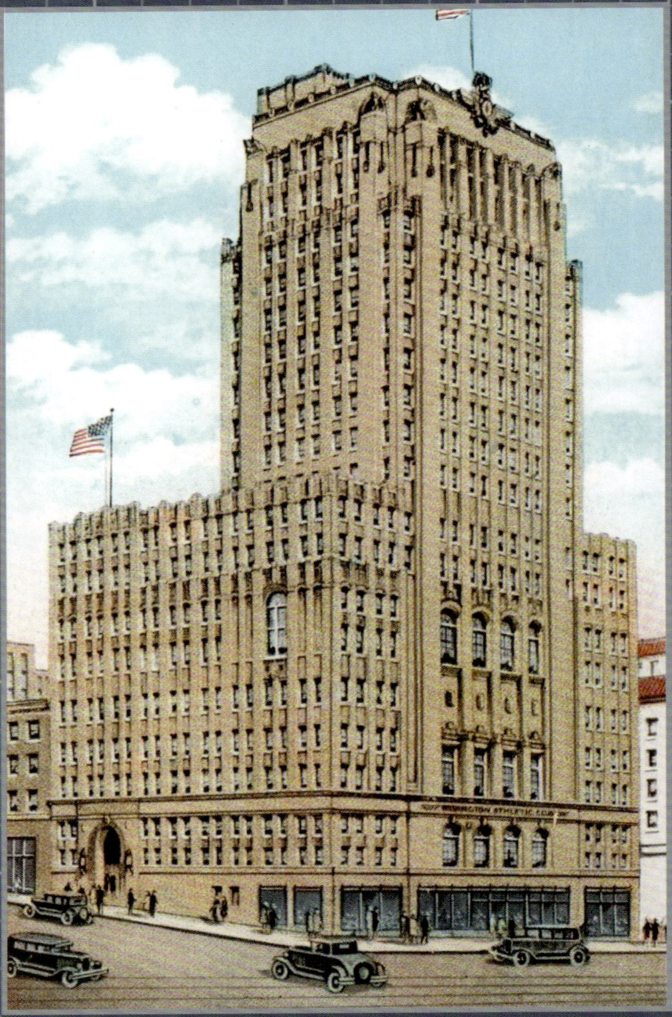

The arched entrance shown in this 1929 postcard no longer exists, but was bricked over in an expansion.

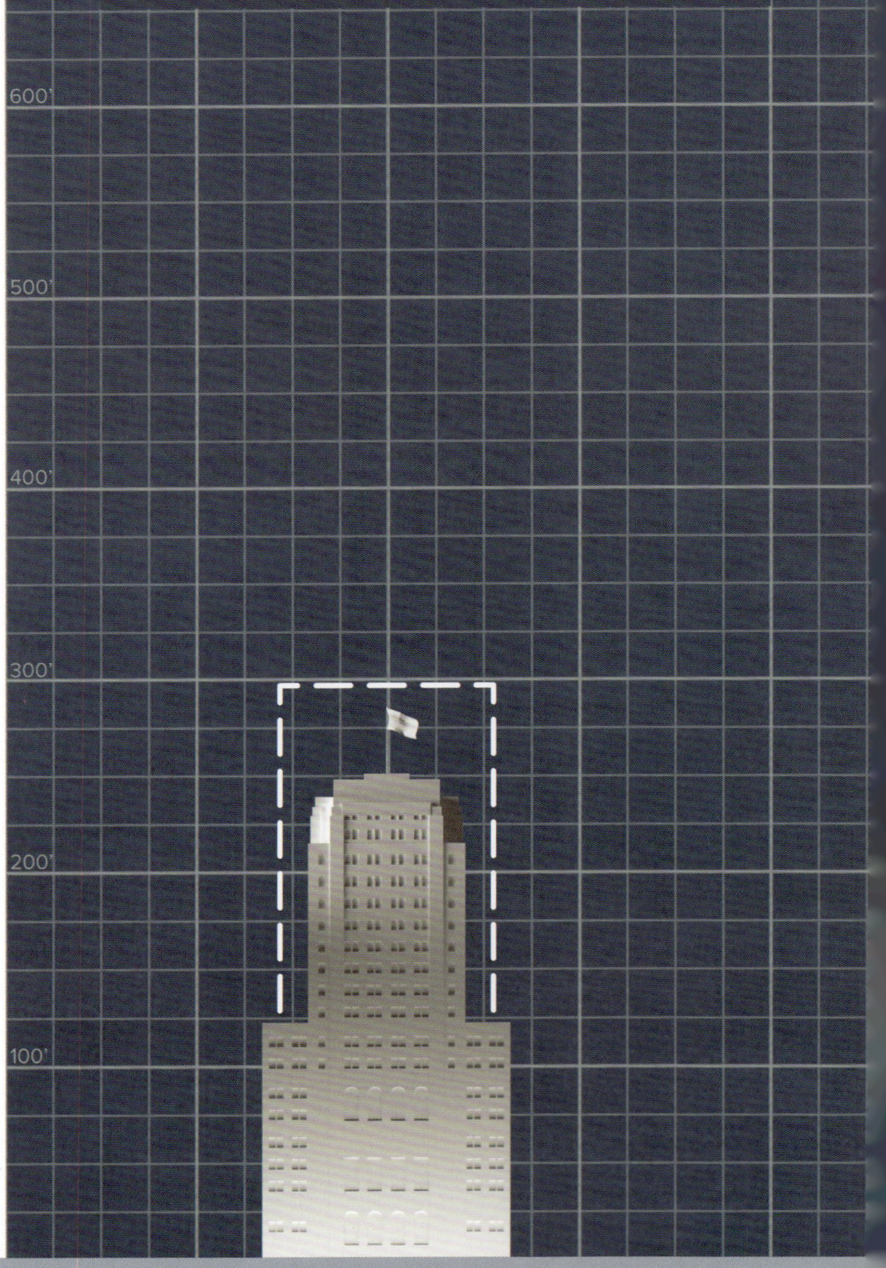

North Elevation *1" = 100'*

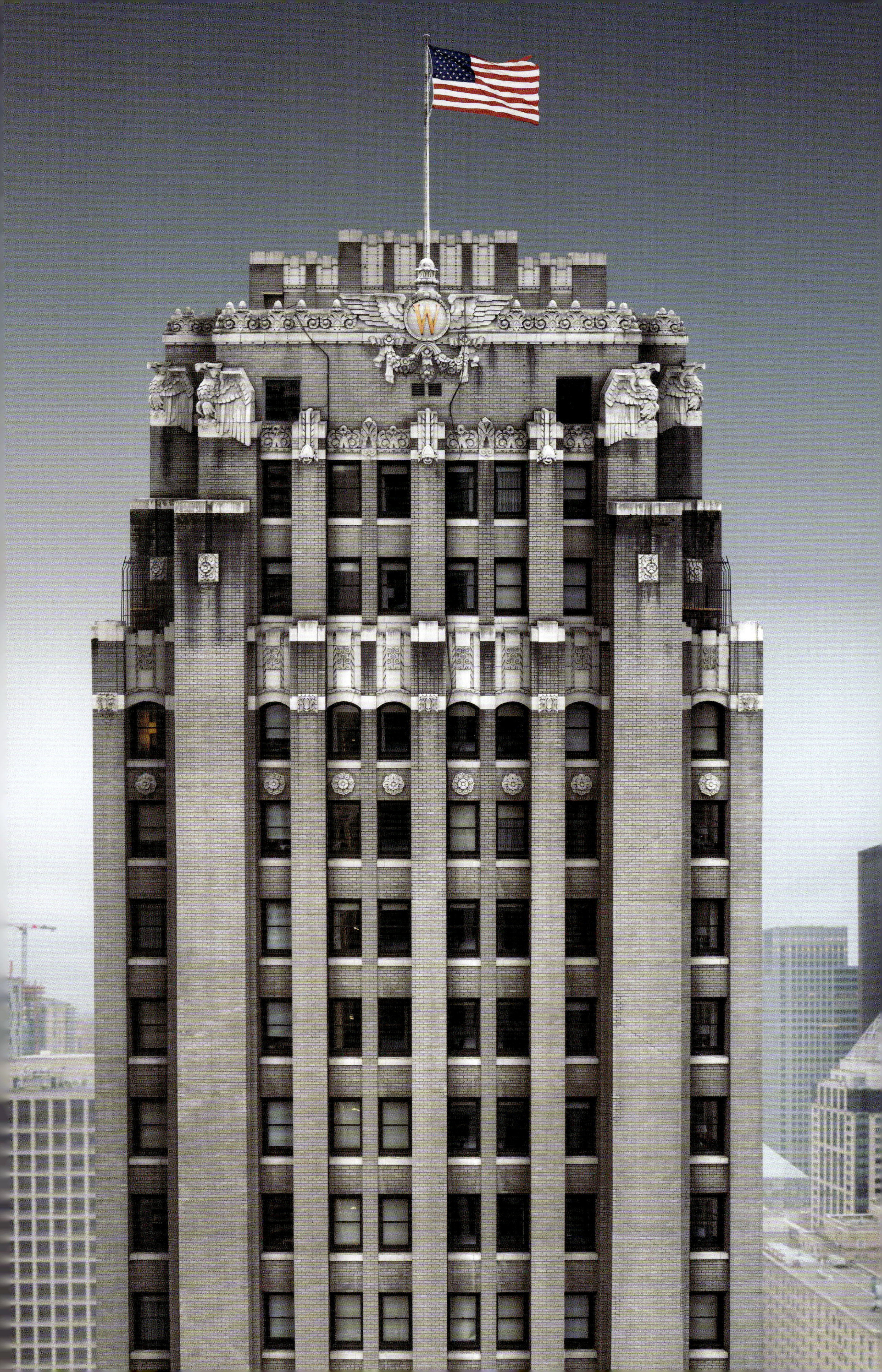
W

Numbers indicate how many buildings are featured in each city.

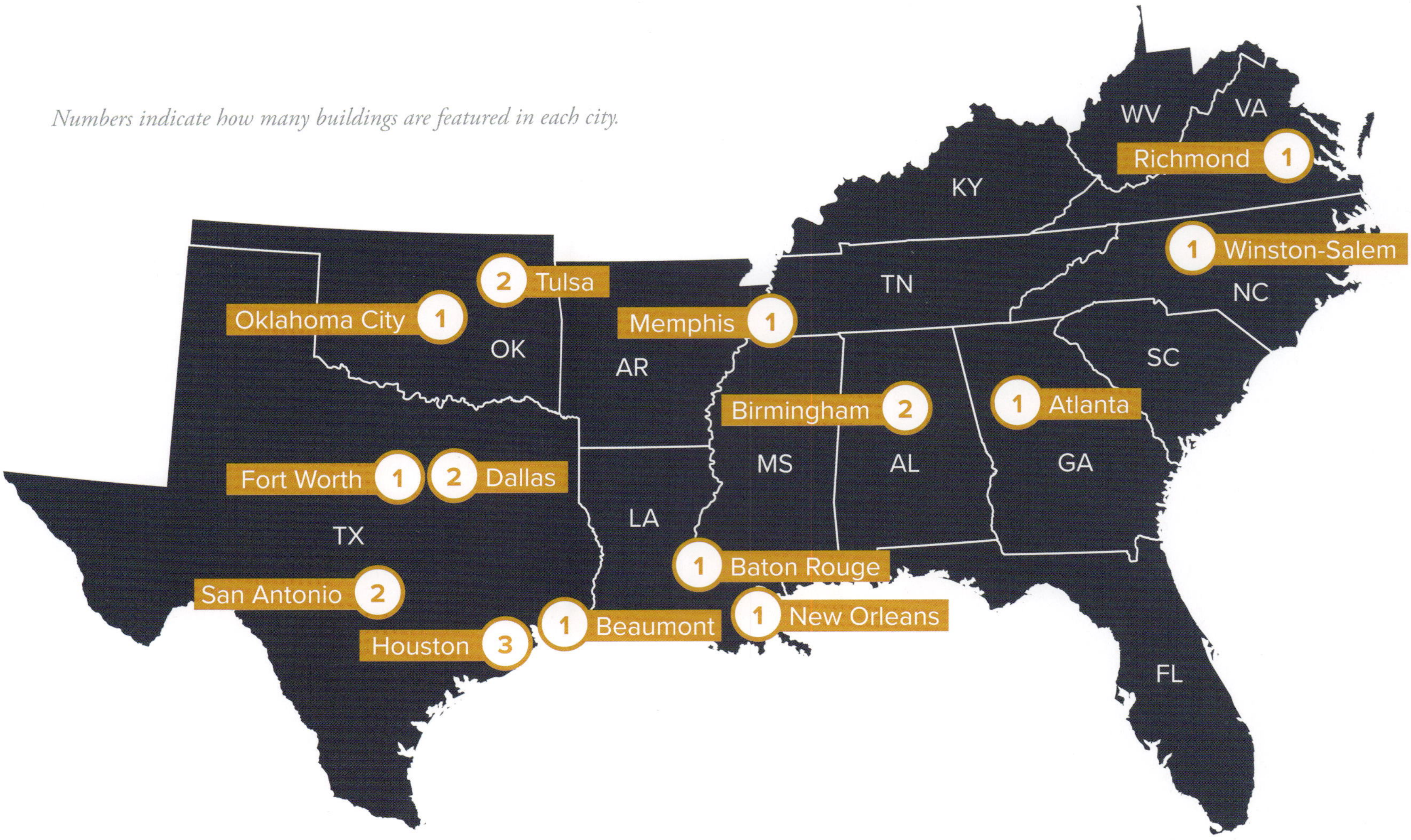

South

Several cities vie for skyscraper supremacy in the South. Many strong contenders abound in the Art Deco category, and while there may be no clear winner, each enjoys passionate support in keeping with Southern tradition.

Take Birmingham, an iron and steel powerhouse founded after the Civil War. Atop its colorful Alabama Power Building stands the goddess Electra, clutching lightning bolts in her fists. Or Baton Rouge, where rabble rouser Huey Long's state capitol blasted past Nebraska's to become the tallest government building in the country — and for a decade, the tallest skyscraper in the South.

It was bested, not surprisingly, by a Texas building. Massive oilfields discovered at the start of the 20th century gushed wealth into the cities of the Lone Star State, fueling skyscraper construction in Houston, Dallas, and elsewhere that continues unabated. Black gold also helped Tulsa to erect its Art Deco highrises, one of them for a church. Tobacco riches, meanwhile, lured a New York architect to design a Winston-Salem office tower a year before he started to sketch what would become the Empire State Building.

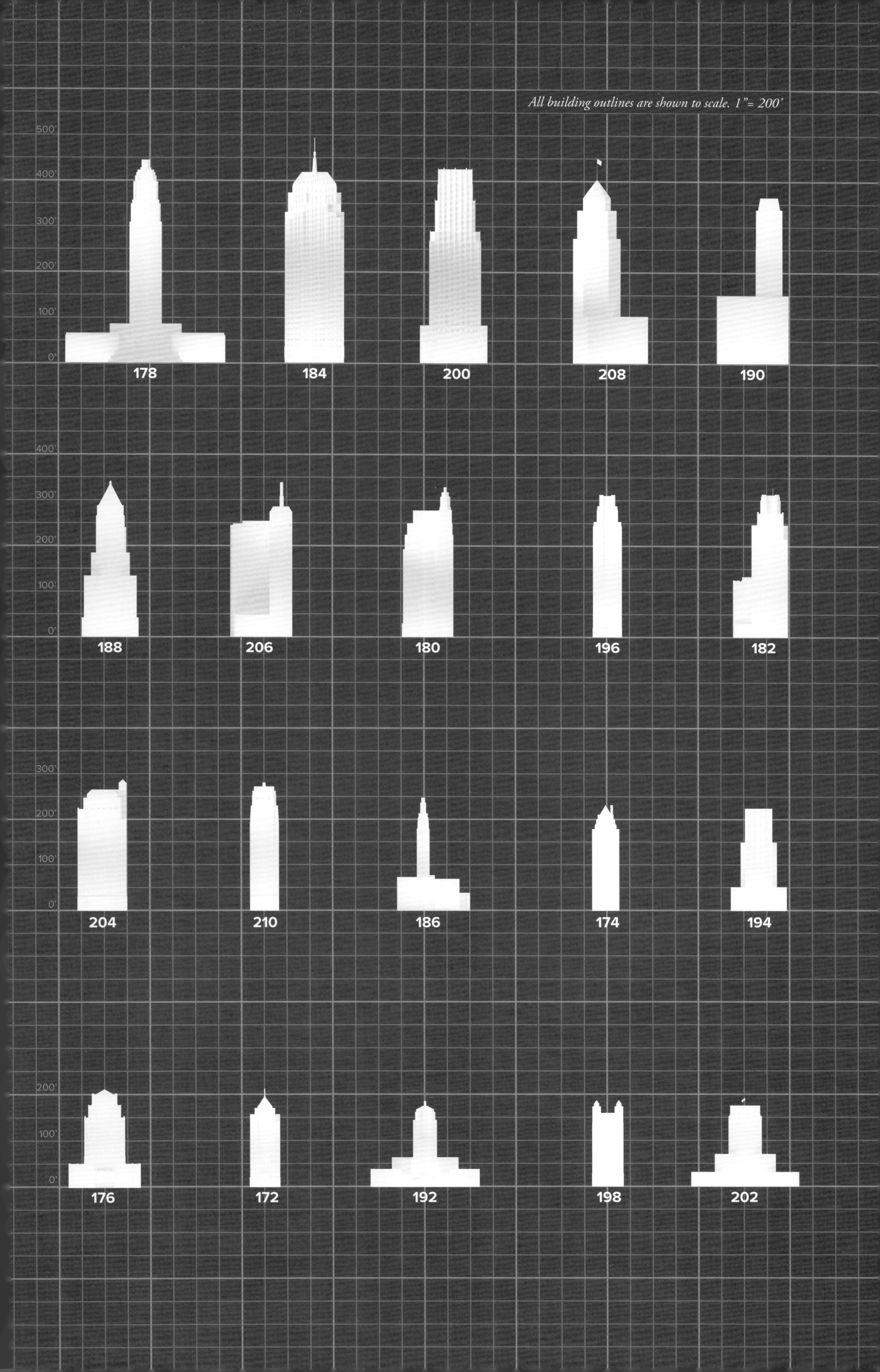

All building outlines are shown to scale. 1"= 200'
500'
400'
300'
200'
100'
0'
178
184
200
208
190
400'
300'
200'
100'
0'
188
206
180
196
182
300'
200'
100'
0'
204
210
186
174
194
200'
100'
0'
176
172
192
198
202

Alabama Power
Building

Birmingham, **AL**

Address	**600 18th St. N**
Opened	**1925**
Height	**217’**
Stories	**13**
Style	**Art Deco**
Architect	**William Warren**

Ever since the 25-foot gold statue of the goddess Electra made her rooftop debut, people have traded tales of a mystical love affair uniting her and the giant iron statue of Vulcan on the ridge overlooking the city. At least the god of the forge has a leather apron to partially shield his modesty.

Alabama Power was founded in 1906 by William Lay, a riverboat captain who mapped out rapids and shoals where hydroelectric dams could go. He started to build one on the Coosa River southeast of Birmingham, but had to hand over control of his company to finance the project, which began service in 1914 and was later named Lay Dam.

Another promising company site, at Muscle Shoals on the Tennessee River, was handed over to the federal government during World War I for a dam meant to power an explosives manufacturing plant. The nitrates factory was eventually built elsewhere, but the dam became the centerpiece of the Tennessee Valley Authority, one of Franklin D. Roosevelt’s most heralded domestic achievements.

Three carved figures over the entrance bearing gifts of a transmission tower, the sun, and a heating coil are labeled Power, Light, and Heat. The utility headquarters complex now fills the entire block, and is still connected to this highrise.

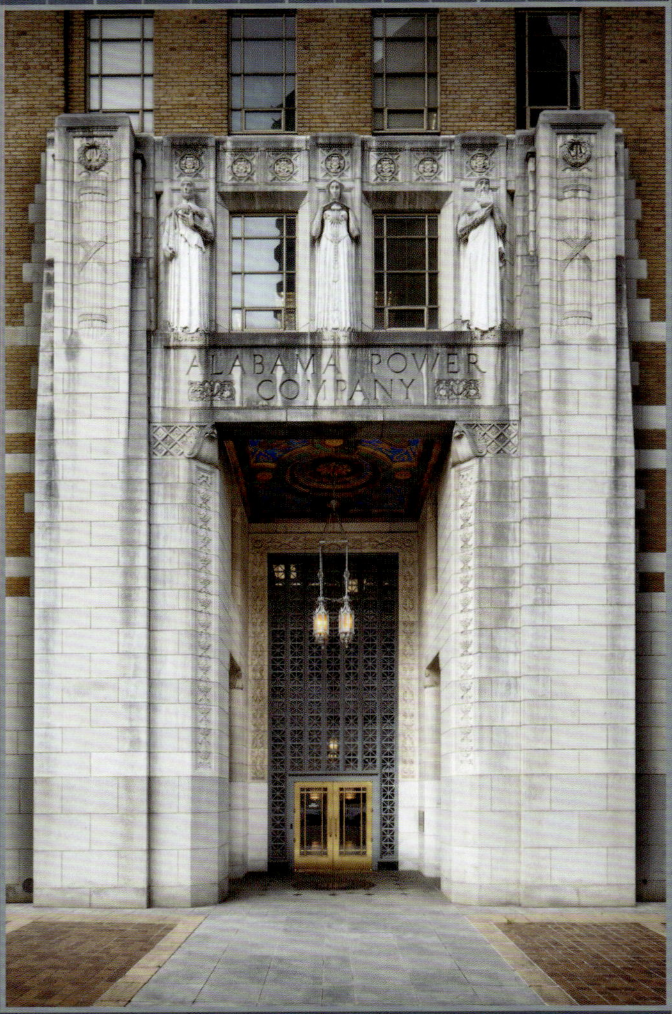

Sculptures of Power, Light, and Heat stand above the arcaded entry and its brightly painted ceiling.

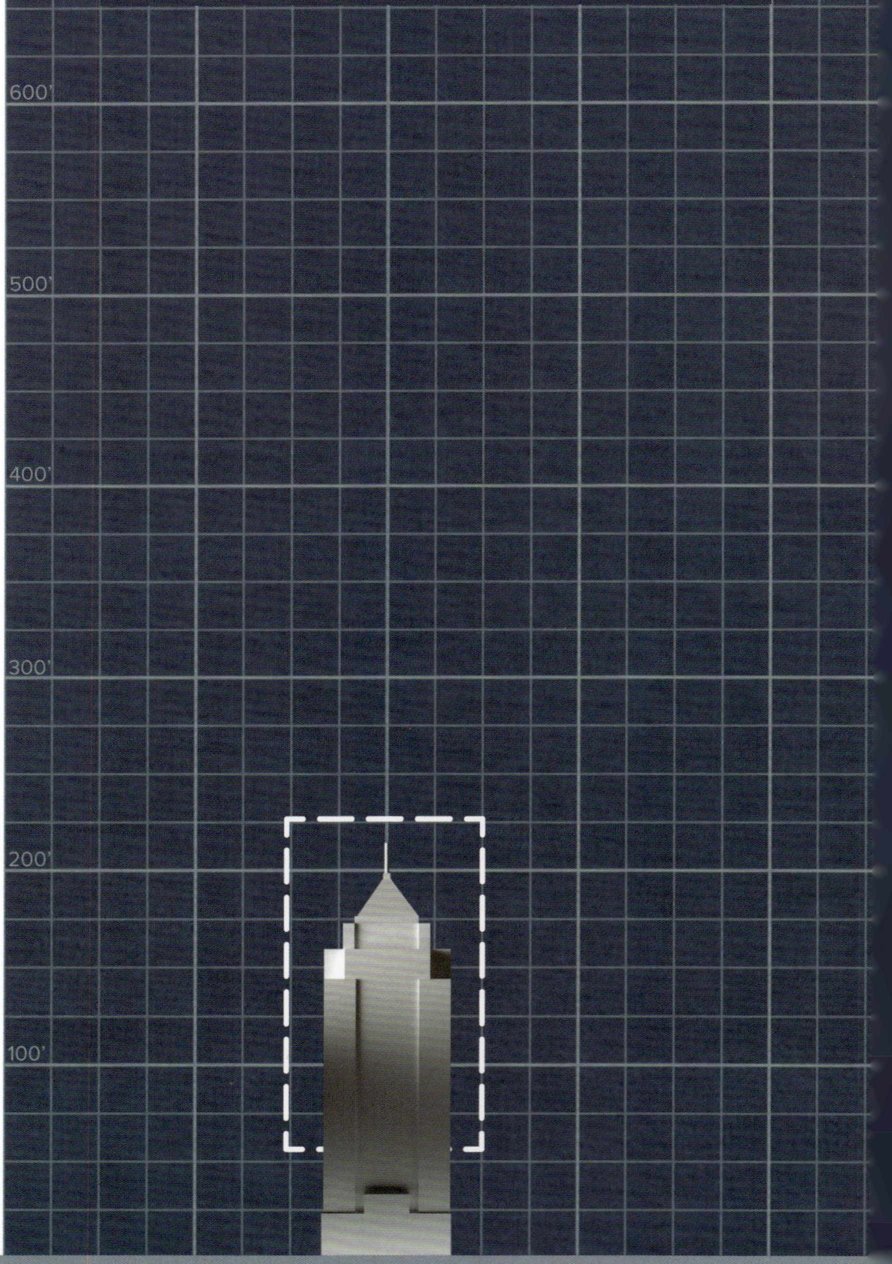

East Elevation *1" = 100'*

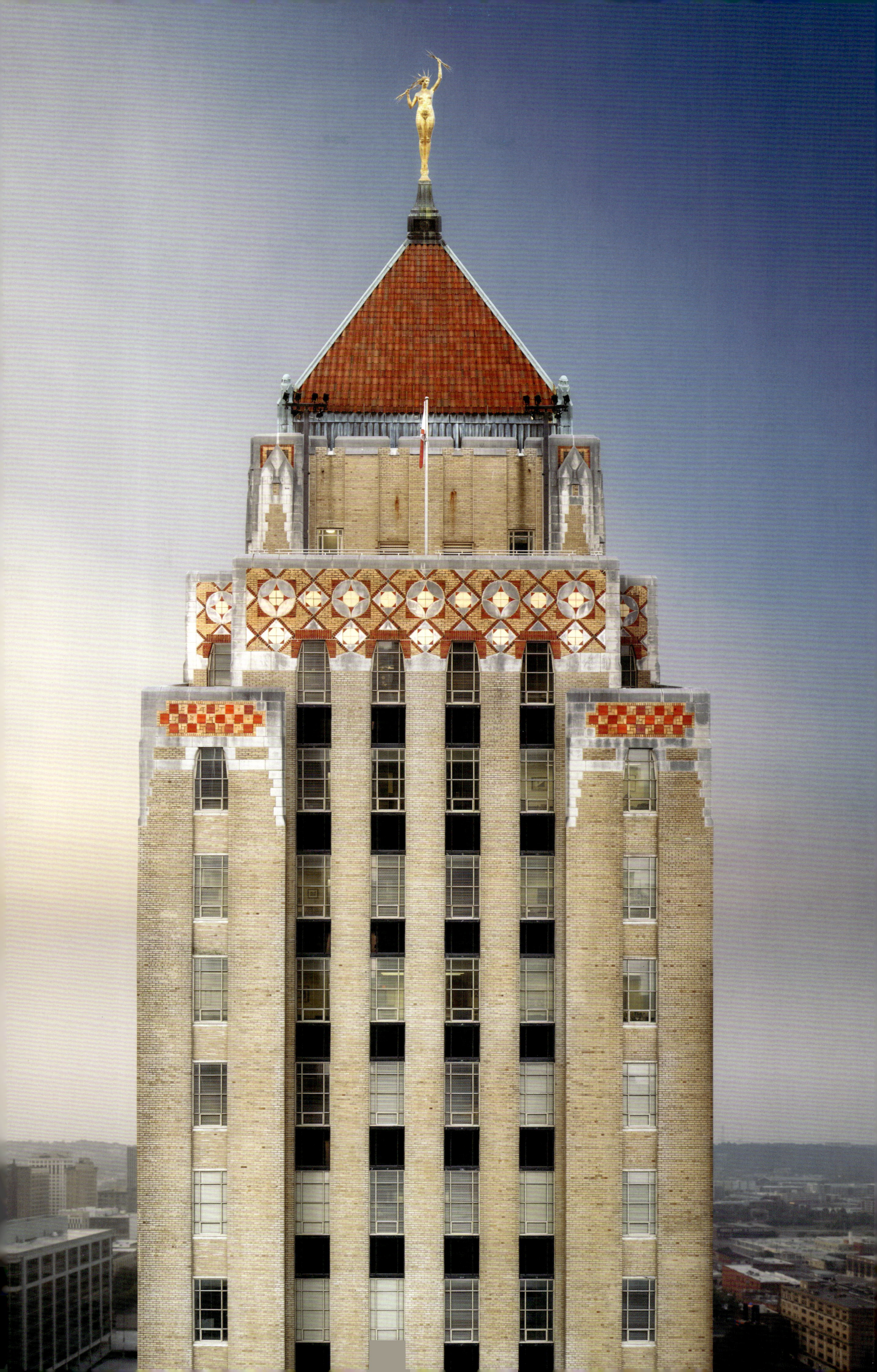

Watts Building

Birmingham, **AL**

Address ················ **300 N. 20th St.**
Opened ························ **1928**
Height ························ **236'**
Stories ························ **16**
Style ························ **Art Deco**
Architect ······· **Warren, Knight & Davis**

Birmingham was not yet two decades old when the first Watts Building, an office block with a tall mansard roof, went up. When the time came to replace it, this new highrise's steep roof was a reminder of its lineage.

The most celebrated person in the Watts family tree was not a Watts, but Charles Linn, a Swedish immigrant who built an iron works and then a bank in the post-Civil War boomtown. The land where the first Watts Building was built was a gift to his oldest daughter, Ellen Linn Watts.

Watts, widowed in her 30s, owned the property for over four decades, leaving it to her son in 1921. Months after her death, he was killed in a hunting accident, so it went to his widow, Julia Glass Watts, and her son, Thomas, a World War I veteran who had started a tire and lube business. They commissioned the skyscraper, but Julia died the next year, so only Thomas saw it completed.

It was the last office building in the city to employ elevator operators, who in 1990 still closed the doors by hand and started the cab with a crank. At the decade's end, it was converted to residential units.

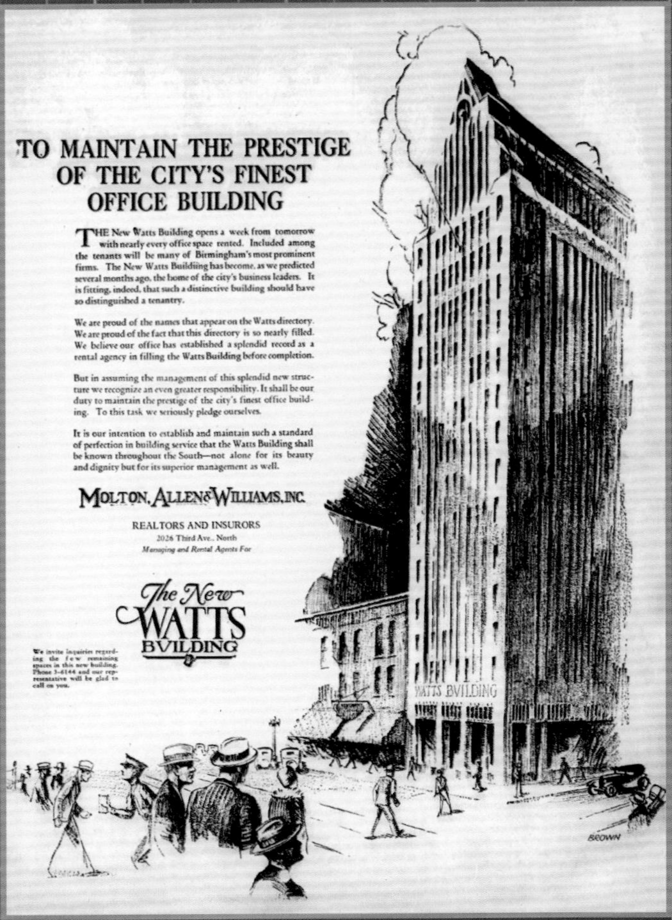

A 1928 leasing ad refers to the "new" Watts Building as the successor of the original office block.

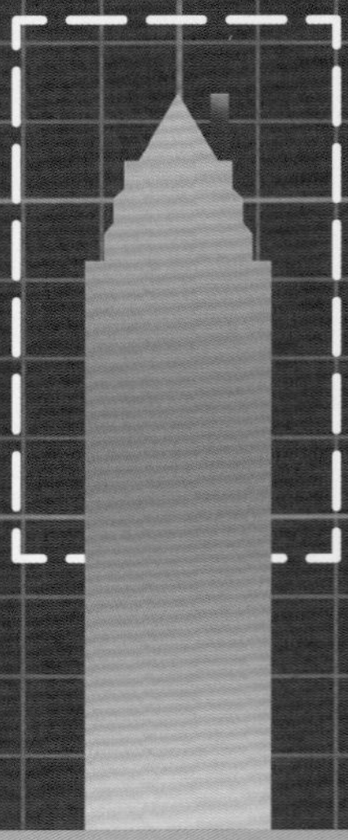

Southwest Elevation *1" = 100'*

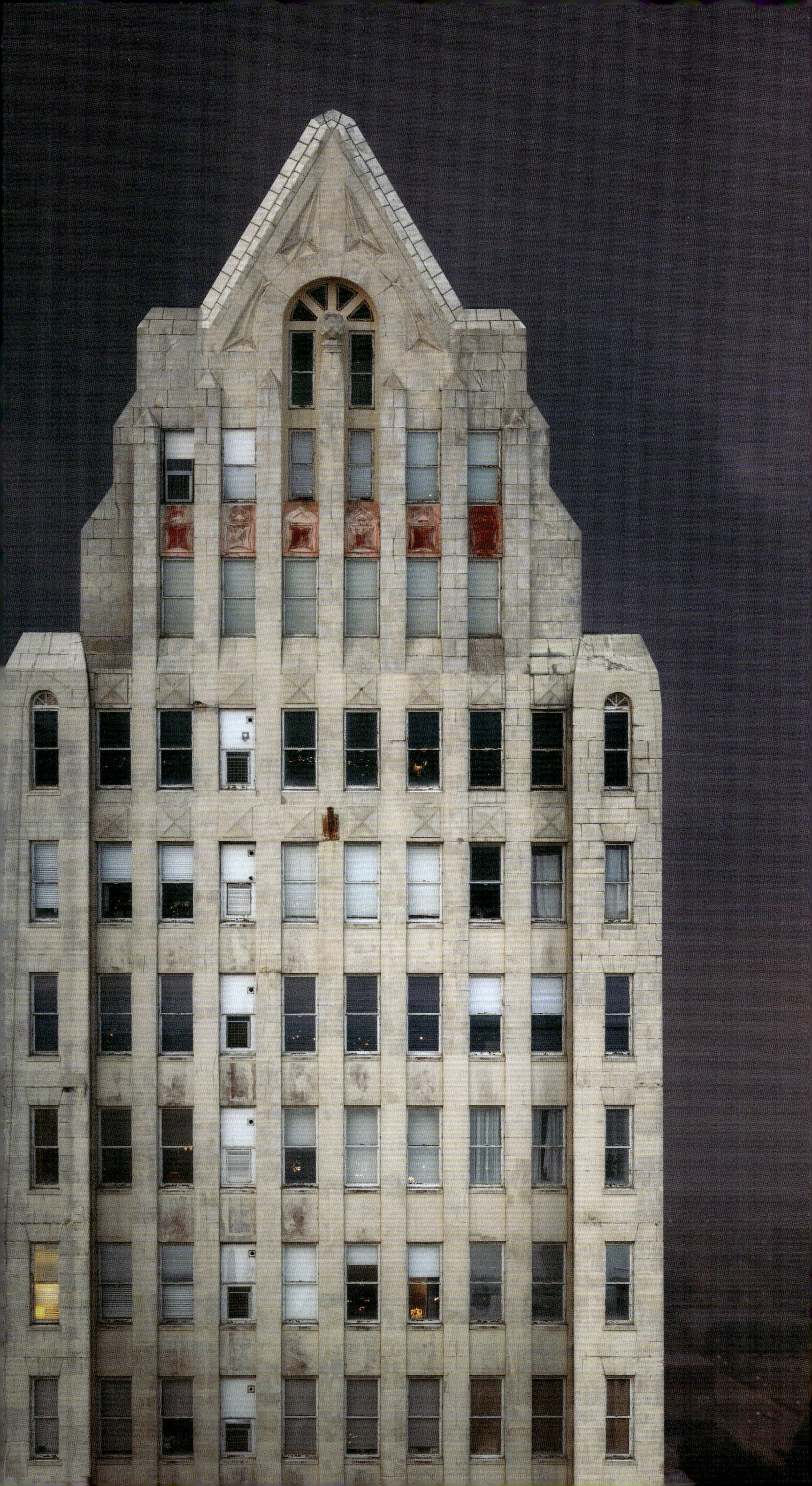

Atlanta City Hall

Atlanta, **GA**

Address	**68 Mitchell St.**
Opened	**1930**
Height	**212'**
Stories	**14**
Style	**Gothic, Art Deco**
Architect	**G. Lloyd Preacher**

It should have been a triumphant moment for Mayor Isaac Ramsdale when he formally accepted the keys to this municipal highrise and toured its gleaming marble halls. But the building by then was also in the spotlight of a graft probe that would send two city council members to prison and make the mayor a lame duck.

A bond to fund it passed overwhelmingly and construction was underway when, during a city council meeting in late 1929, an alderman griped about council wanting payoffs to pick a wiring contractor. Councilman Harry York berated the man, who recanted. That did not satisfy the publisher of the Atlanta Constitution, Clark Howell, who immediately penned an editorial demanding further investigation.

A grand jury report finding widespread corruption was issued the month before the new city hall opened, and York was the first of several officials convicted in the trials that followed. A year later, the Atlanta Constitution won a Pulitzer Prize for its role in uncovering the scandal.

The mayor and council moved to an adjacent annex in 1986, but the city still uses this highrise. Its lobby features extravagant Gothic decorative elements, such as pointed bronze arches above the elevator doors.

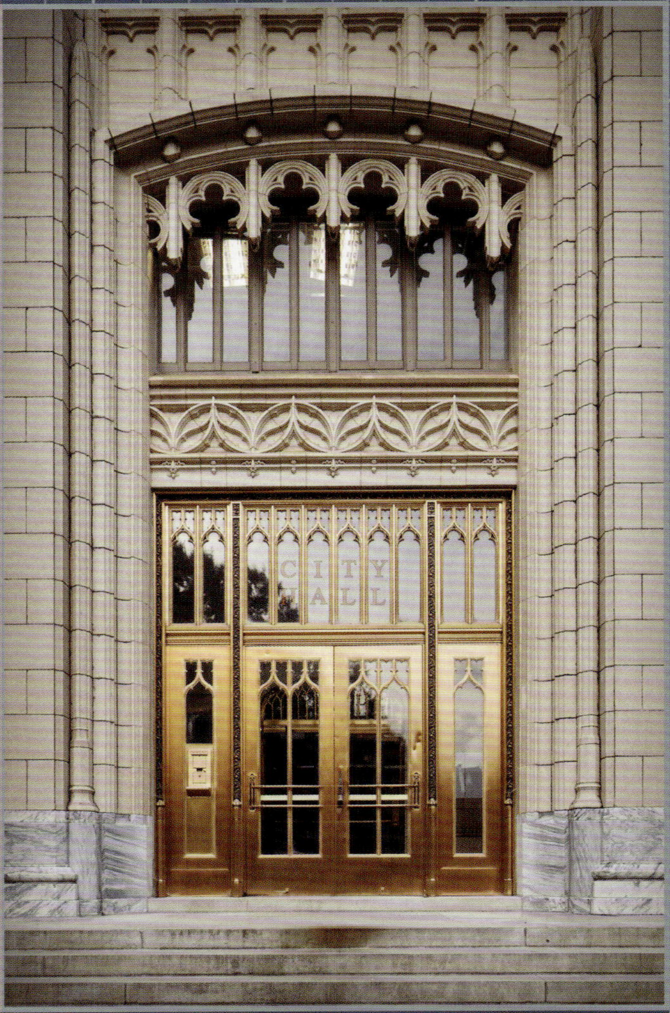

City officials also considered a Neoclassical design by another architect before settling on the Gothic motif.

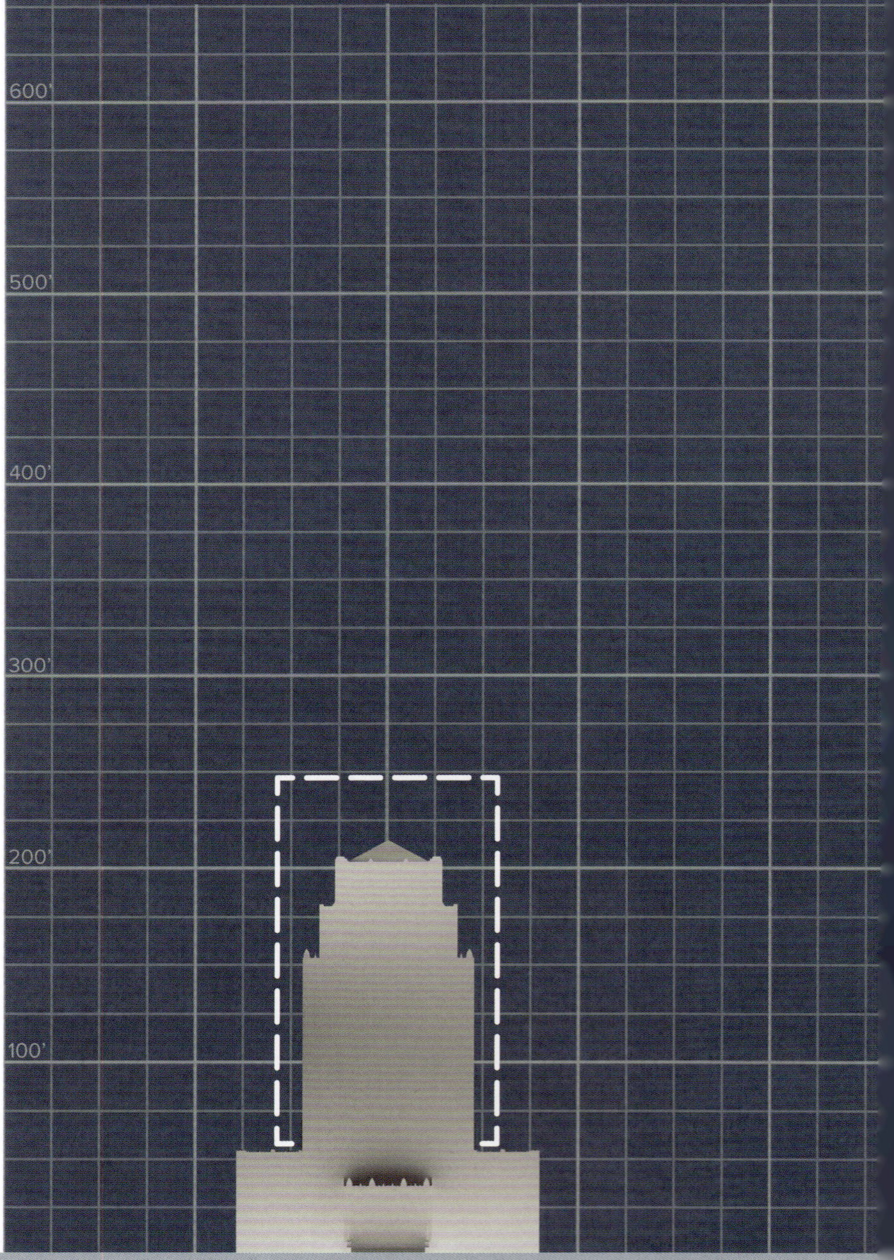

Northeast Elevation *1" = 100'*

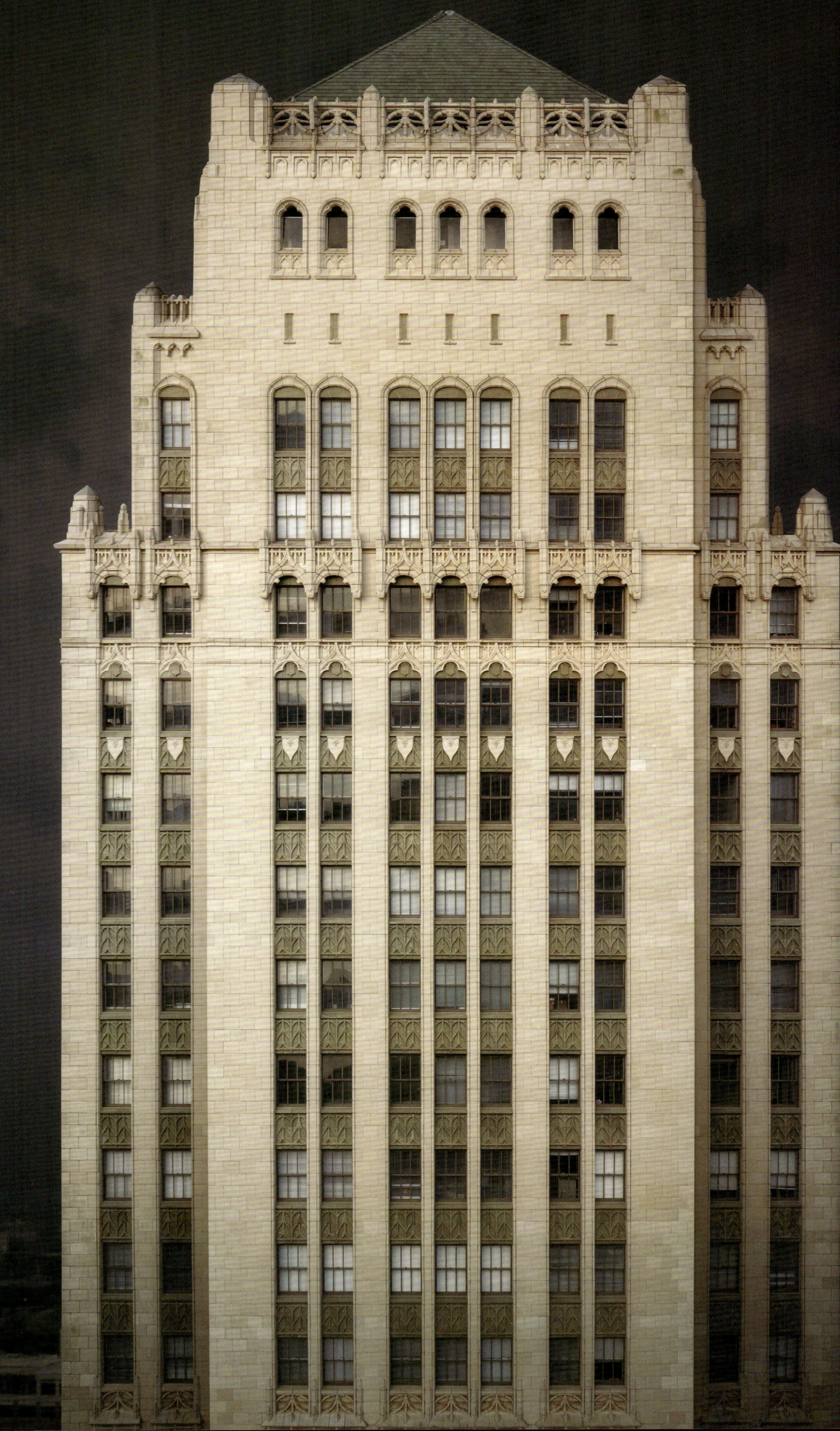

Louisiana
State Capitol

Baton Rouge, **LA**

Address ·············· **900 N. Third St.**
Opened ······················ **1932**
Height ························ **460'**
Stories ························ **34**
Style ······················ **Art Deco**
Architect ················· **Leon Weiss**

The tallest state capitol in America suits its champion, the grandiloquent populist Huey Long, who became governor and then senator in no small part due to big public works projects like this. Ironically, just as Long seemed on a path to the White House, he was gunned down in this very building.

A lawyer on the state public utility commission who honed his oratory arguing before the Supreme Court, Long played up his humble country origins to voters. Elected at age 34 as the state's youngest governor, Long made plenty of enemies, including Standard Oil, which he tried to tax to fund a raft of progressive social programs. An impeachment of Long for abuse of power failed, and he pushed through funding for free textbooks, hundreds of miles of highways, a railroad bridge over the Mississippi, and the new capitol.

Louisiana's state skyscraper supplanted Nebraska's in height; like its Midwestern cousin, the Baton Rouge tower is also richly carved with allegorical figures, friezes, and historical statuary — plus a passel of pelicans, the state bird. Visitors can scan horizons from the 27th floor observation deck, observe bullet damage in the main hall's marble walls from Long's assassination, and make a pilgrimage to the martyred leader's grave in the formal gardens, where a replica of the skyscraper rises from his pale marble tombstone.

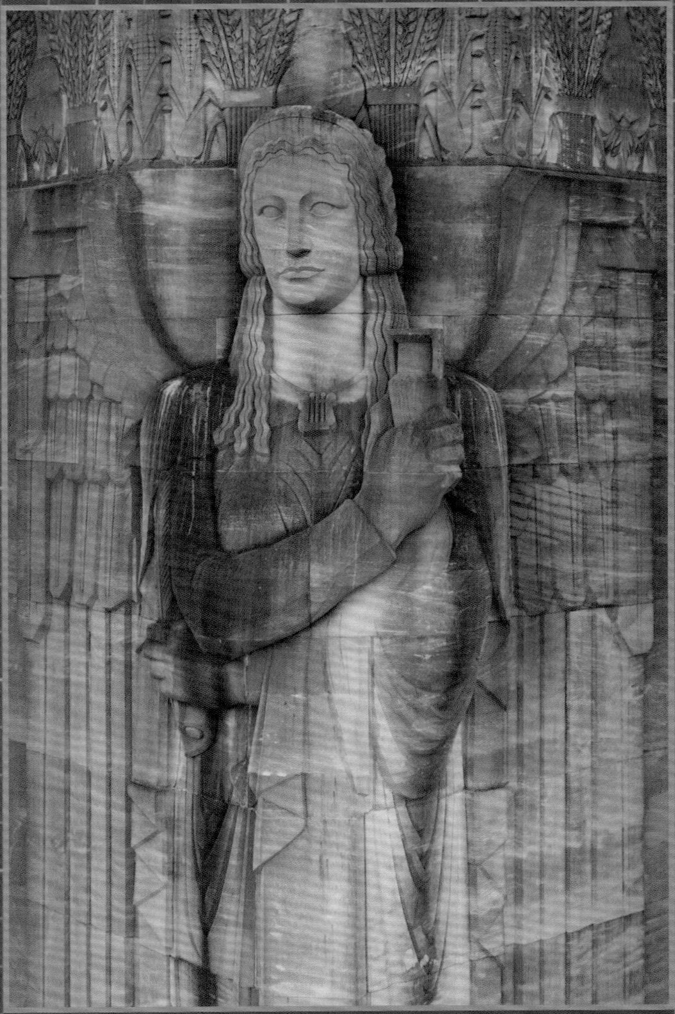

Allegorical busts carved in the corners near the top stand for Law, Science, Philosophy, and Art.

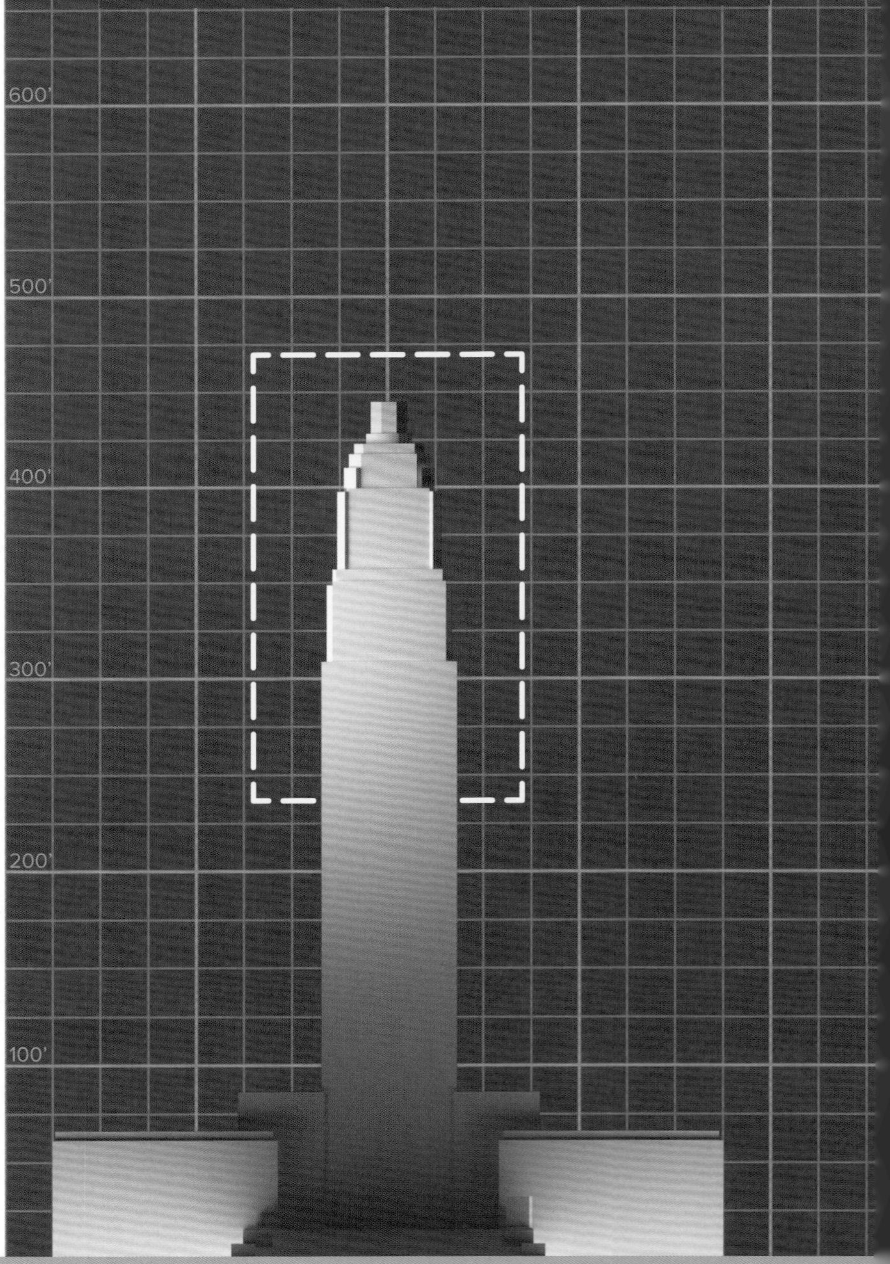

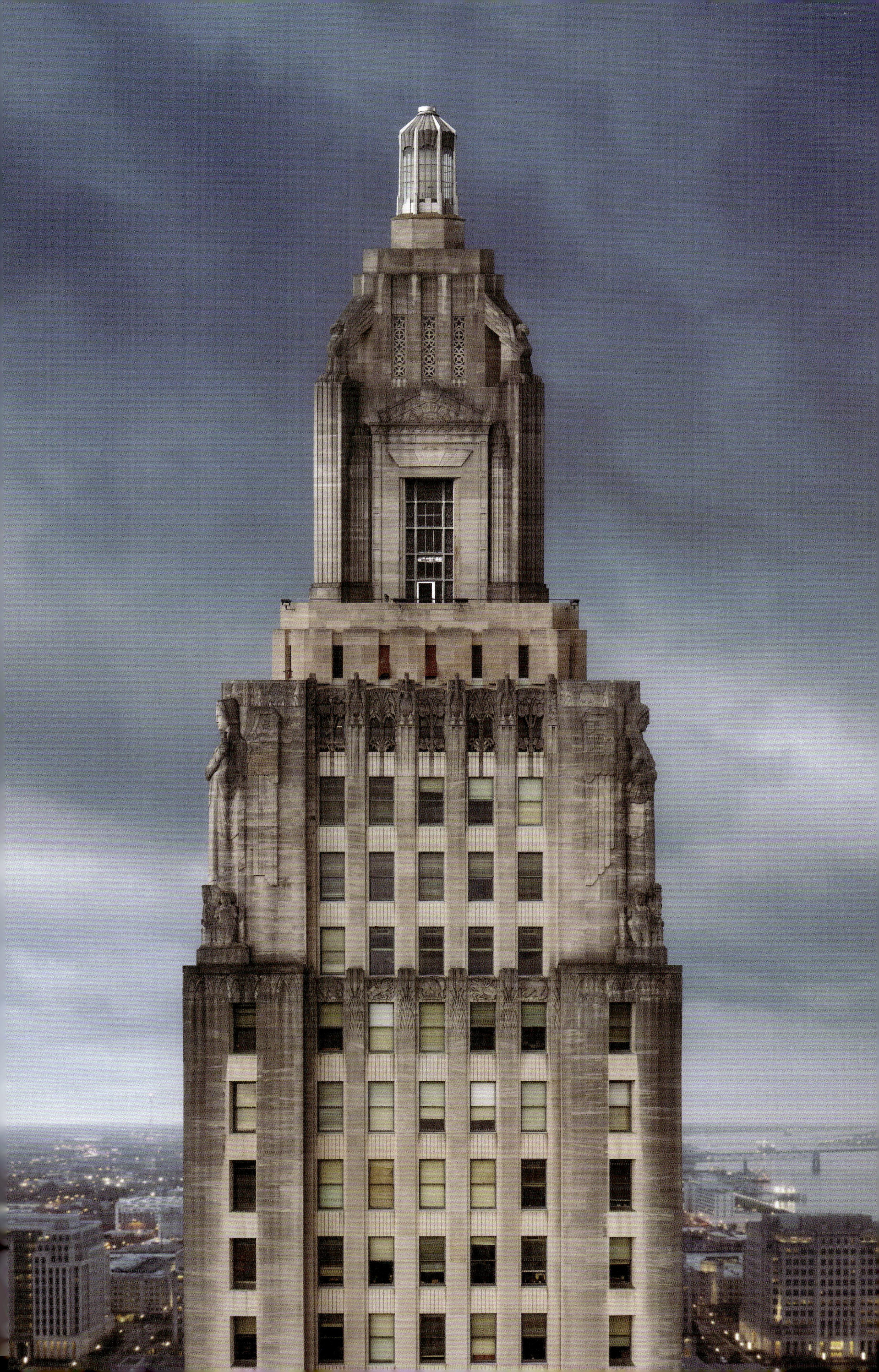

American Bank
Building

New Orleans, **LA**

Address	**200 Carondelet St.**
Opened	**1929**
Height	**330'**
Stories	**23**
Style	**Art Deco**
Architect	**Moise Goldstein**

Late night revelers on Bourbon Street can use the illuminated tower of this highrise as a beacon to guide them out of the French Quarter. The copper-topped cupola, designed to hold the water tank with panache, provides a modern contrast to the classical one on the slightly older Hibernia Bank a block away.

Another neighbor, the 10-story Hennen Building across the street, dates from 1895, laying claim to the title of the South's first skyscraper. Much changed in the intervening three decades from its erection to this highrise, but both were built on top of an underground forest of wooden pilings driven into the swampy soil. So stands steadily the sole Art Deco skyscraper in a city whose architectural style usually hews to tradition.

The original American Bank & Trust brass entrance gate leads from the marble elevator lobby into the banking hall, which is no longer in use. The institution was renamed National American Bank in 1949, and later spent time as a Bank One before it emptied out. Destruction caused by Hurricane Katrina led to huge demand for replacement housing, and the vacant tower was converted into an apartment complex.

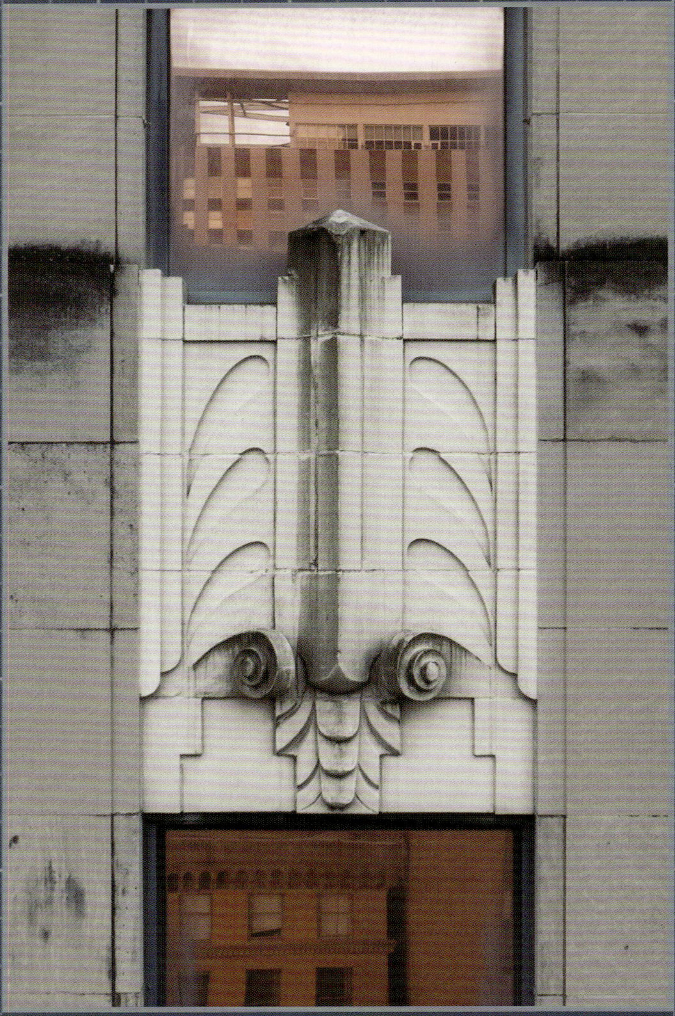

White molded forms above the windows at each setback help to draw the eye upwards to the copper cupola.

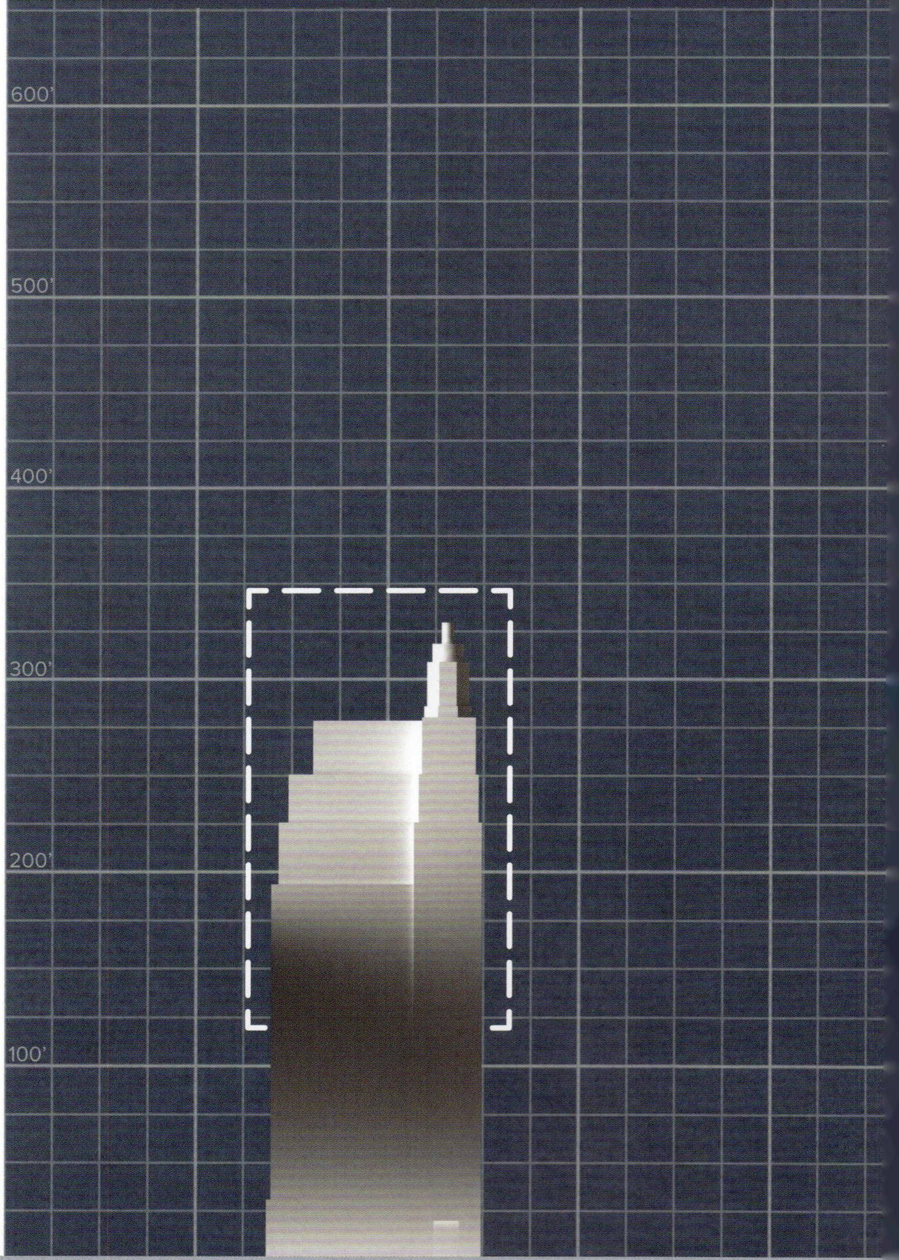

West Elevation *1" = 100'*

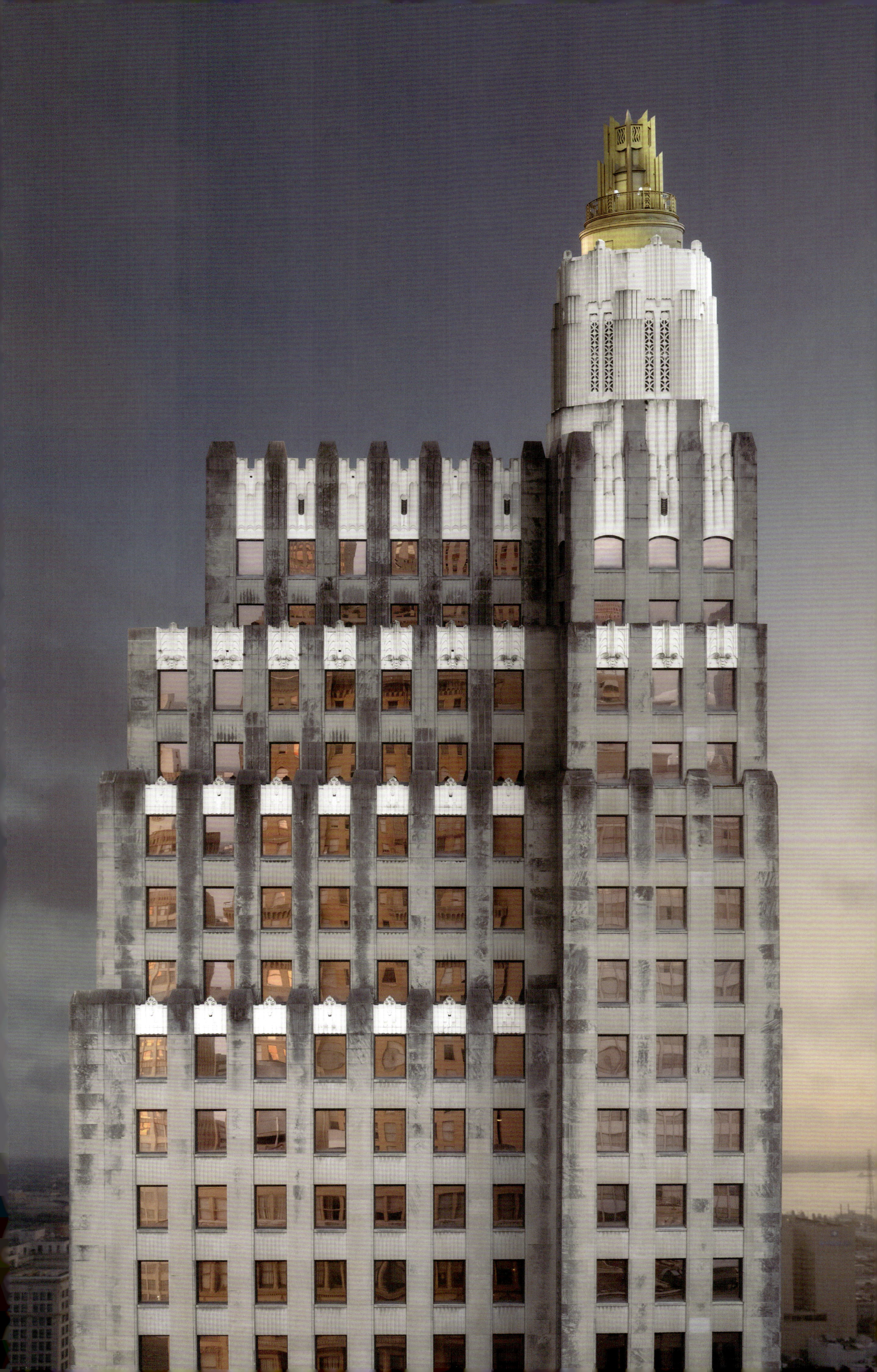

R. J. Reynolds
Building

Winston-Salem, **NC**

Address	**401 N. Main St.**
Opened	**1929**
Height	**314’**
Stories	**21**
Style	**Art Deco**
Architect	**William Lamb**

When this tobacco company highrise turned 50, an executive at the firm managing the Empire State Building sent a card inscribed “Happy anniversary, Dad.” That’s because William Lamb, the New York architect who designed what was once the tallest skyscraper in North Carolina, shortly thereafter drew up plans for the tallest one in the world.

Richard Joshua Reynolds grew up on a Virginia tobacco plantation and started a factory in North Carolina making plug tobacco for chewing or smoking in a pipe. In 1913 he launched a new product, a pre-rolled cigarette blending American and Turkish leaves. His assistant went to the traveling circus in town and got a photograph of their dromedary, “Old Joe,” that became the logo for Camel cigarettes.

Marketed nationally and priced below the competition, the popular brand drove the company’s rapid growth. Its new headquarters had custom plumbing and wiring installed on two floors to entice doctors to lease offices there.

Carved wooden ceilings in the marble elevator lobby still have a tobacco leaf motif, though the company moved out in 2009 to new quarters on the same block. Now its old highrise is part residential, part upscale hotel — with a no smoking sign in every room.

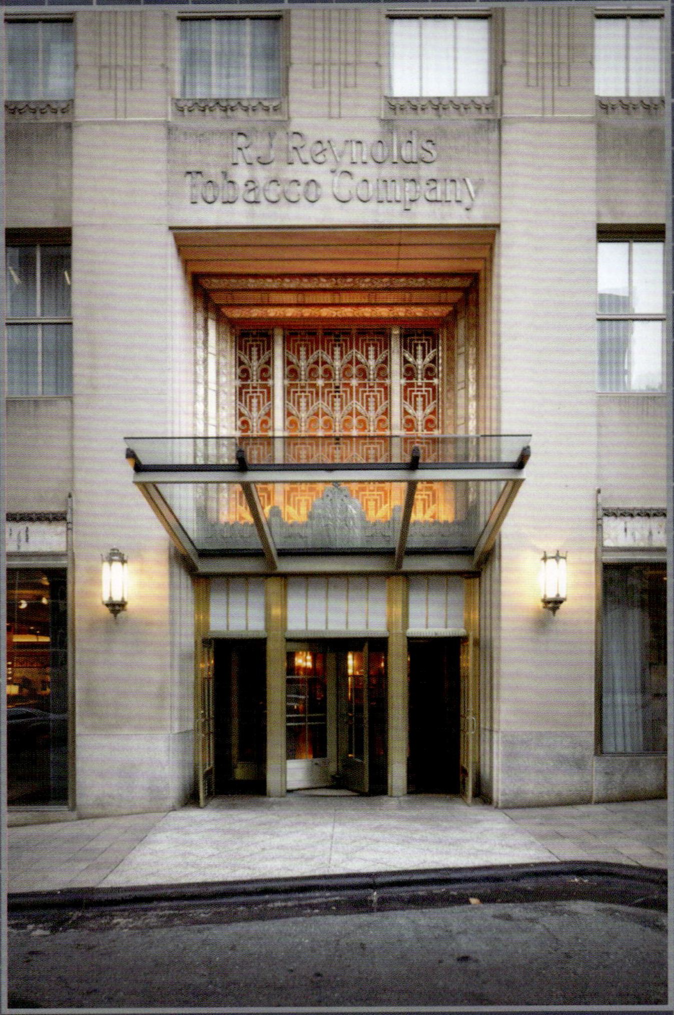

Original molding beneath the grille features a large tobacco leaf flanked by two models of the building.

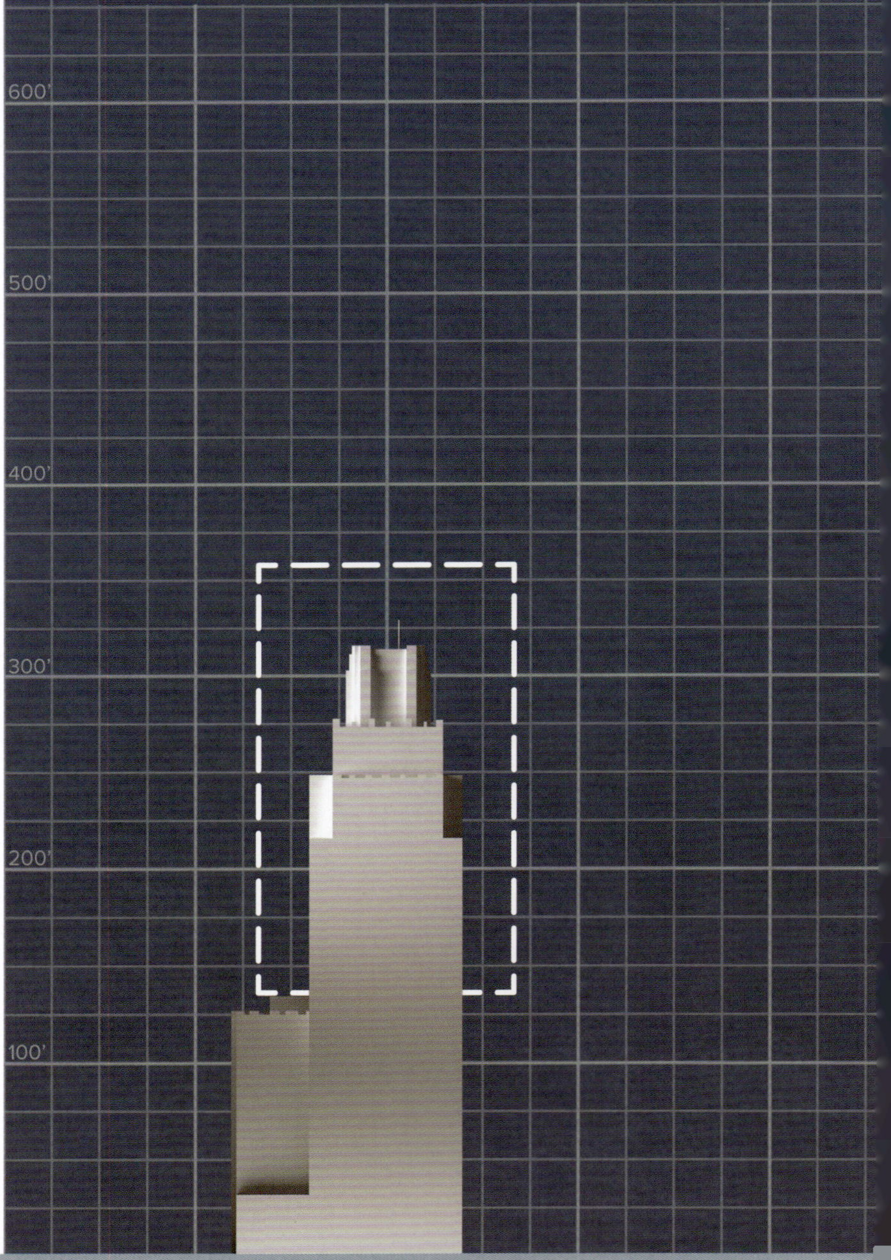

West Elevation *1" = 100'*

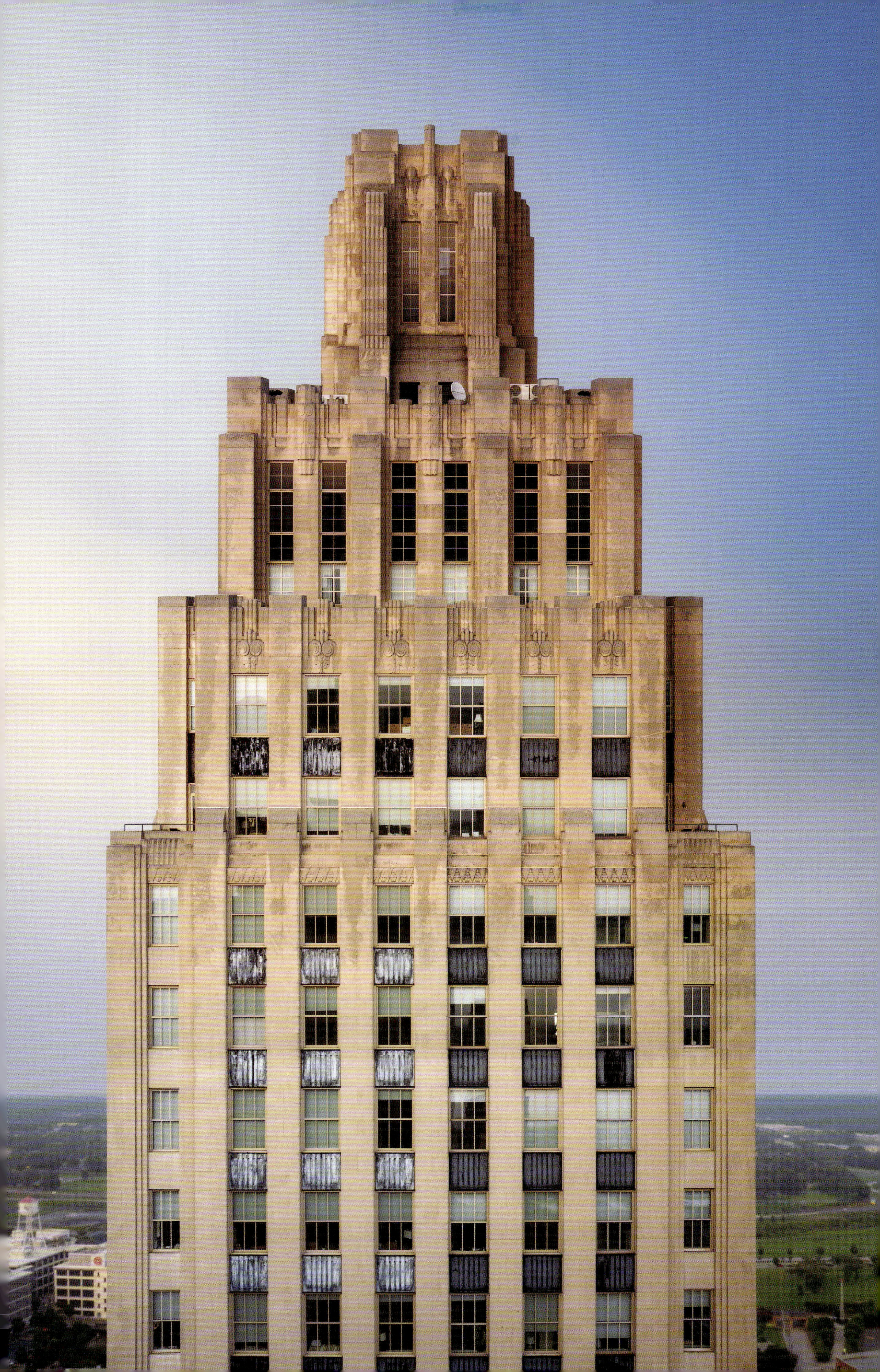

First National Bank
Building

Oklahoma City, **OK**

Address	**120 N. Robinson Ave.**
Opened	**1931**
Height	**443’**
Stories	**32**
Style	**Art Deco**
Architect	**Weary & Alford**

Murals in the banking hall of this highrise depict pivotal moments in the state formerly known as Indian Territory. One shows the arrival of a caravan of indigenous people forced from their ancestral homelands on the “Trail of Tears.” Others depict the wild 1889 land rush when the territory was opened to settlers.

Two brothers, Frank and Hugh Johnson, merged their competing Oklahoma City banks in 1927 and commissioned the state’s tallest skyscraper for their First National Bank & Trust. It was their second cooperative venture; as teenagers they ran the family newspaper and printing business in Kosciusko, Mississippi, after their father died. They moved to Oklahoma soon after the original Sooners and made separate careers in banking before joining forces.

Their bank survived the Great Depression but failed in 1986 in the aftermath of an oil bust that torpedoed its commercial loan portfolio. After a long vacancy, the property was converted to a residential and hotel complex. Penthouses occupy the glass-enclosed 31st story, originally an open-air public observatory that then spent decades as a private supper club. Fancy diners now sup in the sumptuously restored banking hall, beneath an enormous skylight flanked by Corinthian columns 40 feet tall.

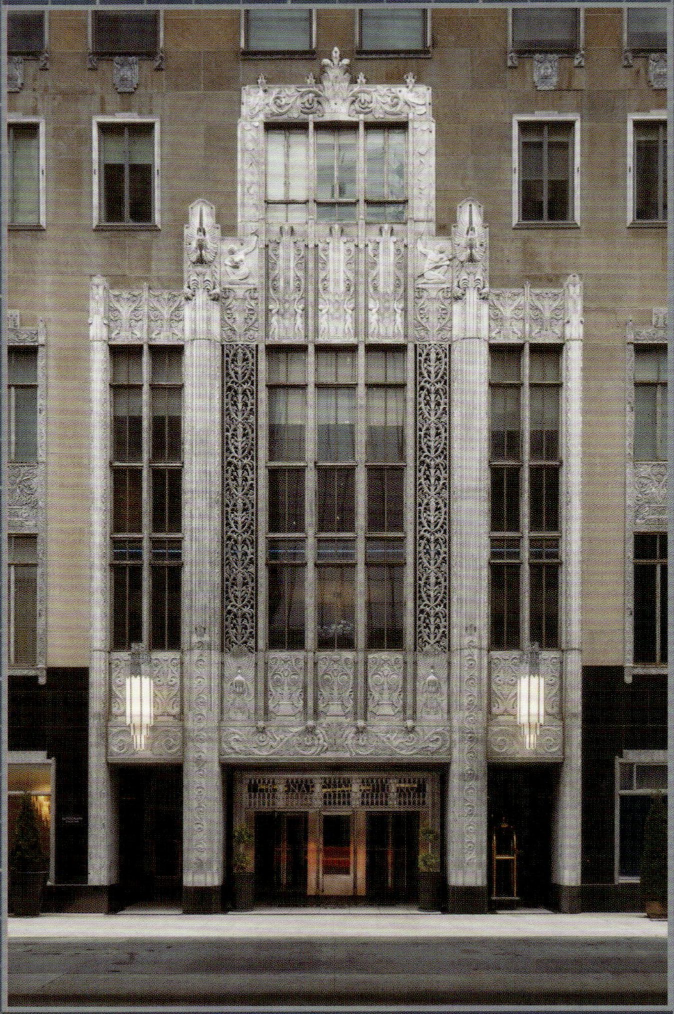

The four-story ornamental entrance of intricate cast aluminum panels gleams against the stone.

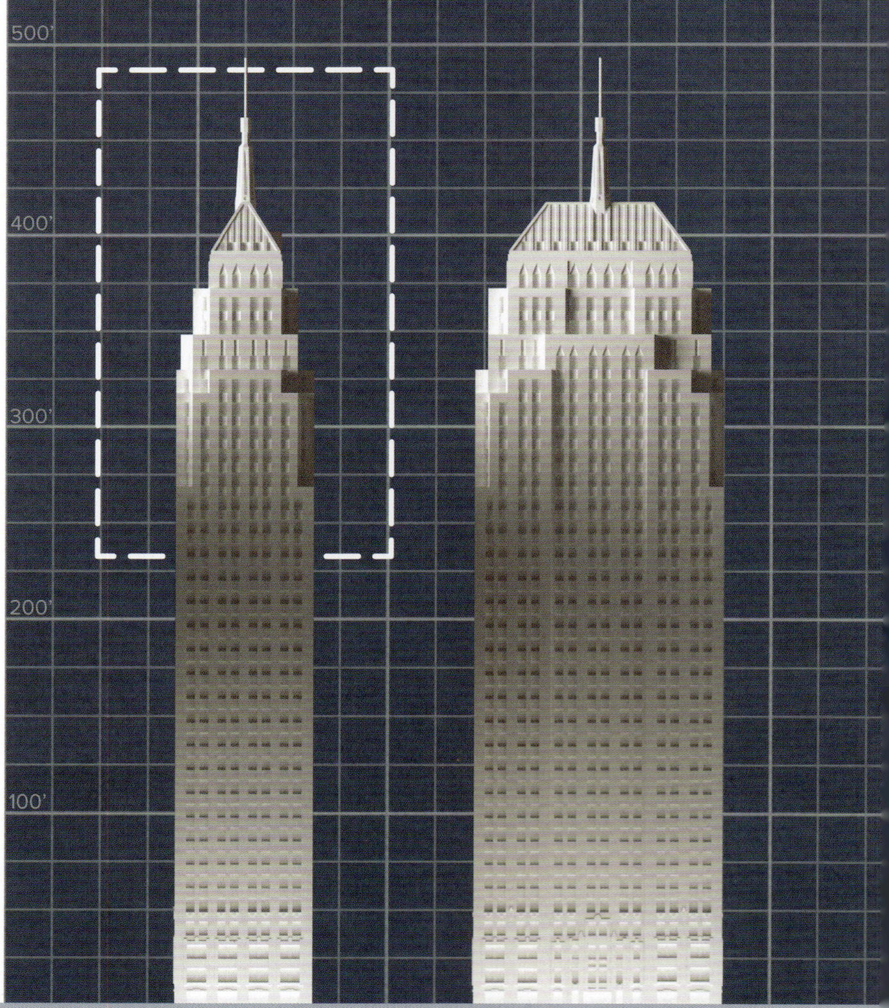

South Elevation West Elevation *1" = 100'*

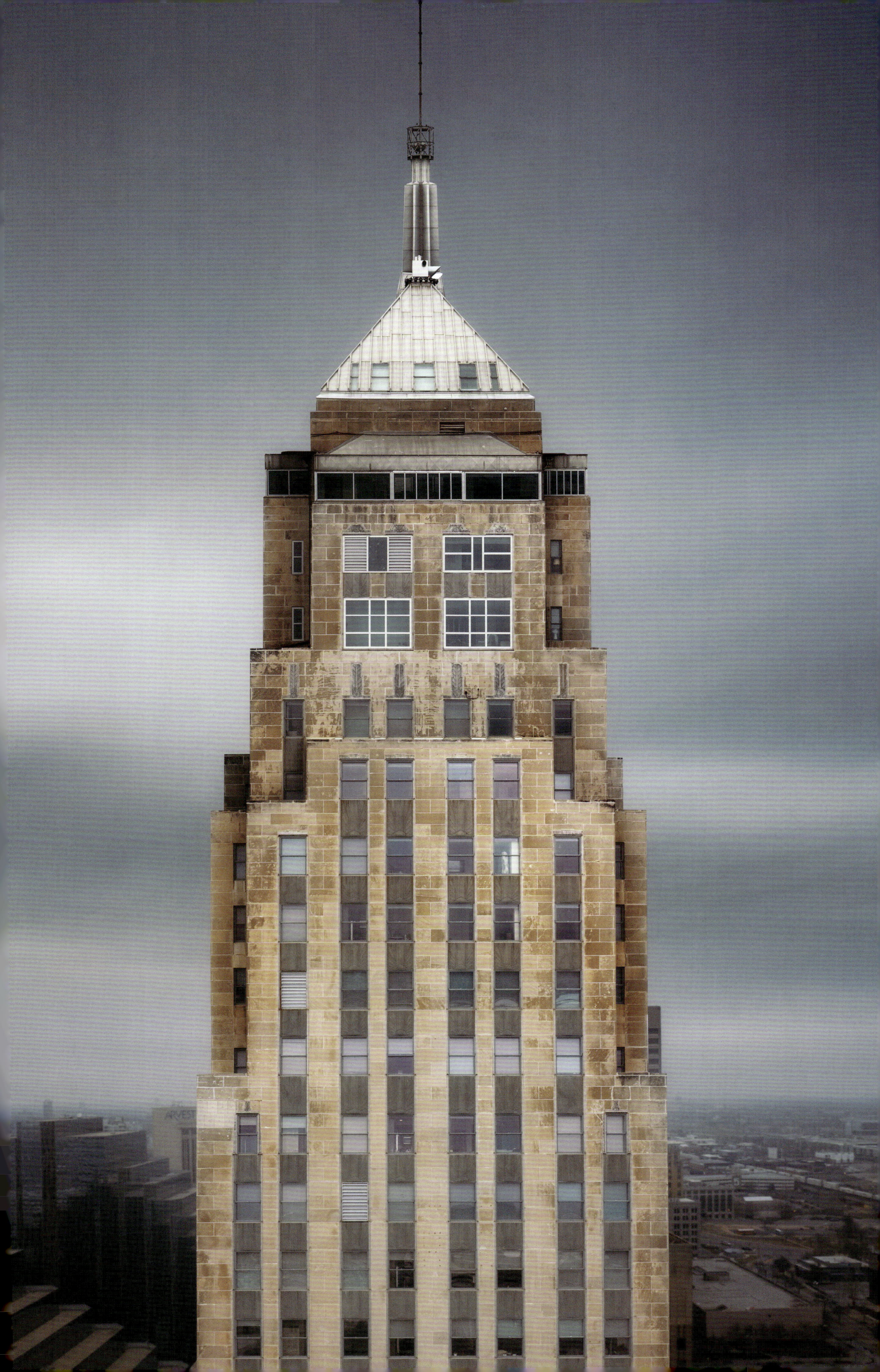

Boston Avenue
Methodist Church

Tulsa, **OK**

Address	**1301 S. Boston Ave.**
Opened	**1929**
Height	**255'**
Stories	**15**
Style	**Art Deco**
Architect	**Adah Robinson**

Praying hands add upward thrust to this inspirational example of an Art Deco skyscraper in service to the sacred. The tower, topped with a prayer chapel, arose during a Roaring '20s spate of ecclesiastical construction.

Two other showy houses of worship were already underway — a stone-walled Methodist one and a strikingly avant-garde Catholic church — when the Boston Avenue congregation resolved to replace their staid 1907 structure with something thoroughly modern. For creative inspiration, the building committee turned to the high school art teacher, Adah Robinson.

A talented painter trained at the Art Institute of Chicago, Robinson won over the committee with imaginative concept and design drawings. Bruce Goff, her former pupil who had become an architect and designed a studio for Robinson, was brought aboard to draft the structure under her direction. Another former student, Robert Garrison, executed the sculptural elements to her specifications.

The project won Robinson an offer from the University of Tulsa to chair its art department. She stayed nearly two decades, but quit when a new president told her he thought Goff was the church's true architect. Boston Avenue has always credited Robinson alone for the design. She also inspired Mary Cole, the teenage daughter of the church building committee chairman, to become Oklahoma's first licensed female architect.

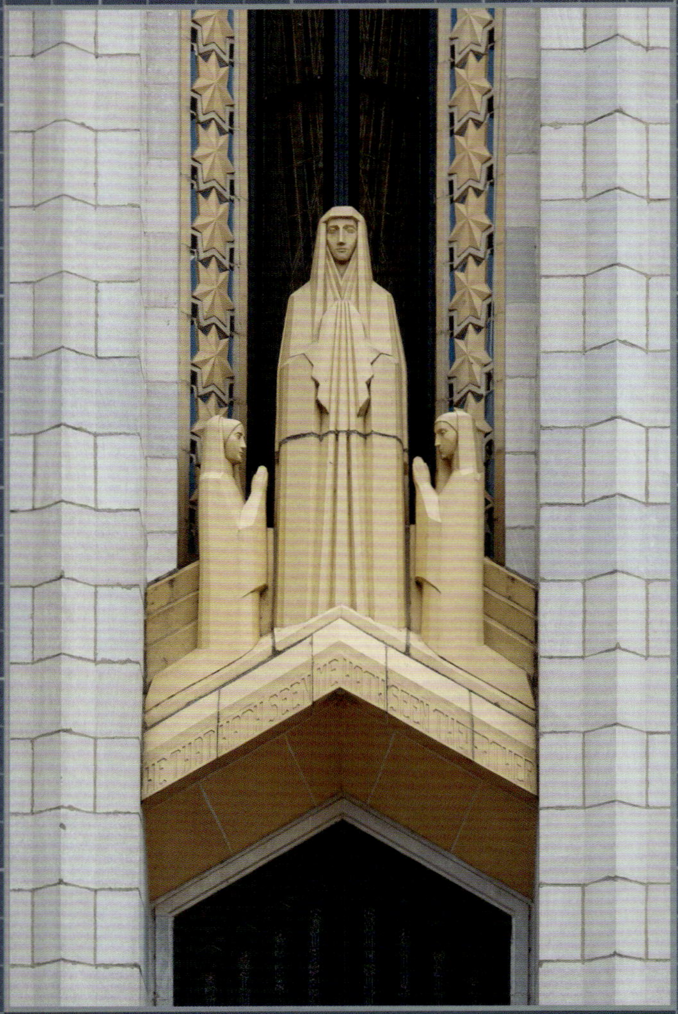

Sculptures honor Methodist leaders and faithful, including worshipers over the door.

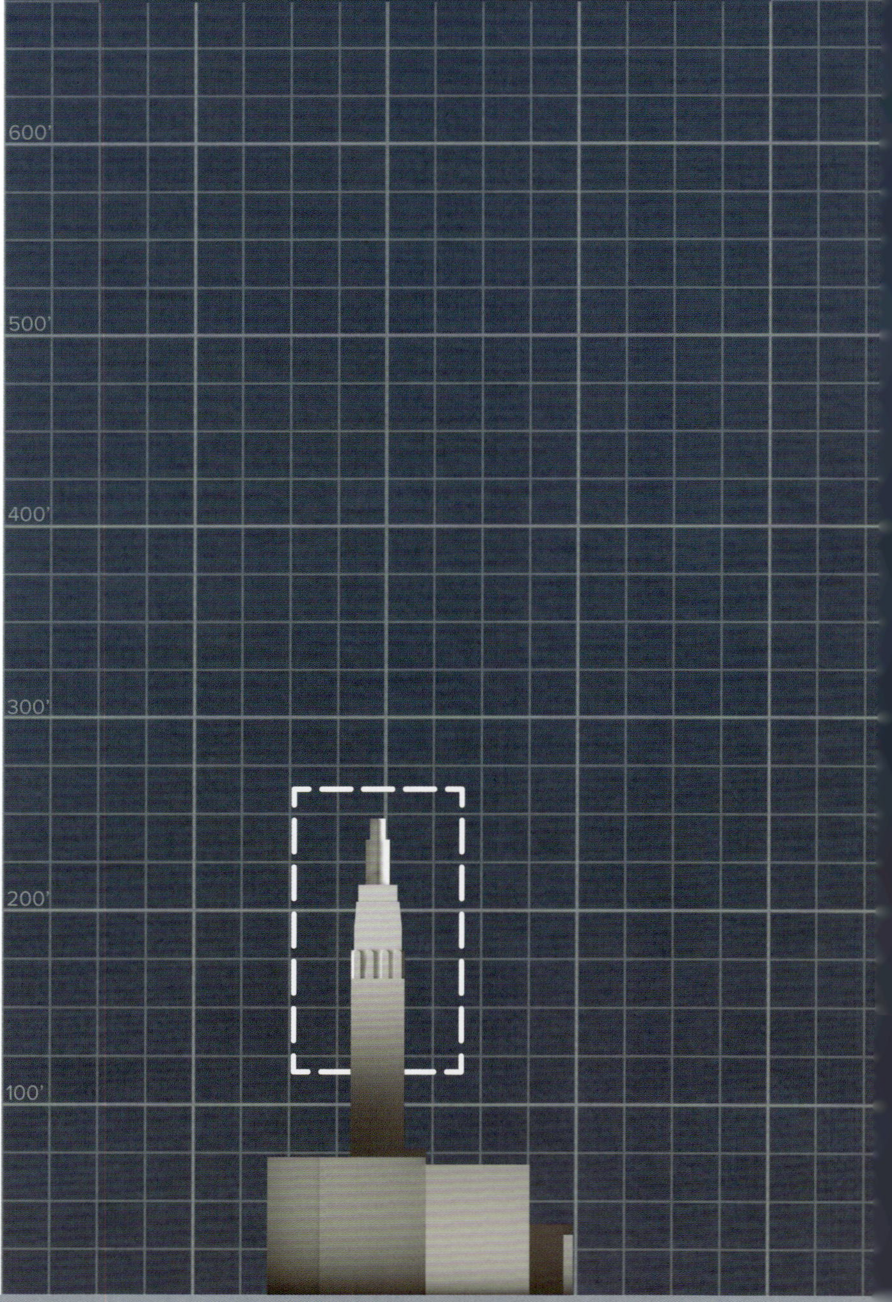

South Elevation *1" = 100'*

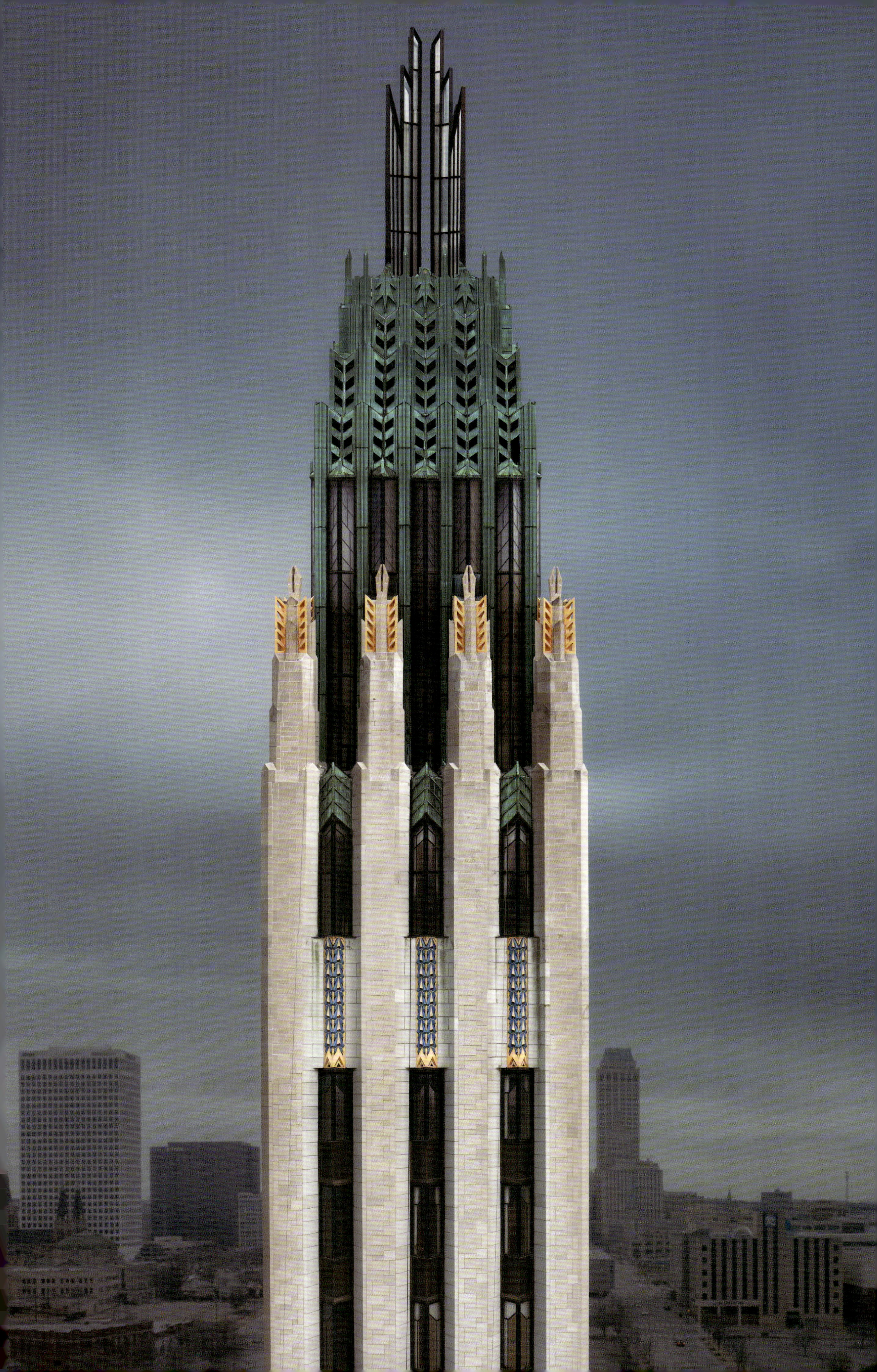

Philtower

Tulsa, **OK**

Address	**427 S. Boston Ave.**
Opened	**1927**
Height	**343'**
Stories	**24**
Style	**Art Deco, Gothic**
Architect	**Edward Delk**

This highrise gets its moniker from oilman Waite Phillips, who also lent his name to his Philcade across the street. A generous if self-referential philanthropist, Phillips donated his Philbrook mansion to the city for an art museum and his Philmont ranch in New Mexico to the Boy Scouts, who still hike its mountain trails.

Phillips and his identical twin brother, Wiate, left the family's Iowa farm in search of adventure when they turned 16, working in timber and railroad camps, in hotels, and as telegraph messengers. Three years into their trek, Wiate suffered a burst appendix in Spokane, and the twins came home on a train, one of them in a coffin.

After working with his older brothers in the oil business for a time, Phillips went solo. He thus missed out on their company, Phillips Petroleum, but nevertheless made a fortune with his own oil operations in Tulsa. Erecting the state's tallest skyscraper, he had its multicolored tile roof marked with an "O" for Oklahoma.

In 1941, Phillips gave Philtower to the Boy Scouts to support their New Mexico camp. They later sold the building, now a mix of offices and apartments. The lobby has elaborate Gothic fan vaults and "WP" monograms on the elevator doors and doorknobs.

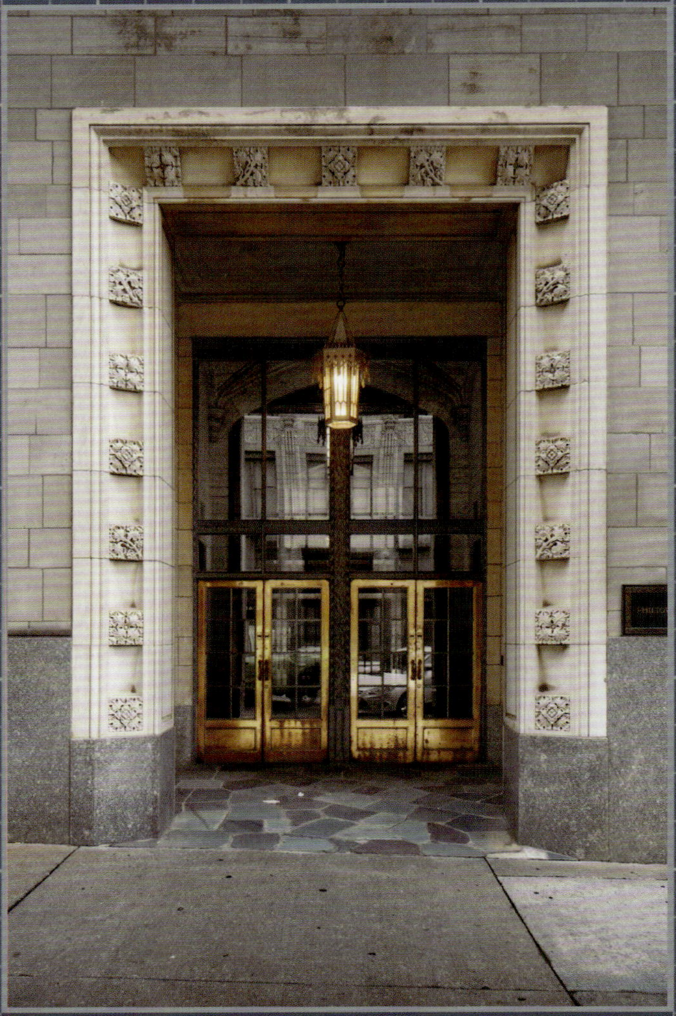

The lobby's Gothic fan vaults can be seen in the shadowy edges of the side entryway transom windows.

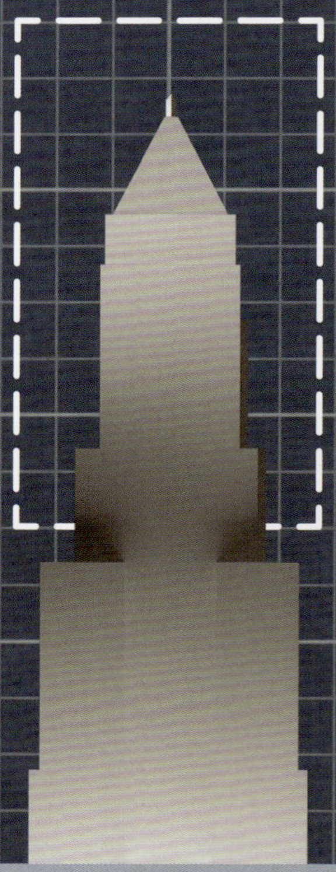

South Elevation *1" = 100'*

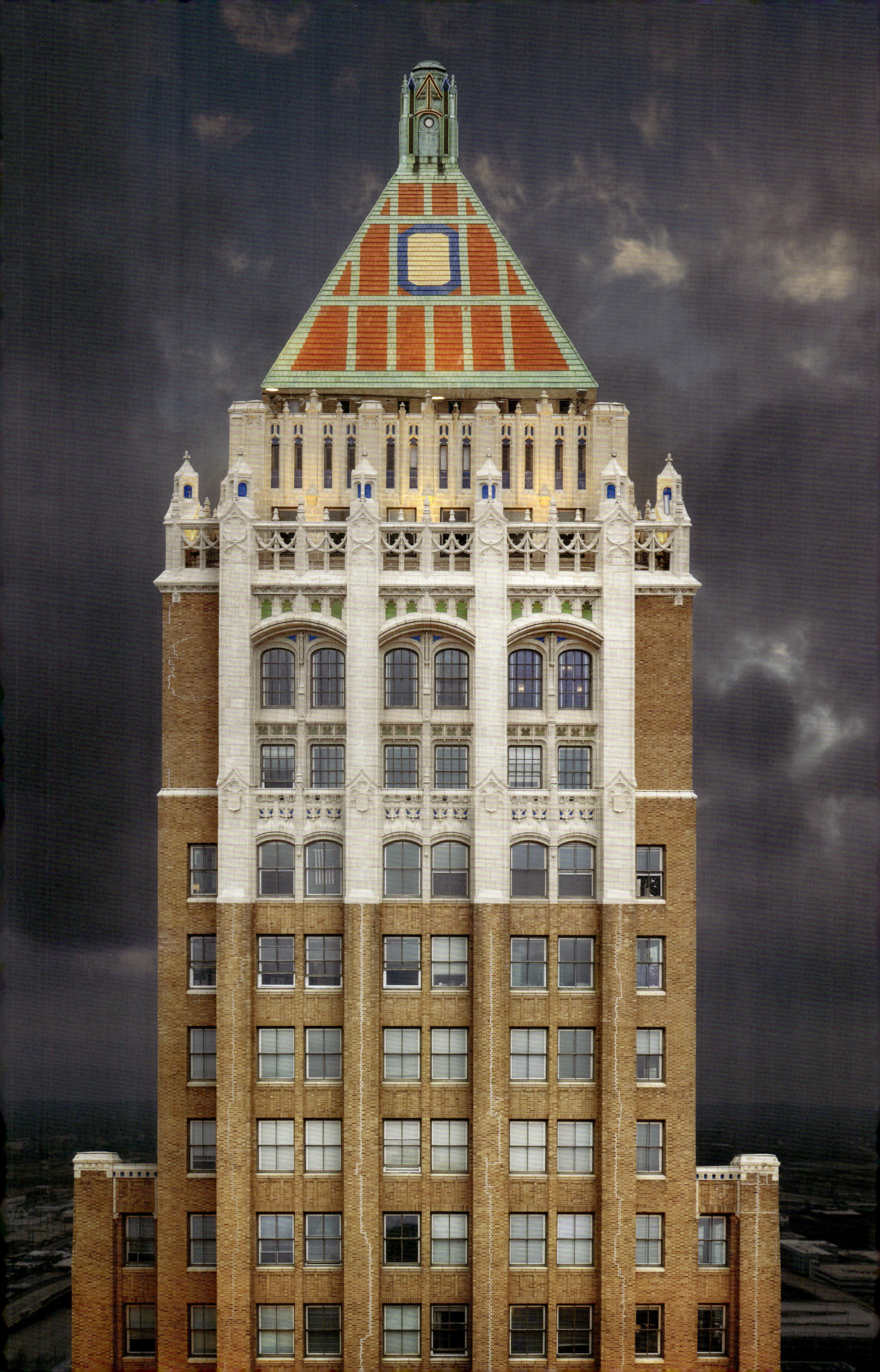

Sterick Building

Memphis, **TN**

Address .... **8 N. Third St.**
Opened **1930**
Height .... **365'**
Stories **29**
Style .... **Gothic, Art Deco**
Architect .... **Wyatt Hedrick**

Empty for nearly four decades, its crumbling concrete skin shedding paint, this speculative skyscraper designed by a Texas architect for his millionaire father-in-law was in trouble almost from the moment it opened.

Sterick is a surname mashup of architect Wyatt Hedrick and Ross Sterling, a Houston oil magnate, newspaper publisher, and chairman of his own bank and the state highway commission. Visiting the construction site in 1929, Sterling joked that his highrise would look better in Houston, and declined to confirm rumors he would run for governor of Texas.

Sterling did run the next year, and won. That same year, the biggest oilfield yet was discovered in east Texas. So many gushers flooded the market that crude oil prices plummeted to two cents a barrel, and the new governor declared martial law to stop drillers from violating production limits. Sterling lost the next election and also his Tennessee tower, which was auctioned on the courthouse steps two years after opening.

Numerous renovation attempts and ill-considered paint jobs by prior owners have failed to restore the Sterick to its intended glory. The new owner plans to convert it into residential units, a project that will take several years.

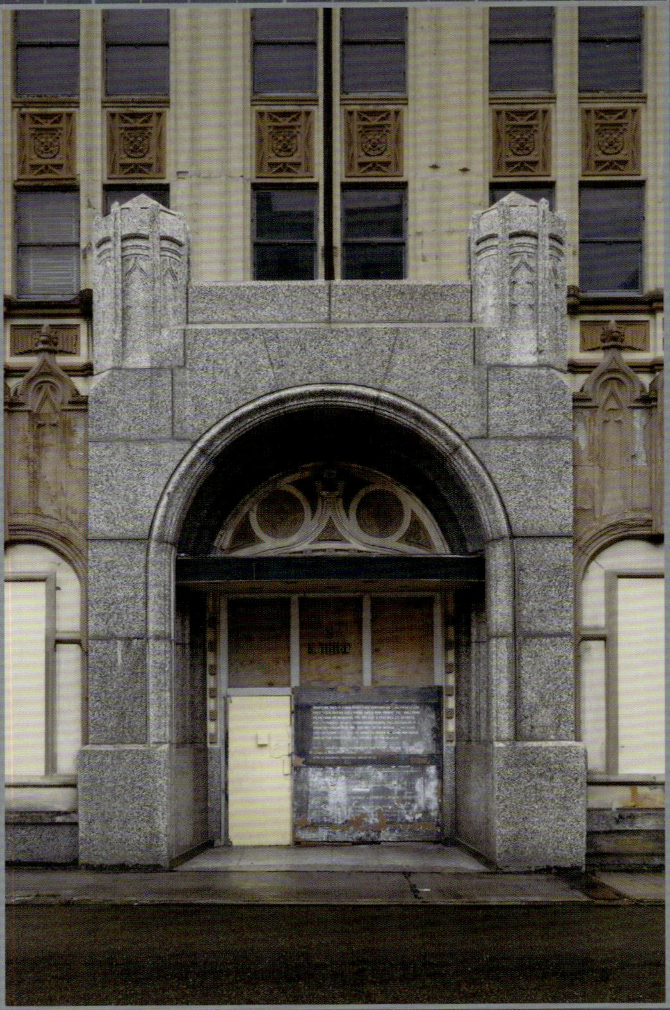

A grand granite archway with Gothic details gives a fortress-like aspect to the vacant and boarded-up structure.

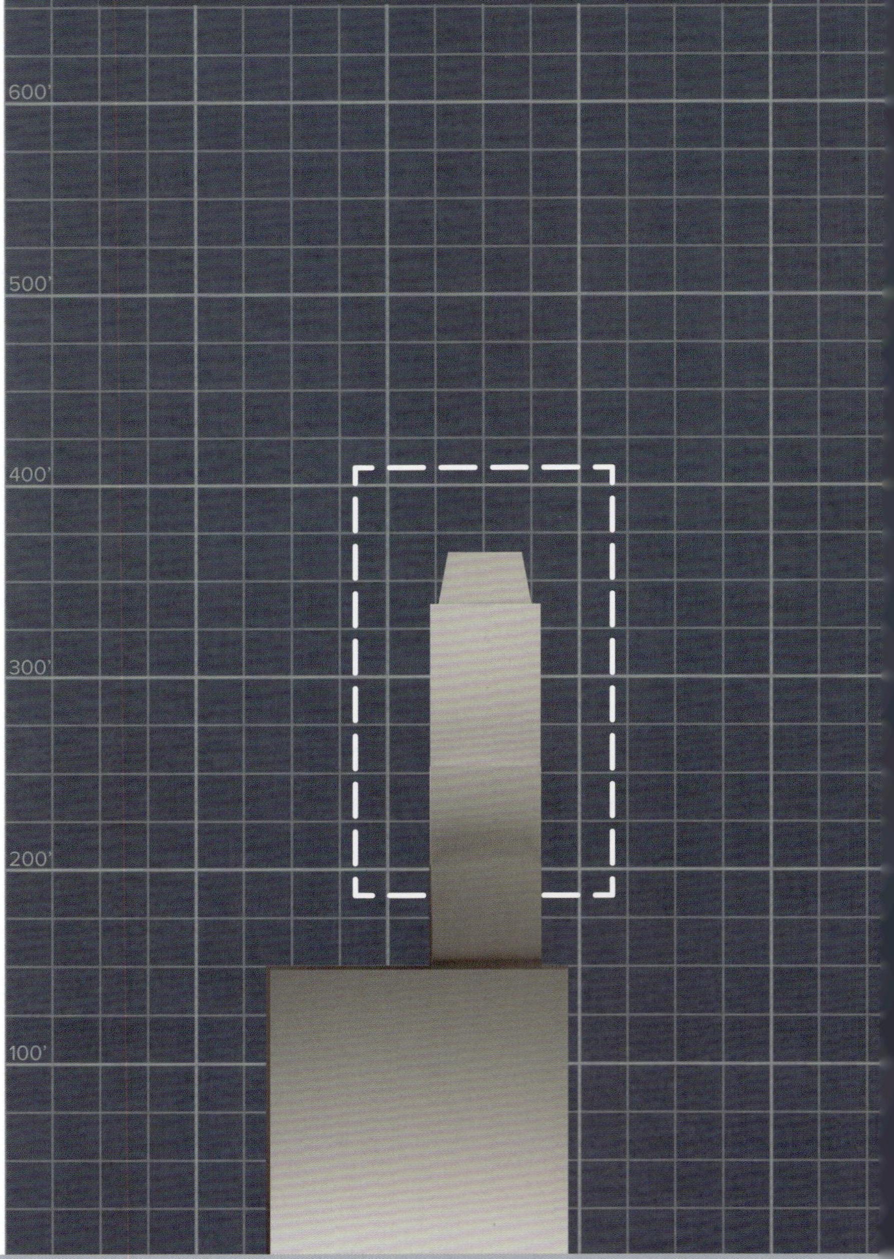

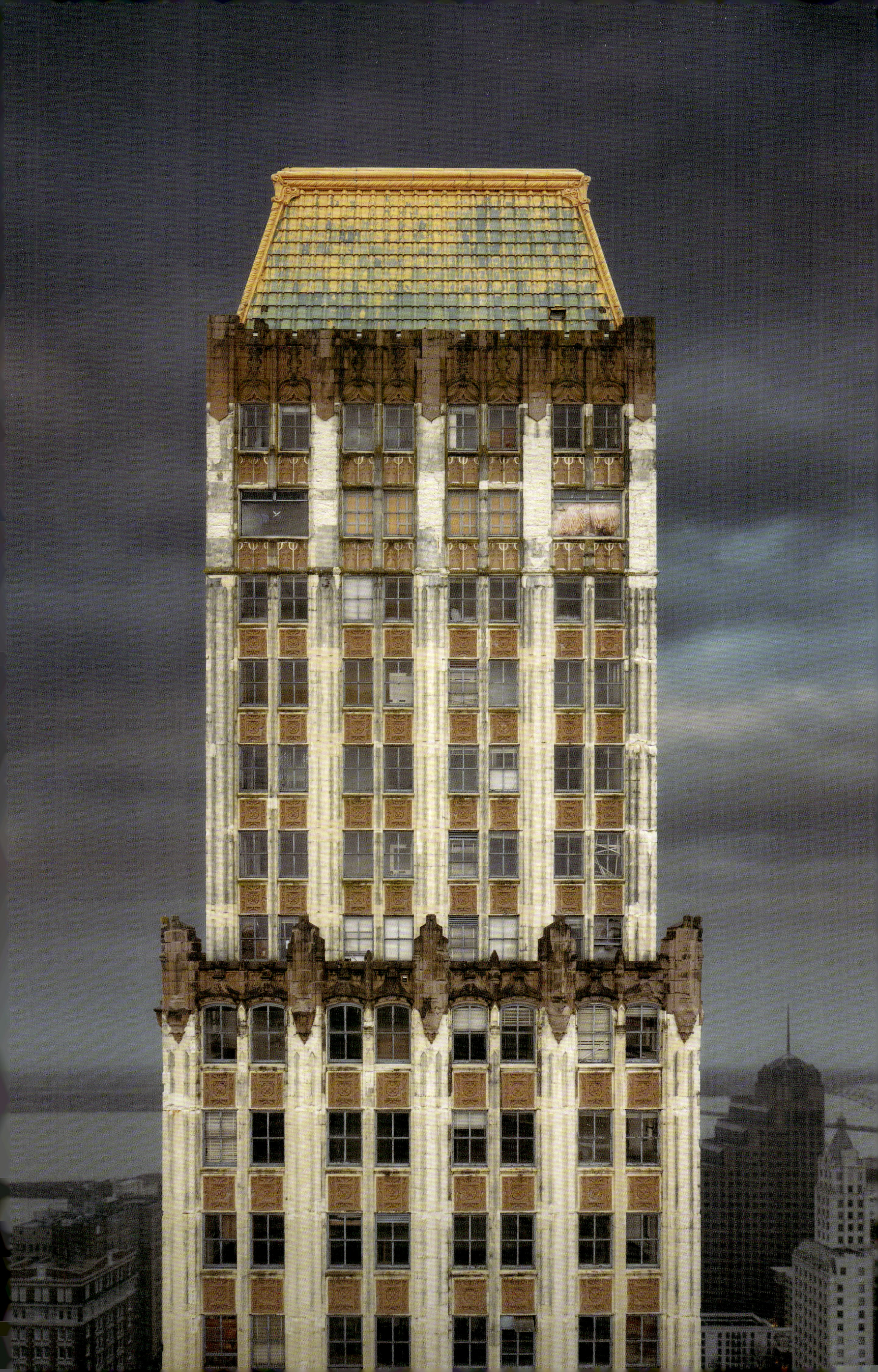

Jefferson County
Courthouse

Beaumont, **TX**

Address	**1149 Pearl St.**
Opened	**1932**
Height	**193’**
Stories	**13**
Style	**Art Deco**
Architect	**Stone & Babin**

The first skyscraper courthouse built in Texas, this highrise originally had a jail in its upper stories. Until the new county jail opened in 1981, keen-eyed inmates might have spotted the derricks four miles south at Spindletop, where gushers first made the state into America’s biggest oil producer.

Friezes of drilling rig workers and a cowboy herding longhorn cattle flank the main courthouse entrance, the first big commission for local sculptor Herring Coe. The artist later did the Art Deco carvings at Houston City Hall (p. 202), and for the state centennial he sculpted a bronze statue of a Confederate artilleryman who repulsed a Union naval invasion at the Sabine Pass, about 40 miles downriver from Beaumont.

Jefferson County Courthouse stands on land once owned by original settler Nancy Nixon Tevis, near the spot on the Neches River where she operated a ferry. Tevis arrived with her husband and children in 1825, when the sparsely populated land was still part of Mexico and Anglo settlers from the United States were welcomed. Widowed around the time the “Texians” revolted against Santa Anna, Tevis later deeded part of her land to found the town, earning her the nickname “Mother of Beaumont.”

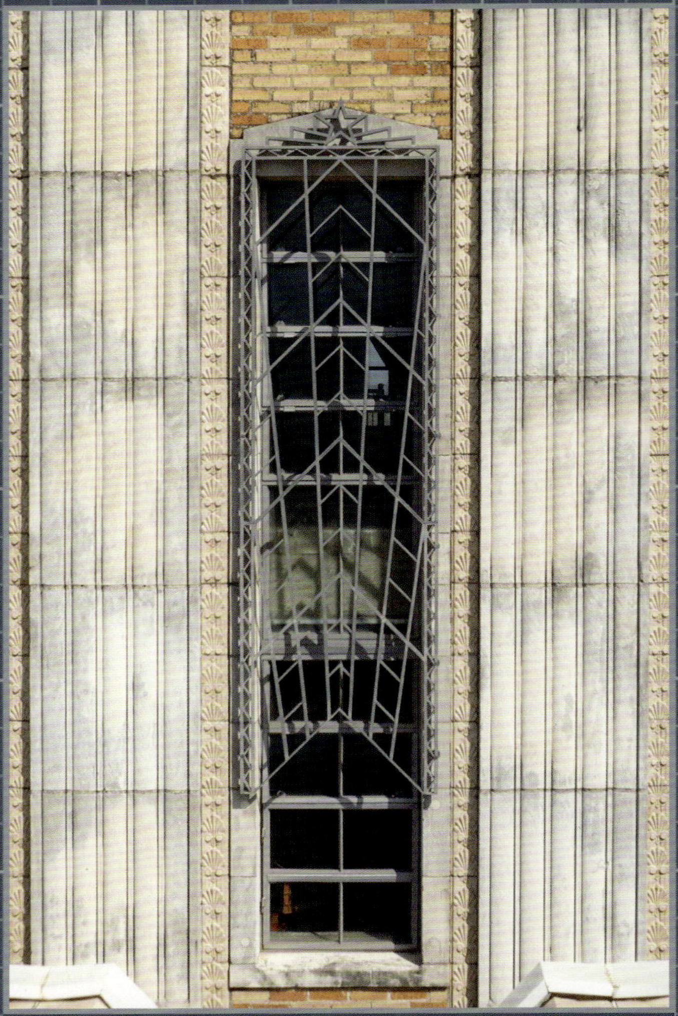

The metal window grilles were likely just ornamental, and not bars to keep the inmates from escaping.

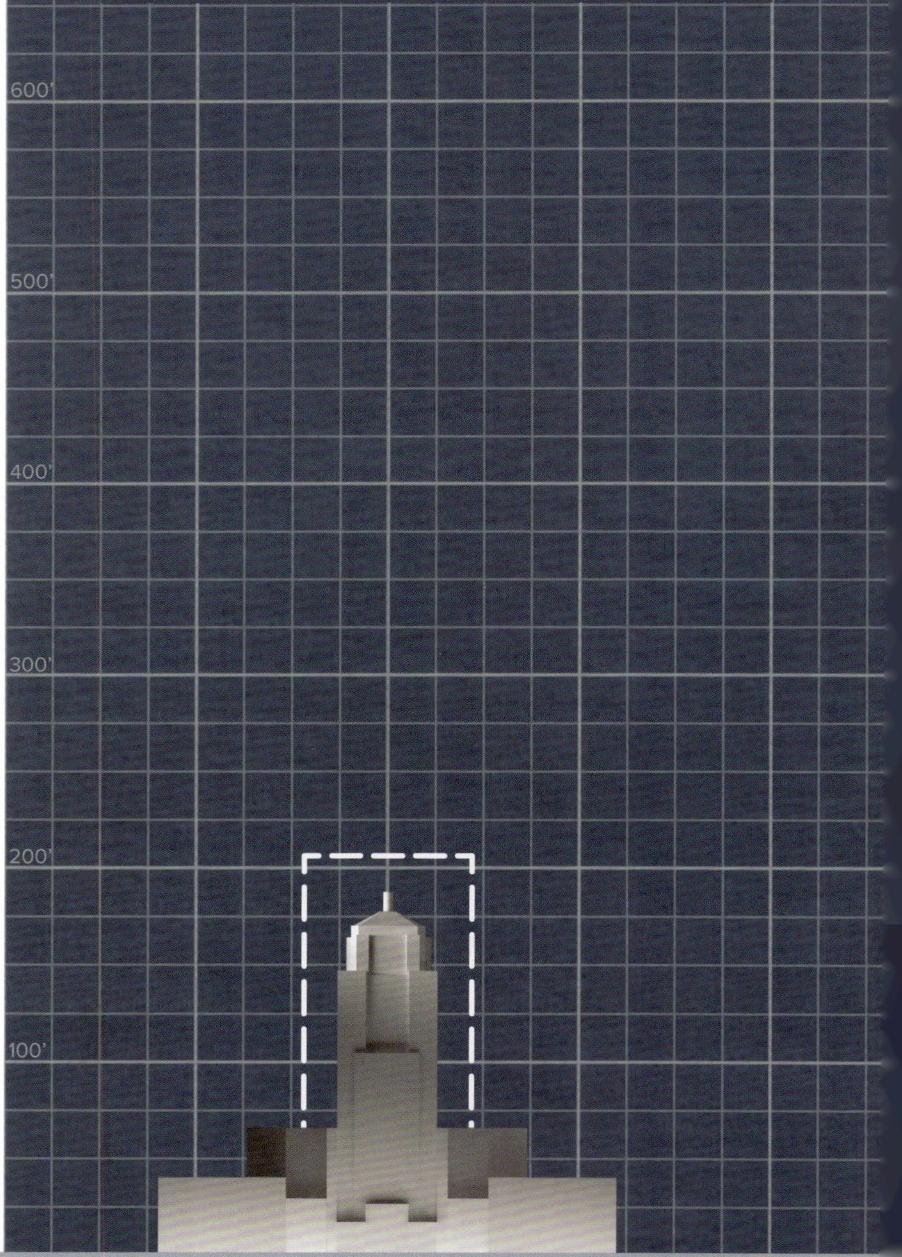

South Elevation *1" = 100'*

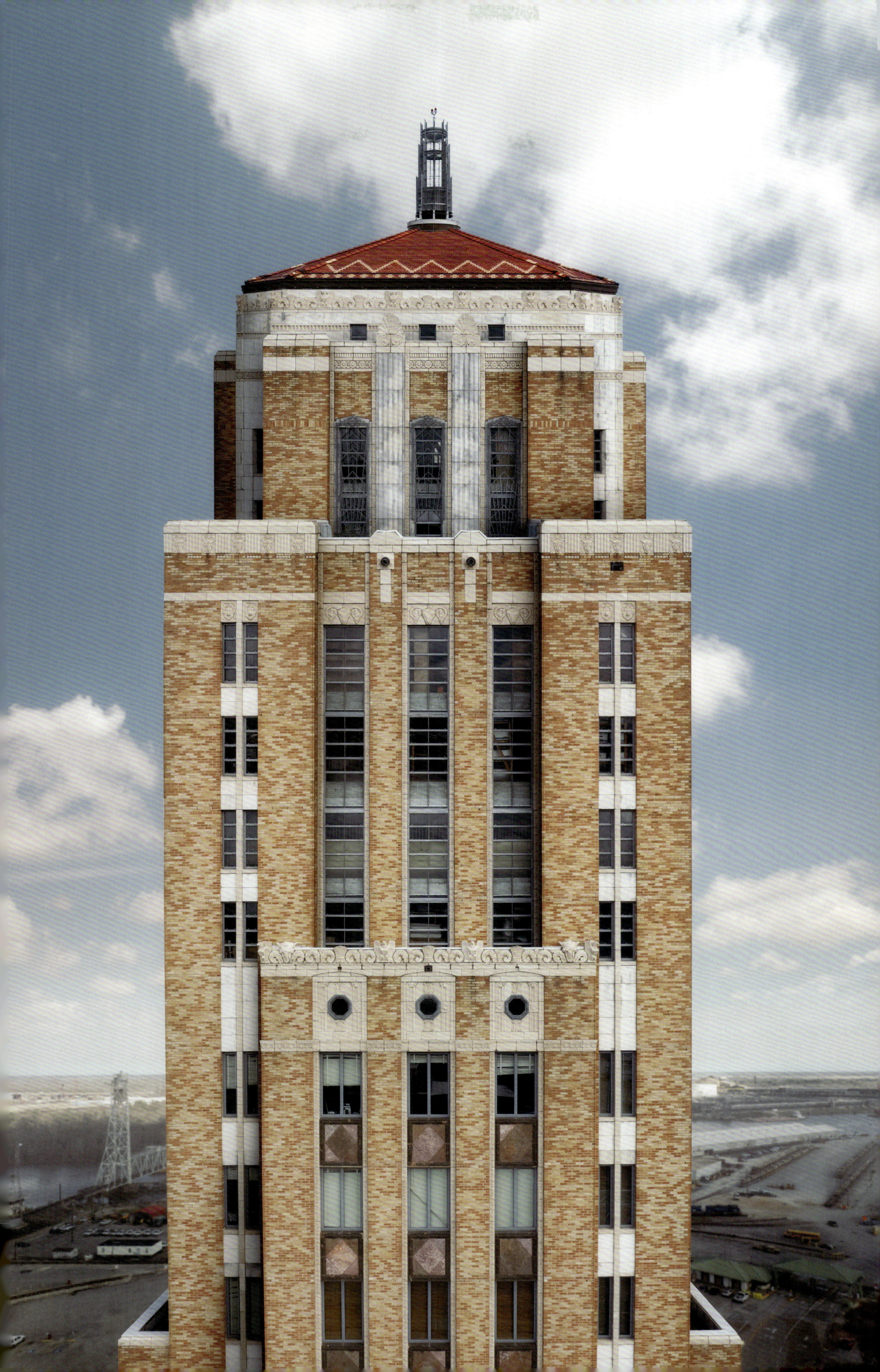

Dallas Power & Light Building

Dallas, **TX**

Address .... **1506 Commerce St.**
Opened **1931**
Height .... **226'**
Stories **19**
Style .... **Art Deco**
Architect .... **Lang & Witchell**

On Thanksgiving night in 1931, red and amber floodlights bathed this highrise as Dallas celebrated adding five new skyscrapers to its skyline in an otherwise gloomy year. Colors swirled too in the stained glass entrance window, portraying a modern Prometheus gripping a web of cables to transmit current to the city below.

The power company was generated by John Strickland, a farmer and cotton gin owner in nearby Waxahachie who tried a grocery and wholesale business before managing the town's electric company. Teaming with investors, Strickland strung five small utilities together to power an interurban trolley line stretching from Dallas south to Waco and north to the Oklahoma border. He consolidated more utilities to create Texas Power & Light and Dallas Power & Light. When Strickland died in 1924, friends said his sole unrealized dream was to build a skyscraper for his companies.

Dallas stained glass artisans Joanna and Robert McIntosh created the original window for the main showroom, now a brewhouse; the office tower has been converted into apartments. Architects Otto Lang and Frank Witchell designed many Dallas highrises, including the first hotel ever built for Conrad Hilton. They honored another prolific duo, inventors Thomas Edison and Charles Steinmetz, with carved busts flanking the limestone facade.

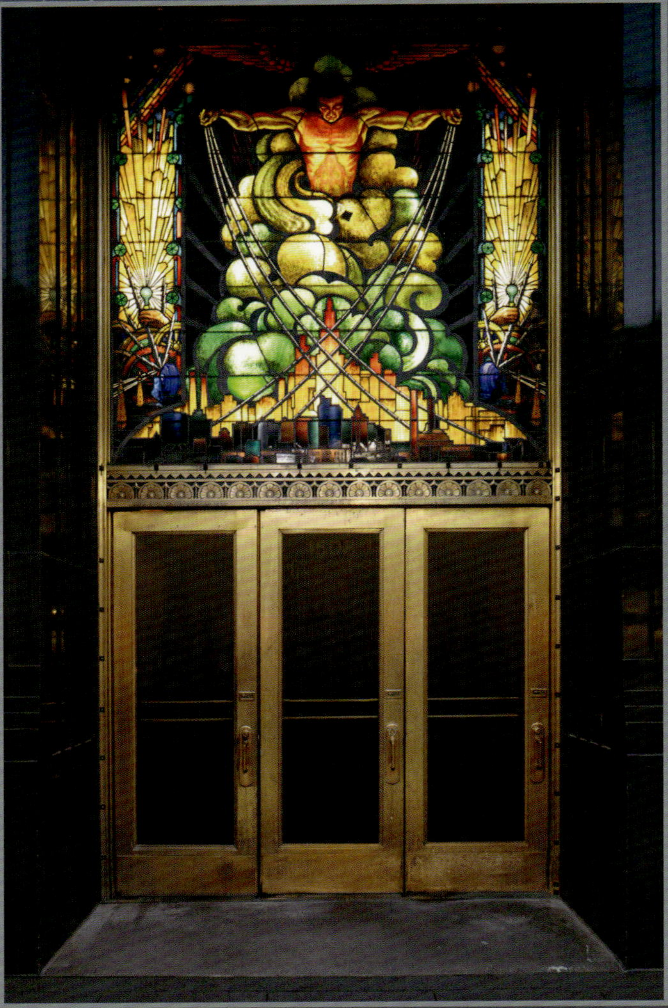

Instead of taking fire from the gods to give to humans, this Prometheus supplies current.

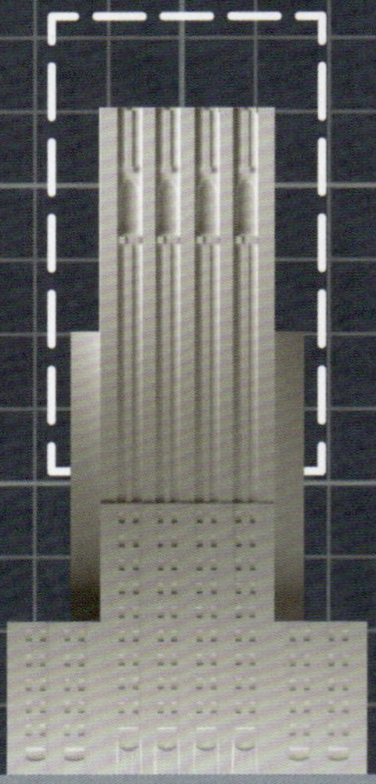

South Elevation 1" = 100'

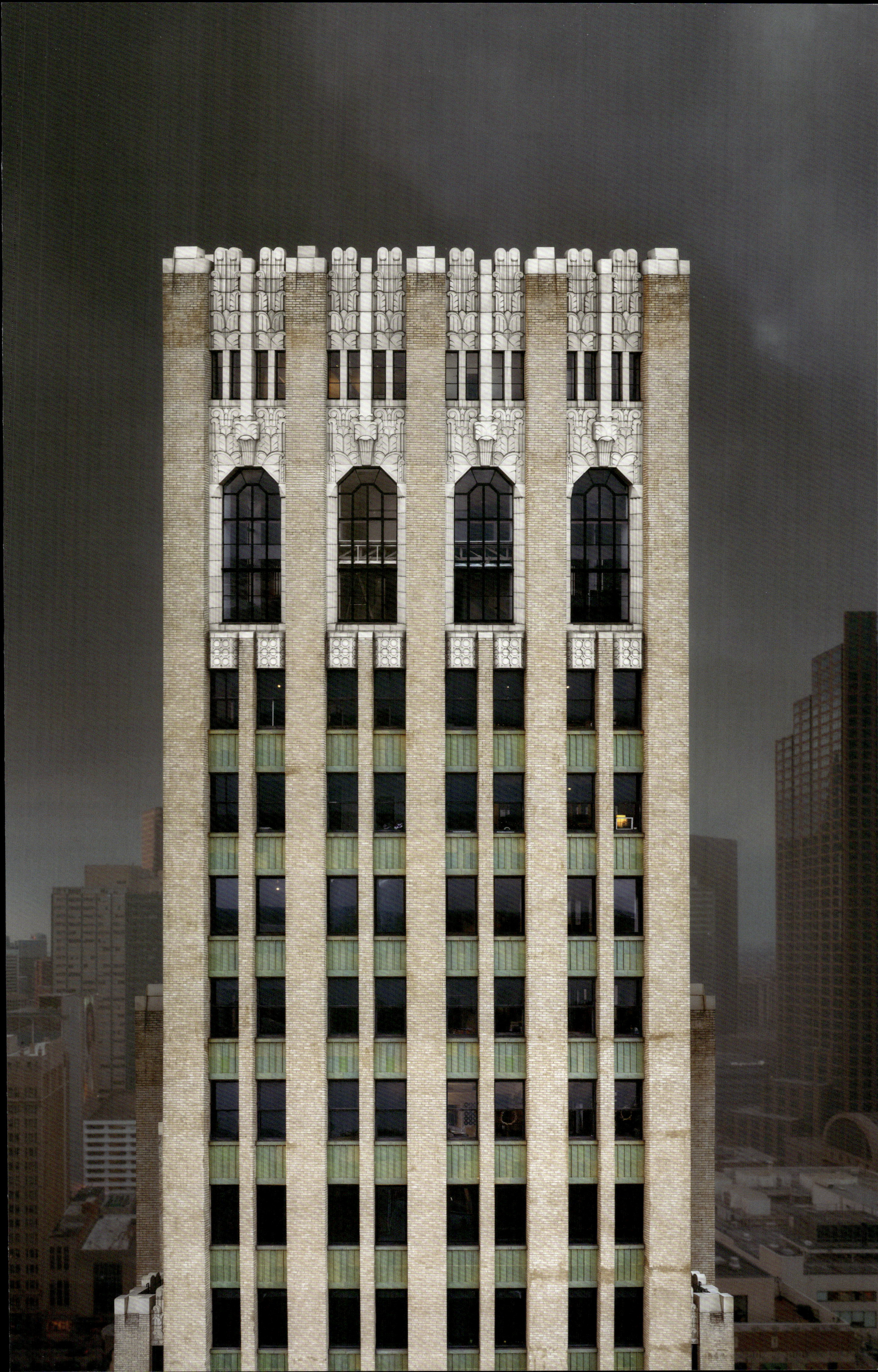

Tower Petroleum
Building

Dallas, **TX** Hotel St. Elm

Address	**1907 Elm St.**
Opened	**1931**
Height	**315'**
Stories	**22**
Style	**Art Deco**
Architect	**Mark Lemmon**

It did not take long for the McNeny brothers to reap the rewards for commissioning this highrise for petroleum companies. Its construction was still underway when geologists discovered the biggest petroleum reservoir in state history.

Thirty years earlier, Fletcher and Frank McNeny had left their family farm in Fannin County to seek their fortune in Dallas. Fletcher first found work with the railroad and Frank in publishing; then they went into business together as McNeny & McNeny, commercial real estate agents. The brothers soon expanded their portfolio to include residential properties, acquiring 100 acres north of the city and developing the suburb of Greenland Hills.

Architect Mark Lemmon also designed Fair Park Stadium, known since the 1936 Texas Centennial by its adopted moniker, the Cotton Bowl. He and the McNeny brothers had offices in this building, which offered its oil industry tenants shared conference rooms, a library, and a lounge.

Now a hotel, the property is owned by music producer John Kirtland, drummer in the Texas band that recorded the 1993 hit "Breakfast at Tiffany's." Guests who remember the film might kind of like that it plays on a loop in an old ticket booth display by the entrance.

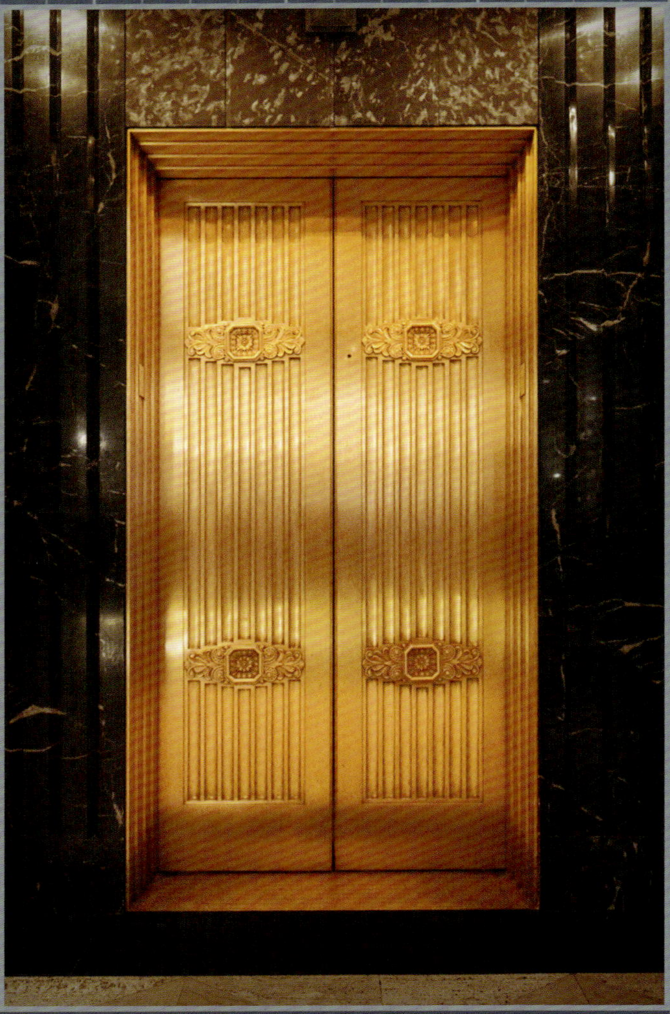

Guests in the hotel can admire the handsome bronze elevator doors framed in fluted veined black marble.

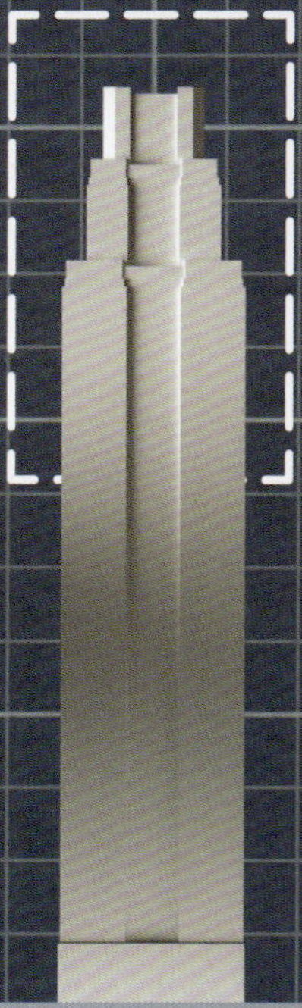

West Elevation *1" = 100'*

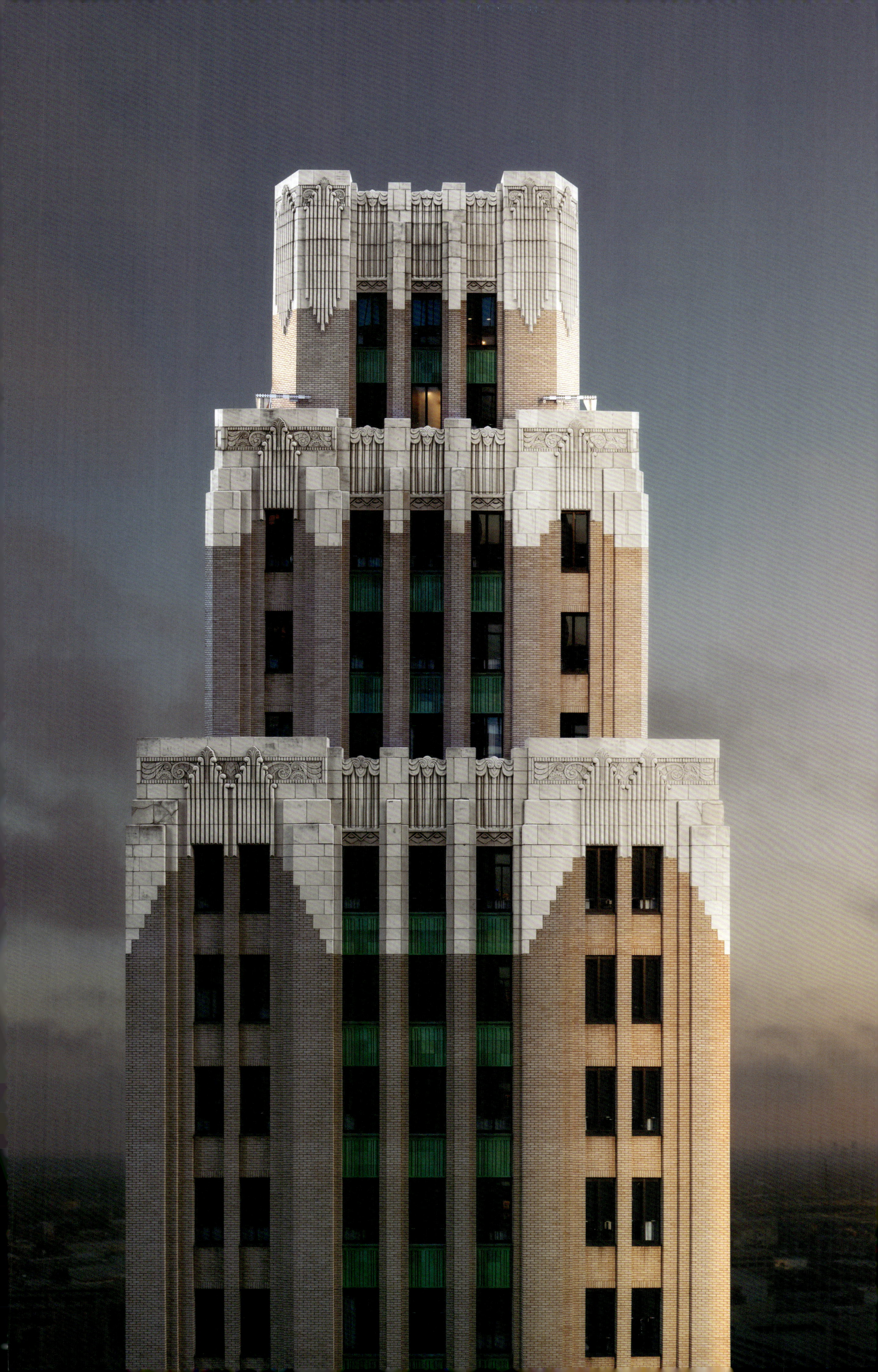

Texas & Pacific
Railway Terminal

Fort Worth, **TX**

Address ·········· **221 W. Lancaster Ave.**
Opened ·························· **1931**
Height ···························· **191'**
Stories ···························· **12**
Style ························ **Art Deco**
Architect ··············· **Wyatt Hedrick**

Railroads were essential to the place called Cowtown, where cattle drivers once rode the Chisholm Trail to get their herds to trains in distant Kansas. So when this highrise opened, grateful officials named the busy road it stands on after John Lancaster, president of the Texas & Pacific.

The railroad's name reveals the ambition of its founders, but the Texas & Pacific never managed to lay tracks to San Diego as planned. It ran out of money and stalled in Fort Worth for several years, until robber baron Jay Gould bought the line and extended it to the state's western tip to meet the Southern Pacific.

Lancaster succeeded Gould's son as president in 1916 after a bankruptcy reorganization. At the banquet for the opening of this passenger terminal and office complex, a rapidly spiraling economy and slumping ridership led the executive to speak bluntly. "If we do not fill up that office building," Lancaster said, "at least it can be seen from a long ways off."

Of many fine Art Deco works by Wyatt Hedrick in Fort Worth, this stands out for its bold massing and rich decor. The tower offices have been converted to condominiums, and the three-story passenger waiting room is now a stunning event venue.

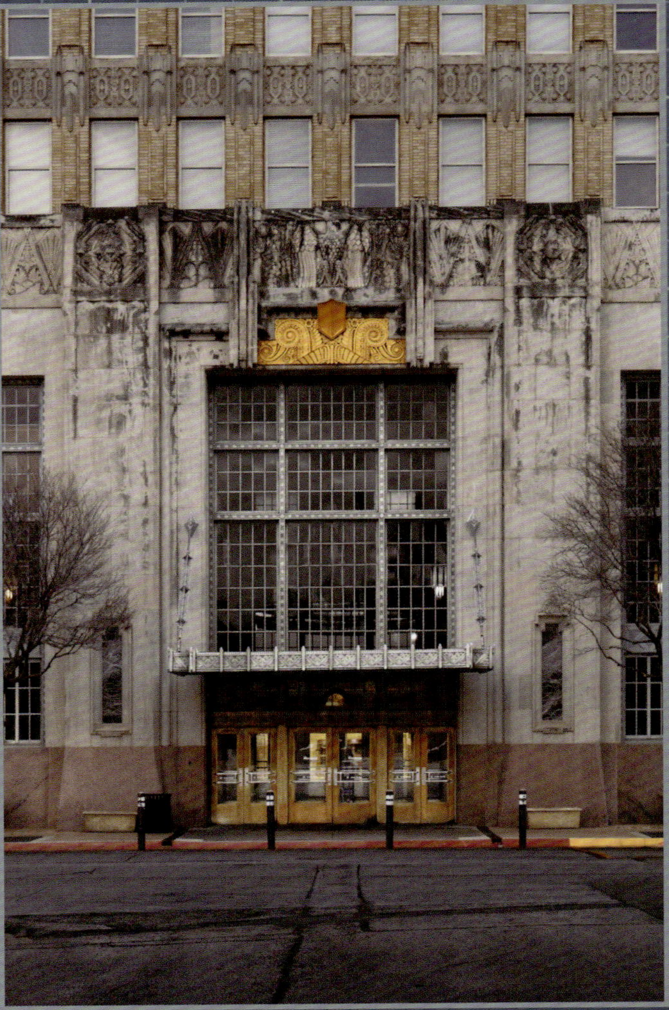

A wall of windows allows light to pour into the vast passenger waiting room, now used for weddings.

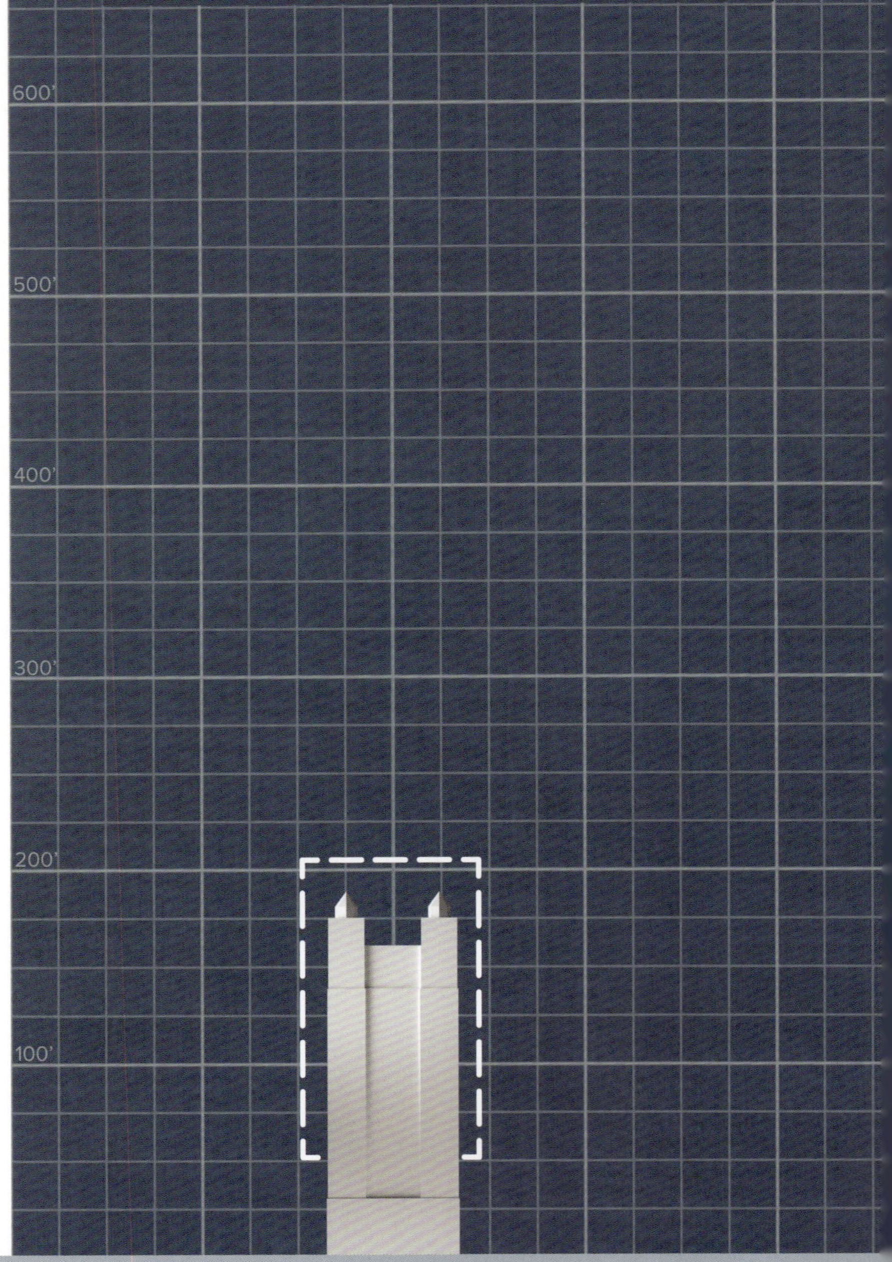

East Elevation *1" = 100'*

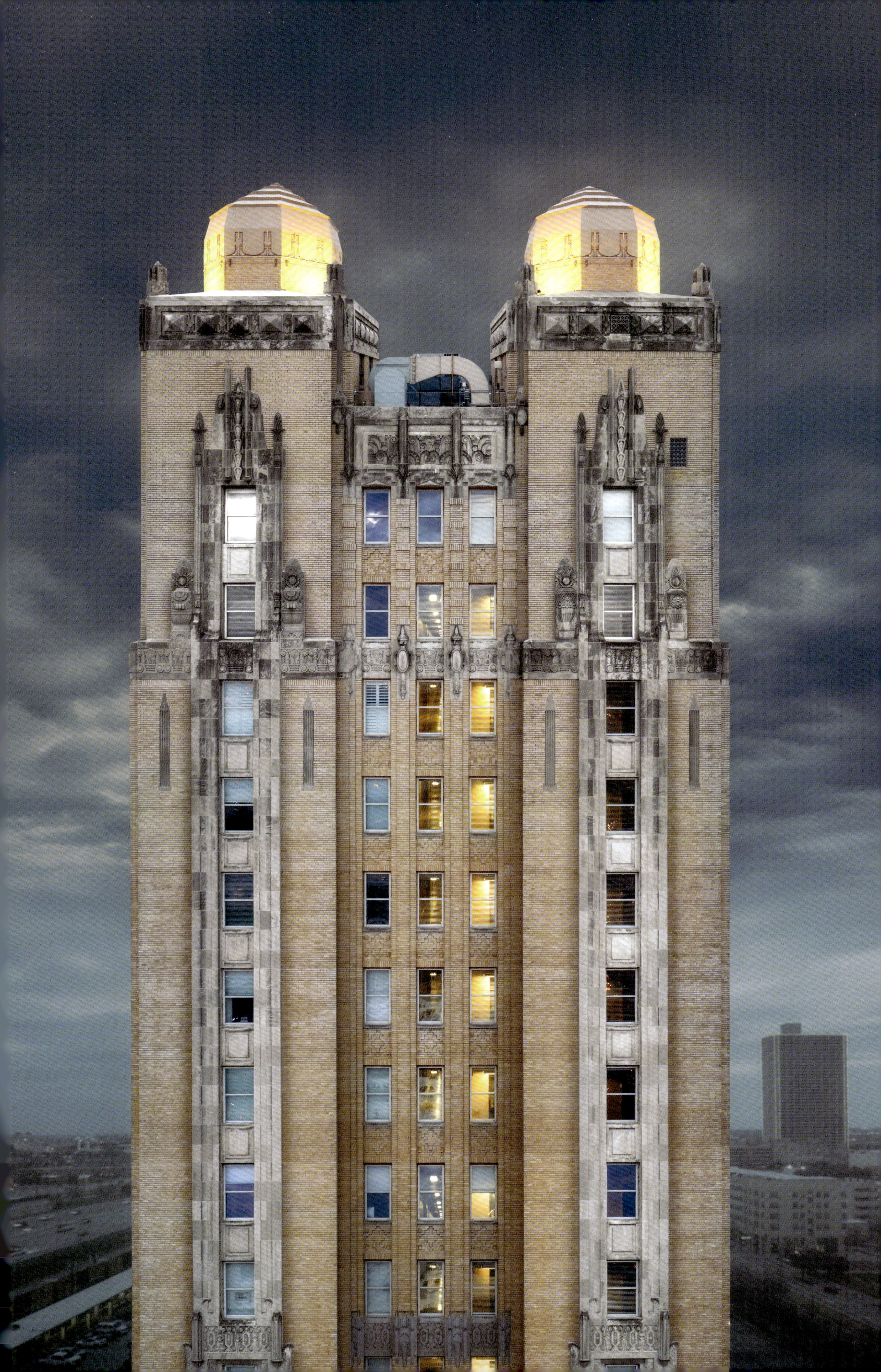

Gulf Building

Houston, **TX** JPMorgan Chase Building

Address ········ **712 Main St.**
Opened ········ **1929**
Height ········ **430'**
Stories ········ **35**
Style ········ **Art Deco**
Architect ········ **A. Finn, K. Franzheim**

This is the most impressive of dozens of highrises that once comprised the real estate empire of Jesse Jones. The developer, banker, and publisher was not only the most powerful businessman in Houston, but also one of the most influential people in Washington, D.C.

Jones managed a Dallas lumberyard for his uncle, and later inherited control of the man's extensive timberlands and sawmills, substantially expanding the business before selling it to go into construction. He built many of Houston's first skyscrapers, including one in 1916 for Gulf Oil and the National Bank of Commerce that they eventually outgrew, necessitating this replacement.

Gulf relocated to Houston after the city got ocean access by dredging a shipping channel through the bayou, a project Jones led efforts to finance. A major figure in the Democratic party, he headed the Reconstruction Finance Corporation during the Great Depression, rescuing banks and funding New Deal projects, and in 1940 he was named secretary of commerce.

Architects Alfred Finn and Kenneth Franzheim collaborated on this highrise, which bears an uncanny resemblance to Eliel Saarinen's influential runner-up in the 1922 Tribune Tower contest. A full-length painting of Jones hangs in the main banking hall, where limestone walls set off a brilliant patterned metallic ceiling three stories high.

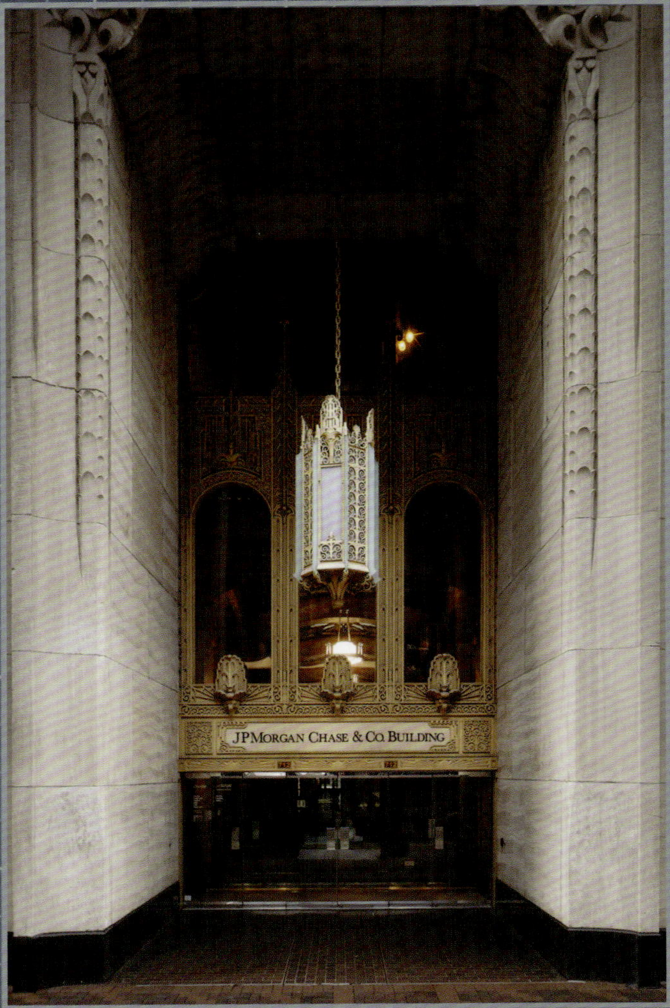

While it is no longer officially called the Gulf Building, the original name is faintly visible in the stone above this entrance arch.

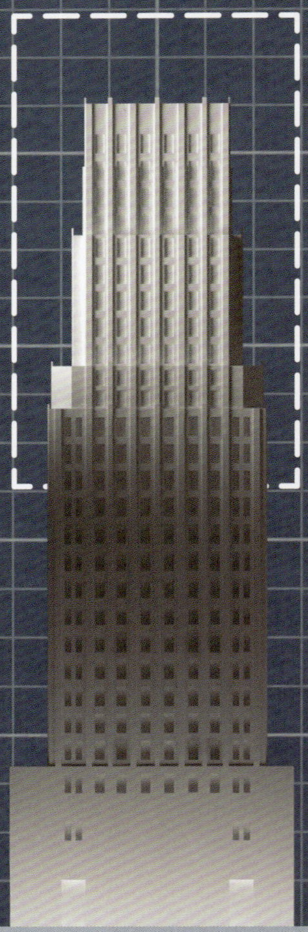

East Elevation 1" = 100'

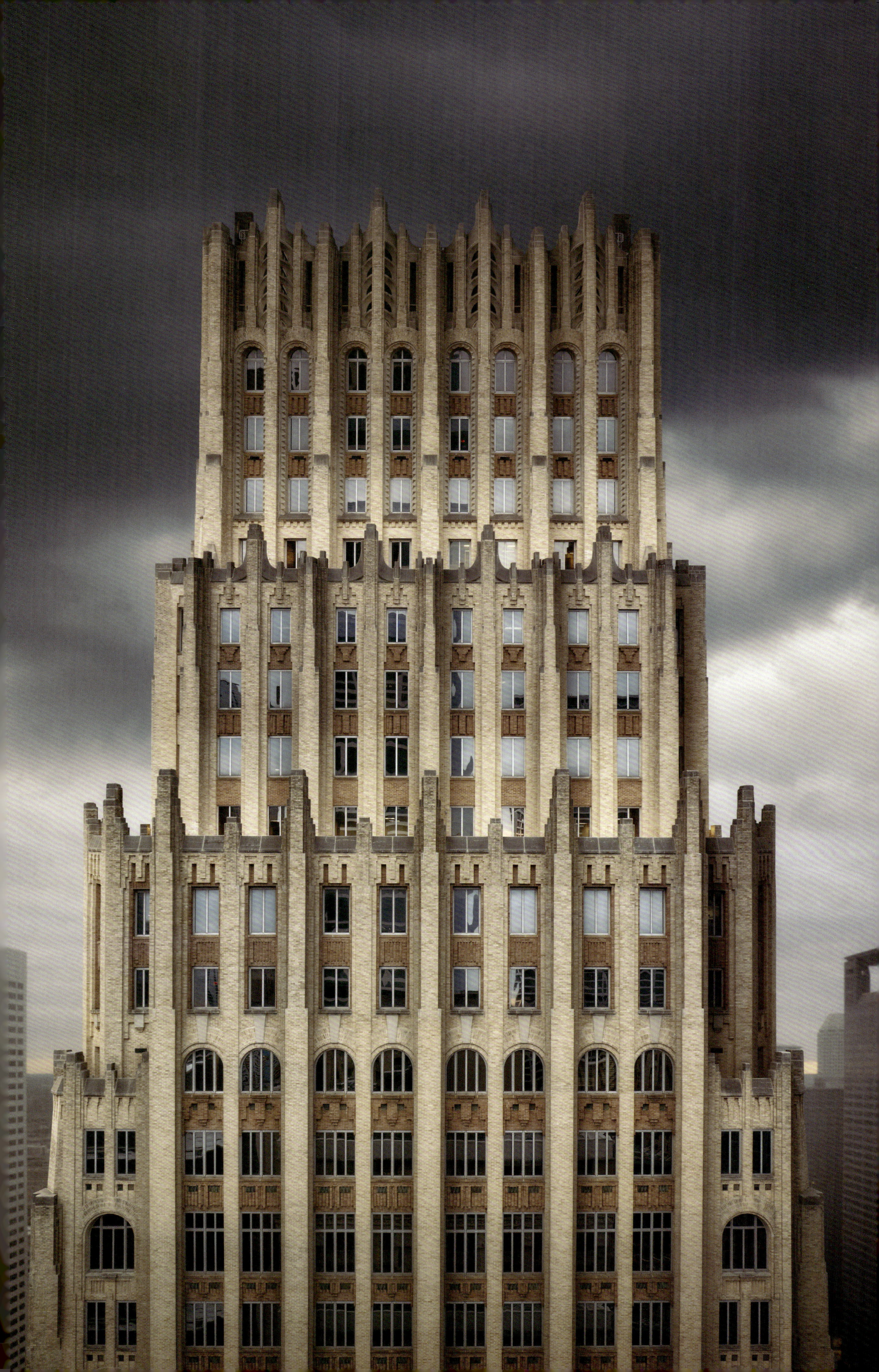

Houston City Hall

Houston, **TX**

Address ·········· **901 Bagby St.**
Opened ·········· **1939**
Height ·········· **175'**
Stories ·········· **10**
Style ·········· **Art Deco**
Architect ·········· **Joseph Finger**

The man who designed this highrise had to overcome a skeptical mayor who wanted city hall to match the Spanish Renaissance look of the city library next door. Joseph Finger, an Austrian immigrant, won the argument by insisting that the modern architecture of his adopted land was "far above that of other countries."

Mayor Richard Fonville preferred to give the job to Albert Finn, who had been selected for the project years earlier before it stalled in the poor economy. In the meantime, Finn had designed the San Jacinto Monument, a towering masonry column for the 1936 centennial commemorating Texan independence. But the mayor failed to persuade the city council.

Simple and boxy in its contours, Houston's fourth city hall depends greatly for its visual interest on a series of friezes carved into the limestone by Texas sculptor Herring Coe, whose work also textures the Art Deco courthouse in Beaumont (p. 192). Ethereal pastel figures in the lobby ceiling mural represent industry, culture, law, and government.

Flanked by sculpted bobcats, minimalist clocks at the top, one on each side, tick the minutes and hours. Mayor Fonville and other anti-modernists might prefer the old city hall clock, which is preserved in a park across town.

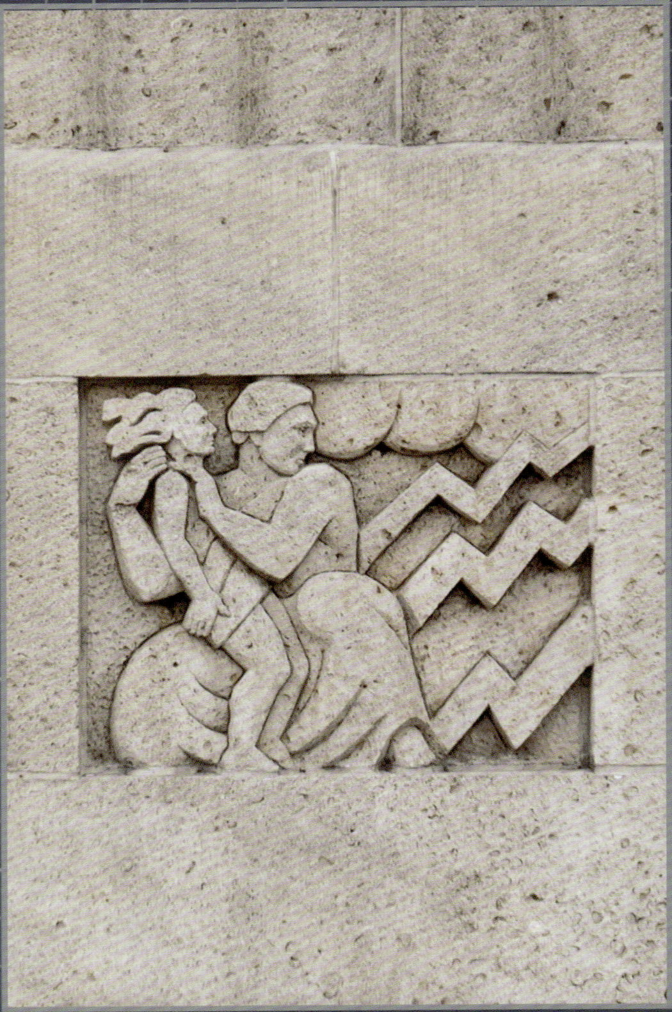

Frieze panels represent the functions of city government, such as protecting citizens from natural disaster.

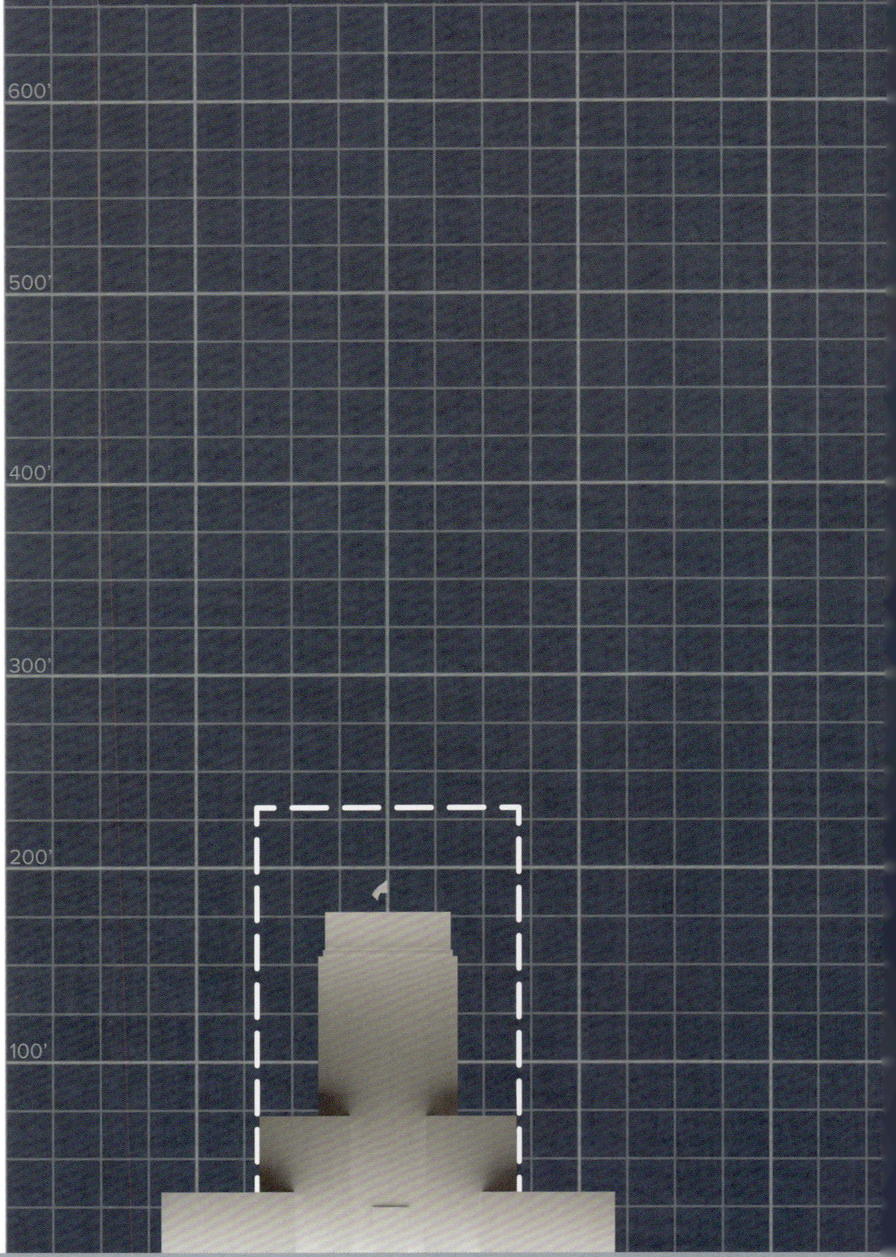

Northwest Elevation *1" = 100'*

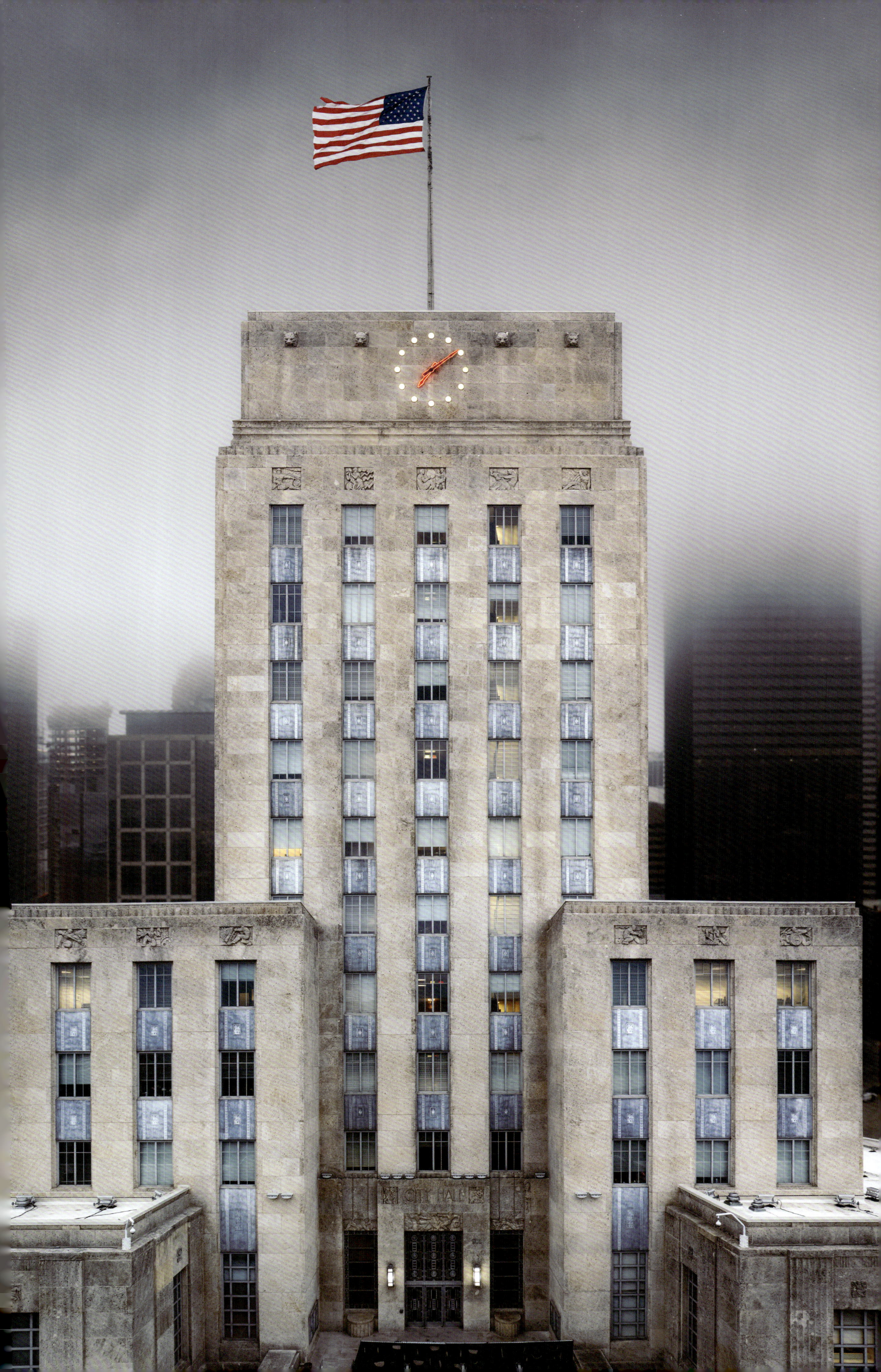
CITY HALL

Petroleum Building

Houston, **TX** — Cambria Hotel

Address	**1314 Texas Ave.**
Opened	**1927**
Height	**291'**
Stories	**21**
Style	**Art Deco**
Architect	**Alfred Bossom**

Mayan motifs adorning this highrise came about after Alfred Bossom took a vacation to Mexico. The stepped stone temples profoundly impressed the eminent English architect, who later wrote that they were the first American skyscrapers.

This building was for Joseph Cullinan, a serial entrepreneur from the Pennsylvania oilfields whose first company made storage tanks. The first oil strikes in Texas lured him in 1897 to Corsicana, which he supplied with a massive tank, and then a refinery, before stepping away in 1902 for a new venture. Called simply the Texas Company, its target was the black gold flowing out of Spindletop.

Cullinan relocated the business — later known as Texaco — to Houston a few years later into one of the city's first skyscrapers. Pushed out by investors in 1913, he formed a new company, American Republics, and commissioned this office tower for it. Known for his temper, Cullinan also showed public spirit, funding a Houston hospital for Black patients in a time of strict segregation. He also chaired the committee that oversaw the creation of Mount Rushmore.

Renamed Great Southwest after an insurance company that moved here in 1968, the building is now a hotel. Its top floor, formerly the private Tejas Club, is now a banquet and meeting hall.

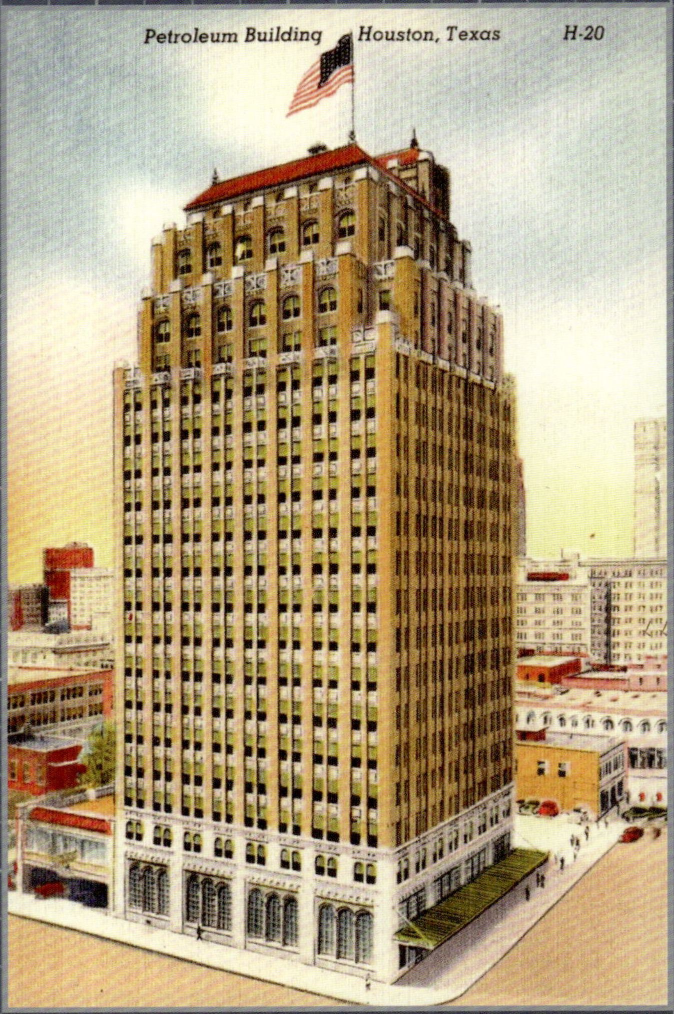

Besides the U.S. flag shown on this postcard, Joseph Cullinan was sometimes known to fly a skull and crossbones on his roof.

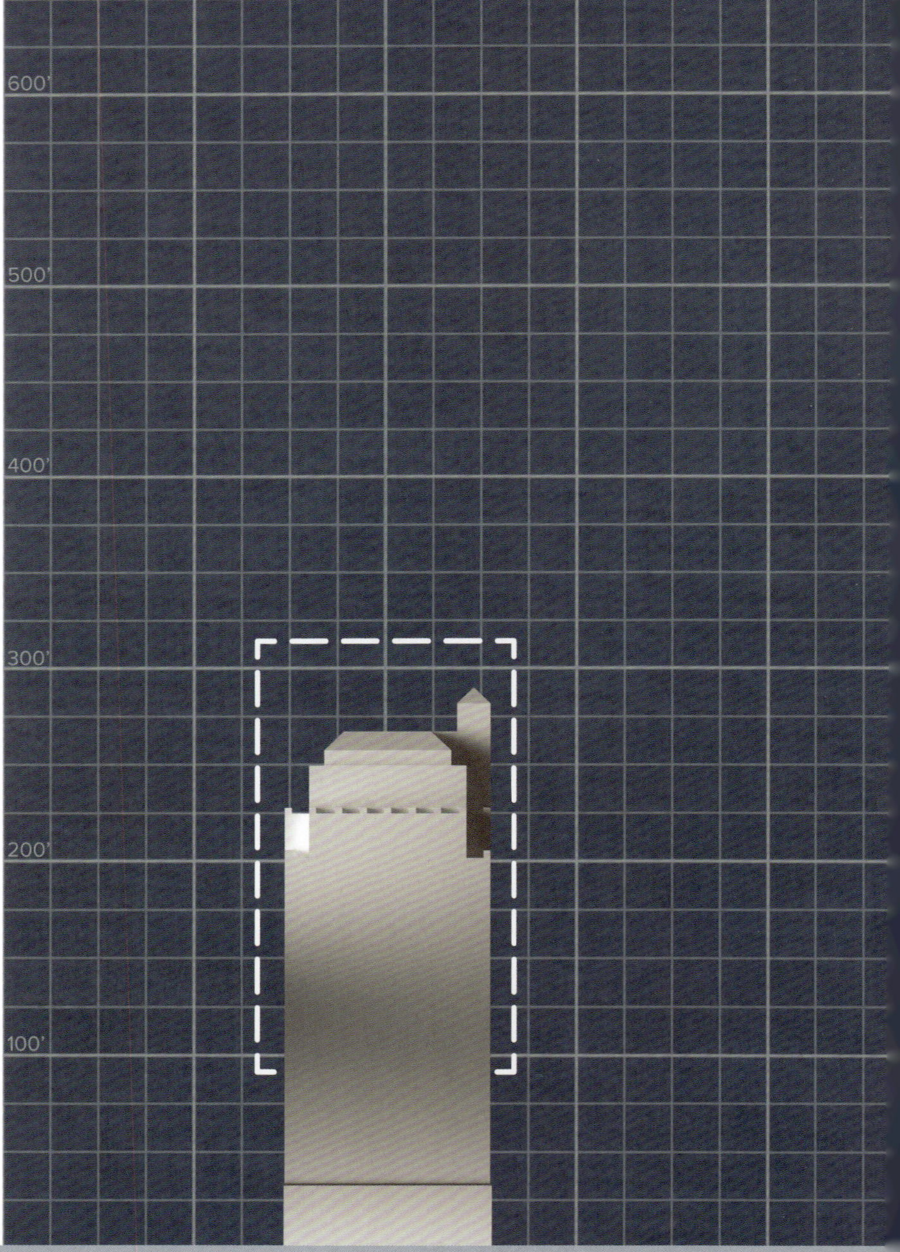

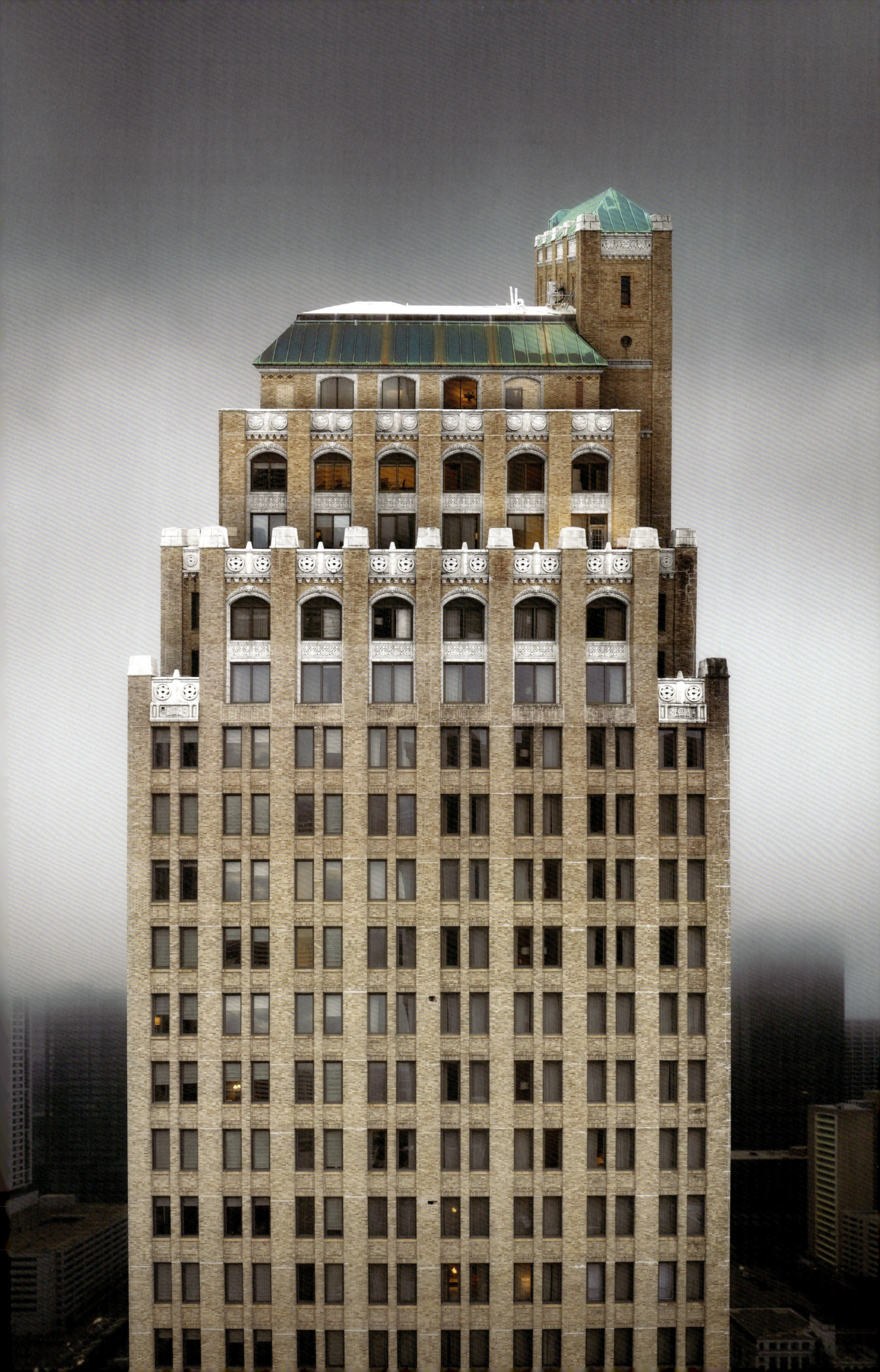

Alamo National
Building

San Antonio, **TX** Drury Plaza Riverwalk

Address	**105 S. St. Mary's St.**
Opened	**1930**
Height	**341'**
Stories	**24**
Style	**Art Deco**
Architect	**Graham, Anderson, Probst & White**

Naming the bank they founded in 1890 after the most hallowed building in Texas was not simply astute marketing for Charles Hugo and Sol Halff. It also illustrated how deeply the two German immigrants had assimilated in the Lone Star State.

Hugo, the bank's first president, owned a large store that incorporated part of the Alamo's original stone walls and abutted the iconic mission church. Preservationists desiring more dignity for the site persuaded the state legislature to buy the store from Hugo in 1905.

Halff, the vice-president, had come to Texas to work at his older brother's dry goods store near Houston. They accepted payment in cattle, and as the herds burgeoned, the Halff brothers relocated to San Antonio, where Sol minded the store business while Mayer became a major rancher.

Hugo and Halff did not live to see this edifice erected two blocks from their original bank, but they surely would have approved of its huge stained glass entry window portraying the Alamo. Its colored light falls on a two-story banking hall ringed with fluted pilasters and gilded trim, now a majestic hotel lobby. Old photos, vaults, and vintage equipment add to the sense of history, while a new rooftop sign replaces one that used to tout the bank.

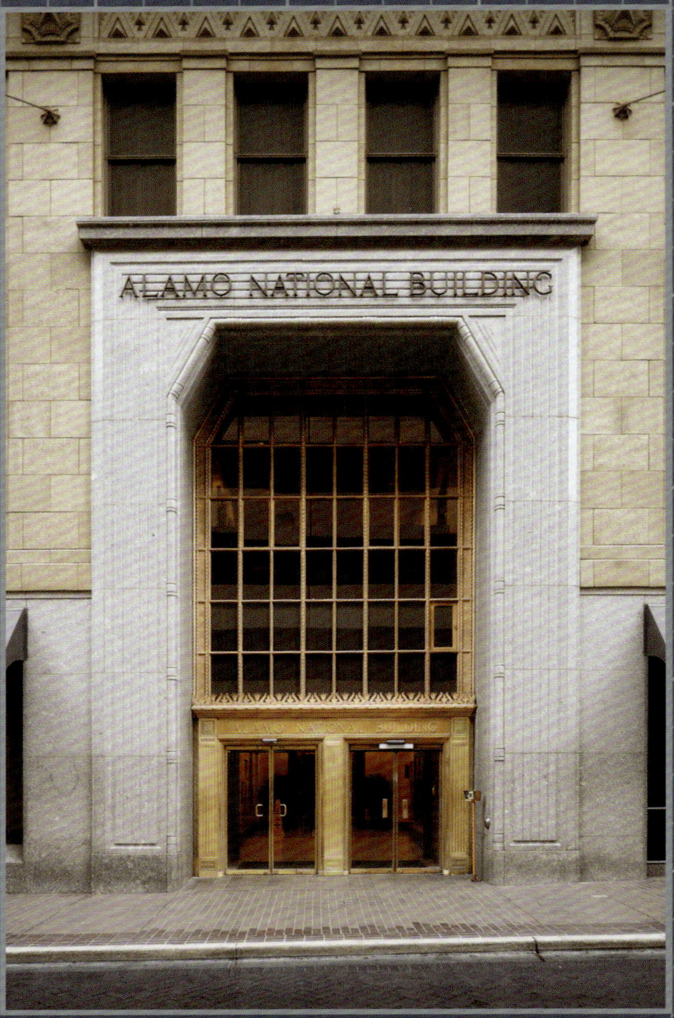

In addition to admitting abundant light, the entryway subtly repeats the shape of the tower's slanted roof.

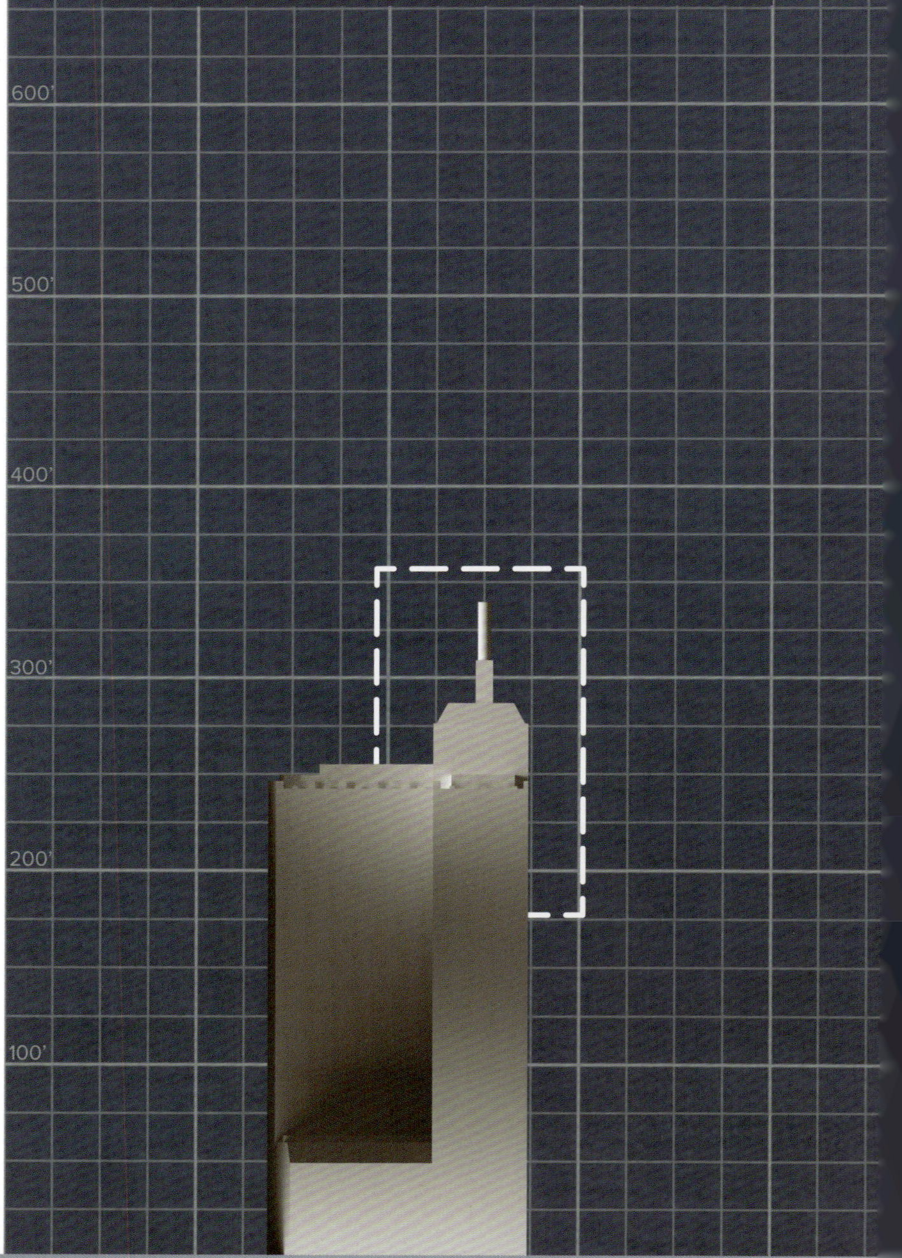

South Elevation *1" = 100'*

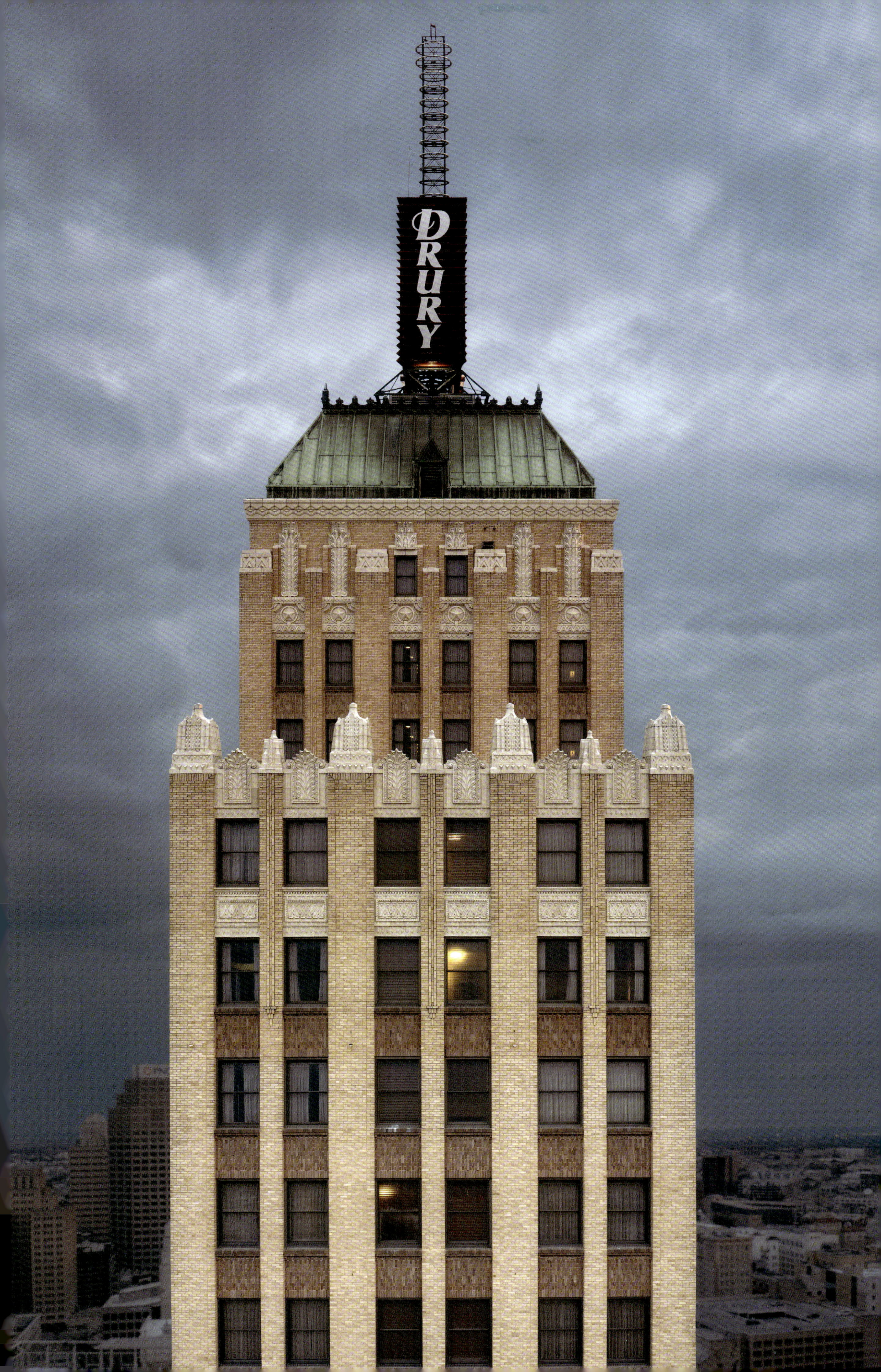
DRURY

Smith-Young
Tower

San Antonio, **TX** — Tower Life Building

Address ··········· **310 S. St. Mary's St.**
Opened ··········· **1929**
Height ··········· **404'**
Stories ··········· **30**
Style ··········· **Gothic, Art Deco**
Architect ··········· **Atlee & Robert Ayres**

Guides on the San Antonio River tour boats puttering past this highrise occasionally say its owner jumped off the roof to end it all. While not accurate in the particulars — Jim Smith shot himself in his Dallas apartment — it does reflect the shocking demise of a skyscraper speculator ruined by the Great Depression.

Smith and his older brother, Albert, were enterprising farm boys who ran a stable and then sold cars before starting up a successful paving business. Rolling the proceeds into real estate development with their lawyer, Jim Young, they erected this eponymous Gothic office tower with its cathedral-vaulted marble lobby. Designed by a local father-and-son architect duo, it was the tallest building in town for decades, offering unobstructed sight lines to its plentiful gargoyles.

After the namesakes lost their building in the crash, it was redubbed Transit Tower for a bus company that moved in. The army also leased space, and General Dwight Eisenhower had an office here before shipping out for World War II and the White House. In 1961 an insurance company rebranded both itself and the building as Tower Life, and that name has stuck since.

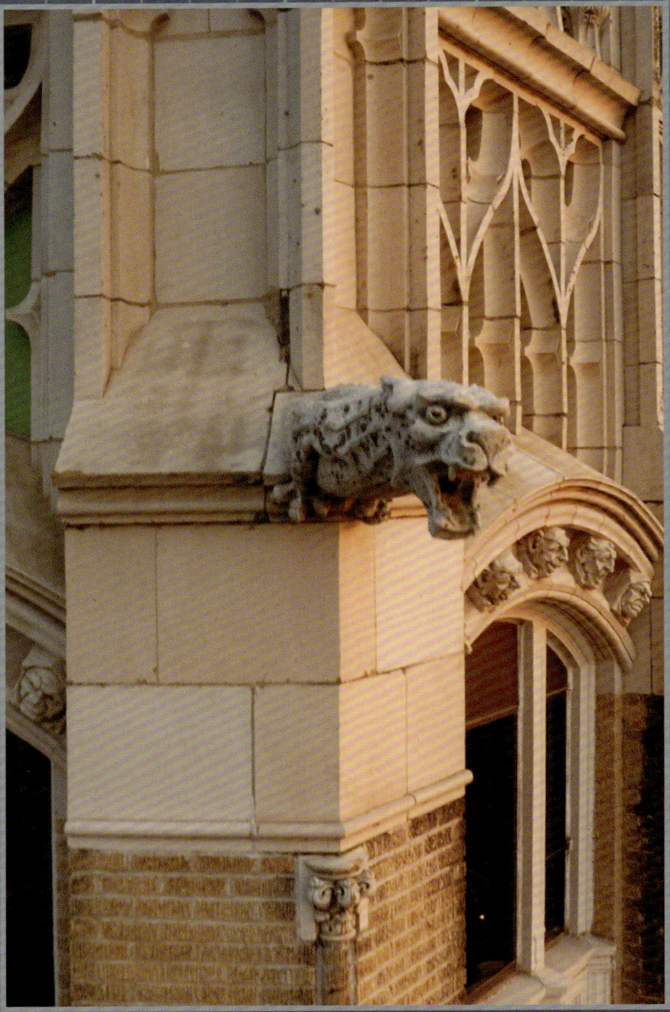

Gargoyles adorn this Gothic tower, along with grimacing peasants and other medieval characters below.

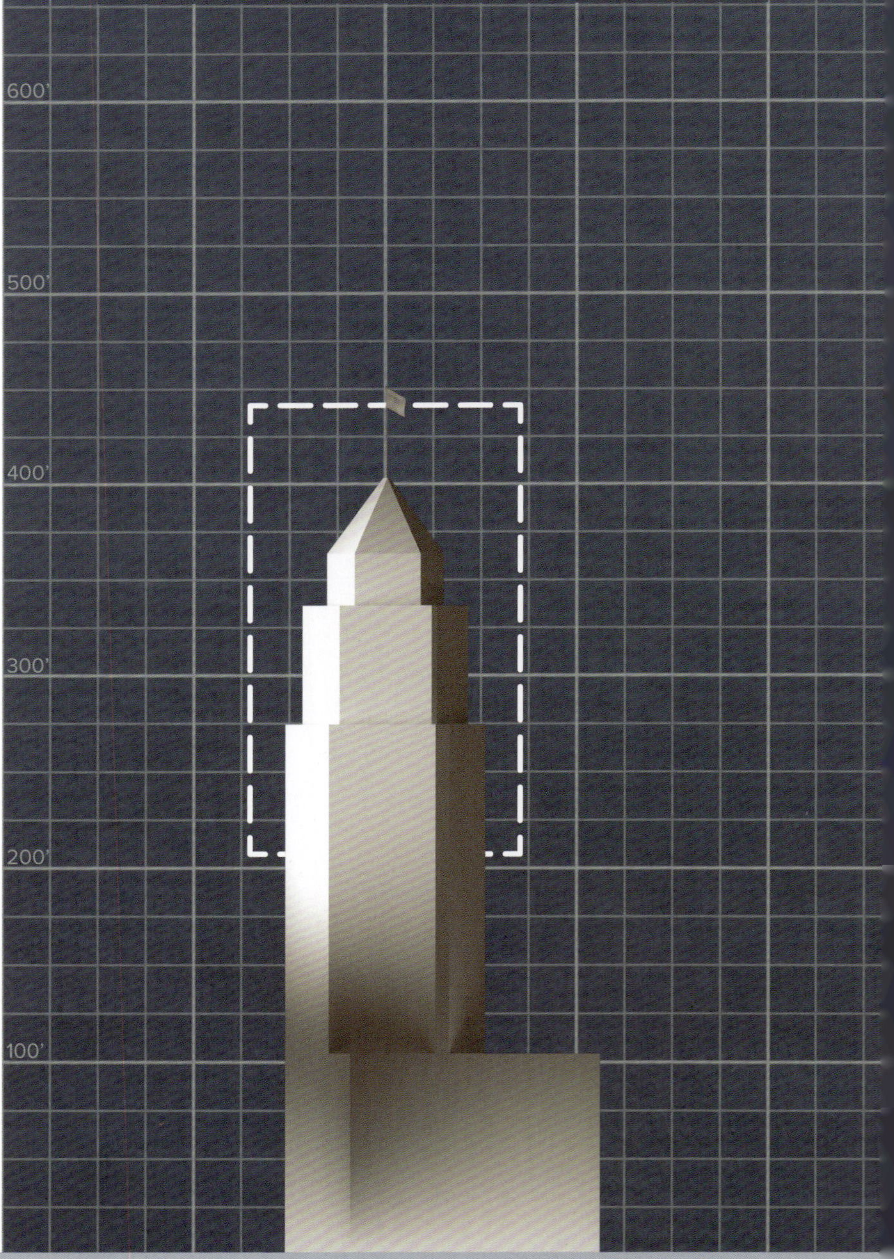

Southeast Elevation *1" = 100'*

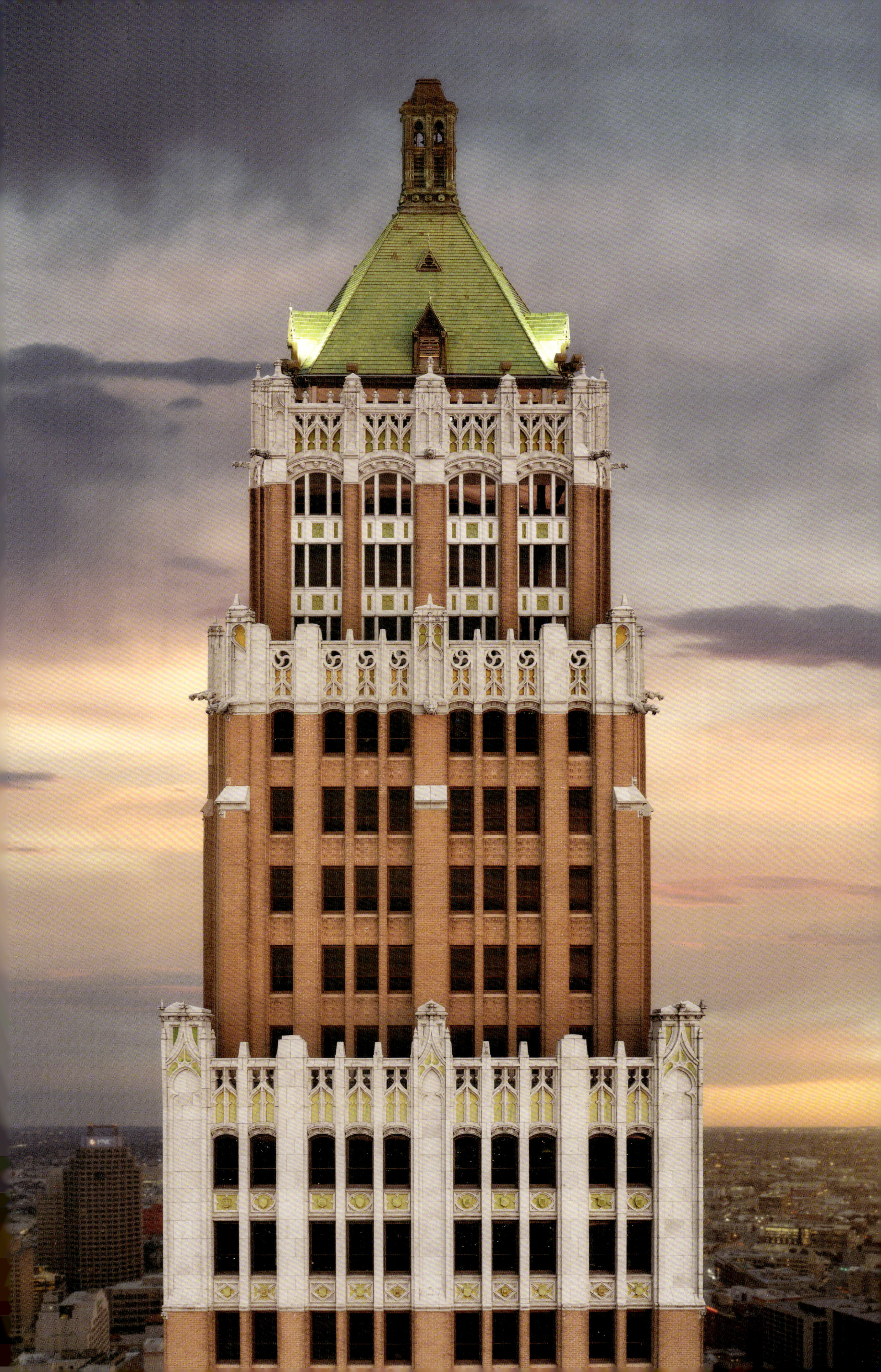

Central National
Bank

Richmond, **VA**

Address	**219 E. Broad St.**
Opened	**1930**
Height	**282’**
Stories	**23**
Style	**Art Deco**
Architect	**John Eberson**

Merchants on the Broad Street retail strip organized this financial institution in 1911 to serve their particular needs, including late Saturday hours so they could do their banking after the last shoppers departed. Founders included a department store owner, a furrier, and a leather merchant.

William Schwarzschild, bank president when the bank opened this new highrise, had grown a watch repair business into a fine jewelry store with his brother, Gus, before taking the reins at Central National. Both he and the bank’s first president, Charles Hutzler, were sons of Jewish immigrants who made a living in the retail clothing business. Schwarzschild was succeeded as head of the bank by his son, Harry.

Patterns of colored tiles along the building’s crown, as well as a splashy multihued coffered ceiling in the main banking hall, are the work of New York architect John Eberson, best known for his movie palaces. He had recently completed one in Richmond when he received this commission, and it is still used today for theatrical productions.

A successor bank eventually sold the building. It stood vacant for more than a decade before being converted into apartments in 2016.

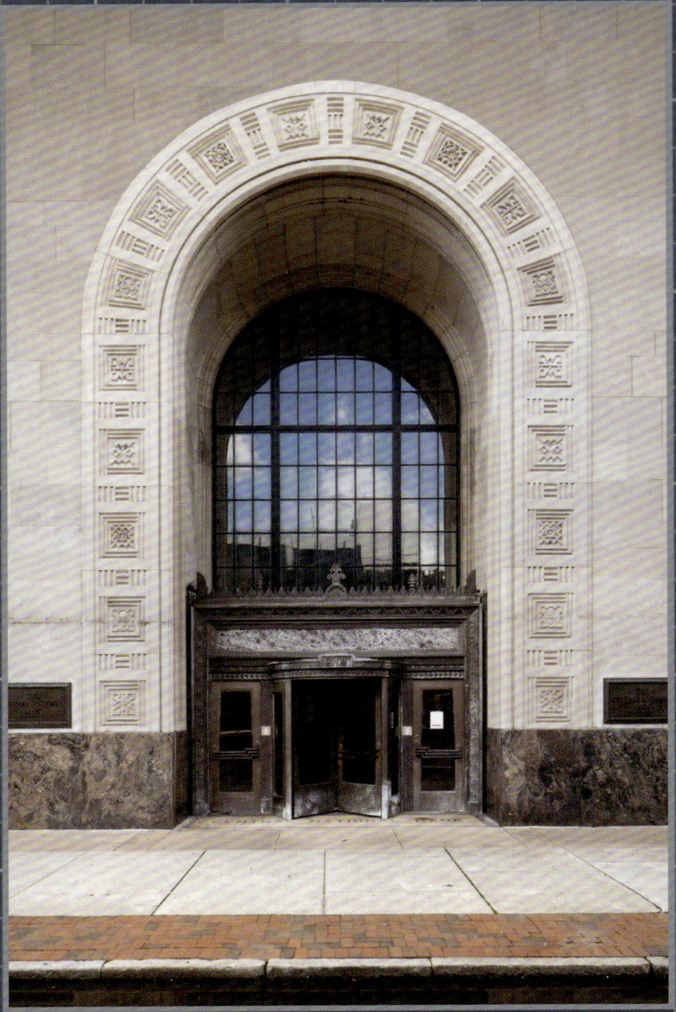

The arch, an ancient architectural form, is made modern with geometric patterns carved along its perimeter.

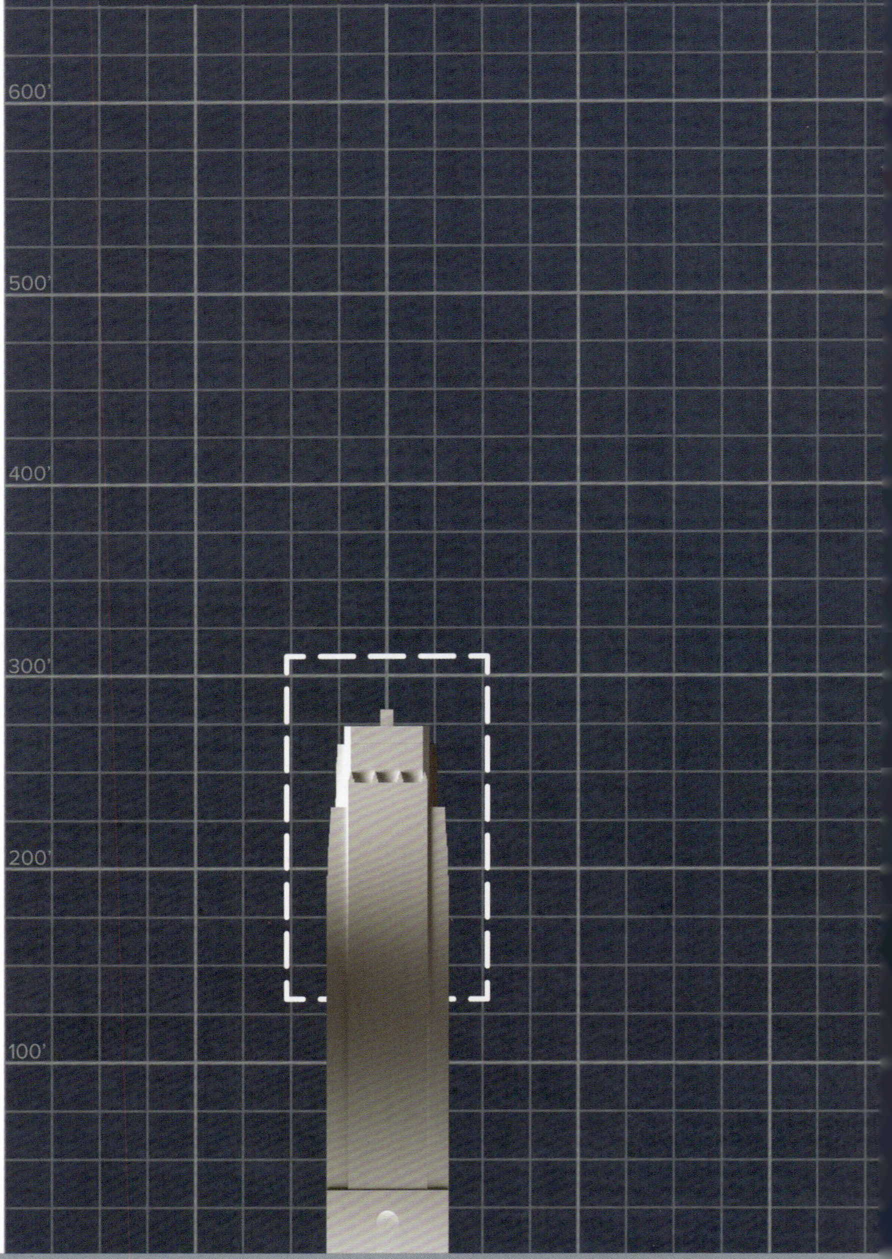

Northeast Elevation *1" = 100'*

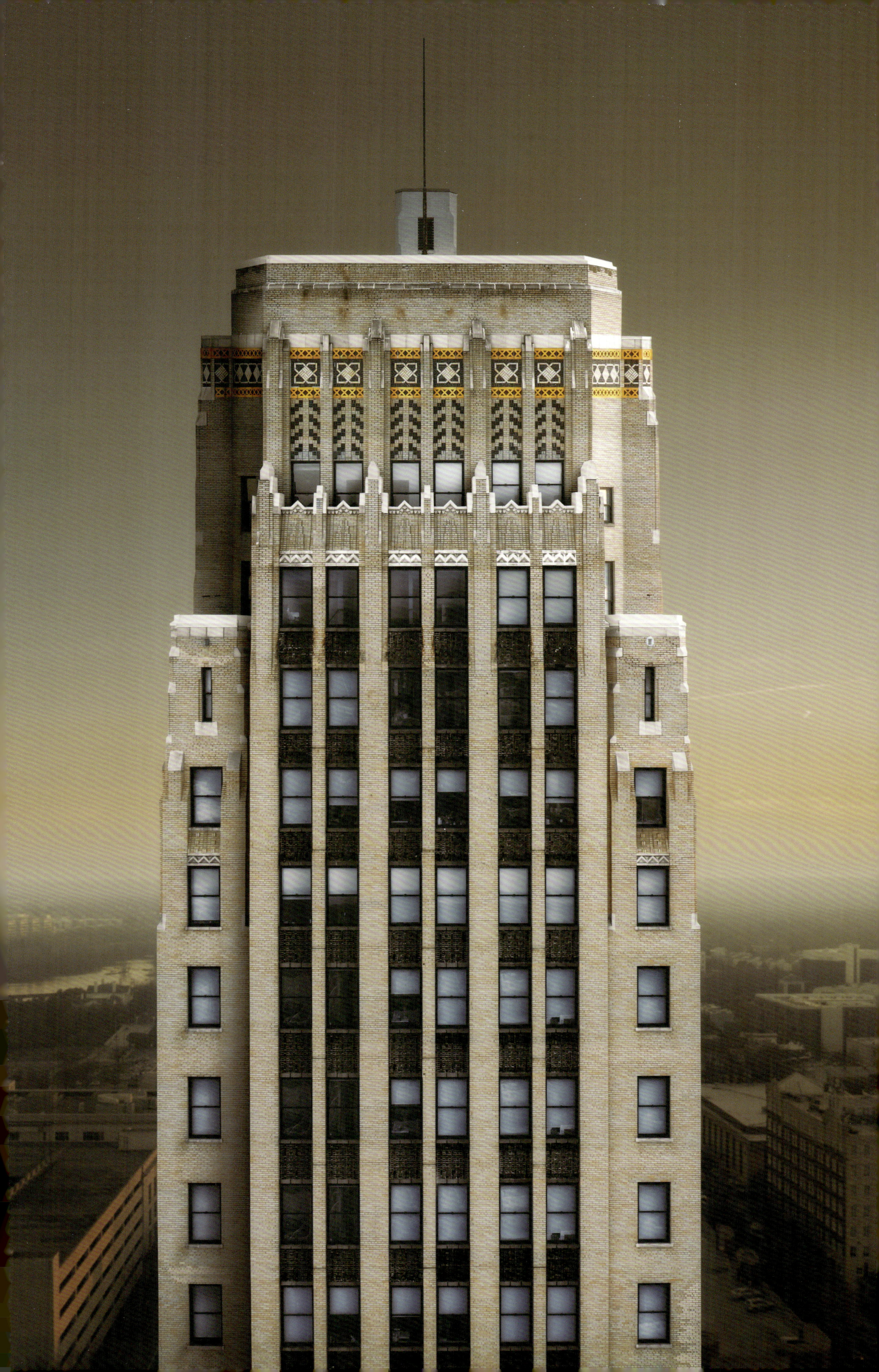

Acknowledgments

Since the Highrises project began almost 200 buildings ago, we have received crucial support from a number of talented and dedicated people. Their care and attention have made this book and the entire collection all the richer.

Andy Gallagher is the genius software engineer behind the Highrises website. Cooper Sherwin has shared valuable strategies as project advisor. Mike Stuart and Ksenia Kudinova both made key contributions when the project was readying for launch. Oriana Leckert offered smart tips for our Kickstarter page, while Colin Giering and Liam Nielsenshultz created a superb video to explain the whole thing. Rachael Houser supplied her sharp proofreading, Rish Vasudevan helped with 3-D models, and Charlie Paixao provided photos of Luhrs Tower. Veb Sharma at Acutrack was instrumental in turning our PDFs into this book.

We are grateful to these people who gave us tours of their Highrises: Maurice Auriemma, Anne Cunningham, Dee Dorochowicz and Erik Nussbaum in Chicago; Robert Caplin in Columbus; Brandon Patterson, Sheila Swanson, Dereck Rascon, Hillary Kane, and Steven Lopez in Los Angeles; Aboudi Kabbani in Oakland; Jessica Black, Karen Besser, Leroy Ball, Bill Benter, Julean Work, and Rob Pfaffmann in Pittsburgh; Jay Furst in Rochester, Minnesota; Rick Rossi in Saint Paul; Wade Brister and Nitin Kasan in San Antonio; Jane Connors and Henry Tsai in San Francisco; and Dennis Williams in Seattle. Special thanks to Sydney Blair in Winston-Salem and Sophie Duquette-Brown in Birmingham for hotel accommodations. We are also thankful for the friendly lobby security guards, building managers, and other helpful people who pointed us in the right direction during our visits and calls.

Chris had the pleasure of meeting these photographers and art lovers who made him feel at home: @Cooper.Visual and @nickdandria in Atlanta, @shanewarephoto in Austin, @avdidit in Boston, @ZachLipp @Daedmorgon @beloveful and @Imgonnabelegend in Chicago, @zkauth in Cincinnati, @Abrahanny and @Streetboxd in Dallas, @Rickapeterson and @imxndr in Detroit, @Valleryphotography in Houston, Josh Braman and @ForestKane in Kansas City, Matt Starr in New York City, David Hytha in Oakland, Jacob Hurst in San Antonio, @IamChasm__ in Los Angeles and Mack Renner in Tulsa.

Highrises research uses hundreds of sources, chiefly archival news coverage on Newspapers.com. Documentation from the National Register of Historic Places, New York Landmarks Preservation Commission, Los Angeles Conservancy, and other preservationists is also invaluable. Many building heights and floor counts are from the Council on Tall Buildings and Urban Habitat, though varying methodology from city to city and building to building led to some adjustments. Eastern Columbia Building image trademark is used with permission.

Special thanks to these leading supporters from our Kickstarter campaign:

Ho Yin Au
Joshua Kagi
Andrew Haley
Timothy Shea
Nicholas Mastracola
Bryan DiSanto
George Eves
Ryan Bowen
Dan Obarski
James Powell
Eric Eymard
Nik Zhang
Lilit Vardanian
Brandi
Andrew Dondero
Christopher Cahoon
Paul S. Morin
Divya Patel
Daniel Tossing
Eli Lever
John Tsentzelis
Raffy Halim
Oliver Dale
Lisa Alfelt
Forrest Moss-Vreeland
Chris Messina
Krystian
Jason Page
Lance Rothstein
Christopher Rauch
James Stapleton
Cooper Sherwin
Robert Brandon
Cyra Uy
Vitalijs Barilo

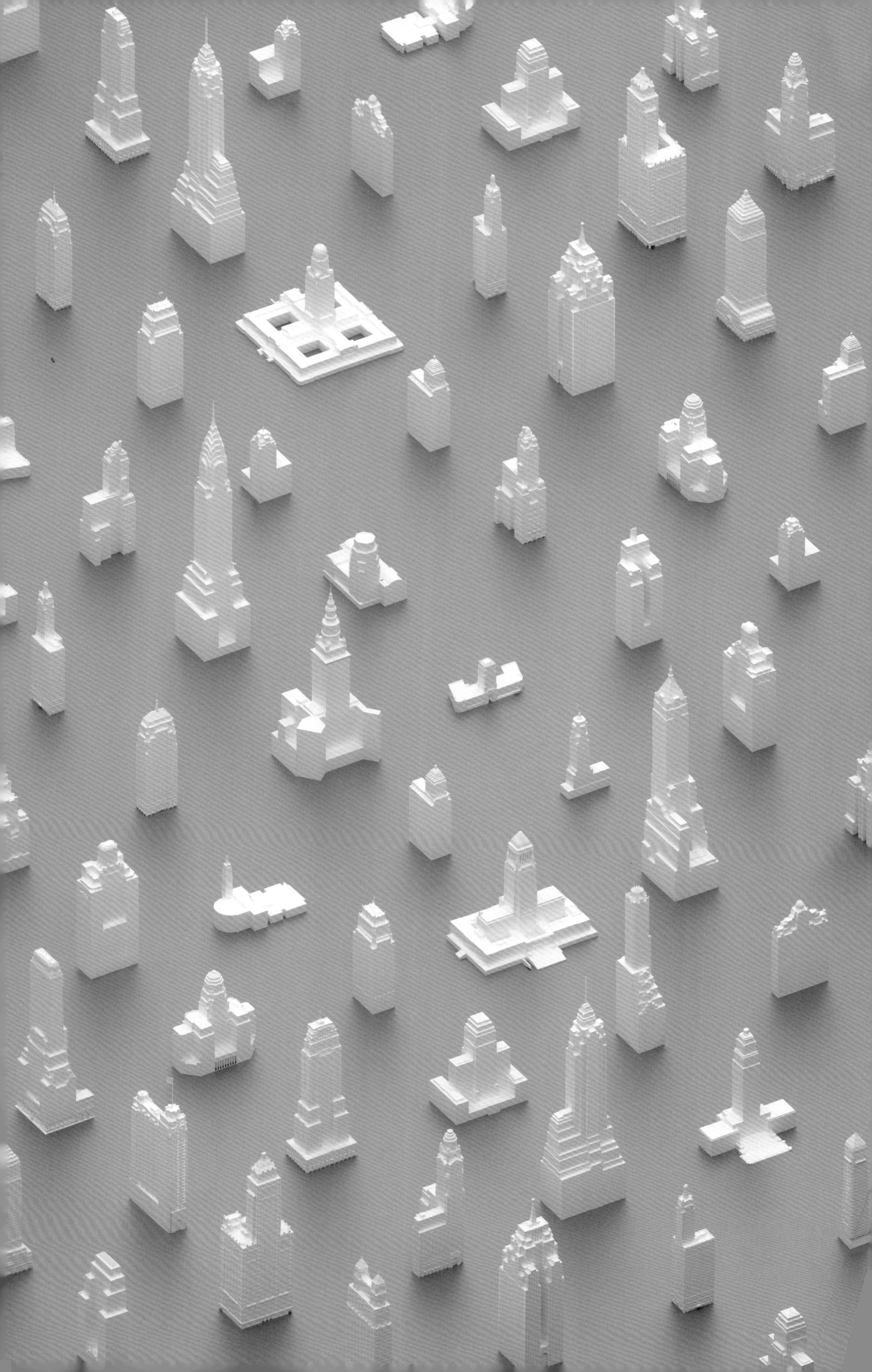

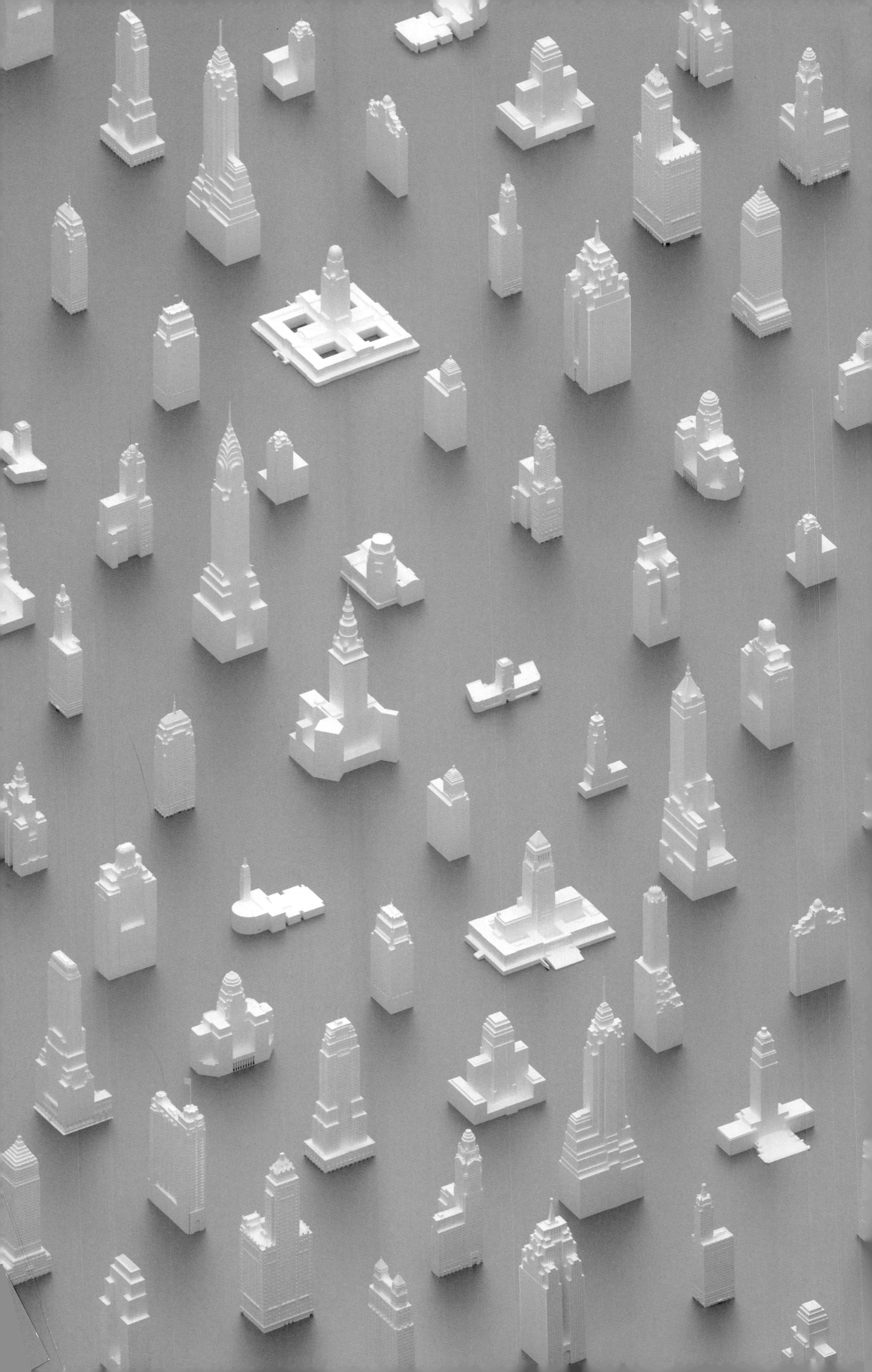